CONTENTS

To

Thomas Shipley Brown

great teacher

and to the memory of

Walter Kahoe

bibliophile

THE
HISTORY
OF
KING RICHARD THE THIRD

THE
HISTORY
OF
KING RICHARD THE THIRD
(1619)

by

SIR GEORGE BUCK

Master of the Revels

Edited with an introduction and notes

by

ARTHUR NOEL KINCAID

ALAN SUTTON
1982

Alan Sutton Publishing Limited
17a Brunswick Road
Gloucester GL1 1HG

First published 1979
Reprinted with corrections 1982

British Library Cataloguing in Publication Data

Buck, *Sir* George
    The history of King Richard the Third.
    1. Richard III, *King of England*
    2. Great Britain — Kings and rulers — Biography
    I. Title II. Kincaid, A N
    942. 04'6'0924   DA260

ISBN 0-904387-26-7 (CASE EDITION)

ISBN 0-86299-008-4

Typesetting and origination by
Alan Sutton Publishing Limited
Printed in Great Britain by
Page Bros (Norwich) Limited

ACKNOWLEDGEMENTS

My thanks for assistance in preparing this edition are due first to R.E. Alton for checking my initial transcript in my handwriting, which is at least as bad as Buck's, and spending many hours working out with me the conjectural emendations and textual problems. And also to C.A.J. Armstrong for his suggestions regarding sources, particularly Continental ones, which I could not otherwise have traced, and for many other kindnesses. For help in tracing the Latin and Greek quotations whose documentation had been destroyed and in disentangling their grammar, I am particularly indebted to the late Robert Levens, and I wish to thank also John Blundell, among many others. Jeannine Alton assisted me in modernizing the French quotations. And Charles Ross called my attention to recently published material. I am especially grateful to Deirdre Barber for help with the immense task of proofreading.

Several individuals and institutions deserve gratitude for giving me access to and information about manuscript material: especially Sidney T. Fisher of Montreal for lending his early manuscript copy of Buck's *History* to the Bodleian Library and for providing information about it; Major W. Halswell for lending his manuscript of Buck's *Commentary* to the Bodleian and the British Museum for my study; Trinity College, Cambridge; the University of Toronto Library; and the Public Record Office. Most of my time was spent in the Bodleian Library — especially Duke Humfrey's Library — the Manuscripts Room of the British Library, and the English Faculty Library at Oxford, so it is to the staffs of these institutions, especially to D.S. Porter of the Bodleian, that I owe most gratitude.

For financial assistance I have especially to thank Margaret Kincaid. And I received research grants from various foundations within Oxford University: Christ Church College, the Meyerstein Bequest, and the Committee for Advanced Study.

Last I must mention several people who assisted me in more general ways when this project was in its infancy and to whom, consequently, it is a monument: Phoebe Neville. Agnes Finnie Hay, the late Fannie Cox Hendrie, and my mother Professor F.B. Jones.

A.N.K.

ACKNOWLEDGEMENTS

ABBREVIATIONS
(see Bibliography for full details)

BIHR	*Bulletin of the Institute of Historical Research*
B.L.	British Library (formerly British Museum)
Bod.	Bodleian
Camden	William Camden, *Britannia*, 1607
Cam. Soc.	Camden Society
Comm.	Buck, *A Commentary upon . . . Liber Domus Dei* (Bod. MS. Eng. Misc. b. 106)
Croyland	[Croyland Chronicle] in *Rerum Anglicarum Scriptorum Veterum*, I, [ed. Fulman], 1648
CSP	*Calendar of State Papers*
DNB	*Dictionary of National Biography*
EETS	Early English Text Society
EHR	*English Historical Review*
GEC	G.E.C[okayne], *The Complete Peerage*
Grafton	Richard Grafton, *Chronicle*, Vol. III, 1807
Pat. Rolls.	*Calendar of the Patent Rolls*
Polydore	Polydore Vergil, *Anglica Historia*, 2nd ed., Basle, 1555
Rot. Parl.	*Rotuli Parliamentorum*
R.S.	Rolls Series
STC	Pollard and Redgrave, *Short Title Catalogue,1475-1640*
Stow	John Stow, *Annales*, 1601

INTRODUCTION
I. THE LIFE OF SIR GEORGE BUCK

There is no purpose in introducing here a long biographical study of Sir George Buck,[1] since the one by Mark Eccles,[2] though its organization makes it somewhat difficult to follow, is nearly exhaustive. It should be sufficient simply to sketch the outlines of Buck's life, filling in only details which have particular bearing on his *History of King Richard the Third* and on his peculiar place in English literature.

Buck traces his own descent in his manuscript *Commentary on the Book of Domus Dei,*[3] and again in the history. Genealogy in an age when its methods were not clearly formulated tended to be based largely on guesswork from philological evidence and to take colour from the wishes of the tracer. In the *Commentary,* Buck lists his own among families such as Percy, Neville, and Vere as examples of those springing from foreign nobility. His is almost the only family below baronial rank which he mentions in the work. In the *History,* his genealogy is introduced as a digression for which he asks the reader's pardon with a moving appeal to the honour we owe our ancestors, from whom we have derived our claims to nobility or gentility (see below, text, p. 115-6). Buck was proud of his status as a gentleman, and his pride extends to the descent from which he derived that status. 'Noblemen', he says in the *Commentary* (f. 58ᵛ), are merely lords, whereas the word 'gentleman' has more honour in it, signifying origin 'from generous paren*tes*'. Buck shared the passion for pedigree which flourished under the Tudors among those newly acquiring court promotion. He needed to feel that in his own promotion at court he was carrying on or restoring a family tradition. For, as he tells us, his family was at one time prominent in service to the crown — under King Richard III.

On Camden's authority, Buck cites as founder of his family in England Sir Walter Buck of Brabant, a descendant of the earls of Flanders, who was one of the foreign commanders serving under King John. The name he derives from Lisle de Buc, a town in Flanders on the River Isle, near which Ludovick de Buck, a much earlier ancestor, built a castle called Castle de Buck. The name, Buck conjectures, comes from the German for beech, a tree very plentiful in this district. Ludovick married the daughter of the King of France who made him governor of Flanders in 621, and his family became earls of Flanders in 880 through a second marriage with the French royal house. After producing the father of Matilda, wife of William the Conqueror, the male line of the earls of Flanders died out in 1119. Walter de Buck was one of its younger descendants.

Buck disagrees with his sources who censure the foreign leaders for their plunder under King John[4] and approves of his ancestor's subduing the Isle of Ely for the king and having 'good spoile' there (*Comm.*, f.451). Lands were given Walter Buck in Yorkshire and Northamptonshire as reward for his service. In the north the family intermarried with another of the same surname, the Lords of Bucton in the Wapentake of Buccross. Buck seems uncertain of this family's origin. In the *Commentary* he sees it as a branch of the Flanders family which came over with the Conqueror, a theory convenient to the theme of that work. But in the *History* he applies the Saxon derivation of the name to this family rather than to the Flemish branch, and suggests that the family had been native in England for a very long time.

The great-grandson of Walter Buck married Agnes, the daughter of Frederick Tilney of Lancaster. This is the earliest association of the Bucks with the Tilneys, the latest being the succession in the post of Master of the Revels of Sir Edmund Tilney by Sir George Buck. A John Buck who lived under Richard II and was married to a Howard served the Earl of Arundel, Lord Admiral of England, and was imprisoned for charging the Spanish fleet without leave of his commander (*Comm.*, f.452[v]; *History*, text,p. 115).[5] About his family's tradition of military service Buck says in his *History*:

> And these Bucks were all soldiers, and so were the rest
> succeeding these, for Robert Buck . . . followed Thomas,
> 2nd Duke of Norfolk, and was with him at the Battle of
> Flodden. And Robert Buck, the son of this Robert Buck,
> my father, served King Henry VIII at the siege of Boulogne,
> and the Duke of Somerset, Lieutenant General of King
> Edward VI, at the Battle of Musselburgh in Scotland. *Et
> nos militavimus et bella vidimus.* G.B.
> (text, p. 116, marginal note)

The early Bucks followed not only the Howards but also the dukes of York, soon to become the House of York. Laurence Buck served under Edward, Duke of York, at Agincourt, and his son John Buck of Harthill died in the Battle of St Albans fighting for Richard, Duke of York. His son John Buck — according to his descendant's account — served the sons of this duke, as a Gentleman of the Privy Chamber under Edward IV and Richard III and Controller of the Household for Richard III. Like his father, he died fighting for his lord. He was taken prisoner at Bosworth and beheaded two days later. Along with others of Richard's followers, among them the ancestor of Thomas Howard, Earl of Arundel, to whom Buck dedicated the *History*, and the great-grandfather of Sir John Harington, he was attainted. His three destitute children, Robert, Joan, and Margaret, were, Buck tells us, taken into the protection of Thomas, Earl of Surrey (later Duke of Norfolk) and brought up 'liberally' (*Comm.*, f. 453) in his house in Suffolk. Robert Buck, who followed Norfolk at Flodden, married the daughter of Clement Heigham and Joan Cotton. His daughter Margaret was given in marriage by the Duchess of Norfolk to Sir Frederick Tilney, a kinsman of hers, cousin to Sir Edmund Tilney, Master of the Revels. His son Robert married Elizabeth Peterill,[6] and their son was George Buck.

Doubt is cast upon Buck's account of his great-grandfather's position in the government of the Yorkist kings by the total absence of any mention of him in either the Patent Rolls or B.L. MS. Harleian 433, the compendium of documents from Richard III's reign. That he was neither a member of the Council nor a Justice of the Peace makes it seem most improbable that he could have become Controller of the Household, and indeed Buck himself in a revision of the *History* (see below, pp. cvi- cvii) retracts his earlier assertion to this effect. The only extant record of John Buck is of his attainder after Bosworth in the Parliament of the first year of Henry VII.[7] Possibly Buck was accepting family traditions at face value, not wishing to know that his family's origins were humbler than he liked to believe. That he does not qualify his statement of John Buck's position in Richard's household until late in the process of composing the *History* and that he fails to cite other records would suggest as much.[8] That no record of a connection with the Bucks appears in the Howard household books during Richard III's reign need not cast similar doubt on this other family tradition, for the association may have originated after the battle.

George Buck was baptized in Holy Trinity Church, Ely, where his father shortly after became Churchwarden,[9] on 1 October 1560.[10] Robert Buck died in Chichester where, in 1577, he had become Steward and Auditor. He had fought in the Battle of Musselburgh and was described as 'vir pius et prudens'. This description, the date of his death, and details of his career and descent appear in his epitaph, to be seen in a draft copied by his son in B.L. MS. Cotton Julius F. XI, f. 97.[11]

George Buck followed his family's traditions in several respects: in adherence to and benefit from the Howards, serving under the Lord Admiral Charles Howard in 1596 on the Cadiz expedition and preferred by him to court favour. He never lost an opportunity of expressing his gratitude to the family, in his historical poem *Daphnis Polystephanos*, in the *Commentary*, and in the *History*. The Lord Admiral, he says, treated him more like a friend and kinsman than a follower (*Comm.*, f. 453ᵛ), and he was in close contact with several other members of the family who, like him, were scholars and collectors. He was indebted to them not only for their patronage of himself and his ancestors, but also for the use of their books and manuscripts and for *viva voce* information he frequently received from them.

He followed another family tradition in his adherence to the House of York, and perhaps he saw the character of the man for whom his great-grandfather died at Bosworth as a reflection on the honour of his own house, just as he seems to find in the glory of the Howards an opportunity not only to show gratitude, but also to rehearse and celebrate his own family. He seems to feel the sting of obscurity and attributes it to the attainder suffered by his family after Bosworth. In the *History* he mentions 'noble and worthy kindred' who will not acknowledge his family because they 'flourish not nor are rich' (text,p. 116). In *Daphnis* he says, 'I am ignorant, I am poore, and I am as obscure as *M. Scaurus* was . . . and so haue been euer since the fatall iourney at *Bosworth*'.[12] Although no evidence exists that documents survived in Buck's family to serve as source material for his *History,* traditions did, for his grandfather was throughout his patron's life closely associated with Thomas Howard, Duke of Norfolk, who survived Bosworth. It is on the testimony of his grandfather that Buck gives his account of Thomas Howard's fortunes after Bosworth, a report which conflicts with those accepted at the time and still in force[13] (see text, pp. 108-09). The Howards too had their family traditions, and they had documents as well.

Buck was educated as a boy at Higham Ferrers in Northamptonshire under his brother-in-law Dr Henry Blaxton, whom he thanks in the Preface to *Daphnis* for showing him charters at Chichester Cathedral (sig. B4[v]). When Buck's family, and Blaxton as well, moved to Chichester, it is probable that Buck continued his studies there at the school of which Blaxton was master. There is good evidence of his having been a student at Cambridge.[14] He proceeded to the Inns of Court, first to Thavies' Inn as a probationer in about 1580, and he was admitted to the Middle Temple in 1585, 'as late of New Inn, gent., son & heir of Robert Buck of Chichester, gent., decd.'[15] He was an envoy to France in 1587 and in the *History* mentions being there when he heard the news of Mary, Queen of Scots' death (text, p. 184). In 1588 he served against the Armada. It was through the Lord Admiral's assistance that Buck became M.P. for Gatton, Surrey, in 1593 and 1597. He tells us that the Lord Admiral preferred him to Queen Elizabeth (*Comm.*, f. 453[v]). In 1595 the queen suggested him for the post of French Secretary or Clerk of the Signet, and Howard recommended him to Cecil for one of these posts. The latter did not fall vacant, and another suitor gained the former. But Buck had already won the queen's attention. While serving with the Lord Admiral on the Cadiz expedition he acted as envoy from the commanders to the queen, thinking it 'an honour & a happines' to be in the expedition, despite having to march in full armour carrying a pike on an extremely hot day, as he says in a letter to Sir John Stanhope,[16] whose favour he is soliciting. In this letter he intimates that his fortunes have taken a different turn from what he had planned and expresses himself beholden to Lady Cecil as well as to Stanhope, and to the Lord Admiral above all.

By 1599 he was Esquire of the Body, and it seems that as early as 1597 there was mention of his candidature for the Revels reversion. He went on a diplomatic expedition to Flanders in 1601, receiving instructions directly from the queen. The praises he bestows on Elizabeth in his works, amounting almost to worship, must have had some basis in personal impression. On the death of his cousin Philip Tilney, who owned lands in Lincolnshire from the Buck side of his family, Buck acquired property as common law heir, since there was no will, after a court case in which Coke supported him as counsel.

In 1603 Buck secured the patent of the Revels reversion, became a Gentleman of the Privy Chamber, and received a knighthood. In 1605 he went on an embassy to Spain. By 1607 he had taken over the work of the Revels Office from Sir Edmund Tilney and appropriated to it the task of being sole licenser of plays for publication. From 1607 to 1615 all licensed plays bore his signature, except for the pseudo-Shakespearean *Yorkshire Tragedy* of 1608. He licensed *Timon of Athens* in 1609, *Coriolanus* in 1610, *Othello* in 1611, *The Tempest* in 1612, and *Twelfth Night* in 1614. Eccles' estimate seems just, that

> From what we know of his acts as Master, Buc seems to
> have been not at all a severe censor, but to have executed
> conscientiously and moderately, rather than with the zeal

> of Herbert, the duties of a difficult office. . . . On the whole
> perhaps it was as well that Elizabeth chose Buc, a gentleman
> poet and lover of plays, from the point of view of the Court
> rather than of the professional playwright, and one who
> had shown the diplomatic qualities necessary to mediate
> between the players and authority.[17]

George Chapman seems to have recognized Buck's learned and gentlemanly qualities
— though there is perhaps a barb in the tail of his letter — even in the heat of his
frustration and anger at the censor's apparent hesitation in licensing *Biron:*

> But how safely soever Illiterate Aucthoritie setts up his
> Bristles against Poverty, methinkes yours (being accom-
> panied with learning) should rebate the points of them,
> and soften the fiercenes of those rude manners; you know
> *Sir*, They are sparkes of the lowest fier in Nature that fly
> out uppon weaknes with every puffe of Power. . . .[18]

The type of censorship exercised was specifically directed against matters tending
to stir religious or political controversy, attacks on government, religion, or foreign
powers, disrespect to contemporary nobility or even to their ancestors (Sir John
Oldcastle is an instance of the last), oaths, and, after 1606, use of the name God.
Buck's own practices of censorship can be seen in the manuscript copies of *The
Second Maiden's Tragedy,* B.L. MS. Lansdowne 807, ff. 29-56) and *Sir John Van
Olden Barnavelt* (B.L. MS. Additional 18653). In the former he begins by correcting a
minor grammatical error of 'hath' to 'haue' (f. 29, 1.2). Several very general
derogatory remarks about courtiers he has altered or marked for alteration. The
phrase 'Frenchmens tortures' (f.55) is altered to 'extremest tortures'. Passages on
lust, most particularly the king's lust, are cut and strong references to tyranny are
marked. A half-line. 'Y*o*ur kinges poisoned' is crossed out, leaving simply, 'I am
poisoned' (f.55ᵛ). An interesting idiosyncracy evident in Buck's censorship as
exercised on this play is his cutting of references denigrating the general character of
women. At the end of the manuscript Buck writes, 'This second Maydens tragedy
(for it hath no name inscribed) may with the reformations bee acted publikely. 31.
October. 1611./. G. Buc.' (f.56).

The alterations in *Barnavelt* are political. Buck usually marks crosses in the margins
where revisions are required, and corrections in his own hand appear in passages
regarding overthrow of governments: 'tooke that course / that now is practisd on
you', which would seem to show too specific a precedent for government overthrow,
is changed to 'cutt of his opposites'; and 'changed to a Monarchie' Buck makes
'changed to another form' (f.26). Against one passage he remarks, 'I like not this:
neith*er* do I think yᵗ the\ pr./ was thus disgracefully vsed. besides he is to much
presented. [here.] G.B.' (f.5ᵛ).[19] The law restricted representations of royalty
onstage. Besides this, Buck seems to be concerned here about a matter of historical
accuracy, unwilling that even popular literature should misrepresent truth.

The Master of the Revels was also responsible for plays performed at court. Buck chose and supervised court performances by the King's Men of *Winter's Tale*, *Tempest, Much Ado, Othello*, both parts of *Henry IV*, and *Pericles*. The Revels Accounts in the Public Reçord Office give some idea of the time he spent in exercising his office.[20] In 1612-13, the year of Princess Elizabeth's marriage to the Elector Palatine, he was in attendance 125 days and 24 nights, then for 10 days and 5 nights he attended the Earl of Suffolk, Lord Chamberlain, to prepare 'for the enterteynment of the said maryed Princes' (2046, no. 18). In addition, he spent 15-20 days airing the wardrobe in the Revels Office. In 1614-16 he was in attendance 115 days and 16 nights between 30 October and 22 February 'as well for Rehersalls and making choice of plaies and Comedies and reforming them' (2047, no 20); 20 days in the summer for airing the garments; and 23 days for triumphs at Easter in celebration of the king's reign. In 1615-16 he claimed expenses for 'wages and Entertaynmentes of Officers Artificers and other ymployed aboute the finishing making and setting forthe of sondry plaies Commodies feates of activity Maskes and Triumphes at Tylte and in ayring the stuffe belonging to the said office' (2047, no. 21). In this year between the end of October and the end of February he attended 107 days and 19 nights, and the next year 127 days and 16 nights, and in addition was on hand for triumphs, Easter celebrations, airing of garments, and the marriage at Hampton Court of Sir John Villiers to the daughter of Sir Edward Coke. The visit of the Earl of Oxford 'to my lodging at Hampton Court' which Buck mentions in the *History* (text, p. 170) must have occurred on this occasion.

From 1615 he suffered difficulties with the Exchequer over payment of back wages to himself and his men, who seem to have been in desperate financial straits and were, he felt, blaming him for not being more urgent in demanding payment. Late in 1621 or early in 1622, Buck went mad. Eccles[21] attributes his madness to his struggles with the government over wages. He died 31 October 1622 and was buried at Broadwater in Sussex.[22]

In 1618, Buck had contemplated marriage with Elizabeth Meutis of West Ham, but his 'humorous and shie proseeding'[23] was said to have stood in his way. Eccles conjectures that his interest was not so much in the marriage itself as in reforming or discomfiting his prospective heirs. His only brother Robert had become a Jesuit. Buck's will, later declared a forgery, stated that if the law should disable his brother, his heir should be his nephew Stephen Buck, a son of his sister Cecilia, who had married a William Buck (no relation to Sir George's family) of Lincolnshire. Since Robert Buck was under indictment for entering the country as a Jesuit, Stephen Buck took immediate possession of Buck's lands and goods on their owner's death, but a general pardon was then granted Robert Buck enabling him to possess his inheritance. There followed a protracted legal battle. Stephen Buck tried to prove that Sir George had conveyed his lands and goods to him and his son George by Deed of Gift, but there were doubts as to whether this was a genuine or forged document and whether it had been made before or after Buck's lunacy had set in. Stephen Buck had at one time been imprisoned for forgery and had since been in collusion with his uncle John Buck, a notorious forger. There was also evidence to show Sir George's dislike of his nephew Stephen. Consequently in 1625, Robert Buck was declared heir. In the meantime, however, Stephen Buck and his son George had acquired numerous of Sir George's possessions, retained them, and were making use of them.

NOTES

1. I have adopted the spelling 'Buck' as more familiar to modern readers. Sir George uses 'Buc' (a classical affectation) with far greater frequency in extant documents, and I can find no justification for A.R. Myers' statement that he preferred the spelling 'Buck' (Introduction to George Buck, Esq., *History of the Life and Reigne of Richard the Third*, London, 1973, repr. of 1646 ed., p. 5.)

2. Mark Eccles, 'Sir George Buc, Master of the Revels', in *Thomas Lodge and Other Elizabethans*, ed. Charles J. Sisson (Cambridge, Mass., 1933), pp. 411-506.

3. Bod. MS. Eng. Misc. b. 106. Folio references to this MS. will be given in the text. See below, pp. xxix -xxxiv for a discussion of this work.

4. See below, p. cxv.

5. Sir John Buck's imprisonment and release into Arundel's custody are documented in *Pat. Rolls* (5 Nov. 1389), p. 146.

6. A detailed family tree will be found in Eccles following p. 506.

7. *Rot. Parl.,* VI, 276.

8. I am grateful to Charles Ross for bringing this home to me.

9. W.H. Challen, 'Sir George Buck, Kt., Master of the Revels', *Notes and Queries,* n.s. III (1957), 326.

10. Ibid., p. 291.

11. There is another copy, differing slightly and in another hand, in B.L. MS. Additional 5699, f. 350.

12. G[eorge] B[uck], Δαφνις Πολυστεφανος (London, 1605), sig. A 4^v. Further references will be given in the text.

13. For the most recent account of Thomas Howard's life, which ignores Buck as a source for his adventure after Bosworth, see Melvin J. Tucker, *The Life of Thomas Howard, Earl of Surrey* (London, 1964), p. 46.

14. See below, pp. 27f.

15. Challen, p. 291.

16. Bod. MS. Eng. lett. b. 27, ff. 106-109, a 19th century copy of the letter written 9 July 1596. No original survives.

17. Eccles, p. 504.

18. Quoted from *Athenaeum,* 6 April 1901, by Virginia Crocheron Gildersleeve, *Government Regulation of the Elizabethan Drama* (New York, 1908), pp. 106ff.

19. 'The pr.' refers to the Prince of Orange, who is shown in the play as being disrespectfully barred from the presence chamber.

20. Public Record Office MSS. A.O. 1, 2046 (16-18) and 2047 (19-22). Specific references will be given in the text.

21. Eccles, p. 481.

22. Challen, p. 291.

23. Letter from Ambrose Randolph to Thomas Wilson, 5 April 1618, quoted in Eccles, p. 470.

II. BUCK'S LITERARY ACTIVITY

Buck has left us several of his minor works, in addition to the three surviving historical treatises, and some references to other compositions which have been lost. For his two poems in English he is given a place in Ritson's biographies of poets.[1] As a poet he is adequate but far from brilliant or inspired. His first extant verse is a quatorzain which leads the group of complimentary verses introducing Thomas Watson's *Hekatompathia, or Passionate Century of Loue,* conjecturally dated 1581. This competent, conventional poem is entitled 'A Quatorzain, in the commendation of Master Thomas Watson, and of His Mistres, for whom he wrote his Booke of Passionat Sonnetes'. In the Folger copy of Buck's *Daphnis*, we have a six line verse expressing gratitude to Lord Ellesmere, to whom the author presented this particular copy.[2] These are Buck's only extant original poems in English, aside from his long poem *Daphnis Polystephanos*, published in 1605. One further long poem was mis-attributed to Buck in 1867 by W. Carew Hazlitt in his *Hand-Book to the Popular, Poetical, and Dramatic Literature of Great Britain:* 'A Poem of St George the Famous Champion of England'; but this was corrected in Hazlitt's *Collections and Notes,* Ser. 1 (1876) with the statement that the poem was actually by a certain Gaudy Brampton of Blow-Norton.

Buck produced several short Latin poems:

1) A manuscript poem on the Armada victory, included in Richard Robinson's *Archippus*. 'newly written oute' (f.2) in 1602 (B.L. MS. Royal 18 A LXVI), 'Vnto whiche ys allso added . . . Collections of English Voyages from 1580 to 1598' (f.14). Robinson describes the poem as 'Certeyne Verses given me by one Mr Buck a gent of my Lord Admiralles to be annexed vnto the Action praecedent, as I sett yt downe in the Booke which I gave vnto his Honorable good Lordship in the yeare aforesayd. 1589' (f.21). Buck entitles the poem 'Aquilae Nigrae Austriacae, et Leonis Albi Norfolcici, pugna, sive Illustrissimi Haerois CAROLI HOVARDI, — Anglia Summi Admirallii, &c Victoria, . . . et Numine DIANAE nostrae ELIZABETHAE DEI GRATIA, ANGLIAE, FRANCIAE et HYBERNIAE REGINAE. AVGVSTAE, FAELICISSIME TRIVMPHANTIS FIDEI DEFENSATRICIS. &ct.'

2) A complimentary verse, one of a group by several authors, prefaced to the 1607 edition of Camden's *Britannia*. It reappears in the 1610 translation.

3) A eulogy of London at the beginning of Buck's own work *The Third Universitie of England,*[3] enumerating the physical attributes, the diversity of arts, crafts,

branches of learning, artifice, culture, wealth and populace of the city.

4) A eulogy in manuscript of Sir Philip Sidney, praising him mainly as a military figure (B.L. MS. Cotton Julius F.XI, ff.93ᵛ-94).

These, like Buck's English poems, are competent and uninspired, rigid in formality and metrical regularity, and conventional in heroic vocabulary.

Buck was also a verse translator from several languages, as numerous examples in his *History* witness.[4] He claims (text, p. 85) the distinction of having preceded Harington as a translator of Ariosto, but he does not say whether he translated the whole of *Orlando Furioso* or merely portions of it. Probably the latter, for in addition to the Ariosto translation in the *History*, he presents a short one in *The Third Universitie* taking this opportunity to express criticism in terms which suggest that in this case Harington's translation preceded his:

> Which verses I haue aduentured thus plainely to turne into English Octaua, and could haue beene well content to haue spared the Laboure had not Sir *John Harrington* discosted from the Author. And yet I must confesse he hath performed an excellent part of a translator in that his English *Orlando*.
>
> (sig. Nnnnᵛ)

The Third Universitie in the section on painting and cosmetology (sig. Oooo 3), includes a verse translation from a Greek epigram by Lucilius about women painting their faces. This particular translation is exceptionallly clever and smooth and reproduces some of the original's wordplay. But ordinarily Buck's translations, which are generally in rhymed iambic epigrammatic couplets, are trite, lame, metrically incompetent, and make no attempt to approximate to the tone of the original.

There is a suggestion that Buck wrote a play. J.Q. Adams[5] presents a late seventeenth century list of early English plays, all probably in manuscript, compiled by Abraham Hill (1635-1721), a book collector. Among those listed is *The Ambitious Brother* by G. Buc. Adams suggests that Hill may have seen Buck's name as licenser and mistaken it for the author's name, and he warns that we should look to Eccles' biography for notice of other George Bucks. He considers it possible, however, that this is a dramatization by Buck of the subject of his *History* and cites Buck's devising the dumb shows for *Locrine* as evidence of his dramatic involvement.

We have Buck's own hand to witness that he devised these dumb shows. The play *Locrine* was published in 1595. In the copy now in the Bodmer collection in Geneva, he has written on the title page, 'Char. Tilney wrote *a* Tragedy of this matter *which* hee named Estrild. *& which* I think is this. it was *lost* by his death. & now *some* fellow hath published *it*. I made du*m*be shews for it. w*h*ich I yet haue. G.B.' Although Tannenbaum has attacked the hand as a Collier forgery,[6] his argument was satisfactorily refuted by R.C. Bald.[7] I see nothing in the inscription to suggest the hand is not Buck's own and consider it unlikely that a forger could have known Buck's hand so well as to have produced so minutely its every idiosyncracy.

Two works of Buck's on artistic subjects are lost. One is his *Poetica,* mentioned by Camden in his *Remaines* in comments on Sir Philip Sidney's epitaph, which he says is 'most happily imitated out of the French of *Mons. Boniuet,* made by *Joach. du Bellay,* as it was noted by Sir *George Buc* in his *Poetica'.*[8] Eccles remarks that in this observation Buck surpasses Raleigh's latest editor, who knows no source for the corresponding stanza of Raleigh's elegy on Sidney.[9] This work of Buck's on poets is probably the one he mentions in *The Third Universitie* in the section 'Of Poets and of Musitians' (Oooo[v]) as 'a particular Treatise', though it is difficult to tell from the context whether he is speaking here of a treatise on poetry or on drama. Chalmers states that Buck 'wrote a treatise — "of *Poets* and *Musicians*," which recent Inquirers have not been able to find'.[10] Presumably this is the same treatise, and Chalmers has simply adopted the section heading. Eccles notes[11] that the reference to Sidney suggests the work discussed contemporary poets. This would not be out of keeping with Buck's interests and activities, for although his antiquarian works and classical education tend to overshadow the other aspects of his career, he was professionally involved with one contemporary art form, the dramatic, was a dabbler in verse himself, and wrote a treatise on contemporary London.

It is fitting that a prolific author who held the post of Master of the Revels and possessed a peculiar sense of the dignity of things pertaining to his own origins and activities should have written about the art of the drama, in which he was so eminently involved. And indeed he did so, but his work is unfortunately not extant. Only this reference to it survives, in his summary of his comments on the craft of dramatic performance:

> I might hereunto adde for a *Corollary* of this discourse, the Art of *Reuels,* which requireth knowledge in Grammar, Rhetorike, Logicke, Philosophie, Historie, Musick, Mathematikes, & in other Arts (& all more then I vnderstand I confesse) & hath a setled place within this Cittie. But because I haue discribed it, and discoursed thereof at large in a particular commentarie, according to my talent, I will surcease to speake any more therof . . . .
> (*Third Universitie,* sig. Oooo 3[v]).

Buck's attitudes to poetry and drama were ambivalent.[12] Poetry was evidently for him, as for other gentlemen of his status and educational background, a fashionable pastime. His various comments in the *History* point to a contempt for fictitious works as frivolous in comparison with history, and his remarks on literary men are few and little concern their literary pursuits. Sidney is mentioned twice in the *Commentary,* both times merely as a valiant soldier (*Comm.,* ff. 354 and 370). The same concentration on Sidney's military at the expense of his literary skill is apparent in Buck's Latin elegy on Sidney mentioned above. Fulke Greville, whom Buck knew best as a fellow antiquary, is called in the *Commentary* 'a very noble & wis & learned gentilman' (f. 408) and of Thomas Sackville, Buck mentions only his honours and offices and an anecdote regarding his death (*Comm.,* f. 248). In a remark in the margin of his own copy of Bishop Godwin's *Catalogue of the Bishops of England* Buck says of Thomas Parkhurst, Bishop of Norwich in 1560, 'hee was a meetly good poet. & his poemes are extant',[13] but there are no other entries of this nature. Buck's comments in the *History* regarding More's poetic ability (text, pp. 121 and 196) are rather backhanded compliments, designed to discredit More as an historian. In the prose preface to *Daphnis,* he quotes Lydgate and Chaucer to support an argument that the terms 'England' and 'Britain' are used interchangeably, but passes from them very quickly to Higden. Like the modern historian, Buck is wary of citing fictional sources for factual information:

> *Ion Lidgate* disertly asseuereth in King *Arthurs* complaint in these words, *Great Britain now called England*: and so likewise doth *Geffrey Chaucer* in the *Franklins* tale (viz.) *In England, that Clepid was Britain*: And *Ranulfus Cestrensis* a grauer Authour peremptorily affirmeth that King *Egbert* . . . commaunded . . . that *Britain* should bee called *England.*
>
> (sig. B 4)

Nearly all Buck's quotations from poets and playwrights are classical, though occasionally he quotes foreign Renaissance writers such as Ariosto.

English translators fare rather better in Buck's esteem. He several times speaks highly of Harington as translator of *Orlando Furioso* (*Third Universitie,* sig. Nnnn^v; *Comm.,* f.417; *History,* text, p. 168). He makes reference once to North's translation of Plutarch (*Comm.,* f. 426^v).

We must be wary of assessing Buck's attitude to the stage, since most of the remarks on it which have been habitually attributed to him may well be editorial additions to the *History,* and it is impossible to tell in some cases whether they represent the author's intention or are merely embellishments. In one case, where we have both the autograph version and the editorial ones, it is clear that a reference to the stage is entirely the editor's addition. When speaking of Richard's calumniators and their attacking him by reference to his bad dreams, Buck himself (text, pp. 128) makes no mention of dramatic versions, nor does the editor in his handwritten copies. But in the printed version the editor, George Buck, Esq., gives us, 'nay, they will dissect his very sleepes, to finde prodigious dreames and bug-beares, . . . which they dresse in all the fright and horrour fiction and the stage can adde.'[14] Consequently, we must not be too hasty in accepting for Buck's final assessment of the stage, as Frank Marcham does,[15] This remark, of which there is no trace in the autograph manuscript, but which appears in some form in all the editorial versions:

> ffor the ignorant, and never-vnderstandeing vulgare; whose faith (in history) is drawne from Pamphlet and Ballad, and their Reverend and learned Autors, the stage, or those that playe the bauds to it, for a liveing, Let them fly their owne pitch, for they are but kytes, and Crowes, and can digest nought (soe well) as stench and filth, to which I leaue them.
>
> (B.L. MS. Egerton 2216, f. 270)

It is natural that Buck should show to some extent a gentleman's contempt for drama, because as fiction it distorts the truth of history, and because it panders to the common people in their ignorance. Buck in his own writings appeals specifically to the learned reader. This attitude toward poetry and drama is evident in his remarks on More, when he says that poetry assists in writing fables and relating fantasies, giving authors licence to tell false tales:

> And that Sir Thomas More was a good poet and much
> delighted with poetry and with quaint inventions, his many
> poems and epigrams yet extant testify; besi[des] the many
> petty comedies and interludes which he made and often-
> times acted in person with the rest of the actors. . . . And to
> these, his practices fantastical and his *Utopia* may be added.
>
> (*History*, text, p. 121)

A contempt for playwrights and actors appears somewhat obscurely in a Latin remark he added to a Revels Office note in his own hand which appears, crossed out, in one of the pages inserted late into the *Commentary*: 'Mimis genua flectuntur ad sagos prophani'.[16]

On the other hand he is moved by the ancient origins of drama and by the honour it bestows on him and on his city to refer to it as 'That first and most auncient kind of Poesy', and to accord the art as practised in his time the highest praise: 'so liuely expressed and represented vpon the publike stages & Theaters of this citty, as *Rome* in the *Auge* of her pompe & glorie, neuer saw it better performed, (I meane in respect of the action, and art, and not of the cost, and sumptousnesse)' (*Third Universitie*, sig. Oooo^v).

Because his place in literature is determined not so much by his own compositions as by the fact that those of so many greater authors passed through his hands and received the imprint of his directions for revision, we should be glad to possess his detailed observations on the arts he supervised. But since these are lost, we can only pursue in as great detail as possible, by picking them here and there from his extant works, the character, opinions, and intellectual bent of the man who touched so many of our greatest dramatic works.

Daphnis Polystephanos

Δαφνις Πολυστεφανος, 'An Eclog treating Of Crownes, and of Garlandes, and to whom of right they appertaine', is an historical-pastoral poem in fifty-eight stanzas in honour of James I's coronation, although Buck says in his dedication to the new king that he began the work 'long since' (sig. A3). It was published in 1605 but seems to have been prepared in 1602 in anticipation of James' accession. The British Library's Grenville copy (shelfmark G 11553), presented by Buck to Henry Howard, Earl of Northampton, which includes a genealogical tree tracing the Plantagenets back to Egbert in 802, has a printed note 'Ioan. Woutneel excud. 1602' at the lower righthand corner of this tree. Buck in pen has altered the '2' to '5'.

Daphnis purports to show the glory of King James' ancestors and sets forth his descent from Henry II through the Tudors. James is reconciler of the intestine quarrel between the sons of Brute, Albanact, and Locrine, as Henry VII was reconciler of the quarrel between Lancaster and York. Faced with the necessity of praising the Tudors as James' ancestors, it is surprising that Buck is able to speak kindly of Richard III:

> Fame hath been sharp to th'other [Richard], yet bicause
> All accusations of him are not proued:
> And hee built Churches, and made good law's,
> And all men held him wise, and valiant,
> Who may deny him then his *Genest* plante?
> (sig. E4ᵛ)

Buck's sense of historical honesty and family pride seem to have combined in compelling him to champion this king. He notes in his Epistle Dedicatory that among the faults others have found in the poem is 'that I haue concealed, and coloured the faultes of bad Princes' (sig. A4ᵛ). He excuses himself on the grounds of Christian charity. That this statement refers specifically to his defence of Richard is suggested strongly by his going on directly to mention on the same page that his own family has been obscure since 'the fatall iourney at *Bosworth*'.

His attitude toward Henry VII is ambiguous. In one stanza Buck praises him in conventional terms:

> This *Richmont* was a very prudent prince
> And therefore was surnamed *Solomon*.
> The world hath seen great works accomplish'd since
> Which were proiected by this *Theodore*.
>   This man of GOD did happily atone
>   The ciuil feud, whidh [*sic*] long had been before,
>   Betwixt the Rose, which first grew in the wood
>   And that which Venns [*sic*] colour'd in hir blood.
>   (sig. F2)

But in a marginal note to this he says, 'hee extinguished the male line of *Yorke*'.

In addition to his defence of Richard, many other themes developed in his later work are struck here. The poem's title and central image are of a garland made from the *planta genista*, whose origins he discusses, citing, as in the *History* (text, p. 15) Leonhard Fuchs as an authority (sig. Dᵛ). Another of his antiquarian interests, the Stone of Scone, to which he returns in the *History* (text, pp. 215f), is briefly mentioned in the dedication (sig. A3ᵛ). His own family history appears not only in the dedication, but also in a marginal note to the verse on King John, where he speaks of Walter Buck's assistance to this king (sig. E3). A very considerable portion of the dedication is taken up with praise of the Howards for fostering his family, and their genealogy is touched upon.

Buck's heroes are the same here as later in the *History*. He shows particular interest in Henry II, spending on him the major part of the Introduction and beginning the poem with him. He is described as 'the greatest King (of whom there is any credible story extant) which hath been in this Isle of *Britain* since the time of the Romaine Emperous [*sic*] . . .' (sig. B3ᵛ). So anxious is Buck to show the magnitude of Henry's empire that he denies James I his claim to be the first ruler of the whole island: 'a late *Anonymous* in a little book dedicated to his Majesty, affirmeth that neuer any Prince was king of this whole Isle vntill now. But he is deceiued . . .' (sig. B3ᵛ). Queen Elizabeth as usual merits an effusion:

> A Queene, whose state so happily did stand
> That men did say (seeing hir greatnesse such)
> This Lady leadeth fortnne [*sic*] in hir hand
> A virgin which did keep hir lamp still light
> And eke for tarenes was a *Phaenix* height.
> (sig. F3ᵛ)

Like his loyalties, his prejudices are the same as in the *History*. He refuses to acknowledge Henry IV's title, but grants him to have been a 'princely Knight' (sig. F). His anti-Catholic feeling is strong: 'To sweep out of this land the drosse of *Roome*; / A worke of worth . . .' (F2ᵛ). He is wary of the 'British History': 'to haue chosen any of the most ancient Kings, I must haue looked so farre backe, as I should not onely haue made this Eclog ouer-long, and tedious, but also haue lost my selfe in the cloudes of obscurity by soring too high amongst them . . .' (sig. B3). He does mention, parenthetically, that the Tudors were descended from Cadwallader, but in general he inclines far more toward the sort of genealogy that can be documented by the heralds.

His methods here are similar to those in his antiquarian prose works. He begins with a genealogical dedication and an historical introduction and accompanies both his prose introduction and his poem with marginal notes which include historical and genealogical information, very exact citation of sources, and classical references. Certain sources cited in the poem are used again in the *History*: Buchanan, Giraldus Cambrensis, Camden, De la Hay, Du Haillan, Fabyan, Froissart, Ingulf, Liber St Stephani (Caen), William of Malmesbury, William of Newburgh, John of Salisbury, Serres, Stow, Walsingham.

This work is interesting as an example of Buck's literary style and interests and as an indication that as early as about 1602 the methods and extent of historical research and the opinions developed in the *History* were already far advanced and firmly established. It has as well a side-line interest because it went through exactly the same process of transformation as the *History*, passing through a manuscript revision and a new edition, published in 1635 under the title *The Great Plantagenet*, by Buck's great-nephew, George Buck, Esq.[17]

The Third Universitie

THE THIRD VNIVERSITE OF ENGLAND. OR A
TREATISE OF THE FOVNDATIONS OF ALL THE
COLLEDGES, AVNCIENT SCHOOLES OF PRIVI-
LEDGE, AND OF HOVSES OF LEARNING, AND

LIBERALL ARTS WITHIN AND ABOVT THE MOST
FAMOUS CITTIE OF LONDON. WITH A BRIEFE
REPORT OF THE SCIENCES, ARTS, AND FACVL-
TIES THEREIN PROFESSED, STVDIED, AND
PRACTISED. Together with the Blazon of the Armes,
and Ensignes thereunto belonging. Gathered faithfully out
of the best Histories, Chronicles, Records, and Archiues,
by G.B. Knight. ANNO DOMINI, 1615.

This work forms part of an appendix to Stow's *Annales* as edited by Edmond
Howes, who includes and expands Stow's own accounts of the 'other' two universities
in England and adds to them Buck's treatise on London. The work is well organized.
It discusses under their headings the numerous 'schools' within the 'university':
divinity, liberal arts, languages, law, medicine, navigational sciences, poetry, music,
dance, painting, heraldry, athletics, and drama. For all these Buck gives origin and
history, gathered from various sources, and where possible he has consulted original
charters. The description and history of each foundation is accompanied by a
description of its arms, collected for Buck by Camden and Charles, Clarenceux and
Lancaster heralds. Probably in Buck's own manuscript of this work the arms were
actually drawn and coloured as they are in his manuscript *Commentary*. So creditable
is this treatise that it earned Buck in William Maitland's estimation a place after Stow
as an early historian of London.[18]

It is useful to survey Buck's research methods in this one published and well-
organized antiquarian work, for the *History* was not published according to his
wishes, never reached a final draft under his hand, and as it stands in his rough draft is
not well organized. In addition to original annals, charters, and records, he relies in
The Third Universitie both on printed sources, historical and literary, and on *viva
voce* information from contemporary antiquarian scholars such as St Low Kniveton,
Sir James Ley, Sir Robert Cotton, Dr Andrewes, and a Dr Palmer who helped with
the chapter on medical studies. One of these *viva voce* references is particularly
interesting, since it is second hand: Buck cites the information of a fellow scholar
whom he trusts, though he himself has not been able to see the document in
question, when he speaks of Wolsey's building plan for Doctors Commons according
to the information of Cotton, who saw it and told Buck about it (sig. Nnnn5). There
is a famous example of similar practice in the *History* (text, p. 121), where Buck refers
to Morton's original of More's *History of Richard III* on the information of Sir
Edward Hoby, who saw it. That this sort of reference exists here in a published work
indicates that such a method of documentation was acceptable practice.[19]

For general information Buck uses a treatise describing London written under
Henry II, Stow's *Survey*, the Statutes at Large of Henry VIII, and the works of
antiquaries and chroniclers. He refers to Du Haillan and Matthew Paris, as he does
often in the *History*. On ecclesiastical foundations, he cites ancient church fathers,
Francis Dilingham's *De Comparatione Petri cum Paulo*, Godwin's *Catalogue of the
Bishops of England*, and 'an old monument'. His discussion of the legal foundations

comes largely from his own experience and through *viva voce* information from his friends and acquaintances who had, like him, been trained in law schools. He refers to a work in private hands, a book of arms, 'enlumined in an auncient manuscripte booke of the foundation, and Statutes of this [templers'] order belonging to the right honorable, and most learned noble Gentlemanne the Lorde *William Howard* of Naworth' (sigs. Nnnn-Nnnn^v).

He quotes Castiglione on arts suitable for a gentleman and cites a series of Italian authors on riding and fencing. He mentions Ludovico Dulce, Georgius Fabritius, and Julius Caesar Scaliger as people who have written on poetry, and on dancing he cites Tommaso Garzoni's *Piazza Universale*, Discorso 45: *De Ballarini*, as well as Plato. Philo and Aristotle are authorities on painting, and on cosmetology, described as a branch of painting, he quotes from Lucilius.

The work is sprinkled with quotations, mainly in Latin, as is the *History*. Often these are documented, but sometimes Buck obviously expects them to be well known, when he mentions an author simply as 'the old poet' or 'our rare countreyman'. Of course many of the quotations may be proverbial, the author simply not known or considered. Buck's treatment of the Lucilius quotation is interesting in illustrating a practice which appears time and time again in the *History*: he states that he 'will set [it] downe in Greeke, because I haue not seen it in Latine' and follow it with his own English translation (sig. Oooo3). Evidently it was usual to find in commonplace books Latin translations of Greek quotations. If a Latin translation were available, it seems to have been proper to give it instead of the Greek original. If none were available, the original was presented, with an accompanying translation written for the occasion.

The Third Universitie is a useful source of information on Buck's personality and certain biographical details, as indeed is every work he writes. Pride of family, profession, and social status lead him to a sense of the dignity and worth of these attributes and a profound regard for and study of their origins. To the Inns of Court, he says, come 'young Gentlemen, the sonnes of the best or better sorte of Gentlemenne of all the Shires of England (and which haue beene formerly bred, and brought vppe liberally in good schooles, and other Uniuersitys)' (sig. Nnnn2^v). A man cannot be made a gentleman simply by being on the register of the Inns of Court,

> for no man can be made a Gentleman but by his father.
> And . . . the King (who hath power to make Esquiers,
> Knightes, Baronets, Barons, Viscounts, Earles, Marquesses,
> and Dukes) cannot make a Gentleman, for Gentilitie is a
> matter of race, and of bloud, and of discent, from gentile
> and noble parents, and auncestors, which no Kings can
> giue to any, but to such as they beget.
> (sig. Mmmm6)

As for his own education, there is a suggestion that he may have attended Trinity Hall, Cambridge, for he mentions 'Maister *Henry Haruey*, Doctor of the ciuill and canon Lawes, maister of Trinitie Hall in *Cambridge*, Prebendarie of *Ely*, and Deane of the Arches, a reuerend, learned and good man whom I being a young Scholler knew' (sig. Nnnn4^v). As we shall see, a remark in the *Commentary* confirms this suggestion of Buck's education at Cambridge. At his 'first comming to London', he was admitted to Thavies' Inn as a probationer and then proceeded to the Middle Temple, to which he wishes 'all honour, and prosperity (for my particuler obligation, hauing beene sometimes a fellow, and Student (or to confesse a truth) a trewand of that most honourable Colledge' (sig. Nnnn2). He describes the process of law study as long and painful, but seems to have had time to hear Dr William Padey read an anatomy lecture. However, of music he can give only second hand reports.

The modesty which balances his self-esteem is winning, when he speaks of himself as a truant, of his translation from Lucilius as 'mine owne homely translation' (sig. Ooo3), and when he confesses that the art of the Revels demands knowledge of more subjects than he understands.

His style of dedication, as can be seen again in the *History* (text, pp. 3-5), is sincere in its professions of friendship and at the same time preserves the author's sense of his own dignity. Very different it is from his great-nephew's weak, subservient, conventional protestations to prospective patrons. Buck writes his dedications to people he knows. To his friend Coke, who was responsible for *The Third Universitie's* publication, he writes, 'and albeit I doe not (in complementing manner) make daily profession of this my obligation (as many vse to doe) yet there is no man shall bee more readie to doe to your Lordshippe any honour, or seruice, then my poore selfe . . .' (sig. Mmmm).

Aside from his description of law study, one of the most interesting items in *The Third Universitie* is Buck's list of proposals for urban improvement, which he provides in case, he says, rich citizens abstain from useful works for lack of knowledge of what needs to be done:

> to build a Theater, for the more safe and certaine, and wholesome hearing of the sermons in Paules Church-yard, *Item* to repaire and beautifie Paules steeple, and to re-furnish the Belfrey thereof. *Item* to make a faire piazza, or Market place within London, such as is and ought to be in euery good Cittie, and to be placed as the manner is, neere to the Towne hall . . . . *Item* to paue Smithfield. *Item* to erect faire arched gates at the bounds of the Liberties, where now beast fences or wooden barres and rayles stand. *Item* to enlarge the cumbersome and dangerous straits of the royall and more publike wayes of this Cittie . . . that the hallowed ground of S. *Pauls* churchyard may no more bee trampled and prophaned with beasts, and Cartes, and Coaches . . . . *Item* to deliuer the wals of the Cittie and the Towne ditch, from the pester and encumbrances of tene-ments, and gardens, & other priuate vses, and to open that Ditch, and to bring a Ryuer or fresh currant into it. And lastly . . . to supplie the suburbes with new parrish Churches, wherein by reason of the exceeding encrease of newe houses and tenements, the people and inhabitaunts are so extremely

> multiplied, as the old churches . . . are not able to conteyne
> the fourth part of the people . . . . Of these projects and
> good workes, the richer citizens . . . may make their choise
> according to their affections, fancies, deuotions, or
> abilities . . . .
>
> (sig. Nnnn 6)

Buck had a gentle sense of humour, too.

The only other printed work by Buck on a contemporary subject is a ten page
abstract of his account of the Cadiz expedition printed in Stow's *Annales* (1601) as
'An Abstract of the expedition to Cadiz 1596, drawne out of Commentaries written
at large thereof, by a gentleman who was in the voyage'.[20] Nothing of the original
treatise survives.

The Commentary, Archigenealogicon, and The Baron

Three antiquarian works preceded the *History* and provided material for it. Two of
them, *Archigenealogicon* and *The Baron,* are lost. The third, *A Commentary on the
Book of Domus Dei*, survives in manuscript. It is not possible to reconstruct either of
the two missing treatises or even to guess at the period of their composition. It is
clear, however, that they all partake to some extent of each other, reproducing and
expanding at many points the same information, relying on the same sources. We
know from *Daphnis* that the research which culminates in the *Commentary* and the
History was well advanced before 1605.

The Commentary

That the *Commentary* was written in 1614 is attested by numerous statements in
the body of the work which mention persons 'now living, 1614'. The manuscript,
some 800 pages of Buck's neatest hand, appears to be in finished form, not, like the
History, still in the process of revision. Additions seem to have been made in the
form of short notes on tipped in pages, on slips pasted over portions of a page, or
above the lines and in the margins of the text, though these practices are much less
frequent than in the *History*. In the later additions the dates mentioned are 1616,
1617, and 1618, and the information in one of them dates from 1621. Occasionally a
name is left out and dots substituted for it. Sources are given carefully, normally
including page numbers, and there is considerable cross-referencing with others of
Buck's own works. He supplies an index. The manuscript is illustrated with shields,
some coloured, some merely sketched in. The shields are described, and elaborate
family trees inserted in another hand — the same hand in which the genealogical
manuscript B.L. MS. Cotton Julius B XII is written — probably that of one of Buck's
herald friends. Later owners of the manuscript have added marginal notes and
additional material, bringing Buck's information up to date in the 1640's and again in
the 1660's, as Buck himself used the margins of his copy of Godwin's *Catalogue of
the Bishops of England* to add information and comments and bring ecclesiastical
appointments up to date.

The title page, in Buck's hand, reads:

> A COMMENTARY Vpon the New Roulle of Winchester,
> Comonly called Liber Domus DEI. &c. Especially con-
> cerning the Baronage, & ancient Nobility of ENGLAND.
> TOGETHER WITH A SVPPLEMENT of other ancient
> noble families of this kingdome not mentioned in the sayd
> Roulle or Book. faithfully gathered out of royall, & publik
> archives, roulles, & charters: & out of private evidences,
> histories, & other monumen*tes* authentik. By George Buc
> Knight one of the gent. of the Kings privy chamber, &
> Mas*ter* of his highnes office of the REVELLS. Wherin the
> Authours chef scope is not to mak exact graduall genea-
> logies but to shew the originall ancesterr & first founder of
> those said noble families w*i*th som*e of* their mo*st* segnall
> posteres & the stat of them & those w*h*ich yet continew &
> florish or els *the* translations & *the* period*es* of the said
> families.

The purpose of the work is to list all noble families in England 'whose ancestors
haue bene at the least simple barons, & to shew the origine & continuance of them'
(f. 3). Buck omits to go into all the alliances and family branches, since he considers
this to be tedious and a task more suited to the heralds. He attempts to confine
himself to families' origins, which he considers much neglected, and only summarizes
their continuance, noting that Glover has traced the genealogies in detail. The work
is divided into three sections: Saxon families, families which came with the Conqueror
and families descending from foreign leaders brought in by King John. His own
ancestors come under the last heading.

Aside from the long discourse on his own family, and a few comments on the worth
of his friends when he cites them as sources for his information, the most important
autobiographical notice regards his studying at Cambridge. Mentioning the name
Pinqueney, he says, 'I rem*em*ber that ther was a yong gentilm*an* of that surname a
[stud] scholler in C*a*mbridg in my tyme' (f. 179). Interesting is his comment on his
intended successor in office: 'S*i*r John Astley now of the Kings pr. chamber & my
successor designed by the Ks patent*es* in reversion' (f. 412). Astley, who was granted
the reversion in 1612, actually did succeed Buck as Master of the Revels when the
latter in 1622 became, by reason of mental decline, incapable of executing the office.
One further bit of interesting autobiographical information concerns his service
under the Lord Admiral, Lord Charles Howard, Earl of Nottingham:

> & as I haue shewed *that* the most noble Howard*es* have ben
> principall patrons & benefactors to my ancestor*es* so I haue
> found them my exceding good & favorable lord*es*: & in
> *pa*rticular & most especially my L. Charles Howard Erl of
> Notingha*m* & high Adm of Engl. whom for more then two
> yeres I followed as a servant, but he of his most noble

> goodnes vsed me rather like a frend & kinsman. then lik a
> servant, & in that anno mirabile viz. 1588 he prefered me
> to Q. Elizab. my most gracious mistress . . . .
>
> (f.453ᵛ)

Buck's use of sources, far more carefully documented than in the damaged and unfinished *History*, is interesting. The majority of sources cited in the *Commentary* are used also in the *History*. Because the incomplete state, the damage by fire, and the editing of the *History* have called Buck's use of sources in question, it would be worthwhile to list here those common to the *History* and to the very carefully documented *Commentary*:[21] [*Axiomata*] *Politica*; Bale; Bracton; Camden; Cicero; Coggeshall; Coke; Du Haillan; Du Tillet; Erasmus; Froissart; Glover; Godwin; Guiccardini; Hall; Heuterus; Holinshed; Hoveden; Huntingdon; Ingulf; Liber Eliensis; Liber St Stephani, Caen; Meyer; Velleius Paterculus; Prateius; El Reusuerq; Rolls; Scaccarii; Stow; Tower Archives; Walsingham; Wendover; Westminster.

In addition, he gives references to several original records and to manuscript books in private hands. He points out the difficulty of documenting such material: '. . . I readd it in an old manuscript book, & nameless as many of them bee . . .' (f.353). He used private libraries as sources of manuscript material: those of Cotton; his cousin Philip Tilney; the heralds Brook, Charles and St George; the Lord Admiral, Charles Howard, Earl of Nottingham; and Lord William Howard of Naworth. At one point he has made a note to himself, probably to express his own excitement about some information he has found in a private collection: he says a charter for creating the Earl of Surrey Duke of Norfolk under Henry VIII 'was the first record *that* I saught in the Roull being sent by the L. Ad. Ch. Howar Er. of Not.' (f.23ᵛ). He crossed this note out when inserting this page as a late addition to the *Commentary*. Nicholas Charles, Lancaster Herald, searched the records (presumably those of the College of Arms) for information on Buck's own family. Camden's *Remaines* is cited in manuscript rather than in its published form. Buck employs a considerable amount of *viva voce* information, both from antiquarian scholars and from representatives of the families whose origins he was tracing, since family traditions, documents, and objects are likely to have been passed down through generations. For *viva voce* information he cites Cotton, Camden, Stow, St Low Kniveton, Ralph Brook (York Herald), Sir Robert Carey, Lord Hunsdon, Sir Henry Wotton, Sir Thomas Vavasor, Lady Mary Vere, Baroness Willoughby, and particularly the Lord Admiral and Lord William Howard. Some of the *viva voce* information has apparently been stored in his memory for many years:

> Sir Tho. Tindale . . . beng a very old knight told me beng
> then a very yong man that the states & barons of Boheme
> sent to N. Tindale an ancestor of his to requir him to com to
> Boheme to take vpon him the Kingdome ᵗherof as beng the
> next heyre, & that in token herof they sent a crown & a
> scepter & a cloth of Estat & other regall ensignes, & the

> which as he told me then wer all to be seen yet at his house
> in Norfolk.
>
> (f.384)

In view of his later use of *viva voce* evidence in the *History*, particularly the instance
already mentioned (text, p. 121), this reference is noteworthy, showing that Buck
considered acceptable documentation in a finished work a reference to verbal
information he had received at some previous time concerning articles which his
informant described but he himself had never seen.

Buck's approach to his sources is critical; he does not simply accept what he reads
but qualifies it in the light of extensive research. Recent authors, particularly, he is at
pains to correct when occasions arise. On many occasions he states that he is
accepting Camden's authority on the basis of Camden's worth as a scholar and
because conflicting information cannot be found. This suggests that he was in the
habit of considering conflicting information before accepting a statement as authoritative. At one point he indicates that reference to a primary source — a deed in the
hands of Lord Howard — proves a statement of Camden's incorrect. On another
occasion he says that Stow is mistaken about a pedigree. Buck's sense of justice to
historical figures who were maligned by his contemporaries appears when he cites in
Matthew Paris a eulogy saying that Walter de Gray, Archbishop of York, was wise,
good, and continent: 'I would haue Dr Goodwin well to mark this, bycaus, he hath
written nothing of him but scandale in his Catalogue of Bishops' (f.206).

Nor does he accept information merely because it is old, but he subjects the source
to scrutiny. He is willing to credit a nameless manuscript book on the origins of the
Herberts 'bycaus I have seen therin many thing*es* carefully, iudiciously & faithfully
collected & observed' (f.353). The Roll of Battle Abbey, on the other hand, cannot
be taken as authentic, because the monks flattered their patrons by adding them to it.
In many places Buck shows a wariness of scribal errors. For example, he knows his
own copy of Domesday Book occasionally to have been corrupted: 'I am in dout *that*
my scribe w*h*ich copied the book of Domus dei w*h*ich I haue hath corrupted these
names, & in sted of Jury hath put Lury, w*h*ich is an error easily committed by reason
of the likenes of j & l' (f.228).

Buck's attitude to the 'British History' is very cautious, for he is speaking as an
historian, not, as in *Daphnis,* as a poet. He declines to present ancient Briton and
Saxon genealogies because 'they ar so high and so remote as that they are either
vnknown or els corrupted w*i*th fables' (f.3). Yet he does employ the traditional myth
in connection with the Tudors to some extent: Tudor, he says, is the oldest of all
houses, and he presents a pedigree deriving it from King Cole,

> for the hon*our* & religious & im*m*ortal loue w*h*ich I beare
> to the most renowned & most Glorious princess Q.
> Elizabeth who was descended & propagated out of this
> great & ancient & royall hous of Britayn. & hir coming was
> foretold by the tale of the return of K. Artur as some & not
> absurdly interpret it.
>
> (f.4ᵛ)

His worship of Queen Elizabeth, constant in all his works, reappears in an auto-biographical passage where he calls her 'my most gracious mistress, who now is in Glory in heaven & shall for her war vertues aboue her sex be euer honored vpon the erth' (f.453ᵛ). He quotes a eulogy, evidently composed by himself, which is written on her picture in his house (ff. 8ᵛ-9). He is not, however, very charitable to Henry VII, of whom he says merely that he was crowned in the right of his wife.

There are mentions of other personages and families which figure in the *History*. Of people connected with Richard III Buck is not always correctly informed in the *Commentary*, but some of the opinions presented later in the *History* seem already well formed. He gives incorrect information about people peripheral to Richard's story, giving Hastings' Christian name as Edward and saying that Rivers became Lord Scales in right of his wife under Richard III. But he has searched carefully the history of Richard's close friend Francis, Viscount Lovell, presenting his titles on the basis of research done for him by Nicholas Charles, Lancaster Herald, and noting that 'this Viscount Lovell was attainted by him who hated all them that his praecessor K.R.3. loved to witt K.H.7.' (f. 141ᵛ). Already Buck seems convinced that Perkin Warbeck was actually Richard, Duke of York, for he notes that Henry VII executed Sir William Stanley for supporting 'Rich duk of York al*ias* Perkin Warbeck' (f.254ᵛ).

In the *Commentary*, between ff. 354 and 355 appears a group of set in pages on the descent of the Herberts which were clearly an early draft intended for the *History*. When Buck, about five years after the completion of the *Commentary*, was involved in composing the *History*, he seems to have discarded these few pages as too digressive and inserted them instead in the *Commentary*, to which they were better suited. He then rewrote the matter on the Herberts which was to appear in the *History*, paring it down to dimensions suitable to that work.[22] In only one other place does this use of a discarded page from the *History* to form a late insertion in the *Commentary* occur. F. 3ᵛ of the *Commentary* is written on the back of an upside down and crossed out draft of the *History*'s title page, a fortunate occurrence, since no title page appears in the autograph manuscript of the *History* in its present state.

The accounts of the Howard family are very similar in the *Commentary* and the *History*, and the same sources are used. The wording is closer to the sources in the *Commentary*'s account, whereas the *History* employs freer paraphrase. The same is true of the accounts of Buck's own family, but in the *History* he corrects some details and makes more plausible conjectures.

Buck mentions the *Commentary* only twice in the *History*. He refers to it as a proving ground for his methods of historical research, informing the reader that he will attempt to discover the origins of the name Plantagenet 'according to my small talent of knowledge and reading and according to the methods I have held for the searching of the originals of the most ancient noble families of England, of their surnames in my *Commentary upon the Book of Domus Dei, or The New Roll of Winchester*' (text, p. 11). He apologizes for his long discussions of the Howard family origins by saying 'I shall be . . . pardoned because I have done the like honour and service to many other the most noble families of this country in my *Commentaries in Librum Domus Dei*' (text, p. 110).

The provenance of the *Commentary* cannot be traced back very far. During the seventeenth century it was owned by persons who continued to make notes in it, and notes tipped in in the eighteenth century show an interest in lawyers and in Berkshire lands, perhaps indicating the profession and residence of the owners. The first owner who can be traced is Major G. Halswell of Devonshire, who died in 1935. R.C. Bald 'discovered' the manuscript in his possession in 1927, mistaking it at first for Buck's lost book *The Baron*.[23] He corrected this assumption when he discussed the work more fully in 1935.[24] Until 1969, Major W. Halswell, son of the previous owner, was unable to trace it and assumed that his father had sold it.[25] In 1969 while moving to a different house, Major W. Halswell rediscovered it. It was purchased by the Bodleian Library in 1972.

Archigenealogicon

Buck refers several times in the *Commentary* to a manuscript work of his own by the name of *Archigenealogicon*. A reference to both it and the *Baron* in the same passage makes us hesitate in identifying them as the same work: Buck tells us that we may see more of the Howard family in 'Baronor*um* Genealogue s*e*cu*n*d*u*m tempora reg*u*m in principio. & in Archigenealogico*n*' (f. 20). What the very few references to it lead us to conclude is that it was a genealogical treatise concentrating on the details of descent and on the various branches of families rather than on the origins of families as the *Commentary* does: 'Ther be divers other Blunt*es* in other shires, the w*h*ich all you may see in my MS. Archigenealogico*n* wher I haue deduced at large all *the* pedegree of the Blounts with their Alliance with some Spanish noble houses, & the rest vndiquaq*ue*' (f.127ᵛ). We are told to look in *Archigenealogicon* under 'Foix' for the family of Geily, evidently a branch of the Foix family. In the *Commentary*, attempting to avoid considering in detail the numerous branches of families, Buck says, 'Vide . . . in Archigenealo. MS.' for Walter Buck's genealogy f. 389), and later he refers us to it for a warrant of Robert Buck under Edward II, 'as also for the orderly descent*es* for here for brevity \& my methode/ sake I omitt many. but thyre ar sett down in a strict gradual succession' (f. 452ᵛ). We are also to see *Archigenealogicon* for all the issue of Philip, Earl of Arundel (f.21ᵛ).

Clearly the two things that Buck attempts to avoid in the *Commentary* so that he may confine himself to origins — branchings of families through intermarriages and a minute cataloguing of descent — he has dealt with in *Archigenealogicon*.

Bald conjectures that this work might be identifiable as the *Collections Historical and Genealogical of Sir George Buck, Kt.*, at one time possessed by John Strype,[26] but this description might equally well apply to the *Baron* or the *Commentary* or, as Bald suggests, 'my Antiquary MS.' to which Buck refers in the *Commentary*, f.59, though this would seem to me to be part of the *Baron*.[27]

The Baron

From the numerous references in the *Commentary* and the *History* to *The Baron, or the Magazin of Honour*, it is possible to some slight extent to reconstruct its history and contents, but it still remains a very great puzzle. We can judge from the references to it in the *Commentary* that it was unfinished in 1614, and was evidently just beginning to take shape then: '. . . I have written largely thereof in my \ Baron / [advertisemen*t*es before Glovers Catalogue, & in my Antiquary MS. sic inscripto.]' (f. 59). This seems to suggest that the work originated as a commentary on Glover's *Catalogue of Honour (*1610) or as material supplementary to it. Again Buck gives a reference 'vt In meis Adve*r*tisemen*t*s ante Glover' (f.254ᵛ). Glover's *Catalogue* does contain considerable prefatory material written by other well known antiquaries such as Camden. It is possible that Buck, too, was writing a treatise for inclusion there, as the *Third Universitie* was included as supplementary material to Stow's *Annales.* The work may have captured his interest so that it grew beyond the bounds of a supplementary treatise and became a manuscript work of several books divided into various chapters.

When Buck was completing the *Commentary,* the *Baron* seems still to have been in process of transition from being a supplement to Glover to being a work in its own right, and Buck has not yet completely settled on its title but sometimes describes it instead of giving it a title: 'Barono*r*u*m* Genealogue *s*ecu*n*du*m* tempora regu*m*' (f.20ᵛ), or 'book of Barons' (ff. 369 and 383ᵛ). Elsewhere there is a reference, 'vide Barone*m* meu*m* in Marchi**' (f. 45ᵛ). The decisive crossing out of the description 'advertisemen*t*es before Glovers Catalogue, & in my Antiquary MS.' to substitute 'Baron' suggests that a Glover supplement and another antiquarian work were joined together under a single title. That there are in the *Commentary* a few explicit references to the *Baron* citing book numbers suggests that the work had crystallized during the final stages of the *Commentary's* composition. By 1619 when the *History* was written, there is no longer any indecision in references to it by title, and book and chapter numbers are given. Still, Buck calls it a 'rude work' (text, p. 6), and the variety of matters mentioned in it to which Buck makes reference in the *History* suggests that it was rather amorphous.

There seem to have been at least sixteen books. Book I was entitled 'Vicomitu*m* et Barono*rum* Catalogus Genealogicis' (*Comm.* f. 383ᵛ) and contained among other things, eulogies of the Howards. A clue to the material in this early section may be gleaned from a table of contents appearing between ff. 349 and 351 of the *Commentary.* The numbers are evidently page numbers, and, except for 153, which appears twice, they correspond to the page numbers that are missing at the beginning of the *Commentary,* whose numbering starts with p. 31. It appears that Book I of the *Baron* was at one time the opening section of the *Commentary.* These early pages seem, from the headings in the table of contents, extremely close in content to the prefatory material in Glover's *Catalogue,* as does Buck's statement in the *Commentary* that he has written at length in the *Baron* of the distinction between nobility and gentry. Camden speaks similarly of his own work on the subject: in an antiquarian discourse, 'The Etymology and Original of Barons', he says, 'I have elsewhere said somewhat of *Barones* [i.e., in Glover's *Catalogue*], therefore if now I be shorter, it may be more pardonable'.[28] Perhaps Buck's work was prevented for some reason — possibly duplication by other scholars — from becoming part of the prefatory material for Glover's *Catalogue.* Such a duplication may have forced Buck to attach these early pages to another work of his own, the *Commentary*. They did not really fit the *Commentary* and so broke off to form part of the *Baron,* which was growing as the *Commentary* was being completed and seems to have served as a sort of catchall. The table of contents refers to material entirely concerned with titles, offices, and estates. Headings include:

Adela ⎫
Adeling ⎬ 4
βαρεις 7.8
Baronis ecclesiast. 15
Barones iurisperiti 29.31
Barones forain̄. 17
Baron &   defined 12. &c
   Baronie 22.16.21.153
Baronia diminuta 23
Baronies claymed
Barons by letters pat.
barons by summons.
Baronetts. 5. Baronuli 5
fief noble quid. 22.153
Honor gift of a Soverain Pr. 19

Judges of the Kingd. 29.31
Knights fee 22.16.153
Marchiae barones
Marchisij ⎫
Marchiones ⎬ 495
Privileges of barons. 25
Principalities inferior to Baronies. 13
Thane 3
Tain 4
Vavasor 5. in marg.
Vnderthane ⎫
Vpthane ⎬ 4
   or Abthane
Writt of Summons. 18.24

It will be noted that the reference on f. 45ᵛ mentioned 'Baronem meum in Marchi∗∗', to which any one of three headings in this list may correspond. That the material to which this index refers was originally part of the *Commentary* is attested by citation of p. 153. On that page in the *Commentary,* now labelled f. 94, Buck crosses out a passage and refers the reader to the *Baron* for information on what a knight's fee was. In the reference to 'Knights fee' in the index, the page numbers 22, 16, and 153 are given. It thus seems that this index was made before the section at the beginning of the *Commentary* was removed to become part of the *Baron.*

Book III — at least in Chapters 11-13 — seems to have been historical in approach. Perhaps it was a history of the House of York or of the Houses of York and Lancaster. The *Commentary* has called the *Baron* 'Baronorum Genealogue secundum tempora regum' (f. 21ᵛ), and this description could perhaps fit this section. Chapter 10 speaks of George, Duke of Clarence's treasons and execution (*History,* text, p. 135), and Chapter 13 is particularly notable as the origin of the *History,* whose 'Advertisement to the Reader' opens thus (text, p. 6):

> Before I enter into the story of King Richard, I must advertise the noble, courteous, and intelligent Reader (for unto such only I write) that the argument and subject of this discourse or story was at the first but a chapter, and the thirteenth chapter, of the third book of a rude work of

> mine entitled THE BARON, or *The Magazin of Honour*.
> But the argument of that chapter being so strange and very
> extravagant and extraordinary (as the affairs and fortunes
> of this prince were), suppeditated strange and extraordinary
> matters, and in such copy and variety as that it diffused
> itself into an extraordinary and unusual largeness, and so
> much as it exceeded very much the laws and the proper
> limits of a chapter.

Buck's only specific reference to the material contained in the particular chapter is to Clarence and Warwick's confederacy and its success in expelling Edward IV from England in 1469(*History*, text p. 137). There is no way of telling whether or not the discussion of the execution of Sir William Stanley and others for aiding Richard, Duke of York (alias Perkin Warbeck), which Buck refers to as existing in his 'Advertisements ante Glover' (*Comm.*, f. 254ᵛ), appeared in this Book as well.

Book IV, at least in part, treated of King Arthur. Buck claims to have 'handled his story' there and to have 'redeemed him & his knights & paladins from fables & scandales' (*Comm.*, f. 2ᵛ). This comment is a late addition, again suggesting concurrent composition of the *Baron* and the *Commentary*. We know nothing of any material in Books V-XII. It is possible that Buck was leading up to the Tudors by a discourse first on their historical ancestors, the Yorkist and Lancastrian families, then on their legendary ancestors, including King Arthur.

Book XIII, Chapter 16 speaks of tortures (*History,* text, p. 152). The last two books mentioned by number are fifteen and sixteen, which '[treat of] matters of [armory]' (*History,* text, p. 81). Since Buck states that he has written of all armorial signs in the last five books, there could not have been many more than sixteen.

There seems nothing to support Eccles' statement that Buck's lost treatise on the art of the revels sprang from the *Baron*.[29]

There is one minor antiquarian work of Buck's which appears in manuscript (B.L. MS. Cotton Titus C.I, f.35ᵛ) and is printed in Hearne's *Curious Discourses*.[30] It seems to be notes for Buck's contribution to a topic under discussion at a meeting of the Society of Antiquaries. The group of manuscripts of which it forms a part considers the office of High Constable of England, on which papers were evidently delivered in the autumn of 1602 (one of the discourses bears the date 27 November 1602). The notes, subtitled 'Justitiarius Angliae' and signed 'G. Buc', comprise a series of factual statements and Latin quotations documented from Camden, Hoveden, Matthew Paris, John of Salisbury, Selden, and others. There are no transitions, and the organization is very loose, but the conclusion to which Buck's observations lead seems to be that at some stage the Chief Justice exercised the duties of Constable, Marshal, Treasurer, and Admiral as well as his nominal function. The manuscript is a fair copy not in Buck's hand, but the marginal documentation and signature are his. In the discourses which make up the collection, use of an amanuensis for the body of the paper with signature and date or other notation given in the author's own hand is not uncommon.

The research involved in composing all his antiquarian treatises and his associations with scholars who assisted him in his searches among original documents made it natural that Lord Darcy should, as Buck says in a letter to Cotton, have 'bene ernest with me to deliuer him some matters concerning the great men of the realm in former tymes' (B.L. MS. Cotton Julius C. III, f. 49). In March 1620, Buck describes himself as actively at work on this research, but no trace of it remains, if it ever materialized. Buck's madness came late in 1621 or early in 1622.

NOTES

1. [Joseph Ritson], *Bibliographia Poetica* (London, 1802), pp. 146f.

2. The authenticity and biographical import of this verse are discussed in Eccles, pp. 438ff. A copy is shown in W.W. Greg, 'Three Manuscript Notes by Sir George Buc', *The Library*, XII (1931), 307-21, Plate V.

3. In John Stow, *The Annales or Generall Chronicle of England* (London, 1615), sig. Llll 6. Buck's work runs from pp. 958-88 (sigs. Llll 5-Oooo 3ᵛ). Since the page numbering is extremely erratic, quotations from this edition will be identified by signatures.

4. See below, present text, pp. 34, 69, 85, 116, 167, 193f, 208.

5. Joseph Quincy Adams, 'Hill's List of Early Plays in Manuscript', *Library*, XX (1939), 71-99.

6. Samuel A. Tannenbaum, *Shakesperian Scraps and Other Elizabethan Fragments* (New York, 1933), pp. 51-74. He reproduces this inscription on Plate VIII. The transcript, with emendations, is mine.

7. R.C. Bald, 'The *Locrine* and *George-a-Green* Title Page Inscriptions', *Library*, XV (1934), 295-305.

8. William Camden, *Remaines concerning Britaine*, rev. ed. (London, 1614), p. 376.

9. Eccles, p. 413. Agnes M.C. Latham's edition of 1929 is the one alluded to. Her edition of 1951 has not benefited from Eccles' observation.

10. [George Chalmers], *An Apology for the Believers in the Shakspeare-Papers* (London, 1797), p. 494.

11. Eccles, pp. 412ff.

12. See below, pp. cxxii-cxxiv.

13. Buck's MS. note in the Bodleian copy of F[rancis] G[odwin], *A Catalogue of the Bishops of England* (London, 1601), p. 355.

14.   George Buck, *History* (London, 1646), p. 78.

15.   Frank Marcham, *The King's Office of the Revels* (London, 1925), p. 4.

16.   See A.N. Kincaid, 'A Revels Office Scrap Deciphered', *Notes and Queries,* n.s. XIX (1972), 461-3.

17.   See below, pp. lxviii-lxvix.

18.   William Maitland, *The History and Survey of London* (London, 1756), II, 811.

19.   See below, pp. ciii-civ and cxiv-cxv for further discussion.

20.   Stow, *Annales* (London, 1601), sigs. Pppp 3-Pppp 8 (the page numbers within which the treatise is included are pp. 1238-93, but extra leaves in this gathering have made for some repetition of pagination). Although Buck's name is not cited in the *Annales,* Eccles, pp. 430f, has produced evidence that the work was his.

21.   See below, pp. cxix-cxi for authors Buck refers to in the *History*.

22.   See below, p. cxxxiv for further discussions of these revisions.

23.   Bald, 'A Revels Office Entry', *Times Literary Supplement,* no. 1,311 (17 March 1927), 193. He printed photocopies of pages from it in 'The *Locrine* . . . Inscriptions', cited above, n. 7.

24.   Bald, 'A Manuscript Work by Sir George Buc', *Modern Language Review,* XXX (1935), 1-12.

25.   Challen, p. 290 and personal correspondence with Major W. Halswell.

26.   Bald, 'A Manuscript Work', pp.3f. See for these references John Strype, *Historical Collections of . . . John Aylmer* (London, 1701), pp. 174 and 332.

27.   See below, p. xxxv.

28.   *A Collection of Curious Discourses,* ed. Thomas Hearne (London, 1775), I, 124.

29.   Eccles, p. 412.

30.   Hearne, II, 88f.

III. ANTIQUARIES AND THEIR LIBRARIES

The rise of antiquarianism[1] during the sixteenth century cannot be traced to any single cause; as is usual with new 'movements', several factors coincided in its origin. The dissolution of the monasteries destroyed libraries, and the dispersal of valuable manuscripts instigated efforts by lovers of learning and of their country's past to collect and preserve them. Archbishop Parker received a royal licence to collect books and manuscripts from dissolved foundations in 1568, and for their own use and interest private men like Cotton, Camden, and Stow made large collections of historical material. With this reorganization of libraries, and as the public records gradually became available and began to be classified, the old dependence on 'authority' in history was no longer possible. Documentary evidence had to be reckoned with, and scholars had to learn, crudely at first, to deal with it critically. The skills of palaeography, philology, translation and transcription, sense of chronology and suitability to period, were in their infancy, but their importance was gradually being recognized. The antiquaries were discovering and applying the rudiments of these skills and were also lending to their studies a particular type of research into earliest precedents and a logical criticism of information peculiar to the law courts, for most of them had a background of legal training.

Search for precedent gave the movement impetus. The burning sense of patriotism and nationalism, the desire to reflect on the country's present glory by revealing a glorious past, and the immediate need to justify Protestantism as a reformed religion based on early Christianity combined in a work like Foxe's *Acts and Monuments,* which looked beyond the common chronicles to seek original sources that could speak in matters of controversy. Old texts were edited so as to make them available for polemical purposes both in theology and in the conflict with Polydore Vergil over the 'British History'. But standards of editorship were lax compared with those we now know. There was a tendency to fill in and embellish texts, and translation and transcription were extremely careless, grammar and spelling freely modified.

Lawyers searched old documents to find the earliest precedents, for the English common law was based on the concept of precedence. In early Stuart times this became a serious issue, when it was necessary to show the precedence of common law over royal prerogative and its consequent immunity from it. To this end Coke's exhaustive study of common law was written. Coke's library was unusually large, but

Cotton, with his immense collection, was in a position to serve as advisor to the Parliamentary opposition on matters of precedent, and in this connection wrote 'A Relation to prove that the Kings of England have been pleased to consult with their Peers in the Great Counsell and Commons in Parliament'. Sir George Buck's arguments for the dignity and prime authority of Parliament are a major side issue in his *History of King Richard III*[2]. R.B. Wernham notes that

> the constitutional conflicts of the early Stuart period took
> somewhat the form of a prolonged lawsuit between King
> and Parliament and, like other lawsuits, it involved much
> search among the records by both parties. But the issues
> raised were so much more generalized that they virtually
> elevated legal searches into historical research.

The pursuit of this debate 'was beginning to arouse a new interest in the public records simply as materials for history'.[3] Legal training and employment in turn assisted scholars in their antiquarian pursuits.

Another group whose profession led them to be antiquaries were the heralds. The Tudors' need to justify their claim to the throne led to the production of family trees traced back to Cadwallader, to Brute, even to Adam. Families, many of them *novi homines* under Elizabeth, sought the ancientry of their origins in deeds and records, some of them inevitably forgeries which, because the sciences dealing with the study of documents were still rudimentary, were often believed even by the most astute of the heralds.[4] Some of the most notable heralds were also notable scholars and collectors: Camden, Dethick, Glover, and St George. Heralds, according to Buck, who, as has already been indicated, was the friend of many, had to be gentlemen and excellent painters for the recording of blazons and ensigns, and 'Their studie also is or ought to be auncient hystorie, Chronicles, & antiquities: they must search old roles & scrowles, and peruse authentike records, Archiues, olde Charters, & evidences' to find and preserve genealogical matter and testimony to alliances, issue, and the honour of ancestors. 'These *Herauldes* bee the ministers of honour, the Antiquaries of the British and English *Heroes*, and the Messengers of Mars' (*Third Universitie*, sig. Oooo 3). The heralds built up libraries to pass on to their successors, and ownership became confused. In 1568 Thomas Howard, Duke of Norfolk, the Earl Marshal, established rules including the foundation of a corporate library which no one could enter unaccompanied by a herald.[5] Further reform and encouragement to scholarship in the College of Arms came in 1597 with the appointment of Camden as Clarenceux. He, with his fellow scholar-heralds, 'found that a firm foundation for the study of national and local history and genealogy could only be laid by a laborious analysis of the public records in the Tower and elsewhere and of charters and other manuscripts in private hands'.[6]

The varied interests of the new historians can be observed in Leland's never-completed research plans: topography, place names, history and geography of individual counties, chorography, tracing of royal and noble families. These subjects were most competently handled by Stow and Camden. Stow's *Survey of London* is a brilliant example of local history. It relies heavily on records and carefully documents statements from manuscript sources. Indeed, Stow's entry into the world of scholarship was impelled by a dissatisfaction with Grafton's adopting wholesale and without documentation accounts from his chronicler forbears. Stow took up the challenge to pursue history based on research and documentation, and though his *Annales* still lean toward reliance on the older chronicles, his use of them is acknowledged, and they are supplemented and often contradicted by references to public records. Camden in his *Remaines* added genealogy to his interests after his appointment to the College of Arms. His *Britannia* studies the whole of the kingdom, county by county, its history, geography, and the origins of noble families. The attack on his accuracy by his fellow herald Ralph Brook[7] caused him to search the records more carefully and document more thoroughly. Buck was thus writing at a time when and among a group of scholars to whom documentation was an exceedingly important issue.

The editor of Thomas Hearne's collection of the antiquaries' papers saw the Elizabethan period as especially fruitful for antiquarian studies, since the queen herself, no mean scholar, was a patroness of learning and preferred learned men to high positions in the church and state:

> At this auspicious period, a set of gentlemen of great abilities, many of them students in the inns of court, applied themselves to the study of the antiquities and history of this kingdom, a taste at that time very prevalent, wisely foreseeing that without a perfect knowledge of those requisites, a thorough understanding of laws of their native country could not be attained.[8]

The Society of Antiquaries, founded in 1586, included lawyers (Sir John Dodderidge, Sir James Ley), heralds (Glover, Dethick, Camden, St George), collectors (Cotton), historians (Stow), and archivists (Michael Heneage, Keeper of the Tower Records).[9] Sir Henry Spelman, one of the original members, describes it thus:

> About fourty two years since, divers Gentlemen in *London,* studious of Antiquities, fram'd themselves into a College or Society of Antiquaries, appointing to meet every Friday weekly in the Term at a place agreed of, and for Learning sake to confer upon some questions in that Faculty, and to sup together. The place, after a meeting or two, became certain at *Darby-house,* where the Herald's Office is kept, and two Questions were propounded at every meeting, to be handled at the next that followed; so that every man had a sennight's respite to advise upon them, and then to deliver his opinion. That which seem'd most material, was

by one of the company (chosen for the purpose) to be entr'd in a book; that so it might remain unto posterity. The Society increased daily: many persons of great worth, as well noble as other learned, joyning themselves unto it.

Thus it continu'd divers years; but as all good uses commonly decline; so many of the chief Supporters hereof either dying or withdrawing themselves from *London* into the Country; this among the rest grew for twenty years to be discontinu'd. But it then came again into the mind of divers principal Gentlemen to revive it; and for that purpose upon the __ day of __ in the year 1614. there met at the same place Sir *James Ley* Knight, then Attorney of the Court of Wards, since Earl of *Marleborough* and Lord Treasurer of *England*; Sir *Robert Cotton* Knight and Baronett; Sir *John Davies* his Majestie's Attorney for *Ireland*; Sir *Richard St. George* Knt. then Norrey, Mr. *Hackwell* the Queen's Solicitor, Mr. *Camden* then Clarentieux, my self, and some others. Of these, the Lord *Treasurer, Sir Robert Cotton,* Mr. *Camden,* and my self, had been of the original Foundation; and so to my knowledge were all then living of that sort, saving Sir *John Doderidge* Knight, Justice of the King's Bench.

We held it sufficient for that time to revive the meeting, and only conceiv'd some rules of Government and limitation to be observ'd amongst us; wherof this was one, That for avoiding offence, we should neither meddle with matters of State nor of Religion. And agreeing of two Questions for the next meeting, we chose Mr *Hackwell* to be our Register and the Convocator of our Assemblies for the present; and supping together, so departed . . . .

But before our next meeting we had notice that his Majesty took a little mislike of our Society; not being enform'd, that we had resolv'd to decline all matters of State. Yet hereupon we forbare to meet again, and so all our labours lost. [10]

We may derive an idea of the antiquaries' interests from a glance at the topics on which members chose to prepare discourses, which include:

The Antiquity of the Laws of England

The Antiquity, Office and Privilege of Heralds

The Antiquity of Houses of Law

The Antiquity of Arms

The Antiquity of the Office of Chancellor

The Antiquity of Seals

The Etymology, Dignity and Antiquity of Duke, or Dux

The Etymology and Original of Barons

Of Epitaphs

Of Motts

The Office of High Steward

The Office of Constable of England

The Office of Earl Marshal

There were also various topographical considerations, and studies of terms denoting measurement and currency.

The Society established and enforced standards and methods of research and documentation. It facilitated access to documents, since many of its members were keepers of official records and there was considerable lending within the Society and its members' immediate circle of friends by those who collected privately. (It may be observed that Buck, throughout his antiquarian works, often applied to friends who were heralds for information in the College of Arms and borrowed many manuscript works from Cotton and other antiquarian scholars.) Emphasis was placed on primary sources, yet without clear critical interpretation: truth was equated with documentation and facts collected without reference to or understanding of the age in which the documented facts occurred. Since dating methods were not well developed, there was a tendency to antedate, and the illogical method was employed of judging the past by what in the present was regarded as 'custom'.[11] On the other hand, 'members were anxious to get behind the chroniclers and explore the masses of original records of English history. Instead of making a virtue of conjecture, as Raleigh did in his *History,* the antiquaries condemned the use of conjecture as an historical technique'.[12]

The treatises read before the Society of Antiquaries and others of the same authors' antiquarian treatises can be seen in Hearne's *Collection of Curious Discourses Written by Eminent Antiquaries upon Several Heads in Our English Antiquities.* The discourses are precedent-orientated and cite as authority Biblical, classical, legal and chronicle references, monuments, and inscriptions. Organization is loose and generally in the form of a barely disguised list tracing a history through records from as far back as possible. The discourses are studded with Latin quotations. Sometimes long sections of the official documents are copied out. Etymological speculation abounds. Most of the antiquaries display great modesty and respect for their fellows in setting forth their opinions. Elaborate documentation is pursued at the expense of style. Allusions to imaginative literature are very few. Sir James Ley appears exceptional in being an excellent stylist, organizing his material systematically under section headings and writing with a fine sense of linguistic balance and conciseness.

The original Society was dissolved in about 1607. In 1614 occurred the attempt related by Spelman to revive it. In 1620, Buckingham presented to the House of

Lords a proposal for the foundation of an English Academy: 'The dissolution of this so well an intended exercise, hath neuerthelesse not happened without the iust griefe of all those worthie patriots who know your Majesties realms afford liuing persons of prime worth, fit to keep vp, and celebrate that round table' (B.L. Harl. 6143, f. 14). Among those listed in illustration were Thomas, Earl of Arundel; Lord William Howard; Greville; Coke; Dodderidge; Ley; Cotton; Spelman; Dr John Hayward; the heralds Segar, St George, and Brook; Selden; 'Incomparable Camden'; and 'Sir Georg Buc knight, Mr. of Reuels'.

It is not known positively whether or not Buck was a member of the Society of Antiquaries.[13] No current work on the subject lists him as such, nor does Spelman or Harleian 6143. But these lists are incomplete and leave out persons who are known from other sources to have been members. The only documentary evidence for his having been so is his notes on the offices of High Constable and Chief Justice bound among the group of members' discourses on that subject prepared for the 27 November 1602 meeting.[14] Since the Society's meetings were closed to non-members, it is not likely that Buck would have prepared a paper on an assigned topic had he not been a member. His close association with so many members and the coincidence of his interests with those discussed by the antiquaries in their regular meetings would seem to support the assumption that he was among their number.

Sir James Ley, a founder member and active contributor to the Society, Buck cites as a *viva voce* authority in *The Third Universitie,* where he calls him 'an excellent antiquarie' (sig. Nnnn 2). Another early member who contributed *viva voce* information to this work was Dr Launcelot Andrewes. The heralds Brook, Charles, and St George assisted Buck with the *Commentary* by giving him access to their private libraries, and Camden and Brook are cited frequently as sources of *viva voce* information. A scholar who does not figure in either list of antiquaries, St Low Kniveton, who wrote a chorography of Derbyshire and assisted Camden in his researches for the *Britannia,* merits from Buck the appellation 'our Greatest Reader of Recordes' and 'our best Archivist' (*Comm.,* ff. 63^v and 452), 'Our best Antiquaries' (*Comm.,* f. 51^v) are Kniveton and Camden, the latter described by Buck as 'a [carefull] \ diligent / antiquary and a very [faithfull] \ iudicious / Genealogist' (*Comm.,* f. 381), and Buck contributes a complimentary verse to the 1607 edition of the *Britannia.* Camden for his part pays tribute to Buck as early as 1600 by including in the *Britannia* a discussion of his ancestry[15] and by twice thanking him for historical information: 'Georgius Buc non minùs maioribus quam bonis studijs clarus notat ex Makerco *Wallon* Gallum dici Germanis'.[16] He describes Buck as 'vir literate doctus & qui (iuuat enim profiteri per quos profeci) multa in historijs obseruauit & candidé impertijt'.[17] It is tempting to wonder to what extent Buck was responsible for Camden's temperate assessment of Richard III in later editions of the *Britannia.* With John Stow, a much older man, Buck was well acquainted, referring to him as a *viva voce* source in the *Commentary* and very prominently in the *History.*[18] Stow for his part includes in his *Annales* Buck's account of the voyage to Cadiz.[19]

Buck obtained both *viva voce* information and manuscript source material from several members of the Howard family. The association was of long standing. It began, according to Buck's account, after Bosworth, when Thomas Howard, Earl of Surrey, who later became Duke of Norfolk, took into his care Buck's grandfather, whose own father, like the earl's, had been killed on Richard III's party. The Lord Admiral, Charles Howard, Earl of Nottingham, a direct descendant of this Duke of Norfolk, was Buck's commander on the Cadiz voyage and preferred Buck to Queen Elizabeth. Buck cites him as a *viva voce* source in the *Commentary,* where he acknowledges also loans from him of several books. To Henry Howard, Earl of Northampton, another noted antiquary, Buck inscribed a copy of *Daphnis.*[20] Lord William Howard of Naworth (1563-1640) was an avid collector of mediaeval historical texts and manuscripts, editor in 1592 of Florence of Worcester, a member of the Society of Antiquaries, and a friend of Camden's, for whom he collected inscriptions.[21] Buck speaks of him as 'an excellent antiquary and Archivist' (*Comm.,* f. 210[v]) and often refers in the *Commentary* to manuscripts in his possession. His nephew Thomas Howard, Earl of Arundel (1585-1646), to whom Buck dedicated his *History,* was a collector of art works, books, and manuscripts. He formed a manuscript collection dealing with history and heraldry which was presented by his grandson to the College of Arms. The remainder of his library went to the Royal Society, which sold it.[22] He also possessed a collection of family relics which was dispersed shortly after his death as a result of family feuding.[23] Despite these dispersals and later damage to the Howard papers, Buck has been severely attacked because one of the Arundel papers to which he refers can no longer be found.[24]

Amongst these numerous collections, Coke's library was outstanding in size, consisting of 1,227 items. It represents the interests of a legal scholar who was interested also in historical studies. Buck, who dedicated *The Third Universitie* to Coke, calls him 'an excellent Antiquary' (sig. Mmmm). It is interesting to note how many of the sources Buck habitually used were among Coke's collection: Camden (in Latin and English), Commynes, Fabyan, Gainsford, Godwin, Glover, Holinshed, More, Newburgh, Paradin, Paris, *Rerum Angliae Scriptores,* Speed, Stow, Du Tillet, Polydore Vergil, Walsingham, Westminster. Also in Coke's library was a copy of Buck's *Daphnis.*[25] Coke lent freely to other antiquaries.

The most famous private library of the age — perhaps of any age — was that of Sir Robert Cotton. It is clearly this library which Buck used most. He refers to manuscripts in the Cotton collection more frequently than to material in any other. He uses it even for information on his own family (*Comm.,* ff. 450 and 451[v]). That Buck's Cotton grandmother might have been related to Sir Robert's family does not in itself explain Cotton's possessing information on Buck's genealogy. Cotton also possessed Howard papers. In 1610 Sir Thomas Wilson was appointed Keeper of State Papers, and his attempt to collect them was, Wernham remarks, 'not, perhaps, made easier by the private collecting activities of Sir Robert Cotton'.[26]

There was considerable lending activity among the antiquaries. This is exemplified in a letter of March 1620 (B.L. Cotton Julius C. III, f. 49) which Buck wrote to Cotton urgently enquiring about a book the Lord Admiral had lent to Buck and Buck had then lent to Cotton, who had not returned it at Buck's request because he in turn had lent it to someone else. Buck now needs to use the book himself and is worried also about betraying his trust with the Lord Admiral should the book be required and he not able to return it at once. He appeals on the basis of his own well known scrupulosity: 'I pray consyder this *that* I haue always bene carefull to hold my credit with good men, & cheefly so good & so great men as my*n* ancient & most noble good Lord the Lord Notingh*am*'. He reminds Cotton that 'when you sent for a book you had giuen me I sent it redely', and presumes '*tha*t if I had desired after, & more & better books to be lent to me *tha*t you (according to yo*u*r woonted noble man*er* & knowing my care in the iust restoring of them) would haue bene willing to haue holpen my studies & labours with the excellent tresury of yo*ur* Cabinet & Library'.

Loans were made by Cotton to Selden, Arundel, Coke, Bacon, Spelman, Greville, Speed, Harington, and Hoby, among others. B.L. MS. Harleian 6018 is a catalogue and notes of lending from the Cotton library to 1653. Books when returned were crossed off the lending list. Several, not crossed off, were evidently not returned, and there is a list of missing books on f. 187^{v} of this catalogue. Evidently, Cotton often gave away and sometimes traded manuscripts, so that, as C.E. Wright says, 'It is not surprising that many manuscripts known to have belonged to Cotton are no longer in the library'.[27] Losses occurred in the later history of the library as well. B.L. MS. Additional 5161 records loans of 1638, among them a book on Glastonbury which was never returned and is now in the Wood collection of the British Library. In the fire of 1731, of 958 volumes supposed to have existed before the fire, 114 were totally destroyed and 98 seriously damaged,[28] one of the damaged works being the original manuscript of Buck's *History*.

In studying the contents of Cotton's library, past and present, we must take into account not only the various opportunities for loss but also the numerous errors in cataloguing. There were several manuscript catalogues: Harleian 6018 was compiled between 1621 and 1653. Additional 5161 is a manuscript catalogue of cartularies in the library. It is of uncertain date, far from complete, and says of itself, 'This booke was made since the book*es* were new plact & therefore imperfect as to find certaine anie booke almost therefore it were very well another Alphabeticall Catalogue in this kind were made' (f. 11). B.L. MS. Harleian 694, a catalogue made in 1674 of several English libraries, lists books under subject headings and gives their numbers in the library. Additional 8926, a parchment roll, is similar, giving the same subject headings but no classification numbers. The first printed catalogue, Thomas Smith's *Catalogus Librorum Manuscriptorum Bibliothecae Cottonianae*, was published in 1696, and Casley's appeared in 1734 as a supplement to it, to show the damage and destruction to the books and manuscripts in the fire. Hooper's catalogue of 1777, derived from Harleian 694, criticizes the 'injudicious manner' and 'many defects' with which Smith's catalogue was compiled and considers itself superior for arrangement by subject.[29] The currently used catalogue was published in 1802.

In formulating all these catalogues there always existed the danger of incorrect copying or printing, listing a manuscript under a wrong number, ignoring an alteration in the library's numerical classification, failing to list a manuscript which had been bound with several others. For example, Sprott's chronicle, consistently throughout the catalogues listed as Vitellius E.IV, is mentioned as lost after the fire; but in fact it is still in the collection, numbered Vitellius E.XIV. One of Ailred's works, listed in Harleian 694 as 'Julius A 2', appears in the printed catalogues as A.XI, its correct number. Obviously the Arabic '11' had at some point been taken for a Roman 'II'. Similar confusions resulting from carelessness and misreading of numbers are frequent. Some items listed in Harleian 694 simply do not appear in the printed catalogues, among them several of the manuscript sources Buck specifically documents as coming from Cotton's collection. Because these works are not correctly listed in the printed catalogues, it has been continually assumed that they were lost or never existed. In fact, despite the numerous allegations that Buck's manuscript sources are in the main no longer extant, there are actually very few not extant.[30] For many of those which do seem genuinely to be lost, either through borrowing or fire, there are records in manuscript catalogues of the Cotton Library to prove that they were there in Buck's time. But the majority of those apparently lost have simply been incorrectly classified, not listed, or too scantily described for identification in the most recent printed catalogues. To locate them it has been necessary to use the listings and descriptions in the early manuscript catalogues of the library and a moderate amount of ingenuity.

Cotton owned copies of Ailred, Bernard André, *Axiomata Politica*, Coggeshall, the Croyland Chronicle, Gildas, Giraldus Cambrensis, Herd, Huntingdon, Malmesbury, Newburgh, Paris, Rous, and Wendover. He had copies of excerpts from the Patent Rolls, the Public Records, and the Treasury records, charters and Papal Bulls, assorted manuscript chronicles of various dates, miscellaneous books of rhymes, apothegms, axioms, and epigrams, and numerous classical works. Ultimately the manuscript of Buck's *History* found its way into the Cotton Library.

Buck's own library was evidently not inconsiderable. He twice invites Cotton to use it: in March 1605, 'if my small library may stand you, or your studies in any stead you shall not fynd the dore shutt against you. for liberall myndes (which exclude none) out not to bee excluded' (Cotton Julius C. III, f. 47). And in March 1620, 'my por library is open to you at your pleasur' (f. 49). Those books which could be traced at Buck's death when the question of inheritance was considered amounted to two trunks full (one a very large trunk), one chest, and one deep drawer full. This would account for about 300-500 books. And during Buck's insanity his nephew Stephen Buck is alleged to have embezzled books, plate, and jewels in great quantity, among them undoubtedly the manuscript of Buck's *History*. Selden acquired a valuable book of arms from Buck's collection, and Eccles believes he would have taken care to secure as many as possible of Buck's more valuable books.[31] The Bodleian Library possesses Buck's copy of Godwin's *Catalogue*, and the Bodleian copy of Bouchard's *Grandes Cronicques de Bretaigne* shows Buck's notation. Although it does not contain his name, it seems fairly certain that it was his property.

Buck's antiquarian activity is well illustrated by his extant works. He seems in addition to have collected epitaphs for Camden. Ff. 93-97 of B.L.MS. Cotton Julius F.XI, a Camden collection, are in Buck's hand, all but the first leaf being filled in with copies of epitaphs. Buck's scholarly methods are evident also in his private annotations to his own copy of Godwin's *Catalogue*. These notes are as carefully documented as anything in Buck's published works. His references are to Bede, Camden, Commynes, Daniel's *History of England,* Liber Eliensis, Erasmus, Florence of Worcester, Foxe, Hall, Holinshed, Hoveden, William of Malmesbury, More, Paris, Parker, Stow's *Annales* and *Survey*, and Wendover. And many references are made also to *viva voce* information derived from his fellow antiquaries and from manuscript collections. Dr Andrewes and Sir Robert Cotton are mentioned as *viva voce* sources. References are made to several manuscripts: to an ancient manuscript book in Cotton's library and to the archives of the College of Arms.

Buck attempts considerable precision in his notes, referring to page and book numbers, but he is often careless with the page numbers and writes over them. He supplies cross references to other sections of the *Catalogue* itself. In the margins he has given regnal years and roughly sketched coats of arms. The notes in margins and the blank pages contain speculation on names, with evidence derived from heraldry and from birthplaces, notes of ownership at different times of lands and houses, correction of names and dates given by Godwin, clarification of the text and addit-ional information on the bishops included. Anecdotes of recent bishops are given, and listing of names and dates of the incumbents of each see from the date the book was published to approximately 1611. Buck seems to have acquired the book in 1606, for he writes on the title page 'Quid retribua*m*? which is evidently his motto, and his signature, 'G.Buc.', then adds to the author's name (given as 'F.G. Subdeane of Exceter') the note '& prebendary of Wells vt videtur fol. 300. 1601. & now Bishop of Landaff. 1606'.

The extent of Buck's notation in the Bodleian copy of Bouchard (shelfmark B. 1. 17. Art. Seld.) would suggest that it was probably his. He has made on the title page a note about the author with a cross reference citing a page number in the book itself, dated the book 1517 (there is no publication date printed) and given the price as £3. It is fairly certain from his quoting the price that the book was his own, and it looks as if some of the blank end papers on which his name might have been written are now missing. At various points throughout the book he translates names of places and persons into other languages and more familiar forms and corrects misprints. He makes a few marginal notes in French and Latin, calling attention to material contained in the text, and underlines items which are of use to him in the *History*.

It is unfortunate that from Buck's complete collection only these two books can be traced.

NOTES

1. For thorough studies of Tudor antiquarianism, see F. Smith Fussner, *The Historical Revolution* (London, 1962); F.J. Levy, *Tudor Historical Thought* (San Marino, 1967); May McKisack, *Medieval History in the Tudor Age* (Oxford, 1971); and Linda Van Norden, *The Elizabethan College of Antiquaries* (University of California at Los Angeles, unpublished Ph.D. diss., 1946).

2. See below, p. cxxv for further mention of this issue.

3. R.B. Wernham, 'The Public Records in the Sixteenth and Seventeenth Centuries', in *English Historical Scholarship in the Sixteenth and Seventeenth Centuries,* ed. Levi Fox (London, 1956), p. 25.

4. See below, General Notes, pp. 249f.

5. Anthony Richard Wagner, *The Records and Collections of the College of Arms* (London, 1952), pp. 9-12.

6. Ibid., p. 31.

7. *A Discoverie of Certaine Errours . . . in the Much Commended Britannia. 1594.* (London, [1596]).

8. Hearne, Introduction, I, iv.

9. Names of members of the original society may be found in B.L. MS. Harl. 6143 and Henry Spelman, *Reliquiae Spelmanniae* (Oxford, 1698), pp. 69f. However, these lists are far from complete, and Harl. 6143 seems to include sympathizers as well as members.

10. Spelman, pp. 69f.

11. Fussner, p. 99.

12. Ibid., p. 97.

13. A.R.Myers, 'Richard III and Historical Tradition', *History* LXXX (1968), 186 states positively that Buck was a member but does not document this assertion.

14. For a discussion of this treatise, see above, pp. xliv-xlv.

15. Camden, *Britannia* (1600), p. 726; in the 1607 ed., p. 668.

16. Ibid., p. 25; in the 1607 ed., pp. 16f.

17. Ibid., p. 726. The 1607 ed., after Buck became Master of the Revels, reads 'vir literatè doctus Eques auratus & à regijs spectaculis . . .', p. 668.

18. See below, pp. cxvii-cxviii for discussion of Stow's influence on Buck.

19. See above, p. xxix.

20. The Grenville copy, B.L. shelfmark B. 11553, mentioned in Eccles, pp. 455f.

21. McKisack, p. 61

22. Seymour de Ricci, *English Collectors of Books and Manuscripts (1550-1930)* (Cambridge, 1930), p. 25.

23. Mary F.S. Hervey, *The Life, Correspondence and Collections of Thomas Howard, Earl of Arundel* (Cambridge, 1921), pp. 456-8.

24. See below pp. xc-xciv and cxiv for further discussion.

25. Information on the contents of Coke's library is derived from *A Catalogue of the Library of Sir Edward Coke,* ed. W.O. Hassall, Yale Law Library Publications, no. 12 (New Haven, 1950).

26. Wernham, p. 22.

27. C.E. Wright, 'The Elizabethan Society of Antiquaries and the Formation of the Cottonian Library', in *The English Library before 1700,* ed. Francis Wormald and C.E. Wright (London, 1958), p. 204.

28. *A Report from the Committee Appointed to View the Cottonian Library* (London, 1732), p. 4.

29. *Samuel Hooper, A Catalogue of the Manuscripts in the Cottonian Library* (London, 1777), Preface, p.v.

30. See below, pp. cxii-cxv.

31. This account of Buck's library is from Eccles, pp. 494f. The estimate of the number of books contained in the trunks and chests comes from my own considerable experience of packing books in large trunks, chests, and deep drawers.

IV. THE TEXTS

There exist several early manuscript versions of Buck's *History*, but discussion and criticism have so far concentrated on the printed edition (see pp. lxxxvii-xcix below), published in 1646, with its reissue in 1647, and again in the edition of Strype (1706 and 1719). In the nineteenth century Charles Yarnold collected materials for an edition from one of the manuscript copies. I shall give a brief description of each of these manuscripts and editions before proceeding to discuss their relationship to each other and the relationship of the printed text to what Buck actually wrote.

British Library MS. Cotton Tiberius E.X. (referred to hereafter as 'Tiberius')

[no title page]

Large folio, probably originally the same size as Buck's *Commentary* (36.5 ×23 cm.), but now badly burnt around all edges, with greater severity toward the end. The largest expanse on the remaining leaves is 30 × 20.5 cm. Tops of pages are better preserved than bottoms. A few pages are greyed by burning, some (ff. 23 and 25) to the point of illegibility. Running heads indicating the number of each book occur at regular intervals. The vertical margins are sometimes ruled, leaving 13-14 cm. between rulings. Considerable revision makes it unlikely that this was intended to be the final copy. Two people have made revisions in it: the author Sir George Buck and his great-nephew George Buck, Esq., hereafter designated as 'the Editor'. Occasionally the author's additions are written on the backs of scrap paper: Revels Office notes, letters, and early notes and drafts for sections of this work. A later binder has sometimes included several versions of the same page or section and has invariably separated portions which have been pasted over passages the author wished to revise. There is considerable revision between lines and down margins of pages, and considerable crossing out by the author and Editor. Several stages of authorial correction appear in different inks, the darkest normally the latest. The author's ink is dull medium brown, with his latest corrections nearly black. The Editor's ink is generally more watery and somewhat reddish. The author has made some of his corrections first in pencil then written over them in ink, having sometimes marked with a pencilled 'X' in the margin sections which he wished to correct. Occasionally sections are bracketed and starred with pencil in the margin, probably indicating the author's intention to revise.

Contents: ff. 1-4ᵛ dedication; ff. 5-5ᵛ Advertisement to the Reader; ff. 6-265 text. Several different hands appear: (1) Buck's normal hand, secretary with some humanist letter forms. Its slope is irregular, and it is not particularly current, although apparently written rapidly; (2) Buck's 'erasure hand', normally in red ink, used over erased portions; (3) a hand, probably Buck's, which attempts to be more formal: ff. 38, 46, and 62ᵛ; (4) a hand similar to Buck's normal hand and probably a variation of it, ff. 31ᵛ, 45ᵛ, 73, and 73ᵛ; (5) a humanist hand which is not Buck's for Latin quotation, f. 49; (6) the hand of a scribe, secretary: there are fifty-five leaves of this in all, and Buck has frequently made alterations on them and filled in blanks with unusual or foreign words; (7) the Editor's hand, evident in revisions on most pages. Ff. 126, 167, 173, 174, and 263 are entirely in the Editor's hand.

Page numbers from the printed edition of 1646 appear throughout in nineteenth century hand, indicating collation of the manuscript with the printed edition, with reference to which the manuscript's pages seems to have been arranged — sometimes incorrectly — for binding. Each leaf has been mounted in guards, and during the nineteenth century the manuscript was bound in calf and buckram.

British Library MS. Egerton 2216 (hereafter referred to as 'Egerton')

The History off Richard / the third / Comprised in fiue books / gathered and written by Geo: Buck / Esq.ʳ / [Quotation from Plato — 2 lines] / [Quotation from D. Ambros.— 2 lines] / [sign apparently signifying a bee]. Folio regularly gathered in eights. Paper, 29 × 19 cm. Twenty-five lines to a page; area covered by text on each page 24 × 12.3 cm. Ink medium to dark brown; later corrections in light reddish brown. Running heads noting the number of each book appear regularly at the top of each page. Catchwords are regular. Paragraphs are of considerably varying length, some indented, some not.

Contents: [f. 1] title page; ff. 2-3 dedication; ff. 4-309 text. Two different hands are apparent. The title page, dedication, corrections, and a few marginal notes throughout the text are in the hand of George Buck, Esq. (the Editor's hand). The body of the text was evidently written by a scribe. Both are individual mid-seventeenth century hands (about 1640), having mixed secretarial and Roman characteristics. The Editor's hand slants to the right; the scribe's is perpendicular. The manuscript was bound in leather in the nineteenth century. Condition is excellent.

Interesting features: Charles Yarnold's notes pencilled in margins pointing out handwriting peculiarities, particular information, and collation with Cotton Tiberius E.X.

Provenance: (1) title page has the signature 'William Ashton' at the top. (2) Below the title on the title page in Yarnold's hand: 'Bibliothecam Caroli Yarnold Mensis Novembbris 23mo 1810 Anno *intravit!*' (3) Yarnold's library was sold at auction by Southgate of Fleet Street in 1825.[1] (4) [b] 'Purchased at Messrs. Sotheby's Jan. Feb. 1873' by the British Museum.

Bodleian MS. Malone 1 (referred to hereafter as 'Malone')

The History of King Richard / the Third: / Comprised in fiue bookes. / Written by Geo: Buck Esqr: / [bee sign] / [Quotation from Plato — 3 lines] / [Quotation from D. Ambros. — 3 lines].

Folio, gathered in eights. Paper, size 28.5 × 19.3 cm. Twenty-five lines to a page; area covered by text 24 × 11.5 cm. Ink dark brown; later corrections medium brown. Running heads noting the number of each book appear regularly at the top of each page. Catchwords regular. Paragraphs of considerably varying lengths, some indented, some not. Contents: f. 1 title page; ff. 2-3 dedication; f. 4 blank; ff. 5-318 text. Interesting features: wormholes near bottom of leaves in ff. 1-114, most serious in ff. 13-30, but in margins, so not destructive to the text. The hand is that of Egerton, with dedication and corrections in Editor's hand. The binding is calf, probably seventeenth century.

Fisher Manuscript, Thomas Fisher Rare Book Library, University of Toronto

The History of King / Richard the 3.^{d} / By Geo: Buck Esqr

Folio, gathered in eights. Paper, size 28 × 18.8 cm. Pages have been trimmed around the edges after binding, and occasionally parts of the marginal notes have been cut off slightly. Area covered by text is 23.5 × 11.5 cm., with twenty-five lines of text to a page. The hand is that of the Egerton and Malone manuscripts, with corrections in the Editor's hand. Ink is very dark brown.

Contents: ff. 1-4 blank; ff. 5-314 text; ff. 315-322 blank.

Interesting features: the title page is not in the Editor's hand. This copy contains no dedication.

Provenance: The manuscript was owned by W.W. Greg, who allowed Frank Marcham to quote from it in *The King's Office of the Revels*. Marcham does not mention Greg's name, describing it only as a manuscript in private hands.[2] It was sold in 1950 or 1951 to Sidney T. Fisher of Montreal by Alan Keen, London, who informed Mr Fisher that the manuscript had been Greg's. Keen's catalogue for 1949 or 1950,[3] p. 6, item 13, gives the following description of it:

> THE FIRST BOOK WRITTEN TO REFUTE WILLIAM SHAKESPEARE'S HISTORICAL ACCURACY . . . . The much corrected holograph draft of this book is in the British Museum and does not contain nearly so much matter as this MS. . . . From this draft it is just possible that a cipher copy of the complete book was made. There are two existing manuscripts of this work, one, formerly Yarnold's, in the British Museum, and the present. The discrepancies between these two can be accounted for if they were transcribed from cipher, as they are both undoubtedly written by the same person. The matter could not legally or even safely have been printed in 1620, and

> even in 1646 it was carefully edited, so that it is but a
> shadow of itself . . . . The above MS. has six blank pages at
> the beginning. These pages were probably intended for an
> address to another friend who would receive the gift. The
> title has been added *c.* 1670.

Keen dates it 1620 and prices it at £200. Mr Fisher gave it to the University of Toronto
in 1973.

Binding is nineteenth century calf. Condition is excellent.

British Library Additional MS. 27422 (referred to hereafter as 'Additional')

The history / of / the life and Death / of / Richard the third. / in / two Bookes / by Geo:
Buck Esq.ʳ / [spiral].

Small folio gathered in eights. Paper 11.2 cm.× 7.4 cm. Number of lines to a page
between twenty and twenty-three. Area covered by text on each page 9.5 to 8.5 ×
4.5 cm. Light brown ink. Running heads giving the number of the book appear
sporadically in Book I, but regularly at the top of each page in Book II. Catchwords
are regular. There are paragraphs, but little punctuation. The manuscript is evenly
written with few corrections in mid-seventeenth century hand. Most of the letters are
in secretary forms, with a generally late appearance because of the short 's' humanist
form which often occurs initially and medially.

Contents: f. 1 nineteenth century description of the manuscript; f. 2 title page; ff. 3-
135 text. Contemporary vellum binding. Condition is excellent.

Provenance: 'Presented by Sir W.C. Trevelyan, Bart, 20 July 1866' to the British
Museum. Trevelyan describes it thus (f. 1):

> This vol: contains Books 1 & 2 of the Life of King Richard
> 3ᵈ which appears to have been all the Author had at first
> intended to write — The 3ᵈ. 4ᵗʰ. & 5ᵗʰ. Books which he
> afterwards added, not being essential to the History, but
> containing principally a defence of King R. The contents
> of this vol. with a short addition at the end of the 2ᵈ book,
> concerning the authors ancestors, is printed with slight
> alterations, in 'The complete History of England vol. 1.
> 1706. pp. 514-545 . . . . It was previously published in
> folio in 1646. —

Printed Edition of 1646

[Within a frame of double rules] THE / HISTORY / of the Life and Reigne of /
RICHARD / The Third. / [rule] / Compoſed in five Bookes / by GEO: BUCK
Eſquire. / [rule] / *Honorandus est qui injuriam non fecit, ſed qui alios eam facere non /
patitur, duplici Honore dignus est.* / Plato de legibus. Lib. 5. / *Qui non repellit a
proximo injuriam ſi potest, tam est in vitio quam / ille qui infert.* / D. Ambros. offic.
Lib. 3. / [rule] / [printer's ornament] / [rule] / LONDON, / Printed by *W. Wilſon,* and

are to be sold by / *W.L.H.M.* and *D.P.* 1646.

Facing title page, a print of Richard III with motto 'Royaulte [*sic*] me Lie' and superscription, 'The true Portraiture of Richard Plantagenest, of England and of France King Lord of Ireland and third King Richard', and signed 'Cross Sculp:'. There are commonly considered to be two early editions, an edition of 1646 and an edition of 1647.[4] Comparison of numerous typographical idiosyncracies which remain constant in all copies examined and notation of the few press corrections, which exist indiscriminately in copies dated 1646 and 1647, prove that there were two issues rather than two editions of this work. Only the date on the title page has been consistently changed in the copies issued later. Both issues were composed from the same sheets.

Small folio gathered in fours (the pages of my copy measure 27.5 × 18 cm). $2°\pi^2$, a, B-O^4 P^2 Q-T^4 V^3 *^{4}. Contents: [i] blank, [ii] title, [iii] blank, [iv-v] dedication, 1-150 text, [151-157] index, [157-158] glossary, [158] list of authors cited. First two leaves of each $ signed, B-N; first three leaves of O, R, S, and T signed; P unsigned; Q$_2$ missigned X$_2$ in some copies. P originally contained 4 leaves: page numbers 108-112 are missing. [P-P$_2$] pp. 105-107; [P$_2$^{v}] blank; P$_3$ and P$_4$, which are missing, were evidently blanks; Q is p. 113. Pagination is otherwise regular, in upper outside corners, arabic numerals ruled all round. Running titles, enclosed in rules: B$_2$^{v}-O '*The History of the Life and Reigne of* King RICHARD the Third'; V$_2$^{v} '*The History of* RICHARD *the Third*'; * - [*4] 'The Table'. Running heads also include the number of each book. The text is enclosed within rules; text area 23.5 × 14 cm. Margins are ruled. Catchwords regular except: p. 21 troubles (trouble); p.23 *Imi (Immisit)*; p. 27 *Solit (Solio)*; p. 58 But (but); p.148 Epi- (EPITAPHIVM); [p. 156] War (Warre). All copies, both 1646 and 1647, have on p. 147, between rows of printer's ornaments, '*Octob. 9. 1646. /* Imprimatur, *Na: Brent*'.

This edition was reprinted from a 1647 copy by E.P. Publishing in 1973 with an introduction by A.R. Myers.[5]

Strype's Edition

In 1706 and again in 1719 was published *A Complete History of England,* which is generally associated with the name of Bishop White Kennett, who wrote the final portion of it. The first volume is a selection of histories from before the conquest up to the end of Henry VII's reign. Authors such as Milton, Daniel, Habington, and Bacon are represented. For the reign of Richard III, we are given both the standard account of the reign, that of Sir Thomas More, and, as a complement to it, Buck's history. This has been done, according to the preface, because Buck's

> Relation is particular, and very remarkable for the Pains
> he takes to wipe off the bloody Stains upon King *Richard's*
> Character, and to vindicate from common Imputation one
> of the blackest Reigns in all our Story. Whether he has
> done it with Reason or not, let the Reader judge; for

there are various Opinions about it, and 'tis upon this
Account that the Booksellers were advis'd to print it. His
Book indeed, tho' it were all Truth, is much too loosely
writ for a History; 'tis pedantick and full of Harangue, and
may more properly be call'd *a Defence of King Richard*
than any thing else; yet as he is the only Advocate of Note
that has appear'd in so odd a Cause, 'tis well worth the
while to give him a Place here, tho' among so many of his
Betters. In some things 'tis highly probable he has done the
King but Justice; yet 'tis strange he'll neither allow him to
have had any Deformity in Mind or Body, for he is angry to
find him describ'd by others crook-back'd, and of an ill
Visage, and seems to be for reversing his Character throughout. 'Twas not fit to let this Work pass without some
Animadversions; and, to set all things as much in the Light
as possible: Mr. *Stripe*, an industrious Antiquary, has added
large Notes and Remarks, from an Authentick Manuscript
which he had by him, and from other Authors.[6]

The text is printed, with no alterations, from the 1646 edition. Obvious printing
errors, misspellings of names (e.g., Bevier for Beaujeu), and incorrect grammar and
spelling in foreign quotations are left uncorrected. The only intrusion Strype has
made into the body of the work is to translate into English occasional foreign
passages. Except for noting one 'patch'd Quotation' from Commynes (p. 562), he
never takes the trouble to check any of Buck's references against their originals.
Neither has he bothered to correct or expand marginal notes to historical works.

Strype's notes to the text, far from extensive, are sporadic, unsystematic, and
often inaccurate. He points out in a few places Buck's more obvious mistakes. He
notes, for example, Buck's incorrect reference to activity performed by Charles,
Duke of Burgundy when this duke was in fact dead (p. 553). But he himself makes
similar mistakes through failing to consult the sources Buck cites. Strype belabours
points which Buck has already made perfectly clear, insisting, for example, upon
calling Lionel, Duke of Clarence Edward III's third son, though Buck has given
reasons for his deliberate decision to style him the second son.

Supplementary illustrative material is occasionally introduced from MS. Harleian
433 — the 'Authentick Manuscript which he had by him' — of which he was at that
time the owner; but his researches extend no farther into original sources. Aside
from these few additions from the 'Journal of Richard III', his 'Animadversions'
consist mainly of contradictions based on the statements of More, Hall, Holinshed,
Grafton, and Bacon. When Buck's statements, no matter how well supported,
disagree with those of the chroniclers, they are censured by Strype as 'notorious
falsity', and the conflicting statement from the chronicles given as 'proof' of the
falsehood. Strype seems singularly uncritical of these authors' authority, assuming
them to be correct because he considers them contemporary with the events they
describe. For example, he counters Buck's statement that no contemporary author

charges Richard with murdering Henry VI by saying that Hall, More, and Bacon all make this accusation (p. 549).

Yet even into these sources Strype's search has not gone far, for although he notices Buck's statement that Richard did not reward Banister is incongruous with the grant of land to Banister recorded in Harleian 433, he neglects to cite Hall as being the source of Buck's misinformation. Similarly he attacks the reference from Camden which states that Richard was a bad man but a good king (see text, p.46) by quoting uncomplimentary remarks which Camden makes elsewhere about Richard and says suspiciously that in any case Buck 'does not tell us where *Cambden* speaks so well of him' (p. 525). Obviously Strype has not wished to take the trouble to look this up in Camden or in Buck's manuscript or even in the Editor's copies of it, all of which give a marginal note on this quotation. When attempting to support a case by using material other than the chroniclers, Strype's reasoning is equally feeble. The identity of the bones found in the Tower as those of the Princes he considers 'proved' by the fact that Charles II was satisfied they were.

Strype ends his extremely shoddy piece of editorial work in a state of some perplexity, unable to reconcile the common chroniclers with the one piece of contemporary material which he possessed, Harleian 433. In his concluding note he gives documentary evidence of Richard's regard for learning, religion, justice, and public welfare, saying, 'Could this King be brought off from the horrid Imputation that lies upon his Memory, of much Bloodshed, Oppression and gross Hypocrisy, to gain and keep the Crown, one might judge him a good King' (p. 576).

Yarnold's Intended Edition

In the first quarter of the nineteenth century, a new edition of Buck's *History,* hitherto unnoticed, went a long way toward completion. The five volumes of collections[7] made by the prospective editor, a surgeon Charles Yarnold, including Egerton 2216, the manuscript on which he based his intended edition, were sold at Sotheby's to the British Museum in 1873, valued collectively at £21. The sale catalogue identified Egerton 2216 as 'GEORGE BUC, Esq. *the original M.S.*', and Buck is styled Master of the Rolls (*sic*), a Gentleman of the Privy Chamber under James I, and 'a distinguished poet as well as historian' (Eg. 2218, f. 1). The final note of the advertisement remarks that 'This Manuscript Volume, edited by the aid of the accompanying materials, would make a suitable publication for a literary club'.

Yarnold's work on this intended edition seems to have extended from 1814 to 1821 and was probably terminated by his death. In 1825 his complete library, amounting to some 573 items, of which the Buck manuscript was the last, was sold at auction by Southgate of Fleet Street. It included Bacon's *Henry VII,* Camden, Cotton's Tower Record abridgements, Commynes, Drake's *Eboracum,* Gainsford's *Perkin Warbeck,* Hall, Habington's *Edward IV,* Hardyng, Hutton's *Bosworth Field,* Lingard, Paradin, Paris, Rapin, Polydore Vergil, Walpole's *Historic Doubts*, Matthew of Westminster, and a manuscript copy of Sir William Cornwallis' *Encomium of Richard III.*[8]

Yarnold's interest in Richard III was evidently of long standing, for he says in his draft for the preface of his intended edition that

> . . . at a very early period a strong interest for research into the manners & history of the 15 Century led me to attend to the several historians who wrote of that period More particularly however the Person & character & [*sic* for 'of'] Richard — was the constant subject of con sideration —
> (Egerton 2218, f. 46).

It is possible that this interest was aroused by Walpole's *Historic Doubts,* published first in 1768. Yarnold acquired MS. Egerton 2216 on 23 November 1810, as he has written on its title page. It is not known how it came to him — for he says in his preface only that he acquired it by 'accident' (Egerton 2218, f. 46), or 'a fortunate occurence' (f. 48).

Egerton 2220, a collection of letters relating to the publication of Yarnold's edition, indicates that part of it was in press late in 1814. A delay occurred in 1815 when the publisher, Richard Rees, retired from business and turned the work over to his brother at Longman's. It is certain that in 1816 the edition was going forward, for in that year Yarnold writes in a draft of a letter to someone possessing original documents that he is 'at this moment editing a republication of that singular Historian & apologizer for the unfortunate Richard, a Prospectus of which I enclose . . .' (Eg. 2218, f. 184). The Prospectus, 'Printed for RICHARD REES, No. 62, Pall Mall', states that the edition is 'In the Press, and speedily will be published', with prices fixed at £1-11-6 for quarto and £2-12-6 for large paper copies (Eg. 2218, f. 2). Throughout the years 1816 and 1817 the printer, Arthur Taylor, attempts to urge Yarnold on, even at one point telling him in a letter of 2 May 1816 that another bookseller had undertaken to publish Buck's *History* from the 1616 edition '& *has actually begun* it!!!! . . . So the world may lose, for Ever, the advantage of a Manuscript which *you,* the *Zealous* defender of Dickon Plantagenest have had sundry years in your possession!' (Eg. 2220, f. 28).

During this time and up to 1821, Yarnold was actively involved in research for the edition. His transcript of Egerton 2216, Books II-V, which takes up the first volume of his collections, is undated, but it includes in the margin collational notes from Tiberius and the printed version. In Egerton 2218, f. 37^v, Yarnold gives the date on which he finished the collation of Tiberius as October 1815. His notes from the Rolls Office are similarly dated (Eg. 2218, f. 243), while his transcripts from the Harleian Manuscripts are dated exactly a year later (Eg. 2219, f. 88), and miscellaneous collections from other sources he has dated 1818 (Eg. 2218, f. 107). A discourse and notes on More, obviously intended as commentary for the edition, are dated 1817 (Eg. 2218, f. 121), and a similar discussion of Howes' edition of Stow is dated 1818 (f. 199). The latest date given in his collections is March 1821, when he records completing his transcript of the *Arrivall of Edward IV* (Eg. 2219, f. 1), and in July 1821 someone sent him an extract on Richard III in French (Eg. 2220, f. 73).

There exist in the collection several corrected proof sheets for Book I, numbered pp. 1-32 (sigs. B1-E4). The corrections perhaps provide some clue to Yarnold's motive for suspending the printing. The transcripts of Books II-V (Eg. 2217) in Yarnold's hand follow the manuscript's spelling, though not its paragraphing, punctuation, and capitalization. The printed pages have done the same. However, in the printed pages 1-8 and 25-32, Yarnold has systematically altered the spelling to modern, and he includes a fair copy manuscript in modern spelling to supersede printed pp. 17-24, in which he had first made only general editorial corrections without modernizing spelling. He evidently had changed his mind or was uncertain about printing the edition 'in the orthography of the writer' as his draft for the preface indicates was his original intention (Eg. 2218, f. 48).

Clearly Yarnold believed at first that Egerton was Sir George Buck's original manuscript, and in his draft for the preface of his edition of it he does not mention and evidently does not yet know of Tiberius. He says of his collating activity at this stage only that

> . . . as it [Eg. 2216] explicitly declares itself the only MS
> — of this historian — I tooke the pains to collate this with
> the printed copy — published in 1646 — the large curtail-
> ments & in many places compressions of which were striking
> — indeed in some instances omissions are to be detected
> perfectly unaccountable — if We consider Buck himself to
> have edited the Work
> (Eg. 2218, f. 48).

In his list entitled 'Arguments for the originality of the M.S.' (Eg. 2217, f. 1), he is clearly pitting it against the printed edition alone. He remarks on the printed edition's references to books (e.g., *Religio Medici*) published after Buck's death and on its blurring of what appear in Egerton as clear personal references (e.g., to Buck's own experiences, to *viva voce* evidence, to other works by Buck). The title page ascription to 'George Buck, Esq.' obviously conflicts with the assumption that the work is Sir George Buck's, but Yarnold tries to resolve this confusion by citing the marginal note in Egerton 2216, f. 153 which speaks of 'this Sir Geo. Buck'.

His conclusion, probably influenced by Malone,[9] is that although Egerton was the work of Sir George Buck, the printed edition was published by his son. In a note (Eg. 2218, f. 37^v), Yarnold conjectures,

> I should think that Buck the Editor [of the printed edition]
> never saw my M.S. [Egerton 2216] — and from the com-
> parison of the Printed Dedication with Sir Georges I am
> led to believe that he crossed out the parts which appeared
> scored — & took out what he chose to insert in his own
> Edition wishing as it should seem to pass for the author as
> in the Pub. Copy he no where acknowledges it to be his
> father's.

Thus Yarnold takes one step toward Eccles' theory of progressive alterations of the text by a Buck descendant. [10] But his eventual discovery of Tiberius led him no further along these lines, for he judges this manuscript to be merely the 'Rough Papers' for Egerton, Buck's own fair copy. In comparing the hands of the two manuscripts he notes that the 'correction hand' of Tiberius, which he assumes to be Sir George's own, is the same as that of the preface and several emendations in Egerton, and hence, he claims, 'the identity of both as Sir G. Bucks is ascertained beyond doubt' (Eg. 2217, f. 1ᵛ). At several points in Egerton 2216 he makes pencilled notes to the effect that the hand of a certain emendation or marginal note is the same as the hand in Tiberius (see for example Yarnold's notes in Egerton 2216, ff. 49 and 64ᵛ).

By the time the proof sheets were printed, Yarnold had collated Egerton with Tiberius and, both in pencilled notes in Egerton 2216 and in the marginal notes to his own transcript of Egerton 2216, Books II-V, had cited certain matters of interst from Tiberius. His notes from Tiberius can be classified as indicating particular interest in autobiographical information; personal, including religious, opinion; strong statements in favour of Richard, and even more frequently and consistently strong statements against Richard's enemies; and expanded information on figures contemporary with Buck or with Richard. These notes appear much more frequently in the earlier stage of the transcript where Yarnold was evidently paying closer attention to Tiberius.

His collections include transcripts of only a small portion of Tiberius, the Dedication and Advertisement to the Reader (Eg. 2218, ff. 35-37 and 50-51). Since he considered the Editor's deletions and additions authorial, there was no purpose in his transcribing more of what he considered only rough papers. His transcripts seem at first glance potentially useful to the modern reader of Tiberius, since some words no longer present seem to have been still in the manuscript when Yarnold saw it. However, since these at times do not accord with the sense of the passage, one must conclude that they are conjectural emendation by Yarnold. His observations on the form of the Tiberius manuscript are negligible. He mentions only that Buck has used the back of a letter for one of its pages. No reference is made to the Revels Office scraps.

Yarnold evidently intended to check the foreign quotations carefully before printing them, for he notes that the Ariosto passage (text, p. 85) is probably not in correct Italian and should be corrected with a good edition (Eg. 2217, f. 23ᵛ). As transcription progresses, his copying of the foreign quotations becomes increasingly careless and incomplete, as if he intended to go back over them all. It is possible that he planned to check and augment the marginal notes throughout the edition, for in the manuscript fair copy for an early portion of Book I he adds a book's title where only the author's name is given in Tiberius, Egerton, and the printed edition.

In Yarnold's collections appear several lists of research plans carried out. Egerton 2218 and 2219 include biographical material on Buck copied from the *General Biographical Dictionary* and from Cotton manuscripts; several of the Paston letters; excerpts from Habington, Rastell, Hutton, Walpole, Drake's *Eboracum*, Strype's notes to Kennett's edition of the *History*, and other printed sources; a discussion of More's authority; and transcripts from the Harleain manuscripts, particularly 433. He has given references to a book by Sir John Jacob, the dedicatee of Egerton 2216, to *The Great Plantagenet* (George Buck, Esquire's revision of *Daphnis*), and to Buck's *Third Universitie*. There are also various notes on buildings and persons of Richard III's period.

Drafts for the Appendix to Book I had been composed. These include the Paston references to the death of the Bastard of Fauconberg; arguments against the existence of a marriage between Anne Neville and the son of Henry VI; Paston evidence of Clarence's aggression; the doubtful death of Edward IV; discussion of Morton's authorship of at least the outlines of More's history (Yarnold makes a note to himself that he intends to try to locate Morton's original); quotations from More and Paston on the hatred by the Woodvilles of Edward IV's family; and statements on the authenticity of Richard's election, including both More's account of the Three Estates' petition to Richard and the confirmatory evidence of the *Titulus Regius* given in full.

Yarnold's assessment of Buck is that he relies for credibility on his own integrity and social position and on his acquaintance with contemporary authorities, and thus that he sometimes seems offhand and unsystematic in citing his authorities. Yarnold imagines that he must have relied very heavily on family tradition, both his own and that of the Howards, for he shows a fondness for 'ancestorial dignity' (Eg. 2218, f. 116^v) and 'a quiet settled sort of contempt' for the common chroniclers, an attitude which 'has much the appearance of being a common one among the better informed or the Noble whose private family records probably were often in direct confutation of the erroneous histories in common circulation' (Eg. 2218, f. 117^v). Nevertheless, Yarnold observes, Buck has taken pains to corroborate these family traditions with evidence from his antagonists, with carefully sought and chosen *viva voce* evidence, and with the resources of the public records. 'His stile is censured and I think justly . . . that he participates in the pedantic spirit of the age is evident . . . ' (Eg. 2218, f. 47).

NOTES

1.   See below, p. lxxii.

2.   Marcham, p. 6.

       Mr Fisher recalls that he purchased the MS. in 1950 or 1951 and that the catalogue came out about a year earlier.

4.   *Sic STC* and Bodleian Library catalogue. A.R. Myers in his introduction to the 1973 reprint of the 1646 edition refers to the reissue as '2nd edition' (p. vi, n. 1), and the publishers speak of reproducing 'the 1647 edition' (title p. verso). The British Library catalogue lists it correctly as a reissue of the 1646 edition.

5.   See below, pp. xcvii-xcix for discussion of Myers' views on Buck.

6.   [?] Hughes, Preface to [White Kennett], *A Complete History of England* (London, 1706), sig. a^v. Further references will be given in the text.

7.   Now classified in the British Library as Egerton 2216-2220. References to these MSS. will henceforth be given in the text.

8.   For discussion of this work's relation to Buck's *History,* see below, pp. ciii-cvi. For further notice of this particular MS. copy (now B.L. MS. Additional 29307) see J.A. Ramsden and A.N. Kincaid, Introd. to Sir William Cornwallis, *The Encomium of Richard III,* ed. A.N. Kincaid (London, 1977).

9.   See below, pp. lxiv-lxv.

10.   Eccles, pp. 485-503.

V. TRANSMUTATION OF THE TEXT

Sir George Buck's manuscript *Hi~'ory of King Richard the Third* had a curious future. Its author never finished his work on it but left it in a rough state of completion, heavily revised and often with decisions not made between revisions, but almost ready for copying fair. After his death it found its way eventually into Cotton's library, by what means it is not known. It is listed in the 1674 catalogue (Harl. 694) as existing in this collection, of which it still forms a part. But this was not before it had undergone considerable revision by another hand and a master copy had been made from it. The other hand was that of Buck's great-nephew who, except for the suffix 'Gent.' or 'Esq.' instead of 'Knight', shared his name and until this century managed to borrow a share of his fame as well. He seems to have been ambitious for preferment, and his methods of seeking it cannot be described as honest.

Mark Eccles suggests that young George Buck got possession of the manuscript through his father's embezzlement of money, books, and other valuables during Sir George's insanity. [1] The younger George's great-uncle, John Buck (no relation to Sir George's family) was a notorious forger who lost his ears and was branded in the business. Quite possibly his father shared the talent for forgery, since Sir George's will, which left his goods to his nephew Stephen Buck's family, was disputed as a forgery. This proclivity seems to have been inherited, with certain artistic distinctions, by George Buck, Esq.

The authorship of the 1646 edition remained a matter of confusion for some time, and the Bodleian catalogue still attributes it to 'Buck (George) son of Sir George' and refers the reader to the spelling 'Buc' for works by Sir George. This error originated with Malone:

> I take this opportunity of correcting an error into which Anthony Wood has fallen, and which has been implicitly adopted in the new edition of the *Biographia Britannica,* and many other books. The error I allude to, is, that this Sir George Buc, who was knighted at White-hall by king James the day before his coronation, July 23, 1603, was the author

of the celebrated *History of King Richard the Third*; which
was written above twenty years after his death by George
Buck, *Esq.* who was, I suppose, his son. [2]

Ritson in his copy of the 1646 edition, now in the British Library, made a note on
the flyleaf:

Wood attributes this history to Sir George Buck (or Buc, as
he himself spelled his name), the father, it is suppose'd of
this George Buck the publisher: and, though he possiblely
[*sic*] confounded the one with the other, there is good
reason, both from the work itself, and from a pamphlet
published by Sir George Buc, in 1605, under the title of
'Δαφνις Πολυστεφανος ... to conclude that he was the
true author. The matter, in short, is place'd beyond a
doubt by the title of a copy in the Cotton library (Tiberius
E.x.) though a few leaves only of the book itself are now
left, and those burnt round: 'The history of king Richard
the third, comprised in five books, gathered and written by
Sir G. Buck knight, master of the kings office of the revels,
and one of the gentlemen of his majesties privy chamber;
corrected and amended in every page.'[3]

In his *Bibliographia Poetica* he states this more succinctly as a direct reply to Malone:
that Sir George Buck was the true author of the 1646 *History* passing under the name
of George Buck, Esq., since the original manuscript, bearing his name, was still
extant in the British Museum.[4]

W. Carew Hazlitt was the first to note that more than one manuscript copy existed:
'The original MS. of his Life of Richard the Third, varying considerably from the
printed copy, 1646, is still extant, and one or two copies of it as well. It was probably
written at least 50 years, before it saw the light in a printed shape'.[5] As we have seen
in the previous chapter, Charles Yarnold owned one of the manuscript copies and
was planning to print it as Buck's original, assuming it to have been a fair copy made
for the author. Frank Marcham in 1925 had access to two manuscript copies (Egerton
and Fisher), yet still followed Yarnold's conjecture that these were fair copies made
for Buck,[6] though he does not adopt Yarnold's palaeographical error of assuming
that the hand of the copies is Buck's own. It was left for Mark Eccles to identify
George Buck, Esq., and discover the relationship of the copies to the original.[7]

Changes in Tiberius

The younger Buck's first step was to make alterations and corrections in the
manuscript itself. These are for the most part stylistic improvements. He simplifies
the tortuous constructions and dispenses with the innumerable 'and's' both in series
and at the beginnings of sentences. By employing subordination, he makes gram-

matical constructions more vivid. He sometimes creates immediacy by changing a verb from past to present tense. While in the first half of the book the Editor sometimes revises sentences and occasionally larger thought units for the sake of compression, he becomes bolder and more ruthless from the middle of Book III onward, and is readier to lop away whole pages of digressive, repetitive, or verbose material, sometimes replacing them with a few sentences summarizing their content, sometimes dispensing with them altogether. His stylistic revisions seem to have the purpose of diversifying and tightening the structure and reducing the size of the work.

Some examples of his stylistic changes are:

(1) diversifying the beginnings of sentences or clauses:
'and the which' becomes 'which'
'and now to proceed' becomes 'to proceed then'

(2) removal of 'and's' in series:
'& the Lord lovell, & the lord Graystok, & Sir William Parr'[8]
becomes 'the Lord lovell, the Lord Graystok, Sir William Parr'

(3) subordination within sentences:
'& he demandeth the erldom of Heryford' becomes
'demanding the erldom of Heryford'

(4) rewording and abbreviating to express more compactly:
'forejudge & hardly censure' becomes 'preiudicate'
'who was a man bredd in good letteres, & well languaged'
becomes a 'man well read and languaged'

(5) making language and construction more diverse and vivid:
'But to proceede with the affaires of these Armies now that thes two armies .i. the army of the king & the army of the rebells Lancastrians were nowe come to Redmore heath, and in viewe the one of the other, & were approachinge and disposed themselues to fight' becomes 'and nowe suppose you see the Kinges Army and the followers of Lancaster at Redmore heath and disposing themselues to fight' (f. 99).
The conversation between Edward IV and his mother (ff. 223-4) is given entirely in direct discourse instead of fluctuating between direct and indirect.

(6) prudery
'lustful' becomes in one instance 'sweetest' and in another 'amorous'
'wench' becomes 'fair one'
'lusts' becomes 'desires'.

Circumstantial detail is deleted, such as that surrounding Dethick's showing Buck the book of sobriquets (f. 10). Some philosophical digressions are reduced or discarded, but this is by no means true of all digressive material. Buck's innumerable pointers to what he has said or what he is about to say, and his cross-referencing of his own statements, are cut.

So far the alterations must in most cases be described as improvements, making the work more compact and readable. One can only regret that Buck did not remain in health long enough to have undertaken similar revision himself. But other types of

revision alter the matter of his work. These are of three main varieties: toning down
political references, particularly with regard to the treason of Henry Tudor and his
followers against Richard III; removing religious references; and concealing the
personal aspects of the work. In doing these things, the Editor begins a process which
he pursues with increasing severity through all his future copies.

In his political revisions he gives special attention to whitewashing Morton:

'all his secret & trayterous practises' becomes 'all his secret practises'

'almost as badd, & fals, & disloyall as himself' becomes 'almost as deadly as
himself'

'Thus the oratour of sedition, & he told his tale so cunningly as that the duke was
agayn, & anew stirred vp *to be f*alse, & disloyal \ & false hearted to his prince/
& hee was with these divelish seditious arguments much \ more / encouraged &
enflamed with the fyre & fury of rebellion' becomes simply 'as that the duke
was agayn incendiated' (f.57^v)

The reference to Morton's gaining advancement through treachery and malice is
omitted, as are suggestions of his complicity in the deaths of Edward, Earl of
Warwick and Perkin Warbeck (ff. 192^v and 202). The remarks about Henry's failing
to punish the Princes' murderers because they were favoured in high places (ff. 205-
206^v) disappear.

Henry's other followers fare better with the Editor than with the author:

'thes noble rebells' becomes 'his partyes' (f. 66)

'Welshe and false knights and Esquires and manie perfidious and rebellious
Englishmenn of all quallities' becomes 'other of all quallities' (f.96).

Criticism of Henry himself is diluted by the Editor. Instead of being ambitious and
egotistical, his temper becomes 'as other men's (f. 21^v). The remark about his risking
his reputation and his soul by following Morton's evil counsel rather than the divine
spirit is deleted (f. 79^v) as is the wish that Henry, although destined to be king, had
awaited the Lord's leisure (f. 263). Instead of disliking combat and being far inferior
to Richard in arms, Henry had 'the advantage other wayes' (f. 103). Examples of
kings keeping the crown from the true heirs are deleted (f. 192^v), and what was
originally a literal translation of the quotation 'prosperum scelus virtus vocatur' —
'*the* wicked act succeeding well is called a vertew' — is softened by judicious crossing
out to '*the* act is called a vertew' (f. 20).

The extensive paraphrasing of the particularly diffuse section on Perkin Warbeck
in the second half of Book III has a serious effect on its content, which seems
intentional: it destroys or dilutes most of the statements that the foreign princes who
aided Perkin believed in the justice of his title, as did the majority of the populace.
Long religious digressions are invariably excised, though brief references are un-
touched. As in his revision of *Daphnis*, the Editor tends to alter or remove the name
of God. Clearly the Editor's intention was to avoid potentially controversial material
in politics and religion.

His alterations in Tiberius take the form of crossing out words, lines or pages,
and rewriting above the lines or in the margins, or very occasionally on scrap sheets,
reworking — primarily for stylistic improvement — the elder Buck's original. There
is no evidence of his adding any factual material of his own, though there is some

stylistic elaboration. The date of this revision must be placed after 1625, since a reference to King James has been altered to read 'our King', and the description of Arundel as young is discarded (f. 239). This work was probably done considerably later than this; probably after his publication in 1635 of *The Great Plantagenet,* his revision of *Daphnis,* the younger Buck felt the challenge of a larger work. Dating the revision of the original manuscript after 1635 would place it nearer the manufacture of the copies, around 1638-40. But there is no internal evidence to permit a closer dating.

In this process of revision an attempt has been made to dispose of the work's autobiographical aspects. The reference to the Earl of Oxford's conversation with Buck about the revenue of his land (ff.209-10) is deleted and the information given with no personal reference. Nearly all the praise of Queen Elizabeth (f.134^v) is cut out. We can see in this only a glimmering of the younger Buck's scheme to pass off the work as his own. He has not dealt systematically with all personal references and indeed does so only gradually through the course of the successive copies. Eccles seems correct in calling his revisions of this type 'haphazard'.[9] These excisions fit his general revision pattern of cutting down passages which are too circumstantial (as in the case of the Earl of Oxford anecdote) or go on too long after making their point (as in the case of the Queen Elizabeth eulogy). All we can say positively at this stage is that the Editor was attempting to update the work.

The 'Literary Career' of George Buck, Esquire

Buck the Younger's life of literary deception seems to have been a succession of appeals to potential patrons in hope of obtaining preferment. He seems never to have met with success. He began at some point after 1625 when Charles I came to the throne, and his first traceable attempt was made on 'Sir John Burrough K*night* principall Kinge att Armes'.[10] The work he dedicated to Burrough is a manuscript revision of his great-uncle's *Daphnis Polystephanos.* Evidently possessing the original manuscript of this work as he did of the *History* (this original unfortunately does not survive), he seems not to have been aware that it had already been published in 1605. The younger Buck's manuscript of *Daphnis,* in a state of revision between the two printed versions, Sir George's of 1605 and his own of 1635, is written in the same hands as the three copies of the *History* made for him. The title page and dedication with its signature are in the same hand (his own) as the title pages, dedication, and corrections in Egerton, Malone, and Fisher. The title of the manuscript version is 'Δαφνι ς *or the Polyanthine Ghirland.* by George Buc. gent.' He signs the dedication with one of his usual formulae: 'Y*our* vnfeigned honorer and humble Servant George Buc:' (f. 3). The dedication is similar to the one in the printed version of t!.e *History,* where he deprecates his own ability and protests his zeal.

He then published the work in 1635, still evidently unaware that it had been previously published; and true to his usual practice in his various copies of the *History,* he dedicates the printed version to someone else, this time to Sir John Finch, Lord Chief Justice of the Court of Common Pleas, a dedication perhaps suggesting that his own training, like his great-uncle's, had been in law. The poem has been revised to focus on Charles I and has been retitled *The Great Plantagenet or a Continued Svccession of that Royall Name*. The dedication includes self-conscious remarks on the 'author's ability: 'There wants nothing in the *Subiect* to make an *Historian* and a *Poet*. And had these *Intentions* met an abler *Pen*, they might (with some desert of Pardon, haue beene admitted the intermission of your *Lordships* more serious Houres . . .' (A3ᵛ). He remarks rather slyly, 'in these *Papers* I have but practis'd like a young Limbner, wipt away the *dust* from some *Antiquities*, and by them drawne these proportions . . .' (A3), and closes, 'Your most humble and unfained honorer, *George Buck*'.

Although *STC*, no. 3997, lists this edition under the works of Sir George Buck, Ritson observed early in the last century that the 1635 edition 'appears to be a reprint of the former, with very considerable alterations, by some fellow who assume'd his name'.[11] In fact, the practice the author follows 'like a young Limbner' is forgery, and his name, except that it lacks the prefix 'Sir', is the same.

The nephew's changes in *Daphnis* are of several types: general reorganization for the sake of clarity; excision of boring and drawn out passages; removal of the original's references to God; and making the whole refer to King Charles rather than to King James. The younger Buck shows himself here as in the *History* a good reviser and organizer of another's material. But wherever he drastically revises existing verse or substitutes verses of his own, he shows himself a poor poet. He has no sense of metre, his language is trite, inappropriate, and insipid. We shall find similar stylistic flaws in his final revision of the *History*.

One would imagine the younger Buck was running some risk in publishing under his own name and with scant revision a work dedicated to the former king which was already published and in the libraries of great men, and which he had presented in a manuscript of his own with a dedication to another prospective patron. And in connection with this or some similar practice with another work, he does — as we shall see — seem to have been censured for reissuing with different dedications works already circulating.

Whether the translation of Lipsius[12] dedicated to Sir John Jacob, one of the farmers of the king's customs, was actually the younger Buck's own work or again a copy of his great-uncle's efforts is not known. That no translation, unpublished or published, is extant under Sir George Buck's name or in his hand does not preclude the possibility of its existence at one time. Lipsius was an antiquary who spoke highly of Camden, and Buck mentions him (but only as an authority on fencing) in *The Third Universitie* (sig. Oooo 2). A translation of Lipsius would have been a natural work for Sir George to have undertaken. However, the fluidity of the language, not laboured as the elder Buck's tends to be, suggests that this very literal translation may really be the work of the man who has put his name to it. The dedication does not involve subterfuges, as do those of the *History* copies, but rather concentrates on the worthiness of the dedicatee, whom young Buck has clearly not approached before:

> Sir: if you aske why this to you, I must appeale to the
> priviledg of you [sic] noble and generall fame, which hath
> improud itself beyond the touch of envy, and plac'd you so

eminently in the esteeme of all good men, that (without
thought of flattery I may avouch it) I haue been vnfainedly
ambitious (in the thronge of those that hono*ur* you) to
offer a zealous vote, to yo*ur* enobled Merritt . . . .

His self-deprecation is expressed in a much more confident tone than that which he
employs later: 'if my zeale hath been too bold and forward, it will not bee much
vnworthy, your fauour and pardon, since (in this) I haue onely sought to expresse
myself your vnfained and humble honoure^r George Bucke'. Young Buck seems to
have employed for most of this presentation the same scribe who was responsible for
the *Daphnis* and three major *History* copies, with the title page and dedication and
corrections, and, as it appears, a few pages of the text in his own hand.

After Lipsius, young George began his manipulations of the *History*. From the
original manuscript, now bearing his own revisions, he seems to have made or had
made for him a master copy which he used in having all his subsequent copies
prepared. The first of these, Egerton 2216, is addressed to Sir John Jacob in a
dedicatory preface which uses some phrases from Sir George Buck's dedication of
the original manuscript to Arundel. As Eccles notes,[13] the presentation would have
had to have occurred between 1638 and 1642, since it refers to the translation of
Lipsius, dated 1638, and Jacob was declared delinquent in his office in 1642. The date
can be fixed even closer by reference to Jacob's publication in his own defence: 'To
be thought rich', he says in 1654, 'was I hope my greatest Crime, and now to be
thought poore, is my greatest Labour', and he claims to have been 'in the midst of
these waves these thirteen years', i.e., since 1641. 1640 would have been the last year
in which Jacob was secure in his position and 'thought rich', for in that year the
farmers had entered into contract with the king and advanced or engaged large sums
for his wars. But Parliament had cancelled the contract, appropriated these sums to
its own uses, then accused the farmers of delinquency and forced them to submit to
composition. From then on, there were for the farmers a series of petitions and
hardships.[14]

It seems that Jacob received the translation favourably but issued a caveat regarding
Buck's having put out a duplicate of some work already in circulation. *Daphnis* is
likely to have been the work in question, easily detected since it was already in print.
Probably Buck pressed the *History* on Jacob very soon after that detection to show
his good intentions, professing that there is no extant copy but his own rough papers:
'I haue nowe aduentured it, to your noble patronage, and giue mee leaue noblest S*ir*
to cleere my self thus farr vnto you (in respect of your former doubt) that (as I respect
your worth and fauour) but my rough papers there is no Copy saue this, which I
present . . .' (ff. 2^v-3). The words 'rough papers' could refer both to his great-uncle's
manuscript, his through 'inheritance', and to his own master copy from which his
subsequent copies seem to have been made. The dedication includes an ambiguous
apology similar to those prefacing the younger Buck's versions of *Daphnis*: he
deprecates his own ability and leads the reader to believe, while not actually saying
so, that he is the author. His words, 'the history laye vnder a rough draught; *which* I

haue hasted to perfect (f. 2ᵛ) recalls the 'young Limbner' remark in *The Great Plantagenet.*

When Jacob's position became insecure, or possibly even before, Buck looked elsewhere for patronage. He next tried Lord Aylesborough, Keeper of the Privy Seal, to whom he dedicated the copy now known as Malone 1. Since Aylesborough died early in 1640, and this was also the year in which Jacob's position became precarious, it is probably early in this year that the dedication was made. There was yet a third copy made, the one now in the Fisher Rare Book Library of the University of Toronto. No dedication exists to show for whom it was intended. Perhaps it was a copy Buck kept on hand in case of future need: indeed Keen's catalogue, as already noted,[15] mentions the six blank pages at the beginning and suggests that they were intended for a dedication. Manuscript peculiarities indicate that Fisher was made almost concurrently with Malone.

Very little else is known of the younger Buck. Of his associates we know only that Robert Codrington contributed to the prefatory material of *The Great Plantagenet* a laudatory poem, speaking of the author in very general terms and in a tone which does not necessarily suggest close relationship. In 1647 young Buck, in company with Waller, Lovelace, Webster, and Habington, contributed some laudatory verses to a volume of Beaumont and Fletcher's works[16] published by John Lowin, Richard Robinson and others, and dedicated to the Earl of Pembroke, to whom he had in the previous year dedicated the *History* in its published form. The Earl of Pembroke was Lord Chamberlain at the time. This may indicate that the younger Buck was pursuing an office in the Revels. The poem is in couplets, the lines not adeptly fitted to the metre, and the wording sometimes awkward or unsuitable. It ends tritely:

> Let *Shakespeare*, *Chapman*, and applauded *Ben*,
> Weare the Eternall merit of their Pen,
> Here I am love-sicke: and were I to chuse,
> A mistress corrivall 'tis *Fletcher*'s Muse.

and is signed 'George Buck'.

His place seems thus to have been that of a very minor literary figure, occasionally admitted to the society of great names, partly on the strength of his uncle's work; pursuing acquaintances similar to his uncle's — antiquaries, heralds, and authors; aspiring to court or government preferment but evidently unsuccessful in obtaining it. After the 1646 publication and 1647 reissue of the *History* and the 1647 poem to Fletcher, nothing further is heard from or of him.

Egerton, Malone, and Fisher

The first three manuscript copies of the *History*, Egerton, Malone, and Fisher, are by the same hand, that of a scribe who clearly had no knowledge of foreign languages or of history, for his errors in foreign quotations and in names of persons and places are numerous. He is obviously following the same manuscript for all three copies, for most of the habitual errors in foreign languages and in proper names are the same in all, and words and names with variant spellings are usually spelled in the same way at the same point in the text of each copy. For example, the spellings 'Beajer', 'Beaugeu' or 'Beauyer', 'Beaujew', and 'Beaujeu' — for a name consistently spelled 'Beaujeu' in Tiberius — appear in their variant forms at the same points in Egerton, Malone, and Fisher.

The Editor has in his own hand gone through the copies rapidly and made a few minor changes in style and matter, sometimes crossing out personal references which would suggest he was not the author, sometimes deleting uncomplimentary references to Morton and other followers of Henry VII. His proofreading seems to have been very cursory, for he corrects only a few errors in names and in foreign words. When making these minor alterations in his own hand in Egerton, he seems to have made many of them simultaneously in then master copy, so that they appear in the texts of Malone and Fisher as well. He has done the same when revising Malone, since the alterations he makes in Malone often appear in Fisher, Additional, and the printed edition. It is not clear that he did so in the case of the Fisher revisions, since Additional and the printed edition seem closer to Malone than to Fisher.

On first glance one would assume that Fisher is a copy of Malone. However, closer examination proves this impossible. The two copies are very close in their use of accidentals. In spelling peculiarities, placement of commas, and tendency to capitalize they are very close to each other, much closer than either is to Egerton. This closeness is shown in the striking regularity with which habitual differences from Egerton in the spelling of common words occur in Malone and Fisher identically:

Egerton	*Malone and Fisher*
authority	autority
howse	house
-*cion*	-*tion*
desimulac*ion*	dissimulat*ion*
Earle	Erle
accompte	account

However, errors and unintentional omissions occurring in one do not appear in the other. Intentional alterations made in Malone, including those made by the Editor above the line, sometimes appear in Fisher, but just as often they do not. Evidence indicates that Fisher is the later copy: Malone is closer to Egerton in accidentals than is Fisher. Whereas Fisher incorporates changes made in Malone, Malone incorporates none of Fisher's deletions or alterations in wording. Fisher proceeds farther than Malone in material changes, in the deletion of personal references and derogatory remarks about Richmond's party, especially Morton. The explanation of their closeness seems to lie in (1) their being done at about the same time; (2) alterations made in Malone often being put into the master copy; (3) simultaneous correction of the two by the Editor.

We may infer something about the nature of the master copy by comparing the corrections in Malone and Fisher. It seems that the crossings out were not always clear, since often in Fisher the copyist does not realize until after he has written in a word or phrase that it was intended to have been deleted or emended, and then he crosses it out or changes it. For example, at one point Egerton says 'Treachery'. In Malone the word is 'practises'. Fisher gives '[treachery] practises'. This change in Fisher is made instantly, appearing on rather than above the line, and is typical of many similar corrections. It suggests that the emendation was made in the master copy with the new word written above the line and the discarded word only very lightly crossed out, or perhaps on occasion not crossed out at all. Some of the Editor's crossings out in his three copies are in the form of pale dashes rather than solid lines through the word, and we can see how unclear these might have appeared to the copyist when he encountered them in the master copy. When he made corrections in the copies themselves, the Editor evidently added many but not all of these to the master copy. And in addition he probably made minor emendations in the master copy between the creation of his various copies. This would account for the fact that Malone and Fisher often produce the same wording in places where Egerton's is different, a factor occurring far too frequently always to be the result of errors in Egerton. That all three copies used the same master can be inferred from the fact that although they are not dependent on each other they very often make the same misreadings in the same places. At one point in Tiberius the word 'contudit' appears. This is given by Egerton and Malone as 'conludit', evidently because of an uncrossed 't' in the master. In several places some error is made at an identical point in the text of all three copies, but not precisely the same error. This clearly occurs in places where the master was difficult to read.

Egerton, Malone, and Fisher are so close that they can be discussed together. What we have in them is a representation at some length of the original manuscript. The three copies differ from each other in that they make different errors at certain points, leaving out short sections by accident or misreading. They differ also in intentional alterations made by the Editor in the copies themselves or in the master between copies. Such changes are not numerous or considerable, but they are progressive except where an alteration has not found its way into the master copy. The copies are approximately two-thirds the length of the original and show progressive stylistic improvement and material alterations along precisely the same lines as those changes, already described, made by the Editor in the original manuscript. As we saw the Editor making changes in the holograph by removing personal reference, religious remarks, derogatory references to Henry Tudor and his followers, so in the copies we see him making further alterations on these points and making more of them as he progresses from copy to copy.

The stylistic revision shows continuing reduction of the innumerable 'and's, both through deletion and through substitution of other linking words. Rearranging of word order ensures that modifications are clear and points are not lost in verbal meandering. Verbs are often made more vivid by changing from past to present or passive to active. Pronouns are substituted for repetitive noun references, and unnecessary repetitions of words or ideas are avoided. Subsidiary or digressive factual information is often relegated to a marginal note. Repetitions and digressions are discarded and diffuse passages more compactly expressed, sometimes in little more than brief summary. But though much is given in summary, little of a material nature is entirely left out, and no new material is added.

The Editor gradually becomes bolder in the introduction of his own style, which is less pedestrian and more flowery than Sir George's. Thus Egerton's '. . . were become penetents, and made Confession thereof' becomes in Malone and Fisher, '. . . became so sensible thereof that at length, there penitence broke forthe ['brake out' in Fisher] into confession'. This tendency increases as the copies progress. Young Buck occasionally tries his hand in these manuscripts as in *Daphnis* at revising his uncle's verses. He makes a minor improvement in the Ariosto translation, where for the awkward first line, 'No man ever whilst he was happy knew', a somewhat more fluent 'No man whilst he was happy ever knew' is substituted. The copies make a few genuine corrections in their reorganization of material, for example deleting the references to *Utopia* and the eulogy of Queen Elizabeth from the list of contents at the beginning of Book IV. In Egerton and Malone these are written in but crossed out, and they do not appear at all in Fisher. The Editor had noticed that material on these subjects does not in fact appear in Book IV.

Since religion was not a safe subject, religious references, especially those which might be misconstrued as betraying Catholic ideology, are deleted. A mention of the Pope's 'spiritual power' is crossed out in Egerton, but since evidently the Editor forgot to cross this out in the master copy as well, it is retained by all the other copies, including the printed version (p. 47). The statement that the Plantagenets all passed one purgatory appears in Egerton and Malone but is crossed out in Fisher.

In these manuscripts, as in his revisions of the original, the Editor's most numerous and consistent revisions occur in passages describing Henry Tudor and his followers. These are reworded so as to soften or eliminate suggestions of sedition and treachery. The word 'treason' becomes 'inconstancy' or 'practices', and the word 'rebellion' becomes 'action'. Where Sir George had at one point revised to make an accusation stronger, substituting the word 'evil' for his original 'mighty', the Editor gradually dilutes this, correcting it in the original to 'cruell' then in Egerton, Malone, and Fisher to 'very insolent and strong'. Circumlocution is stretched almost to the breaking point when a statement that Richmond's followers were all rebels in Egerton is in Malone and Fisher turned into a comment on their loyalty: they 'could not be called soe' — i.e., loyal — 'beinge worse'.

Morton himself, once 'perfidious and treacherous' to Richard (Egerton) becomes 'extreamely his Enemy in harte' (Fisher); from 'Malitious Morton', he becomes 'B*isho*pp Morton'; from 'this politique prelate' (Egerton and Malone), simply 'hee' (Fisher). Derogatory descriptions of him, such as 'How Covetous hee was, those examples may giue a taste' (Egerton) are deleted (this one disappears in Malone but reappears by accident in Fisher). There is even perhaps a mild attempt to whitewash More by calling Bale's account of More 'Legend' in Malone and Fisher, whereas it appeared in Egerton as 'truth'.

Henry Tudor's practices, 'seditious & Ambitious' in Egerton and Malone, are only 'Ambitious' in Fisher. King James IV's ill affection to him disappears. At the end of Book III, revision of the criticism of the Tudor monarchy for destroying the rightful heirs who stood in their way is extensive in Fisher, and the statement that the Lancastrians were 'soe vehement, that they regarded noe title, how iuster, or better soever' is crossed out.

Considerably less deletion of personal references is made in Egerton than in the later copies. That Egerton leaves so many of these intact is extremely useful for filling in gaps burnt out of the original manuscript. As he progresses in his deception, the Editor becomes more careful. But one very interesting personal recollection, the mention of Mary, Queen of Scots' death, the end of which is burnt away in Tib., f.227, does not appear even in Egerton.

In Egerton there is a fascinating alteration, made by scraping rather than the usual crossing out. This concerns Buck's consultation with Dethick. All copies omit the personal detail surrounding this consultation. However, in Egerton the Editor has allowed himself to write the name 'William Dethick', only to erase 'Dethick' and write 'Segar', the name of Dethick's successor in office. Yarnold's pencilled note opposite this substitution in Egerton (f. 8ᵛ) observes the original manuscript's reading of 'Dethick' and says 'Segar is here evidently on an erasure and \ its Insertion / apparently some time subsequent. I think that part of the h. and the final letter k is visible.' Part of the initial 'D' is visible as well. In later copies the Editor is more careful and says merely 'in the rich studdy of a noble, and learned freind, I mett with a Catalogue of such Setbriquetts' (Malone and Fisher). In Additional he reduces it further: 'from a Catalogue of many I have translated these . . . .'

Other examples of *viva voce* information have been tampered with. The marginal note on Don Duarte de Lancastro which describes a conference at which Buck was present reads in the ensuing text, 'Don Duarte de Lancastro, a noble gentleman of Portugal, came to my Lord Admiral ambassador to the King of Spain, and to[ld] him that he was descen[ded] from the Duke of La[ncaster in] Valodolid. G.[B. *teste*]' (see below, text, p. 75). Changes have been gradually introduced into this note by the Editor. He has not touched it in the original manuscript and copies it *verbatim* in Egerton. But in Malone he alters 'came . . . and told him' to 'averred', and 'my Lord Admiral' to 'my Lord Howard'. Fisher repeats the change to 'averred' and deletes 'G.B. teste'.

A reference to material Buck has seen in Cotton's collection, which was shut down in 1629, is revised in Malone and Fisher, but not in Egerton, Additional, or the printed version. Malone has 'which Charter [is] \ was / in the hands of Sir Robert Cotton, [wherof I have read it and]\ from which I haue / transcribed, these summarye notes'. Fisher reads 'which Charter [is] / was / in the hands of Sir Robert Cotton, and / from thence / transcribed, these summarye notes, from'. As can be easily seen the revision was made carelessly, and it was obviously not copied carefully into the master script.

Viva voce information from Stow regarding Richard III's personal appearance is deprived of its firsthand nature. Egerton gives as they stand the words 'as he himself told me'. But in Malone, the scribe wrote these words in then crossed them out, changing them to 'protested averring', and a marginal note was added identifying the recipient of the information as Cotton: 'ad D: Rob: Cotton'. In Fisher again 'tould me' is written in but crossed out and altered to 'averred', and the marginal attribution to Cotton is retained. Thus where we originally had a personal confrontation between Stow and Buck, we now have a vague report that Stow averred to Cotton that Richard was not deformed, with no indication of how this hearsay might have reached Buck. Later on the same page another reference to what Stow 'told me' is retained in Egerton, but Malone has corrected this to '[tould mee] \ likewise reported /', and Fisher to '[told me]\ added /'. Again we have no indication of how this information reached the author. A later discussion with Stow, when Buck pressed him to know his opinion of the evidence for the murder of the Princes, is altered in Egerton to the nonsensical wording, 'Mr John Stowe affirmed confidently vpon occation, pressing to knowe', making it unclear who was pressing to know. Malone and Fisher remedy the structural awkwardness but do not improve credibility by saying Stow 'hath affirmed confidently to some'.

References to Buck's own works disappear. That not one reference to the *Baron* of the five which appear in Egerton exists in Malone and Fisher may indicate that the *Baron* was widely known. The excisions in the master copy of all references to it must have been very plain indeed. A single reference to the *Commentary* remains in all three copies, perhaps as an oversight, possibly suggesting that it was not so widely known. The translation from Ariosto, its first line improved, appears in Malone and Fisher with the comment, '\I / haue adventured thus to translate, without any forfeite to Sir Jon Harington as I hope', though in Egerton the remark that the author made his translation before Harington's stands.

Mentions of Sir George Buck himself are tampered with. The instance of deleting 'G.B. teste', indicating the author's presence at a conversation, has already been described. Two marginal notes regarding Buck's family at the end of Book II are emended: 'this Sir George Buck' is changed to 'this Author' in Malone and Fisher but not in Egerton. The printed version omits the note altogether. In the note which refers to 'Robert Buck my ffather', 'my father' appears in Malone but is crossed out there and reappears in Fisher. The same thing happens with Buck's reference to his participation in the Battle of Cadiz: it appears in all three copies but is crossed out in Malone. It does not appear in Additional and the printed version. In addition to these changes, the younger Buck becomes bolder in assuming authorship, changing the note on the title page from 'gathered and written by George Buck Esq.' in Egerton to 'Written by George Buck Esqʳ' in Malone.

Contemporary references or remarks bearing on contemporary situations suffer changes, both for political reasons and for the purpose of updating. In Malone and Fisher, though not in Egerton, the Editor is careful to avoid offence by deleting the note that James I was descended reputedly from a bastard son of Fleance. In speaking of Charles Howard of Effingham, who died in 1624, he changes Egerton's unaltered 'there is one liveing' to 'there was one lately liveinge' in Malone and Fisher. The master copy seems before Egerton was made to have altered a reference to Dr Godwin, 'now Bishoppe of Hereford' by removing 'now Bishoppe', so that Egerton and Malone read 'Dr. Goodwin, of Hereford.' Fisher ignores the crossing out in the master copy and replaces the phrase. A marginal note at this point gives the date 1620. This is crossed out in Malone, and it seems simultaneously to have been crossed out in the master as well, since Fisher does not include it. Thomas Gainsford is described in Book V of Egerton as still alive. Actually, he had died in 1624, and Malone and Fisher delete 'yet liueing'.

Though James I was king when the original was composed, he died in 1625. Consequently, though Egerton as usual makes few changes, Malone and Fisher in Book V alter the several present tense references to this king to the past tense. 'But had Sir Tho. Moore, liued in these dayes, hee had knowne a kinge, whose sacred temper, would not haue admitted such an Act' becomes '. . . liued in these latter dayes'. And the ensuing 'hee' is clarified in Malone and Fisher to refer to 'our late kinge of euer famous memory'. But these changes do not indicate that King James died between Egerton and Malone's composition, for even in his alterations of the original manuscript the Editor has changed a reference to King James by name to 'our king', indicating that James was no longer king when the editorial alterations were made in the original.

Additional and the Printed Version

The alterations made in the master copy between Malone and Fisher's composition and the printed stage were drastic. Additional, a fair copy of Books I and II, represents a state of revision very close to the printed edition, but it is neither its direct source nor derived from it. It is in a different hand from the earlier copies, and the Editor's hand appears nowhere. The purpose for which it was made is not known. The revisions which led to Additional and the printed version do not take account of Fisher: many corrections appearing in Fisher but in neither of the previous copies are not taken up by Additional and the printed edition. That in some places the wording of Additional is closer to that of Fisher than to the earlier manuscripts may represent minor revision made in the master copy between Malone and Fisher. Of the three early copies, Malone is the one to which Additional and the printed edition are closest. It seems that they were based on a master copy into which some of the changes the Editor made in Malone but in no later manuscript had been incorporated. There is no reason not to assume that this was the same master which served as the basis for the three earlier copies.

The alterations in Additional and the printed edition consist most obviously in reduction of material and in drastic stylistic revision both for the sake of extreme compression and to give the Editor's own style freer rein. Since Additional is an offshoot which has no important connection with the other copies and seems merely to represent a state very close to that of the printed edition, and also because it includes only the first two books, there is no purpose in discussing it separately in any detail. Differences between Additional and the printed edition are infrequent up to p. 26 of the latter but increase thereafter. They are changes in wording rather than in material. This pattern can be observed in all the copies, the wording in the early pages being very close to the preceding copy and growing more divergent as the copy progresses. Where differences exist, Additional is closer in wording than the printed edition to Egerton, Malone and Fisher, and the style of the printed edition is much more flamboyant and careless of sense. Both paraphrase the material in the three earlier copies, but more words and phrases of the earlier copies are retained in Additional. The style of the printed edition is smoother at certain points, carrying further the tendency to eliminate conjunctions and to subordinate. And there is further elimination of apparently inessential detail, of introductions to passages and statements of intention. This suggests that the printed edition was made after Additional, from the same master copy which had been further emended. Two examples of stylistic divergence appear on p. 28 of the printed edition in the description of Richard's progress, which reads in Egerton, 'All things thus established, in good order' and in Additional, 'All things thus in good order', becomes in the printed edition, 'All things thus in a happy presage and good order'. And Egerton's 'where hee was very honorably, and delightfully entertained of the Muses' is again reduced in Additional: 'where he was delightfully entertained of the Muses', and elaborated in the printed edition: 'where the Muses Crown'd their browes with fragrant Wreathes for his entertainment'. If we were to fall into the error of assuming that the printed edition represented the elder Buck's work, we would think that we had here an interestingly specific reference from the Master of the Revels.

Whereas Egerton, Malone, and Fisher are about two-thirds the length of the original, the printed edition is less than half its length The outlines of the work remain, and what we have in the printed version is in some sense a summary of the original. Paragraphs and even pages are summed up in sentences or phrases. Elaboration, explanation and digression are eliminated. Strict cutting removes all apparently extraneous phrases and sentences. Sentence structure is tightened: connectives are eliminated, pronouns substituted for repeated nouns, and pairs of adjectives and verbs reduced to single words. Narrative elaborations are omitted. Whereas Buck the elder has, using More as his source, created visual setting and action for the scene in which Richard is petitioned to be king, Buck the younger removes the dramatic elements and gives only the speeches, in slightly reduced form, one after the other, with no scene visualized. The original's descriptions of emotion, mood, tone, quality, character, and situation are rejected, as are statements of opinion. So that where Buck represents a speech and asks us to understand that the character speaking it is undergoing emotional or intellectual turmoil or has scruples about what he says, Buck, Jr., does nothing more than present the speech. Where the elder Buck in citing his sources states their qualifications and describes the authors as wise, learned, or specially experienced; or where in mentioning an historical personage he describes him, for example, as honourable or courageous, Buck the younger merely mentions the name and leaves all description out.

The Editor's creative urge was evidently released in the extended revision process, for he shows at this stage a tendency to add his own stylistic elaborations. Sometimes these are of structural value. He writes short transitional and introductory passages when new material is introduced. And he begins and ends books with a greater flourish than does the original author. He closes Book I, for example, with the words, 'And thus farre King *Richard*, in the Voyage of his Affaires had a promising Gale; wee will therefore here cast Anchor a while, and claspe up this first Booke, with the Relation of his better Fortunes' (p. 37). He opens Book II with a much more intrusive metaphor: 'We left King *Richard* the Third in the growth of a flourishing and promising Estate . . . . But Fortune that lends her smiles as Exactors do mony, to undoe the Debtor, soone cald for the Principall and Interest from this Prince . . .' (p. 41). He has a tendency to add moralistic comment, remarking, for example, that Fulke of Anjou's courage and strength are 'two of the best Principles when they have good seconds, and make too a glorious man, where they serve his vertues, not affections, as in this Prince they did' (p. 5). Not a word of this comment is in the original or early copies. The Editor's flourishes are usually incongruous and very often incomprehensible. He describes Richard's decision to offer single combat thus: 'this might taste of a desperate will, if he had not afterwards given an apodixis in the battaile, upon what plat-forme he had projected and raised that hope, which as it had much of danger in it, so of an inconcusse and great resolution, and might have brought the odds of that day to an even bet . . .' (p. 60)!

But despite tendencies to clog the sense by incongruous and incomprehensible rhetorical flourish or puzzle the reader by too drastic summarizing, he is sometimes able, when employing his flair for clarifying and organizing in conjunction with his own euphuistic tendencies to produce a clearer, stronger, and better turned passage than the author has given us. Where we get from Buck a plodding, diffuse, and unvaried construction we sometimes get a varied and interesting construction from the Editor's summary.

Not all his additions are purely stylistic. Whereas in the manuscript copies it is striking that the Editor does not make additions, he gives himself a bit more licence in the printed edition. He adds marginal notes, two purely explanatory and one giving illustrative information, and in one Plutarch reference and one Suetonius reference he specifies the particular life from which the example is drawn. He adds one classical quotation and makes two additions to the material of the work, one a letter relating to Don Sebastian's identity (pp. 98-99) and the other a lame discourse, based on uninformed guesswork, on the etymology of the word 'Parliament' (pp. 124-5), which he substitutes for the original's discussion of God punishing Edward IV for his sins.

But his excisions are far more numerous than his additions. They exhibit the same intentions as do the revisions in the earlier copies: to reduce length; to remove derogatory comments about the Tudor faction; to avoid religious questions; to eliminate sexual suggestion; and to destroy personal references. In matters of religion he seems to want to stay clear of all controversy, since he cuts out a reference to the massacre of Protestants as well as removing references to the Pope.

Discussions of Morton are very drastically cut, since the original had very little good to speak of Morton. The lists of men Richard III ought to have destroyed are removed. Henry VII is treated more tenderly at this stage than at any other. His responsibility for destroying the Yorkist heirs and the emphasis on the Yorkists' right are minimized as far as possible. The discussion of Perkin Warbeck's tortures is shortened. Henry becomes confident, pure, and manly, and the discomfort Perkin causes him is reduced. His ability in amorous speech disappears. His government is given the Editor's approval in his deletion of the discussion of bad Parliaments and the suggestion that the Parliament in which Henry had Richard attainted was self-abrogating; and then most strikingly in the alteration (p. 149) of Richard's reign from two years, fifty-two days to two years, fifty-one days, and the date of the Tudor reign's inception from 22 August to 21 August, the day before Richard's death — an adherence to Henry VII's own device of backdating his reign to make Richard appear to have been the traitor against the true king at Bosworth.

References leading to awareness of the author's period, identity, associates, and interests are further deleted in this copy, though the Editor still misses a few. A mere mention of Queen Elizabeth's name (p. 77) is substituted for Buck's first long eulogy, and another eulogy of this queen is cut out altogether. The marginal reference about all the Bucks, including the author, having been soldiers is gone.

Because it is in the form of the printed edition that the work has always been known and criticized, it is important to take account of those alterations which reflect on the author's research methods, care and thoroughness in documentation, accuracy, and presentation of his subject. For changes introduced by the Editor, which make the work exhibit an apparent lack of scholarship, have been largely responsible for Buck's failure to be taken seriously from his own century to the present time.

Changes in documentation, both intentional and careless, give an incorrect impression of Buck's research methods, which are made to look extremely shoddy and far less thorough than they actually were. His long description of how he went about his research into the origins of the name 'Plantagenet', perusing many books and monuments, consulting heralds, ultimately receiving from Dethick the information he quotes (see text, pp. 11-12) is reduced to 'In my Inquiry . . . I met with an ancient manuscript' (p. 5). This makes Buck's research look haphazard and deprives it of any sense of method or authority. Another example of Buck's careful method is lost in the mention of Richard III's charter incorporating the College of Arms (see text, p. 204), when the Editor excludes the words 'I have seen it' and also the marginal reference to Ralph Brook, York Herald, through whose agency Buck evidently saw the original charter. What Buck says is that the charter was once kept in the College of Arms, but its now being elsewhere is of no importance since he has seen the original in its new place — he gives Brook's name to corroborate this — and there is a duplicate in the College. The printed edition on the other hand simply says the lack of the charter is not important because there is a copy of it in the College. Buck had very painstakingly demonstrated his care to see the original and indicate that his seeing only a copy would have been of less value. The Editor makes him seem easily content with a copy and to consider viewing the original unimportant.

Again, a statement of Buck's that he will transcribe a charter 'as I have seen and read it in the archives and records kept in the Tower of London' (text, p. 79) becomes 'which Charter . . . I shall exhibite, as it is taken out of the Archives and Tower

Records' (p. 48). There is no indication in the printed version that the author ever saw this document himself or that it was of any importance to him whether he had or not.

The references to Cotton's library, closed for some fifteen years, necessarily suffer. Whereas Buck had said specifically 'this charter *is now* [italics mine] in the hands of Sir Robert Cotton, where I have seen and read it and transcribed these summary notes from thence' (text, p. 81), the printed edition can give us only the impression of a vague situation in the past: 'This Charter I saw in the hands of Sir *Rob. Cotton,* & from it took these Summary notes' (p. 50). Buck knows the material from recent examination and knows its collector well enough to inform the reader of the present whereabouts of the document. The printed edition does not enlighten us on the present status of the document and makes it appear that the notes were taken not recently but some time in the past. This is only one example of what frequently happens in the case of Cotton material.

The errors and omissions in marginal documentation are numerous:

p. 5   marginal reference to Du Haillan and Paradin documenting a quotation from Fulke of Anjou is left out

       marginal documentation of Zosimus for reference to Constantine and Aegyptus is left out

       marginal reference 'Georgics II' is left out, only a general attribution, 'Virgil', remaining in the text

  7   the laudatory citation of Glover is replaced by references in the text to 'Master *Brookes* genealogies of England', but the marginal note, 'In his Catalogue of Honour' confusingly remains

17   'Nyerus' is given for 'Meyerus'

24   only 'Camden' appears in the marginal note for 'Camden in Dobuni' (which the copies had corrupted to 'Dolucu'). Strype criticizes Buck here for not stating where in Camden the reference occurs (Strype, p. 525)

28   the references to the Cotton MS. and Fabyan are so misplaced as to seem to refer to the appointment of John of Gloucester as Captain of Calais, not, as they actually do, to Richard's pacifying the country

29   only 'Ioan Maierus' is given in a marginal note without the original's specific citation of *Annales Flandr.* Lib 17

43   textual documentation citing More, Polydore Vergil, the histories of Brittany, French writers, and the common chroniclers as the sources on which the account of Henry's first invasion is based is left out

45   reference to Salisbury, Epistle 89 is given as '85'

58   citation of Polydore Vergil for information on Henry Tudor's problems about marriage is left out

80   'Sir *Thomas Moor apud Harlington*' is the reading given for what must originally have been '. . . Hardyng et Grafton'

81   'Majerus' is twice given for 'Meyerus'

      a marginal reference to Holinshed documenting the chronicles' account of Edward, Prince of Wales' death is left out

93   the reader is not referred to 'Grafton, Hall, etc.' for further information on Perkin Warbeck's confession
94   in a reference to St Augustine's *Civitas Dei,* 'Lib. 19' is left out
117 the lost work *El Reusuerq* is made to appear part of the Duke of Milan's title: 'Duke *of Millain el Rueseur.'*
121 a marginal reference to Ovid for a quotation from that author is left out
128 '4. *Evang. Harmon. Evang.'* is given for '4 Ebr. Harmon. Evang.'
130 a marginal reference to Prateius is left out
141 a marginal reference to Çurita and Garibay for information regarding Henry VII's 'capture' of Philip, Duke of Burgundy is left out
146 'Edwardus Ethelredus' is confusingly given for 'Edmerus Alvredus'

Buck's *viva voce* references are so tampered with as to be reduced to the level of apparent hearsay. All awareness of his working closely with other eminent scholars and personally gleaning information from people whose professional positions or historical connections made them more authoritative than any published matter on certain subjects is lost. In the original, Buck, speaking of bastards, says 'I have been informed by a very learned and signal judge of the laws of this land', whom he identifies in the margin as Coke (text, p. 78). The printed edition depersonalizes this: 'as a Learned and eminent Judge reports' (p. 48) and retains the attribution to Coke, so that one assumes the reference is to a printed work. Buck was able to present his story of Surrey's adventures after Bosworth by the testimony of his grandfather, Robert Buck, who was with the earl from his own childhood until Surrey's old age 'and was well acquainted with all his actions and his fortunes' (text, p. 108). The printed edition says merely that the information comes 'by the warrant of one that well knew him' (p. 64). The information on the value of the Earl of Oxford's lands is given, but without any documentation. This had been conveyed to Buck in personal conversation when the earl visited him (text, p. 170). Instead of the detailed face to face discussion with Stow about Richard's lack of deformity, the printed edition says only that Stow 'acknowledged *vivâ voce*' that he had spoken to old men who affirmed Richard not to have been deformed (p. 79). Another conversation between Buck and Stow we can almost visualize as the original gives it: 'when pressed much to know and understand' Stow's opinion on the death of the Princes, 'his answer was this, and as peremptory as short . . .' (text, p. 173). The printed edition robs this confrontation of all immediacy: Stow 'being required to deliver his opinion . . . affirmed . . .' (p. 106). Not once in all these statements of personally derived information is there the slightest indication of how they reached the author, and we can only assume that they were little more than hearsay and not credit them. It begins to appear hardly a wonder that Buck's reputation has suffered so seriously as a result of his great-nephew's tamperings.

The disputed letter from Elizabeth of York to the Duke of Norfolk regarding her love for King Richard is in the printed edition made to look both more important and more unreliable because of the rearrangement of material and exclusion of all details regarding the research which uncovered it. First of all, the question of Elizabeth's objecting or not objecting to marriage with Richard is given prominence it does not possess in the original. The Editor in reorganizing material has begun the discussion of this contemplated marriage with two forcefully stated points, as if they are the main things he is aiming to disprove:

> Item, *That all men, and the Maid herself most of all,*
> *detested this unlawful Copulation.*
> Item, *That he made away the Queen his wife, to make*
> *way for this Marriage, and that he propounded not the*
> *Treaty of Marriage, until the Queen his wife was dead*
> (pp. 126f).

This is quite differently stated in the original, where Buck observes that Richard has been accused of wanting to marry Elizabeth 'and they add' that she opposed the match and that he killed his wife (see text, p. 192). The original gives subordinate rather than primary emphasis to the two latter points. In the original, the letter appears as a sideline, a matter of interest, not as crucial proof. It is a digression within the argument that Richard, if he had wished, could have procured a divorce, and the information derived from it is primarily that Elizabeth spoke like a young girl in her letter, in ignorance that a man could remarry without his wife's dying. One may easily suspect that Buck's intention in including the letter was as much to pay tribute to Arundel by citing material derived from his splendid collection as to exhibit the young lady's feelings, which he seems to view with gentle amusement. But in the compressed printed version the letter seems to take on much greater importance, particularly since it stands there in a different relation to the surrounding material: it has suffered only slight reduction, but the material around it has been very much compressed. From the letter itself are cut only the important references to Norfolk's loyalty to Richard III and to the sons of Edward IV. These are replaced by a mere '&c' (p. 128). The words 'in body, and in all' are left out as well. But, aside from minor stylistic changes, this is all. Yet the circumstantial detail surrounding Buck's viewing of the letter is reduced to a mere statement that this is the sum of what Elizabeth said, in her own words, and the letter 'remains in the Autograph, or Original Draft, under her own hand, in the magnificent Cabinet of *Thomas* Earl of Arundel and Surrey' (p. 128). There is no statement that the author actually had *seen* the letter. And the expressions of gratitude to Arundel for his kindness and favour in allowing Buck to see it are gone, as are the descriptive details of Arundel's 'rich cabinet' and collection. The fact that Arundel is a direct descendant of the letter's recipient is not mentioned.

Rewriting and excerpting is sometimes careless of the sense, and often the details omitted are important ones, Some of the details of Archibald Quhitlaw's acquaintance with Richard III are left out, so that we are ignorant of the personal knowledge on which his eulogistic address was based. The Editor also leaves out the perceptive suggestion that More transfers to Richard III his own deformity (the inequality of shoulders mentioned by Erasmus).

Some violence is done to Buck's methods of argumentation. Compression and omission in the printed edition create a very abrupt leap from the deploring of Hastings' execution to parallel cases in modern times: 'Let us leave it up on that accompt, and but consider how much more wee forgive the fames of *H*.1. *E*.3. *H*.4.

E.4. *H*.7. because they had their happy Starres and successe . . .' (p. 13). The Editor then goes backward to cite ancient examples, which in this position appear mere pedantry, and cites reason of state at the end. The original, on the other hand, presents a carefully constructed discussion leading from Richard's specific action, which it accepts instead of putting it aside, then discusses reason of state at some length, illustrating it by examples proceeding logically from ancient to modern times and hence back to Richard. In Book III the same abruptness is constantly apparent because of the compression and deletion. Pressing together of accusation and defence deprives Buck of his gradual rational argument with its occasionally whimsical character and makes his defences appear more polemical.

Revision badly distorts a description of the relationship of More's narrative to the chronicles which followed it. The printed edition says merely that the chroniclers trusted what More said and followed him; not, as the original explicitly observes, that they went so far as to copy his narrative entirely into their own works. Buck's caution to the reader about the unreliability of common chronicles and critical discussions of their authority are left out. Since Buck uses these statements about contemporary historiography to introduce his defence and explain its necessity, the omission not only deprives us of all awareness of Buck's critical acumen but is structurally quite crucial. In the original he tells us, in historiographical terms, why a defence of Richard III is needed. The printed version gives no inkling of any such perception.

Errors in the printed text are numerous. Some of the foreign words and proper names which are incorrect in the earlier copies are corrected in print, but as often as this happens a new glaring error is made in another place. These errors lend the work an appearance of carelessness and ignorance. Some of the most glaring mistakes in factual information and proper names can be listed, but the errors in foreign quotations are too numerous.

pr.ed.p.   9 'Exon' for 'Hexham'
         20 'Elizabeth Butler' for 'Eleanor Butler' (in Additional also)
         25 'Norfolk' for 'Suffolk' (all other copies are correct)
         27 'John Hide' for 'John Herd'
         30 'Fieries' for 'Fiennes'
         52 'Pe.' for 'Pontus' (Heuterus)
         61 'Sir Charles Brandon' for 'Sir William Brandon'
         63 'Billington' for 'Pilkington'
         67 'Gadys' for 'Cadiz'[17] (Additional gives 'Cadish')
         79 'Juliola' for 'Tulliosa'
             'Totheringham' for 'Fotheringhay' (copies give 'Fotheringham')
         83 'Loualto melie' and 'Loyalty bindeth men' for 'Loyaulte me lie' and 'Loyalty bindeth me' (the latter is also in the earlier MS. copies)
         91 'Aylau' for 'Ayala'
         92 'Beanely' for 'Beaulieu'

93 'Shrene' for 'Sheen' (Egerton gives 'Shrene', Malone 'Shree', Fisher 'Shreeue')

97 'Walter Blunt' for 'Walter Blewyt'

100 'York' for 'Essex'

129 'Don Alde Mendoza' for 'Don Alonzo de Mendoza' (in copies given as 'Don Al: de Mendoza')

141 '1493' for '1485' as Richard's date of death (*sic* in all copies)

'Edward' for 'Edmund', Earl of Kent, uncle to Edward III

The word 'fifth' is misread as 'first' in all copies except Fisher, and so the printed version absurdly states that Edward III was 'the first King in a Lineall descent' from Henry II (p. 4). A careless compression makes the Bastard of Fauconberg Earl of Kent rather than son to the Earl of Kent, an error for which Strype criticizes Buck (Strype, p. 517n). All the Editor's copies, including the printed edition, duplicate the designation 'of Ross' and attach it to Sir William Parr as well as to Lord Parr. Strype attacks Buck for misquoting More in saying that Richard resembled his father physically as well as facially (Strype, p. 548n). In fact the original says the resemblance was 'in the lineaments and in favour of his visage' (text, p. 130), but the printed edition says 'in the lineaments of his body and in the favour of his visage' (p. 80). Instead of stating that Morton and a certain countess were contemplating the death of King Edward's sons by poison, a more likely proposition, the printed edition states that they were plotting the death of King Edward (p. 102), thus depriving Richard's defenders of another rumour which might add grist to their mill.

The structure of the printed edition is neatly finished with the inclusion of 'The Authors Scope; Peroratio & Votum', a heading which had appeared in the original's list of contents for Book V but had puzzled the Editor in his previous copies and been removed from the list of contents for that book in the manuscripts. He has found it now in Buck's diffuse summing up of Richard's case near the end of Book V and has cut, organized, and placed it in a prominent postion. He provides a not very painstaking index and a list of sources, a practice Buck had considered unnecessary because, as he says, he cites his authors everywhere. He gives the authorship on the title page: 'Composed in five Bookes by George Buck Esquire'.

This reduction of Buck's *History* was published about twenty-six years after work ceased on the original, and after several revised copies had been made to serve the Editor's purposes. No scholar seems as yet to have observed the significance of its publication date, 1646. It was in this year that Lord Arundel, the original dedicatee, died. It appears that George Buck, Esq., had learned a lesson from his detection in the *Daphnis* publication or some similar action and had cautiously waited until there was no one alive who could call him soundly to account for publishing under his own name a work not his own. Still cautious in the dedication, however, he refers to his 'Having collected these papers out of their dust' (sig. a), implying but not actually stating his own composition.

Sir George Buck's diffuse work, well-documented and researched through various original documents with the personal assistance of the most eminent antiquaries of the age had been reduced to a concise summary, careless in its documentation and spellings of proper names and foreign words and giving as hearsay what is firsthand information. All traces of the original author's identity, his period, his associates and assistants, his opinions of scholarship, of the Lancastrians' treachery, of Morton's evil nature, have been erased. The style, which in the original was plodding and repetitious, has become in places clear and varied, but often shows extreme carelessness and incongruity. It is in the form of this edition that the work is still commonly known.

NOTES

1. Eccles, p. 495.

2. Edmond Malone, 'An Historical Account . . . of the English Stage', prefaced to William Shakespeare, *The Plays and Poems* (London, 1790), I, pt. ii, 46f.

3. Joseph Ritson, MS. note in Buck, Esq., *History*, flyleaf of B.L. copy, shelfmark 610. 1. 5.

4. [Ritson], *Bibliographia*, p. 147.

5. Hazlitt, *Hand-Book*, p. 66.

6. Marcham, p. 3.

7. Eccles, pp. 485-503.

8. Tiberius, f. 13ᵛ. Square brackets in these examples indicate crossings out by the Editor, George Buck, Esq., and italics my conjectural filling in of gaps. Folio numbers from Tiberius will hereafter be given in parentheses in the text when the material in these examples is of any magnitude or interest.

9. Eccles. p. 503.

10. George Buck, Esq., Δαφνις *or the Polyanthine Ghirland,* Bod. MS. Rawl. Poet. 105, f. 2.

11. Ritson, *Bibliographia,* p. 146.

12. Justus Lipsius / his two bookes / de Constantia / englished / by George Bucke Esq.ʳ 1638. Trinity College, Cambridge, MS. O. 3. 17.

13. Eccles., p. 501.

14. John Jacob, *Publicanus Vindicatus* (London, 1654), pp. 1-2. There exists also a petition signed by Jacob and others, 'A Remonstrance of the Case of the late Farmers of the Customes, and Their Humble Petition to the Parliament', 1654.

15. See above, p. lxvi.

16. Beaumont and Fletcher, *Comedies and Tragedies* (London, 1647), sig. C3.

17. Marcham inexplicably seems to consider this spelling acceptable: 'Buc tells us that he was at the siege of Gadys', p. 3.

VI. BUCK'S *HISTORY* AND ITS CRITICS

Buck himself expected that his book 'would find many censors and critical essayers, and those of divers kinds: some curious, some jealous, some captious and peremptory, some incredulous, some scrupulous, and some haply malevolent and malicious. But the fairest censure would be that all was a paradox or contr'opinion' (text, p. 3).

And indeed this censure began to be entertained shortly after the publication of the work, which has been subject ever since to conflicting evaluations on the grounds of both content and style. Bishop Fuller in his *Church History* (1655) is very severe upon it:

> . . . I confess it is no heresy to maintain a paradox in history; nor am I such an enemy to wit as not to allow it leave harmlessly to disport itself for its own content and the delight of others. . . . But when men shall do it cordially, in sober sadness, to pervert people's judgements, and therein go against all received records, I say singularity is the least fault can be laid to such men's charge.

Fuller expresses moral indignation that whereas Richard was

> low in stature, crook-backed, with one shoulder higher than the other, having a prominent gobber-tooth, a war-like countenance; . . . yet a modern author, in a book by him lately set forth, eveneth his shoulders, smootheth his back, planeth his teeth, maketh him in all points a comely and beautiful person; nor stoppeth he here, but, proceeding from his naturals to his morals, maketh him as virtuous as handsome . . . , concealing most, denying some, defending others of his foulest facts, wherewith in all ages since he standeth charged on record. [1]

His note identifies the modern author as 'George Buck, esq.' In so short a time all consideration of the original author Sir George Buck and his reputation for scholarship, learning, integrity, and dignity have vanished. It is perhaps ironic that most subsequent accounts should assume that 'George Buck, Esquire' is a misprint for 'Sir George Buck'.

On the other hand, an anonymous writer, whose comments were seen by Chalmers in the margin of Ulpian Fulwell's *Flower of Fame,* 1575, in a hand Chalmers claims to be of James I's era, speaks highly of the author's treatment of his subject: '. . . a just confutation of all their unjust and false imputations are clearly and with truth wiped of from that inocent prince by the thrice noble and famous scoller S.ʳ G. Buc: in v bookes which hee hath (with special knowledge) written in King Richard's defence . . . .'[2] Certain antiquarian scholars, probably influenced by Buck's defence, presented favourable accounts of Richard's life and reign, a prominent example being William Winstanley in *England's Worthies,* 1660.

The conflict of these opinions inspired the republication of Buck's *History* in 1706 and 1719 — directly from the printed edition of 1646 — in Kennett's *Complete History of England.* Hughes, who wrote the Preface, mentions that on the grounds of content 'there are various Opinions about it, and 'tis upon this Account that the Booksellers were advis'd to print it.'[3] He goes on to criticize the *History* particularly on stylistic grounds: it is 'much too loosely writ for a History; 'tis pedantick and full of Harangue, and may more properly be call'd *a Defence of King Richard* than any thing else'. The word 'harangue' obviously alludes to the florid style of Buck's great-nephew, for Buck himself cannot be accused of it. The suggestion that it is more properly described as a defence, too, is applicable to the printed edition, with its jamming together of accusation and defence which obliterates Buck's leisurely reasoning methods.

In the 1748 edition of *Biographia Britannica,* the annotator Morant agrees with these stylistic criticisms and adds that the *History* 'abounds with faults, which, in a man of his learning, is something unaccountable'.[4] It is accountable, of course, only by the alterations the Editor and his scribe made intentionally and accidentally in Buck's original, of which Morant was not aware. Nevertheless, he states that the *History* was the work by which Sir George Buck most distinguished himself.

Andrew Kippis, reviser of *Biographia Britannica,* gives, in 1780, this addition to the stylistic criticism, tempering it with appreciation of Buck's ability:

> . . . though Buc writes very pedantically, which may partly be attributed to the fashion of the times, he displays considerable abilities. His digressions, in particular, though they are introduced in an improper place, manifest a good portion of antiquarian knowledge. In his Vindication of Richard the Third, he hath offered some things worthy of attention; but he writes in so declamatory a manner, and with so much of the air of a professed panegyrist, rather than of a cool enquirer into truth, that he makes, on that account, the less impression upon the minds of his readers.[5]

Again it would seem that this reference to panegyric style describes the nephew's in the printed edition, for Buck's own could be well described as that of 'a cool enquirer into truth'.

During the eighteenth century Buck's *History* was not without influence. His most important general influence on all historians of the period seems to have lain in his calling attention to the Croyland Chronicle, and to a lesser degree in his use of other original documents in public repositories and his discussion of Perkin Warbeck. Rapin in his *History of England* (1728), though generally following More, advises caution in accepting reports of Lancastrian historians when they criticize actions by Yorkists and notes that 'George Buck, Esq.' has tried to represent Richard better than tradition esteemed him.

Carte in *A General History of England* (1750) is of all historians the one who follows Buck most closely. He uses Buck as a source for factual material, for the order of events, and for interpretations. He follows Buck's assessment of Richard's character and his judgement that it was obscured by the interest which Tudor historians had in calumniating him. He makes explicit Buck's point that it was necessary for the Princes to be believed dead if Henry's plan to take over the throne was to succeed. He points out the inconsistencies in More's account of their death, adducing the same arguments against Richard's being the murderer and concluding as Buck does that Edward died naturally and Richard escaped to reappear as Perkin Warbeck. Carte cites Buck's various manuscript documents without quibble.

Hume in *The History of England* (1763) is severely traditional and disapproving of Richard's apologists. But his friend Walpole wrote the first full-scale defence since Buck. In his review of Walpole's *Historic Doubts on the Life and Reign of Richard the Third* (1768), Gibbon has this to say of Buck: 'Un seul critique (Buck) s'est élevé contre le sentiment général, mais son ton de panégyriste a révolté tous les esprits'.[6] Evidently Gibbon had not read Buck.

Walpole, like Buck, is sensitive to the risk of being considered a paradoxicalist, and he defends Buck against this imputation: 'Buck, so long exploded as a lover of paradoxes, and as an advocate for a monster, gains new credit the deeper this dark scene is fathomed' (p. 20). And he ends his defence with an apology similar to Buck's opening one: 'I flatter myself that I shall not be thought either fantastic or paradoxical, for not blindly adopting an improbable tale . . . ' (p. 122).

Compared with Buck's, Walpole's is a paltry effort, too flippant in style to be taken seriously, basing its argument less on original records than on Tudor historians, on Buck, and on logical assumption. But what Walpole considers logic is not critically informed, and his arguments tend to be flimsy and capricious, based on uninformed, idiosyncratic personal opinion. He uses the Croyland Chronicle, but he has not Buck's gift for assessing his sources. To Walpole, the chronicler, merely 'a monk who busies himself in recording the insignificant events of his own order or monastery, and who was at most occasionally made use of, was not likely to know the most important and most mysterious secrets of state' (p. 16). He follows Buck in pointing out (not quite accurately) that More was a young man in low office when he wrote his *History* but denies Buck's statement that More had most of his material from Morton, because Walpole's own sense of social position does not admit of intimacy between 'so raw a youth' and 'a prelate of that rank and prime minister' (p. 18). He joins Buck in pronouncing More's *History*, like his *Utopia*, 'invention and romance' (p. 19).

Like Buck, Walpole makes mistakes in the literary quotations he occasionally inserts as illustrations, and his mistakes are so considerable as to prove his memory far inferior to Buck's. Like Buck he is careless in attributing to More material which actually comes from the post-More sections of Hall and the other chroniclers. He uses Buck uncritically, incorporating the errors of the printed edition into his own references. Walpole says that Buck 'has gone too far; nor are his style or method to be admired. With every intention of vindicating Richard, he does but authenticate his crimes, by searching in other story for parallel instances of what he calls policy' (p. 20). This is a method Buck uses not as a defence but rather as evidence that irrationally disproportionate blame is being attached to Richard by his calumniators. Walpole follows his criticism of Buck's method almost immediately by using reason of state as a defence. Like Buck, Walpole uses classical parallels, at one point listing beautiful men who have done atrocious deeds.

Walpole follows Buck's lead on the question of Perkin Warbeck, which he examines at length. And he is the first to refer to the letter from Elizabeth of York which Buck cites. Since critical opinion against Buck has focused on this letter to such a large degree, it will be instructive to trace responses to it from Walpole to the present day before returning to consider nineteenth and twentieth century assessments of Buck in more general terms. Walpole cites it incorrectly, stating that Buck says the physicians predicted the queen could not live until April, and Elizabeth 'expressed doubts that the month of April would never arrive' (p. 74). What Buck actually says is that the physicians projected February as the date of the queen's demise, and Elizabeth in her letter complained that most of February was past and she feared the queen would never die. Walpole defends the existence of this letter: 'Buck would not have dared to quote her letter as extant in the earl of Arundel's library, if it had not actually been there: . . . others of Buck's assertions having been corroborated by subsequent discoveries, leave no doubt of his veracity on this' (p. 129).

The nineteenth century, however, was not so generous to Buck and ignored the evidence of his integrity and careful methods in order to heap vilification upon him for his audacity in bringing to light a paper which appeared to cast aspersions on the honour of young English womanhood. 'If this letter really existed', says N. Harris Nicolas, 'and if Buck has cited it fairly, it would be vain to contend against such testimony, and Elizabeth's fame would be irredeemably affected'. However, we are told,

> The character of Buck as a faithless writer is well known;
> and even if his notorious inaccuracies and prejudices do not
> justify the suspicion that the letter itself was never written,
> it is not too much to suggest that the interpretation which
> he has given it is at variance with truth. As Buck has
> inserted copies of several documents of much less interest,

> it may be asked, why did he not give this most important
> letter at length?[7]

The answer to this is of course that Buck as an antiquary found legal charters of much more interest than domestic gossip and more worthy of preservation in exact detail. He does state that he is giving Elizabeth's own words. And why, Nicolas asks, did none of the other famous antiquaries — Dugdale or Wood — copy it? He does not consider whether this was a matter of particular interest to them, what were their terms of intimacy with the Howards, and what the state was of the Howard papers when they wrote. Nicolas goes on in his notes to expound, just in case the letter did exist, some tortuous theories of how Buck might have misinterpreted it, since he regards it as too prejudicial to Elizabeth to be true as reported.

  Nicolas' absurdities on this point are adopted by numerous other writers of the succeeding decades. John Heneage Jesse in his *Memoirs of King Richard the Third* says,

> Buck is acknowledged to have been a highly prejudiced,
> and not always trustworthy, chronicler. . . . On the other
> hand, admitting Buck to be a faithless chronicler, and the
> disappearance of the letter to be a very suspicious circum-
> stance, there is still the difficulty of believing that anyone
> could so grossly and impudently outstep his duty as a writer
> of history, as to interlard it with positive fiction.[8]

So in defence of Buck's honour this time rather than Elizabeth's, Jesse follows Nicolas' arguments of possible misquotation. He has already 'proved' Buck to hold an 'unscrupulous partiality'[9] in showing how his quotation of Richard's epitaph differs in several places from Sandford's. He ignores the fact that Sandford and Buck copied the epitaph from different manuscripts, and takes no account of editorial corruption or printer's errors in Buck.

  Caroline Halsted speaks very oddly of this letter:

> If Sir George Buck had himself seen the letter, and
> spoken of its contents from his own knowledge, —if either
> himself or any other writer had inserted a copy of it, or
> even a transcript from the 'original draft,' then, indeed, it
> would have been difficult to set aside such testimony. But
> considering that every search has been made for the alleged
> autograph, — that no trace of such a document has ever
> been discovered, or even known to have existed, — that no
> person is named as having seen it, or is instanced in support
> of its validity, — and moreover, that Sir George Buck
> throughout his history of Richard III. inserts at full length
> copies of almost every other instrument to which he refers,
> or gives marginal references to the source whence his

> authority was derived, but, in this instance, contents him-
> self with merely stating the fact, and giving the substance of
> a letter which he appears to have received from rumour or
> hearsay information, the conviction cannot but arise that
> the letter in question was either not the production of
> Elizabeth of York, or, if so, that the insinuations referred
> to in it were misconstrued, and that its contents had re-
> ference to some other individual, and not, as was supposed,
> to her uncle.[10]

She then goes on in a note to quote Nicolas' conjectures as to possible mis-
interpretations of the letter. Halsted seems curiously unaware even of the statements
of the printed edition, let alone Buck's own writing on the subject. For even the
printed edition *does* have a marginal as well as a textual reference stating that the
letter is in Arundel's cabinet. Had Halsted taken the trouble to examine Buck's
original — readily available at that time in the British Museum — she would have
found that Buck clearly states he *did* see it and was shown it by Arundel who must,
consequently, have seen it as well. Halsted exaggerates Nicolas' statement when
she says that Buck gives copies of almost every other document he uses. This is far
from true.

With James Gairdner we return to the sense of outrage perpetrated against
English womanhood and a consequent ambivalence in his disposition on one hand to
respect Buck and his unwillingness on the other to accept Elizabeth's humanity. He
begins by saying the letter cannot be ignored, 'however revolting and opposed to
natural expectation'. But there are, he says with relief, grounds for incredulity in
this. His statement of them, incorporating the errors made by Nicolas and Halsted, is
too silly to avoid quoting in full:

> Buck does not expressly say that he had seen the letter
> himself; and we might, perhaps, rather infer the contrary,
> from the fact that he only gives the substance of it in his
> own words, whereas he has quoted at full length many
> documents of less importance. On the other hand, if it is not
> clear that Buck saw it, there is not a tittle of evidence to
> show that anyone else did. No reference is made to it by
> any of the great antiquaries and historians of Buck's day —
> by Stow, or Speed, or Holinshed, or Camden. No person
> appears to have seen it before, no person appears to have
> seen it since, and nothing is known of its existence now.
> Add to this the fact that Buck, even though not altogether
> dishonest (and I see no reason to think him so), was by no
> means an impartial historian, but an essayist bent on justi-
> fying a paradox, and that such a letter, if it really existed,
> was of very great service to his argument. Taking all these
> circumstances into consideration — together with the fur-
> ther possibility that the letter, even if it existed, may have

been misconstrued — we ought certainly to be pardoned
for indulging a belief, or, at all events, a charitable hope,
that Elizabeth was incapable of sentiments so dishonourable and repulsive.

At the same time it must be remarked that Buck's
abstract of the letter is very minute, and such as would
seem to follow pretty closely the turns of expression in a
genuine original; that he expressly declares the MS. to be
an autograph or original draft; and that the horrible per-
version and degradation of domestic life which it implies is
only too characteristic of the age. Still, it would certainly
appear from the little we know of her after life that
Elizabeth of York was not destitute of domestic feeling;
and that she could have been eager to obtain the hand of
her brothers' murderer is really too monstrous to be
believed. [11]

In case, however, the letter should happen not to be a forgery passed off on Buck 'or
by him upon his readers', Gairdner attempts to explain how it may have been written
(with a few minor 'errors' such as the substitution of the word 'father' for 'husband')
by Elizabeth Woodville.

This account reaches almost the limit of absurdity. Gairdner sees no reason to
assume Buck dishonest, yet this may be a forgery palmed off by him on his readers.
'Not a tittle of evidence' exists that anyone saw the letter, but Gairdner has not
bothered to look for this evidence in the most likely place — Buck's original work.
He fails to consider the interests and methods of Stow, Speed, Holinshed, and
Camden (whom he arbitrarily substitutes for Nicolas' Dugdale and Wood): how far
in advance of them Buck was in his treatment of this subject; and his association,
which they did not share, with the Howards. The description of Buck as 'an essayist
bent on justifying a paradox' can result only from Gairdner's confusing him with Sir
William Cornwallis. Buck wrote in diverse forms, but the essay is not one of them.

These nineteenth century absurdities led to even greater twentieth century ones.
The attacks on the letter seem to have gained such great authority through repetition
and accretion that in order to attack the letter it seems to have become unnecessary to
read Buck at all by the time David MacGibbon wrote in 1938:

There does not seem to be an atom of truth in the letter
printed by Buck in Kennet's [sic] *History of England* . . . in
which he quotes a so-called 'authentic' letter written by the
Princess Elizabeth to Richard III stating that she was willing
to become his wife. It seems rather peculiar that Buck is
the only person to mention this letter, and that its contents
were invaluable to him in his attempt at defending Richard
III's character. [12]

Because of his stylistic carelessness, it is necessary in part to guess at what MacGibbon means. We are expected, it seems, to imagine Buck alive in 1706 and 1719 printing his letter in Kennett's history. Even this, the most distant text from Buck's original, states quite plainly that the letter was from Elizabeth to Norfolk, not to Richard, and makes no overt statement 'that she was willing to become his wife' (this is, if anything, an understatement of what actually is communicated by innuendo in the letter as Buck cites it). The contents have assumed such importance only because so many people have used them as a vehicle for attacking Buck. They were far from 'invaluable to him in his attempt at defending Richard III's character' but were presented as little more than a sideline in his arguments relating to one of the more minor accusations against Richard, the possible truth of which he is not unwilling to concede.

These attitudes resolve themselves most recently, stripped of their grossest absurdities, into A.R. Myers' statement that 'it is hard to accept Buc's testimony on this, for no one else has ever seen this document.'[13] It would be interesting to see how Myers would go about proving that no one has ever seen any document. Gairdner managed at least to say that no one appeared to have seen it.

The nineteenth and twentieth centuries have shown a close battle between two extremes — Richard's defenders and Richard's attackers. Attitudes to Buck have affected as well as reflecting these extremes. Halsted, the nineteenth century's major defender, follows Walpole closely in appraising Buck, except that she credits him because he agrees with Commynes and the Parliament Rolls, whereas Walpole had credited Commynes because he agreed with Buck and the Parliament Rolls. She observes that Buck 'appears to have had access to documents no longer extant',[14] but she does not seem to have looked for them. She uses Buck as a serious source, though she feels she must apologize for doing so by citing Walpole's approval of him. But she, like Walpole, uses him haphazardly and uncritically, incorporating into her own references both the errors of the printed edition and Buck's own paraphrases of other authors. Her organization is an improvement over Buck's, following chronological order and dealing with accusations according to the order of events. This entails digressing for the purpose of arguing cases in defence, but the basic structure is clearer. She follows Buck's method of study, pursuing old histories and original manuscripts, but she is less critically acute than Buck in using these, despite the distance of over two hundred years. Her documentation, too, though copious and more standardized is not much more careful or thorough than his. She follows Buck's method and arguments in defending Richard against the numerous accusations, particularly in the case of the deformity, adding to his arguments further evidence discovered at a later date. That this is also the method employed by Markham in 1906 and Kendall in 1955 shows how firm is Buck's groundwork in establishing methods and arraying evidence for later defenders to build upon. Halsted follows Buck and Walpole in pursuing the question of Perkin Warbeck.

Gairdner's ambivalent attitude has already been amply demonstrated. He uses the same sources as Buck, with the addition of Harleian 433, but no more critically than does Buck. He does not differentiate between More and Polydore Vergil and their followers (Hall, Grafton, Holinshed, Stow) who copy them. He gives whole passages of More's invented speeches and Hall's battle orations as factual quotations. An example of his ignorance in the use of both primary and secondary sources is his lack of awareness that Buck derived the information that Eleanor Butler rather than Elizabeth Lucy was Edward IV's betrothed from the *Titulus Regius* and his statement that another century and a quarter elapsed after Buck before the *Titulus Regius* was discovered![15] Gairdner was the first to undertake a large scale discussion of Perkin Warbeck with intent to prove that he was *not* the Duke of York. He is the only historian who ever set about trying to prove Richard guilty by use of historical evidence, and he fails because he cannot or will not examine his sources critically. This is a skill in which Buck, nearly three hundred years earlier, far surpassed him.

Markham, Gairdner's antagonist, couples Buck with Hall, Grafton, Holinshed, and Stow as authors who copied from earlier writers and therefore cannot be considered authorities except when they introduce documents as evidence. This is just to a degree, though it ignores Buck's differences from the other four, in that he exercises critical judgement in the use of his secondary sources, deciding which are most authoritative on which subjects, rather than copying them wholesale as do the other historians in the list; and it ignores also Buck's explicit assessment of his sources. Markham is the first to take cognizance of the original manuscript of Buck's *History*, saying that the work was published in 1646 under the name of George Buck, Esq., but the existence of the manuscript in the British Museum, giving Sir George as author, proves the substitution of 'Esq.' for 'Sir' an error. This is, unfortunately, an incorrect guess and permits the identification of the printed edition with the original manuscript to continue, both ascribed to Sir George Buck. But at least Markham is able to see Sir George in his own right, as a man Camden praises for distinction in learning.

Markham follows Buck's structure in dividing his book: half is a chronological biography and half a discussion of the 'authorities' and a defence of Richard against his accusations one by one. Like Buck, he discusses Tudor sources and 'proves' that Morton wrote More's *History*. Thereafter he gives all references to More's *History* as 'Morton', as Buck gives many of his More references as 'Morton and More'. As Buck vilified More to prove his unreliability, Markham vilifies Morton. He agrees with Buck in making Morton the author of all slanders against Richard and even enlarges on this, showing how the slanders travelled with Morton wherever he went, both in England and abroad. Like Buck, he hates Henry VII and praises Queen Elizabeth. His general assessment of Richard is the same as Buck's: he attributes to him the same virtues on similar evidence. Buck occasionally sentimentalizes his picture of Richard. Markham sentimentalizes it even further. He deviates from Buck, however, on the matter of Perkin Warbeck, for his theory that Henry VII murdered the Princes after Richard's death invalidates Warbeck's claim. This theory of the murder is certainly as speculative a case as the most speculative Buck propounded. As for the letter, 'Buck no doubt was prejudiced, but not more so than the Tudor chroniclers. He blunders and is uncritical, yet there is no reason to impugn his good faith.'[16]

Shakespeare scholarship was not kind to Buck. Furness in the Variorum says dogmatically, 'the character drawn by that mighty hand is the one which all of us

remember and accept as true, in spite of all apologists'. [17] And he quotes Bishop
Fuller's abusive remarks (see above, p. lxxxvii) to apply to all defenders of Richard,
among whom he lists Buck, Walpole, Halsted, and Markham. As an assessment of
Buck's style Furness quotes R.G. White:

> As history, it is neither more nor less interesting than the
> older chronicles. At times the excess of quotations from
> Latin authors is not only bewildering, but exasperating. Sir
> George apparently belongs to that class of writers to whom
> the effort of recording their thick-coming fancies presents
> but slight difficulty. . . . [18]

Paul Murray Kendall's criticism in the mid-twentieth century is not far from this.
He considers Buck's *History* 'so desultory in organization as to make for grim
reading'. [19] Some of Kendall's criticisms seem just, others curiously inappropriate:
the style is, as he says, 'tiresome', and 'cumbersome'. But it is certainly not 'capricious'[20] nor is Buck 'blundering and uncritical',[21] as Kendall says, echoing
Markham. Despite Walpole's scholarly inferiority and stylistic inanity, Kendall
considers More and Walpole 'the original antagonists of the Great Debate'[22] on
Richard III, bypassing Cornwallis and Buck. Yet a few pages later he says that Buck

> composed the first full-scale attack on the Tudor tradition.
> . . . For all his Yorkist partisanship . . . Buc was a friend of
> the best antiquaries of the day, John Stow, William
> Camden, and Sir Robert Cotton; he conscientiously
> searched old records, and was the first to make use of the
> late fifteenth-century 'Second Continuation' of the *Croy-
> land Chronicle,* a source of great importance, in attempting
> to discredit More's *History.* [23]

It was Buck who first pointed out 'some of the inaccuracies of Vergil and More, who
sought sources more nearly contemporary with Richard than the Tudor writers, and
who thus was the first to reveal that the tradition was not inviolable'. [24]

Kendall notes that Buck 'is driven, like Cornwallis, to dispose of the Tudor
tradition by dismissing its charges as improbabilities or justifying them on the basis of
raison d'État'. [25] This is exactly what Kendall himself does on occasions in his own
biography when he is unable to prove a point conclusively yet wishes to promote a
balanced judgement of Richard III. Kendall solves the problem of organization by
using chronological order and relegating the defences and debates to footnotes and
appendices. This means one must read with one finger in the corresponding page of
notes, but it allows for an uninterrupted narrative. Also he manages at last to achieve
near perfection in standards of quotation and documentation. Yet he is not unlike
Buck in that he invents, to fill out his picture, speeches, scenes, and conjectured
emotions and thoughts for which his sources give no basis but which are not incongruous with them.

A.R. Myers has written most recently on Buck, in articles published in *History Today* in 1954 and in *History* in 1968, and in an introduction to a reprint of the 1646 edition published in 1973. In the second article, Myers indicates awareness that the composition of Buck's *History* significantly predates the publication by his nephew. And he is aware to some extent of the work's nature:

> Buc clears the king of every charge made against him; he denies that Richard was a villain and asserts that on the contrary he was a good king whose memory had been blackened by Tudor historians. Buc was an antiquary of some note, a member of the first Society of Antiquaries; and it may be through the contacts of this society, especially Sir Robert Cotton, that he was able to consult many of the Cotton MSS. and the public records. [26]

While professing to assess Buck's *History,* Myers has not read the first pages of the original carefully enough to *know* that it was through Cotton, Camden, and Brook that Buck gained access to the records mentioned. Myers' tendency is to quote from the printed edition and ignore the author's original, saying that no one has ever seen manuscripts which Buck carefully documents and at one point attributing to him a bizarre etymological discourse which is actually an editorial insertion in the printed edition, appearing in no other version. Myers' conclusion is that Buck's use of documents is sometimes careless, and hence likely to be unreliable where it cannot be checked, and that consequently, 'except for his criticism of More, Buck's defence of Richard III does not amount to much'.[27] It is, he feels, more interesting an example of contemporary scholarship, which showed 'great erudition, but little critical method'.[28] But Myers fails in arguing this case because he then presents a jumble of examples from both Buck and his great-nephew, without distinguishing between them, to illustrate the point.

Myers' introduction to the reprint appears extraordinarily careless. It relies heavily on Eccles for factual details, but again by only glancing at the author's original and depending on the printed edition for illustrations makes out a case for the *elder* Buck's irresponsibility. Ideas referred to as Buck's own are represented by quotation from his great-nephew's version, with all its alterations and misprints. To discredit the elder Buck, Myers cites *Biographia Britannica's* criticism of the younger's style. Once again he speaks of 'far-fetched etymologies', but this time is wise enough not to support the statement by quoting from the printed edition: he gives no instances.

Three examples are given to illustrate Buck's unreliability, the first two quotations from the printed edition, one of them cited by an incorrect page number. One is the omission from a quotation from Croyland Chronicle of the word 'violenti', which Myers calls the 'crucial word'.[29] Setting aside the fact that this word is not particularly crucial in its context, and that Buck was using a manuscript no longer available to us, Myers has neglected to note that there is no way in which we can determine whether or not Buck *did* omit the word, since the section of the passage in which it would have occurred is burnt away in the original manuscript: the deletion may have resulted from an error on the part of the Editor or his scribe. Myers neglects also to adjust his frame of reference to the period in which Buck was writing and the conventions of that period. Very rarely does Buck indicate that he is quoting exactly. His tendency is to paraphrase, a practice for which he makes no apology because he does not claim to do otherwise.

The second illustration is so blatant an example of either carelessness or perversity on Myers' part that it vitiates anything else he may have to say in this essay. It is a claim that Buck 'quotes a statement in Camden which no one has seen since'.[30] Setting aside the impossibility of proving that no one has seen a document, the *Britannia* is still Camden's most widely read work, existing in several editions. The quotation to which Myers refers — one for which Buck cites the particular section of the *Britannia* where it occurs — can most easily be located in that work by looking up 'Richard III' in the index and turning to the page numbers there listed. It seems that in both this and the previous illustration Myers has done no more than follow Strype, an editor he himself has criticized, not bothering to check the *Britannia* himself.

No page number is given for the third example, so it is impossible to trace its source. It is a statement that Buck 'says that Bishop was condemned in Richard's parliament in 1484 of necromancy along with Thomas Nandik and William Knyvet', an assertion which misrepresents the information given by the Parliament Roll. No one by the name of 'Bishop' is mentioned in Buck's *History,* in any of its versions. It may have been Myers' intention to refer to Bishop Morton. But this we can only conjecture, since Buck, like the Act of Attainder he cites, describes only Nandick as a necromancer (see text, pp. 54, 121, 163, and 188).

Some of Myers' points on texts are extremely confusing or confused. His perversity in referring to the great-nephew's work carries over even to comments on *Daphnis,* and here no argument of accessibility can support him in choosing the version he does, for he chooses the least accessible, referring to the work not in Buck's printed edition or even in his great-nephew's printed version, but inexplicably in the great-nephew's manuscript reworking. The purpose for this selection is not made clear. Myers claims that the younger Buck dropped the lines on Richard III from *Daphnis,* though he himself has quoted them from the younger Buck's version only two pages earlier. As for the *History,* erasure by the great-nephew is cited but no folio references given, so this statement cannot be checked. Malone is said to precede Egerton, but no evidence is given for this or for the assertion that Egerton's dedication to Jacob dates from 1640. No mention at all is made of the Fisher manuscript and its place in the stemma. On the basis of the existence of the 1647 reissue (termed an 'edition'), Myers judges the work to have been popular. A reissue may indicate unpopularity in a work, certainly never its opposite. The 1646 edition is referred to as scarce, which is far from the truth.

Myers' claims for the usefulness of the 1646 edition are unsupported, and he leads the reader astray by failing to describe in any detail the significant differences in content between the original and the printed version. Once again we are led to judge Sir George Buck's methods, style, and intentions by virtually total reliance on criticism of his great-nephew's version in its latest state.

Only Mark Eccles, Buck's biographer, writing in 1933 — the one author under-taking a discussion of Buck who knew his work well in the original — is willing to examine content dispassionately and take account of stylistic conventions current in an earlier period: 'Buc is original in his sturdy defence of the character of Richard, whose annals were written under his Tudor enemies. . . . The *History* is a scholarly performance, well buttressed from public records in the Tower and in "the chappell of the Convertites in Chancery lane". . . .'[32]

From 1646 to the present day we have had criticisms of Buck muddled not only by worship of More, of the Tudors, of Elizabeth of York, of Shakespeare, and of tradition in general, but also by the identification of the 1646 edition as Buck's original work, or the arbitrary use of either the original or the printed editon under the assumption that they are similar enough for it not to matter which is attended to. Yarnold in the nineteenth century never published his intended edition of Egerton 2216. But he was aware that a clarification of inaccuracies would result from the substitution even of this, the earliest extant copy, for the garbled and truncated edition of 1646,

> An imperfect edition of this important work . . . which, defective and incorrect as it is, is now rarely to be met with, and at considerable price. The intended edition, given literally from the ORIGINAL MANUSCRIPT of Sir George Buck, will be found to contain considerably more of interesting matter than the former one. Several omissions, which in the prior edition had occasioned some plausible cavils at his integrity as an historian, or obtained for him the character of a 'lover of paradoxes,' are now fully rectified; and the imperfect marginal Notes of the printed copy, which had given rise to charges of misquotation, will be supplied by the original references to personal and oral testimony.[33]

It was in 1925, over fifty years ago, that Frank Marcham, speaking of Sir George Buck's *History of Richard III,* said that because 'the edition of 1646 is nearly worthless', and the original 'contains a good deal of interesting information on literary matters', the *History* 'should be carefully edited'. [34]

NOTES

1. Thomas Fuller, *The Church History of Britain,* ed. J.S. Brewer (Oxford, 1845), II, 490.

2. Quoted in [George Chalmers], *A Supplemental Apology for the Believers in the Shakspeare-Papers* (London, 1799), pp. 206f.

3. Hughes, Preface to Kennett, I, sig. a^v.

4. [Philip Morant], 'Buc', in *Biographia Britannica* (London, 1748), II, 1005n.

5. Andrew Kippis, 'Buc', in *Biog. Brit.* (London, 1780), II, 677.

6. Edward Gibbon, 'Doutes Historiques sur la Vie et la Regne du Roi Richard III. Par M. Horace Walpole', in *Miscellaneous Works* (London, 1814), III, 333.

7. Nicholas Harris Nicolas, 'Memoir', in *Privy Purse Expenses of Elizabeth of York* (London, 1830), p. li.

8. John Heneage Jesse, *Memoirs of King Richard the Third and Some of His Contemporaries* (London, 1862), p. 316.

9. Ibid., p. 226.

10. Caroline A. Halsted, *Richard III* (London, 1844), II, 388f.

11. James Gairdner, *History of the Life and Reign of Richard the Third* (Cambridge, 1898), p. 203.

12. David MacGibbon, *Elizabeth Woodville* (London, 1938), p. 183n.

13. A.R. Myers, 'Richard III and Historical Tradition', *History,* LIII (1968), 186.

14. Halstead, I, 95.

15. Gairdner, p. 92.

16. Clements R. Markham, *Richard III: His Life and Character* (London, 1906), p. 229n.

17. Horace Howard Furness, Jr., in Shakespeare, *The Tragedy of Richard the Third,* Variorum, 3rd ed. (Philadelphia, 1908), p.x.

18. R.G. White, quoted Furness, pp. 458f.

19. Paul Murray Kendall, *Richard III* (New York, 1955), p. 506.

20. *Richard III, the Great Debate,* ed. Kendall (London, 1965), General Introduction, pp. 8f.

21. Kendall, *Richard III,* p. 506. See Markham, p. 229n, quoted above.

22. *Great Debate,* p.5.

23. Ibid., p. 8.

24. Kendall, *Richard III,* p. 506.

25. *Great Debate,* p.9.

26.   Myers, 'Richard III and Historical Tradition', pp. 185f. It is unfortunate that Myers fails to document his assertion that Buck was a member of the Society of Antiquaries.

27.   Ibid., p. 186.

28.   Ibid.

29.   Myers, Introd. to Buck, Esq., p. vii. See p. 139 in the present text and note thereto. Myers cites it as being on p. 46 of the printed ed.; it is on p. 84.

30.   Myers, Introd., p. vii.

31.   Ibid.

32.   Eccles, p. 474.

33.   B.L. MS. Egerton 2218, f.2.

34.   Marcham, p.3.

VII. BUCK'S ATTITUDES AND USE OF SOURCES
IN THE *HISTORY*

Origin and Genre

Generically, Buck's *History of Richard III* is related both to biography and to the paradoxical encomium, and it is divided into two halves of equal length along these lines of influence. Based on classical and contemporary Continental models, the biographical form in England took its impulse from national consciousness, which inspired the searches of antiquaries for the sake of exalting the glories of England's past and England's great men, as the Protestant reformation led to the study of ecclesiastical figures. Donald A. Stauffer cites Buck's *History* as an example of 'biographies of historical figures in the past published [*sic*] as parallels and precedents for present political action'. [1] Whatever motives led to publishing the work, [2] this can be seen as in some measure influencing its composition. Buck enhances the purity and sanctity of kingship by clearing the reputation of a defamed king. And as a sideline he uses the story of Richard III, in particular the legality of his accession, in support of Parliamentary authority. The defence of a maligned monarch would have engaged Buck's strong sense of justice and of historical accuracy, and it would also have appealed to his philosophical awareness, for, as M.M. Reese says, 'in theory the Elizabethans believed that no one could be a good ruler who was not also a good man'. [3] Buck's activity as censor was at one with his life as historian: 'The manuscripts he has censored', says Eccles, 'show curiously mingled his reverence for truth and for princes'. [4] This description could apply equally well to the *History*.

At least one other matter had engaged Buck's interest in Richard III: his sense of his own personal worth and his 'interest in the quality gentle or noble' (text, p.116-17). His own ancestors, from whom he derived his status as a gentleman, were partisans of Richard III. The current passion for genealogy led the antiquary Buck to search into his own family's past as into his country's and prove it equally glorious. To do so he needed to exculpate the monarch in whose service his great-grandfather had lost his life.

The subject seems to have been in the air, ready for Buck to take hold of. Interest in the House of York as an extant entity had been aroused in Elizabeth's time, though it is uncertain how strongly or openly. *Lord Leicester's Commonwealth,* a subversive tract widely circulated, indicates that the Earl of Huntingdon, a friend of Leicester and open competitor for the sceptre, based his claim on descent from the House of York, specifically from Clarence, and that Leicester was performing for Huntingdon the role of Warwick the Kingmaker. Comparisons are made with the events of Richard III's reign: the possibility is raised of Leicester's marrying Queen Elizabeth when he is already married, and Richard's giving out that his wife was dead, after which she really did die, is mentioned in this connection. The current Hastings is considered likely to suffer his ancestor's fate. Huntingdon's supporters follow Richard III in debasing Edward IV's line as illegitimate to give his own derivation from Clarence precedence. Since this faction reopens the whole question of Lancaster and York, their history, including Richard's reign, is rehearsed in full.

Further interest in Richard III existed among three groups of scholars with whom Buck had associations. There were the antiquary-historians Stow and Camden, whose works began, though only slightly, to liberalize the view of Richard. Stow was apparently making investigations, as we can see from Buck's *viva voce* references to him, and finding many of the charges unjustified. In his *Survey,* he describes Richard's accession as an election, not a usurpation, and in his *Annales* he lists Richard's good works. This is as far as he goes in his published writings, but as Buck's *History* shows, his private researches went much farther. Buck's friend Camden in the later editions of his *Britannia* (1607 onward) has to concede Richard's potential position among the best of kings, although he still finds him among the worst of men, and describes the liberality, affability, wisdom, and justice he displayed as Protector, which persuaded everyone, especially lawyers, to petition him to be king. Camden judges the marriage of Edward IV to Elizabeth Woodville invalid, not because of the precontract, but because it occurred without asking of the banns and without the nobility's consent. Thus, with Clarence's children debarred by attainder, Richard was legal heir to the crown. Camden still does not exonerate Richard of the various murder charges, but only of the great political charge of usurpation. There is no way of knowing how much of this enlightenment concerning Richard, whom Camden had described in 1600 as seizing the realm, is due to Buck's influence, or how much Buck owes to Camden in this respect. The heralds, of whom Camden was one, and many of whom were Buck's friends, had a natural interest in Richard because that monarch had incorporated their foundation, the College of Arms. They gave Buck considerable assistance in his antiquarian works.

Another focus of interest in Richard III found its first outlet in Sir William Cornwallis' *Encomium of Richard III.* This interest seems to have existed among a group of literary men, all of whom were aware of the existence of a pamphlet by Bishop Morton on which More's history is based. This Morton tract is mentioned by Sir John Harington in *The Metamorphosis of Ajax* (1596)[5] as well as by Buck, though neither seems actually to have seen it. It is quite likely that Harington, like Buck, received his information from Sir Edward Hoby, his closest friend.[6] Hoby died in 1617 and Buck's *History* is dated 1619, but Buck had this information about the Morton tract considerably earlier and gives documentary evidence in a statement — clearer than the one in the *History* — which he wrote in the margin of his copy of Godwin's *Catalogue*: 'This Morton wrote\ in Latin / the life of K.R.3. which goeth in Sir Th. Mores name — as S. Ed. Hoby saith & *that Sir* W. Roper hath the originall'.[7]

Buck's entries in his copy of Godwin were made between 1604 and 1611, most of them around 1607-9. Buck and Hoby were acquainted at least from 1596, when they were on the Cadiz expedition together.[8] A reference to a non-extant work of Hoby's, the *Anatomia de Espagna* (text, p. 160) suggests that Buck remained close enough to Hoby to be among the readers of a work he must have circulated privately in manuscript.

Hoby was evidently so much impressed by the similarity of this tract to More's *History* that he told Buck, as Harington was also informed, that the two works were all but identical. The Ropers, heirs to both Morton and More, were certainly the likeliest possessors of such a tract. But their status as recusants may have made consultation of the work difficult. Although around 1609 Buck knew that Roper had the manuscript, in 1619 he can say only that he knows Roper has it 'lately'. He documents its existence and nature after his usual fashion by naming someone who had seen it. He trusts Hoby's description so completely that he frequently documents something he has derived from More as emanating from Morton and More. These references unfortunately have no significance in tracing the similarity of the Morton tract to More, since Buck is relying on someone else's word rather than on his own observation when he assumes their identity in factual material.

Cornwallis knew Harington and probably Hoby, and he could hardly have avoided knowing the Ropers, since the Cornwallises and Ropers, two of the most prominent recusant families, were neighbours and relatives by marriage. Cornwallis therefore had an opportunity to know about and read the Morton pamphlet. W. Gordon Zeeveld makes a case for Cornwallis' *Encomium* being a direct reply to the Morton tract, though he believes the origin of the *Encomium* to be much earlier and Cornwallis to be only the reviser rather than the author, a theory against which I have argued elsewhere.[9]

But Cornwallis' authorship of the *Encomium* was not known to Buck, who did not use it in connection with the Morton tract. He was not even aware that it had been published, and invariably speaks of it as an anonymous manuscript in defence of Richard III. He refers to it several times, and the structure and argument of his last three books, particularly the beginning of Book III, depend heavily upon it. There is certainly no reasonable foundation in Zeeveld's suggestion that this tract was written by a member of the Buck family.[10] Had this been the case, Buck would hardly have referred to to it as anonymous, and had he possessed this document through family sources his strong family pride and care in documentation would have led him to say so. He would probably also have known of its publication in 1616. And if he had had private access to an earlier verision, as Zeeveld argues, he would not have used — as he consistently does — one of the later versions, which incorporates the later additions by Cornwallis himself and by others who evidently took over the tract for their own political purposes.[11] Many manuscript copies of it were in circulation. Buck probably saw one in the collection of an antiquarian friend. All he appears to know of the author is that he was a lawyer, for he calls him 'Anonymus juris peritus' (text, p. 199).

Cornwallis, a writer of paradoxes, seems to have written this essay as a refutation of the accusations against Richard and tried to fit it into paradox form. The concluding remark of the *Encomium*, 'yet for all this knowe I hold this but as a Paradoxe',[12] which appears only in the later versions of the work, is almost certainly the basis of Buck's fear, expressed in his dedication, of the worst possible censure his work could incur: that of being taken for a paradox (text, p. 3). A paradox was a rhetorical device of classical origin whose purpose was to show off the orator's skill in choosing an absurd topic for defence and his expertise in defending it. R.E. Bennett in his thesis on Cornwallis[13] cites praises of historical or mythological figures not generally considered praiseworthy as being among the oldest types of paradoxical encomium. Rosalie L. Colie in her study of paradoxes gives Cornwallis' *Encomium* as an example that fails because it does not 'surprise or dazzle by its incongruities',[14] for it strikes the reader as an all but serious defence. Instead of appearing skilful, many of its arguments give the impression of being sincere but lame efforts at exonerating Richard.

Buck in his last three books follows the method of Cornwallis' *Encomium*. After the first two books — a biography of Richard which, though digressive, is chronological — he spends three books taking up and replying one by one to accusations levelled by the chroniclers. In this second section of the *History* too he is extremely digressive, but in general outline he uses as his basic structure Cornwallis' technique of posing accusations and following them by apologies. In Book III between pp. 127 and 137 we find Buck taking up in order similar to Cornwallis' the accusations regarding Richard's birth with teeth, his deformity, his mother's pangs, then the murders of Henry VI, Edward, Prince of Wales, and Clarence. These accusations form groups in Cornwallis; they form groups also in Buck, who, however, arranges them within the groups in more strictly chronological order. Both Cornwallis and Buck pass on to Shaw's sermon and Richard's charging his mother with adultery, and again Buck retains Cornwallis' grouping but reverses the order. Shortly thereafter both take up the death of the Princes. As Buck follows the first half of Cornwallis' essay in Book III, he follows the second half in Books IV and V. In Book IV he deals with the death of Queen Anne and Richard's intention to marry his niece. Both use the argument that Richard could have divorced his wife had he wished to be rid of her. The accusation of unjustly killing Colingbourne follows soon after. Book V deals with Richard's good qualities — his mercy, justice, care for religion and for his people's safety, his eschewing of taxation, luxury, epicurism, and riot. Again Buck follows Cornwallis in general grouping but not in the precise order in which he takes up particular virtues.

In certain general ideas Buck seems to have been influenced by Cornwallis: that Richard should have been less merciful and dealt more harshly with his enemies (Cornwallis mentions only Stanley and the Countess of Richmond; Buck expands the list considerably). That if Richard had won the battle his fame would have been good. That Richard has been made infamous in pamphlets and plays. And that even if he did commit the crimes with which he is charged he is excused by reasons of state.

The debt is primarily structural. Buck expands and improves on Cornwallis in use of argument. He seems to have assimilated Cornwallis' technique of posing and answering accusations, and at times he uses in a very general way a similar argument as defence (as in the case of the divorce suggestion, cited above). But where both authors give examples to support their arguments, Buck's are far more numerous and invariably different. And whereas Cornwallis' tendency is to accept the accusations against Richard as true and then argue that they are tolerable, Buck's in most cases is to try to prove the arguments untrue. By so doing he is not, as is Cornwallis, forced to produce ridiculous arguments proving crimes laudable. As a paradoxical essayist Cornwallis attempts to prove praiseworthy something that remains not praiseworthy, not to prove that unpraiseworthy facts are not facts at all, though he shows considerable ambivalence. Buck, though he adopts the accusation-defence technique, does so with the purpose of proving the accusations false. Thus he avoids the danger he fears of his *History*'s being dismissed as a mere paradox. Whereas Cornwallis' arguments are intellectually ingenious, Buck's are carefully researched accumulations of evidence from a wide range of primary and secondary sources. This basis of scholarly research rather than intellectual dexterity makes his structure much looser, as of course does his tendency to digress and the scope which the length of his work allows for digression. Cornwallis, writing a short, tightly argued essay, could not afford this luxury.

Organization

Buck's organization is far from haphazard, nor is it purposelessly rambling, as it may seem at first glance. He sets out in the Advertisement to the Reader his plan of organization and the scope of his work. First he describes Richard's lineage, birth, youth, training, and private life; then he proceeds to his public life, his coronation and reign; and lastly he tries to redeem him from the slanders with which he has been taxed. He is conscious of a certain decorum or prescription in this organization, for he describes his following Richard's early and private life with the story of his public life as being 'as it ought according to method and due order'. His scope is 'to write this unhappy king's story faithfully and at large, and to plead his cause, and to answer and refell the many accusations and calumniations brought against him' (text, p. 8).

In the first two books he feels so dependent on chronology that he sees a chronological interim between Richmond's first and second invasions which he must fill up. He interposes mentions of certain events of Richard's reign and a discussion of Henry VII's claim, in case 'for lack of them there would be a silence here until we come to the second invasion of the Earl of Richmond' (text, p. 73). He feels the conflicting needs of giving background material on Henry VII so that his invasions may make sense in the context of Richard's story, while at the same time keeping this material in check, since it is not of central importance.

Book I ends with Richard at the height of his prosperity, and Book II starts with the beginning of his downfall and the shift in Fortune's favour to him. Buck makes this structure, influenced by the *de casibus* tradition, stronger in revision. The second book proceeds to Richard's death, and with the treatment of his body after death introduces the theme of calumny which will dominate the next three books. Although in the first book chronology now and again compels him to mention Richard's supposed crimes, he touches on these only briefly and says that he will reserve full discussion of them until he comes to the 'fit place' where he intends to clear Richard fully. When he actually begins his refutations, he prepares the way for them by discussing the unreliability of the sources which have so far dealt with Richard.

Buck's style differs considerably from what Camden propounds as his own ideal: 'Short Sentences I have seldom interlaced, nor adorn'd my Discourse with those nice Observations which the *Greeks* aptly term ΕΠΙΣΤΆΣΕΙΣ. . . . Digressions I have avoided'.[15] Buck, as will be shown, uses 'short sentences' to support his statments and ornament his work, and he is extremely digressive and repetitious. He is aware of this tendency and defends it in his Advertisement to the Reader as 'a tacit persuasion to the reader or author to remember better, and better to mark the thing so repeated and its causes' (text, p. 7). And he is aware also of his tendency to multiply evidence. In the section on Perkin Warbeck he allows that he has already given enough evidence to prove that Perkin was the Duke of York, but though more is not needed, more is available, and 'according to the *ancient* principle, *abundans cautela non nocet*' (text, p. 160), he will add it. He does tend to allow his enthusiasms sometimes to get out of hand. His long genealogical digression on Hamelin Plantagenet has at best a tenuous connection with the matter in hand, but his discussion of Hamelin's false shield has not the slightest relevance in context, although to us it is an interesting testimony from one acquainted with heraldic practices of the heraldic malpractices of his period.

Buck contrasts himself with an author he criticizes by saying, 'I am here rather prolix than brief' (text, p. 7). He is objecting undoubtedly to the annalistic style which gives facts without explanations, and thus he considers it better to say too much than too little in an historical work. This does frequently prove a virtue, for he tends to heap up evidence rather than citing only one authority in support of his assertions, and by so doing he not only arrives at a clearer awareness of the relative reliability of his sources but often in his research uncovers new information which is an original contribution to his study. His digressiveness is annoying in itself, but interesting in that he gives information, often firsthand, on sidelines of the story about which there is little or no other contemporary information extant. His sentence structure, strung along with unvaried series after series, 'and' following 'and', with little subordination, is distracting.

Family Tradition

In the case of an author like Buck who has family associations to connect him with the cause of Richard III, we might wonder first of all whether he had access to any private family data which were not available to others. The answer is without question that he did not. He did possess a few family traditions. One was that his great-grandfather was Controller of the House under Richard. In his manuscript he gives this as Sir John Buck's office, in a late addition in his own hand to a scribal page, qualifying it by the remark 'as the tradition of \t/his family is' (Tiberius, f. 52). He must have begun to wonder at once about the accuracy of this family tradition, for he crossed the reference out. His confusion probably arose from his research, when he found Sir Robert (he gives the name erroneously as Thomas) Percy listed as Controller under Richard. But by the time he came to rewrite the page he had resolved the question, perhaps by guesswork, stating that Buck succeeded Percy in the office. He cites family tradition in the testimony of his grandfather, who was brought up by the Earl of Surrey, about Surrey's adventures after Bosworth. Aside from this there is nothing.

The Howards, it seems, managed to preserve little more. A letter from Elizabeth of York to the Duke of Norfolk is one of Buck's unique contributions to the study of Richard III. This document Buck has derived from the Howards, but only this. The extent to which family tradition had failed among the Howards to preserve Richard's memory is indicated by the following quotation, expressing gratitude for Richard's generosity but for a report of his actions relying entirely upon the popular chronicles:

> Rycharde duke of Glocester, finding that so longe as his brother George of Clarence, stoode betweene him & the gole, he coulde not gette the prise, . . . caused a certaine prophecie to be suggested to the kyng his elder brother, that G. shoulde one day were the crowne, not doubtinge but the king would rather look to Glocester, then George, aswell in respect of the sayd Dukes former trespasse, and alliance, with the house of Warwicke . . . as because the manner of these prophecies, hath beene rather to regarde the proper name then the dignity. I speake not this to quicken or reuiue the memory of king Rychards heinous fault, which in respecte of all the bountifull and princlye benefites bestowed vppon the family from whence I come, I could rather wish to be drowned in the blacke deepes, and folded vppe in the darke clowdes of obliuion for euer. [16]

This is by Henry Howard in 1583. Here family tradition has preserved only a strong sympathy and sense of gratitude, baffled by what had been written about Richard by the 'authorities'. Buck speaks of the Howards' gratitude to Richard in the dedication of his *History* to Thomas Howard, Earl of Arundel (text, p. 3). He possessed a similar sympathy, and it remained for him, as an antiquary versed in methods of scholarly research, to approach the authorities critically and combat them with evidence of greater authority.

Sources

Buck's use of classical and religious sources is both decorative and illustrative. His style seems to be very little influenced by classical examples, though of course in following the genre of biographical writing he is influenced by classical historians, as his numerous references to them show. Aside from this we see some specific influence in his rarely indulged tendency to invent speeches, a classical technique adopted by many other English historical writers who preceded him and were his contemporaries. Examples of Buck's enlarging on a small hint to create brief scenes and speeches can be seen in the conversation of Henry Tudor and Pierre de Landois (text, p. 36) and in that of Alexander and Medius in one of the illustrative passages (text, pp. 166-67). He adds visual details to the scene in which Richard is petitioned to accept the crown and constructs speeches using More's phraseology where More's account is in indirect discourse. He adds to this scene a second attempt on Richard by Buckingham and a speech by the Lord Mayor. We may imagine from this tendency that he may have done something similar with the encounter between Surrey and Henry VII: relying on his grandfather's report of the general facts and perhaps a few of Surrey's heroic utterances, he imagined the setting and the conversation as a rounded whole. At no point does he distort sense by taking creative liberties. What he does is essentially to convey factual information through direct discourse, creating vividness and immediacy. Because the work is so rambling, these short scenes or speeches have an effect only where they occur and not for the work as a whole.

Buck uses the Alexander and Medius scene, mentioned above, as an illustrative parallel to the case of Richard III, showing how persons in power make innocent men culpable by fastening on them false accusations. Similar anecdotes are drawn from Roman historians, Roman and Greek tragedians, and the Bible. Sententious comments, proverbs, and apt quotations are taken from a number of classical, mediaeval, and Biblical authors. This sort of decorative and illustrative quotation is typical of prose writing in Buck's time. At school, pupils learned texts from which they were supposed to 'gather the flowers', the phrases useful in rhetoric. There existed numerous commonplace books, collections of useful quotations, to assist authors and speakers. Erasmus, whose *Chiliades* is probably the most famous of these, gives reasons for their use: they strengthen and clarify the argument and they add ornament and elegance. [17] Buck seems to rely on his own memory for many of his rhetorical flowers, for he sometimes ascribes them to the wrong authors and changes words to synonyms of the same quantities. He probably used a commonplace book when arraying a long series of quotations on a single subject as, for example, on tyranny at the beginning of Book V. But I have not been able to locate a precise book from which he drew his casual quotations. Three collections he mentions which are apparently no longer extant are *Anthologia Sacra, Sententiae Arabicae,* and *Axiomata Politica.* He does use and document Erasmus' *Chiliades.* Sometimes he gives translated into Latin a quotation which was originally in Greek, an habitual practice of the commonplace book. He drew on his legal background for legal maxims and had some knowledge of commentaries on the scriptures.

By far the largest number of Buck's illustrative references and quotations comes from the Bible. Seneca is next, with half the references to his tragedies, half to his prose works. Then Vergil and Cicero, the former used largely for ornament, like Ovid, another author Buck quotes frequently, the latter often for political sentences. Plutarch, both *Lives* and *Moralia,* is used for long illustrative anecdotes, as is

Suetonius, whose lives of the Roman emperors provide Buck with political parallels. Terence merits three citations, Plautus none at all. Euripides is the Greek dramatist Buck knows best, though he quotes once from Sophocles and once from Menander. Aristotle and Homer are the Greek nondramatic authors with whom Buck seems most familiar, and he draws a few references from Plato.

Among the authors he uses less often the largest number are historians: Quintus Curtius, Diodorus, Dion Cassius, Herodotus, Julius Capitolinus, Aelius Lampridius, Livy, Trebellius Pollio, Trogus Pompeius, Valerius Maximus, Velleius Paterculus, and Flavius Vopiscus. Next come religious commentators: St Thomas Aquinas, St Augustine, John Chrysostom, Andreas Osiander, Philo, Strigelius, and Zosimus. And finally legal authors, first Ulpian, then Vulteius and Prateius, all the legal references being almost certainly from memory. Other classical authors who supplied Buck with one or more 'flowers' or anecdotes are Ausonius, Claudian, Demosthenes, Horace, Juvenal, Lucan, Lucretius (not documented), Lycurgus, Philostratus, Pliny, Polybius, Quintilian (not documented), Strabo, Suidas, and Publilius Syrus (referred to as 'the old Mimographus').

In his antiquarian pursuit of origins, Buck searches the ancestry of Richard III, of the Howards, of his own family, and of James I. He has done this at much greater length for a larger number of families in the *Commentary,* and he uses similar sources, mediaeval histories of Britain: the ledger book of Ely monastry, Radulphus de Coggeshall, Gildas, Giraldus Cambrensis, Roger de Hoveden, Henry Huntingdon, William of Malmesbury, William of Newburgh, Matthew Paris, John of Salisbury, Thomas Walsingham, Roger Wendover, Matthew of Westminster, and the early part of the Croyland Chronicle. Many of these he could at the time have seen only in manuscript, and he uses other manuscript mediaeval histories in Cotton's library as well: a Benedictine history of Henry II (incorrectly documented because two manuscript histories were bound in one book) and the history of the Abbey of St Stephen, Caen. Most of these he had already used in *Daphnis* for his genealogical excursions through early Britain.

He uses more recent sources, Hector Boethius and George Buchanan, for early Scottish history. Continental references, Claude Paradin, Jean de la Haye, and Gerard du Haillan, trace the genealogy of the Plantagenets abroad. Another small group of sources which Buck uses only once appear in his discussion of More: John Bale, John Foxe, Germain Brie, George Courinus, and Erasmus' letters.

His references to modern legal works are to Henry Bracton and William Staundford. Aside from these he relies on *viva voce* information from famous contemporary lawyers. He uses Bishop Godwin's *Catalogue,* a relatively recent work of which he owned a copy, for ecclesiastical biography.

The continental side of the Yorkist and Tudor story he supplements by use of continental sources, relying most heavily on Philippe de Commynes' *Memoirs,* Alain Bouchard's *Grandes Cronicques de Bretaigne* (his own copy), Johann Meyer's *Annales Flandriae,* Jean du Tillet's *Recueil des Roys,* and Monstrelet's *Chroniques.* For Spain, he refers once each to Çurita, Garibay, Sir Edward Hoby's unpublished and non-extant *Anatomia de Espagna,* and a no longer extant work called *El*

Reusuerq, to which he had referred once in the *Commentary*. He occasionally glances at Froissart, demonstrating an easy familiarity with that author, and refers once to Guicciardini (for his own family history), and once to Jean de Serres (for Edward IV's death).

British topographical references are primarily to Camden, aside from the historians of mediaeval Britain already noted, and a few historical comments are drawn from Camden as well. For English genealogy he uses Glover. The sources on which Buck relies most heavily throughout, however, are the Tudor histories. One of his greatest contributions to the history of the period is his use of Croyland Chronicle as a source. He would have been able to find the whole of this work, including all the continuations, only in manuscript form. It is a valuable discovery in that it does not depend, as do all the other available sources, on More or on Henry VII's official sources. It was written by a member of Edward IV's council, probably John Russell, Bishop of Lincoln,[18] and although it expresses the attitude of one politically opposed to Richard's accession and becomes increasingly less informative and reliable, probably because the author was no longer so constantly present at Court after the coronation, it represents more authoritatively than any other source the events preceding and to a great extent following Richard's accession. Buck may be said to have discovered this most valuable source for Ricardian history. He uses it frequently to add to the information of the Tudor chronicles, to substantiate them or to correct their bias. There are more references to it than to any other source except More.

More and Polydore Vergil are the historians upon whom Buck most relies for the general story of Richard III and Henry VII. He often couples these with reference to other histories derived from them, Grafton, Hall, Holinshed, and Stow, and he links Morton's name with More's assuming Morton to be More's source. How he kept up with contemporary material is shown in his use of Thomas Gainsford's *True and Wonderfull History of Perkin Warbeck,* published in 1618 (and also dedicated to Arundel). Other Tudor historians he uses are Fabyan (one reference), Rous (one reference through Stow's *viva voce* information), and André. The reference to André does not appear in the present edition because it occurs in a passage Buck deleted for fuller development later on. In his later version he does not repeat the reference.

He has received *viva voce* information from Coke on a legal point. John, Baron Lumley, is cited for the description of the Duchess of Salisbury's execution under Henry VIII. Arundel is witness that James I had been heard to deplore the execution of Edward, Earl of Warwick and is cited also for the amount of the fine imposed on the Earl of Oxford. The present Earl of Oxford told Buck that he had been offered £12,000 annually for the use of a part of his lands. Baron Darcy is the *viva voce* source of information regarding Don Sebastian of Portugal. Sir Edward Hoby told Buck about the existence and nature of the Morton tract which was reputedly the basis of More's *History*. Stow on several occasions is cited as imparting to Buck information, existing in none of his published works, from his own independent enquiries about Richard III. Buck's grandfather has given him the story of Surrey's escape and pardon, and Buck himself was witness to the conversation between Don Duarte de

Lancastro and Charles Howard, Lord Admiral.

Considering the length of his work and that it exists in a rough state, Buck's accuracy is amazing. He documents frequently and regularly, and, despite the serious damage by fire to the margins of his manuscript, it is rare that his references cannot be located. I have failed to find the sources of some of the occasional Latin quotations which he uses for ornament and illustration, but I have found so many, often accidentally, that the failure is more likely to be my fault than Buck's. Many, of course, are proverbial and their authors unknown. It is noteworthy that the ones I have failed to trace are concentrated mostly toward the end of the book where Buck's marginal documentation is totally destroyed and the copies are most divergent from the original. Judging from the copies' habit of progressively omitting marginal documentation, we may assume that many of the references now apparently un-documented were once documented in the margins.

I have already discussed the use of antiquaries' collections and the general hazards to manuscripts residing in them (see above, pp. xlvi-xlviii), citing C.E. Wright's remark that it is not surprising so many manuscripts once known to have been in Cotton's collection are there no more. Loss, borrowing, exchange, sale, division of property, recataloguing, fire, or the activities of rodents and insects could cause a document to disappear. Many of the Cotton manuscripts which appear to have been lost are actually still there under a different number or bound with another work. Under these circumstances it should not be a matter of amazement to the reader or of discredit to Buck that of the huge number of sources he mentions, only eight or nine — not counting commonplace books and collections of proverbs — cannot now be found. Of these less than half can be considered of material importance. It should of course be kept in mind that my failure to locate these sources does not prove that they do not or never did exist. Those missing are:

a copy of a commission for truce and peace with Scotland, giving certain of Lord Howard's titles;

letters about truce and peace between Richard III and Charles VIII;

El Reusuerq, from which Buck derives a brief marginal reference to Bona of Savoy's eventual marriage;

Sir Edward Hoby's manuscript history *La Anatomia de Espagna,* to which he makes one passing reference in a generalization about Spanish kings;

a list of sobriquets shown to Buck by Sir William Dethick, mentioned in a digression on the name 'Plantagenet';

the letter from Elizabeth of York to the Duke of Norfolk on her plan to marry King Richard, shown to Buck by Arundel;

the tract by Morton which is reputedly the source of More's history, not seen by Buck but by Sir Edward Hoby, who reported its whereabouts;

'an old manuscript book' from which Buck derives a reference to a plot by Morton and 'a certain countess' to poison the Princes;

a 'chronicle manuscript in quarto' in Cotton's collection, to which Buck makes six brief references, usually to material that can easily be found elsewhere; possibly the same work as the 'old manuscript book' mentioned above.

That so few of his sources have been lost through fire, lending, and the destruction of his own marginal references, cannot be considered evidence that Buck is a careless or irresponsible author, especially bearing in mind the work's unfinished state. It is not sufficient warrant for Myers' implication[19] that since Buck is occasionally careless, his testimony in the few instances where the source cannot be traced is auto-matically unreliable. Nor does it justify Myers' curious statement that 'no one else has ever seen' some of Buck's sources, a statement subject to disproof, never to proof. Of those few of Buck's sources which I have not seen, we may assume that Cotton himself and others of his readers saw the manuscript chronicle in quarto in his collection to which Buck refers as many as six times, about which Myers specifically says, 'No one else has ever seen this document',[20] prejudicing his statement by failing to cite Buck's marginal documentation which gives the work's location. All other items to which Buck refers as being in Cotton's library can still be found there, with the exception of one, *Axiomata Politica,* whose existence is plainly recorded in the Cotton borrowing list, which designates it as a quarto. It was lent to Mr (Auditor) Povey (Harl. 6018, f. 156ᵛ), who passed it on to a Dr Hickman. The record of borrowing is not crossed out. The Editor has found in one of Buck's citations of it a specific reference, 'cap. 129', which, though now lost from Tiberius E.X, appears in all the copies. To assume that the manuscript history, the only one of the many works Buck cites from the Cotton collection which has been lost without sufficient identifying trace to prove its existence at one time was an invention of his is not plausible. Information derived from this document is rarely of great importance. On one occasion Fabyan is cited in conjunction with it as supplying the same information. Fabyan, an extant work, can be checked, and this particular reference (text, p. 52) proves to be correct. Several manuscript chronicles covering this period were lost in the fire. Catalogue descriptions are insufficient to identify the one Buck used.

The commision for Scotland still exists in several copies, but none gives as many of Howard's titles as Buck's source did. The precise copy to which Buck refers was at the time, he says, extant in the Rolls, and the letters about the French peace were extant in the Exchequer. He states that he has seen them, and his citing their whereabouts suggests that he is attempting to aid others in seeing them (see text, pp. 46-47 and 58).

Dethick saw the list of sobriquets (text, pp. 11-12), for he owned them and showed them to Buck. The Morton tract Buck never claims to have seen, but he refers to a re-liable person who has seen it, and if we question this reference in the *History,* we should note that Buck recorded it with greater detail and clarity about ten years earlier in the margin of a book in his private library (see above, p. ciii). Buck refers to *La Anatomia de Espagna* on the assumption that some of his readers have seen it: 'he who hath read the book of Sir Edward Hoby entitled *La Anatomia de [Espagna]* . . .' (text, p. 160).

Arundel showed Buck the letter from Elizabeth of York, so obviously, despite Myers' claim that 'no one else has ever seen this document', [21] Arundel saw it himself, as, no doubt, did his ancestor, to whom it was directed. There is no reason to doubt the existence at one time of this letter. If it were not available at the time in the place where Buck said that it resided, he would not have documented it as existing there. Cooperation in revealing information to each other was a habit among antiquaries, and there is no reason for Buck, contrary to his usual practice of giving very explicit documentation according to the standards which the Society of Antiquaries attempted to foster, suddenly to have falsified it, misleading his readers rather than trying to lead them, as was his habit. Such a fabrication would have been pointless here, since this letter is of no great importance to his case in this section: his main subject is Richard's disposition to the marriage, not Elizabeth's. He was bound to be especially careful in this particular citation, since the owner of the document was the person to whom he dedicates the work in which he cites it. That the letter cannot at the present time be traced is not extraordinary. Much of Arundel's collection was given away and sold by Henry Howard, sixth Duke of Norfolk. It had already been split up on Arundel's death in 1646 because of family feuding. Naworth Castle, where certain of the Howard treasures were preserved, was burned in 1844, along with many of the treasures it contained. Numerous of these are, however, still in the possession of the various branches of the Howard family. It may still have been available in 1750 when Carte speaks of it as 'preserved in the Arundel collection' [22] without citing Buck as his source, as he normally does in the case of information found in no other place. This may, however, be simply a slip of Carte's. Henry Howard of Corby, 'who had access to many secret sources of information respecting his house', [23] says, 'there is no reason to doubt his [Buck's] veracity in what must then have been so easily contradicted. I think it very possible that this letter, if sought among the mass of papers at Norfolk House, may still cast up'. [24] Scholars of the present day express frustration at not being permitted to explore the Howard papers. [25] As for the letter's interpretation, Arundel, himself a scholar and collector and a descendant of the recipient, must have been convinced of its authenticity, provenance, and meaning or he would not have shown it to Buck as historical evidence.

Still unaccounted for are *El Reusuerq*, to which Buck had made one reference in the *Commentary*, and 'an old manuscript book' which says that 'Morton and a certain countess, [conspirin]g the deaths of the sons of King Edward and some other, resolved that *these treach*eries should be executed by poison and by sorcery' (text, p. 163). For this last no documentation remains, but that is not to say there was none.

Buck is consistently concerned that others should be able to locate his sources, as has already been seen (for above, p. lxxx) in his reassurance concerning the charter of incorporation for the College of Arms which is no longer to be found in the College itself, where a reader might naturally look for it. In other cases he refers as specifically as possible to the present whereabouts of a document: often he states that a particular manuscript is *now* in the hands of Cotton, and in the case of the Morton tract he specifies that it *was lately* in the hands of Mr Roper. When he has been unable to view a primary source, he makes this clear and gives the word of a reliable colleague, such as that of Hoby about the Morton tract, as the best alternative documentation. This form of second hand reference by report to document a work the author has not himself seen is usual and acceptable. Buck uses it in a published work, *The Third Universitie* (see above, p. xxvi). Description of the circumstances in which information was obtained seems to figure as an important part of its documentation. It may be partly pride of his acquaintance that led Buck to describe the Earl of Oxford's visiting him at his Hampton Court lodgings and there telling him about the value of his lands, but also the circumstantial detail serves to support the information.

Buck's documentation is amazingly copious and painstaking for a period in which documentation was still in its earliest stages. At the beginning of the work, in the Dedication and Advertisement to the Reader, he comments on his method, saying that he has followed other authors in his history, 'And because I follow other men, I cite their names and their authorities either in the text or in the margent, and it maketh more for the credit of the story' (text, p. 4). He goes on to criticize authors whose histories 'are of little cred*it* because they deliver all their matters . . . upon their own bare and worthless word' (text, p. 4). Later he attacks a particular author for 'neglect of citation of authors and quotations, thus concealing of their names and vainly taking all upon himself'. He himself, on the other hand, claims, 'I cite mine authors everywhere' (text, p. 7).

It would be a mistake to impugn Buck's accuracy on the basis of his failing to quote the authors he uses word for word according to our own standard practices of three and a half centuries later. He does not profess to do so. Buck's references are generally accurate in terms of sense, but he takes the liberty of introducing synonyms, of paraphrasing, of omitting unnecessary words and passages, of making corrections, of changing from direct to indirect discourse or *vice versa*, of adapting the style or grammatical construction to fit his own. He makes corrections where his sources 'write false and incongruous English' (text, p. 179). Quhitlaw's speech is improved by omission of digressive material, some transposition, and grammatical corrections, but there is no change in basic content. Richard's epitaph, found in a manuscript book in Guildhall, is quoted 'the faults and corruptions being amended' (text, p. 217). Herd's poem is followed very closely, and the longest quotation from it is on a separate sheet pasted in, suggesting that Buck had copied it carefully from the manuscript. But he has made improvements, filling in an incomplete first line and introducing an emendation for an illegible section. As E.E. Reynolds says, 'Our strict rules of transcription were unknown in the sixteenth century and for long afterwards'.[26]

Yet despite this licence, Buck's paraphrase rarely distorts sense. An example of his actually slanting an argument occurs when he cites Coggeshall, Westminster, Wendover, Walsingham, Paris as witnesses of his ancestor Walter Buck's worthiness (text, p. 115). In fact, all these references are unfavourable and use Walter Buck's activities to illustrate the destructiveness and violence of King John's foreign mercenaries.

He also sometimes eliminates derogatory references to Richard. When Camden says that Richard would have been worthy to reign if he had not obtained the throne by criminal means and to have been numbered among bad men but good princes, Buck alters the verb to say that Richard *was* worthy to reign, and omits mention of his devious means and of his being among the worst of men (text, p. 46). In a reference to Johann Meyer, he neglects to mention Gloucester as the owner of the sword that killed Henry VI (text, p. 134). It is possible to comment on these distortions because they refer to works Buck used in print. But in the case of Croyland Chronicle we can make no such judgements, for Buck used manuscripts no longer extant. So when he uses the verb 'immisit' where Fulman's printed text says 'intrusit', to refer to Richard's taking his seat in Westminster Hall (text, p. 46), this may be an example either of Buck's softening the attitude to Richard or of a difference between manuscripts. The same caution must be observed with regard to the epitaph which he and Sandford quoted from different manuscripts (text, p. 217).

Buck's inaccuracies are few considering the size and state of his work. About matters relating to the House of Burgundy, however, he tends to be careless, undoubtedly because he is working from memory. He once calls Margaret of Burgundy Richard's aunt rather than his sister, and on two other occasions he refers to Charles of Burgundy in situations which occurred after his death. The errors about Richard's early military career, giving him an active part in battles that occurred in his infancy (an error Shakespeare shares), probably have basis partly in mistaken recollection, partly in the miscalculation of Richard's birthdate. Buck cannot be blamed for this latter error because there was no objective evidence available at the time, and Buck was forced upon his own conjecture to establish the date. His methods of conjecture, though they produce an incorrect result, are judicious and intelligent.

When Buck is in doubt he checks and makes corrections, and when in the process of revision he discovers a mistake, he changes it. For example, on f. 38 in the original manuscript he attributes to the Croyland Chronicle information on Sir Thomas Stanley's part in Richard's Scottish campaign. But on more careful consideration of the source, Buck discovered that although it does mention the recovery of Berwick, the Croyland Chronicle does not mention Sir Thomas Stanley's part in it, so he crosses out the attribution.

He sometimes falls into a trap by taking one source as authority and searching no further. One such occasion is in his reference to Banister, who betrayed the traitor Buckingham to Richard. Buck relies on Hall for his information about Banister. Hall's account is inaccurate. The greatest danger occurs when Buck assumes the accuracy of a document because it is old and in manuscript. In these cases he has not, as with printed sources, much basis for critical appraisal. He often has no way of telling how much of the information he takes from old manuscript chronicles is hearsay. But though his practice with original documents is imperfect, his using them at all is an advance in historical writing of this period. He uses *Titulus Regius* to support the justice of Richard's title, to set forth the circumstances leading to his assumption of the throne, and to correct the chroniclers' references to Elizabeth Lucy. He uses it also, however, in an attempt to prove the Princes still alive early in

1484, neglecting to observe that what he is reading is a petition of the previous summer which has been bodily incorporated into the business of Richard's first Parliament. And he takes the *Titulus Regius* at face value because it has the status of a legal document, not pausing to consider that political machinations might have affected it. Buck's palaeography is good, though he sometimes misreads names which are not very legible in manuscripts.

Buck is seldom guilty of wildly absurd reasoning, and never in connection with his main theme. The wildest is his derivation of the Howards. So anxious is he to prove them descendants of Hereward — a notion with which for some generations they flattered themselves — that he must postulate Hereward's having had illegitimate male descendants, since he can find recorded only the existence of a daughter. He says that Hereward's having had illegitimate children is probable because he was so noted for physical strength and hardihood. Buck then goes on to give examples of great men descended from bastards (including Jesus Christ) to prove to the Howards that this conjectural descent is no shame to them, and finishes by saying he is sure that if Hereward's arms could be found they would be seen to be the same as the Howards'.

Buck's documentation from memory is sometimes faulty. In his discussion of the name Plantagenet he cites several sources to indicate that it was used prior to the time of the Yorkists. He thinks he has documented this assumption adequately, but only one of his sources — Glover — contains the frequent mention of the name which he claims for four other sources as well. His memory sometimes fails him in the use of More and his followers, because he knows that Hall, Grafton, Holinshed, and Stow have copied More, but he does not keep careful track of where the parts derived from More begin and end, so that sometimes we find him ascribing to More, along with Hall, Grafton, Holinshed, and Stow, what are actually inventions by Hall or matter translated by the later chroniclers from Polydore Vergil.

Antiquarian Methods

In methods of research, Buck seems most influenced by 'honest John Stow, who could not flatter and speak dishonestly' (text, p. 129). In his own tireless researches, Stow, 'a man very diligent and much inquisitive to uncover all things concerning the affairs or works or persons of princes' had been finding out things about Richard III. And Buck, whose *Daphnis*, in which a charitable view is taken of Richard, was published in 1605, the year Stow died, had been questioning him about them. Buck knew Stow as a 'good antiquary and diligent searcher [of] *kno*wledge of the obscure and *hi*dden things appertaining to our story' (text, p. 173) — and Stow's collections, now in the British Library, contain a number of tracts and histories of Richard's time. So it was to him that Buck went to seek the most authoritative opinion about Richard's deformity and about the Princes' murder (see text, pp. 129 and 173). It is fortunate for our knowledge of Stow that we have Buck's report of his opinions on these matters, for Stow does not make use of them himself. In his *Annales* he describes Richard's accession as an election rather than a usurpation, yet he refers the reader to More's account of his reign, which he prints in his own history. But he was at the time Buck began considering Richard obviously the authority who had gone farthest in original research on him. He was 'apparently the first to recover from the fascination' of More, says Pollard, [27] who attributes this to the form of the *Annales,* which relied on research into documents as well as on accepted authorities.

Buck seems to follow Stow's methods, in which — though Fussner points out that they were not original but those required by the Society of Antiquaries [28] — there was not a more exemplary practitioner to serve as model. Edmond Howes, Stow's literary executor, describes him thus:

> his sight and memory, very good, very sober, mild, and courteous to any that required his instructions and retained the true vse of all his sences, vnto the day of his death, being of an excelent memory, he alwaies protested neuer to haue writt*en* any thing, either for malice, feare, or fauour, nor to seeke his owne particuler gaine, or vaine glory, and that his only paines and care was to write truth . . . .' [29]

He was conscientious in documentation. The feud with Grafton into which he was pressed was founded on and brought into prominence the importance of documentation and critical examination of sources. His collecting of unprinted as well as printed material from various sources proves his awareness of the necessity for acquiring evidence and judging its accuracy by comparison. His careful observation and collection must be attributed to his own zeal and acuteness, not wholly to externally imposed standards. He helped to form these standards, and it was in them that Buck grew.

By his tendency to discuss matters about which there was current disagreement among antiquaries, Buck gives us a view of the sorts of subjects they were considering and how they went about attempting to resolve them. An example of this is his discussion of the origin of the surname Plantagenet, about which there were conflicting opinions. After having 'read and searched many books and perused many written monuments', he went to his friends 'learned in heraldry and in history'. Sir William Dethick showed him an old manuscript book on sobriquets, tracing them to the practice of penance. One penitent, an earl of Anjou, took the name Plantagenet. Buck seems to assume this is true not only because the book told him so, but also because there existed an oral tradition to that effect. However, English and French antiquaries cannot identify the particular earl. Buck disagrees with those who identify him with Geoffrey of Anjou and gives brief details of Geoffrey's career to prove him unsuitable. He fastens on Fulke, whose history he sets down, using French antiquarian sources. Having proved this earl a penitent, he discusses the nature of the plant and the soil around Jerusalem, according to Leonhard Fuchs, Pliny, and Strabo, to establish the likelihood of its use as an instrument of penance. Buck's conclusions may be incorrect, but his methods are thorough.

Legal argumentation is brought to bear on the question of Henry VII's right. Again Buck starts from a controversy: whether the Somersets or Beauforts were of the House of Lancaster. He first discusses the families' history, then their legitimation, of which he exhibits Richard II's and Pope Urban's charters. He then considers whether or not legitimation granted the use of royal names and a right to the throne. He presents evidence to contradict the genealogists' citation of Hamelin Plantagenet for use of the royal surname by illegitimate children. He discusses legal scholars' opinions on the Pope's ability to make bastards capable of heritage, citing *viva voce* evidence from Coke. He counters the argument that the term 'principatus' makes the Beauforts capable, saying that 'principatus' cannot be taken for 'regnum'. In opposition to the arguments that the charter was meaningless because Richard II was a reckless king, he notes that Henry IV too excluded the Beauforts by entailing the crown on his sons and refers to the charter of entail which he has seen in the Cotton collection and from which he has 'transcribed these summary notes' (text, p. 81). His conclusion is that the Beauforts had no right to the crown before Henry VII became king and by his sovereign power took all royal titles to himself.

Critical Approach to Sources

Buck has a clear idea of historiographical principles and practice. He claims no bias. His intent in attempting to clear Richard is to make truth emerge:

> . . . the historiographer must be ve[ritable and free from all pro]sopolepsies and partial respects. *He must not a*dd nor omit anything, *either of partiality* or of hatred. [All which I have endeavoured to observe in] the writing of this story, so that [if my authors be sincere and faithful, my Muse is pure and innocent. For I have imitated the sceptic philosophers,] who of themselves affirmed nothing, but liked the doctrine of the other more renowned and more learned philosophers. *For that* which is said and related in this history is the *true te*stimony *of* honest and faithful writers of former times.
>
> (text. p. 4)

His tendency is to rely for the general thread of his argument on particular main sources, well known histories, using them according to the extent of their completeness and authority for the period or circumstances he is discussing. This involves considerable critical acuity, which Buck admirably displays, and which allows him safely, according to his intentions, to follow the common histories 'so long as they err not in the m*atter* . . .' (text, p. 179). In all the details of Henry VII's early years and his invasions of England, Polydore Vergil is Buck's basic source. Polydore was Henry's official historian and must have had this particular information from Henry himself. All historians to the present day have used him as the basis for their discussions of this part of Henry's life. [30] As his main source for events from Edward IV's death to Richard's accession, Buck uses More, who was assumed to have had his information from Morton, a participant in these events.

Buck supports, adds, and fills in with other sources which have a prime claim to authority. He fills in the sections which use Polydore as main source by referring to Commynes, useful because he was in France, moved in high circles, and knew Henry VII. The English sections are backed up and filled in by reference to the Croyland Chronicle, also derived from a person in high office during the events Buck's history covers. His bolstering More or Polydore by citing the numerous chroniclers who include these authors' histories in their own is generally meaningless, except insofar as it may be said that the chroniclers who copy others add authority to the original accounts by copying them.

Aside from his main references and main supporting references, he uses subsidiary ones to add and confirm details. For matters concerning France he uses Tillet, Meyer, and particularly Bouchard, in addition to the sources already cited. He occasionally brings in Stow and other English chroniclers for dates, and Glover for genealogical excursions. For matters concerning England, he derives considerable support from legal, ecclesiastical, and heraldic manuscript sources. He has done research in the Tower Records, in the College of Arms, and in the Rolls, and from the last he gives details of various Parliaments, particularly that of Richard III and the first Parliament of Henry VII. He had access to material in the College of Arms through the help of his herald friends, whom he thanks at the beginning of the work. Someone, probably one of the heralds, has copied out for him the commission for the Vice Constableship. He uses a few memorials: the inscription on Surrey's tomb at Thetford, and the inscription on the Stone of Scone.

Most of Buck's manuscript sources for the *History* are in Cotton's collections, though he once cites Lord William Howard, of whose private collection he made use in the *Commentary,* and he once cites a document owned by the Earl of Arundel. The Herd poem, the anonymous manuscript chronicle mentioned six times, the Benedictine history he cites in error as Ailred, the book of St Stephen's, Caen, the list of Richard's officers, many of Richard's foreign treaties, the Bull of Pope Urban for the legitimation of the Beauforts, the charter for entailing the crown on Henry IV's sons, the Bull of Pope Innocent VIII granting Henry VII's titles, the charter showing the Buck family's participation in the founding of Bridlington Abbey, Quhitlaw's speech, and the Croyland Chronicle all come from Cotton. Harl. 6018, Cotton's borrowing register, records the loan to Buck of a Calendar of Papal Bulls in the Treasury, a Collection of the Cinq Ports, Liber Wigornensis, Radulphus de Coggeshall, and Roger Wendover (ff. 160, 173, and 174ᵛ).

His treatment of More is the most complex. Buck has perceived something about More which no one had perceived before: More writes ironically, and if the irony is ignored and his statements taken seriously, we have a picture of Richard as a good man and a good king which accords very closely with the objective records of his life and reign. Although he is well aware of More's irony (More 'useth so much to speak ironically and in jest', text, p. 132), Buck ignores it in his use of More's statements, and habitually quotes him as if he wrote in all seriousness. For example , when More says that the Protector was so much moved with the words of Buckingham persuading him to the crown that 'else as euery man may witte, would neuer of likelyhood haue inclyned to the suit,'[31] he means the opposite; he speaks with a knowing sneer. Buck ignores the sneer. In discarding More's stylistic overlay of irony, Buck uncovers the basis of information on which More's history is based. Buck quotes More to give favourable evidence when More in context meant to indicate by his quotation of a good sentiment in Richard's mouth the extent of Richard's dissimulation. The facts remain stable; only the interpretation varies, as Buck demonstrates. More chooses to attribute to these facts vicious motives, Buck to apply charity. Any good deed, Buck says, may be depraved by a foul interpretation (text, p. 127).

Introducing a passage in which More is to be his main source, he recommends Morton and More as 'men of nea*rest* [authority, and] b[y all ou]r chroniclers and historians held to be veritable. And it may be thought [they would] *not* [w]rite anything favourably or partially of the Lord Protector nor of [his cause, being the chiefest of those who loved him not]'(text, p. 40). This assessment shows (1) that Buck has a good grasp of the subjects about which Morton and consequently More are likely to be most authoritative; (2) he assumes that what they say in Richard's favour must be true because they hated him. When More praises Richard he is 'loath to speak much in his favour, yet occasion forced him to speak his knowledge, though coldly and sparingly' (text, p. 202). In the last three books Buck deals minutely with the unfavourable things More says about Richard, showing them to be absurd or self-contradictory.

He attributes the origin of More's history to time-serving in a period when it was meritorious to publish slanders of Richard and an offence to write well of him. Buck postulates that Morton, in revenge for his political grievances, had written a book in Latin reporting Richard's actions, accusing him of numerous crimes and suppressing his virtues. This book came into the hands of More, who, desiring preferment, 'translated and interpreted and glosed and altered' it (text, p. 121). He left it incomplete because he grew tired of practising the detracting style, but he was favoured by fame, which reputed his learning and holiness higher than they deserved — a reputation which Buck misguidedly proceeds to shatter — and the book was accepted while it was safer to criticize than to praise Richard (Buck thus implies that this time is past). Yet even now, Buck cautions, More has so many friends in England and abroad that they will excuse him anything.

The English chroniclers followed More 'step by step and word by word, not having the judgement nor discret[ion to] consider his affections, nor his drifts, nor his arts, nor his placentine manners, nor his ends, nor to examine [the truth of] *the* relations which he maketh, nor to search out the truth of his writings' (text, p. 124). Because of their credulity, they 'could swallow any gudgeon and never examine the [style or faith] of those aforesaid authors nor bring th[em to the touchstone of verity]' (text, p. 125). Although Holinshed, Hall, Grafton, and Stow were honest men, they were at fault in incorporating More's story into their works. Yet they have some excuse in that Morton and More were so highly reputed. Buck is the first to have perceived a common source for More and Vergil,[32] claiming that Polydore is at fault in the extent to which he follows Morton's pamphlet. In general, Buck's opinion of Polydore is favourable: he was 'neither of the House [of York] nor of Lancaster, but only an honest man' (text, p. 204). 'Ma[ny are jealous of him,]' says Buck, 'and yet in my opinion not for any *or many* just causes' (text, p. 179). He uses André, in the crossed-out reference mentioned above (p. cxi) to bolster the credibility of Polydore, 'whoe was an honest, and \a / Learned *man* and liued in the tyme of King Henry:7: . . . (as **Be**r*nardus* Andreas Tolosanus the Annalist of this King Henry 7 writeth)' (Tiberius, f. 58ᵛ).

He has made observations on the authors he uses

> by way of caution, because they which read their books should be we*ll advised to consider* and examine what they read, and make trial of such doubtful things as are written before they give credit unto them. . . . *For it* is a hard thing to find that prince's story truly and faithfully written, who was so hateful to the writers th*en; for when they* wrote they might write no better. And therefore, *t*hese reasons being considered, their writings must be *re*garded and the authors censured accordingly.
> (text, pp.125f)

Buck is ready to correct his sources where they are wrong. By using the *Titulus Regius* he points out the chroniclers' error in citing Elizabeth Lucy rather than Eleanor Butler as Edward IV's betrothed. He uses his own knowledge of royal ceremony to correct Polydore's notion of why Richard wore the crown at Bosworth. Using his grandfather's testimony, he disputes the chroniclers' statement that Surrey submitted directly after the battle. Commynes is a 'noble and veritable historian' (text, p. 82), praised several times by Buck, but at one point, Buck wonders, is he not mistaken in saying Stanley's force numbered 26,000 men, since the English historians mention only 5,000?

It is interesting to see how Buck deals with a contemporary historian in his response to 'a new writer', Gainsford, who affirms Perkin Warbeck and Don Sebastian to be counterfeits and yet 'would have it thought he knew much, and especially matters of [histories] as of other nations and countries. . . . And yet he shows himself p*lainly ignorant in* stories. . . .' Gainsford 'would have us think that he took much pains in perusing and sifting [of authors; and indeed I think he did sift them]' (text, p. 156). There is some excuse, Buck says, for his not knowing about Don Sebastian: when he was in Spain the Spaniards concealed the truth, 'for they are close and wary and [most politic,] and will give many gudgeons to tramontane travellers' (text, p. 156). Buck's criticism is in part an expression of contempt for an author writing at the same time as himself whose conclusions are different from his own. But it is also a fact that Buck's methods of research are generally far superior to Gainsford's.

'Since the censor constituted one influence on the formation of a play's printed text, the question of Buc's attitude and practices touches upon the history of most of the Jacobean plays before 1622'.[33] This statement by Eccles applies not only specifically to Buck's expressed attitude toward dramatic literature, but also more generally to the details of his life and his attitudes and interests.

It may seem amazing that a Master of the Revels should give so little heed to the drama of the time. We should like him to refer to Shakespeare's *Richard III,* but he does not. Yet this apparent failure is not remarkable. Buck was writing an historical work based on serious research into historical texts and original documents. Popular literature, which included the drama, could contribute nothing to his research and could only evoke his scorn at its frivolity. He uses theatre imagery in the course of his work, viewing to some extent, as his contemporaries tended to do, the events of history as acts played out on a stage, in this case scenes of a tragedy. But his position as censor does not make him more liable to this practice than his contemporaries. He is, if anything, less liable to it, being extremely literal-minded and not often given to flights of fancy.

His references to imaginative literature are either damning or supercilious. He speaks of irresponsible historians as delivering all matter

> upon their own bare and worthless word, and after the manner of fabulous and trivial romancers. And who for *the* most part being idle and sensual persons, will no*t* take the pains to read the ancient and la*rge* histories, but epito*mes* of them, and vulgar pamphlets only. And therefore their stories or ta*les or* romances are accounted as things ambiguous and fabulous.
> (text, pp. 4f)

Because he had a talent for poetry, More is to be dismissed as a serious historian: 'many of these accusa*tion*s are but fables and fictions and poetical inv*entions*. Besides, he had much intelligence of the *kingdom* of Utopia, and perhaps many of those imaginary *accusations were* advertisements from that strange and uncouth land . . .' (text, p. 196). Stow has told Buck that it was never proved by any evidence 'nor yet by any fine fiction or argument or poetry' that Richard killed his nephews. Buck might have taken this to refer to dramatic representations, but he does not: 'And whereas Mr *S*tow added fiction and poetry to the proofs, he alluded (as I conceived) to the poetical disposition of Sir Thomas More, because he was a poet and wrote *a poetical boo*k, to wit, *Utopia* is a fable' (text, p. 173). And yet Legge's play on Richard, not to mention *The True Tragedy* and Shakespeare's play, was well known at the time.[34]

The only mention Buck makes of plays — and it is uncertain whether he or the Editor makes it — is the one quoted previously (p. xxii) about 'the ignorant, and never-vnderstandeinge vulgare' who take their history from the pamphlets, ballads, and the stage. This attitude accords with the usual one among men of Buck's class and educational status. Cornwallis' was similar: Bennett points out that although he spent some time in the playhouse, in his essays he refers to the stage only through metaphorical figures, often contemptuous. And as for vulgar literature he remarks that it is his custom to read it in the privy and then use it as toilet paper. [35]

The pamphlets which are linked with plays as vulgar literature are thus described by Stauffer: the 'popular interest in sensational and strange lives . . . produced broadsides and short pamphlets on the disagreeable deaths of every murderer and Newgate criminal, and turned over the pages of old chronicles and foreign histories for lives incredibly criminal or heroic'. [36] This is how Buck would have regarded the sensationalizing technique of Shakespeare's *Richard III*.

Autobiography and Personal Opinions

Of all of Buck's works, the *History* contains most biographical information. Yet this is still not considerable. Buck speaks of his presence with the Lord Admiral at Cadiz and of taking part in the events there. He notes that he was in France when Mary, Queen of Scots died and heard general remarks there on the cause of her death, which seem to have been (this section is burnt away) that she died of a catarrh, the polite way of saying in France that she had been put to death. He speaks of his ancestors, of his great-grandfather who may or may not have been Richard's Controller of the House and was executed and attainted after Bosworth for siding with Richard; of his grandfather, orphaned by the battle and taken into the care of the Howards, by whom the Bucks had ever since been favoured, who told him the story of Surrey's fortunes after Bosworth; of his father, that he like all his forebears and like his son had been a soldier.

His acquaintances are revealed in the sources of his *viva voce* information, and we have firsthand descriptions of a number of important personages of the day who were his personal acquaintances: Sir Charles Howard, the Earl of Arundel, the Earl of Oxford, and Queen Elizabeth herself. He is flattered that the Earl of Oxford 'vouchsafed me his familiar acquaintance' and came to visit him. He saw the private collections of Lord William Howard of Naworth and his nephew the Earl of Arundel, to whom he dedicates his book, and Arundel relayed to him information by word of mouth, as did Baron Lumley and Baron Darcy. He was assisted by his fellow antiquaries and close friends, Cotton, Camden, and Brook, and also by the herald Dethick, and he records regard and respect for all these men, some of whom were enemies of each other. He is generous in his praise of them and also of recently dead scholars such as Stow and Glover. His respect for their learning and wisdom is profound, and his own attitude is humble rather than competitive.

But more than in mere biographical details, Buck is characterized by his attitudes and scholarly methods. His stated intention in his history is a generous one: to allow truth to come to light. And he proceeds not in an opinionated and emotional manner but in a rational and charitable one, tempered by the lawyer's objective sense of justice. His plea is that a well-balanced, just and charitable assessment be accorded Richard, and this is the treatment he himself gives his subject. Occasionally he is carried away by hatred of Morton, and he dislikes Henry VII (a dislike which, ironically, he shared with More), he is unfair to More, but he had his sources to blame for this, just as he allows that the historians whose faults he is attempting to unravel have their sources to blame for their view of Richard. He has no sympathy with sloppy, careless, incomplete and inaccurate research in others and displays contempt for authors of whose methods he disapproves. He himself carefully follows the methods he upholds as more responsible. He is proud of this, but at the same time humble, deprecating his own 'mean reading'. He has the highest regard for chivalry and honour, the lowest for 'policy', cunning, and treachery. Upholding the sanctity of kingship he must condemn rebellion against it.

Buck's attitude to James I is interesting and subtle. He is aware of the risk involved in his present study in that it criticizes Henry VII, from whom James is directly descended, and praises the king whom Henry destroyed to usurp the throne. Buck counters this at the outset. He first makes a humble apology to the king in his dedication, saying that this 'rare and peerless One' without equal in judgement, justice, and clemency, may rightly take exception that a man of not very high rank or fame or learning should presume to write of the king's 'royal ancestors and to examine their actions, to rip up their vices, and to treat and to d*iscourse of* crowns, of majesty, of *kingdoms,* of royal rights and tit*les*' (text, p. 5). Then in the Advertisement to the Reader he explains that he is allowing the truth, long suppressed, to come to light 'by the opportune taking of the fair advantage of these happy and just times of a king by whose favour and furtherance Truth hath here safe conduit and free passage and prevaileth and flourisheth'. A marginal note describes this exemplary time as *'Beatum Sancti Regis Jacobi regnum'* (text, p. 6).

Buck clearly considers the greatest risk to lie in his rehearsing of Richard's title according to the rediscovered *Titulus Regius* which Henry VII had ordered suppressed and destroyed. Twice in speaking of the illegitimacy of Edward IV's children — James' ancestors — he adds a disclaimer, protesting that these opinions are not his own but those of the times of which he speaks. He takes pains to show the various methods by which the defects in Henry VII's claim were 'cured'.

Buck flatters James by rehearsing his title to the throne, and under this cover does two things. First he observes that the breach caused by Edward IV's marriage was repaired by Richard III's accession, thus placing Richard in the scheme of history not in his traditional role of the interrupter of succession but as the restorer of it, and making James dependent on Richard for his unbroken title. Second, he defends the power and authority of Parliament, saying the title to the throne was reinforced by many Parliaments so that Henry VII (from whom it descended to James) was able to bear it as if it had never been broken. And James has another important claim in his descent from the ancient British kings through Henry VII who 'would have all the titles of this kingdom confirmed to him by the strongest and greatest authority', and so had them settled in himself and in his heirs by Parliament.

This is the culmination of a thread which runs through the entire work. Buck is using the *History* partly as a tract on the authority of Parliament. To suggest that Richard's accession was unlawful was to cast aspersions on Parliament, which 'is or should be a general assembly of all the most [noble] *and m*ost honourable and most just, the most godly and the *most* [rel]igious persons of the kingdom' (text, p. 186). This attitude is useful equally to Buck's defence of Richard and his defence of Parliament.

Buck's judgement of Henry VII and his followers is harsh, but he tries to assume an ambivalent attitude toward Henry himself, partly by using qualifying statements, partly by pushing off as much blame as possible onto Morton. About one thing he is clear: those who bore arms against their sovereign in the field were traitors, and their wars were sedition and rebellion, crimes against God as well as against man and against their king. He states this very emphatically in general terms and reinforces it by frequent remarks on the treachery of Henry's accomplices.

At the beginning of the work he claims that one of his intentions is to distinguish between true and false barons and show Morton and More and their followers in their true colours. He uses Morton as a general scapegoat: he is the instigator of rebellion against Richard (this exonerates Henry), and he is the ringleader of Richard's detractors in writing (this clears the historians on whom Buck must rely for general outlines). He sees Morton as an avatar of evil, 'that evil spirit transformed into an angel of light and wearing the habit of religion and of sanctity' (text, p. 83). It is he who turns Buckingham against Richard (More gives good evidence of this), who stirs up Pembroke, Oxford, and Devon, who poisons Henry's heart with ambition. That Morton, as Buck says, devised the death of Perkin Warbeck and Edward, Earl of Warwick, there is no evidence, but the suggestion does remove the blame from Henry. Although Buck admits that the Lancastrians would have been forced to kill the Princes in order to have a king of their faction, he points the accusing finger away from Henry himself by giving evidence from an old manuscript book that Morton and 'a certain countess' (obviously the Countess of Richmond) were plotting the death of the Princes and others of the House of York. It may not be carelessness or lack of critical facility which keeps Buck from saying more about this particular document (if indeed he did not — there may have been marginal documentation now lost), but rather wisdom.

On the other hand, Henry VII's fault — 'and almost [his] only fault' — was that of hearing and following evil counsel, and for his credulity 'he beareth the blames of other men'. What Buck is really doing, however, is making other men bear the blame for Henry's actions. The account of Henry's early life is straightforwardly factual. Buck's compliments almost invariably have a reverse side: he was 'a wary and a very circumspect man, and also somewhat timorous' (text, p. 70). He was obviously good and wise because many people reputed him so and because Queen Elizabeth was said to resemble him. 'Although a very good king' he was guilty of *crimen regale* in disposing of young Warwick, Perkin Warbeck, and other claimants. Buck does not at all mislike his having the crown , but only his not awaiting the Lord's leisure to gain possession of it. His title was made strong by Parliament, so he bore it as if it had never been 'broken by mischance and cunning' (text, p. 214). Henry had faults, but he was nevertheless wise, provident, and religious, the restorer of the British kings, the nephew of Henry VI (Buck takes pains to note that this is a tenuous connection through the female) and an offspring of the House of Lancaster (Buck takes pains to note that this was by grant of the Pope).

Subtler than these backhand compliments is another method Buck uses to cast aspersions on Henry and exalt Richard by comparison: that of analogy. He will sometimes adduce a fable or an anecdote from ancient history as an illustrative instance, heap abuse on the character who tacitly parallels Henry in the illustration, and leave the reader to make the comparison. An example of this is the fable of the Eagle and the Scarab (text, pp. 101-2). The ostensible motive for including this story is to show the danger of underrating one's enemy. But in addition to this it draws a judgemental parallel between Richard as the royal Eagle ('the king of birds and the chief esquire of the God Jupiter') and Henry as the vile Scarab ('a base and contemptible insect and of no power nor credit') who scores by treachery. Buck disclaims all harm, saying, 'This *is only* a fable, and the moral is easy to be conceived by the Reader'. The perceptive reader will have gleaned from it, in addition to his moral, his attitude to the antagonists at Bosworth.

Buck does not mince words about what he sees as Henry's serious faults. He was cowardly and unchivalrous in battle and inferior to Richard in skill of arms. His Parliament, which attainted of treason the rightful king and his followers, was evil and self-abrogating. He probably would not have resigned the crown to Perkin had he known him to be Richard of York, for he (tyrannously, Buck implies) destroyed other royal claimants. On the other hand, Buck's remarks about Henry's grand-daughter Elizabeth are, as usual in his works, couched in terms almost of worship. He presents in the middle of the *History* a long eulogy of this queen, in which her heroic qualities are exalted, and a shorter one at the end.

Buck's general picture of Richard is a temperately favourable one, slightly senti-mentalized at times. He sees him as a good and loving brother, husband, and father, deducing the gentleness and faithfulness of his nature partly from his service to his brother as compared with Clarence's treachery. He loved his childhood home and had no ambition other than to remain in the north as King Edward's servant, a life in which he was well reputed by all as generous and hospitable, wise, courageous, and loyal. This attitude in Richard Buck sees confirmed by his initial refusal to take the crown. Buck considers him sincere in this, feeling that love for the father dictated loyalty to the son, and putting thoughts — for which there is no evidence — in Richard's mind regarding the reasons for his dislike of sovereignty. But he was forced, by the risk that the Queen Mother's relations would seize power, and also by the threat of foreign invasion, reluctantly to accept. Buck presents evidence of Richard's moderation and temperance in private life and his wisdom, justice, fortitude, bounty, magnificence, temperance, and piety — which are, he considers, the ideal attributes of kingliness — in public life, listing his good works and documenting his exemplary legislation in support of these virtues. By discussing the *Titulus Regius* he justifies Richard's title to the throne, indisputable because it was passed by Parliament.

His arguments against some of the attacks on Richard are based on common sense tempered by a certain degree of ridicule: idiosyncracies of gesture do not constitute a crime. Nor does being born with teeth, being deformed in body, or for one's mother to have suffered pain in childbed. And he gives examples of noble and famous men born with teeth, others who were deformed, others whose mothers actually died in childbed. By using ridicule he points up the absurdity of one accusation in particular, the one about the teeth, saying that he does not think Morton or More ever spoke with the Duchess of York's midwife. The deformity he is able to disprove by reference to Stow's firsthand evidence, the failure of all authors who actually knew Richard to mention it, and personal observation of portraits.

Buck's historiography is as morally orientated as was that of his predecessors, but in a different way. He is original in introducing into history the concept of charity. He seems to be one of the first English historical writers to take into account the differences (if only apparent) between his own and earlier ages, and to see consistently and clearly the distinctions between his own highly chivalric code of honour, which he attributes to his times, and what he interprets as the more opportunistic morality of the fifteenth century.

Buck cannot exonerate Richard of Hastings' death and personally deplores the '*Artes Imperii*' which justified it. But he dislikes the tendency to blame Richard disproportionately for employing these tactics when other famous and well-reputed men, of whom he gives many examples, are not so harshly censured. He uses the same argument in regard to the general attitude toward Richard. Although he has to his satisfaction cleared Richard of most of the crimes of which he is accused, he reminds his readers that others have committed similar crimes and not been so harshly reputed, and he gives examples of several other kings, including Henry VII, whose disposing of rival claimants is not a matter of mere suspicion but firmly proved. Buck's method is that of a lawyer: he exonerates where possible on the basis of available evidence, and where not possible he pleads for mercy on the basis of precedent. 'All King Richard's guilt', Buck pleads, '[is but suspicion. And suspicion is] in la[w no more guilt or culpableness than imagination]' (text, p. 193). The accusations against Richard are not to be credited, because they cannot be proved.

Richard is poorly reputed, Buck reminds us, because he lost the battle: 'ill fortune is accounted a vice in military adventures' (text, p. 100), and when fortune is adverse in battle the loser is considered reprobate, whereas the winners are renowned as brave and valiant. Buck voices his rational objection to the argument of Richard's enemies that his death in battle betokened divine wrath. His view of history is in a sense providential. Earlier writers had explained Richard's downfall as punishment for his misdeeds. Buck from his Protestant standpoint sees God's determination to destroy the house of Plantagenet and transfer the crown as the basis of Richard's downfall. Richard's actions, good or bad, would have had no effect in altering God's plan and could only serve to bring it about. It is presumptuous to assume that man's choices and actions can have weight enough to sway God's intentions.

Buck sees Richard occasionally as a parallel to Christ, but only in that both, having sacred status, were betrayed and vilified. He is far from setting up Richard as a Christlike figure, and in all cases he deals with Richard's reputation by shrewd analysis rather than emotional harangue. Upon dispassionate examination, one finds not a heated, emotional defence of a hero but a surprisingly cool examination. Buck's passion appears to be rather for accuracy than for Richard III. He shows the same regard for minor historical inaccuracies as for Richard's reputation. His defence springs not from hero worship but from a concern over the illogical and inaccurate nature of the traditional portrayal. His final assessment of Richard is balanced and judicious:

> [although this prince was not so superlative as to assume the name of holy or best, you see him a wise, magnificent,] and a valiant man, *and a* [just,] bountiful, [and temperate;] *and* an eloquent *and magnanimous and* pious prince; and *a benefactor to the holy* church and to the *realm.* [Yet] for all this it ha[th] been his [fortun]e to be aspersed and foul*ed and* to fall into this *malice of those who have* been ill-affected *towards him* . . . .
>   (text, p. 208)

NOTES

1. Donald A. Stauffer, *English Biography before 1700* (Cambridge, Mass., 1930), p. 229.

2. See above, pp. lxiv-lxxxvi.

3. M.M. Reese, *The Cease of Majesty* (London, 1961), p. 101.

4. Eccles, p. 505.

5. Sir John Harington, *The Metamorphosis of Ajax*, ed. Elizabeth Story Donno (London, 1962), pp. 107f: 'the best, and best written part of all our Chronicles, in all mens opinions; is that of Richard the third, written as I have heard by Moorton, but as most suppose by that worthy, and un-corrupt Magistrate, Sir Thomas More'.

6. The associations among the persons involved with this tract are studied by Kincaid and Ramsden, Introductions to Cornwallis, pp. ii-iv. See also Kincaid, 'Sir Edward Hoby and "K. Richard": Shakespeare Play or Morton Tract' *Notes and Queries*, n.s. xxviii (1981), 124-6.
    Kincaid and Ramsden, Introduction to Cornwallis, pp. ii-iv.

7. Buck's handwritten note in Bod. copy of Godwin, p. 115.

8. In his account of the expedition Buck describes Hoby as bearing the Lord Admiral's ensign: Stow, *Annales,* 1601, sig. Pppp5^v.

9. See W. Gordon Zeeveld, 'A Tudor Defense of Richard III', *PMLA,* LV (1940), 946-57; and Kincaid and Ramsden.

10. Zeeveld, p. 957.

11. Kincaid and Ramsden, p. v-vii.

12. Cornwallis, p. 32.

13. R.E. Bennett, *The Life and Works of Sir William Cornwallis,* unpublished Ph.D. diss., Harvard, 1931, p. 342.

14. Rosalie L. Colie, *Paradoxia Epidemica* (Princeton, 1966), p. 8.

15. Camden, *The History . . . of England during the Whole Life and Reign of Elizabeth,* in Kennett, II, 362.

16. Henry Howard, *A Defensatiue against the Poyson of Supposed Prophesies* (London, 1583), sigs. Hhiii^v-Hhiv.

17. Desiderius Erasmus, *Proverbs or Adages,* trans. Richard Taverner, facsimile of 1569 edition, ed. De Witt T. Starnes (Gainesville, 1956), Introd., p. viii.

18. Kendall, *Richard III,* pp. 512. The case for this authorship is argued persuasively by Ira. J. Black, *A Study of Changing Historiographical Trends as Illustrated in the . . . Chronicles of Croyland Abbey,* unpublished M.A. thesis, Ohio State University, 1965. See also J.G. Edwards, 'The "Second" Continuation of the Crowland Chronicle', *BIHR,* XXXIX (1966), 117-28.

19. Myers, 'Richard III and Historical Tradition', p. 186.

20. Ibid., p. 187.

21. Ibid., p. 186.

22. Carte, II, 815.

23. Gerald Brenan and Edward Phillips Stratham, *The House of Howard* (London, 1907), I, 50n.

24. Howard, *Indications of Memorials . . . of the Howard Family* (Corby Castle, 1854), 'Memorials', p. 20n.

25. Tucker, p. 42.

26. E.E. Reynolds, *The Trial of St Thomas More* (London, 1964), p. 1.

27. A.F. Pollard, 'The Making of Sir Thomas More's *Richard III',* in *Historical Essays in Honour of James Tait* (Manchester, 1933), p. 228.

28. Fussner, p. 223.

29. Edmond Howes in his continuation of Stow, *Annales* (1615), sig. Yyy^v.

30. See S.B. Chrimes, *Henry VII* (London, 1972), p. 19.

31. Sir Thomas More, *The History of King Richard the Third,* ed. Richard S. Sylvester (New Haven, 1963), p. 79.

32. This is most recently discussed by Sylvester, Introduction to More, *passim,* and by Alison Hanham in *Richard III and His Early Historians* (Oxford, 1975), pp. 164ff.

33. Eccles, p. 413.

34. See the reference in Harington, 'A Briefe Apologie of Poetrie'.

35. Bennett, pp. 207f.

36. Stauffer, pp. 224f.

VIII. METHOD OF COMPOSITION AND THE PRESENT TEXT

Buck completed the dedication of his *History* in fair copy and dated it 1619. Nearly all internal evidence supports this date of composition, but there is some suggestion that Buck continued to revise and make additions to the work in 1620. This is indicated by the date '1620' in the margin (text, p. 184), elucidating a remark that Francis Godwin is now (i.e., at the time of writing) Bishop of Hereford. There seems to be a vestige of another such dating on p. 98 of the printed edition above the marginal note which attributes to Baron Darcy *viva voce* information about Don Sebastian of Portugal. This note reads '162.' and has no meaning or purpose if it is not assumed to be the remains of a marginal dating '1620', the year in which Buck was doing research for Darcy (see above, p. xxxviii).

One may for assistance in dating examine the various scraps Buck has used for late insertions. These are printed in Frank Marcham's *The King's Office of the Revels* and have been discussed by E.K. Chambers in his review of that book.[1] Many of them are scraps from the Revels Office which Buck has crossed out in order to use their blank versos for late additions to his *History*, following his practice in the *Commentary*,[2] where most of the scraps can be proved to be slightly later than the main composition of the work (see above, p. xxix). Chambers in examining the names of the plays on these scraps points out that they cannot be notations of licensing for performance or publication, since some were performed and published before Buck became Master of the Revels. He believes that they were probably being considered by the Revels Office for court performance, and he presents evidence pointing to the likelihood of 1619-20 as the period of their revival.

The *Commentary* seems to have been composed within a limited time span. Probably the same is true of the *History*. Most of it is in rough draft, but at an advanced stage, near completion. No gaps are left to be filled in, and the author has gone through the text revising it more than once. In 1619 he seems to have begun making a fair copy. The dedication he has written in a large, neat, rounded hand. Corrections in it are few and are written in very clearly. He begins a fair copy of the Advertisement to the Reader as well, but starts to correct it at the end of its first page (f. 5). The next page (f. 5^v) is more heavily corrected and ultimately crossed out, probably because the author intended to rewrite it. Book I too begins as a fair copy. Ff. 7-7^v are written with few corrections in a small, neat hand until the end of f. 7^v, where some rewriting first took place over an erasure, and the last few lines so rewritten have then been crossed out. From then on corrections are numerous, and a very few pages in fair-copy appear among the others which are in various states of revision.

What probably happened is that Buck, having completed to his satisfaction a rough draft of his *History* and having made many revisions in it, began to write a fair copy for presentation to its dedicatee, dating the dedication 1619 but leaving blanks for the day and month. But he found when he began the fair copy that he needed to revise even further and make further additions. This he continued to do into 1620, probably not long past the beginning of that year, and work gradually ceased altogether because of his encroaching illness.

Buck's methods of composition and revision are difficult to trace, more difficult to generalize about. In his Advertisement to the Reader he states that the 'argument and subject' formed the thirteenth chapter of *The Baron*, a work of Buck's now lost (see above, pp. xxxiv-xxxvii). He mentions *The Baron* frequently in the *History,* but we have not nearly enough evidence about it to reconstruct what he might have included in this chapter and how much he added later. He has expanded the material from chapter to complete history because, as he says, it existed 'in such copy and variety as that it diffused itself into an extraordinary and unusual largeness, and so much as it exceeded very much the laws and the proper limits of a chapter', and hence he has 'much enlarged' and transferred it to the *History* (text, p. 6). Now, he says, the chapter can serve as argument for the *History* and the *History* as gloss on the chapter. Evidence of this enlarging and transferring process is lacking. Buck does say specifically that he intends to 'transcribe hither from the said thirteenth chapter some particular matters, and especially the beginnings and first times of this Prince Richard, comprehending *the princ*ely image of the king and his parentage, his birth, his education, his [tirocin]y, and all the conditions of these acts, and of his youth, and of his [private] life' (text, p. 6). But aside from this, and even within this section, we have no way of knowing which is newly written material and which is old.

Buck has left a small page of notes, Tiberius f. 145ᵛ (see Plate I), including page numbers, referring to material in Gainsford. It is impossible to surmise from this one page much about Buck's note-taking practice, particularly since Gainsford was a very recent publication (1618). One may only observe that on this page he organizes his notes according to source rather than subject, and the ordering of it in various parts of the *History* occurs at a later stage. Aside from this, we can observe the markings in his own books, his notes in his copy of Godwin and underlinings in his copy of Bouchard, and in some of the Cotton manuscripts his underlinings and pencilled 'X's in the margins opposite material he intends to use. Once he inserts a whole page which he has apparently had copied by someone else: f. 19, the charter for creating the Vice Constable, is in another hand, but occasionally he pastes in a quotation he has copied out separately in his own hand.

What we lack is anything to represent his intermediate organizing stage. Probably his lists of contents were written before the books to which they refer were completed, as an attempted outline, from which the material in the book itself sometimes deviates. At one stage in composition he employed a scribe to make fair copies of some pages from f. 55 to the end, perhaps intending that the scribal pages should form part of the presentation copy. Fifty-five of these scribal pages remain. Buck has gone over them and filled in or corrected foreign or difficult words for which the scribe has left blanks or in which he has made mistakes. His proofreading, though far more painstaking than the Editor's in his own scribally composed manuscripts, is not perfect, and many more errors have occurred on the scribal pages than on those in Buck's own hand. Hence I have in the ensuing text marked the scribal page numbers with an asterisk, so that errors which might otherwise be attributed to Buck may be seen as copying errors by the scribe. Frequently he was not satisfied with the scribal pages and began to cross out and revise in them. Often his revision was so heavy that he was forced to make another copy of the same page, incorporating his revisions, for the sake of legibility. Thus at times we have at least three representations of a passage or page: Buck's first draft, revised by him in the process of and after composition, discarded by him but retained in the manuscript because he had later used its back for rewriting something else; a more legible and coherent rewriting, often scribal, in which Buck makes heavy revisions between the lines; and then a further copy in his own hand, incorporating further revisions made by him either during or after writing it.

Thus the manuscript is a collection of pages in various states: Buck's own early drafts, discarded pages whose material has been rewritten but which have been preserved because Buck wrote on their blank backs and pasted them over other material he wished to revise (these have been taken apart in the binding process and bound as separate pages); scribal pages, which make up one fifth of the collection; Buck's own revised versions of these pages, themselves bearing revisions between the lines and in the margins; at the beginning and infrequently thereafter, fair copy pages in Buck's hand; and a very few pages in other hands; material copied for him from a manuscript; and Editorial reworkings.

Buck rewrites to reorganize material, to put ideas in better chronological order, or to bring together separate discussions of related topics. He rewrites to make expression smoother and more vivid, or to make a cleaner and expanded copy of a page in which a series of small and not always complete revisions above the lines and in the margins have destroyed coherence and left him no further room for expansion. His revising of large sections is effected by crossing out, by rewriting whole pages, or by rewriting portions of a page on separate sheets or fragments of paper and pasting these over the part he wishes to replace.

When transferring material which fits better elsewhere, he sometimes writes new transitional passages on separate sheets and pastes them in, but sometimes he fails to create new transitions. An example of such failure occurs in Book III, the book in which, because of the extreme difficulty in organization, most rewriting occurs. Originally the anecdote about the Earl of Oxford followed the story of Perkin Warbeck directly, but Buck has revised so as to insert more material before it and has failed to write a new transitional passage when he introduces it later, so it appears stuck on. On the other hand, he improves the transition from Book I to Book II, making the opening of the second book an induction rather than the abrupt plunge into a continuation of Book I's events which he had originally given.

Plates II and III show material twice rewritten. Buck originally intended his description of the coronation to end with mention of the creation of the Knights of the Bath, and he planned to go on directly from there to the French tribute. However, after roughly beginning the French tribute, he finds it constitutes a false start. He wishes rather to enlarge on Richard's rights and to describe the coronation in greater detail. So later, on ff. 45-45^v (text, p. 52) he rewrites the French tribute material in compressed and organized form, and in between he continues the description of the coronation, taken from Grafton. He introduces this with a brief discussion of Richard's right, which justifies him in placing greater emphasis on the coronation and giving it more expanded treatment. His first attempt at composing this can be seen in the margin of the crossed out section on the French tribute (f. 38^v; plate II), but this was given up for lack of space. It was then rewritten at the end of f. 39, where it was drastically revised above the lines (Plate III). The final rewriting, on f. 40 (Plate III, flap) compresses and organizes the material. F. 40 is a fragment with a blank back and was originally pasted over the end of f. 39. Paste marks where it began on f. 39 can still be seen. The first two lines are rewritten yet again on f. 41.

Buck rewrites the story of Hereward on ff. 115-16 to give it in much greater detail. But in other cases, Buck feels he has given too much detail for the context and rewrites so as to reduce it. An example of this is the discussion of the Herberts, which deals in detail with the family history from the fifteenth century to the present. He crosses this out and reduces the material on the Herberts to a short paragraph employing considerable subordination (f. 25). There was originally in the *History* an even more expanded discussion of the Herberts, but Buck discarded this and inserted it instead in the *Commentary* (see above, p. xxxiii), where he considers it more appropriate to deal with the origins of families at length.

Buck rewrites the Morton-Buckingham intrigue. He had originally given only pure facts, and had not organized them well. The rewriting on ff. 56f is expanded to make the scene clearer, smoother, and more immediate, giving details of the story and direct discourse. Psychological and conversational steps are followed in a clear and logical order, so that the stages in the process of Morton's convincing Buckingham become clear.

Buck's smaller revisions are stylistic ones, tending toward expansion. He seems obsessively concerned with stating everything as completely and explicitly as possible. Toward this end, he substitutes one word for another or adds one or two words above the line as possible alternatives for one which he finds not perfectly satisfactory, and in doing so he often neglects to cross out any of the alternatives. He does the same with phrases. He adds explanatory clauses above the line in an attempt to eliminate vagueness and duplicates nouns, verbs, and adjectives to reinforce his meaning. He must designate, explain, and specify, often more than once, Frequently he makes these revisions and expansions in the process of what started out as a simple attempt to make a clearer copy of a page. On f. 69^v he has the words 'But if it be here obiected that albeeit *that* this be the law of france yet it is not obserued in England'; which in revision on f. 70 become 'But if it be obiected that albeeit this be the law & custome of france, yet it is not in vse nor \hath it bene/ observed in England'. F.95ᵛ, rewriting part of the scribal f. 96, has in place of 'Countryman' the words 'frend, & countryman, & kinsman'.

Revisions occur for the sake of accuracy. Buck had, in discussing Surrey's fortunes on f. 111ᵛ, originally stated that he received his promotions in the time of Henry VII. These promotions were in fact rewards for the Flodden victory. When Buck realized that they were events of Henry VIII's reign, he tried to rectify the error by making above-line additions, which produce a very confused and awkward effect. Had he rewritten the page, he would certainly have made this section smoother and integrated the revisions. On f. 8 he corrected an error in the text but apparently forgot to correct the same error in the marginal note. He alters '*this* was foulk the first erl of Anjow' to '*this m*an was the first foulk w*hich* was erl of Anjow'. The marginal note (which now exists only in the copies) was left to say 'Foulke first Ear. of Anjow' (Egerton, f. 10ᵛ).

Buck very occasionally revised his own material to remove indecorous references, on f. 224 changing 'prostitute' to 'yeld', for example. This is in keeping with his practice as censor (see above, p. xv). It is a tendency which the Editor carried much farther.

When the manuscript was damaged in the Cotton fire of 1731, the report on the library after the fire describes Tiberius E. X thus: 'A few Leaves of this Book are left, burnt round'.[3] This pessimistic view of the state of the text is echoed in Casley's 1734 catalogue — 'Bundles of Leaves so burnt as to be of little use'[4] — and Hooper's of 1777.[5] It was inset and bound in the mid-nineteenth century. 265 leaves survive, and only a very few (indicated in the textual notes) can be shown to be entirely missing — whether because of fire it is not known. Only two pages have been almost obliterated by fire, f. 23 and f. 25; they are intact, but the pages are so greyed with smoke that the writing has faded away.

My intention in the present text has been to produce something as close as possible to what Buck would himself have written had he made a fair copy of the work. The manuscript as it stands presents a number of problems to an editor: the manuscript has been severely damaged by fire; the author has made portions of the text illegible by striking out and revising; the author's revisions are often incomplete and produce duplications and syntactical breakdown; the author has frequently failed to make a final decision — normally stylistic — among alternative wordings; finally, George Buck, Esq., has made his own alterations in the manuscript and has thus provided two sets of crossing out, and it is sometimes difficult to ascertain whether his or the author's hand was responsible for a particular deletion. In addition, the manuscript has been rebound in modern times. The binder has guarded each leaf and has removed from the place where Buck had pasted them down revised sections which have now been bound in as separate leaves, separated from their proper place in the text sometimes by several leaves (see Plate III). There are ninety-eight such leaves.

I have dealt with these problems in the following ways:

A) Damage by fire:

All leaves of the manuscript are burnt round the edges, more and more as the text progresses from beginning to end, so that a large proportion of the marginal notes and the beginnings and ends of pages are lost. I have restored these lost portions whenever possible by reference to other versions of the same material which Buck sometimes gives in his numerous rewritings. Where there is in the original manuscript no representation of the missing material, as is usually the case, I have made reference to the early editorial copies in order of their composition. Hence Egerton has supplied nearly all the additions which derive from the copies. When because of obvious errors or omissions in Egerton, Malone and Fisher have been used, this has been indicated in the textual notes. Additional has made no contribution to filling in the gaps, but sometimes the printed edition has made a correction in the reading of an obscure word or the grammar or spelling of a word in a foreign language.

In Egerton, George Buck, Esq., sometimes makes minor stylistic revisions in his own hand. In these cases the unrevised version more closely resembles Sir George's style than the revision does, and hence when these editorial stylistic revisions have occurred in Egerton, I have adopted the unrevised version as closer to Sir George's original and given in the textual notes the Egerton passage as it stands, showing the process of revision.

George Buck, Esq. has a habit of tightening the author's constructions. This means that sometimes a short emendation from Egerton will not fit the structure of the sentence into which I have inserted it without the omission of a word or two, generally a relative pronoun. In these cases I have considered that nothing could be gained by placing dots in the emendation from Egerton to show where the excision was made, since it is the syntax of Tiberius, not Egerton, which I am following and attempting to reconstruct. An indication of how Egerton has changed the author's style in minor points is of no interest in the creation of a text as close as possible to the original author's intention, and such an indication of omission could only break the continuity to no advantage. Aside from these occasional small omissions, I have cited in the textual notes any changes I have made in sections taken from Egerton.

The copies, as previously indicated, are about three-fifths the length of the original. This means that there are portions of the original which they do not represent at all. In such cases, where no other source represents the destroyed material, I have supplied short passages by conjecture based on the sense of the surviving parts of the passage and on knowledge of Buck's ideas and style. Some marginal notes have irrevocably vanished without any possibility of discovery or reconstruction. There are a few short passages without other representation in the original or copies which are so badly damaged that only a word or two survives here and there, and conjecture regarding their meaning, purpose, or the author's intentions to retain or reject them, is impossible. I have omitted these from the text and given them in the textual notes.

B) Incomplete revision:

Buck often leaves sections in a state of partial revision, with portions partially crossed out, additions above the line, and several alternatives given. Revision in these cases is invariably stylistic and not material to the sense of the passage. Buck's style is his weakest point, and to have noted all these partial revisions would have produced far more notes than text. Where Buck gives several alternatives of the same page, word, or phrase, I have had to decide which to accept. Whenever possible I have used the latest version given.

I have not invariably followed the order in which the folios are bound in Tiberius because: where several alternatives exist, one or more have been crossed out or pasted over by the author; the clearer and later alternative has sometimes been bound before the less clear and earlier composed alternative; the pasted-on fragments have not been bound in logical order, since they have been separated from the pages to which they were attached, and their backs and fronts come from different parts of the work; whole folios are occasionally misbound. I have decided among alternative pages by comparing the various drafts to see which seems most complete and finished and includes the revisions made in other drafts. On rare occasions where two drafts for a page are so close as to necessitate consideration of them as alternatives rather than as revisions one of the other, I have chosen the one containing the fuller information more fluently expressed. Drafts which formed the backs of pasted-on sections I have excluded, since Buck by using their reverse sides for new material and pasting them down onto other pages has rejected them. I have matched the pasted-on revisions with the pages to which they were originally pasted, by observing subject matter, position of paste marks, size, and shape. In arranging the text I have considered the early manuscript copies, since George Buck, Esq., who was responsible for them, saw the original intact, as I have not been able to do. I have sometimes been guided by and often received corroboration from them and have thus been able to achieve a continuity of material not always evident in the order in which the folios are bound.

A few pages have been bound in the wrong order and make more sense if their order is shifted. F. 4 is clearly the conclusion of the Advertisement to the Reader rather than of the Dedication. Ff. 10-10^v was almost certainly intended to precede f. 8 in the author's original, and all manuscript copies arrange them thus. The binding, however, follows the printed edition's reversal and destroys clarity by placing the more specific adoption of Fulke of Anjou as founder of the name 'Plantagenet' before Buck's description of the research which led him to posit the qualities requisite to the possessor of a sobriquet and to reject Geoffrey of Anjou, the usual candidate, for not possessing these qualities, thus making necessary a search for someone more likely.

In the case of Buck's incomplete revisions, his intentions are usually obvious from the partial revisions he has made. Such incomplete revisions occur in the following ways: (1) He has made his revisions so hastily that they are syntactically incongruous with the unrevised portions. (2) He has begun revisions but failed to complete them: dissatisfied with his original wording, he has given several alternatives of a word or phrase, intending at some later point to make a final decision among them. (3) In the process of revising all or part of a page he has crossed out most of it, having cluttered it too much to complete his revisions where he began them, or having decided to remove the material to another place. His intention was certainly to rewrite the whole passage later, but since he never does so, I have had to depend on the incomplete existing versions and to select the clearest, most coherent, and most informative wording. And I have attempted to create coherent grammatical constructions in passages Buck left partially revised by restoring words he has crossed out, deleting words he has failed to cross out, and occasionally reversing the order of phrases. In so doing I have not altered the sense but merely made its expression coherent by continuing a revision along lines suggested by the author.

In the present text I have modernized spelling and regularized punctuation. This has been necessary because of the number of hands, all with different spelling and punctuation conventions, which have contributed to the present text: the author in various moods in which he is more or less careful and in which his spelling is more or less formal; the author's scribe; another hand in which a document has been copied for the author; George Buck, Esq. in his revisions in the original manuscript; his scribe in the copies Egerton, Malone, and Fisher; his own corrections in these copies; the compositor in the 1646 edition; and the present editor. There are in the original manuscript numerous gaps which have had to be filled in by non-authorial material, either from copies or from conjecture. It would have been foolish either to present a conglomeration of spelling styles or to arrange all the insertions so that their spelling approximated Buck's own. Modernization of spelling eliminates yet another confusion and difficulty from a text already complicated with emendations.

I have followed the same procedure with foreign languages: I have modernized French and normalized Latin spelling. The scribal pages in Tiberius and the emendations derived from manuscript copies show a very large number of errors, whereas those in the author's hand show almost none. Buck himself makes two minor grammatical errors in Latin, the language from which he quotes most frequently, none in French, from which he quotes very often, three very minor ones in Greek, from which he quotes a few times, and none in Spanish and Italian which he quotes rarely. He made attempts to correct his scribe's numerous errors in foreign passages, but he missed many of them. The Editor's scribe in the copies distorts most of the foreign passages. When grammatical errors occur in foreign passages, I have corrected them in the text and given the erroneous version in the textual notes. However, these alterations apply to grammar only, and when Buck documents a passage as 'Cicero', what he gives is more often than not his paraphrase of Cicero, adapted grammatically to suit his own context. In these cases I have not substituted in the present text the correct quotation for Buck's paraphrase, but I have given in the General Notes a reference to the correct quotation. And to aid the reader in weaning himself away from looking at Buck's references as if they were quotations in a modern historical work, the present edition does not use quotation marks except for direct discourse: it does not turn Buck's references into quotations.

I have corrected Buck's few accidental misspellings without citing them individually in the textual notes. Proper names which vary in spelling throughout the manuscript I have regularized, and names whose habitual spelling in Buck differs from that to which we are now accustomed, such as 'Richmont' and 'Plantagenest', I have given as they are normally seen today. To avoid confusion, I have invariably given 'Joab' as 'Joas'. But if Buck has mistakenly given 'Thomas' as the name of a man who is in fact Robert, I have let the error stand in the text and given the name correctly in the General Notes.

In keeping with the modernized spelling, I have regularized the punctuation and other accidentals. Buck's punctuation is irregular, sometimes non-existent. I have had, consequently, to try to punctuate the whole work so that thought units stand out as clearly and distinctly as possible and so that sense is as clear as possible in so diffuse a work.

As the reader can see from the samples shown on Plates I-III which follow, the manuscript is not very legible. These examples are, of course, more legible than average, or they could not have been exhibited at all. Fire, constant and often incomplete revision, and sloppy handwriting make reading difficult. I have no doubt that despite my several checkings of my transcripts against the original I have made some errors and omissions. I cannot claim that my conjectures filling in areas of text damaged beyond recovery always represents Buck's exact wording. These are inevitable hazards in dealing with a badly damaged manuscript in rough draft. All one can do is exercise the greatest care and attention in hope of recovering something as close to the author's intention as possible.

NOTES

1. E.K. Chambers, review of *The King's Office of the Revels, Review of English Studies,* I (1925), 479-84.

2. See Kincaid, 'Revels Scrap'.

3. *Report on the Cottonian Library,* p. 35.

4. David Casley, *A Catalogue of the Manuscripts of the King's Library: an Appendix to the Catalogue of the Cottonian Library, Together with an Account of the Books Burnt or Damaged by a Late Fire* (London, 1734), p. 314.

5. Hooper, sig. R^v.

In the transcripts which follow,
    bold type indicates a revision by George Buck, Esq. in the original MS.
    square brackets surround passages crossed out
    braces indicate that one word is written on top of another
    asterisks fill in a gap, a destroyed, damaged or illegible portion of the MS.

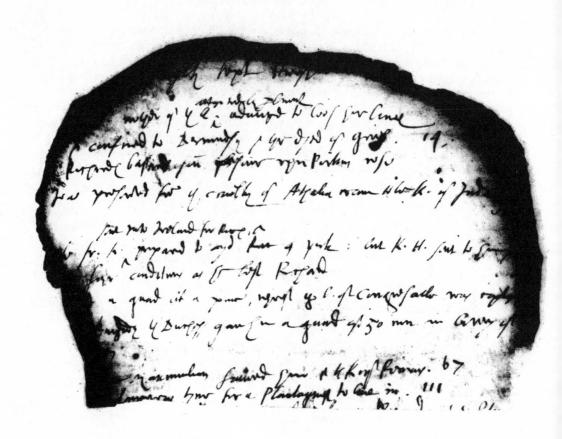

PLATE I (f. 145v)

Willoughby kept Shery hutton cast

attaynted by parlmnt

Elizab. mother of the Q. adiugd to loos her landes 13

& confined to Bermndsy & ther dyed of grief.   14-43/ 18

K. Richardes bastard sonn prisoner when Pirkin rose   lig

Joas preserved from the cruelty of Athalia cam to be K. of Juda so

sent into Ireland for Rich, &

The fr. K. prepared to ayd [Ric] of York: but K. H. sent to him & off

so fayr conditions as he left Richard

e had a guard lik a prince, wherof the L. of Congresalle was captyn

Burgundy the Duchess gau him a guard of 50 men in livery of h

urry.

emper. Maximilian fauored him & th K. of Romans. 67

a dangerous tyme for a Plantagenest to liue in. 111

[This is upside down in the original and forms the back of a revision of the latter half of f. 143v which was originally pasted down on that folio.]

Doctor Tho: Kitterram L: Chauntler of
England (& archbyshop of Canterbury Hubrt beē
comitted to prison for delivering ye great seale
to ye Queen widow) was now ydeml, & sett
at liberty, & restored to grace; & to his place.
& in briefe many knyghtes now created, & adublished
of yo old order, & of ye new order, or habet of
ye Bath. these names I have fully sett dowen them

about this tyme ye king demanded ye
forme kny the tribut, wch was payed yerly
by ye kings of to K: Edward, & ye tribut
partcularly ye forme would rather seue it
as follows: to Comines infuccably, was
& proudly & rightt meonspderates of lff
of Aquitayne, & of Normand, & of ober ser
beng y̅ never cōfirtaunt of ye kinge of
pey wth ye foluer kinge by force of armes,
but sold, & as usurpers & dissessors did
tyme for ye king of england their king
cept propritaries & thy to these yoluney
pougaments in fraue wth k: did send, &
m̅ his oracon to ye land, promising to see
all redens to wrongewr, & to re order for
& before k: Edward made
not fraue perfect did & pceued, &
sword, & a great army demanded wth the
ys o dayes, & countyos of k: kyns
ye enforced jm̅ to ene to compe
s̅ly forme kny way over

PLATE II (f. 38ᵛ)
LIB

& Doctor Tho. Rotheram L. Chancellor of

England, & archbishop of Canterbury (having bene

committed to prison for deliuering the great seale

to the Quene widow) {was / were} now pardoned, & sett

at liberty, & restored to grace, & to his place

[&] in breef many knightes were created & adubbed
                              seventene knightes
of the old order, &ˏof the new order, or habit of

the Bath. whose names I h{aue / ere} [follow,] here sett down,[&]

[ly]

[yd]

[K.]

[es]

[& about this tyme the King demanded of the]

[french king the tribute, wch was payed yerely]

[by K. Lewys xj. to K. Edward; & the tribute or]

[pension (as the french would rather haue it ca]

[as Philipp de Commines insinuateth) was ye]

[& granted, & payed in consyderation of the du]

[of Aquitayn, & of Normandy & of other seign]

[beng the ancient enheritance of the kinges of En]
                          [tort &]
[& the wch the french kinges byˏforce of armes h]
                       vniust
[long held, & as vsurpers & desseysors det]

[them from the kinges of England the[ir] true &]
                      therof
[iust proprietaries ˏ : & thes be those provinces &]

[seigneuries in France wch K. Richard pro]
          vowed
     ˏ [in his oration to the Lordes & commons to seek]

r regularly, &
Item.
rue & faithfull rela
[vsed] in all publik
at the coronation of this
as orderly a coronacion
celebrated
at any tyme before
spoken much for the
fulnes & pomp
the relation &
storie

all meanes to reconquer, & to recover for
      & for the bringing of this to pass the sayd
[&] [befor]ˏK. Edward [in his raigne] made a io

into France [for that end & purpose,] & wth h
      in his hand & attended wth
sword, {&} a great army demanded restitut

those duchies & countyes of K. Lewys x

he enforced him to come to composition

& then the French King was very we

had to promise

... they ... what reyard was ... of ye ... hey
of ye ... in his tyme ... ...
to ... and ... ...

Sr Edmund de la pole son of ye duke of Suffolk .
George Grey son of ye Erl of Kent
Will Howse son of ye L. Sands .
Harry Vaule son of ye L. Abergaveny .
Christopher Willoughby . Will Baskervile .
Hen. Baynton . Tho. Arundell
Tho. Bohen . Bryan of Clifton
Will Say . Edw. Bedingfield .
Will Enderby . Tho. Loukenor
   verenon
Tho. ... . Jhn. Brown
Will Bashley & another Bastley . is ... be ...

... ...
   ... this ... I am ... ...
... ... say it ... ... into the kyngdom ...
... ... fitt for ye ... ...
... ...
... ... with ... ... John as many ...
... ...
... ...
... ... of the kyngdom ...

A

& nd bycaus it is com*m*only thought & sa

that the king came indirectly to the crown
hee   craf
(as it wer) crept into the kingdom ([& I hau]

wthout due order & prop*er* ceremonies, refelling fa
hinke it fitt for the better [answer] of that
tion of the due & solem*n* pomp & of all the maiestica
{ ll }   [coronation of]
& lawfu{ to } [transcribe hether the report of the

& magnificent & [a] publik & [a] solem an inauguratio

              (it shall) also be necessary to repor
in this kingdome. &{   } [as it shall appere &]

[coronation of the K. & of the Queen An

  [description therof I wyll   follow the best write
[therof I will [therin] cheefly follow Sr Tho. M]

PLATE III (f. 39)

to show what reguard was had of the choys
kind
of thos of knight*es,* in thos tymes wch are accounted

to be so evill, [&] disorderly & tyranous

Sr Edmund de la poole son*n* of th. duke of Suffolk.

George Gray son*n* of the erl of Kent

Will' Souch son*n* of th^e L. Souch.
Henry Nevill son*n* of L. Abergaven*n*y.

Christopher Willoughby. Will' Barkeley.

Hen. Baynton.   Tho. Arondell

Tho. Bolen.   Breus of Clifton.

Will' Say.   Edm. Bedingfeld.

Will' Enderby.   Tho. Leukenor
Vernon
Tho. of [Vermon].   Jhon. Brown

Will' Barkley .i. another Barkley
                              it cannot bee vn

& now [I think it very convenient & necessary] **to make a ful**   (f.40)
                                              ^

true relation of all the solem ceremonies & Regall pom

wch were vsed & exhibited at the consecration & corona
                    first to make a good
of this king [Richard 3.] & [for two causes, the one for] th
                    [formerl]
of my word bycaus I haue [in some places here] before

med [& avowed y^t] the coronation of this King was
                                        [regularly]
lawfully [&] authentically [&] solemly, & publikely [&] accord
          [vsed therin)]   **secondly**
ancient custome celebrated & p*er*formed [& the other ca]
    those
that [they] may see their errour, & the wrong wch they ha

to the king [&] to all the barons [&] nobles & people o
                              & irregularly
who say that this king came indirectly to the cr
                                    ^

t he crept in at the wyndow, [secretl]

        treacher

The following notations have been used in the present text:

Conjectural emendations are in italics.

[ ] surrounds an emendation made from another copy of the work. These are from Egerton unless designated in the Textual Notes as being from Malone or Fisher.

[ ] surrounds a portion bracketed in the original manuscript.
A series of asterisks in the text indicates a lacuna for which no satisfactory conjectural emendation can be made.

/ indicates the end of a folio in the original manuscript. Folio numbers are given in the margins in bold type.

* following a folio number in the margin indicates a page in the hand of Buck's scribe.

** follows the folio number of a page entirely in the Editor's hand.

The numbers of folios in Tiberius from which material is taken are given in the margins throughout. When a long section, such as a whole page or leaf, has been lost, the text has been given from Egerton and the folio numbers from Egerton given in the margin.

THE HISTORY OF KING RICHARD THE THIRD

Comprised in five books.

Gathered and written by

Sir G. Buc, Knight,
Master of the King's Office of the Revels
and one of the Gentlemen of His Majesty's Privy Chamber

****

**Honorandus est qui iniuriam non facit, sed qui alios
eam facere non patitur duplici honore dignius est.**

Plato, **De Legibus,**
Lib. 5

****

**Qui non repellit a proximo iniuriam si potest, tam est
in vitio quam ille qui infert.**

D. Ambrosius,
De Officiis,
Lib.3

To the Most Illustrious Lord, Sir Thomas Howard,
Premier Count of this Realm, Earl of Arundel and of
Surrey, Baron Howard, Mowbray, Segrave, Breus,
Fitzalan, Maltravers, etc., Knight of the Garter, etc.,
5 a Marshal and Counsellor of the King and of the Kingdom
of England.

*Mo*st illustrious count, and my most honourable *good* lord: when I had
finished this strange and uncouth [story] of King Richard III (and the which
had been *forme*rly, and often, written by sundry men, and [in a
10 s]tyle and character very different and *very* contrary to this, and yet
received for the *story* of this king), I began to suspect [*that this* my book
would find many censors *and cr*itical essayers, and those of diverse
*kinds: som*e curious, some jealous, some haply malevolent and malicious.
But the fairest censure would be that all was [a pa]radox, or countr'opinion.
15 It *seemed* very necessary and behoveful for *me to s*eek the protection of *a
patron who is noble not only* / in blood, but also in mind *and in vir*tue: that
is, wise, learned, judicious, and magnanimous; *and who* must be potent:
that is, great in authority, in grace, and *in honour.* And all these, in mine
opinion, and without flattery, concur copious*ly and* completely in your
20 lordship, and as I could demonstrate if this place *and* your modest ears
would admit.

And this is one cause, and a chief cause, why I should appeal to your
lordship, and why your lordship should with a good will and with all
noble alacrity entertain this charge and undertake this honourable office.
25 And one is in regard that the prince whose story is here related and whose
cause is here pleaded was a most magnificent and a most gracious patron of
your most nob*le* and illustrious ancestors. For he (besides many other
prince*ly* bounties and benefits bestowed upon them) advanced th*em to* the
estates and titles of earls and of dukes, and to the quality of *princes.* And
30 for these causes, he may by good right and by due *merit have* all the honour
and right and good offices which your lordship ma*y afford* him.

Another cause why I dedicate and give this boo*k to your* lordship is
because I hold it to be proper and due unto you, *for that* you are more
interested than any other noble person *of this* kingdom. For herein be many
35 honourable mentio*ns and* fair eulogies of your heroical progenitors and of
your *ancestors,* and to whose honours, dignities, titles, fortunes *you* most
worthily succeed and rightly inherit. And yo*u are not only the* lineal and
immediate heir and successor, but a*lso the* lively image, so that whatsoever

lv
Construere est mani-
*fes*tis et irrefragibili-
bus argumentis
et testi*moni*is solidis
rei cogniti ****
veritatem indi*care.*
Johannes Veteranus
talis **** huius verbi
ubique.

is said *to be* theirs is also yours.

And the fourth and last cause *of this my* dedication hereof to your lordship groweth from the ancient and *noble* custom of offering and dedicating the spiritual *fruits and* the offspring of the best and divine part of men, and *the rewards of* their long and painful studies to   5 honourable person*s to be* esteemed a token and testimony of the reverent *care and* affection which they bear to *them. And this represents the esteem* and love which I bear, and am bound to bear, to the *noble* house of the Howards, and chiefly to you, as the *p*rince or head thereof, for the many great favours and good benefits which mine ancestors and myself have   10 received of your most illustrious and magnificent ancestors, and whereof (as I might conveniently), I have made honourable and thankful mentions in some places of this book.

And now that I have declared the many good causes which I had to pray your protection and to grave your most noble name upon the frontispiece of   15 this historical fabric, I doubt not of your most noble and favourable propensiveness to the patrociny and *p*rotection hereof, against the sharp and sinister censures and against the *jea*lous and calumnious spirits of such men as I suspected and *form*ulated in the beginning. For I fear not the generous, *nor the* learned, nor the candid, nor the judicious readers, *for*   20 they out of the goodness and justice of their dispositions are *r*espectively and modestly careful not to mistake nor *mis*construe anything, and much less to forejudge and hardly *censu*re the honest endeavours of studious persons. But, *being* wise, they will rather find means not only to resolve and to *satisfy the*mselves, but also any other curious, scrupulous, *malicious* and   25 ill-affected men.

I know not what he is who can justly take *any of*fence at this work, if he know what a story is [and ought to be,] for, as your lordship well knoweth, a story must be true [and faithful], must be a plain and perspicuous narration of [things memora]ble and remarkable which have been done or   30 [execute]d before. And the historiographer must be ve[ritable and free from all pro]sopolepsies and partial respects. *He must not a*dd nor omit anything, *either of partiality* or of hatred. [All which I have endeavoured to observe in] the writing of this story, so that [if my authors be sincere and faithful, my Muse is pure and innocent. For I have imitated the sceptic philosophers]   35 who of themselves affirmed nothing, but [liked the doctrine of the] other more renowned and more learned philosophers. Fo*r that* which is said and related in this history is the *true testi*mony *of* honest and faithful writers of former times.

Bu*t* I use (and that seld*om, and only* upon necessity) to make some   40 illustrations, and not *inter*pretations, and som*e appa*rent and probable conjectures, and to no other end but for the better un*der*standing of some obscure passages and of some ambiguous words. And that is common and commendable licence and of very ancient use. And because I follo*w* other men, I cite their names and their authorities either in the text or in the   45 margent, and it maketh more for the credit of the story.

Whereas on the other side the relations of stories of some other writers are of little cred*it* because they deliver all their matters of what time and antiquity soever upon their own bare and worthless word, and after the manner of fab*u*lous and trivial romancers. And who for *the* most part being   50

idle and sensual persons, will no*t* take the pains to read the ancient and la*rge*
histories, but epito*mes* of them, and vulgar pamph*lets* only. And therefore
their stories or ta*les or* romances are accounted as things ambiguous and
fabulous. Where*fore I* like very well the counsel of the wise Cicero and
5 follow it as [occasion] requireth. And *t*hat is this: **Testimonia et exempla ex** *Cicero*
veteri memori[a et mo]numentis antiquis deprompta plurimum solent
auctoritatis [habere].

And thus much for the account which I held myself bound to r*ender of*
my style in this work. And here I purposed to end this dedica*tion.* But in the
10 passage to the close thereof, I was admonished by my Genius, *firmly* to
answer (and by way of the orator's preoccupation) an objection *and*
*ex*ception which may be made to me for a general word which I *said* but
now and too peremptorily, as I confess; and I recant it. And that was *where*
I said that I know not any man who might justly take excep*tion to this*
15 history. And wherein it might be said that this my case was like to *that*
famous Mantuan shepherd who was reprehended by Apollo for dealing too
high for him:
Cum canerem reges et proelia, Cynthius aurem
Vellit et admonuit: 'Pastorem, Tityre, pingues', etc.   **Vergil in** *Eclogues*
20 And I confess that my s*t*yle reached too high and was too general *to* have
excepted ONE, and that *is* a rare and a peerless One, and [of a singular] and
sacred quality, for he hath no peers nor paragons eith*er* in *nature or in*
condition. Neither hath he any peers or equals *in judgemen*t, in justice, and
in clemency. And *this* one may take exceptions at me as at one who *without*
25 *a great share* or portion in fortunes and in fame and as small in lear*ning* and
but slightly initiated in the mysteries of poli*cy should presume* to write of
his royal ancestors and to examine their actions, to rip up their vices, and to
treat and to d*iscourse of* crowns, of majesty, of *kingdoms,* of royal rights
and tit*les,* and of those *who a*re supposed to be nob*le.*

AN ADVERTISEMENT TO THE READER

5

Before I enter into this story of King Richard, I must advertise the noble, courteous, and intelligent Reader (for unto such only I write) that the argument and subject of this discourse or story was at the first but a chapter, and the thirteenth chapter, of the third book of a rude work of mine entitled THE BARON, or **The Magazin of Honour.** But the argument 5 of that chapter being strange and very extravagant and extraordinary (as the affairs and fortunes of this prince were), suppeditated strange and extraordinary matters, and in such copy and variety as that it diffused itself into an extraordinary and unusual largeness, and so much as it exceeded very much the laws and the proper limits of a chapter. *Wherefore* being also 10 much enlarged and transferred hither, it may pass here *under* the title of a discourse or historiola, and it may serve *as a* gloss and a paraphrase of the foresaid chapter, and that chapter for an *argum*ent of this story of King Richard III; and not of Perkin Warbeck, *as mine* host of *Westminster* (and now a worshipful shallow magistrate) hath idly and add*ledly alleged.* 15

But to let these sycophantisms pass, and to proceed, I must now draw out *and* transcribe hither from the said thirteenth chapter some particular *matters,* and especially the beginnings and first times of this Prince Richard, comprehending *the princ*ely lineage of the king and his parentage, his birth, his education, his [tirocin]y, and all the conditions of these acts, and of his 20 youth, and of his [private] life. And this being done, and as it ought according to [meth]od and due order, I will next address my style and my *labour*s to the story of his public person and of his regal state, *and to* relate his election and coronation and affairs and actions and the more signal acci[dents of hi]s reign and time until his death. 25

And lastly, and because he hath been accu[sed of] great crimes, and slanderously (as I verily believe), and even at such times as envy is accustomed [to cease barking] and malevolence *to leave men* at rest in their graves, *I shall make* [endeavo]ur to answer for him, and to clear and [redeem] *him from those improbab*le imputations and strange and spiteful 30 [scandals] *and rescue* him *entirely* from th*o*se wrongs, and *to make truth* (*hereby* / concealed and oppressed and almost utterly suppressed) present herself to the light, according to her desire, and by the opportune taking of the fair advantage of these happy and just times of a king by whose favour and furtherance Truth hath here safe conduit and free passage and 35 prevaileth and flourishes. And these shall also see the calumniators and false accusers of this prince detected and convinced of slanders and of lies. And the good and loyal barons shall be distinguished from the bad and false barons. And Morton and More and their apes shall be delineated and painted in their own colours, every *one* of them, and shall receive here and 40

Publica [persona est] prince[ps, vel magistratus,] qui Re[ipublicae vel parti eius] praeest. [Heironymus Vulteius]

Beatum Sancti Regis Jacobi regnum.

hereafter **propriam mercedem** and **referet unusquisque propria corporis prout gessit sive bonum, sive malum,** if I might so say.

And as truth and justice shall direct and help to answer by way of *refuta*tion an objection against some repetitions which shall occur in this
5   story by the curious carpers, battologies and tautolog*ies*, I answer and I say confidently that such repetitions as are here are not *only proper* and allowable, but also needful. And they be such as the ancient *and* grave jurisconsults defended thus in their axiom: **Verba gemina repetita enixam et constantem voluntatem indicant.** And such that other repetitions are a tacit
10 persuasion to the reader or *author to* remember better, and better to mark the thing so repeate*d, and its* causes. The divine Plato was of opinion that   *Plato* **Quod bene dicitur,** *repetere* **non nocet;** and it is much used by him. And in brief, repeti*tion was* allowed in the Holy Scripture and authorized by good reasons. And thus for my repeti*tion*s.
15 I must not for*get* gratefully to commemorate the courtesies and ingenious prompt*ings of* some of my learned friends to help and to further my studies and *labours* on this enterprise and by whom *I have* profited, besides the nomenclation and quotation of the names of mine *authors* and records which I have followed, and for my better warrant. For I like not that *the*
20 *right* and privilege of **ipse dixit** should be allowed to any *but* Pythagoras, or to such another, whose words were as ora*cles.*

****

[*There follows here a criticism of an individual historian, the beginning of which is missing. Buck has evidently made two points already: that the unnamed author reports events too briefly, and that he neglects to*
25 *give the dates of the occurrences which he relates.*]

****

******** year and of the years of the reigns of kings. The third wa*s* his   **4** neglect of citation of authors and quotations, thus concealing of their names and vainly taking all upon himself.

Therefore, I have avoided their faults. For as concerning brevi*ty*, I am
30 here rather prolix than brief, and I observe times and years, and I cite mine authors everywhere. And therefore I shall not need to make here a catalogue of them as many do vainly also and to no purpose. But as I in*tend* to make a thankful remembrance of the more signal courtesies and of the better help which I have had of some of my more learned and better-booked friends, as
35 namely Mr Camden, Clarensius; and the good herald Mr Brooke, York; and chiefly the noble and learned knight and baronet, Sir Robert Cotton, whose rich and plentiful library hath still been open to me, and very freely and friendly, and as *in* like manner it is to all his honest and studious friends and lovers of good monuments and of rare antiquities. And therefore his
40 cabinet *and* library may worthily have the same inscription and title which *was* set upon the gate of the School of the Sacred Muses, and *to their* immortal honour and glory: **Apertae semper Musarum ianuae.**

And if it be objected that I have omitted anything of *the* story of King Richard, I answer that I have omitted nothing of *great* matter or moment,
45 nor anything else but some slight *matter*s, and such as are to be seen in the

common and vulgar chroni*cles* and stories, and which are in the hands of
every idiot or mere *fool*ish reader, *and to no pur*pose, and for the most part
not worth the reading. And my scope was to write this unhappy *king's* story
faithfully and at large, and to plead his cause, and to answer and refell the
many accusations and calumniations brought against him. And if I have   5
performe*d this as* I hope and I *believe* I have, then I have done a work of
charity and won the goal and prize *which I sought.*

The just and intelligent and generous and judicious Reader must be
there*fore satisfied,* and so wishing him all right, and that with favour, I bid
him farewell.   10

From the King's Office of the Re*ve*ls, Peter's Hill,
the .... of ....1619.

The Argument and Contents of the First Book

The lineage, family, birth, education, and tirociny of King Richard III.
The royal house of Plantagenet, and the beginning of that surname.
What sobriquets were.
The antiquity of surnames.
5	Richard is created Duke of Gloucester; his marriage and his issue.
His martial employments; his prowess and skill in military affairs.
His journey into Scotland and his recovery of Berwick.
The death of King Edward IV.
The Duke of Gloucester is made Lord Protector, and soon after King of
10	England by the earnest and importunate suits of the barons and of the
people, and as the right true and lawful heir.
Henry Tudor, Earl of Richmond, is suspected of practice against the king
and the state, and not only by King Richard, but also [long] before by the
king his brother.
15	He is conveyed into France.
The noble lineage and [wor]thiness of Sir William Herbert; his employment;
he is made Earl of Pembroke.
King Edward IV first, and after King Richard, solicits the Duke of Brittany
and [treats] with him for the delivery of the young Earl of Richmond, his
20	prisoner.
T[he success] of that business.
The quality and title of the Beauforts and Somersets.
[The] lineage and family of the Earl of Richmond.
The solemn coronations of King R[ichard] and of the queen his wife, his
25	first at Westminster and his second at York; the no[bles,] knights, and
officers made by him.
The Prince Edward his son is [invested] in the principality of Wales, and the
oath of allegiance is made to him.
King R[ichard] demandeth a tribute of France.
30	His progress to York.
His careful and godly [charge] given to the judges and magistrates for the
administration of justice.
He hold[eth a] Parliament, wherein the marriage of the king his brother
with the Lady Gray is decla[red and] adjudged to be unlawful, and their
35	children to be illegitimate and not capa[ble of] the crown.
Morton, Bishop of Ely, and Dr Nandick, a conjurer, and the Earl of
R[ichmond] and divers others are attainted of treason, and many good
laws are m[ade,] and the king is declared and approved by the Parliament
to be the only true and lawful [heir] of the crown.
40	The king h[ath secret] advertisement of seditions and of treasons.
He createth a Vice-Constable of E[ngland.]
His sundry treaties with foreign princes.
Dr Morton an excellent politician [and a] chief sower of sedition.
The Duke of Buckingham is corrupted by Morton and en*vious and*
45	*malcontent,* and he entereth into disloyal practices, and he demandeth the
earldom of Hereford, [with the] Great Constableship of England.
He taketh arms; he is taken and put [to death] by martial law.

THE FIRST BOOK OF
THE HISTORY OF RICHARD THE THIRD,
OF ENGLAND AND OF FRANCE KING,
AND LORD OF IRELAND

Richard Plantagenet, Duke of Gloucester and King of England and of
France and Lord of Ireland, the third King Richard, was the younger son
of Sir Richard Plantagenet, the fourth Duke of York of that royal family,
and King of England designate by [King] Henry the Sixth and by the High
Court of Parliament: that is by the most noble senate and by the universal 5
[syn]od of this kingdom.

The mother of this Richard, Duke of Gloucester, [was] the Lady Cecily,
daughter of Sir Ralph de Neville, Earl of Westmorl[and] by his wife, Joan
de Beaufort, the natural daughter of [John] Plantagenet (alias de Gand),
Duke of Guienne and of Lancaster, [King] of Castile and of Lyons, and the 10
third son of King Edward the Third [(for in t]hat order this duke is best
accounted, because William of Hatfield, [the seco]nd son of King Edward
III, died in his infancy). And this Duke of York [and King] Designate was
propagated from two younger sons of the same King Edward III. And
whereby he had both paternal and maternal title to [the crow]ns of England 15
and of France. But his better and nearer title was the [materna]l title, or that
which came to him by his mother the Lady Anne de [Mortim]er, the
daughter and heir of the Lady Philippa Plantagenet, who was the sole
daughter and heir of Lionel Plantagenet, Duke of Clarence, [secon]d son to
King Edward III, according to the account and order aforesaid. And this 20
Lady [Philipp]a was the wife of Sir Edmund Mortimer, the great and
famous Earl [of Marc]h. And that Duke Richard, King Designate, by his
father Richard Plantagenet, Duke [of York (surnamed also de Conisburgh),
issued directly and in a masculine line [from Edm]und Plantagenet (alias de
Langley), [the] first Duke of York, and the [fourth son] of King Edward III. 25
And thus much briefly for the princely house [and title of] York.

[And here it] may [se]em fit and convenient to make a report of the stem
and lineage [of that most r]enowned and glorious progenitor of these
princes of York and [Lancaster,] namely the often before mentioned King
Edward III, [which is thus: this king] was the fifth king in a lineal and 30
masculine descent [from the great Henry surnamed] Plantagenet, famous
for his great [prowess and many victories. He was the second Henry, King
of England, in the right of his mother the Empress Matilda, or Maud,
daughter and heir of King Henry I, and styled **Anglorum Domina,** and
sometime wife of the Emperor Henry V, whereupon he was] / also 35
surnamed **Filius Imperatricis.** And the Frenchmen called him Henry **du
Court Manteau,** or Curtmantle, because he wore a cloak shorter than the
fashion was in his times. And by his father Galfrede, or Geoffrey,

The [house and] tit[le of York]

[Plantagenet]

7v

Plantagenet he was Earl, or Duke, of Anjou (for then **Dux** and **Comes,** and **Ducatus** and [**Comitatus**] were synonyms and promiscuous words). And he was also Earl of Maine and of Touraine, and hereditary Seneschal or High Steward of France. And by his marriage of Eleanor, Queen of France

5 repudiate, and the daughter and heir of William, Duke of Gascoigne and of Guienne and Earl of Poitou, he was duke and earl of those principalities and signories, and he was also by the empress his mother Duke of Normandy. He was Lord of Ireland by conquest, and confirmed by [Pope Adrian.]

[The empire of King Henry II]

10 But these were not all his signories and dominions. For after that he was King of England he extended the limits of his empire and principate so far as they were bounded in the south by the Pyrenean Mountains (the confines of Spain and France), and in the north with the Isles of Orkney, and in the east and west with the oceans. And for his greatness he was styled **Regum**

15 **Britanniae Maximus** (as Giraldus Cambrensis, Gulielmus Novobrigensis, and Johanne[s] Sarisberiensis, grave and creditable authors, affirm). And doubtless he w[as] the greatest King of Britain since King Arthur reigned.

[Giraldus in **Topographica Hiberniae;** Sarisberiensis in **Policratico;** Neubrigensis, **Liber** 2.]

But whereas some say that the foresaid Geoffrey Plantagenet, [Earl of] Anjou, father of this Henry, was the first Earl of Anjou which bore the

20 sur[name] of Plantagenest (or Plantagenet, after the common and vulgar [orthography])], that must not be allowed. For certainly that surname ha[d the] beginning from a much more ancient Earl of Anjou, and [for other reasons and better causes] than can be found in the foresaid Geoffrey, as it shall be made apparent.

25 It is controverted amongst the antiquaries and the heralds which Ear[l of Anjou] first bore the name and sobriquet of Plantagenet. And upo[n what] occasion and for what cause it was so taken and borne, and also [in what] time or age it had beginning, I think I shall be able to determine according to my small talent of knowledge and reading and ac*cor*ding to the methods I

30 have held for the searching of the originals *of the* most ancient noble families of England, of their surnames in my *Commentary* **upon the Book of Domus Dei, or The New Roll of Winche*ster*.** And for the accomplishment hereof, I must not only use the he*lp of* good historians and learned antiquaries, but also of traditions and of proce*d*ures, and those

35 fortified with reasons and with arguments of force and credit sufficie*nt* for the beginning of this surname of Plantagenet.

For after I had read and searched many books and perused many written monuments for the knowledge of this matter, I went to some of my friends learned in heraldry and in history, and I conferred with them and desired to

10

40 be better informed by them. And amongst these, I addressed myself to Sir William Dethick, Principal King at Arms, who was a man bred in good letters, and well languaged, and a generous person, and one of the best heralds of his time. And he had good means to be a good antiquary and a good herald, for he had a library very well furnished with rolls and good

45 books, manuscripts and other and diverse monuments and stories, and such as were fit and proper to a man of his profession.

And I desired this honest officer of arms to declare to me the first beginning and first bearing of the name of Plantagenet. And he answered very courteously that he both could and would show *me* much good matter

50 for that purpose. And he took me with *him* into his library, and he took

down a fair old book written *on p*archment, wherein he said there was some
matter concerning *the be*ginning of the name of Plantagenet. And he turned
to a brief *glos*s or paragraph, which was written of those strange and
fantasti*cal n*ames or words which the Frenchmen call sobriquets, *which*,
according to the learned Nicot and other French writers, *were used* 5
sometimes seriously and in good part, and sometimes as *nick*names and
names of scorn. And there was a jolly catalogue *of* sobriquets in that book.
And I made choice of some of *them,* and I transcribed them into a piece of
paper and from thence hither, and these they are.

[Sobriquets]

Berger: shepherd   10
Grisegonelle: grey coat
Teste d'Estouppe: head of tow
Arbuscula: shrub
Martell: hammer
Grundeboeuf: oxface   15
La Zouch: a branch upon a stem
Houlette: sheephook
Hapken: hatchet
Capelle: hood
Sansterre: lackland   20
Geffard: **iuvencus,** or heiffer
Malduit: ill taught
Filz de Fleau: the son of a flail

and many othe*rs*. [And amongst them] was Plantagenet: that is, the plant or
stalk [of a broom.   25

[And the g]loss upon the text was that anciently these so[briquets and the
like base and ridiculous] names were taken by great persons [and by other
noble and signal persons who had been great and heinous sinners, and had
committed murder, blasphemy, treason, sacrilege, incest, perjury, rapes,]

10v

and all kind of sins and abominations; and now at the last, by the merciful 30
goodness of God, were become penitent for them, and in all humility and
hearty sorrow confessed them to God and to the holy priest, their confessor
or ghostly father; and whose manner was to enjoin them some penance for
the better appeasing of the divine wrath, and for some amends and

[After this manner, satisfaction for their so great and enormous offences, as they supposed. 35
and long after, King   And the priests also enjoined them to punish their bodies with fasting and
Henry II, the heir   with sackcloth and with whipping and with other kind of rigours and
and successor of this austerities, and also to undertake some hard and painful labour; or to go a
Earl Fulco, was en-   long and dangerous journey upon their bare feet; or to take the cross and to
joined by the Pope to bear arms against the Saracens, Turks, and other infidels; or to go in 40
go to the Holy Land   pilgrimage to some far remote saint's temple or shrine of some special saint,
and to fight against   as to St Iago of Compostella, to our Lady or Gua*da*lupe or of Loretta, etc.;
the infidels. Hove-   but chiefly to the Holy Sep[ulchre] of our Lord and Saviour in Jerusalem.
den, Rievall, etc.]

And furthermore, these lords which [undertook] these penances, to the
end to show by this ou[t]ward sign their great hu[militation] and inward 45
direction wrought by their contrition and hearty peniten*ce* did not only
abstain from all matters of pleasure and of po[mp,] of delicacy and of
bravery, but also took upon them the c[onditions] and qualities and habits
of mean and base and ignoble pers[ons.] One of them would be apparelled
and disguised like to a carpen[ter,] and another like to a smith, and another 50

like to a fisherman, *or* like to a mariner, and another like to a shepherd, and
another like to [a mourner,] and another like to a woodman, and another
took the title and habit and the ensign [of] a broom man. And he was the
ancient Earl of Anjou befo[re intimated.]

5   And this opinion is general. But none of the heralds nor antiquaries,
French or English, [tell how that earl] was called, nor when he lived, nor
whose son he was. These be the doubts which remain, *and* I shall be able to
unfold and resolve them. And, as I intim*ated,* I m[ust dissent] from them
who make Geoffrey Plantagenet, who was the f[ather of King Henry II, to

10   be the first which bore the broom stalk or took the device thereof, for it will
be found, I doubt not, that he which first took it was a much more ancient
Earl of Anjou, and a man more religious, one that had been in pilgrimage at
Jerusalem.]

       But Geoffrey Plantagenet was never so pious nor so religious, nor had   **8**

15   never so much remorse of his sins, for he was an amorous knight and a
jovial, and a gallant courtier, and spent his time in the courts of princes,
and in feasting and in tournaments, and in courting of fair ladies, and those
of the highest quality, for Lewis le Gros, King of France, suspected him
with the queen his wife, and not without cause. And he did not only make

20   love to the Empress Matilda, but also won her favour and love with his
amorous devices and married her. And doubtless he neither had nor would
have any leisure [for] such humble and penitent and mortified thoughts,
nor had he any so goodly disposition as to resolve to go in a poor and
perilous pilgrimage to Jerusalem.

25   Therefore I will let him pass and find another and more ancient Earl of
Anjou, who was doubtless the man we seek, and his ancestor. And he was a
great sinner, and in the [end] repented himself of his sins and vowed to do
bitter and austere penance. And for his penance, he undertook *a* poor and
vile and obscure and hard pilgrimage to the Holy Sepulchre. *This m*an was

30   the first Fulke which was Earl of Anjou, and who lived above a hundred   [Fulke, first Earl of
years before the Norman Conquest of England. And I will [set] down his   Anjou]
story briefly, as I find it in the chronicles of [Anjou.]

       This Fulke was the son of Godfrey, or Geoffrey, Grise[gonelle,] the first
Earl of Anjou, according to du Haillan. [And] *he* was an ancestor and

35   progenitor to the foresaid Geoffrey Plan[tagenet,] and some seven or eight
degrees in the ascending line (as Para[din] accounteth). And he was a man
of great courage and of much strength, *and* [of] a warlike disposition. And
he was also very ambitious [and] covetous, and would do anything to fulfill
and to satisfy his [desires] And, amongst other crimes, he committed two

40   more heinous than the rest, and the [one was a wilfu]l perjury, and the other
a treacherous murder of his young [kinsm]an Drogo, Earl of Brittany. His
perjury was for the defrauding and spoiling of a [church of certain] rights.
[And he caused his nephew Dr]ogo to be murdered to the end that he might
have and possess his lands and [his co]unty and principality.

45   And he, being grown old and having much solitary time [and man]y
heavy and sad thoughts, which naturally accompany old age and suggest
better considerations of a[man's] former life and of his sins committed in
his y[outh], *he bec*ame much grieved and troubled in mind, and he was
tormented [with the s]ecret scourges and stings of these his great and

50   heinous [crimes.] And at shrift, or confession, he discovered his grief to his

confessor and made his *obeissance,* and desired him (as great Constantine did Aegyptus) to devise some means to help him [in his trou]bled and afflicted mind.

And this good priest, perceiving [his remorse], (*which* is a token of God's grace), bade him be of good comfort. And he t*old him that to cure him* of   5
his soul's diseases was not hard, if he *would undergo a penance.* / And forthwith this earl in all humility and sorrow confessed his sins and professed to be most heartily sorry for them, and that in taking his true penitence he would endure any pain or penance to have pardon for his sins and to be absolved of their great guilt. Then this priest told him that he   10
should be pardoned and absolved, but with the condition that for the making of some amends for [satisfaction] of Almighty God, he should go in humble and hard pilgrimage to the Holy Sepul*chre* of our Lord and Saviour at Jerusalem, and there most humbly and peniten*tly* to make his confession of his sins and to crave pardon for them.   15

And the earl gladly and willingly accepted this penance and resolved to perform that pilgrimage, and in all lowly and contemptible manner. And the better to express his humbled and dejected spirit, he clad himself in the habit of a peasant and base fellow. And he left and dismiss*ed* all his gallant followers and courtly train, and went his jour[ney as a private m]an, and   20
took with him only two of his meanest but honest servants. And not to th*e* end to be holpen or eased anything by their services in his poor *pilgri*mage, but rather that they might be witnesses of his true *and* faithful performance of the penance enjoined on him and of s*ervice to* be done by them to him when he was come to Jerusalem.   25

And he was come to Jerusalem, and then he made the first use of those two f*ellows,* and that was a very strange use. For he employed the one of them [to get] a strong cord, such as is used for the strangling and hanging o[f] *traitors* and criminals. And he commanded the other to provide a bun*dle* of such twigs as wherewith there might rods be made*;* and they   30

[Accoutré en] crimi-
nel [et condamne.]
Paradin
[The second] Henry
King of England
*from these sc*ourges
of his [ancestor] took
example to [submit]
his body to be
scourged [by the]
monks of Canter-
bury [for the death]
of Thomas Becket.
[Du Haillan;
Paradin]
9

fulfilled his will and commandment. And then he caused [them] to strip him and to accouter him as a condemned person. And then *he* willed the one to put the halter about his neck and to draw *and* lead him to the Holy Sepulchre. And he commanded his other serv*ant* to follow him close with his rods and to scourge him most sha*mefully,* and without any favour, until   35
he came to kneel before the [Holy] Sepulchre.

And when he came thither, he bowed himself and [prostrated] himself before that sacred monument of Jesus Christ. And he said to the Lord in this manner: '*I have been wa*ndering from thy holy ways, and I am here as an assassin or traitor to be hanged for my spiritual treasons commit*ted'.*   40
And anon, and after much sorrow and many tears, he raised himself upon his knees and confessed all his sins; and chiefly and with most remorse these his two great [sins] of per[jury and] of murder, and in all sincere and hearty repentance, he p*rayed for mercy* and pardon for his sins. Amongst other his zealou[s and devout words, he u]ttered these: **Mon die[u et seigneur reçois**   45
à pardon le parjure et homicide et misérable Foulques.] / And he returned home w[ith a sa]tisfied [conscience,] *and lived* [many] years in his country in all [prosperity and honour of all men.]

And there be many more exa[mple]s, and they *be* of many princes [and noble persons who] lived about the year of our Lord 1000, and somewha*t* in   50

some three or four ages after; who, having been great and famous
[offenders, and after,] feeling by the divine mercy a remorse of their gr*eat*
*sins in t*heir consciences, ha[ve under]taken long and painful pilgrimages to
sundry holy places, to *Canterbury and* to Jerusalem, the holy city, where
5 the shrine or glorious sepul*chre* of our Lord and Redeemer Jesus Christ was
and is. And amongst thes*e* sinful and penitent princes, this first Fulco (or
Fulke), Earl of Anjou, and the son of Godfrey Grisegonelle, earl of that
country, w[as] one of these noble sinful and penitent persons [who went this
pil]grimage to Jerusalem, and expressly to visit *the Holy Sepulchre,* about
10 the year of our Lord 1000.

*And in con*sideration *thi*rdly, we may observe here that as they did wear
an outward habit of *humility, they wrought and* laboured to have the true
and perfect humility in their hearts and souls. But *the signs of* their inward
humility and of the*ir outward submission* were in their plain and coarse and
15 p*oor attire, and* in their base disguises of shepher*ds, peasants,* and the like.
And we find also that according to this dis*guise they took* igno*ble* and
contemptible names or nicknames and ca*lled themselves by sobriquets. And
it* hath also been made apparent that this old Earl of A*njou* then *took* the
sobriquet of Plantagenest, **ut supra.**

20   And to conclude, by all these particulars being *com*pared and considered, it is apparent and mani*fest* that the foresaid Fulke, the first Earl
of Anjou, and the son of *Geoffrey* Grisegonelle, was that noble *person*
which first took that sobriquet of Plantagenest, or *Broomstalk.* And that
now it remaineth that we seek *the* reason why the Count Fulke chose the
25 genet [plant or broomstalk] before any other vegetable or other thing; *and
this may* also be resolved. And the reasons of *it* [which I conceive] may be
[first in respect the] / broom, [in the hieroglyphical learning, is the] symbol
of hu[mility,] *because it grow*eth not in high, but in low places. [And
therefore the] poets, and parti[cularly] Vergil, the best poet, [giveth it] the
30 epithet of **humilis: humilisque genista.**

[And the etymolo]gists say that it is derived from the word **genu,** [the]
knee, [which of] all the parts or members of man is most applied, and (as [it
were]) dedicated unto lowliness and to humble offices, and to the chief act
[of rev]erence: that is, kneeling (as all men know). And the natural
35 philosophers affirm [there] is so mutual a correspondency and so natural a
sympathy [betw]een **genu** and **genista,** as that the broom is of all other
plants [or] vegetals the most comfortable and the most medicinable thing
[to] the pains and diseases of the knees. And Pliny, a great master amongst
[them, sai]th, **Genista tusa cum,** etc., **genua dolentia sanat.**

40   *Moreover, b*room is a natural and actual instrument of pur*ifying and
c*leansing places which are foul, and therefore it may serve well for a type of
the *instrumen*ts which are proper to purge and to cleanse the soul, *which
c*orrections and chastisements be distasteful and b*ring forth evidence of
cleansing in th*e flowers of the genet. Or in consi[deration] *the stalk*s or
45 branches of the broom m[ay be made a fit instrum]ent of correction (such as
the rod [is), it may be defined and conclu]ded [that the] rods or scourges
wherewith the n*ewly* [penitent earl was chastis]ed were made of broom
tw[igs, and not for that cause only,] but for the necessity the which the[re
was to make rods of broom.] For in regard that the earl wa*s a penitent,*
50 *there were* rods necessarily to be provided, and t*here* could *good quantity*

9v

Geo[rgica,] **Lib.** [**II**].

Leo[nard] Fuch-
[sius.]

Pli[ny,] **Lib.** 2[4]
cap. [9]

of rods be made at or near to Jeru[salem.] And those trees which are the most proper to such uses (as namely [the] birch and the willow and the withy) because they covet to be in *rich* and watery and moist soils, or else they will not grow, and the so[il] o[f] Jerusalem was contrary to their nature, for (as Strabo, [a fa]mous geographer, writeth) the soil about   5
Jer[usalem] is stony and sandy and dry and barren; and that kind of soil is [grate]ful and very pleasing to the genet; and therefore, as it is most like, the earl's m*en who* provided and prepared the rods made them of the stalk *or the* twigs of broom about Jerusalem, as the virtues and *strengths of that plant* were well known to the Earl Fulke.   10

    [And from hence, it must take the beginning of that honour which afterward his noble and princely posters continued in making it their chief surname of all other. Nor had they reason only to honour, but also to maintain and continue the fame and honour of the demise of that good earl, because they prospered and lived in greater felicity for his sake, as the pious   15
people of that age, and long after, said and verily believed and observed, that God so blessed him and his progeny that they became afterwards dukes and princes in sundry other places. And some of them were kings, namely of Jerusalem, of England, France, Ireland, and Scotland, etc.

    And now give me leave to say with Mr Camden, for the continuance of   20
this device, that the father of Henry Plantagenet, King of England, would wear a broomstalk in his bonnet, as also many other nobles of the House of Anjou did, and used it for their surname. But because some men make a doubt and question of the continuance thereof, I will say something which shall be of sufficient importance to determine the question.]   25

    Some men (who pretend to see furt[her and better in the dark than]/other men as clearsighted as they) [affirm that the name or surname of] Plantagenet was not used by the kings and [princes of] the Angevin race in the ancient times, but [to be taken of late time.] But *that* [is] a false opinion, [and the] contrary is so tr[ue and manifest, and the testimonies] so   30
many [that it were tedious] to cite and to adduce them. And whosoever shall be [pleased but to] fo*llo*w and pursue the excellent collection of a[ll the princely and] royal genealogies of England in the **Catalogue of Honour** made by that learne[d and diligent] antiquary, and one of the best and most skilful heralds which [have been] from the first foundation and institution   35
of the College of Heralds and of the officers at arms, and namely Robert Glover, Somerset Duke at Arms, he shall see nothing more obvious nor more frequent in the deductions of the princes of the House of Anjou than the [a]ddition of the surname of Plantagenet to their forename, or Christian name. As for example there you have Thomas Plantagenet, Edmund   40
[Plan]tagenet, George Plantagenet, John Plantagenet, Edward Plantage-net, [Lion]el Plantagenet, Humphrey Plantagenet, and a great many more such. And in the French [histori]ans and antiquaries, and namely in John du Tillet and Gerard du [Haill]an and Claude Paradin and Jean, Baron de la Hay, and in others, you [shall] very often meet with Geoffrey   45
Plantagenet, Arthur Plantagenet, [Rich]ard Plantagenet, and divers the like, all of the first age, and when the [Angev]in princes first became English, and some before.

    And Mr [Cam]den, a very learned and judicious writer, maketh mention of some [ancient Plantagenets, as of Rich]ard Plantagenet, and of John   50

[Strabo, **Lib.** 16]

[Du Haillan]

11

[The surname of Plantagenet very ancient and contin-uate.]

Plantagenet, and of others more in his [immor]tal **Britannia.** And many
more such authorities and such [exam]ples might be brought for the ancient
use of the surname [P]lantagenet, but it were in vain and needless *to do this,*
for the case is so clear, and not called in question by any. *So much for the*
5 bearing and use of the surname Plantagenet. And *nevertheless, we* may not
leave the name of Plantagenet, *and of wh*ich *I sha*ll have other occasions to
speak in the [next book, where] also I will by the way show, and by good
authority, [that the surname] of Plantagenet was continually borne by all
the [lawful sons, nephews, and] legitimate posters and progeny of the
10 foresaid [king, and the second Henry,] surnamed Plantagenet and
FitzEmpre[ss, and that none else] might bear that surname.

Enough has been said for the genealogy and *lineage* of *Plantagenet.* And   11v
whereunto might be added that [those earls of Anjou were] descended out
of the great house of Saxon [in Germany, which h]ath brought forth many
15 kings and emperors [and dukes, and that they] were of kindred and alliance
to the ancient [kings of France] and to sundry other princes. [There nee]d no
more to be said here therein, but to conclude for the great and high
no[bilit]y of King Richard, as the good old poet did for another noble and   [Ovid]
heroical person, **viz:**
20   *Deus est in utroque parente.   [*Deus, id est Rex.]

And now to proceed with other matters of the king's private story, and
the first as concerning his birth and native place. He was born in the Castle   [The place and time
of Fotheringhay, or, as some write, in the Castle of Berkhamsted, both   of the birth of King
castles and honours of the duke his father, *and* about the year of our Lord   Richard.]
25 1450. And the which I discover by the cal[culation] of the birth and reign
and death of the King Edward his brother. For Edward was born about the
year of our Lord 1441 or 1442, [and he] reigned twenty-two years, and he
died at the age of forty-one years, [**Anno**] **Domini** 1483. And the Duchess of
York, his mother, had five [children] betwixt King Edward and King
30 Richard his brother, so that R[ichard] could not be less than seven or eight
years younger than King Edw[ard]. And he survived him not fully three
years.

And this Richard Plantagenet and the other children of Richa[rd, Duke]
of York were brought up for the most part in the Castle of Middleham in
35 Yorkshire, until [the duke their fathe]r, together with his son Edmund
Plantagenet, E[arl of Rutland,] were slain in the Battle of Wakefield, **Anno**
D[omini, 1461. And then th]e Duchess of York, their mother, much fearing
that [her two] sons could not be safe in any part of England, [by reason th]e
faction of Lancaster, after the slau[ghte]r of the Duk[e of York, was gr]own
40 very insolent and also very strong and evil, and di[d] bear [a mortal hatred
t]o the House of York, she secretly and sudden[ly conveyed her two son]s,
the Lord George Plantagenet and [the Lord Richard Plantagenet, and out
o]f this land, and sent them / [by shipping into the Low Countries, to their   **Egerton 16v-18v**
aunt, the Lady Margaret, Duchess of Burgundy, wife of Charles, Duke of
45 Burgundy and Brabant, and Earl of Flanders, etc., where they were very
kindly and honourably received and were brought to Utrecht, the chief city
then in Holland, where they had liberal and princely education, the young
Lord Richard being about the age of ten years at his going into Holland.
And there they continued until Edward, Earl of March, their eldest brother,
50 had revenged the death and slaughter of his father and had put down King

Henry VI and got possession of his kingdom and crown, as it was his right.

[Then he recalls his two brothers, and being desirous to make them soldiers, caused them to be entered into the practice of arms, and was not long ere he made them knights, of which honour their towardliness and aptness to military affairs made them worthy, time making them very valiant and expert captains, especially the Lord Richard, who in his riper years was reputed one of the best captains and greatest soldiers of his time. Soon after the king had made these two young princes knights, being desirous still to demonstrate his affection towards them, he gave to them the most honourable titles and estates of dukes and earls, investing the Lord George into the duchy of Clarence and the earldom of Richmond, and the rather conferred that title and earldom of Richmond upon him because he was in great mislike of the young Earl of Richmond, Henry Tudor. The Lord Richard, his brother, had the dukedom of Gloucester and earldom of Carlisle, as I have read in an old manuscript story, but the heralds do not acknowledge this creation.

[The king was also very careful in their advancement other ways, as well as giving lands and signories unto them, as in procuring most noble and rich marriages for them. For after the great Earl of Warwick and Salisbury, Richard de Neville, was reconciled to the king's favour, these two brothers obtained, by the king's means, to marry the two daughters and heirs of this Earl of Warwick. George, Duke of Clarence, married the Lady Isabel (or Elizabeth), the elder daughter, and Richard, Duke of Gloucester, married the Lady Anne; which ladies, by their most noble mother, the Lady Anne de Beauchamp, daughter and heir of Sir Richard de Beauchamp, Earl of Warwick, were also heirs of that earldom.

[But Anne, the wife of Richard, although she were the younger sister, was the better woman, having been a little before married to Edward Plantagenet, Prince of Wales and Duke of Cornwall, only son to King Henry VI, and was now his princess and dowager. The Duke Richard loved her dearly and had by her a son called Edward, who after, when his father was king, was created Prince of Wales, as it shall appear in another place.

[And here I may insert the great difference between the disposition of these two dukes, George and Richard, the Duke of Clarence being of a sullen and mutinous disposition, very apt to quarrels, nor would forbear to offend the king his brother, raising slanders of him and of the good duchess his mother, becoming an utter foe and professed enemy to the king,]/and confederated and joined with the disloyal and rebellious adversaries of the king. And he took arms against the king and fought a battle against him, and he practised with the French king to break league with the king his brother and to send forces against [England,] and he obtained his *effect* with these French forces and with those of other rebels. He assaulted the king and fought a battle with him and overthrew him, and made him fly into Flanders, *and of which I* shall say hereafter and in a more convenient place.

But the Duke of Gloucester was of a more kind and gentle nature, and very loving and obsequious to the king his brother, ever conformable in all *humble* and dutiful manner to the will and pleasure of the king. And he ever followed him with all fidelity and love in all his fortunes, adverse and prosperous, and never departed from him but when the king employed him

[The crimes of the Duke of Clarence]
12

Richard, Duke of [Gloucester,] his [love and constancy to his brother.]

5

10

15

20

25

30

35

40

45

50

[in] some honourable and weighty affairs, civil or military, *so* much as that
when all the king's friends forsook him, the duke was still as [his] most
faithful and perpetual Achates, and willingly partaked [of a]ll the calamities
and troubles of the king his brother, so [truly] and so equally and so nobly
5 his love and his fidelity and his [cour]age and magnanimity were tempered
together.

And as he accompanied the king in all his troubles, quarrels, conflicts,
and *batt*les, so he was most forward and most adventurous *in the* bloody
and perilous congresses and encounters *of war*. And witness hereof are the
10 many battles wherein he fought with and for h[is brother:] in that battle and
victory *which the* king had at Barnet, where the duke entered so far and so
boldly into the enemy's army that two of his esquires, [Tho]mas Parr and
John Millwater, being nearest unto this *duke*, were slain instantly; but the
duke by his great courage [and val]our and skill not only saved himself, but
15 also put the most part of the enemies to flight and the [rest to the sword.]
And so likewise he behaved himself at [the bat]tles of Hexham and of
Doncaster, and at St Albans and at Blore Heath and at Mortimer's Cross
[and at Te]wkesbury, and still thought that he could never essay or attempt
to *encounter* perils enough to succour and defend his brother and to
20 advance his cause and his fortunes. [And when he] was employed in any
expedition sent forth by [the king,] *who commanded* above in chief, he so
behaved himself and showed his [skill and courage that he still returned with
good success] and with honour and with victory.

And in this manner and in this kind, this duke did many good services to
25 the king and to the commonwealth, and especially in the expedition into
Scotland, whereof I will write more particularly by and by. And he also in
this did very good service, taking of the seditious rebel, the famous and
mischievous pirate Thomas Neville, alias Fauconberg, the base son of Sir
William de Neville, Lord Fauconberg and Earl of Kent. And who, being
30 well entertained and much caressed by Sir Richard de Neville, Earl of
Warwick, and the near kinsman of the Earl of Kent, his natural father, he
w*ould undertake* any adventure, how difficult soever, for that proud earl
and for his friends. And Warwick esteemed him the *more* because he was a
skilful and valiant soldier either by land or sea, and where*of King Edward*
35 had had good trial. For he had by his prowess and valour done good service
not long before to King Edward and the House of York, and from where he
was nor basely nor *dishonourably descended*.

But being become a Lancastrian, he followed the part of King Henry VI
and rebelled against King Edward and bore arms against him. And King
40 Henry VI, by the counsel of Warwick, who feared much the forces and help
which King Edward might have from his friends beyond the seas, and also
being desirous to rob and to spoil the subjects and [parties] of the king
passing along or through the narrow seas, and to take or to destroy their
ships, made th[is Fauconberg] admiral, or chief captain, of a warlike fleet.
45 And *this* Admiral Fauconberg did not fail the hopes of the k*ing* and his new
friends in this service, in this employment, but robbed and spoiled and took
and sunk as well the ships of the king as of his [friends and subjects,] and
put very many of the men to the sword.

Edw[ard] had no means then to subdue or to suppress him at [sea,]
50 whereupon the Duke of Gloucester found out another way to meet with him

12v

The Bastard of
Fauconberg.

and [to prevent] his mischiefs, rapines, and slaughters. And that was by the
means of *an a*dvice and strategem which he had to catch Fauconberg
suddenly and unawares. And he had advertisement that the Captain
Fauconberg came sometimes ashore and lurked in some of the ports of the
south, and where he had good friends. And the king, understanding hereof,   5
committed *the taking* him to his brother Gloucester. The duke went *in*[to
Ha]mpshire, and there he understood that Fauconberg would ere long
[privily visit;] and he lay in wait for his landing. And ere long he came
ashore to Southampto[n,] and there Gloucester suddenly surprised and
apprehended *him* and brought him to London, and from there he was   10
c[onveyed to] Middleham Castle. And after that he had told some ta[les,
and being] well sifted and sounded, he was put to death and *executed.*

[But for the most part the employment] of th[is Duke of Gloucester was

13   in the north parts, where] / he much lived and did good service according to
his charge and duty. For he was Lord Warden of all the marches, eastern,   15
middle, and western, and earl and governor, or captain (as they then said)
of Carlisle. And he liked well to live in those parts of the north for sundry
good causes. For besides that Yorkshire was his native country; and that is
clear to every man, and most esteemed, for the birth in any place breedeth
especial love and affection to the place, and that by a natural instinct, as the   20
poet said well:

[Ovid]   **Natale solum dulcedine cunctos mulcet.**

And for that they were the native country both of the duke his father and of
the duchess his mother, and by whom he had most noble alliance and very
many great friends, and mu*ch* love in those parts. And certainly he was   25
generally well beloved and honoured of all the northern people, his
countrymen, not [o]nly for his greatness and alliance, but also (and chiefly)
because he was [a] valiant, a wise, and a bountiful and liberal prince, and a
good and a magni[fic]ent housekeeper, and the which bringeth not the least
love of the people, but rather the most and greatest good will, for they and   30
all men love and admire liberality and good [hosp]itality. And thirdly, he
liked best to live in these parts *because* his appanage and patrimony was
there chiefly and he had [besid]es goodly possessions and lordships by the
hereditary right of [the du]chess his wife in the north parts.

[G. Camden in   And amongst them he had the signory of [Penri]th (**vulgo** 'Perith'), a   35
Cumberland]   chief port in Cumberland, and where he either built or very much [repa]ired
[D. William   the castle, and there he much resided; and much also at the city [of C]arlisle,
Howard]   and where he was made **Comes** by his brother, as [I sa]id before. But
Co[mes: id est]   whether he were **Comes** after the [anc]ient Roman understanding — that is,
Praes[es.]   the governor — or **Comes** [or c]ount after the common taking it by us   40
Englishmen and other nations now — and that is for [a special titular lord —
I] will not take upon me to determine. But I boldly affirm *that* I have
[Liber MS. in quarto   read he was **Comes Carliolensis.** And lastly, he had the *love of* these
apud D. Rob.   countries because the noblemen, and of the greatest, much honoured
Cotton]   and loved him. And especially the Earl of Northumberland professed much   45
love [unto him.]

And for these many good causes, he was so much in *the* good liking of the
north countries as that he desired *only* to finish his days there and in the
condition of a subject and of a servant to the king. And his ambition and
other worldly *aims extende*d no further. And he governed those countries   50

very [wisely and justly, both] in time of peace and of war, and preserved
[concord and amity between the] Scots and English so much as he could.
[But the breaches between them could not so strongly be made up to
continue long.] / And especially the borderers, whose best means of living

5   grew out of mutual spoils and common rapines, and for the which cause
they were ever very apt to enter into brawls and feuds. And whilst the
Duke of Gloucester lay in these northern parts, and in the last year of the
reign of the king his brother, the quarr[els] and the feuds and despoils were
much more outrageous and more extreme than before. And thereby there

10   grew so great unkindness, and so great enmity, and such hostile hatred
between the kings of England and of Scotland, and so irreconcileably as
that nothing but the sword and open war could compose or determine and
extinguish them. And the cause hereof [was] the unjust detaining of the
tribute which King James was bound yearly to pay, as Polydore [thus

15   writeth.]
And [King Edward] IV took it very ill at the hands of James IV, King of
Scotland, that he [refuse]d to pay the tribute whereunto he was bound by
covenants. And therefore he resolved by arms to [com]pel him to perform
and pay it yearly. But King Edward being di[strac]ted with the care of his

20   watching of the practices of France, neglect[ed that] business of Scotland.
And in the meantime, Alexander, Duke of Albany [and brother] to King
James, pretending to go upon some earnest business into Franc[e, passi]ng
through England as his nearest way, he came to King Edward and s[olicited
him] to take arms for the wrong which the king his b[rother] *did* him. And

25   he promised to return soon out of France and to raise a pow[er in Sco]tland
for his aid.
And hereupon King Edward sent his best brother, the Duk[e of
Gloucester, with] a good army into Scotland. And he marched master of the
[field, even near to] Berwick, having a little before sent thither Sir Thomas

30   Stanley to besiege it. And the duke came and soon took [it.] But the Duke of
Albany fail[ed him,] for he secretly made a peace with the king his brother.
But yet Richar[d of Gloucester] accomplished the business of the Scottish
expedition very honourably and happily. Thus [Polydore.]
But to proceed in the narration of that story which I instituted, to enlarge

35   that which Polydore abridgeth and reporteth defective[ly:] King Edward,
notwithstanding his negligence, noted before by Polydore, *caused* good and
great forces to be levied. And the King of Scotland was as diligent there in
that business. And King Edward, as was said before, made his brother
Richard Captain General of all the English forces. And under him the chief

40   commanders were sundry noble person*s*, as namely S[ir Henry] / Percy, Earl
of Northumberland, and the Lord Stanley (after [Earl] of Derby), and the
Lord Lovell, and the Lord of Graystock, and [the Lord] Scroop of Bolton,
and the Lord Fitzhugh, and Sir W[illiam] Parr, a [noble] and a valiant
knight, and father of [the] Lord Parr of Ross, Kendal, and Fitzhugh, and

45   grandfather to Sir William Parr, Earl of Essex and Marquis of
No[rthampton.] There was also in the army Sir Edward Wood[ville,] Lord
Rivers and brother to Queen Elizabeth, with many other signal and noble
and worthy men, and too long to rec[ord.]
And the duke marched with this army to the borders and to the frontier,

50   *and met* with those which encountered or resisted, overthrew them, and then

13v

14

[An army sent into
Scotland under the
Duke of Gloucester.]

— Polydore

[**Anno** 24 Edward IV]

14v

13v

he went [to the] strong town of Berwick, which was then possesse[d] by the
King of Scotland, and by the folly and base surrend[er of] King Henry VI.
And he, having beaten and slew or else chased those tr[oops of the] enemies
which he met and found about the town, he *came to* Berwick and battered
it, and he summoned the tow*n and* the defenders thereof to yield. And   5
[after a short siege, the besieged, upon summons and parley, finding

15

themselves not able to resist so strong a power,] / were easily persuaded to
be at quiet and in safety upon very ordinary poor conditions, to render the
town and the castle of Berwick and themselves into the duke's hands.

Chronicle Croyland   And thus he got and recovered Berwick, as it is recorded in the Chronicle   10
of Croyland. And this was held a very honourable and very acceptable
achievement by the king and by all the English nation. And after the duke
had placed a captain and officers and soldiers in that town, forthwith
he marched towards Edinburgh, the chief city of Scotland, and with
a purpose to besiege and to take, and also to sack it. But before he was past   15
the half way toward that city, there were certain signal persons sent as
ambassadors to the duke, and they craved and they obtai*ned* audience, and
it was [granted] them. And they told him that the city *of* Edinburgh, and
that furthermore the king and the whole nation of Scotland,desired the love
and friendship of the duke and of the [King] of England, and to have league   20
and peace made, or at the [least a tru]ce made [bet]wixt both the kingdoms.
And they offered so fair conditions for [it] that the general favourably
hearkened unto them, and after [some] ripe deliberation and consultation
he granted [to] suspend or to cease or intermit his hostile proceeding. And
he [gave] good and courteous entertainment and audience to these   25
ambassadors, and then instantly he commanded and gave order [by] public
edict proclaimed throughout all the army that no [Eng]lishman should offer
any violence to any Scot, *nor* to make any spoil of them nor of their goods,
nor to do the least offence or hurt unto them. And thus the great [mischief]s
of war and bloodshed (which then seemed terribly and heavily [to   30
impend)] were stayed and prevented, and there was a truce taken, [which
truce] was the preface of that famous league [after]ward made and
concluded by this duke (and that was after [he was king) and James IV,]
King of Scotland.

15v   There were other martial accidents and exploits and military actions   35
which were put in practice and acted in this expedition made by the Duke of
Gloucester into Scotland. But I will willingly omit them, as well because they
were not needful in this work, as also because they are written copiously and
largely by Polydore Vergil, Ralph Holinshed, Edward Hall, John Stow,
Richard Grafton, and other public and vulgar historians and chroniclers,   40
and all that which I desire therein (and *be*cause it maketh best for my
purpose) is that *the* indifferent and judicious Reader will take knowledge

16   of those said writers of the affairs and actions of this duke in the north
parts ten*ding* to his praise and honour wholly and entirely. And it is so
certain as that it may not be denied that this wise and valorous prince had   45

15v   still good success and good fortune in the execution of his designs/and
services of the king his brother, and with love and true affection undertook
such designs, and *to* perform and act such deeds. And undoubtedly the love
and faith of this duke to the king his brother was most inviolable.
Wherefore he was very careful and *diligent* for the safety and honour of the   50

king and for his welfare and prosperity. Therefore it was an unhappy thing
for the king that the duke was absent so long, and especially when he fell
sick. For he would have pried so narrowly and cunningly into all the
practices and treacher*ous* machinations against the king as that he might
5   have discovered and prevented the practices thereof and so have saved the
king's life, the which (as som*e* authors write) was shortened by violent
treachery, which shall be discuss*ed* more at large in another place.

[The doubtful death
of King Edward IV:
vide **Lib.** 4]

But so unhappily it fell out that when the king died, the Duke of
Gloucester was in [Scotland,] and the news thereof came very speedi[ly
10   unto] him (for, as the proverb is, ill news flyeth apace upon the wings of
fame). The barons and [nobles] who were at London and in the south parts
seconded that fame, and they sent secret letters in [post] unto him, wherein
they advertised him that the king his brother [had] committed the guard and
tuition of his sons, Prince Edward and his brother Richard, Duke of York,
15   to him and had ordained him to be the Lord [Protector] of them and of the
kingdom: **Rex Edwardus IV filios suos Ricardo duci Gloucestriae
[in tutelam] moriens tradidit,** as Polydore testifieth, and those lords also
that they approved the [king's election.]

[The Duke of
Gloucester made
Lord Protector]

Hereupon the d[uke] *became* the more careful of the good and safe estate
20   of the young prince and of the kingdom, and made the more hasty return to
London. For he stayed no*t, but* [dispo]sed of the army and set in good order
the affairs [of these parts, and came to York, where, for some good respects
of honour] / and of piety, he made a stay for some few days. And in that
time he performed certain charitable and religious offices to [his] brother
25   deceased, and with such honourable and sacred ceremonies proper to
princes as the place and the shortness of time would afford. And this being
done, he hastened to London, and he was very nobly attended. For besides
his own and ordinary train and followers, he was guarded or accompanied
all the way to *London* with six hundred voluntary gentlemen of the north
30   parts, and who were brave horsemen of Yorkshire, and of *good apparel* and
gallantly mounted, as he passed in his train. So great their love and devotion
were unto this duke.

17

And upon the way he dispatched *cer*tain signal and trusty gentlemen
toward the prince *or* young king, who was then at Ludlow Castle in Wales.
35   [And the] duke very carefully provided for his more safe conveyance and
for his more honourable *repute on coming* into London. And the Lord
Protector was not long there arrived *when* also the prince came thither. And
he was with all honour and state [receiv]ed at London, and conducted to the
Bishop's Palace, *where* he was lodged and entertained some days very
40   magnificently *in a* manner as *was* fit and due to such a prince.

[Prince Edward
cometh to London]

And being there, he desired to see [his br]other, the young Duke of York,
and to have his company, *and he* sent for him. But the queen his mother,
being then in the [Palac]e of Westminster, kept him with her, and would not
[let hi]m depart from her. And because she would be the more [assure]d of
45   him, she took sanctuary in the Abbey and carried [the y]oung duke her son
with her. And then the Protector sent to her to pray and to require her to
send or bring the young duke to the [king] his brother. But they could not
prevail. And then the Lord [Protec]tor, by the advice of the Duke of
Buckingham and of the [other gr]eat lords, made choice of Cardinal
50   Bourchier, [Archbishop] of Canterbury, for their messenger, as a man of

more authority by reason of his call[ing.] And they sent him to the queen and willed *him to entre*at and to persuade her by all means to send the Duke of York to the *king at Lon*don. And with much mediation and very earnest persuasions, at length *he made her* consent to deliver her son to him, and he [brought him to the king] his brother in London.　　　　　5

[But the king could not make any longer] abode in the Bishop's House, [and ancient manner and custom being that the prince] / who was next to succeed the deceased king and to possess and to enjoy *the* crown should go to the Tower of London, being n*ot only* the chief house of the king, but also the castle of the greatest strength and of the most safety i[n this] kingdom.　　10 And he was to keep his court there until such time as the more weighty affairs of the kingdom were well ordered and settled and the troubles and seditions, if any happened (and the which often happen at the alteration of reigns and at the death of princes) were composed and appeased. And of which kind of evils some were discovered and reformed before the Protector　15 came to London, and as you shall understand more particularly anon. And moreover, this new king was also to stay in the Tower until all things of royal ap[parel] and of pomp, and necessary and proper to his consecration and co[ro]nation were duly prepared.

And here the Protector attended the king his nephew very dutifully and　20 carefully and very reverently, and he wa*s not* only very kind and loving unto him, but also most obseq*uious* and serviceable, as to his master and to his liege lord and sovereign. And he mos*t humbly* did homage unto him. And this is testified by the good and honoura[ble] Philip de Commynes, and in these words:**Le duc de Gloucestre avait fait hommage à son neveu comme à**　25 **son roi et souverain seigneur.** But the testimony of that and other obsequious duties will be of mor[e credit] being made by one who loved not the Protector, but much hated him.

When the young king approached near to London, the Lord [Protector] his uncle rode barehead, and in passing before the king said [in a] loud　30 voice to all the people which stood to see and to [welcome] their new king, 'Behold your prince and sovereign lord'. [And] in brief, there was no humble nor dutiful office, w*hether* of the lowest and meanest kind, and due from any se[rvant] or vassal, which he did not readily yield and perform to this [young king. And] all is affirmed and confirmed by a man of good　35 cr[edit, and] a religious man, and one who lived in those times, and n[amely] the Prior of the Abbey of Croyland. And thus he write[th]: **Ricardus Protector nihil reverentiae quod capitis n[udato, genu] flexio, aliusve quilibet corporis habitus in subdito [exigit regi] nepoti suo facere distulit aut recusavit.**　40

[And as I believe these relations so I also believe the duke performed those humble and officious services faithfully and sincerely. Whereof he gave good] / testimony hereof soon afterward, and that was when he was very earnestly and importunately solicited and prayed to take the crown upon him: whereunto his answer was (and with solemn protestation) that he　45 much rather desired to serve his nephew as his humble vassal, holding it to be much more safe and more happy to be a subject and in good favour with the king than to be a king. So true and clear he was from aspiring to sovereignty and from ambitious thoughts.

And it is also manifest that the duke was drawn by earnest persuasions　50

17v

[The b]usiness [of the Lord Protec]tor *for* [the king his neph]ew

[Philip de Commynes in **Lodovicus** xi]

[Sir Thomas More]

[Chronicl. Abbatiae Croyland]

18
The Lord Protect[or] prayed to be [King]

and, as it were, enfor[ced] by continual importunities to hearken to their
motion [and] to raise his thoughts so high as to a crown. And when the
barons saw that their requests would not serve, they used threats [and]
menaces of imminent evils, and which should soon fall upon him. And the
5 reasons for these their importunate persuasions to have him to be king were
these, as they intimated. And first in respect that they utterly misliked that
the son of King Edward should reign [o]ver them, and not only because he
was too young to govern his kingdom, but also, and chiefly, because they
held him and the rest of [t]he children of King Edward to be illegitimate,
10 and not born [i]n lawful matrimony, and therefore not capable of the
crown.
    [But] on the contrary side they esteemed the duke to be not [o]nly the true
and next heir of the crown, and his title to be pure [and] right and without
crack or flaw; but also they knew hi[m] by long and tried experience to be a
15 wise, a just, a bountiful, a valorous, and a religious prince, and in regard
there[fore, they held him] to be the most worthy to wear the crown. [And they
did not only] desire most earnestly and required importunately that he would
be their king, [but they] seem[ed in an imperious manner to call] him to the
crown. But still the Protector withstood and refused their election of him to be
20 king. And he stood a long time upon those wilful and ingrate and distasteful
terms, but yet then he rendered many good reasons in excuse of his refusal —
of his obstinacy, as the barons censured it. And here I give but a taste of these
aff*airs; but pa*ssages of them shall be related and discoursed at large anon.
    And in the mea[ntime i]t must be understood that the Protector during
25 these his *continual* refusals of the crown, and, as it were, in the interreign,
omitted not any business of the state nor any service to the [young king] *to*
be done, and he was very careful, and doubtless, / as I said before, he was
very dutiful and obsequious to the young prince, and very careful and
studious of his safety and welfare. And I think verily that he was so far
30 from seeking to hurt him as no man could justly and directly charge him
that he gave any offence to the p*rince* or practised or attempted any ill
against him. And the reason thereof was because his love was so kind and
constant to the king their father as that he could not nor would *not* entertain
or nourish any evil and treacherous thought against this prince his son. But
35 contrariwise, he was an utter enemy to all such practices and to all such men
as were suspected to be guilty of them or were apt to sedition and tumults,
or might be dangerous members of the commonwealth and pernicious or
mischievous to him or to his estate.
    And in due consideration of the premises, he began betimes to remove
40 some dangerous stumbling-blocks out of the prince's way. And he
dispatched and made short work with these men whom he vehemently
suspected to be over-ambitious, and m[en] insolent, and who arrogated and
usurped such high authority and great power as was not proper unto them.
And therefore he made clean riddance of such persons as were not *only*
45 ill-affected to the prince or to the government, but also to the governors,
and of whom he was the chief. And therefore he had the more reason to fe*ar*
*those that h*ated him and were turbulent and seditious persons, and who
extremely ther*efore* envied and maligned and hated him for his very high
authority and greatness, but also, and most *of* all, for his justice.
50   And long before, in the time of King Edward, th[ere was] great mislike

18v

and enmity between those of the Duke of Gloucester's blood, [whose party]
the most ancient and most noble barons of the kingdom favoured and
defended, and between those of the queen's kindred for the many wrongs
and outrages done to the nobles and gentlemen of England. And this was so
notorious as that all the people murmured and mut[inied] against them. For 5
besides the pride and insolency of these Reginists, they were so malicious
and so evilly affected to the princes of the blood and to the great and chief
noblemen, as th*at* they, by false tales and slanders, many times incensed the
king against them and alienated his love and favour from them and
provoked his displeasure and wr*ath*. And these were chief[ly] the Grays and 10
the Woodvilles and their kinsmen and partisans, and they made full
accompt to have greater power and greater au*thority* with the young king
their kins[man than] they had before. And then there was no doubt but that
[they would have acted more and higher rhodomontados and injuries] than
before, and would *have* [removed the princes of the blood and at their 15
pleasures swayed and ruled all things during the minority of the king; after,
too, so long as the Queen Mother could usurp the sovereignty.] Wherefore
the Duke of Buckingham and some other of the more ancient nobility,
consulting of these dangers and mischiefs hanging over their heads and
threatening dangers and evils to the state, resolved to give timely remedy 20
unto them.

And Sir Thomas More acknowledgeth all this to be true, and he confesseth
that the nobles of the kingdom had reason to suspect, and also to fear, that
the kinsfolks of the queen would bear more sway and do more mischief
when their young kinsman was king than before, in the king his father's 25
time, although their insolencies and outrages were then intolerable. And
further, the author acknowledgeth that there had been a long time a grudge
and an heartburning between the queen's kindred and the king's blood in
the time of King Edward, and the which the king, although he were partial
of the queen's side, yet he endeavoured to compose that hatred which was 30
between them, and yet he did what he could by all means to reconcil*e them,
but he* could not effect it.

And Master More further telleth that after that king was dead, the Lord
Gray, Marquess of Dorset, and the Lord Richard Gray, and the Lord Rivers
made full accompt to rule the young king and to usurp the government of 35
the kingdom. They had learned that it was best fishing [i]n a troubled sea.
They therefore, the better to accomplish their plots and designs, practised to
set variance and debate amongst the great men of the kingdom, and that
then whilst th*at* they were occupied in their own quarrels and particular
revenges, these cunning and ambi[tious] politicians *by the* [opportun]ity 40
thereof might assault the noble barons, whom they hated, and supplant and
destroy the ancient noble blood of the realm.

Moreover, Sir Thomas More intimateth that those proud and *haughty
kindred of the* queen, for the better effecting their designs, had made
warlike preparations and were purposed to use means of for[ce] to bring the 45
plot to effect and to maintain it by force and by arms and bloodshed; and
for the better provision of such warlike instruments, the marquess had
secretly taken great quantity of the king's treasure [o]ut of the Tower; and
also that the Woodvilles had provided [goo]d store of armour, and whereof
some part was soon after [ta]ken upon the way, as it was carried close 50

[The insolency of the
queen's kindred]

19

Sir Thomas More in
[Edwa]rd V [et]
Richard III.

packed [up] in carts.

It was therefore high time for the Protector [and] the ancient nobility to look well to themselves, and to neglect *no* [o]ccasions to prevent the mischief of these treacheries. And in their consultation they found that
5 there was *no way* to prevent and avoid these evils but by taking away the lives of those noblemen. *It was* therefore resolved that the Marquess Dorset and the Lord Richard [Gray, and their uncle] Sir Anthony Woodville, Lord Rivers, and some [other of the queen's kindred and faction] should be suddenly a[pprehended and safely guarded until their heads paid the forfeit
10 of their seditions.] *And justice* / was executed upon them all except the   **19v** Marquess Dorset, who, as it was *thought,* was by a friend of his *who was* present at the Council secretly advertised of their plot. And hereupon he presently fled to sanctuary and so was saved. But the rest were taken and sent to Pomfret and there put to death.
15   And at the same time the Lord Hastings, one who much honoured and   [Lord Hastings] favoured and loved the queen and her kinsfolks, and especially the marquess, and he was therefore the more suspected to be dangerous, and for that cause he was arrested of High Treason in the Tower, and instantly his head was chopped off upon a block in the Green yard. And this may
20 seem a more strange and a barbarous and a tyrannous act than the other, he being supposed to be a good subject, and also generally thought to love and to honour the Protector and the Duke of Buckingham. And Sir Thomas   Sir Thomas Mor‹ More affirmeth also that the Protector undoubtedly loved the Lord Hastings very well and was loath to have lost him, had it not been that they
25 feared that he might take part with [their] enemie[s and so] his life might dash and quench their purpose. Thus Sir Thomas More. And this was a dilemma. But he telleth n[ot] disertly what that particular purpose was, and what they had in hand at that instant again[st the Protec]tor and against his friends. But by other places of his story and of his followers' it may be they
30 well understood [that they suspected ve]hemently the Protector's affection of the sovereignty and the practice of the making away of the young prince and of his brother. For these be the crimes which Sir Thomas More and the rest of the calumniators continually objected against the Prote[ctor.]

But let us admit it to be so, and we will also acknowledge that the Pro-
35 tector [was] now grown very suspicious and jealous of the Lord Hastings. And it is true that for tha[t cause] he sent Sir William Catesby, [a man] in gre[at] favour and credit with Hastings, to sound him and to learn what conceit or opinio[n he held] of the title and claim which the Protector might have to the crown and to be *king. And he perfor*med this task.And the Lord
40 Hastings, presuming of Catesby's secrecy and aff*y*ing in his love and in his fidel[ity] (*for* Catesby had been advanced by him), told Catesby without any colours or circumstances, and also plainly, and eve[n with some] indignation, that he utterly misliked the plot and the title, and that he would resist it and withstand it by all the means and power which he had.
45 And he [added peremp]torily that he had rather see the death and destructions both of the [Protector] and of Buckingham than to see or to suffer the young king *to be* deprived of the crown and of the sovereignty of the kingdom by *them.*

[Now] Catesby, forgetting the dutiful respects which he owed to the Lord
50 Hastings, and the [regard of his safety,] made report of this answer to the

Protector, who was much troubled and perplexed therewith, as well bec*ause* he loved the Lord Hastings, and for good *reason that he* [knew no man could stand him in more stead than he, could his faith and love be assured. But being his adversary, and opposing] / his power and his authority and his council and his friends and his forces, he knew or vehemently suspected 5 that Hastings was able not only to resist him, but also to oppress and to suppress him and Buckingham and all their confederates. And hereupon these two dukes resolved to dispatch Hastings out of the way, and he was presently arrested and beheaded, as is aforesaid. And this is the greatest bloody crime of King Richard, and whereof there may weak proof be made. 10 And yet proofs be not so clear but that there may be packing and juggling and frauds in them.

But admit that this bloody deed was the practice and plot of the Protector, yet in reason of state and of policy, and by the rules of those arts which are called **Artes Imperii**, this also may be excused, and it may also 15 *be* authorized or countenanced by many great examples. For it hath been usual for many ages, and even since the Ogygian times, for these men which affect and seek reign and sovereignty never to strain courtesy at the doing of a*nything, or to* forbear to take the life of any man who standeth in their way or is against them and their attempts, insomuch as the father 20 cannot be a servant of his son, nor one brother of another, and whereof there be too many examples, and even in our own stories. And this is an old observation, and general in all foreign countries:

Regnum furto
Et fraude adeptum antiquum est specimen imperii.   25

And as King Atreus said by his own experience,

Ut nemo doceat fraudis et
Sceleris vias, regnum docebit.

This is the censure of a king. [But] when these fraudulent and bloody practices succeed well, *and* when the actors prevail, then **prosperum scelus** 30 **virtus vocatur:** the wicked act, succeeding well, is called a virtue; and the actors are held to be wise, valorous, and most renowned and happy men.

I would have the virtuous and discreet Reader to think that I write not this as approving and allowing such cruel and perfidious practices *as pertain* to sovereignties and principalities; but I abhor them. So on the other side, *I* 35 *dislike that* the prince King Richard should of all men *besides b*e condemned in such *manner* for the exercising and practice of [these Imperial Arts, and even above all other, considering others have used them with credit.

[And it is a very ancient axiom in politic philosophy that] / **Via ad potentiam est tolere aemulos et premere adversarios**. And the great master 40 of policy disalloweth not this manner of proceeding, as he intimateth, and not obscurely, in a similitude taken from a painter and a prince or an ambitious man. For he saith that a painter, when he maketh a horse, must take heed that he make not one leg longer than another, nor one buttock higher than another, and that if he happen to commit such a fault, that he must 45 make these members shorter and take them down. And that so likewise a prince must not suffer any man who approacheth near to him in authority or in titles, or rivalleth him in his ambition, to overtop him, nor to outgrow him, nor in any wise to suffer him to be higher nor greater than himself, but straight to lop him.   50

Marginal notes:

20

The Lord Hasting[s] his power

[Artes Imperii]

[Seneca, in tragedies]

[Idem Seneca]

20v
[Axiomata Politica]

Aristotle, **Politics**

And this reason made Julius Caesar to take arms against the great
Pompeius, and wherein he prevailed and was and ever shall be reputed a
wise captain and a great conqueror, although his emulation cost an infinite
quantity of excellent human blood. And in like manner his nephew Octavius
5 Augustus never ceased proscribing and banishing and massacring until he
had dispatched all his proud emules, rivals of sovereignty, and all his
danger*ous* adversaries out of the *way*.

And our King Henry I and Edward III and Henry IV and Edward IV and
Henry VII took the like courses and used the same arts of empire, as all the
10 world knoweth. And yet these fa[ults] ar[e forgiven them, and they are]
reputed and renowned for good and wise and virtuous princes. And only
Richard, who is an innocent in comparison of some of them, is cried down
and utterly condemned for cruel practices of taking away his rivals in
authority and in empire, and such as *threatened him,* and al*though* there
15 were never yet any lawful proofs made that he *committed those* crimes
whereof he is accused. Yet he of all men hath been in those matters so
injuriously and so slanderously dealt with, and that in so grossly false a
manner as that he *hath not only* been suspected, but also charged and
directly accused of the slaughter of his two nephews and of *others,* albeit
20 some of them *were* living many years after that King Richard was dead and
buried, which will be hereafter, and in the third book and elsewhere,
declared.

But suppose that he took away some of his most da*ngerous* adversaries,
and such of the nobles as are before named. *Notwith*/standing, he may be
25 taxed of gross error and also condemned as a man guilty of his own
blood and ruin and much more reproved and blamed for not taking
away the other his impediments and his other emules and adversaries than
for his cutting off these lords and nobles aforesaid. For if he had dealt with
Dr Morton, Bishop of Ely, and with Peter Courtenay, Bishop of Exeter,
30 and with the Marquess of Dorset, and with the earls of Richmond, of
Pembroke, of Oxford, and of Northumberland. And likewise with some
principal gentlemen, as namely Hungerford, Bourchier, Digby, Savage, and
Talbot, Mortimer, and Rice, and [Blount, wh]o, although they were no
lords, yet were lords in their lordlike possessions and in their noble
35 alliances. To these may be added Bray, Poins, Sanford, the young Stanley,
Fortescue, and the crafty doctors Morgan, Lewis, and Urswick. And if King
Richard, I say, had dealt with his enemies and foes entered into conspiracies
against him as he did with the Grays, Woodvilles, Hastings, and
Buckingham, he had been out of danger and had preserved in safety his life
40 and his fortunes and his crown; and of all the which they afterwards
deprived and utterly bereaved him.

Therefore it is plain that his error in sparing them was in politic
consideration and in human providence a much greater crime than the
killing of the other. But I confess that he spared some of them because he
45 suspected them not, nor did he fear them, for he had no cause to suspect
Northumberland, by reason of the old acquaintance and amity and good   [Northumberland]
correspondence which was between, and had long been between, King
Richard and him. And albeit he knew that Oxford hated him in his heart   [Oxford]
and was a nobleman of such power and riches and greatness as that he was
50 to be feared, yet because he was a prisoner in the strong Castle of Hammes,

21

and very safely and strongly guarded, he was secure of that earl and did not
fear him nor his forces. But he feared and suspected Jasper, Earl of
[Pembroke]   Pembroke, and his nephew Richmond, and not without good cause, and as
was apparent to all the world afterward. But they were out of King
Richard's reach and were in safely in France.   5

And the king feared Morton, and he had greater cause and reason to fear
him than any other man, for he was not only treacherous and perfi[d]ious,
and one who much hated the king, but he was a subtle and a chief
persua[d]er of others to be seditious and treacherous; and in a word he was
of all [the m]ost practick and politic **boutefeu** in those affairs of treachery 10
and of sedition and *re*bellion. And although the king had no certain
intelligence of all his secret [workings] *and* traitorous practices, yet he knew
enough to hold him [suspected and also] to remove him from the council
table [and restrain his liberty,] and to commit him to prison. And all this the
king did, [committing him to the custody] of one whom he suspected to be 15
his close and inward friend, the Duke [of Buckingham; though he was
deceived and betrayed in trust by the duke, who was then secretly
21v   malcontent and alienated in his heart.] / And he did continually plot
treasons against the king, and as you shall see and know at large anon and
in the next book, when I come to speak of the rebellion of that duke.   20

And when Morton had made the duke almost as bad and as false and
disloyal as himself, he stole away from Brecknock Castle and went to Ely,
and there he found good means for good store of coin and safe means for his
passage into France. And whither he had a great desire and vehement
longing to go, and to the end that he might fashion and confirm an   25
ambitious and seditious wind in the Earl of Richmond, and under the
pretence and colour of a Lancastrian title in him to the crown. And for the
achieving and acquiring whereof, he persuaded and counselled and
vehemently animated him to take arms and to invade England. And for his
better encouragement, he assured the earl that he had so many and so 30
mighty friends in England as that the enterprise would be facile and of very
little danger or difficulty, and this politic prelate did with so many artificial
22   and eloquent words recommend this design and attempt to *persuade* / the
earl.

And he that being, as other ambitious men, apt to be persuaded of his 35
own virtues and powers and titles and to hope well of his own fortune, as
that he did not only hearken unto him and accept well his persuasions and
counsels, but also he soon put on a resolution to take arms and to invade
this kingdom and to put down King Richard. And this purpose was not held
in any great secrecy, but it was well known to very many as well in France as 40
in England. And the King Richard himself had certain intelligence thereof,
and also of some particular practices and plots which we[re] kept more
close. And he came to understand what friends and confederates he had,
and amongst them he found some who professed great love and fidelity to
him, as namely the Duke of Buckingham, the Countess of Richmond, and 45
others whose names shall be seen afterward.

And now, therefore, the king had good cause to have a watchful eye upon
the Earl of Richmond and upon his confederates and the conspirators
against him and his estate, and he now well considered that albeit the king
his brother su[spected] and feared the Earl of Richmond, and had sought by 50

su[ndry means to get him into his hands,] / yet that king had not so great
cause to observe and to watch the earl and to provide defences against his
designs as Richard had, because now the practice of the earl had taken deep
root and was spread very far; and by this time the earl had drawn many
5 noblemen and gentlemen of England into his conspiracy, but also he had so
cunningly in[sinu]ated himself into the good favour of some foreign princes
as that he obtained their promise and their me*ans* to aid and to assist him in
his enterprise of the conquest of England.

But during all the time of King Edward this conspiracy and practice was
10 not of any strength nor of any danger, as well because he was very strong
and rich as also be*cause* [the earl's title] of no man w[as preferred.] But yet
King Edward without that had cause enough to use means to take and to
seize upon Richmond, in respect that he and his friends had adventured to
report and give out that he was an heir of the House of Lancaster, and the
15 nearest kinsman to King Henry VI. And thereupon King Edward, and as
John Hardyng hath well observed, was in fear that the young Earl of
Richmond would claim the crown as the nephew and next heir of the blood
of King Henry VI. And the king in regard of these vaunts, albeit he knew
well that the barons and the gentlemen and the wiser sort of Englishman,
20 and also the French King Louis XI, and Francis II, Duke of Brittany, and
the other foreign princes knew and understood of how little worth the title
of Richmond was, and he could in right claim little in the crown by his
blood of Lancaster, and that on the other side they also knew that the title
of York, whereof King Edward was the head and the most true and certain
25 heir, was a title sound and fair and just and without all default or exception.

But yet this prince, being very wise and provident, conceived well that
some foreign princes ill-affected to him, and some of his own falsehearted
and seditious subjects, bearing envy or malice or both to his house and to
his blood and to his prosperous estate, would make use of any pretended or
30 defective title to trouble his [pe]ace, and to raise seditions and rebellions in
his kingdom. Wherefore, this king was desirous to have the Earl of
Richmond *safe* and to hold him fast in his own custody. And he put this his
plan in practice very early, for / when the earl was very young, [the king
committed him to safe custody. And Philippe de] Commynes saith that
35 [when he] came first [acquainted with this earl, being then a prisoner in]
Brittany, [he] told him he had been either in a prison [or under strait
guard ever since he was] five [years old. And I believe it. For I find he was]
but yo[ung] when he [was committed to the custody of Sir] William
Herbert, [Lord of Raglan Castle in Monmouthshire, where he was] not
40 long.

For [Jasper, Earl of Pembroke, uncle to Henry Richmond, being then in
France, whither he fled after the overthrow of the Lancastrians at
Tewkesbury (as John Stow), having advertisement that his nephew was a
prisoner with Sir William Herbert, with whom he had alliance and
45 friendship, came secretly out of France into Wales, to Raglan Castle, where
he] found the Lady Herbert, [her husband being with the king.] But in the
meantime, [the earl] so cunningly practised with the lady of the castle as
that he got his nephew out of that castle [and conveyed] him to his own
castle of Pembroke, the young earl's native place, presuming that he should
50 be a*ble* to keep him safe there, *because it was* a strong castle, and also

24

23v

[The flight of
Richmond with his
uncle Pembroke]

[The Earl of Rich]-
mond [born in Pem-
broke] Castle

beca*use* the people [of] that country [were much affected to] him and his [nephew.] But he overweened in this opinion and hope. For as soon as [the king was adver]tised of the [escape, he commanded Sir William Herbert to levy forces and take both the earls.]

25 This Sir William Herbert was a wise and valiant knight [of] rich and of 5 fair and large possessions, much beloved in those parts because he was of a very noble and ancient family and descended from Herbertus, who was Chamberlain and Treasurer to the kings William Rufus and Henry Beauclerk. And this Sir William was created Earl of Pembroke afterward. And from this noble Herbertus are also descended the noble Herberts, earls 10 of Pembroke and of Montgomery, and many other worthy Welsh gentlemen of that surname and family.

But to proceed with the employments of this noble knight Sir William Herbert for the surprising and apprehending of the two *a*foresaid earls of Pembroke and Richmond, and who then held the Castle of Pembroke for 15 their better safety and more security. As soon *as* those two earls had advertisement *th*at Sir William Herbert was coming, and with a good and strong *po*wer of soldiers, and was near at hand, they, distrusting their own

Th[is flight of theirs was in **anno** xi] Edward IV. [John Stow.]

strength and forces, fled *secre*tly in the night out of the castle and rode in great *post* to the port of Tenby, and there lurked and kept *the*mselves close 20 and unknown until they had gotten [fit] opportunity for their transportation and escape of this kingdom.

And they soon [got] a ship and [pu]rposed to go into France and to land at [Diep]pe, and from thence to go to the French court, [wher]e the Earl of Pembroke had been not long before, and very [well] entertained. But they 25 failed of this purpose by rea[son of a v]iolent and unhappy storm which arose in the night whilst they [were at] sea [and forced upon them] to run [another course upon the coasts of Little Britain, which fell out as a sad disaster and cross to them and their fortunes for a long time after, the Duke

26v of Brittany being not their friend.] / And how they sped, you shall hear 30 more hereafter. And of this their flight and of many other noble Englishmen which followed the unlucky and unju[st] party of King Henry VI and were fain to fly when he was overthrown by King Edward IV, there is this memorial in the histories of Brittany: **Plusieurs des seigneurs d'Angleterre qui tenaient le parti du roi Henri VI s'en fuyant par mer hors** 35 **du royaume et entre autres le comte de Penbroke fuyant sauva un jeune prince d'Angleterre nomme Henri comte de Richmont.**

And whilst these earls made some stay in St Malo to refresh themselves after their tempestuous and dangerous passage, Francis II, Duke of Brittany, was advertised in post of their landing and arrival. And he sent in 40 as great post and haste a commandment to the governor of that port to

[Earl of Richmond prisoner in Brittany]

arrest those earls and to keep them so surely as that they might not escape nor depart. And this commandment was duly executed accordingly. And because it seemed strange and also an injurious act of the duke thus to make

[The last duke of Bri]ttany [who was Earl of Ric]hmond and [possessed the earldo]m was [John de Monfort, who]

prisoners those noblemen, being the subjects of a prince with whom the 45 duke was in league and good amity, therefore to give some colour to the arrest, the duke pretended that he had good cause to detain the Earl of Richmond until he had received satisfaction of him for the wrong which he did [to] him in the usurping the title and state of Earl of Richmond and in detaining that earldom from him, which was belonging to the ancien[t] earls 50

and dukes of Brittany, his progenitors (and whereof they had been disseized
by the spac[e of thirty years)] whose heir and successor he was. And for this
cause he resolved there to detain them both as his pris*oners* until that he had
restitution of his earldom of Richmond, or composition and satisfaction for
5 it.

And for their more safe custody, he took order for conducting of these
earls to his city of Vannes, where he often resided, and he cau*sed* them to be
put into the castle and to be kept as prisoners w[ith] a good guard, and the
rather and in truth because the duke h[ad] advertisement that the young
10 Earl of Richmond was a *prince* of England, and nephew to King Henry VI,
and that he [laid claim] and title to the crown and kingdom of England [by
the blood of Lancaster, for which he, notwithstanding, made their
imprisonment more honourable, as is testified by Philip Commynes: **Le
duc**, saith he, **les traita doucement pour prisonniers.** And this their
15 imprisonment was such] / an one as Jean Froissart calleth, and fitly, **Prison
Curtois.**

And now when the duke considered and deliberated what good use he
might make of these his noble prisoners, and what benefit and profit might
arise to him by them, he conceived that this their captivity would be very
20 acceptable to the King of England, especially the holding and safe-guarding
of the younger, to wit, the Earl of Richmond, because his liberty might turn
the thing to great trouble and prove very perilous and pernicious unto him
and to his estate. And he hoped not only to have great rewards and great
sums of money of the King of England for keeping of the Earl of
25 Richmond, but also that he should be assured of his love and amity. And
which is [more,] if you will believe Jacobus Meyerus, that King Edward
should stand so much in awe of him by this means as that he would not
dare to displease nor to offend the duke: **Propter Henricum Richmontiae
comitem non audebat Anglus ab amicitia Britanni discedere.**
30   And that author was not much mistaken. For it is true that the king
would have done anything to have had Richmond delivered unto him. And
he was much troubled when he heard that these earls were fled, for he
suspected that they would go to some of his enemies, who would make such
use of the young earl as *might bring to* him danger and damage. For from
35 hence might spring an invasion, and whereby all should be in tumults and in
combustions. But when the king heard that they were in Brittany, his mind
was not only well quieted and his cares well eased, but also he was glad that
they were in the hands of his friend and ally, the Duke of Brittany, and
detained by him as prisoners. And the king had so good affiance *in* the
40 duke's love and friendship as that he presumed that he would, especially
[upo]n some good and golden conditions to boot, send them home to him *to*
England.

But if the earls had gone to any of the king's enemies, *and* especially to
the French king Lewis XI, the king must [have expe]cted any evil which the
45 French king could contrive for and in the behalf of the young earl, who
pretended title to the crown *of England, as has* been before declared. For
King Lewis, although he [were then in truce and league] with King Edward,
yet he was but in hollow ho*pe. For* he was a mere politician, and studying
only to his own ends, yet fearing King Edward, *who was very valiant* / and
50 very famous for his prowess and for his victories, and also for that withal he

flourished [**Anno
Domini** 1440] and had
sons, [but no Earl] of
Richmond, [as Rob-
ert Glov]er writeth.
[And now this] Fran-
cis II [renewed the]
claim to the *earldom
of* Richmond, and
[a]bout thirty [years
after] John de Mont-
[fort, Duke of]
Brittany.

27

[Jacob Meyerus in
**Annales Flandriae,
Lib.** 17]

King [Edward treat-
eth] for [the delivery
of the Earl of Rich-
mond]

27v

was very rich and very well stored with treasure, as also because he had
threatened to enter France with fire and sword for the recovery and
reconquest of his ancient hereditary principalities and signories: namely, the
duchies of Normandy and of Aquitaine, and counties of Poitou and of
Touraine, and other lands. And for these causes King Lewis did not only   5
fear but also hate King Edward in his heart, and so consequently wished and
desired his ruin and destruction. For as the good old Ennius said, and it is of
the credit of an oracle,

Quem metuunt oderunt;
Quem oderunt perisse expetunt.   10
Whom men do fear and dread, they hate likewise,
And wish them to fall, and never to rise.

Wherefore doubtless the French king would gladly have taken the
protection of the Earl of Richmond and his title and cause into his hands,
and he would have furnished him with money and arms to attempt the 15
conquest of England, or at the least to have so occupied the king with so
many and so dangerous seditions and rebellions as that he should not have
had leisure nor been able to invade France, nor to enterprise anything
against King Lewis or his kingdom.

And therefore the king, to prevent and to avoid the said dangers and 20
mischiefs which might happen by the practices of the French king or any
other his enemies with the Duke of Brittany for the de*livering of* the Earl of
Richmond to them, or for making him an instrument of any troubles,

dispatched with all speed a wise and discreet gentleman to the Duke of
Brittany, and sent by h*im* a rich present to the said duke. And partly by his 25
kind letters and partly *by the* speeches of his messengers, he earnestly
entreated and solicited the duke to send the two earls, of Pembroke and of
Richmond, into Eng*land* and to him. And for the which favour he made
offers of furth[er] *and* better gratifications, together with his love and the
best offices of friend[ship] that he could do to the duke.   30

The duke received [the commendation of these] letters to him, and his
present, and the recommendation of the king's love and *friendship in*
honourable thankfulness, and entert*ained* [the messenger, assuring him that
he was as ready to do the King of England any pleasure as any other

whatsoever.] / But he prayed the king to excuse him that he granted not his 35
request nor fulfilled his desire for the delivery of the earls and for the
sending them to England to his highness. Because it was a thing which he
might not do with his credit and honour saved, in regard that it was against
the law of nations and scandal to princely hospitality and to the privileges of
sovereignty. Besides that, it were a kind of discharity and impiety for him or 40
for any other prince to deliver to any man, and much less to their enemies
and persecutors, such d*istressed* persons as fled to him for succour and
craved his safeguard and protection. He was of opinion that if any wrong or
violence were offered unto them, that he should be guilty of their afflictions
and pains, and also of their blood if it were shed or if they were put to 45
death. But therefore excepting and setting aside this sending of them home,
the duke promised faithfully that he would do anything that might be most
advantageable and most agreeable and most safe to the king, and that he
would keep them so safe as that they should have no more power to hurt or
offend the king than if they were his close prisoners in the Tower of 50

London.

When this answer of the duke was returned to the king, albeit [i]t was not according to his desire nor to his expectation, yet because *he* perceived and considered in his wisdom that the answer was not *unre*asonable, but
5 agreeable with honour and with reason, he well accepted it. [And] thus this cause rested by the space of eight years, as I calculate. [F]or the king made this request and propounded this suit to the duke in the twelfth year of his reign, and **Anno Domini** 1472. And the king was careful all this while to preserve mutual love and his league with the duke, and he entertained the
10 duke's promise bountifully and *to* his great cost, for he sent to him into Brittany every year [g]ood sums of money and fair presents. And all the time the king was *o*ut of any fear of danger or hurt that might come to him by the earl.

[After,] in the twentieth year of his reign, and **Anno Domini** 1480, the
15 king having [inte]lligence of certain new and secret practices and con-spiracies, the which the Earl of Richmond and [some of his frie]nds had in the French court and in England, and that he was grown [every day] more and more ambitious, and much aspiring to the crown of England, [the] French king by the solicitations and mediations of the Earl of [Pembroke]   [Histoire de
20 and of his other noble friends practised to get [the Earl of Richmon]d into   Bretagne] his hands, and had already offered great sums of money for him to the Duke of Brittany, and had promised to aid and assist the [earl in his enterprises] of England. The king then was afresh [trouble]*d* with [this news,] and he presently resolved to [renew his old suit to the duke by the
25 best means that he could.]

The king made choice of Dr Stillington, Bishop of Bath, a very wise and   **28v** learned and eloquent man, and the king's secretary, and one who had ancient acquaintance and good credit with the Duke of Brittany, whither he   Dr Stillington sent was sent with convenient speed. And he came to the duke, who entertained   for Richmond
30 him very honourably and with all courtesy. And the bishop forthwith declared the cause of his employment by the king unto him, and that was, in brief, earnestly to pray the duke to send the Earl of Richmond into England. And the bishop did not only persuade and press this suit with good and artificial words, but also with precious presents and with golden
35 rewards, and at that instant presented the duke with a very rich and sumptuous gift from the king. And the duke liked well the present and also the promise made of more and better gifts. But he liked not the suit, but contrariwise he distasted it much, as before, and was very averse unto it. But the bishop would not leave him so, but with more eloquence and with
40 more importu*nate* persuasions and mediations, he pressed the duke.

And to make yet hi*s* suit more acceptable and plausible, he told the duke that the king his sovereign gave him in charge to tell him that in token of his *goo*d will toward him, and to make their mutual love and amity perpetual and durable, he had chosen him into the noble society of the Order of the
45 Garter. Moreover, and to captate the duke's good will, and also the earl's, he told the duke that the king was des*irous* to have the Earl of Richmond with him for the love which he b*are* unto him, as well because he was his kinsman, also for the desire which he had to advance him and to bestow one of his daughters upon the earl in marriage.
50 And to be brief of the eloquence and rhetorical flowers and the fair

presents, of the charm of gold and jewels which this orator offered and gave to the duke, so farfor*th* and at the length *he* prevailed with the duke as that he faithf[ully] promised and also firmly covenanted that he would deli[ver] the Earl of Richmond to him, and that he would see him sa[fely] conveyed to the port of St Malo, and where four good sh[ips] *of* the king waited and 5 attended upon the bishop's embassa*ge a*bout these affairs. And the bishop with his letters [sen]*t* the king this word, which came not without exceeding welcome to the king.

[And the duke forthwith cause]*d* [the earl] to be strongly guarded from the castle of] / St Malo's. And all the way as the earl passed he was very 10 heavy and sad. And that was well observed by some of the convoys, and especially by Pierre de Landois, a noble gentleman of Brittany, and treasurer to the duke, who had the chief charge of bringing the earl to St Malo's and to deliver him to the English deputies and captains who were to receive him there. And this Monsieur de Landois, being a kind and a 15 courteous and honourable gent*l*eman, had compassion of the sorrow of the earl. He would needs know the cause thereof, and promised to give remedy unto it if it lay in his power. And the earl, being thus happily and fairly provoked by M. Landois to discover the cause of his grief and sadness unto him, willingly exposed and imparted it unto him, and in this manner: 20

'Sir, it is true, and as you have observed, that I am very sad and sorrowful, and I have great cause to be so, for I am now enforced to return into England, where I shall find and feel nothing but prisons and bonds and captivity, or else the lesser and the last evil, that is, death. For although the King of England, knowing well how to dissemble, pretendeth to love me 25 and to have a purpose to do me good and to advance me (as he hath insinua*ted* to the duke your master by his ambassador), [y]et I know most assuredly that he hateth me, and so mortally and irreconcileably as that he will never receive me to favour *or* ever be satisfied with anything but with my blood and death'. 30

[And] thus this sorrowful earl, with many tears and deep sighs, discovered and reported the cause of his heaviness and pensiveness to the treasurer Landois. And he at the hearing thereof was much moved and greatly [piti]ed him. And he exhorted the earl *to put aside* his [fears] and *doubts* and to be of good comfort, and he assured him that [he woul]d find means 35 to free and deliver him from these evils and calamities which he *feared. W*ith which Monsieur de Landois made relation by writing to the duke of this [lam]entable and miserable estate of the earl, and being pressed *for time,* and because he knew that the Baron of Chandait [stood well affected to the earl, and that there had been a long and reciprocal love betwixt them,] / and 40 also that this baron was a man in great favour and credit with the duke, he went to him (having a house near to St Malo) and acquainted him with the fears of the earl, and he desired him earnestly to go to the duke and to persuade him to have compassion of the earl and to stay him, or else he was utterly lost and cast away. 45

And this noble and friendly Baron Chandait rode in post to the duke's court at Vannes and recounted to the duke the lamentable tale, and with such passion and vehemence as that he moved much the duke, and brought him to have commiseration of the miserable state of the earl. And then the duke had remorse of [his contrac]t made with the king, was very sorry that 50

29
The heaviness of the
Earl of Richmond

29v

he granted to the king's request, and he was much offended at the king for
having so cunningly drawn him into these false trains and so much abused
and wronged his credulity and his good affection to the king. And the duke
sent a messenger in post to stay the earl and not to suffer him to be shipped
5 for England.

And in the meantime, Peter Landois, studying how he might help the
earl, devised that the earl should make an escape from his keepers, whom he
would corrup[t,] and that he should fly to the Abbey Church in St Malo's,
and there to claim and crave the benefit and privilege of the Holy Asyle *of*
10 *that* place, and the which he obtained easily. And the duke also, bec*ause* he
would not be suspected for some packing and impostures used in this
business by him, and be*cause* he would not have the king preoccupied nor
possess*ed by any mes*senger before with any distasteful or reproachful news
of this business and of prejudice of himself, he presently sent [Maurice]
15 Brumel, one of his most discreet and honest servants, to the king, to a*dvise*
him that according to his promise and covenant he had sent th[e] Earl of
Richmond to St Malo's, and that he was there delivered to the serv[ants] of
the king, and that they had negligently let him to escape, and that he had
taken sanctuary. Then the duke further intimated to the king that he had
20 sent to the [abbot] and to the king to require or pray them to deliver the earl
ag[ain] unto his officers in St Malo. And that the abbot's answer w[as] that
he neither might nor would deliver the earl to them nor to the king of
England, nor to any man unless he have sufficient caution and security that
the earl should [not be ill entreated or delive]red nor put into the hands of
25 his enemies, but at the w[orst, to be sent back] to Va[nn]es and to be kept
[a prisoner, but with as much courtesy as formerly.   **Egerton 46-50**

[And being the case was fallen into such strict and peremptory terms, and
within the contumacy of such lawless persons, he prayed the king to rest
contented. And although he could not send the earl into England, he
30 faithfully protested there should be so watchful a guard placed upon him as
should prevent all means of escape or ability to offend and hurt him, and
that no suit from the French king nor any other should move him to the
contrary. The king was content perforce to take this answer in good part,
and the duke kept his word religiously, still holding the earl as a prisoner
35 whilst King Edward lived, his imprisonment being, as Philip de Commynes
writeth, for the space of twelve years. In which vicissitude of time, as you
may observe, how strangely the earl was preserved, and doubtless **Provi-
dentia Dei,** though some thought according to Lucanus,
multos servat fortuna nocentes,   [Lucan]
40 and made it Fortune's fantastickness.

[Soon after King Edward died, the Duke of Gloucester, being crowned,   [King Richard
renewed and continued the suit and treaty with the said Duke of Brittany.   reneweth the suit to
And in this negotiation the king employed Sir Thomas Hutton of   the Duke of Brittany
Yorkshire, a wise and worthy gentleman, giving him all fit instructions for for Richmond]
45 his embassy, with such sums of money and with presents as he thought
might engage the continuance of his former promise. But nothing could
overcome him to deliver the earl. But perceiving the king's fear of his claim,
and the importance of such trouble as might arise that way, he again
solemnly promised and assured him there should be no liberty given to the
50 earl which might in any way give him advantage to disturb his peace.

[Yet not long after, the duke broke his promise, and so dishonourably that it then appeared he had kept it with Edward more for fear than love or honour. And indeed the name of Edward and of the Earl of March was counted terrible, and he esteemed the thunder and lightning of arms where his keen and victorious sword was drawn. Nor was this perfidious dealing of the Duke of Brittany left unpunished by a divine revenge. For he having married Margaret, daughter and coheir of Francis de Montfort, Duke of Brittany, she dying without issue, he married another Margaret, the daughter of Gaston de Foix, King of Navarre, by whom he had one only daughter, Anne, who was married to the French king Charles VIII. And the Duke Francis died thus without issue male, the duchy being swallowed up and drowned in the lilies or crapauds of France irrecoverably. And so his family ended, and the duchy of Brittany was lost and absorbed eternally.

[And thus much for the fears and jealousies of those two kings and their endeavours to get the earl in their custody. But all their counsels and practices were vain and against the ordinances of heaven. For as Henry the Saint foretold, the Earl of Richmond must be King of England, to which it pleaseth God to bring him safe through all those hazards, dangers, and difficulties. And no doubt he was animated and prompted by his better genius.

[But it must be supposed here that the House of York flourished and reigned, and that, King Edward being dead, his brother, the Duke of Gloucester, constituted by his brother Lord Protector, was soon after made King of England. Now because his adversaries have censured him very harshly and bitterly for his wearing the crown and for the sinister means by which, as they pretend, he obtained it (in which opinions I verily think they have cast much wrong and slander upon him), to clear the truth whereof I will make a plain and faithful declaration of the manner and means of his getting and coming to the crown, that by a direct and lawful way, not by such frauds and practices as is charged upon him by his enemies. For it is most manifest that he was freely chosen to be king by the estates of the kingdom, and was also very earnestly solicited to take the crown —nay, in a manner constrained, as shall be proved by irrefragable testimonies.

[And the better to prepare the way, first it must be understood that the barons and commons, with one common and general dislike and with an universal negative voice, had utterly refused to have the sons of King Edward to be their king, for diverse reasons, as shall be produced; the sum of which was that neither the barons nor commons held those children to be legitimate, nor the Queen Elizabeth Gray (or Woodville) to be the lawful wife, nor yet a woman worthy to be the wife of a king, in regard of her so extreme unequal quality. And therefore they would in disdain say, as Sarah did, **Eiice ancillam hanc et filium eius.** And it is most certain the nobles and people were so resolute in this opinion that no arguments could persuade them to the contrary.

[And the Protector was as difficultly persuaded on the other side to take the crown, though some have made it his only aim and practice, which objections are without sense and against reason. For it was not possible, and therefore not credible, the Lord Protector could by any practices attain so suddenly to so great power and credit that he should be able to procure and persuade all the barons spiritual and temporal and all the commons and

[Edward IV **fulmen belli, ut Seleucus. Rex inde ceraunus, i., fulmen dictus.**]

[Claude Paradin]

[The Earl of Richmond ordained to be king]

[That the Duke of Gloucester came lawfully to the crown]

[Know, Reader, those assertions be not mine, but of those times.]

clergy, as it were in a moment, to renounce and abandon the sons of King
Edward and become vassals and liege people to him, and make an only and
unanimous choice of him for their king with such continual and instant suit
to him to take the crown, and then to put it on his head with all due
5 solemnity and authentical public ceremonies proper and due unto a
legitimate and true inauguration. But this will not seem strange if their
reasons both for the one resolution and the other be well considered, which
will appear to be very important and just. For they rejected those children
not for any ill will or malice, but for their disabilities and incapacities of the
10 crown, as also because they had known his wisdom and valour and that he
was a magnificent and worthy prince, able to rule and govern the kingdom,
which opinion was afterward allowed and confirmed by the high and whole
court of Parliament, which I shall come to by degrees.

[But first you must know how the noble barons, the prelates, and the rest
15 came to the Duke of Buckingham, who was a very wise, honourable, and
well-spoken man, with one voice and general consent, and solicited him to
go to Baynard's Castle (then York House) to the Lord Protector, who was
newly removed from Crosby Place, where he lay before, to the Tower,
where the prince was. According to the request of those prelates, the duke,
20 accompanied with many of the chief barons and other grave and learned
men, went to the Protector, humbly desiring access unto him, who came
into the Great Chamber, and saluting the duke and the rest, sat down,
giving respective audience to the duke, their orator.]

And first of all, the duke in all humble manner prayed the Lord Protector
25 to give him leave to propose to his grace the intent and cause of their
coming, of himself and of the rest, and withal insinuating that without his
Grace's licence and pardon they durst not to offer nor to report that matter
to his Grace's ears. Because albeit they meant as well all good and honour to
his Grace, as also welfare and wealth to the realm, yet because they would
30 prevent his displeasure, they most humbly required that his and their
pardon might be before granted by his Grace. The Lord Protector then in
answer hereof, and briefly, told them that he well loved them, and that he
knew that they well loved him also, *and* that he was content that they should
declare their business free and securely. And then the duke, this leave and
35 pardon being obtained, and most reverently, and first making humble
obeisance to the Protector, spake in manner as followeth:

'Sire, may it please your Grace to be informed that after much and grave
consultation and long and well-advised deliberation being had amongst the
noble barons and other wise and worthy persons of the realm, it was
40 concluded and resolved that the sons of King Edward should not reign, as
well because it was a miserable fortune and a most dangerous state for the
kingdom where a child was king, and the which was by a wise and holy man
observed and thus testified: **Vae tibi terra cuius rex est puer.** And as also,
and chiefly, because they were not born in lawful marriage, the king their
45 father having then another wife alive, namely Dame Eleanor Butler,
besides the great dishonour and reproach which he incurred by
dispa[ra]ging his royal blood with a woman so full unmeet to match *with*
him. And for these and other causes, they have refused and utterly renounce
to have the children to reign over them and to be king of the realm. [And]
50 because they would not have the realm unprovided and destitute *of* a king,

30
The Duke of Buc[k-
ingham] orator to the
[Lord Protector in
behalf of the three]
estates

Sir Thomas More

[Bishop Morton, Sir
Thomas More,
Holinshed, Grafton,
Stow, Hall]

[The common pub-
lished] st[ories have
Elizabeth Lucy] but
[that is false.]

and that of a good king, these nobles and knights *and* worthy and grave persons have made choice of your Grace to be king, and with [whom no subjects more w]illingly nor with more alacrity concur than the lords and people of the northern [parts. And in like manner,] the Lord Mayor and the aldermen and commons of the City of London [have a]ll [a]llowed and 5 gladly embraced this general choice of your Grace. And in testimony thereof they [are come h]ither and are desirous to join with us in the said humble [suit, well un]derstanding that now the crowns of England and of [France, with the] *just course* of inheritance, the right and title of the same, and the [which were by the high authority of Parliament entailed] to the 10 [royal blood and issue of Richard, Duke of York, father unto your Grace, are by just course of inheritance,] / and according to the common laws of the land, devolved and come unto your Grace, as to the very lawfully begotten son and heir of the fore-remembered most noble Duke of York.

'And the thing being well considered and pondered, together with the 15 great kingly and knightly virtues which in your Grace singularly abound, the nobles and also the commons of the realm, being not willing (as hath been afore showed) that any bastard blood should have the rule of the land, have agreed and resolved and fully determined to make your Grace King of England. And they pray your Grace most earnestly to accept their choice, 20 and for that they have made me their advocate and solicitor of this their weighty and great suit to your Grace, deputed me *the*reunto with one voice and common consent and general suffrage of them all. Wherefore I must *beg* humbly before your Grace, in the behalves of all, that you will be pleased of your accustomed goodness and of your wonted zeal unto the 25 good of the realm, now with your eyes of pity and compassion to behold the long and continual distress and decay of the same estate, and set your happy hands to redress and amendment thereo[f.] And the which work is only to be done and to be effected by your takin[g] the crown and by taking upon you the governance of the realm, acc*ording* to your right and title lawfully 30 descended unto your Grace. And this shall be to the l[aws] of God, and to the profit of the land, and to your Grace's so much the more honour, and so much the less pain by how much that never any prince reigned upon any people which was so gla[d] to live under his obeisance and in his allegiance as the people of this land are and will be glad to live under your rule and 35 governance.

'And again and lastly I am bold in their n[ames] most humbly to pray and beseech your Grace to take the crown and government of this kingdom upon you. And we hope and desi*re* and humbly, most earnestly, to have your gracious and favourable answer'.   40

This speech was made thus by the Duke of Buckingham, and sincerely and truly, as we oug[ht to think.] And it is recorded by the Bishop Morton and by Sir Thomas More, men of nea*rest* [authority, and] b[y all ou]r chroniclers and historians held to be veritable. And it may be thought [they would] *not* [w]rite anything favourably or partially of the Lord Protector 45 nor of [his cause, being the chiefest of those who loved him not. And therefore,] whosoever shall detract from [the sincerity and ingenuity of this oration, it may justly be conceived and censured to proceed from envy and malice.

[And it is] *not only* [most uncharitable,] / but also very injurious to judge 50

30v

31

so hardly of any man not detected of falsehood and forgery, and much
more of this noble duke, who was a man which much respected his honour
and his word and the credit thereof, and for many years might not speak
anything but as he thought it just, according to the truth. And it is to *be*
5 *credited.* And certainly (as we must believe that he did) in his secret
thoughts *he* held and accounted the Lord Protector to be a wise and a just
and good man, and never said other[wise] until he himself became false and
a malicious and a perfidious man.
   But to let these censures and observations to pass, we will now make
10 report of the answer of the Lord Protector to this speech of the Duke of
Buckingham, and the which answer was very distasteful and unpleasing to
the duke and to all the nobles and commons, because that the Protector
accepted not their election of him to be king, but refused it and profess*ed*
much mislike thereof. And he stood up, and with a sad and discontented
15 countenance spake these words, and as they are set down by the credible,
gracious, and much appli*ed* authors aforesaid:

   'My most noble lords and my most loving friends and dear countrymen. [The answer of the
Albeit I know and I must confess that I hold your request and suit made Lord Protector] to
now to me is both reasonable and favourable, and that the things therein [the Three Estates]
20 and the necessities alleged and urged are true and certain, yet because I bear
such entire and faithful love and tender respect unto my most noble and
most dear brother, the king deceased lately, and to his children, my sweet
and princely nephews, for his sake I cannot find in my heart to yield to your
favourable motion nor to condescend to take the crown and the kingdom
25 unto myself. [And] because also I much more regard mine honour [an]d
good fame in other realms and foreign countries *which* are round about this
land than I do a crown, *or to* take the kingdom or any sceptre.
   'For if I should [accept] the crown and take the kingdom into *my*
possession and into my own hands, it would *distaste and disg*ust those
30 foreign nations [where the truth and certain proceedings herein are not
known, that it may be] / my plot and politic device to procure the rejecting 31v
and deposing of the young prince, King Edward, and to the end to take the
crown unto myself. But these be such matters of infamy and of reproach as
that I would not have mine honour and good name stained therewith for all
35 the crowns in the world. Besides that (I have long perceived and well
observed it) there is more labour and more pains in the government of a
kingdom than pleasure or delight, especially to the prince who would use
the kingly authority and royal office as it ought to be used. And therefore,
and for these and the like causes, I protest I never desired the crown; neither
40 can I now find in mine heart to take it, nor to incline to your desires.
   'But yet I think myself much beholding to you all for your favourable
election of me, and I give you all most hearty thanks for your great good
will and true hearty love, which I find hereby you bear to me. And I promise
here that for your sakes, it shall be all one whether I be your king or no, for
45 I will serve the young king my nephew faithfully and diligently and carefully
and will live under him his subject and vassal; and I will endeavour with my
best counsels and with my sw[ord] to defend him and to preserve him and
this kin[g]dom in peace and prosperity. And furthermo[re,] I will be willing
and ready to attempt the recov[ery] of the hereditary signories and
50 provinces in France which belong to the King of England, and lately and

negligently unhappily lost'.

And here the Prot[ector] became silent and sat down again in his chair, and thought [not] safe nor a politic course to tell them all the distastes and dislikes which [he] had of the condition of sovereignty and of reigning, and *especially* in England, because that would have been a matter of 5 exprobation of [the barons] and would have much offended them. And

32

therefore, he *concealed his* dislike. / *And* they many times much afflicted and vexed the kings, and brought them into great distress and fear of their lives. And further yet, all their raging fury was sometimes so outrageous and excessive as that they ceased not until they had either deposed or killed 10 and utterly destroyed their sovereign lord. And he knew well, and there were fresh examples hereof in the reigns of his brother King Edward and of King Henry VI, and not long before in the time of King Richard II and of his grandfather, King Edward II. He knew that more anciently the troubles and desperate distresses and calamities of the kings John and Henry III, 15 caused by their barons, were dreadful warnings and [monu]ments of the insolencies and of the rhodomontados and of the disloyal levity of those seditious Bashaes. This was **alta mente repositum** with this wise prince. And he was desirous to avoid and to prevent the dangers and miserable mischiefs following it. But for the causes here showed, he concealed his objection and 20 supposed that he had said enough in his foresaid speech and should not need other arguments.

[Tha barons, etc., press the Lord Protector to take the crown]

But the barons and the other grave and worthy persons would not admit any answers or excuses of the Lord Protector, nor rest satisfied therewith, but they continued resolute in their purpose, in their choice of him to be 25 king, and then instantly they conferred with the duke their orator, and they gave him instructions and directions sufficient to answer and to refute all the objections. And the duke prayed audience again, and did very fully and eloquently answer and confute the Protector's objections and avoided all his tergiversations and refelled all his arguments and exceptions, as it may 30 be seen in our stories, and in effect as tedious and super*fluous to re*peat. And then in silence the duke attended the answer of the Protector.

But he was also silent and mute, and he *neither* [repli]ed nor said anything to him (as at the least in public), but he [turned to] the Lord Mayor of London and to the Recorder, being [near unto] him, and that which he said, 35 and in a low voice, [tended to] *the* dislike and disgust which he had of their *entreating con*cerning his taking of the crown and had *delivered already. And* [the Lord Mayor, with reverence and discreetly, repre]hended the *which,* [intimating how much the change of his opinion would give requital

32v

and satisfaction to the] / barons and to the commons and to the City of 40 London, who all had so earnestly and so importunately besought his Grace to take the kingdom and to be their king and only sovereign lord.

And when the Lord Mayor had ended his short speech, and which the Duke of Buckingham had overheard with close and diligent listening, and thereby had observed and perceived how slightly the Protector entertained 45 the Mayor's advice, and how lightly he regarded his good and grave speeches and his profitable persuasions of the Mayor, and also with the like careless manner he heard those speeches which more at large and more effectually had been uttered by himself, he seemed to have much mislike and indignation thereof, and, as it were, in indignation and in a kind of 50

scorn of the Protector's neglect and of the many repulses and many
obstinate refusals of their love and of the election of the *barons and*
commons of him to be their king. And being also wearied, and even tired
with the perverse and cross proceedings herein, stood forth and craved leave
5 of the Protector to sp*eak* but two or three words more. And he said that he
would from thenceforth cease from troubling of his Grace any more in that
vein. And the duke, being licensed to speak what he would for his epilogue
and his **ultimum vale** to this motion and suit, spake in this manner:
    'Sire, since it hath pleased your Grace to give me leave to speak again, the
10 which leave I have ta*ken,* it must also be allowed to me in a bolder and   [The bold and round
rounder style, because I am bound by this mine employment and by my   conclusion of the
duty to my cou[ntrymen] to declare plainly in this cause, and to the end to   Duke of Buckingham]
rid the noble barons and the commons out of suspense and out of doubt,
quia dubia plus torquent mala (i.e., doubtful things more torment the
15 mind), and I must therefore finally and peremptori*ly* advertise your Grace
that the most constant and final determination and last and irrevocable
resolution of the barons and of the people are that the line of King Ed[ward]
shall not reign over them, and for the reasons before *stated,* and also
because these estates have entered so far and [proceeded so off]ensively
20 to other men and so dangerously to t[hemselves as is now too late to recant
or retire. And therefore they have fixed their election upon you, as on the
man whom they think most able and careful for their safety.
    'But if there be no end of these your repulses and denials and of your   **33**
contempt or light regard of our suit, and you be so obstinate and so
25 inexorable and inflexible as that you will never be persuaded nor by any
petitions or by any reasons or arguments inanswerable, or by any request or
solicitation, nor by prayers and humble petitions be brought to like and
embrace and to put on the condition of a king, then we hope and we desire that
you will be pleased to declare once more your mind plainly and sincerely
30 and definitively therein, and to give unto us your peremptory and final
answer. And if there be no remedy but that it shall and must be as it hath
hitherto been — that is, very distasteful and discomfortable and very bitter
and grievous unto us — then we humbly pray your Grace that you will be
content and give your consent that we seek out some other most noble and
35 princely person who shall be fit and worthy to undertake the great and
stately and imperial charge and will gladly and willingly accept our offer
and our election of him to be king. And this request we trust that your
Grace will grant, considering our great necessity and desperate case. And we
hope yet that by these means and by God's good favour to find out one, and
40 such an one, and so well affected unto us, and so princely qualified as
aforesaid. And this is all, and the last that we have to say or will say in this
matter. And all that we crave and desire now is that you will be pleased once
again and finally to give to us your perem*p*tory and definite answer, and
instantly and without delays'.
45   The Protecto[r] *considered the* matters of this speech, and he was much
troubled also, and almost distracted with this plain and round and braving
conclusion *and as it were from* a castle of defiance. And he seemed as one
that had been roused out of a drowsy slumber or awaked out of a frightful
dream. [For] certain it is that the Protector was much altered with the bold
50 speech of the Duke of Buckingham. As Sir Thomas More disertly

confesseth tha*t* the Protector was so much moved with those words as that otherwise and of likelihood he would never have inclined to their suit of the barons and of the commons. This Mr More, and the same author proceeding herein, saith that when the Lord Protector saw that there was no other remedy but that he must [e]ither take the crown now and at this 5 instant, or else that both he and [his] heirs forever forgo it and lack and lose it irrecuperably, *and th*at it also should pass to another, who might be his enemy and a scourge and ***malus genius*** to him and to his. And especially (and so it is to be understood) if the crown went to the *Earl of* Richmond, between whom and this prince Richard the hatred and the malice was 10 equaliy extreme *and* irreconcilable, he might be assured that he should *have care*s and evils and mischiefs greater and more than he could conceive. And *when he had his* desire now therefore at last considered and forecast and forefeared, then almost too late for th*e safety of sovereign*ty and of empire,

now, therefore, *with* better and more advised judgement he / signified unto 15 them in these words:

'My most noble good lords and my most loving and faithful friends, I

must confess that upon better considerations of your offer and of the dangers and evils which were insinu[ated] now at the *last* to me by your noble speaker, and also upon the plain and wise words which he last spake, 20 I better apprehend the benefit of your offer and election and [proffer,] *and* I find some alteration in my mind, as well for the causes aforesaid, and also because I perceive and consider that all the realm is set against the sons of King Edward, and which much grieveth us, and will not suffer in any wise King Edward's line to govern them; and that I likewise know that the nation 25 is a people of that stout stomach and courage as that no earthly man can govern them against their wills; and also forasmuch as that we certainly understand there is no man to whom the crown can by just title be so due as to ourself, being the very rightful and lawful gotten son and heir of our most dear and princely father, Richard, Duke of York, and unto which true 30 titles of blood and of nature now by your favour is joined another title, and that is the election of me, made by you, and the which title we take and hold to be the most safe and the most strong and the most effectual title of all other titles. And because also I cannot *nor* ever will endure that that one at whom you glanced, mentioned and without a name in your last speech, 35 being mine utter enemy, should sit in the throne of my kingdom and usurp my royal heritage; and that so I should become a vassal to mine unworthy and hateful subject.

'And therefore, according to the necessities of those causes, there is no remedy but that w*e* must needs consent and agree, and to take your 40 favourable offer of the cro[wn,] and to incline to your petition, and to accept your election of us, and to yield to your earnest and importunate requests to have me to be your king. We therefore, according to the same requests and suits and to our right, do now in the place and at the instant accept your choice and take upon us the royal state and the regal 45 preeminence and the r*ule* of these two noble kingdoms of England and of France from this day forward, and by us and by our heirs to rule and to govern and to defend the one (that is, England), and by God's grace and by your good aid to redeem and recover the other (that is, France) and to resubdue it to the rea[lm,] and to restore it to the ancient allegiance of the 50

kings of England, and to es[tablish] it in due obeisance of this kingdom
forever. And we ask not of any longer to live than so long as we intend and
endeavour to [procure] and labour the advancement and flourishing estate
of this [kingdom'. At which they all cried 'Go]d save King Richard', [and
5 thus he] became king, and so all *the people departed.*

And here the ingenious and judicious Reader may see how much the
detractors and cavillers wrong and slander the noble prince Richard, and
also all the proceedings in the business before related, and who are not
ashamed to say that all that hath been said and done, and all the
10 proceedings of state in these affairs of the election and making of him king
were but dissimulations and tricks and arts of impostures. And if that be
true, then they may as well say **(adsit reverentia dicto)** that all the barons
and all the worthy and grave gentlemen and all the better commons, who
were the only actors herein, were fools and knaves, **aut utrumque.** And that
15 were a most impudent and an intolerable scandal, and the which also would
light upon all the high and most grave and wise and religious court of
Parliament, for it was not long after ere all that which was handled and
alleged and persuaded and acted and concluded in the same treaties and
colloquies and suits aforesaid was allowed and approved and ratified and
20 confirmed by the court of Parliament. But these be so gross cavils as that
they serve for nothing but to discover the extreme envy and malice of the
contrivers and patrons of them. And therefore they need no answer nor
refutation. Then to let them pass with this passport, and to proceed with the
story.
25 And for it is not to be omit[ted] that whilst these matters of the election of
King Richard were hand!ed (as is aforesaid) that the northern gentlemen
who had joined with these southern friends of the Protector's had an
advertisement that there were some difficulties and some obstacles and
crosses in the effecting and accomplishment thereof, and those proceeding
30 out of the will and w[ilfulness of the Protector.] Whereupon they caused a
bill supplicatory to be made and to be directed and addressed to the barons
spiritual and temporal which were at London or near abouts and were
occupied in the foresaid business of the election. And in this bill they
signified to them their great desire to have the Protector to be their king, as
35 well for his good title and for his virtues and princely worthiness as also
because the children of King Edward and his marriage were unlawful, and
also that the blood of the young Earl of Warwick was attainted and his title
confiscated by Parliament. And they intimated that for these causes, they
had chosen the Duke of Gloucester to be their king.
40 [He]re, and once for all, because I shall have occasion to speak often of
this [mar]riage of King Edward and of these children's birth, and how that
they were reputed *unlaw*ful and illegitimate, I pray the noble and discreet
Reader to conceive that [I em]brace not those hard opinions, but I only
relate that such opinions and such *beliefs* [were the censures of those times
45 generally believed, and they were of good use for the better effecting of that
great business in hand. For to the world it is all one to seem and to be.]

This bill was delivered to th[e] lords being assembled in the Great Hall at
Westminster, and the Lord Protector sitting in the chair [of] marble
amongst them, upon the 26th day of Jun[e,] and which was some six or
50 seven days after the Protector had accepted the cr[own and was] proclaimed

34

T[he general caution
of] th[e author.] E[t
vide in Lib. 2.]

36v

king. And this is the tenor of this bill, as I *have seen it* written in the Chronicle of the Abbey of [Croyland]:

[Lib. Abb. Croyland]

37

Ricardus Protector eodem die, quo re[gimine sub] titulo regii nominis sibi vendicav[it, viz., 26] die Junii, anno Domini [1483, se apud magnam Aulam Westmonasterii, in Cathedram Marmoream] / immisit, et tum mox 5 **omnibus proceribus tam laicis quam ecclesiasticis et ceteris assidentibus et astantibus,** etc., **ostendebatur rotulus, quidam in quo per modum supplicationis in nomine procerum et populi Borealis exhibitae, primum quod filii regis Edwardi erant bastardi, supponendo illum praecontraxisse matrimonium cum quadam domina Alienora Boteler antequam reginam** 10 **Elizabetham duxisset in uxorem. Deinde quod sanguis alterius fratris Georgii (scilicet) Clarentiae ducis, fuisset attinctus, ita quod nullus certus et [i]ncorruptus sanguis linealis ex parte Ri[ca]rdi ducis Eboraci poterat inveniri, [n]isi in persona Ricardi protectoris, ducis [G]locestriae, et tum eidem duci supplicabant, [ut] ius suum in regno Angliae sibi assumeret, [et** 15 **c]oronam acciperet,** etc. Thus that *Ch*ronicle of Croyland.

[Bu]t this suit of the northern men was not then very n[eedful, for the barons] were all accorded before the bill came and was presented, all went [well,] and all men were [contentedly] and cheerfully disposed. And now there were preparations of festival [solemn]ity and pomp *ma*de for the 20 coronation. And in the month [of Ju]ly next following, and in the year 1483, all things being r*eady,* [with all st]ate and magnificence, the Protector was very solemnly and most [lawfully] crowned and consecrated, with all the *ancie*nt and pompous rites and royal and sacred [ceremonies apper]taining to the crowning, [anointing, and inaugur]ation of a sovereign 25

37v

king, [and received] / for king with so joyful and general applause, in such favourable acclamations, as any other king was or had been in England for many years before. And that doubtless was done and yielded heart*ily,* without dissimulation, by good right and reason. For as a grave man writeth

Cam[den] in **Dobuni**

of this king, **Fui[t dign]issimus regno, et [non in]ter malos, sed inter bonos** 30 **principes prudentum consensu connum[erandus]:** He was most worthy to be numbered a[mongst the g]ood and not [bad pri]nces.

The Queen Anne also, his wife, was there crowned with him. And she accompanied him with pompous proceeding all the way from the Tower to Westminster. And besides the nobility, greater and lesser, of the south parts 35 which attended at this solemn inauguration feast, there were fou[r] thousand gallant gentlemen of Yorkshire [and of] the north parts in the train. And for the more magnificent and more honourable celebration of this great feast, there were creations and investitures of noble perso[ns] and of knights. 40

And first the king, some days befo[re] the coronation (viz., 28th day of June) invest[ed] Sir John Howard, who was made Lord Howard and a Knight of the Garter by K[ing Edward IV], in the duk[e]dom of Norfolk, in a favourable ad[mi]ssion of the right of the Lady Marg[aret] his mother, and daughter of Sir Thomas [Mowbray,] Duke of Norfolk, and heir 45 gen[eral] of the most noble Mowbrays, [dukes] of Norfolk and earls of

38

[Surrey,] and descended from the Lord Th[omas Plantagenet,] / the first Earl of Norfolk and Marshal of England. And he was also as well and as

Style of the Duke of Norfolk

rightly Lord Mowbray and Lord Segrave and Lord Breus as Lord Howard, and so I have seen him styled, and by good and royal warrant, namely in a 50

commission in a treatise of truce and peace with Scotland, in the Rolls kept   [In Rot]ulis [in] domo
in [t]he Chapel of the Convertites.   [conver]sorum
      And then also the king created Sir [Th]omas Howard, eldest son of the
[sa]id duke, Earl of Surrey, and he made him a Knight of the [Garter.] And
5 this king [ma]de William, Lord Berkeley, Earl [of] Nottingham; and the
Baron [Lo]vell was made Viscount Lovell and [Lo]rd Chamberlain; and he
took the [Lo]rd Stanley out of prison and made [him] Steward of his house.
And Sir Henry Stafford, Duke of [Buc]kingham, was made Constable of
[En]gland for term of life, albeit [he] claimed that office as belonging [to
10 hi]m by inheritance. But Sir Thomas More writeth that the Lord Thomas
Howard, Earl of [Surrey,] executed the office, and after the Duke of
[Buckingham was] dead the king gave that office [of cons]tableship to the   [Rotuli in capella
Lord Stanley, [with an] annual fee of £100, and *who* [became a most]   conversorum]
ingrate, and fatally *served* [the king, his good master.]
15   And Dr Thomas Rotherham, Lord Chancellor of England and Arch-   38v
bishop of Canterbury, having been committed to prison for delivering
the Great Seal to the Queen Widow, was now pardoned and set at liberty and
restored to grace and to his place. And in brief, many knights were created
and adubbed of the old Order, and seventeen knights of the new Order or
20 habit of the Bath, whose names I have here set down, / to show what regard   39
was had of the choice of those kind of knights in those times which are
accounted to be so evil and disorderly and tyrannous:
            Sir Edmund de la Pole, son of the Duke of Suffolk   [Knights of the Bath
            George Gray, son of the Earl of Kent   made by King
25   William Souch, son of the Lord Souch   Richard III]
            Henry Neville, son of the Lord Abergavenny
            Christopher Willoughby   William Berkeley
            Henry Baynton   Thomas Arundel
            Thomas Boleyn   Breus of Clifton
30   William Say   Edmund Bedingfield
            William Enderby   Thomas Lewkenor
            Thomas of Vernon   John Brown
            William Berkeley i.e. another Berkeley
      And now I think it very necessary to make a ful[l and] true relation of all   40
35 the solemn ceremonies and regal pom[p] which were used and exhibited at
the consecration and corona[tion] of this King Richard III. And for two
causes, the one for th[e credit] of my word, because I have in some places
here before [affir]med the coronation of this king was [most] lawfully and
authentically and solemnly and publicly and regularly, and accor[ding] to
40 the ancient custom used therein, celebrated and performed. And the other
cause, that they may see their error and the wrong which they ha[ve done] to
the king and to all the barons and nobles and people o[f this kingdom] who
say that this king came indirectly and irregularly to the cr[own and like a
thief] he crept in at the window secret*ly*, [climbing to the throne by]
45 treacher[y and evil acts. The authors which I will follow herein be all the
best chroniclers and writers of our stories, all public and well allowed.]
      Richard, the third of that name, took upon him to be King of England the   41
19th day of June, **Anno Domini** 1483, and in the twenty-fifth year of the
reign of the French king Lewis XI. And the morrow after, viz., 20 June, he
50 was proclaimed king, and he then made for London to Westminster, with

More, Grafton, Hall,
Polydore, **Croyland-
ensis**, Holinshed,
Stow, etc.

great solemnity, and there sat in the seat royal and called before him the
judges of the realm, straightly commanding them to execute the law without
favour or evil will or delay, and with many other good exhortations. And
then he departed toward the Abbey, and at the church door he was met with
the procession, and the sceptre of St Edward was delivered to him by the   5
abbot. And then he went to St Edward's shrine and offered there, the
monks in the meantime singing **Te Deum.** From the church he returned to
the palace, where he lodged until his coronation.

Upon the 4th day of July, he went to the Tower by water with the queen
his wife, and being there upon the next day, he created Edward, his only   10

[Monstrelet,
Commynes, **Anglicos**
Scriptores]

son, being ten years old, Prince of Wales. And then Sir John, Lord
Howard, a man very loyal and of great knowledge and experience, and as
well in council as in bat[tle, and deservedly therefore in gr]eat favour with
King Edward IV, and by him made Lord Howard, was created Duke of
Norfolk. And Sir Thomas Howard, his eldest son, was created Earl of   15
Surrey. And William, Lord Berkeley, was then created Earl of Nottingham.
And Francis, Lord Lovell, was then made Viscount Lovell and Chamberlain
to the king. And the Lord Stanley was delivered out of durance and made
Steward of the King's [House]hold. And Thomas Rotherham, Archbishop
of York, [was pardone]d and set at liberty. But Bishop Morton was sent for   20
[his treachery to Brecknock C]astle, and to be kept safely [by the Duke of
Buckingham. And that same day the king made those seventeen knights of
the Bath before named.

[The next day he rode from the Tower through London in great state and
pomp, most gallantly attended. The Duke of Buckingham was of most   25

41v

eminent note and most extraordinary rich and gallant,] / his habit and
caparison of blue velvet embroidered with golden naves of carts burning,
and trappings, were supported by footmen in brave and costly garments
suitable to the rest.

And on the morrow, being the 6th day of July, the king proceeded in state   30
toward his coronation, and he came into Westminster Hall, where all the
prelates, mitred and in their **pontificalibus,** to his chapel received him. And
there attended upon the king in this proceeding three dukes, nine earls, and
twenty-two viscounts and simple barons, and about eighty knights, and
esquires and gentlemen without number.   35

And the great officers of the crown and of the king which had special
services to do upon that Great Day went in their order and manner, viz.:
next after the procession followed the Earl of Northumberland with a
pointless sword naked. The Lord Stanley bare the mace of the
Constableship, but he waited not for Constable there, as you shall see by   40
and by. The Earl of Kent bare the second sword naked upon the right hand
of the king. The Lord Viscount Lovell bare another sword on the king's left
hand. Next came the Duke of Suffolk with the sceptre; and the Earl of
Lincoln bare the ball and cross. Then the Earl of Surrey with the sword of
estate in a rich scabbard, and in the place of the Constable of England. His   45
father the Duke of Norfolk went upon his right, bearing the crown. And
now next came the king himself, clad in a surcoat and a robe of purple
velvet, and over his head there was a canopy borne by the barons of the five
ports. The king was between the bishops of Bath and of Durham. Next the
king came the Duke of Buckingham, bearing up the king's train, and he   50

served with a rod and staff for a Seneschal or High Steward of England.

And now the queen came in her estate, *and* in the forefront of her attendants cam[e the Earl of Huntington, bearing the queen's sceptre, and the Viscount Lisle, the rod with the dove. The Earl of Wiltshire] / bare the

5 queen's crown. Then followed Queen Anne in robes like to those of the king, between two bishops likewise, and also with a canopy borne over her head by the barons of the ports. And upon her head she wore a rich coronet set with precious stones and pearls, and the Lady Margaret Somerset, Countess of Richmond, bare her train. And then followed the Duchesses of

10 Suffolk and Norfolk and many countesses and baronesses and other ladies, etc. And in this order this whole procession passed through the palace to the Abbey and entered at the west door.

And then the king and queen took their seats of state, and they stayed there until divers holy hymns were solemnly sung. And then they both

15 descended and went to the high altar, and they shifted their robes and put on others, which were voided and open in sundry places for their anointment. And they, being anointed, put on other robes of cloth of gold and returned to their seats, and where the Cardinal of Canterbury and other bishops crowned them, according to the ancient and solemn customs of the

20 realm. And these prelates put the sceptre in the left hand of the king, and the ball and cross in his right hand. And they put the queen's sceptre in her right hand, and the rod with the dove in her left hand. And on each hand of the king there stood a duke, and before him stood the Earl of Surrey, bearing the foresaid sword in his hands. And upon each hand of the queen

25 stood a bishop and a lady kneeling.

The cardinal said mass and gave the **pax,** and then the king and queen descended, and they were both housled, with one host parted between them, at the high altar. And this being done, they [bot]h offered at St Edward's shrine, and there the king laid down [St] Edward's crown and put on

30 another crown. And these [cere]monies of inauguration and royal consecration being thus *performed,* [t]he king and queen and the nobles and all the train returned to Westminster Hall in the same [order as they we]nt forth, and then they dispersed themselves [and retired for a little season to] their chambers. And in [the meantime, the Duke of Norfolk, Marshal of

35 England, came mounted upon a brave horse richly trapped with cloth] / of gold down to the ground, and he submoved the press of the people and voided the hall.

And by this time it was near four of the clock, and then the king and queen came into the hall and sat down at the royal table to dinner. And the

40 king sat in the middle of the table, and the queen sat upon the king's left hand, and she had two countesses attending upon each side of her, holding a cloth of pleasance (or rat[her] of essuyance) for her cup. And upon the king's right hand sat the Archbishop of Canterbury. And all the ladies sat on one side of a long table placed in the middle of the hall. And over against

45 them at another table sat the Lord Chancellor and all the nobles and barons. And at the table next to the cupboard sat the Lord Mayor of London and the aldermen. And at another table behind the barons of the kingdom sat the barons of the ports. And there were divers other tables, whereat also many noble and worshipful persons sat and dined.

50 And after that all were set, then again came in the Duke of N[orfolk,]

42

42v

Marshal of England, and the Earl of Surrey, his son, Constabl[e **pro ille vice tantum,**] and next came the Lord Stanley, Lord Steward, and Sir William Hopton, Treasurer of the Household, and Sir Thomas Percy, Controller. And they served the king's board with one dish of go[ld] and another of silver. And the queen was served all in gilt vessel*s*, and the   5
Archibishop Cardinal had all his diet in silver dish[es.] And as soon as the second course was served into the hall, there came Sir Robert Dymock, the King's Champion, making proclamation that whosoever would say that King Richard III was not lawfully king, he would fight with him at all outerance. And for the gage hereof, he threw down his gauntle[t.] But then 10
all the hall cried, 'King Richard, God save King Ri[chard.]' And in this manner the Champion acted the part in three several parts of the hall. And then an officer of the ki[ng's] cellar brought to him a gilded bowl, covered and full of wine. And the Champion drank some of the wine and ca[st] out the rest, and carried the cup away with him as his a[ncient fee.] And after 15
this, the heralds cried 'largess' thrice and retu[rned to] their scaffold. And lastly came the Mayor of L[ondon and the sheriffs with a voider,] and served the king and queen, [and with sweet wine, or hippocras. By this time the day was spent and it grew somewhat dark, when the king and queen rose from the table and went into their lodgings.   20

[And this is a brief and true relation of this solemn coronation, which I have the rather reported because (as I intimated before) the malicious adversaries of the king have not shamed to say he was not lawfully and rightfully crowned and anointed king.]

44   And the king gave strait charge to the justices, magistrates, and officers 25
of courts and jurisdictions that they would deal so uprightly as that there might be no corrupting nor frauds nor injustices nor abuses found or used in them. Moreover, and as he had done before, and as it hath been
[Sir] Thomas M[ore] remembered before, he gave strict commandment to the lords spiritual and temporal who were then to take their leaves of the king and to return to 30
their countries, and had charge of justice and jurisdiction in the countries, and all other magist[rates] which had like charge of justice, to be careful to distribute justice and right to every man, as well to the poor as to the rich and great, and equally and indifferently. And also that they would have great and chief regard that God might be duly and rightly served and 35
worshipped in all places.

When the judges of oyer and terminer were [to] depart from Westminster and to ride their summer [circu]its, the king sent for them and gave them *direction, and* required and charged them to administer indiffe[rently] justice to all his subjects and liege people. *And of* all these good and godly 40
exhortations and *instruc*tions given by this king to the honourable *cou*rtly magistrates and to the judges and justi*ces,* this testimony was made by Mr John Herd, a learned m[an and Docto]r of Physic, and a good poet, in a manuscript poesy of his which I have seen:

43   **Solio Juris [rectique minist]ra**   45
Ille sedens alte, tali sermone profatur:
Moses consilio soceri persuasus Ietro,
[So]lus quod populi nequiit componere lites,
Constituit populi praefectos atque tribunos.
[Sic] cum me praecelsa premant fastigia regni,   50

[Ardu]a magnarum teneatis munera rerum.
[Et] primum a vobis p[ra]vos secludite motus,
[Aequis Just]itiae tratinis appendite causas.
[Ob paupertatem,] miserum ne spernite civem;
5   [Nec vota in cassum fundat pu]pillus in auras,
[Denique largitio, ne vos corrumpat iniqua, etc.]

All things being set in good order, the king departed from London, being **44v**
accompanied with the queen his wife and with Edward, Duke of Cornwall,
his son, and attended upon with many lords and ladies and other worthy
10   servito[rs,] and amongst other, and chiefly, with the Duke of Buckingham.
And the king made the castle of Windsor the first gifts of his progress,
where he for some few days took the pleasure of the fresh air and the green
woods and of the red and fallow deer of that forest, as he did also at his
manor and park of Woodstock, which was his next place of lodging. And
15   from thence he went to the University of Oxenford, where he was very
honourably and delightfully entertained of the noble and courteous Muses.
And he visited soon after his titular city of Gloucester and thanked the
citizens for the love and loyalty which they showed in defending and
holding the castle and town, and so constantly [and] stoutly, against the
20   Queen Margaret and the forces of King Henry VI for him and for the king
his brother. And he bestowed large privileges and immunities upon that
city. And here the Duke of Bu[ckingham took his leave of the kin]g and
went a[way to Brecknock, very] well content, [as it seemed.]
The king made small stay anywhere, saving only [at] Coventry, until he
25   came to the goodly and ancient [city] of York, a place much esteemed and
beloved of [him.] And whilst he was in York, he was crowned the [second]
time by Dr Rotherham, Archbishop of York, with gre[at solem]nity and all
festivity in the cathedral, where also his son Edward was invested in the
principali[ties of] Wales, and with all due pomp and ceremonies, and as it
30   [is] reported by the Prior of Croyland, and thus:

Eodem die [quo] Ricardus coronatus est rex in ecclesia metr[opoli]tana
Eboracensi, mox filium Edwardum in [princi]patum Walliae cum insigniis
virgae aureae, et se[rti in] capite erexit, et pomposa et sumptuosa festa [et]
convivia ibi fecit.

35   And indeed, this was a day [of great] state and of great pomp, and very
glorious. For u[pon this] day (as saith Polydore) there were three princes
adorned with crowns, namely, the king, the q[ueen and prince. In
acclamation whereof,] there were stage plays and tournaments and other
triumphal sports, as Sir Thomas More writeth. And at this city also, as   [Richard the bastard
40   some say, [the king] made Richard of Gloucester, his base son, [Captain   of] Gloucester [Cap-
of] Calais, who was a valiant young gentleman, and of whom I shall [have   tain of Calais]
occasion to speak more anon.]
In this progress, the king graced many worthy gentlemen of the north   **45**
parts with the title and order of knighthood. And albeit this was a time of [Chronicle MS. **in**
45   great feasting and of revelling and of pleasure, yet the king neglected not the **quarto apud** Robert
duty and charge of his royal office, but still as he travelled he had a care that Cotton, **et** Robert
justice should be duly done, and in sundry places, and gave commandment Fabyan]
that the more facinorous malefactors should be executed. And after some
convenient time bestowed in this progress to York, he bade farewell, and as
50   it unhappily happened, **longum aeternumque vale**, as the poet said of   [Vergil, **Aeneid**]

Aeneas, to that good city of York so much beloved of him, and to all those northern countries and people. And he came to Nottingham Castle, and from there to London.

And being returned, and whereas he had admonished and friendly warned the [Fre]nch King Lewis XI to continue the payment of the tribute 5 [and] pension which he was bound to pay the king and some noble [and] worthy persons of England, now he went more roundly [to] work and required that payment with threat and stout menaces, the which tribute was raised by King Edward IV. But / the Frenchmen would not have it called a tribute but a pension, as Philip Commynes insinuateth. And the 10 tribute and pension was paid in lieu of the profits and revenues of the duchies and counties of Aquitaine and of Normandy and of Maine and of Poitou and of other signories in France, ancient heritages of the kings of England, and whereof the French had disseised the kings of England and usurped the title and right and possession of those said lands and signories. 15

And King Richard vowed that he would either have the said tribute paid or else he would adventure to recover those lands with his sword, and by such means as his brother the king had before obtained and gained that tribute. For he enforced King Lewis XI to acknowledge his right unto those lands and provinces and to pay a tribute to him for his occupation [of] 20 them. And he made him to give good caution and security [for] the payment thereof in the city of London, and it was covenanted and agreed that / the King of France and his heirs and successors should yearly pay to the King of England and to his heirs and successors the sum of fifty thousand crowns (or after John Tillet and John Meyerus, seventy-five thousand crowns), 25 and that to be brought in the Tower.

And the French king granted to give or to pay certain chief noblemen and other men of special credit and favour with the king the sum of sixteen thousand crowns, and that in the name of annual pension, and to these noble persons by name, viz.: to Sir Thomas Gray, Marquess of Dorset, 30 [t]o William, Lord Hastings, Chamberlain to the king, [to D]r Thomas Rotherham, Bishop of Lincoln [and] Lord Chancellor of England, [an]d to John, Lord Howard, and to Sir [Jo]hn Cheyney, Master of the Horse, and to Sir [T]homas Montgomery, and to the Master [of] the Rolls, and to Mr Challoner and others. And the chiefest of these had [two] thousand crowns 35 apiece per annum. And [bes]ides these pensions, King Lewis gave [gr]eat rewards and rich presents to [ce]rtain of those lords to whom he was most beholding for their good affection to him [and] their advancing of this accord and agreement.

And Enguerrant [de] Monstrelet writeth that the Lord Howard and the 40 Master [of the] Horse were the chiefest of the English medi[ators] of this accord and peace. And his reason is because, [as he sai]th, they were the most in favour with [King E]dward. And this is also another great reason that the Lord Howard might be one of them. [And King Edward IV made this Sir John Howard a baron and a Knight of the Bath: he was installed in 45 **anno** 17, Edward IV. Philip de Commyn]es writeth that King Lewis gave to the [Lord Howard in less than two] years the value of [2400 crowns in plate and coin and jewels, over and above his annual pension, and that this] king gave to the Lord Hastings at one time to the value of 2000 marks in plate, besides also his pension. And to these may be added Sir Richard de 50

Marginal notes

45v

46
Du Tillet saith that this French tribute or pension was three score and fifteen escus or crowns, and **chaque écu valant trente-trois sous.**

Joannes Meyer, **Annal. Fland. Lib.** 17, *p.* 469

The Lord [Howard] favoured h[ighly of King] Edward IV

[Du Tillet]

46v

Neville, the great Earl of Warwick. For if it be true which I have read in the French stories, the King of France gave much greater rewards to him than to any other English noblemen. And the author of the Chronicle of Brittany saith that the Earl of Warwick cost King Lewis very great sums of money.

5   King Richard, according to his promise and protestation in this behalf to the Lords and Commons (and before remembered) demanded this French trib[ute] *of King Lewis* and his son, King Charles VIII, if my memory fail me not. And if he had not been by horrible sed[ition] and most unnatural treason prevented, he would have compell[ed] the kings of France to have
10   performed and continued the due paym[ent] thereof, and of the pensions besides, or else he would have transported and led a new *expedition* into France for the recovery of those duchies and sig[nories,] the ancient heritage of the kings of *England,* as is aforesaid. But yet as cross and as thwart as fortune was to this king, he brought King Lewis to give him good
15   words, and seemed but to [crave respite] and longer time for the payment hereof, as Commynes not obscurel[y intimates.]

      [Not long after] that, by the good, honest, and charitable mediation of [som]e honourable and good persons, the king and the Lady [Eliz]abeth, Queen Dowager, were reconciled, and a friendly accord and mutual amity
20   was made between them. And then she, being out of fear and in secu*rity,* *left* the sanctuary. And in token of her good affection, she sent her five daughters soon afterward to the court, where they were very [honou]rably entertained, and with all princely [kind]ness, as you shall understand in a *more* fit place hereafter.

25   [The] king kept a very great and magnificent Christmas feast this [year] at Westminster, and as soon as that was ended, [he s]ummoned a Parliament, viz., 23rd day of January, [in] the first year of his reign, to be holden at Westminster. [In] that Parliament, many great and grave and honourable matters [were] handled, and many very good laws were made, and *of which*
30   *I shall give* instances hereafter. [And in this Par]liament, the marriages of King Edward were de[ba]ted and tried, *and* his marriage with the Lady Gray was declared [and] adjudged to be unlawful, and his children [begotten upon her] to be illegitimate and bastards be[cause he was formerly contr]acted and also married to the Lady [Eleanor Talbot, daughter of the
35   old Earl of Shrewsbury, and relict to the Lord Butler of Sudeley, then living and long after.]

      And all the foresaid matters objected and pleaded by the Duke of Buckingham in his speeches and orations made in the name of the nobles and commons against this marriage of the Lady Elizabeth Gray, and against
40   the unlawfulness and bastardy of the children of King Edward, and against the attainder and incapacity of reign of the children of the Duke of Clarence; also the matters contained in the bill supplicatory of the deputies of the northern people were rehearsed, and those, and all the foresaid objections and accusations, were approved and allowed, and judgement
45   was given and pronounced against that unlawful second marriage of King Edward and against the illegitimacy and bastardy of his children and against their incapacity of reigning, as also of the Earl of Warwick and his sister, the Lady Margaret Plantage[net.] And this judgement and sentence was decreed, ratified, and confirmed b[y] Act of Parliament. And therefore it
50   must be thought that this court o[f Parliament] dealt justly and rightly, or

47
The Queen [Mother and] King Richard [made friends]

The Parl[iament] of King Ric[hard III]

47v

else the detractor may say (and which were an extremely foul sca[ndal) t]hat
there was [neither one hone]st or [just nor godly man in that] Parliament,
but *all were corrupte*d.

Moreover, in this Parliament public knowledge was taken of the
[seditious] and highly ambitious practices of Henry, Earl of Richmond and 　5
[of his] treasons, and of his false claim made to the crown and king*dom* by a
title derived from his kindred to the House of Lancas[ter,] and how that this
earl was at that time in France, practi[sing] and labouring by all means to
persuade and to draw [the] French king and the Duke of Brittany to enter
into his quarrel and to aid him to inva*de* this land, and to put down and to 　10
destroy the lawful and rightful king.

[It was fur]ther declared in the court of Parliament that he to the
effecting hereof, and for the better colour and pretext [to] bring his disloyal
purpose to pass, practised, and by all me[ans] sought and promised to
marry the eldest da[ughter] of King Edward, supposing thereby to join the 　15
titles [of] York and Lancaster together, and pretending by *means* of this
marriage to compose and atone *and bring* to an end all the quarrels and
questions which had been between those tw*o* [princely] Houses. But it
rather proved to be the end of the line of th[e House] of York. And yet the
true and rightful Lancaster had no fi[nger in it. For it] was not then granted 　20
this earl was of the House of Lancaster until the Pope by hi[s Bull had
given him the style of Lancaste]r, and that he himself, after he was king,
had by his prerogative royal made himself [of that house, which I will *turn*
to in the next book, when I come to report all the titles of this Earl of
Richmond. 　25

[But] in the meantime, whilst this earl was most busily occupied in his
seditious practices and treasons [again]st the king and his estate, he was
attainted in this Parliament [of High Treason, as also many of those English
noblemen and gentlemen who were] / his confederates and had entered
falsely into the conspiracies and treacherous practices with him and for him, 　30
and namely John, Earl of Oxford, Thomas, Marquess of Dorset, Jasper,
Earl of Pembroke, Lionel, Bishop of Salisbury, Piers, Bishop of Exeter, the
Lady Margaret, Countess of Richmond, mother to the earl, Thomas
Morton, Bishop of Ely, and jointly with him one Thomas Nandick (by the
style of Thomas Nandick of Cambridge, conjurer), and William Knevet of 　35
Buckingham, smeared with the like pitch. Then George Brown of
Beckworth, Thomas Lewkenor of Tratton, John Guildford, John Fogg,
Edward Poynings, Thomas Fiennes of Hurstmonceux, Nicholas Gains-
ford, William Clifford, [J]ohn Darrell, and many other gentlemen and
knights of Kent and of the West Country and of other parts. All these were 　40
attainted of treason with the Earl of Richmond in the Parliament. Then also
for the approbation and confirmation of the true [and law]ful title of King
Richard to the crown of England, there [is thi]s clause or sentence enacted
by the whole court of [Parli]ament, viz.,

[It] is declared, pronounced, decreed, confirmed, and esta[blish]ed by the 　45
authority of the present Parliament that King [Richa]rd III is the very true
and undoubted king of [this r]ealm, as well by right of consanguinity and of
heritage, [as by] lawful election, consecration, and coronation.

[T]hus much briefly of the Parliament of King Richard. And whereunto
[I will] add that I observe in a place of the Roll of [Par]liament that there is 　50

48

The friends and con-
federates of the Earl
of Richmond

argument to be gathered from thence [that the] two sons of King Edward IV
were living in [the time] of that Parliament, and that was (at the least) nine
[months after the] death of King Edward and six months after Richard was
crowned king. And hereof we [may make also this] observation that if King
5 Richard, being [then lawfully and quietly possessed of] the crown, had
suffered them [to live so long after his coronation, there is no reason why he
should after make them away; [for their lives could not rectify their bloods
nor their titles, so that their lives could not hurt him nor their deaths
advantage him. Neither are the lives of bastards dangerous or prejudicial to
10 the just and true titular lords, nor to the lawful and rightful proprietary,]
be he prince or subject. Witness France and other countries, and even
England itself, as I could demonstrate by many examples. For bastards a[re]
not capable of heritage nor of honour nor offices. But I will say no more of
this matter, because it is handled, and more properly, in another place of
15 this story hereafter.
To proceed then in those causes. In the month of February and toward
the end of that Parliament aforesaid, the king, out of a tender fatherly love
of the prince his son, and in a provident care of his future royal fortune and
sta[te], and to establish the succession of the kingdom in him, and to draw
20 and to build the affection and love of the barons and of his liege people
unto him, thought it very important and needful in this case to require the
prelates and the noblemen and many knights and gentlemen of quality to
come to the Palace of Westminster, and there in **interiori caenaculo** (as mine
author saith) to offer unto them an oath of fealty and of allegiance in
25 writing, and ten*dered unto t*hem by the Duke of Norfolk; and they took and
swore the oath willingly and readily. And then the Duke of Norfolk prayed
and required them to put their hands and subscribe their names unto this
writing, and the which also they will[ingly] accomplished.
The special occasion and cause of the tenderi[ng] and of the requiring this
30 oath proceeded and grew from the jealous[y] and fear which the king had of
the secret and seditious practices *of* the Earl of Richmond and of the Duke
of Buckingham, and whose con[sorting] and conspiring with the Earl of
Richmond was now discovered, and more plainly and certain[ly] known, as
also their confederates. And because these conspirators and their
35 confederates were many, and fit to be *sought out,* and in that it was time
that they were apprehended and suppressed, therefore the king *had* erected
a new and a great officer some months before [in] the name of Vice-Constable
of England, to whom he [gave] ample power and authority to search and to
seek and also *to* chastise and to suppress all such persons as were known [or]
40 vehemently suspected to be of the said traitorous conspira[cy.] And this
office was committed to the wise and stout and val*iant* knight, Sir Ralph
Ashton, by the king's letters pa[tents,] and made by the king himself **ore
tenus.** And because [the] precedent is rare, and the office very great, I think
fit [to let] the reader see a true copy of the said commission o[r letters]
45 patents, and taken **verbatim** as they stand recorded [in the] Chapel of the
Convertites, or Rolls:
Rex dilecto et fideli suo Radulpho Asheton militi, salutem. Sciatis quod
nos de fidelitate, circumspectione, et probitate vestris plenius confidentes,
assignavimus, deputavimus, et ordinavimus vos hac viceconstabularium
50 **nostrum Angliae ac Commissarium nostrum dantes et concedentes vobis**

The sons [of King
Edward] living [in
January and Feb-
ruary following the
death of King
Edward IV]

48v

[Vice Constable of
Eng]land

49

[Vi]ce Constabulario
[Ang]liae constituto.
Patentes de anno 1,
Richard III, parte 1,
mem. 2

tenore praesentium potestatem et auctoritatem generalem et mandatum
speciale ad audiendum et examinandum ac procedendum contra
quascumque personas de crimine laesae nostrae regiae Maiestatis suspectas
et culpabiles, tam per viam examinationis testium quam aliter prout vobis
melius visum fuerit ex officio mero seu promoto, necnon in causis illis 5
iudicaliter et sententialiter, iuxta casus exigentiam et delinquentium
demerita, sine strepitu et figura iudicii appellatione quacumque remota
quandocumque vobis videbitur procedendum iudicandum, et finali
executioni demandandum cum omnibus etiam clausulis, verbis et terminis
specialibus ad executionem istius mandati et auctoritatis nostrorum de iure 10
vel consuetudine requisitis, quae etiam omnia hic expressa habemus,
assumpto vobiscum aliquo tabellione fide digno, qui singula conscribat una
cum aliis quae in praemissis vel circa ea necessaria videbuntur, seu
qualitercumque requisita mandantes et firmiter vobis iniungentes quod aliis
quibuscumque praetermissis circa praedicta quotiens et quando opus fuerit 15
intendatis, causasque antedictas audiatis examinetis, et in eisdem procedatis
ac eas iudicetis et finali executioni ut praefertur demandetis. Damus etiam
omnibus et singulis quorum interest in hac parte tenore praesentium
firmiter in mandatis quod vobis in praemissis faciendis pareant assistant et
auxilientur in omnibus diligenter. In cuius, &c. Teste Rege apud Coventr., 20
24 die Octobris, anno regni primo. Per ipsum Regem ore tenus.

50

[What] / success this commission and new office of Vice-Constable of
England [had, I] have not found reported. But I doubt it came too late, or
that the new officer was *negligent*. For the [faction]s and conspiracies of the
king's enemies, or rather traitors against King *Richard*, [sough]t to corrupt 25
and to win all men to them, and [were] secretly and suddenly grown to such
a strength and such [height tha]t nothing then but more mighty forces and
greater armies and a sharper sword *could have the powe*r to oppress and to
extinguish them, *and to which I shall give further considera*tion in the next
boo*k*. 30

50v

[Yet surely, in my opinion, the institution of this new office] / was very
politic and of great importance, howsoever it succeeded. And it is a pl[ain]
portrait and ritrat or image, and hereafter, of the office and authority of the
Great or High Constable of England, and the which office being in the
hands of a valorous, wise, and faithful baron and exercised in fit and due 35

Other officers of
Richard III

time is of great good use and of the highest importance. And sithence that I
have made mentions of these offices and of the officers exercising and
enjoying them, and also of some other officers of this King Richard, it shall
not be a parergon in this void place, but rather a just and necessary work, to
add and supply the rest of the king's officers, and not only the chief, but 40
also the rest, at the least if their offices were places and charges of honour
or of dignity, or the administrators thereof were men of some special
quality. And I have already told who was the High Constable, the Great
Marshal, the High Admiral, the Lord Chancellor, and the Lord
Chamberlain of this king, and therefore I shall not need to ma*k*e repetition 45
of them. But the rest (not mentioned before) are th[ose] which follow:
namely, Sir John Wood, knight, the eld[er,] was Lord Treasurer, J[ohn]
Touchet, Lord Audeley, was Lord Treasurer during the rest [of] the reign of
the king. The Great Seal was committed to Dr Russell, [Bishop of Lincoln.]
Thomas Barowe was Master of the Rolls. And because he was a very 50

sufficient and serviceable minister, and a wise man, King Henry VII, *successor* to King Richard, retained and continued him in his office and place, [and made] him one of his Privy Council. Mr John Kendall was principal Secre[tary, Sir] William Hopton was Treasurer of the Household,
5 and Sir Thomas Percy was Controller to King Richard, and after [him,] John [Buck] *was that* officer. And John Gunthorp was Keeper of the Privy Seal. Sir William Hussey was Chief [Justice,] Thomas Tremain and Roger Townsend were the King's Serge[ants,] and Morgan Kidwelly was his Attorney, and N. Fitzwilliam [Recorder of London.] And I have already
10 remembered that his base son was Captain of Calais.

And now I will treat of the rest of the treaties which were *en*tertained betwixt this king and some foreign princes concer[ning] matters of state and of honour and also of profit. I have found a memorial of a treatise for intercourse [and] commerce between King Richard and Philip, Duke of
15 B[urgundy] and the estates of Flanders, and who in the record are called **[mem]bra Flandriae.** And these princes and states had each [of them] three commissioners to confer and to treat and to deter[mine the] affairs. And I find also that they came to good [agreement] and dispatched and concluded those affairs [with approbation of the princes, their masters. And there]
20 was about that time also a commission directed to certain grave and learned men to hear and redress the complaints made to the king by the subjects of the kings of France and Denmark, and they were well expedied.

In the next year of this king, viz., **anno regni** 2, that treaty of peace and league with Scotland, and begun before (as I have intimated) was continued
25 and finished by [ce]rtain ambassadors and commissioners sent from James IV, King of Scotland, and by other commissioners [d]elegate for the King of England. The ambassadors *and* commissioners for Scotland were these: Coli, [Ear]l of Argyle,* Chancellor of Scotland, N., Bishop [of] Aberdeen, the Lord Lisle, the Lord Drummond [of] Stobhall, Mr Archibald Quhitlaw,
30 Archdeacon [of] Lodon and Secretary to the king, *item,* Lion [K]ing at Arms, and Duncan of Dundas. And *they* were honourably received by the king in the [Gr]eat Chamber in the said castle, where the said [M]r Archibald Quhitlaw, stepping before the rest, and somewhat [ne]arer to the king, who then sat under his Royal [Cl]oth of Estate, and attended by many
35 noble barons, knights, and other worthy persons, made a very [elo]quent oration in Latin, and for the most part [in] the praise of martial men and of the Art Military. [And bec]ause there is also much in it tending to honour and praise [of] King Richard, I have chosen and selected some of *the choic*er flowers thereof. And I will reserve them *until I dec*lare of the other his
40 particular honours, and that toward the end, *and where I wi*ll make it the corollary of them.

And here I will proceed with the occasion of *the visit* of these ambassadors, and the which was to treat [partly about m]atters of truce and of peace, and partly [about a marriage of James,] the prince of Scotland,
45 [with the Lady Anne, daughter of John de la Pole, Duke of Suffolk, and niece to King Richard. The] / commissioners of the King of England who treated with these Scottish ambassadors for this truce and peace were John, Bishop of Lincoln; Richard, Bishop of St Asaph; John, Duke of Norfolk; Henry, Earl of Northumberland; Mr John Gunthorp, **Custos Privati Sigilli**
50 (i.e., Keeper of the Privy Seal); Sir Thomas Stanley, Lord Stanley; Sir N.,

[**Thesau. Scaccar.** 1 Richard III]

*Artic*les for league [and comm]erce with [Flanders,] etc.
52*

[In] Roll [anno] 1 Richard III

A[nno Domini 1484, a treaty with the] King [of Scotland]

*Erg[ile in record]

52v*

Lord Strange; Sir N., Lord Powys; Sir Henry, Lord Fitzhugh; Sir
Humphrey, Lord Dacres; Mr Thomas Barowe, Master of the Rolls; Sir
Richard Ratcliff; William Catesby; and Richard Salkeld. And the other
English ambassadors for the other treaty (and concerning the matter of
alliance and of marriage) were Thomas, Archbishop of York; John, Bishop   5
of Lincoln; John, Bishop of Worcester; John, Duke of Norfolk; John, Earl
of Nottingham; John Sutton, Lord Dudley; N., Lord Scroop of Upsall; Sir
William Hussey, Chief Justicer of the King's Bench; Sir Richard Ratcliff;
and William Catesby.

And this treaty had had good success if the manifold troubles, tumults,   10
and seditions [of the] fickle barons had not come on so fast as that they
interrupted the treaty of the marriage, and man[y] other good works. And

[The Lady Anne de
la Pole a nun]
the Lady Anne de la Pole, being discouraged with the ill success here[of,]
resolved to hearken to no more motions nor [trea]ties, but forthwith took a
religiou[s] habit and became a nun in the monastery [of] Sion.   15

[Treaty] with the
[Duke of] Brittany
There was also a treaty of truce and pea[ce] in this second year of King
Richard between him [and] Francis, Duke of Brittany, or at least gi[ven out
to] be held for a peace; but that was but a part, and ra[ther] a pretext and
colour of the treaty, for the ma[in] negotiations of the king's part was about
the means to get the E[arl] of Richmond out of his hands and to have h[im   20
de]livered to him, or else kept a[s he] was in the time of the king his brother.
The chief [negotiators] and mediators in this t[reaty were the Bishop of
Lincoln and Sir Thomas Hutton for the king, and the Bishop of

53*
[Ibi]dem in
[Sc]accario
Lyons and others for the duke.] / This treaty for the truce and peace was
begun **Anno Domini** 1484 and finished and ratified in the year following. 25
But yet the duke broke and violated it immediately. For he gave aid to the
king's enemies and rebels, **ut supra.**

Treaty with the King
of Fr[ance]
And in the same year there were letters made (and are yet extant in the
Treasury of the Exchequer) about matters of truce and peace moved
between King Richard and Charles VIII, King of France, and wherein [it]   30
must be understood that the matter of the tribute aforesaid was one article.

Trea[ty of marriage
of] King [Richard]
with [the Lady]
Eliz[abeth]
There was also in the year before passed another treaty, and the which I
may not omit, and that also was a treaty for marriage, and that a close and
secret treaty, and it was for the marriage of the Lady Elizabeth, eldest
daughter to King Edward IV, and even with King Richard himself. And   35
what the success of this treaty was, and how far it proceeded, I will defer to
declare until I come to the scandals and crimes objected against King
Richard, because this treaty is accounted and reputed amongst them,
though very unjustly.

[Th]is place and time also require that I should here make commem-   40
oration of the charitable and good works of [this] king, and of his founding
of churches and colleges, and of the erecting of other good and beneficial
monu[men]ts, but I have determined to reserve them for the [end,] and to
the end they may accompany his other [pio]us, honourable, and
magnificent and profitable works, and other matters of his praise and   45
honour. And the chief or special cause why I have thus deferred the report
of those his good deeds and virtues is because they will have small credit and
small grace to be reported and to be remembered in such honourable wise
until the many slanders and false criminations brought against this king be
answered and confuted.   50

This is a fit time and place to relate the conspiracy and treason *and* rebellion of Henry, Duke of Buckingham and *the* other inconstant and seditious barons and *those* who joined with him. For this was the **preparatif** [and] **fourrier** of the rest. This [duke, togeth]er with his complices,
5 pretended the [cause of their] discontentment and mutiny [to be for the reformation of the ill government and tyranny of the king, and under this colour (for treason is ever] / fairly palliated) they resolved to take arms against the king and to bereave him both of crown and life. And here they discovered their ancient and native vice and fault and taint, to wit, their
10 inconstancy and disloyalty and variableness, and also perfidiousness, and the which the prince supposed in the beginning, as I intimated *before.* And herein those false barons imitated the ingrateful and perverse Jews, who one while cried very kindly, **Osanna,** and **Osanna in altissimis** and **Benedictus qui venit in nomine Domini,** and anon they cried, **Crucifige, crucifige.**
15 **Tolle, tolle, crucifige eum.** Thus inconstant are men, and even to the best of men and most deserving love and loyalty.
And this duke, who made the first overture and demonstrations of the false heart of a seditious baron, departed malcontent from the court and retired himself to his strong castle of Brecknock in Wales. But he made not
20 that general and publicly pretended cause of sedition, to wit, the king's great crimes and tyranny, to be all his quarrel, but he also challenged the king for some private wrongs, as namely for the king's denying to give o[r] to restore (as he would have it) to him the earldom of Hereford and the Constableship of England (for they went together a long time), and the
25 which he said belonged to the partage which fell to his grandmother, the Lady Anne, daugh[ter] and heir of Thomas de Woodstock Plantagenet, alias Duke of Gloucester and Earl of Buckingham, and of his w[ife] Eleanor, daughter and coheir of Humphrey de Bohu[n,] Earl [of] Hereford and Constable of England.
30 But this claim of the duke was not unjust. And because that clai[m and] this [con]troversy may the better be understood, I wi[ll] set down the cause and case according to the truth t[hereof,] and the rather for the king's justification. An*d of this* kind of good offices this story hath most need. This is the case: Humphrey de Bohun, Earl [of] Hereford, of Essex, and of
35 Northampton, and Lord of Brecknock, and Constable of Englan[d] in the time of Edward III, and the [last] earl of the family of the Bohuns, had by th[e] Lady Joan his wife, daughter of Rich[ard] Fitzalan, Earl of Arundel, two daughters and heirs, Eleanor and Mary. E[leanor was] married to the same Thomas P[lantagenet, **alias** de Woodstock, youngest son of King
40 Edward III, and Duke of Gloucester and Earl of Buckingham.]
Mary, the second daughter, was married to Henry Plantagenet, Duke of Lancaster, and after King of England by the name of Henry IV, and the earldom of Hereford fell to his wife. And in regard and favour thereof, he was created Duke of Hereford by King Richard II. And this earldom (now a
45 duchy) and the rights thereof, remained in the king and in the king's heirs and successors until the death of King Henry VI, who died without issue. And then all the estate of Lancaster escheated to King Edward IV, and from him it came to King Richard, as heir to his brother the king, and to all the kings his ancestors.
50 And this Duke of Buckingham craved and required that earldom of King

The treas[on of the] Duke of Buc[king- ham]

53v

Mat. 21. John 19.

[The Duke of] Buck- ingham [first riseth in] rebellion

[The quarrel of] the [Duke of Bucking]- ham [against King] Richard

[The titl]e of the [earldom] of Here- ford [and of t]he Constable[ship o]f England

54*

Richard, pretending a title to it by his said grandmother Anne, who was one of the daughters and heirs of the foresaid Lady Mary, wife of Thomas de Woodstock, Duke of Glou[c]ester and Earl of Buckingham. And she was the wife of Edward Stafford, Ear[l of Stafford, and grandfather] to this duke. The [d]uke the rather presumed to make the claim because, [th]e issue 5 of the other sister, Eleanor, being extinct, he took hi[mself to be] her heir. But King Richard, not liking this suit because it savoured of the like secret ambition and [aff]ectation of royalty and sovereignty as was in Henry of B[olingbroke, ans]wered the Duke of Buckingham and told him that [th]e earldom of Hereford was the inheritance of *King* Henry IV , and which was 10 also King of England *and France,* but by tort and by usurpation. 'And will you, my [Lo]rd of Buckingham', quoth the king, 'claim to be heir to [King Henry IV? Then you w]ill also haply assume his spirits, and then you will also [cla]im the crown, and by the same titles'.

The answer was very displeasing and bitter to the duke, and it was doubly 15 [ill] taken of him, first because it came with a repulse of his suit, *and* then next because it seemed to proceed from a [sus]picion which the king had of his high ambition and *affec*tation of the crown, and as a tax also of his disloyal mind. [With this, the] duke pretended another cause of grievance *and of* injury, and that was the breach of the king's promise and *declaration* 20 whereby he bound himself to join the prince [his son] *in* marriage to the Lady Anne Stafford, daughter [of the Duke of] Buckingham. But these exceptions and challenges [were but pretences] of his revolt, and [the true cause was well divined and found out by the king, which was his ambition and aim to be sovereign, springing from that] / overweening which the duke 25 had of the royal blood which he supposed to [be] in himself and in his descent from the said Thomas of Woodstock, Duke of Gloucester, and son of a king.

54v

The ambition of the
Duke of Buckingham

But he was not resolutely determined to make his claim to the crown, nor to attempt the kingdom by rebellion and seditious arms until he was 30 earnestly incited and animated and persuaded thereunto by the factious and seditious clerk, Dr Morton, Bishop of Ely, and the[n] also a Privy Counsellor, but in disgrace, and committed to the custody of the duke as a prisoner (as hath been said), and for his treachery and seditious practices against the king. And at this time, and particularly, amongst other offences 35 of the prelate, one offence of his was greater, for because that he, being a Privy Counsellor, gave secret advertisement to the Earl of Richmond of all that passed in the secret council of the king; and that is double treason.

[And] thus he, being ill affected to the king and perceiving the duke's discontentment and his ill affection also to the king by sundry of his 40 speeches which passed in the often conferences betwixt them, as also finding his aspiring mind and ambition and his great good opinion of his royal

[Dr Morton persu]-
adeth [the Duke of
Buck]ing[ham to
rebel]

bl[ood] *and* stem, took the advantage thereof, and finely fed his vain and proud humour, and wrought diligently upon th[ose tickling] grounds. For the drift and chief desire of Mor[ton] was to prepare the duke to rebellion at 45 any ha[nd,] but not that he should seek to get the kingdom and comp*ass* the crown thereby for himself. For Morton had [destined that to another, whom he] loved much better, and as you have heard and shall hear better. But this prelate, to draw the duke on the faster into his net and to *make him* apt to rebel, first he persuaded earnestly the duke to claim his title to the 50

crown and to take the advantage of the presen[t] times, in respect that now
he which reigned was [an] usurper and a murderer and a tyrant, and hated
of all men, and that he would ere long be pulled fro[m] the royal throne by a
most noble and worthy person.

5   The ambitious and silly duke bit at this cunning, deceitful bait and
swallowed it. And in a word, he was much encouraged and incensed [by]
these mutinous motions and treacherous exhortations of the bishop. And
after he had a while ruminated or meditated of the b*ishop's* speech, he
desired to know of him who [that] brave and noble and worthy person was
10 who would pull the ty*rant* King Richard out of his royal throne. [The
bishop] answered that it was the noble Earl [of Richmond,] and who, upon
his certain k[nowledge, was resolved to invade this land. And] *to help him
to* / accomplish this his enterprise, it was resolved by the Queen Widow of
King Edward IV to give her eldest daughter Elizabeth to him in marriage
15 and therewithal to bring all the friends and lovers of the House of York who
were at her service and devotion into this action, and that by the means also
of this marriage, the titles of York and Lancaster should be united, and so
all claims should cease and vanish away. And further, this prelate added
that many great and potent lords and many worthy and valiant knights and
20 resolute and adventurous gentlemen were entered into this confederacy (or
rather conspir*acy*) and faction, and had faithfully promised to the Earl of
Richmond and to his mother and to the queen and to his other chief friends
that they would join their forces to his forces and assist him to their
uttermost and at all hazards in this attempt for the crown of England, and
25 that also some foreign princes ha[d promised to assist him.]

And as it hath been intimate*d*, when the bishop had spoken these words
and thus [wi]th much art and treacherous and crafty rhetoric set forth,
declared, and advanced the cause and the forces and *promis*ed and
accomplished power *and the* greatness of the titles of the Earl of Richmond,
30 York and Lancaster being so *conjoined, and* then had *urged an*d insinuated
the great hope and fair possibility of the good success of this earl in *his*
*en*terprise of England.

The duke withdrew a little *and* was much troubled and perplexed with this
a*d*vertisement, and he then, being [entered into] a wrong way, *be*gan to
35 consider, and more advisedly, and that his titles and claim would be
nothing. [If] the titles of York and Lancaster were united and joined
together, *they* would be so mighty *and* be so strong — because then they
would draw all the *factions together* — as that neither he nor any much
more mighty m*an* should by no means be able to resist and *to* encounter
40 with them, and much less to prevail against them. And he *had wandered*
*into a fool'*s paradise, and he apprehended that the grass was [cu]t under his
feet, and in a word, he doubted that he was abused. And thereupon he
grew out of liking with his [ow]n cause and of his title, and into utter
despair of the *goo*d success thereof, as well because the Earl of Rich[mon]d
45 was not only so resolute to attempt the gaining of the *roya*l goal, and at all
perils, but also, and chiefly, because he was so strong and w*as we*ll
furnished with arms and with forces and guarded *and* aided with such
multitudes of great and puissant friends as well foreign as *native.* And when
this duke had weighed well the state of these affairs and well considered, he
50 found plain*ly and conc*eived that to contend with the Earl of Richmond and

***of the Earl *of*
*Rich*mond

55*
[Sir] Thomas More

be his rival for the crown were but to seek his *own* ruin and destruction, and nothing else to be hoped or expected.

And now it may be conceived that the duke, after due consideration and meditation upon these plots and evil counsels, could have been content to have been silent, and doubtless that he wished to have been reconciled to the 5 king and to have his love again and to enjoy his favour as he had in former times, and his *trust*. The duke in his reply to Morton somewhat discovered all this in effect, for therein he bewrayed his disgust and distaste of the prelate's counsel and perilous *arguments* and persuasions, and that he suspected that they were not only cunning and ambiguous, but also very 10 dangerous. And he smelled some spice of fraudulent practice, in that the prelate first persuaded and advised him to take arms against the king and to make his title to the crown to be the pretense and colour thereof; and after that he had brought him to resolve to undertake that great business, the duke thought it strange that Morton should anon use such arguments to 15 divert him [and] *terri*fy him with the amplification of the greatness of the great aspirer and with the impossibility [to resist him]; *and* [so] from thence to come by degrees to persuade the duke to be the earl's follower and his fellow conspirer: he would have the duke to love and to join with him in his rebellion and perfidious enterprise. And in brief, the duke thought (as he 20 had *reason to think,*) that these things did not well hang together. And the duke acknowledged that he should not be ab*le to* over*come these doubts,* for∗∗∗∗∗∗∗∗∗∗∗∗ he∗∗∗∗∗∗∗∗∗∗∗∗ and∗∗∗∗∗∗∗∗∗∗∗.

And therefore, as soon as the subtle prelate perceived the dislike and the alteration of the duke, and having a ready and a nimble wit and an eloquent 25 tongue, he found instantly a device to salve the disgust of the duke and to correct and *over*come that his alteration, and then to retain still the duke in his former false purpose and inclination to rebellion. Wherefore he insinuated *to this* duke that albeit [he knew his title] to the crown was very good, and that he wished with all his heart that he might possess it, but yet 30 h[e would] not conceal the plot and the power of the Earl of Richmond from him, because as he said there was no reason to suppose that so great strength and forces which that no*ble earl possessed,* and so *many* great and powerful friends as he had abroad and at home, should fail or not happily and absolutely prevail in that his enterprise of England and of his getting of the 35 crown. And that therefore on the other side it was not to be hoped that the duke should be able to make forces sufficien[t to encounter] with him and to resist, and much less to suppress him and thereby to catch or snatch the gar*land* or crown from the earl's head, there being no hope or possibility thereof. Yet he would not have the duke to change his mind and to forbear 40 to take arms for any such doubts of *hazards* or losses and so high and great fortunes as seemed to trouble and to alter him.

Because (he tol*d* the duke) that albeit he forbore his claim, yet there were other reasons, and very important, although he had no cause or [claim to the crown,] why he sh[ould] be resolute in his taking of arms against the 45 king and to join [with] the earl, and to assist him in his attempt and royal ambite. 'For', quoth he, 'by [this] enterprise, and by the most certain victory which will ensue, you [shall be] revenged of Richard, and you shall have full satisfaction of all *the* wrongs done to you by him. And besides, I dare assure [you] that the earl, as soon as he is king, shall in all kinds of 50

h[onourable] and princely gratitude acknowledge his great obligation,
[and] shall not only restore all the honours and titles, [office, and signories
to you which you] claim, which Ri[chard hath unjustly detained, but shall
advance you above any other nobleman'.

5   [Further, he engages the duke] / that as he was a great man and a chief
peer of the realm, so in regard thereof, his principal and most honourable
obligation was to help and to relieve the oppressed subjects, and to reform
abuses, and to purge the land of impiety and of tyranny, and to provide
carefully for the good and prosperous estate of the kingdom. And he then
10   inculcated that by how much a man is greater, that by so much the greater is
his obligation and bond to do good to his country and to redress wrongs and
oppressions, at any hazard of his person and f[ortune. And he, being the]
grea[test and most eminent person in the kingdom, was therefore] bound in
honour to be the most forward in this work, and that for what difficulty or
15   danger somever, he ought to exp*ect* to use his power and his forces for the
defence or preservation and of the commonwealth.

And then again and afresh this prelate urged and, [as it were, refr]icated
[t]he sundry and particular wrongs done to him by King Richard. For [h]e
finely found that argument to be the most vigorous and forcible, and the
20   sharpest *s*ting to incense and stir up the duke to rebellion; and the which
wrongs he un*d*erstood partly by his often conferences with the duke and by
the duke's many and bitt*er* *c*omplaints of the injuries done to him by the
king, and partly by his own observations thereof, and by other means. And
he intimated *and* aggravated the greatness and the extremeness thereof, and
25   that [t]hey were so intolerable as that they were cause enough alone *for* him
to endeavour and to seek by all means the overthrow *and* ruin of the king.
And that therefore, although neither he (nor y*et* *any other* *s*traight and clear
eyes) could see that by his taking of arms in the cause of [his] title and for
the advancement of his claim to the kingdom *th*at he might prevail in his
30   hope and attempt thereof, *for* the reason of the ever strong and mighty
opposition and vehement and violent ambite of the Earl of Richmond
(which would be *irresisti*ble and insuperable (and as was before intimated
more than once). Yet he would in no cause have [the duke] be an idle
spectator in so great and so *noble and* so meritorious an action, especially
35   considering disturbing the king from the throne and his overthrow, and *that
it promised* a good amending and fair satisfaction [for his wrongs, and his
more assured and greater honours.]

Thus the orator; I will not say the **primus motor,** for that were to profane
a hol[y word, but he may be sa]id to be **primus molitor,** and in French, **le
40   premier mutin,** and chief mover of sed[ition.] And he told his tale so
cunningly as that the duke was again and anew stirred up t*o be* false and
disloyal, and he was with these argument*s* much more encouraged and
inflamed with the fire and fury of rebellion. And now therefore he entered
into the conspiracy and plots and practices of treasons, and he became a
45   chief actor in them, all*owing* both the reasons of his **malus genius,** as well
for the taking of his own revenge, as also f*or* the assisting and advancing of
the Earl of Richmond.

And it was not long ere the duke made a journey to visit the C[oun]tess of
Richmond, and to confer with her about these treacher*ous* matters. For she
50   was entered far into them, and none better plunged in them and deeply

57
**Nobiles sunt spes
miserorum.** Seneca
Declam. 12

57v

[This Margaret,]
Countess [of Rich-
mond, was d]aughter
[and heir to John

Beauf]ort, first Duke
[of Somerset, and]
Margaret [Beaufort,]
mother of [the Duke
of] Buckingham,
was [daughter of]
Edmund, Duke [of
Somerset.] And thus
were [the Earl of
Richmond] and the
Duke [of Bucking-
ham ak]in. Robert
[Glover, in **Ca**]tal-
ogue.

58*

acquainted with th*em*. And she was a politic and subtle lady. And he made
open to her of the propositions and motions Dr Morton had made to him
concerning the royal design of the earl her son for England, and of the great
and mighty means which he had to accomplish and effect it. And he told
h[er] also how earnestly the bishop had dealt with him, and how the bishop 5
had persuaded him to ass*ist the* earl in his said enterprise for England. And
then the duke *told the* countess of the intelligence of the prelate in these
[design]*s, to know if they* might be credited.

She answered and pr[otest]*ed* [it was really true, yet short of the full,
which she then report]*ed,* [and fell into a cunning captation of the affection 10
and endearment of her son ever towards him, closing her argument upon
the nearness of blood and kindred betwixt, affirming the duke's mother was
a Somerset, concluding that consanguinity, a great and just bond of mutual
love and friendship — for that cause and the ancient and constant affinity
and respects] / which was between the Duke of Somerset, her father, and 15
the Duke of Buckingham, his father — that he would be kind and loving to
her son and join his love and his forces with those of her son and of his most
noble friends, and who were very many and very great and mighty, etc., and
who had determined and vowed to put down King Richard, the tyrant and
usurper, and to put her son up in his place and to make him king, but 20
provided and upon condition that he would marry the Lady Elizabeth, and
the which to perform he had taken solemn oath. For it must be understood
that this cunning countess had, by the mediations and the ministry of Dr
Lewis, conciliated the love and friendship of the Queen Mother and
persuaded her t[o acc]ept that alliance by marriage, and also drawn her into 25
this conspiracy. And yet in that time the countess, knowing well to
dissemble great love to the king, to desire and to effect the love of King
Richard, came in all h[umility] *and* besought him to call home her son and
to be gracious to him and to vouchsa[fe him the honou]r as to marry him to
any of King Edward's daughters. 30

But to pr*oceed* with this conference of the duke and of the Countess of
Richmond and ret[urn. She,] having prevailed with him (he being apt to
rebel against King Richard) as that he promised her faithfully that *he* would
join with her son and give him all the *hel*p and succours that he could. And
then he took his leave of the countess *and enter*ed forthwith *into* 35
consultation and conjuration with the chief friends of *the* Earl of
Richmond: namely, the Lord Stanley, [the] Marquess of Dorset, Edward
Courtenay, Earl of Devon[shi]re, and his brother, the Bishop of Exeter, Sir
John Bourchier, [Sir J]ohn Wells, Robert Willoughby, Edward Woodville,
Thomas [Aru]ndel, and others, and they resolved the rebellion, and they 40
made ready their [force]s in all haste, and they appointed their rendezvous
[nea]r to Gloucester. And the duke with his Welshmen and *othe*rs, and the
marquess with his northern men, and [the] Courtenays with their western
men, and Sir Richard [Gui]ldford and Sir John Cheyney and other knights
of Kent [and] of the south parts, marched towards Gloucester. And if 45
[thei]r power had been joined, it was so very great as that it had been very
dang[erous.] And they made full and sure account to have given [King]
Richard a terrible and fatal blow.

But the king, having good intellige[nce of all the plots and] counsels of
this rebellion, and he having a good army, made as much haste to meet 50

The con[spirators
with the] Duke of
[Buckingham] for
the [Earl of
Rich]mond

them, and before all their forces were united and a*lso before* the Earl of Richmond should c[ome to the coast of D]orsetshire, where [he was to fight] with them. But the armies never met, for by strange accidents, and both by the element of water, their designs and attempts thereby [were]
5 checked and made frustrate. For the English forces were kept asunder by [a su]dden and very huge inundation, which not only [overflowed] the ways and passages so deeply and so dangerously as the forces *of Buckingham* [c]ould not come together nor pass the River [Severn; but] besides which, the suddenness and strangeness and fright thereof [struck such a terror into] the
10 soldiers that [the most part of them] forsook the duke and came away, leaving him so weak and slenderly guarded that himself was glad to fly too and provide for] / his safety with the swiftness of his heels.

And the accident which overthrew the earl's *attempt* by sea was a great storm and tempest which took him upon the coasts of England, as you shall
15 hear an*on* and at large. But the king, who was an excellent captain, took the advantage instantly which was offered him, and he pursued the disarmed duke, and not only with posting and galloping armies, but also with edicts and proscriptions, offering thereby to give a thousand pounds in money (and whereunto some writers add so much land as was worth £100 by the
20 year) to any man who would bring in the duke.

. And thus first by that disastrous inundation, and next by the diligent chase of the pursuit, and thirdly by the golden charm of reward, this rebellious army and enterprise was defeated there. And the duke was taken and brought to the king (being then at Salisbury) by Humphrey Banister,
25 the duke's false servant. And there the duke being examined, he freely and foolishly confessed all the treason and he discovered all the conspirators, as well the Earl of Richmond as the rest. And this being done, his head was struck off, [according to] martial law used in armies and in the field in November, **Anno Domini** 1484 and **anno** 2 of King Richard III.
30 And this unhappy end had that seditious and inconst*ant baron,* and by the means of Bishop Morton, who, as Sir Thomas More confesseth and affirmeth, [by his politic drifts and] pride [advanced himself and brought the duke] to destructi[on.] And the rest of his fellow conspira[tors] fled, some into sanctuaries, and some into Brittany to the Earl of Richmond, and
35 some into Flanders. And all were glad to hide thems*elves.*

And because that hitherto all things have gone well [with] King Richard, and that his affairs have well prospe*red,* we will close here these his good fortunes and this fir[st] book together.

[The overthrow of the Duke of Buckingham]

58v

Polydore, **Lib.** 25

[King Richard shar]-ply rebuked *and* [re]-prehended [Banister for] apprehending [his master] which argued [a noble min]d.

Explicit Liber I

60

THE SECOND BOOK
OF THE HISTORY OF KING RICHARD THE THIRD

The Contents of this Second Book

[King]s go not now to the wars.
Cruelties executed [upon] the corpse of King Richard.
He was attainted of treason (though against the laws of [nature and of royal] majesty, and hereof see more **Lib.** 4), with many noble and
5   faithful and valiant gentlemen. [His fol]lowers and servants and subjects also attainted.
The Earl of Surrey, how released [out of pris]on.
[Hi]s genealogy from Hewardus.
His goodness to the children orphans [of Sir John Buck.]
10 The description of Hewardus.
[The nobility and grea]tness of the House of Howard.
[Walter de Buck and his progeny.]

THE HISTORY OF KING RICHARD III
THE SECOND BOOK

61v

We left King Richard III in a flourishing and glorious estate, and reigning in peace (*a* never enough desired and blessed state), and he enjoyed all worldly prosperity for a time. But Fortune, that inconstant and variable and unfaithful dame, will suffer no joys nor honours nor pleasures, no prosperity nor any worldly good thing to last long, and much less to be 5 permanent and perpetual in this world. And therefore this was well called by the expert **Heros** in Euripides, **Fortuna diurna:** fortune of a day's life; and especially if she be extraordinarily gracious and favourable, for then she is most wavering and inconstant. And when she is in her best mood, she is brief in her favours and tedious in her mischiefs, as it was well observed 10 by a grave man: **fortuna adversas res cupido animo inducit secundas parco.** And she is a mother but a little while, but a stepdame a long time, and ever to s[ome.]

[Euripides in **Heraclides**]

[Valerius Maximus, Lib. VII]

And indeed she was very sparing and very brief in her favours towards this King Richard, and merely nov[ercal to him.] For he enjoyed them but a 15 little while, and then she changed her countenance, and she frowned upon him, and she much and grievously afflicted him. And times of calamity and adverse chances came galloping and posting upon him. And in this *way* they oppressed and accabled him — but not forever. For Fortune hath no interest no*r* estate in perpetuity; neither can she give permanence or any 20 hig*h* time to anything in this world. But that is only proper to Virtue; for she, like to a go*ddess,* maketh the men which serve and honour her to live long and to flourish still, and to leave a true fame and name of their virtues behind them, according to that wise sente*nce,* **Efficacior est ad b***reve* **tempus Fortuna, ad longum Virtus.** 25

But it may haply be thou*ght that I neglect the will of God* in ascribing so much to Fortune. But yet I pray you to think that I know *not that puni*shment which is not the will of God and by his divine privilege.

Bu[t] now we are ent*ering* [into] *the story o*f the troubles and tumults which angry Fortune hath raised, [which were the end and period] to the 30 story of the unhappy times [of this king and of his reign.] / The invasions of this land of England attempted and made by the Earl of Richmond were the formal and efficient and final cause of all the mischiefs and calamity. I will begin this second book with his invasions, and I say invasions plurally because he twice invaded this kingdom, but through error and ignorance or 35 negligence of our common chroniclers and vulgar historians, they are confounded and made one journey or one invasion. And these have thereby corrupted and maimed the story and concealed or omitted some things well

62

worth the knowing and very remarkable. And particularly by error and by this negligence, the true and certain cause of the ill success of the enterprise of Buckingham and his defeat is misunderstood or not at [all] known. Wherefore I think it necessary to make a brief relation of those first
5 preparations and of the first attempt of invasion made by the said Earl of Richmond.

First then, it must be understood that after it was resolved by him and by the Duke of Buckingham and by the Lord Stanley and other that he should come to make his claim of the crown, and that they assured him by Bishop
10 Morton and other their secret treacherous instruments that he should lack no means nor friends for the accomplishment of his design and for the attaining to the crown, and he were able to bring but so much power and force with him as thereby they might land safely, and to defend himself in any sort until his friends of England came to him, and who would be with
15 him with all speed possible.

Hereupon he propounded this his cause and enterprise to the Duke of Brittany, and told him what good friends he had in England and how great possibilities he had to win the crown and the kingdom. The duke gave him favourable hearing and wished good success unto him and to his designs,
20 but he pleaded first h[is amity and leag]ue with the King of England, which in honour and justice he might not violate; and then *he* alleged his poverty and want of growing, by the long and cruel wars which he had with his barons of Brittany; and he *t*old the earl that therefore he was not able to furnish him as (at the least) [in] any short time, and as his cause required.
25 But the earl, having a great affiance in h[is] own [good] fortune, would not leave the motion and suit thus. But he resolved to renew it to the duke by some of his most honourable and most gracious and po[werful friends.] The truth is that the earl had many and great friends. / But yet I must   **62v**
confess for that the ingenious behaviour, and with sharp and pleasant wit,
30 and the fine, insinuating, also courtly arts of the Earl of Richmond were such, and so agreeable and so plausible to all these noble persons with whom he conversed and to whom he had favourable access, as that he won the favour and the good will and well wishing of them and of many private persons of the best estimation and of the greatest authority; and in brief, of
35 all men and of women likewise.

And he was so good and so cunning an Amoret as that when he came amongst ladies, [he ob]tained and (as I note) he stole their affections and favours from them, so that he was with them very gracious. And he could not only speak French well, but also excellently and best in the amorous and
40 courtly and insinuating style. And to grace that the better, he was, as Philip Commynes, who knew him, testifieth, a very complete and well-featured gentleman. And then the rule is certain and well-ominating: **Gratior est**   Vergil
pulchro veniens e corpore virt[us]:
　　The beauties of the mind more gracious are,
45 　　Whereas the body's features are more fair.

And amongst the many ladies with whom he became acquainted during his fair and courteous imprisonment, he obtained the favour of tw[o] ladies, and these great ladies, and in great *esteem*. And the one, and the first of them, was the Lady Margaret, Duchess of Brittany, and the daughter of
50 Gaston de Foix, a great man in those western parts of France, and whose

ancestors were very well affect[ed] to the English nation, as John Froissart
and Pa[radin] / and sundry French historians report. And the other lady
(and his most gracious lady) was Madame de Beaujeu, and of whom I will
speak in the second invasion.

And it pleased this Lady of Foix, the Duchess of Brittany, to be so   5
favourable to him and to his cause as to afford and to yield [him] help and
succour of men and of money and of ships and of arms and of other
necessary provisions for his enterprise of England. And the duke consented
and granted to furnish the earl with all these things, and in such quantity as
his store and ability would afford, and all the bonds and cautions and   10
pledges which the earl gave and put in for these aids and succours were only
that the earl was to go to the cathedral and chief church of Vannes, and
there, kneeling at the high altar and before the Lord's sacrament, should
faithfully and religiously promise and vow that he would justly and truly
observe such covenants and promises for restitution or satisfaction as he   15
had made to the duke and to the duchess. And the protestation was
accordingly made by the earl.

And then, and immediately thereupon, these warlike implements and
instruments were delivered unto him: to wit, three great ships, well-
equipped and ready rigged and copiously furnished with arms, men, and   20
victuals, and as in these few words of my British author it may be seen: **Au
comte de Richemont furent aux dépens du duc trois gros navires de
Bretagne chargés de gens, d'armes, etc., et qui se mirent en mer.**

[But] by the favour and leave of this British writer, I must tell you that the
earl stayed many days at the seaside and at St Malo. And the cause of his   25
stay was that [in the meantime he might] give advertisement and warning to
the Duke of Buckingham and the rest of *his* loyal barons and other his
consorts in this conspiracy that he was *furnis*hed with soldiers and with a
convenient fleet for his invading this land and for landing *in Englan*d, and
that his best and most experienced friends had advertised him to land in   30
[Hampshire] or in Dorset, because he might descend so near to London and
[in] such plac[e] *of safe*ty and convenience. And he also advertised them
that he would [loose from St Malo's in] the beginning of October, and
prayed them [to have the forces ready at his landing,] and without fail. And
thus h*e advised them,* [and had answer from them that they were ready and   35
would not miss nor fail] to receive him [with good power in those western]
parts, according to his direction and desire.

The earl being thus satisfied in all things, to wit of the English sides there
for the observing of their time and of the place, he weighed anchor and
departed from the port of St Malo in the beginning of October, **Anno**   40
Domini 1484, and accor*ding* to his promise. And he sailed toward England,
and he came before the port of Poole in Dorset, and he cast anchor in the
road or harbour and prepared to land there with all convenient speed, but yet
with safety, or else not. For he was a very wary and a very circumspect man,
and also somewhat timorous.   45

And therefore, and to prevent and to avoid all dangers and damages, he
made choice [of] some stout and well-experienced soldiers to go ashore in
their [skiff]s or cockboats, and in the manner of explorers or spies to go
spy into the *situation* on land and to survey the coasts, and to learn what
news there was ashore, [and get some intelligence] where [the] armies of his   50

friends were, how near they were, and what *King Richard did,* and where he was, and how armed; and other such instructions he gave to them. In the meantime, the earl stayed aboard.

5   But these messengers could [l]earn no certainty, especially of those matters whereof the [e]arl desired chiefly to hear. But they understood that there were many armed men in [the] country and thereabouts — no news of the Duk[e of] Buckingham nor of his forces in those parts. Hereupon the earl grew susp[icious] *and un*happy, and was [weary of] staying in that harbour, and resolved to go to some other port.

10   And it happ[ened] *suddenly* [the] night following an unhappy and adverse accident, but it was very, very happy to him and to his fleet. For there arose so wh*irling and so* terrible a tempest of winds and of foul weather as that he was driven for the safety of his fleet and for the safety of himself and of the life of all his companies to weigh anchor and to go into the wind and main.

15   And with this storm the ships in the darkness of [the ni]ght were severed and dispersed in the sea, and some were driven upon the coasts of Brittany. And the earl's ship fell upon the coasts of Normandy, and the first invasion failed and quailed.

But this storm (as I noted even now) was a happy disaster for the earl, for
20   if he had gone on land at Poole or thereabouts, or if he had stayed but till the king's ships came, and which were not far of[f,] he had been a lost man every way, and he had been brought to the king, and then all his high and ambitious hopes had been cut off, and his head also, without all doubt. For *the* king hated him exceedingly, and was well provided to be revenged of
25   him, and that was *by* the good intelligence which the king *had* of the *p*lots and counsels of the earl and of his consorts at that time from a faithful and secret friend. And thereby the king so well ploughed with their hay for as that he knew all that they either debated or deliberated and resolved. And by this means and at this time he was too hard for the earl and [the Duk]e of
30   Buckingham and for the Earl of Devon and for the other conspirators. And *thus he over*reached them and overshot them in their plots and practices.

For after that he understood what their counsel was, and where their rendezvous should be, and where they were appointed to meet and when, the king by his great wit and industry and skill in martial affairs found good
35   and certain means to prevent all their plots. For whereas it was resolved by these noble rebels that first the forces of the Duke of Buckingham and of the Earl of Devon and others should meet in Gloucestershire and near Gloucester, and that as soon as they were joined, they should march in their full and united strength toward the seacoasts of Dorset, there to receive and
40   to entertain the earl with all their forces — him whom they had chosen and ordained to be their chief captain and also their king, to wit, the Earl of Richmond — the king finely, and like to a skilful captain, prevented and crushed all these purposes and designs. For first, and as soon as he heard that the Duke of Buckingham was armed and that his army was afoot, the
45   king made all haste to meet and encounter him before his forces of his friends and fellow rebels were joined. He perfor[med] *all this* according to his project and desire: for he made such haste to meet with the Duke of Buckingham and to fight with him, and [he encountered him] and beat him, and cut off his head before his friends could come to him.

50   And the king also, to prevent that the Earl of Richmond should not do

66

any harm at his landing, nor join with the said duke and with the rest of the
rebels, he took order that the ordinary bands of the   West Countries should
be appointed to guard the coasts. And he gave directions to the [sold]iers
and guards of the coasts that if [the] Earl of Richmond or any of his French
forces came ashore, that they should entertain them courteously, and to say 5
that they were soldiers and bands of the army of the Duke of Buckingham,
and how that he (having overthrown the king and chased him away) had
sent them thither to receive the earl and his companies and to conduct them
to London. And then the earl had been caught and [ensnared] if the sudden
*a*ccident of the great storm aforesaid, together with the good fortune of the 10
Earl *of* Richmond, *had* not preserved and saved him from that trap which
the king had set for him so subtly.

But yet [this] first expedition and first invasion by sea miscarried and all
was lost, as also the Duke of Buckingham. *But the* earl and the rebels and
the conspirators mended all these faults and errors of th*is first invasion by* 15
the other *and* second invasion. And for the better accomplishing thereof
then, they kept their counsel and purpose so *secret that neither the* king nor
any of his true friends could come to any matter of moment of their designs,
*and as you sha*ll better know when I come to the relation thereof.

[And for my warrant of this] *which I have* here written, I have followed 20
[Sir Thomas More, Polydore Vergil, and the authors of the story of
Little Britain] and some other [French writers, and our common
chroniclers.]

66v
And now here very fitly the strange fortune of the Earl of Richmond
may be considered and observed. And it is very remarkable, for he did not 25
only thrive by the good success and by the prosperous events of his practices
and enterprises, but also by the adverse accidents and by the evil and cross
fortunes thereof. For it was good and happy for him that the storm arose at
Poole, and that it scared and chased him from the coasts of England.

It was also good for him that the Duke of Buckingham was overthrown 30
and defeated in his absence, and utterly. For if the duke had then prevailed
in his rebellious attempt and had overcome the king in the battle and utterly
vanquished and suppressed him, and in the absence of the Earl of
Richmond (for here he was to be not only present in person, but also chief
commander and Captain General of all the for*ces which we*re levied and 35
assembled for him and in his behalf). But he being absent, then the Duke of
Buckingham (who pretended title to the crown and claimed the kingdom as
due to him by right of blood and by lawful inheritance) without doubt
would not have reserved the honours and the fortunes and the glorious and
rich prize of the victory and of such a conq[uest] to the earl, but he would 40
have kept all and seized all to his own use and for himself, and put the
crown upon his own head, and made himself king.

And the reason hereof is ready, and not to be contradicted: and that is
that great men have not been accustomed to part with such stately purchases
nor to surrender any such princely requisitions nor any sovereign 45
possessions to any man during their lives — and n*o*t to any man then but to
their own sons and to their next heirs. And not to go far for any examples,
we have a very famous example thereof: this very Earl of Richmond, who,
when he had gotten the kingdom and, albeit he knew that the children of the
Duke of Clarence and others h[ad] better right to the crown than he, yet he 50

would not resign it to any of them; no, not yet his own son so long as [he]
could hold it. He had many precedents for his warrant and authority, as a[ll
men know who know anything.]

5 And now I will proceed with the other matters of *the* story which
happened in the times following these acc*idents* and occurrents herebefore
related. And if for lack of them there *should be* silence here until we come
to the second invasion of the Earl *of Richmond* (and which is the main
matter of all), we will discourse *at this* time of other things, and which shall
not be impertinent to thi*s* [story] *and* [may well supply the interim and the
10 Reader's observation.]

And first I must declare and relate that in the interim, amongst many
other accidents, there happened unhappily the untimely death of the most
towardly young prince, and the king's most dear and only son (at the least
legitimate), viz., in the month of April, **Anno Domini** 1484. And he died in
15 the Castle of Middleham in Yorkshire. And when [the] heavy news was
brought to the king and to the [qu]een, they were then in the Castle of
Nottingham, and they took the death of this their only son so grievously
and so impatiently that (as mine [auth]or saith) **subitis doloribus insanire
videbantur** : that they were ready to run out of their wits [and] be mad for
20 grief.

But yet the king, being [a] man of much moderation and temperance, and
abounding with great courage and true magnanimity, did as easily a*n*d in as
short time *o*vercome the grief and the care as he had done many adverse
*acc*idents and worldly calamities before; [and a]s it was said of Julius Caesar
25 when the evil and *heavy* news of the death of his dear and only daughter
[Ju]lia was advertised to him, he soon passed it over. **Et tam facile
dolorem [hun]c, quam omnia vicit.** And the King Richard, [as t]he Prior
of Croyland [tell]eth, neglected not his business. Notwithstanding this cau*se
he* [did] all things as gravely and as orderly as before: **Rex Ricardus [nihilo]-
30 minus tamen suarum partium defensioni vacaveri**t.

But the queen, being [more passionate, according to the] tender sex, took
the death of her son so grievously and so passionately, *and it* pierced her so
far and afflicted her *so deeply that there*withal she grew very sick and very
weak and in such extremity *as that she neve*r recovered her health, but she
35 *languished until she* died, and that was not long after this [prince's] *death,*
[and added not a little to the king's sufferings and sorrows, though his
adversaries belied him in that, as in the rest.] *And* [I will not only prove
against them this] / assertion anon when I come to the fit place for it, but
also I will show how much they slandered him who reported that he
40 poisoned or otherwise treacherously made away the queen his wife. And
because this is a great crime, I will also reserve the answering thereof to that
place where I am purposed to do my best to clear him of the false
accusations and unjust criminations and slanders which are brought and
laid against him.

45 But now we will return to this government of the state. And there we
shall find that notwithstanding h*is grief* and great sorrow, yet his care for
matters of importance, and even then (and as I noted before) was well
discovered, and that he was a man not only endowed with true fortitude and
void of passion, and a wise man, but also that he was a true lover and father
50 of his country. For as soon as his son was dead and he issueless, he

67
The [death of
Edward,] Princ[e of
Wales, son of] King
R[ichard III]
[Croyland Chr]on-
i[cle]
[Ibidem]

[Seneca]

67v

delibe[rated] of his successor in the kingdom to himself, and his care was to
nominate such an on[e that was] not only next heir of the crown, but also a
man worthy for his [virtues.] And thereupon without delays he nominated
and chose, with the cons[ent] of the barons, Sir John de la Pole, Earl of   5
Lincoln, son and heir of John de la [Pole,] Duke of Suffolk, and of the
Lady Elizabeth Plantagenet, Duch[ess of Suffolk, the sister and heir of this
King Richard. And he was forthwith [de]clared and proclaimed heir
apparent of the kingdo[m.]

But this was a **countrecoeur** to the faction of Ric[hmond,] and it much
troubled and offended them, and it was as a *thorn* or pin in the eye of   10
Buckingham, of Pembroke, of Morton, and of the Countess of Richmond,
and *as a* crown of thorns set upon his head who affected *the party* of the
golden Richmond, *who lan*guished after the golden and precious crown and
imperial diadem of this kingdom. And what mor*e* extreme and intolerable
injury might b[e] offered to the Earl of Richmond if these gentlemen of the   15
House of Lancaster or of [Beaufort] w[ere] the next heirs to the crown (as
the friends of the Earl of Ri[chmond] a[ffirmed]), and that he was **caput et
princeps familiae gentis Lancastriae.** But [they could not prove] that, nor
hardly that he was **membrum illius familiae,** until he was [king.]

And this is a question heretofore much arg[ued] and disputed, to wit,   20
whether the Beauforts or Somersets were of the House of [Lancaster or no,
and never determi]ned so long as the House of York flourished. But how it
was decided and determ[ined afterward, I could say something,] but I will
not pre[sume to speak indifferently] of this controversy, but I will deliver
the argu[ments which] have been brought about it, and about the claim   25
[which those of Somerset or Beaufort] made [to the crown by the title of
Lancaster.]

And first, and if I may be bold to tell mine opinion, I will first say that
there was much difference held to be between Lancaster and Beaufort, alias
Somerset, and that so long held to be such until pride and usurpation on the   30
one side, and parasitism and gross error on the other side confounded them
and made them one and the same. For there is no doubt but that the houses
of Lancaster and of Beaufort differed as much as royal and feudal, as much
as legitimate and illegitimate, and as sovereignty and suzerainety.

For the children of the House of Lancaster, being lawfully born, and   35
after Henry Plantagenet, Duke of L[ancaster, had conque]red and also
[deposed Richard II,] were held to be princes of the blood royal, and
capable of the crown in their natural and due order. But those of Beaufort
(or Somerset) were, as people say, **filii populi,** or as the imperial
jurisconsults say, **liberi vulgo quaesiti;** and who by the old Greeks were   40
termed ἀπάτορες: **sine patre;** and as the doctors of the spiritual law say,

these kind of children had their **originem ab illicito et damnato coitu,** and
of the polluted and adulterous bed.

And those Beauforts, begotten by John of Gaunt, as he believed and said,
were according to the laws to be reputed the children of Otho Swinford, for   45
Catharine, the mother of these children, was the wife of Sir Otho Swinford,
and the daughter of Sir Payen Rouet, a Frenchman dwelling in Beaufort, a
town in Anjou, and he was Guienne Herald to the Duke of Lancaster. And
albeit this duke was straitly bound by the sacred bands and duties of holy
and honourable matrimony to his most noble and virtuous wife, Dona   50

Constantia, daughter of Don Pedro, King [of] Castile, yet nothingstanding
that zealous religious bond and that solemn vow of conjuga*l faith* at his
marriage, this duke kept as his **pellex,** or leman, or concubine *the* said
Catharine a long time in the life of the noble and virtuous lady his co*nsort,*
5 in which time he begat his four Beauforts, three males [and one fe]male,
upon the said Catherina, and whose husband also, [Sir Otho Swinford,] was
then also living.

And because the Duke of [Lancaster might not] give to these children the
princely [name of Plantagenet nor of Lancaster, he surnamed them from
10 the town of Beaufort, a town of his own where they were born. And they
bore that name of Beaufort,] / and with good liking and contentment, until
that the children of that John de Beaufort, the eldest brother of those base
children of John of Gaunt being made Earl of Somerset, assumed the name
of their father's greatest honour and earldom for their surname, viz.,
15 Somerset. And the rest afterward, following their example, left the name of
Beaufort and took that of Somerset.

And to speak a word more of the frailties of their father, he added error
to error and crime to crime (as the poet saith), for he, after his wife the
duchess and after Sir Otho Swinford were dead, and when he was old and
20 had lived out all the time of his life within one year, he would needs marry
Catherina Swinford and make her a duchess, and against the liking of the
king and of all his noble friends. Besides that, such a marriage as this, and
between such men and women as have lived in adultery, is forbidden by the
common law. And there was much wondering and scoffing at it in the
25 court, as Thomas Walsingha[m writeth.]

And albeit that these base children of John de Gaunt were made
legitimate first by Pope Urbanus VI, and next by the charter of King
Richard II, and both of these indulgences and graces afterward allowed and
confirmed and enlarged by Parliament, yet neither these four legitimated
30 children of the Duke of Lancaster, **Nec qui nascebantur ab illis,** were
allowed and permitted to take the princely familiar title and the gentilitious
surname of Plantagenet, for that was the p[eculiar or] capital surname or
surname in chief, of the kings of Engla[nd and of their] lawful children,
since the time of the second King Henry, son of the Empre[ss Matilda,] and
35 surnamed Plantagenet, and the founder and author of that sur[name] in the
royal family of England, **ut in Libro Pri*mo*.** And [none] but the princes and
princesses of the blood royal and of le[gitimate] birth might take the
surname of Plantage*net*, [(as all our] *goo*d heralds and antiquaries), [of
which honours were partakers the princely families of Wales, of
40 Brotherton, of York, of Lancaster, of Clarence, of Woodstock, of
Gloucester, and others.

And there be yet some noble gentlemen in Portugal who, being descended
from John, Duke of Lancaster, bear that surname and are called and
written de Lancastro. And other having the like origin and title may do the
45 like, and not else. And thereof this is a good argument and testimony: to
wit, that neither King Henry IV, nor King Henry V, nor King Henry VI, all
being kings of the line and race of Lancaster, and albeit they much
respected and favoured these their kinsmen of the house and lineage of
Beaufort or Somerset, and advanced them to many honours, and called
50 them cousins, yet these kings would not endure that those base children nor

68v

Thomas Walsingham
in R[ichard II]

[Parliament **anno** 20
Richard II]

[Plan]tagenet

69
Don Duarte de Lan-
castro, a noble
gentleman of Portu-
gal, came to my Lord
Admiral ambassador
to the King of Spain
and to[ld] him that
he was descen[ded]

from the Duke of
La[ncaster in] Valo-
dolid. G.[B. **teste.**]

their posters should bear the name or surname of Lancaster; for they held
that to be an arrogation and usurpation of royalty and of royal right and
title, and not due to them.

And herein these kings followed the example of their royal ancestors,
who would not suffer their base children to bear the royal name of 5
Plantagenet, but óther surnames were devised and appointed to them. And

Th[e particular sur]-
na[mes of the] b[ast-
ards of the] an[cient
kings of England]

as, for example, the divers bastards of sundry kings were called Fitzroy
Oxenford, Fitzherbert Clarendon, Fitzhenry Longuespee Cornwall, as after
the same manner the base children of the foresaid Duke of Lancaster were
called Beaufort and Somerset, **ut supra,** and not Plantagenet nor Lancaster, 10
and for the reasons before showed.

And this ancient manner and laudable law of [giv]ing meaner names to
the bastards of kings was an imitation of the kings [o]f France, as I
conceive. For I have observed that the kings of France since the time of
Hugh Capet never permitted nor vouchsafed any of their base [so]ns either 15
to be capable of the crown of France or to have the **[ad]veu,** as they call it, or
approbation of lawful children, nor the surname of France. [B]ut the
female bastards or illegitimate daughters of these [kin]gs may take and bear
the surname of France, or 'de France'. This is thus witnessed by Mr Jean
[de Tillet, a] learned man and one of the best antiquaries of France: [**La** 20
**troisième lig]née a du tout rejeté les bâtardes non seulement [de la
couronne, mais aussi] de l'aveu et surnom de France, [quelle concession est
permis aux bâtardes des rois,]** etc.

70

But if it be objected that albeit this be the law and custom of France, yet it
is not in use nor hath it been observed in England. And for the better 25
maintenance and authority of this their objection, they bring the example of
Hamelin, whom some silly and negligent heralds who have forged his arms
call Hamelin Plantagenet. This therefore importeth nothing, nor may have
any more credit than an error or a fiction. For the truth is that the said
Hamelin (who was the base son of Geoffrey Plantagenet, Earl of 30
Anjou) was simply called Hamelin, and bastard of Geoffrey Plantagenet.
And his son William took the surname of his mother, Dame Isabel de
Warren, daughter and heir of William de Warren, Earl of Surrey. And their
posters were also called Warrens, as Johannes de Warrena the first, and
Johannes de Warrena the [second, both earls of Surrey,] and Isabella de 35
Warren, and Eleanor de Warren, etc., as I have seen in charters and good
records — and never Pl[antagenet.

[This is confirmed] plainly by our best herald and our most learned

[Camden in **Surrey**]

antiquary, Mr William Camden, whose words be these: /Isabella/ [fi]lia sola
Gulielmi de Warrena comitis Surreiae, Hamelinum nothum Galfredi 40
Plantegeneti, etc., **titulo comitis Surriae maritum adornavit: Hamelinus
Gulielmum Surriae comitem genuit, cuius posteri ascit[o] Warrenorum
nomine eundem titulum gesserunt.** And I make no doubt but tha*t* they took
the name of Warren because they might not be suffered to b[ear] the royal
surname of Plantagenet, it seems.   45

71v

But if it be further objected / the base son of Edward IV was commonly
call[ed] Arthur Plantagenet, this example, if it be well and duly considered,
can give no authority nor credit to their assertions. And the reason is
because that in the time wherein this Arthur lived, the name of Plantagenet,
being only left in the House of York (for the Lan[castrian Plantagenets] 50

were extinguished), was of little or no reputation nor of any honour, but
rather held in contempt, and they which bore [it] were despised and hated,
and the White Rose daily faded and withered and *perished.* So that the case
stood then with the Plantagenets as it stood with the unhappy children of
5 Baby[lon] when the prophet said, **Beatus qui tenebit et allidet [parvulos tuos**   Ψalm. 1.36
ad petram. And as a learned gentleman hath well [ob]served, it was not
safe in that time to be a Plantagene[t.] He was held in disgrace and scorned   [Thomas Gainsford]
and oppressed with wrongs, and *others* were imprisoned, and anon they were
made away by one mischief or a*nother,* and as it shall be better
10 demonstrated in th*e next book.*

   And it also shall be fit to note and to advertise that [our poetical heralds
have forged and given a false surname to Hamelin and to his posters. So
they have also assigned to him by the like fabulous] / art a shield of familiar   73
ensigns, which he never bore, nor yet any of the ancient earls of Anjou nor
15 any of their progeny. And that is the arms of France, bordered with an orle
of Normandy or of Guienne, albeit that not any earl of Anjou of the
antique lineage, nor any of the progenitors of our kings of England ever
bore the arms of France — that is, the l[ilies of gold] in the azure field —
until King Edward claimed the crown of France and assumed the arms of
20 France in the right of the Queen Isabella de Valois, his [m]other. And he
first of all bore them, and quarterly with [his] arms of England.

   But the arms of the [ancie]nt earls of Anjou were a scarboucle: that is, a
golden [buc]kle of a military scarf or belt, set with precious stones, and not
a car[bunc]le, or more precious ruby, for that is erroneous, and also
25 [absu]rd if the form be considered, as I have demon[stra]ted in the fifteenth   [15] B[ook of]
book of my **Baron.** And the princes of Anjou bore this [sc]arboucle in a   **Ba[ron, etc.]**
shield, **parti per chief,** argent and [g]ules. This will not be denied by any
good an[ti]quaries and learned heralds, either English or French.

   And the heir[s of this Hameli]n, and who took the surname of Warren (**ut**
30 **supra**) bore also the arms of the house of Warren in the[ir shields and
capar]isons. But in token that they were descended out of the house of
Anjou, they bore the **epipo[ma] scarboucle** upon their [helmets for] their
crests: and [this I have] seen upon a [seal of John] de Warrena, Earl [of
Surrey,] at a charter dat[ed 20] Edward III, **Anno Domini** 13[46] **apud**
35 **Dominum** Robert [Cotton.] And you shall see at large in the 16th [Book of   [16th Book **Baron**]
my] **Baron,** where I [treat of] matters of [armoury.]

   [Bu]t the herald or painter which forged that coat of flower de [lis and]
lions for [Hame]lin was but a silly and ignorant animal. For [the fo]rgery is
so gross as it may easily be detected by [any] mean armorist, and who was,
40 or would be able to say that [neither] Hamelin nor Geoffrey Plantagenet his
father could by right [and jus]t title bear the arms of France or Normandy,
or of [Guienne,] either simply or compounded. And thus much for this error
[and fiction.]

   And now I will return to the Beauforts or Somersets, [and in
45 comm]endation of their modesty and discretion I must [needs acknowledge]
that they have not to my knowledge and in my [mean reading anywhere
adv]entured / or presumed to take the surname and title of Lancaster until   73v
Henry Tudor, descended from the Somersets, and Earl of Richmond, came.
And what would not he presume to do, being a man of so high ambition?
50 And in the end, what might he not do, or what and how great and royal

titles might he not take upon him when he had won the crown and when he was King of England and lord of all the regal titles and rights thereof? And whereof more anon.

The first Beauforts which were legitimated by the Pope and by King Richard II have no other surnames but Beaufort in either of the instruments 5 apostolical or royal for their legitimation, nor any words to give or to ensure to them any capacity of royal title or state of sovereignty in the crown. As for that Bull of the Pope Urbanus which he made for the legitimation of these Beaufort[s,] the which I have seen, it conferreth no honours nor titles up[on them] but only purged and cleansed them by his 10 spiritual pow[er from] the foulness and infamous note of bastardy. And he a[llowed] them to be held and reputed as children legitimate [and] lawfully born. And in that Bull they have no other sty[les] but these: Joannus de Beaufort, **Miles;** Henricus de Beauf[ort,] **Clericus;** Thomas de Beaufort, **Domicellus;** Joanna de [Beaufort,] **Domicella,** and in brief, only dispensed 15 with thei[r bas]tardy.

And more the Pope cannot do, as the doctor[s] of [Sorbonne] and some other of the best canonists hold and affirm. For [they] say peremptorily that the Pope cannot make bastar[ds] capable of any succession or heritage, nor of any [office] or magistracy. Neither can he give to them any power/to 20 ordain and constitute any successors or heirs. And the civil and imperial law agreeth herein with the ecclesiastical law, for that law suffereth not bastards to inherit the patrimony and hereditary lands of their father, not admitteth them to be capable of offices or dignities or titles without the special grace and dispensation of the prince. And the same law is in force in England, as I 25 have been informed by a very learned and signal judge of the laws of this land.

But some grave men are of opinion that these laws are too strict and too hard, and they hold it agreeable to reason and also to law — because law much affecteth and observeth reason — that bastards, being honest and 30 worthy men, and the rather if they be allowed by their fathers, may be admitted to be partakers of such honours and dignities and titles and feuds and other ornaments and rewards of virtue as with other virtuous and worthy m[en.]

Of this indulgence or connivance we have had in England some 35 ex[a]mples, and not long since. For two worthy and good men [flourishi]ng in this age, being bastards, were admitted to be the greatest officers, to wit, Chancellors of England. And the foresaid King Richard II in his charter of the legitimation of the Beauforts, insinuateth that men of desert, and avowed by their fathers, should be well esteemed and are fit to be advanced 40 to honours and dignities and to possess feuds and signories, etc. And this King Richard and other kings of England, as also the kings of France, called and call the bastards of the princes of the blood cousins. And this is a great honour unto them. But yet it certifieth not their blood, nor inureth any title *to* the crown unto them. Neither doth it give any increment [or] 45 advancement to their fortunes and estates, for they may be and are many times poor, notwithstanding [their cousinage to the king.] But to prevent that evil, this king [made the eldest son, John de Be]aufort, Earl of Somerset and Marquis of Dorset. And from them descended Henry, Duke of Somerset, f[ather natural] to Charles Somers[et,] Earl of Worcester by 50

74
The civil and imperial law against bastards

Sir Edward Coke

Dr [Stephen Gardiner,] Sir Thomas [Egerton Chancellors of England]

[King Henry VIII,] **ut supra**. And it is w[orth the] noting that this Duke Hen[ry Somerset left the] faction of Lancas[ter and follo]wed King Edward IV.

[B]ut to leave these extravagant disputations, I will here [ex]hibit the true
5 copy of the charter of the legitimation of [the] Beauforts and the confirmation thereof by Parliament, and [let] the gentle and learned Reader judge thereof. Only I prepare his way by a short advertisement, and necessary [in this cas]e.

First, then, the Reader must understand that in the Act of Parliament
10 [there is a pream]ble or preface to the charter, and it was made by Dr Edmund [Stafford, brother of the Earl o]f Stafford, and Bishop of Exeter and Lord Chancellor of England, and in the [20th year of King Richard II.] This Lord Chancellor [intimateth that Pope Urbanus VI, at the earnest request of the king, vouchsafed to legitimate these Beauforts,] / the   74v
15 foresaid base sons and the daughter of the Duke of Guienne and of Lancaster. And that the king, also having power to legitimate and to enable bastards in the same kind and in as ample manner as the emperor hath or had (for so he professeth and avoweth in the Act) was pleased at the humble request and suit of the duke their father to make them not only legitimate
20 but capable of lands, heritages, titles, honours, offices, dignities, etc. And that this king, for the more authority hereof, craved the allowance and the favourable assent of the barons and lords of the Parliament and obtained it. And now I will transcribe hither the charter, as I have seen and read it in the archives and records kept in the Tower of London:

25   **[Charta legitimationis spuriorum Joannis Ducis Lancastriae:**

[Ricard/us Dei gratia, rex Angliae et Franciae, Dominus   75v
Hiberniae, [car]issimis consanguineis nostris, nobilibus
viris Joanni de B[eaufort] m[iliti, Hen]rico de Beaufort
clerico, Thomae domicello, et nobili mulieri Joannae
30 **[Ricard]/us Dei gratia, rex Angliae et Franciae, Dominus**   [*patrui]
nobilis viri Joannis duci[s Aqui]taniae et Lancastriae
germanis natis, et ligeis nostris, salutem. [Nos] pro
honore et meritis, etc., avunculi nostri congruum
arbitramur [ut merit]orum suorum intuitu, vos qui
35 **magnae probitatis, ingenio, ac vitae, [ac morum hone]s-**
tate fulgetis, et ex regali estis prosapia propagati, etc.
Hinc e[st quo]d Joannis avunculi nostri genitoris vestri
precibus inclinati vobiscu[m qui (ut) asseritur) defectum
natalium patimini ut huiusmodi defectu et e[isdem
40 **qua]litates quascumque praesentibus, vos haberi volumus**
pro sufficientibus [ex]pressis non obstante. Ad
quaecumque honores, dignitates, praeeminentias,
[status,] gradus, et officia publica et privata, tam
perpetua, quam temporalia, [atque] feudalia et nobilia
45 **quibuscumque nominibus nuncupentur, etiamsi du-**
[catus,] principatus, comitatus, baroniae, vel alia feuda
fuerint, etiamsi media[te] vel immediate a nobis
dependeant, seu teneantur, praefici, promoveri, elig[i,]

assumi, et admitti, illaque recipere, retinere, gerere, et
exercere proinde li[bere] ac licite valeatis, ac si de legitimo
thoro nati existeretis. [Quibuscumque statutis] seu
consuetudinibus regni nostri Angliae in contrarium
editis, seu [observatis quae hic] habemus pro totaliter   5
expressis nequaquam obstantibus, de ple[nitudine nostrae
reg]alis potestatis et de assensu Parliamenti nostri [tenore
praesentium dispensamus, vosque et] quemlibet vestrum
natalibus [restituimus et legitimamus. Die Februarii,
Anno Regni 20, R. II]   10

76

In this charter there be great graces and great honours and privileges
conferred upon these Beauforts by the king. For here the king calleth them
consanguineos suos. And he doth not only most graciously allow and
confirm their legitimation, but also his making them (and by the help of the
Parliament) capable of baronies, of earldoms, of principalities, and of all   15
honours, titles, and dignities. And he also enableth them to bear and to
exercise all offices, public and private, temporary and perpetual, and lastly
to take and to hold and to enjoy all feuds, as well noble as other, and all
heritages and lands and signories hereditary, and to hold and to exercise and
enjoy them as lawfully and as firmly and as rightfully as if they had been   20
born in lawful matrimony. And these be as great honours and great
privileges as may be given (at the least to a subject).

But they confer no royal interest nor any right or title to the crown, at the
least [acco]rding to the observation and caution of these men, which
disallow the claim of the Beauforts and Somersets to the crown. For they   25
say that to enable a man to have title to a sovereignty and to be an heir of a
kingdom, there be higher and greater words required, and words of empire,
of majesty, and of sovereignty, and as such as **regnum, summa potestas,**
corona, sceptrum, diadema purpura, maiestas, and the like. But there be
neither these words nor [an]y other importing sovereignty or empire or   30
reign, nor any grant or permission to bear *arms* in this charter. And
hereupon they conclude that without such words no title to the crown, nor
sovereign quality, nor royal ensigns could pass to them.

To these objections are made these answers by the friends and favourers
of th[e Somersets:] first, that whereas the opposers to the claim of the   35
Beaufor[ts affirm] that there be no express or nuncu[p]ative words in the
said charter to confer upon these Beaufort[s] a capacity [of] reign and of
empire in this kingdom, the defendants for the Somersets *deny* that, and in
their answer they say that there is a word in the charter which
Prin[cipatus]   [com]prehendeth empire and reign and sovereignty, and that is **princi-** 40
Pri[nceps]   **[patus,]** and whereof the king and the Parliament make the Beauforts
capable. And they *explain,* as the scholars know, that **principatus** is the state
of **princeps,** [the] title of the highest and most absolute sovereign prince. [For
the Roman] emperors in their greatest height were called [**princeps.**
Therefore, **princeps** is thus defined:] **Princeps [est pen]es quem summa i[n** 45
76v   **rempublicam potestas est, et qui primus omnium dominatur.]** / And
principatus and **dominatus** are used as synonyms.

But the other adverse parties and opponents replying said that it was an
error that the word **principatus** for **regnum** or for **supremus dominatus,**

because that the word **principatus** in the age of King Richard II and long
before, and ever since, hath been restrained to the estate of the primogenite
and heir apparent, not only of kings, but also of dukes and marquises, as
well feudal as sovereign. Furthermore it was objected by them that the king
5 which made the charter was reckless and irregular, and so prodigal a
distributor of all things, as well of lands as of honours and offices, and that
he would give anything, although it were not to be given. So that he may be
said to have be*en* rather a [dissipator than a] dispensator of honours and
treasures, and such an one as the good Emperor Severus was.

10   But on the other side *they* say that the next king, namely Henry IV, who
was a wise and a discreet and a wary prince, although he loved these
Beauforts dearly (as being his natural brethren by the paternal side) and was
willing to do them any honour or grace that might be lawfully done to them,   [The charter of King
yet he discovered plainly enough in a certain charter in which he entailed the   Henry IV] for [en-
15 crown to the heirs of his own body, and namely to his four sons and to   tailing the crown]
t[hem] successively, and to the heirs of their bodies, that he reputed not the
Somersets nor Beauforts to be Lancastr[ians, nor heirs of the crown] and of
the kingdom of England. For there is not any one word to lead a remainder
[thereof] to any of his said brothers the Beauforts, nor any one word [nor]
20 mention of them.

For first he entaileth the crown and kingdom to his eldest son Henry,
Prince of Wales, and after him to the heirs of his body. Then to Thomas of
Lancaster, his second son, and to the heirs of his body. And thirdly to his
third son, John of Lancaster, and to th[e] heirs of his body. And lastly to
25 his fourth son, Humphrey, and to the heirs of his body. For still, and for
every estate, the words are, **Post ipsum successive haeredibus suis de ipsius
corpore legiti[me] procreandis.** And this is all. And this, though implicitly,
is a plain and express exclusion of the Beauforts from the crown.

And this charter was confirmed by Act of Parliament held at Westminster
30 by this King Henry IV upon the 22nd day of December, in the eighth year of
his reign. And it was sealed with the seal, and upon the dexter side of the
seal hung the [seals] of sundry lords spiritual, and upon the left side h*ung*
the seals of the temporal lords and noble barons, the wi[tnesses thereof.]
And this charter is now in the hands of Sir Robert Cotton, [where I have]
35 seen and read it and transcribed these summa[ry notes from thence.]

And this is also here fitly to be noted, that the bastards of the kings of   **77**
England bore not the arms of the kingdom, but they had other new arms   Arms of bastar[ds] of
devised for them, or else they were permitted to bear the arms of their   the kings of England
mothers if they were gentlewomen and to whom the ensigns of gentility and
40 nobility appertained. But if the bastards were tolerated to bear the arms of
England, then they were diversified in a checking and debasing and rebating
manner, and were not differenced with such honourable notes as the arms
of the princely legitimate sons were, but with other differences which were
marks of baseness, of rebatement, and of obscurity and of novelty, as
45 namely basters, bends sinisters, bars, bordures, and such like marks, and in
such manner as that they might be borne by any new gentleman, such as the
learned call **filios terrae** and **novos homines** (and we vulgarly call them
upstarts). But I will say no more of these things here now; besides, I have
touched them already. I have written of them at large, and of all armorial
50 signs, in the last five books of my **Baron.**

And as the Beauforts, alias Somersets, had never the surname of
Plantagenet, nor yet of Lancaster, so they never bore the arms of England
but d[ifferenced, as aforesaid.] Neither did or durst any of them assume or
take these royal arms and royal surnames until Henry, Earl of Richmond,
vehemently aspiring to royalty, came, and albeit that he could not so well   5
and so rightly bear the names of Beaufort or Somerset, be[ca]use he was a
Tudor by his father, and so to be surnamed Tudor or some other Welsh
surname, if there were any in his family; but by his mother's side he was

descended from the Beauforts. For the Lady Margaret, Countess of
Richmond, was the daughter and heir of Sir John de Beaufort, Duke of   10
Somerset, and grandchild to John de Gaunt by Catharine, the wife of Sir
Otes de Swinford. And this John de Beau[fort] was first Duke of Somerset,
and created by King Henry V and his wife *Cathar*ine, Queen of England. He
descended from the kings of France.

And I have [seen a] pedigree made for this earl since he was king, wherein   15
he is [derived from] the ancient kings and princes of Great Britain, whose
[princely posters being] chased out of the chief countries of Britain by the
Saxons, they occupied Wales. / And I also acknowledge that he was near
akin to Henry VI and that the king called him nephew, and that he called
the king **avunculum nostrum** (instead of **patruum**): our uncle — as it is in the   20
records of the Parliament of **anno 1,** Henry VII. And he was to King Henry
VI **ex fratre nepos,** as Polydore writeth him.

But he was not that king's nephew, that is as we, and erroneously, take it
now: his germane younger brother's son; for then he had been a true
masculine issue of the House of Lancaster and of Plantagenet, and of the   25
royal house of England. But he was nephew to King Henry VI by his
brother uterine, Edmund Tudor, Earl of Richmond, the son of Owen Tudor
or Meriodoc and of the said Queen Catharine, daughter of Charles VI, King
of France, and widow of Henry V, King of England. And this was well
known in France, and he was in respect of his blood of France the better   30
respected and the more honoured in France. But he was not content with
that honour, but he would also be reputed to be a prince of the House of
Lancaster, and so then of England, and to be a near kinsman to the crown.
And he had much grace thereby.

And this error passed so currently in France as that Monsieur Jean du   35
Tillet, who was otherwise a very learned and faithful writer and an excellent
herald, and the antiquary of France in his time, **ut supra,** was so far abused
with the fame of this cousinage as that he hath committed this error to
writing, and recorded in his book entitled **Le Recueil des Rangs,** etc., Part
II. For there he writeth that John, Duke of Somerset, father of the foresaid   40
Lady Margaret, Countess of Richmond, was the true and lawful son of
John de Gaunt, Duke of Gui[enne] and of Lancaster, and begotten by him
upon his first wife, and his right noble and virtuous wife, the Lady Blanche
Plantagenet, daughter and heir of Henry and of the earldom of Lancaster.

But the noble and veritable historian Philip de Commynes, Lord of   45
Argenton, had better intelligence of the pedigree of the Earl of Richmond
and also of his title to the crown, and of either of which he conceived but
slightly and lightly, as these his words show, albeit the earl was king when
Commynes wrote this; viz: **Il n'avait ni croix ni pi[lle] ni nul droit, comme je
crois, à la couronne d'Angl[eterre.]**   50

But suppose that the Earl of Richmond had been one [of the lawfu]l
progeny of the said Duke of Lanc[aster. Yet he could not rightfully and
lawfully claim the crown of England] / nor make any title to the kingdom so   78
long as the royal family of York flourished and continued, because that
5   Richard Plantagenet — Duke of York and King of England designate by
Act of Parliament holden [in the] thirty-ninth year of King Henry VI, and
to whom the titles of Prince of Wales, Duke of Cornwall, Earl of Chester,
and Protector of England were given by the Three Estates in the same
Parliament — descended from the daughter and heir of the second son of
10   King Edward III (for as before, so still I leave the infant William of Hatfield
out of the catalogue). And King Henry IV and his progeny descended
from the third son of the said King Edward III, as it hath been here declared
in the first book. And King Henry VI, being the best of the House of
Lancaster then living, did acknowledge in the Parliament aforesaid that the
15   title of Richard, Duke of York, was the only just and lawful title, and so
consequently it was the true and next title, therefore better than that of
Lancaster or any other.
    And all this was known well enough to the Earl of Richmond. And there
was a time that he would have been content and glad with all his heart but to
20   have possessed peaceably and *in* safety his earldom of Richmond and to have
enjoyed the hon[ours and] dignities and signories thereof *with the* good
grace of the sovereign. And he had reason, for it was a much better state
and condit*ion than* that of a bandit or prisoner in a foreign country or
*any*where else. [Besides that, the issue] of the two daughters of John, Duke
25   of Lancaster, Philippa and Catharine, married to the kings of Portu[gal and
of Castile, were to be preferred before any Beaufort or their heirs, if foreign
titles be not excluded by Parliament.]
    But after that Morton had infected his ears and *pois*oned his heart and his
desires and affections with the ambitious aff*ectation and* aspiring to the
30   crown and to the sovereignty, then nothing would *content* him but the
crown, and his haste and impatience were such as that he m*ust* have and
possess it forthwith, **quo iure quaque iniuria.** And he would imita*te the*
insatiable ambitious thirst of Great Alexander, and therefore he would cut
the sa*me* Gordian knot profanely and rudely, and not to regard to do it
35   orderly and in due and convenient time, and time ordai*ned by God.* I make
not doubt but that he was ordained to be king (as I intimated before,) *albe*it
he ought by the laws of Christian religion to have attended God's leisure.
And it had been better for his / honour and reputation in this world, and   79v
more for the safety of his soul in the next world.
40   But he followed the advice and counsel of that evil spirit transformed into
an angel of light and wearing the habit of religion and of sanctity, and
whose malice was so extreme toward King Richard as that nothing could
appease it but the deturpation of the slaughter and the blood and the utter
destruction of this prince. And that must not be delayed, but it must be
45   performed and executed in all haste, albeit (as the Italians say proverbially)
nothing is well done in haste. And according to the saying of Augustus   Suetonius in
Caesar, that which is well done enough is soon enough done. But Morton   **Augustus**
hastily prepared and raised great instruments for this monstrous and
impious work, and he hastily brought and, as it were, he precipitated the
50   earls of Oxford and of Richmond and of Pembroke and the Duke of

Buckingham and other men fitter for better employments, and he incited them to undertake this enterprise *and enter* into this conspiracy unduly and unseasonably.

And it was the greatest fault, and almost the only fault of this noble Earl of Richmond, that he would hear evil counsels and too much follow them. 5 And the reason was because they were given by such men whom he better loved, and of whose virtue and honesty and learning and prudence he had a much better opinion than there was cause. And such were Morton, Dudley, Empson, Bray, Urswick, Knevet, etc. And for that, his partiality and credulity, he beareth the blames of other men. 10

There be two extrem[es] in the case of the counsel of princes. The one is when the prince will consu[lt] with no man, nor hear the counsel of the wisest and best experienced men. And such a prince was Charles the Hardy, Duke of Burgun[dy,] who was so self-wise and so overweening of his own wit and judgem[ent] as that he thought no man to be so wise and so 15 intelligent, and of which his madne[ss] there is the monument, **Carolus**
[Pontus Heuterus;   **Pugnax aliorum consilia, et rationes (ne dicam) sequi, vix audire volebat,**
John Meyerus]   **ignominiae loco habens ab aliis discere, et iudicavit se proprio cerebro omnia consilia habere recondita.**

[Sententiae Arabicae]   But this is a better opinion, and it passeth for an oracle: **Vir optimus eget** 20 **consilio**: the best man needeth counsel. But yet therefore the fault or extremity before mentioned is worse: that is, to hear and follow evil counsels, and such especially as are given by men who are held to be envious, malicious, and wicked and impious persons, as much worse or most unhappy. 25

And such an one (if you will c[on]sider the testimonies and notes and censures which Mr More, [the old] servant of Bishop Morton, maketh of this said bishop his master) w[as] this Dr Morton. And because I will not be
[Dr Morton's   his accus[er,] I will set down Morton's character as it was dra[wn and]
character]   portrayed by the said Sir Thomas More and by other. 30
80   I will begin with his studies of policy and with his natural inclination to
82   that kind of learning. / And first as concerning his skill in policy, Sir Thomas More declareth that in these words and shortly, **The Bishop (Morton) had gotten great experience in politic affairs and in worldly drifts.** And that is as much to say as that Dr Morton was a much better politician 35 or Machiavellian than a divine or churchman. And according to this character, Dr J. Herd in his metrical history of England bringeth in the Bishop Morton speaking thus as an observer and worshipper of the pagan idol Fortune, and as a variable Proteus and Ambidexter, one while Yorkizing and another while Lancastrizing or Somersetizing, and in all 40 Satanizing. And thus he brings him to describe himself and to characterize himself:

81   **Si fortuna meis favisset partibus olim**
   Et gnato Henrici Sexti diadema dedisset,
   Edwardi numquam venissem regis in aulam. 45
   Sed quia supremo stetit hac sententia regi
   Henrico auferre ac Edwardo reddere sceptrum,
   Tanta meam numquam lusit dementia mentem
   Ut sequerer partes regis victi, atque sepulti
82   **Adversus vivum, etc.** 50

And this prelate used sp[eeches] to the same effect in his discourses with
the Duke of Buckingham. And this is well said by a mere politician. But an
ho[nest] man and a truehearted friend will love his friend or lord in
adversity, and also when he is dead, as the divine Ariosto hath well
5 observed, [and] maketh the descript[ion] of the one and the other in this
elegant stanza:

> **Nessun può saper da chi sia amato**   [Ariosto, Canto 19]
> **quando felice in su la ruota siede;**
> **però ch'ha i veri ed i finti amici a lato,**
> 10   **chi monstran tutti una medesima fede.**   **83**
> **Se poi si cangia in tristo il lieto stato,**
> **volta la turba adulatrice il piede,**
> **e quel di cuor' ama riman' forte,**
> **ed ama il suo amico dopo la morte.**

15 Translated by me long before the translation of Sir John Harington was
*pu*blished, and thus as follows:

> No man ever whilst he was happy knew
> Assuredly of whom he was beloved;   **82v**
> For then he hath both feigned friends and true,
> 20   Whose faiths seem both alike till they be proved.
> But he is left of all the flattering crew
> When from his happy state he is removed;
> But he who loves in heart remains still one,
> And loves his friend when he is dead and gone.

25   But as they say in the proverb, the devil is good to somebody, and
certainly this politic prelate was very kind and very friendly and faithful *and*
firm to the rebels. And he took great pains for the advancing of their *cause*
and for the seditious designs of the barons. And he crossed the seas betwixt
the Earl of Richmond and these rebels and conspirators against King
30 Richard; oftentimes and dangerously he adventured his liberty or his life for
them. And all was for the love of the Earl of Richmond and of his mother
the Countess of Richmond, and whom he visited often and observed, and
with all devotion. And he seemed as their creature, for he had been the
countess' chaplain, *a*s I have heard, and also the tutor of the earl her son
35 when he *w*as young.

And he was well re*w*arded for his love and service, *for t*he earl, a*s soon as*
he *w*as king, made this man Archbishop *of* Canterbury and Lord
Chancellor of England, and by the king's means [he] was also made
Cardinal. And that was to be a better man [t]han the king himself, according
40 to the order of Roman marshalling of states. For in the Pope's list of ranks   [Ranks of the chief
and of precedence, the Pope hath the first place and the emperor the next,   prelates]
and next to him a cardinal, and then a king.

And this doctor had other good politic gifts, and well worthy the   **83v**
rewarding. And if they were not rewarded here in this world, there is no
45 doubt but they shall be considered and rewarded to their uttermost merit
when every man shall receive his reward according to his worth: **Omnes
enim nos manifestari oportet ante tribunal Ch*r*isti, ut re*f*erat *u*nusquisque
propria corporis p*r*out gessit sive bonum sive malum.**

And that he was not only a seditious and treacherous man, but also a   **85**
50 covetous, bloody, cruel, and ambitious and a proud prelate, I will briefly

here demonstrate. And first that he was treacherous and a traitor to the king his master, and his good master as long as he was true, that hath already been clearly demonstrated and proved by his many false and seditious practices and persuasions of disloyalty and rebellion to the Duke of Buckingham and to the earls of Oxford, Pembroke, Devon, Richmond, and 5 to a great many other noble persons and worthy gentlemen of this land. And this crime of sedition and stirring of rebellion against the sovereign is not only a crime of **laese majesty,** but a deadly and damnable sin. Witness St Thomas Aquinas: **Seditio est semper de se peccatum mortale.** And certes, as I think, of all men, yea, even of all villains, a traitor is the wo[rst.]   10

And as this was thus seditious and treacherous, so that he was as cru[el] and bloody, his many conspiracies and practices, not only against the life of King Richard, and the cruel counsel which he gave to put Edward Plantagenet, Earl of Warwick, to death, and also Perkin Warbeck (alias Richard, Duke of Yo[rk)], and his bloody thirsting after the destruction of 15 all the princes of the House of York [are] great and pregnant testimonies thereof.

Now we will take a view of his covetous*ness*. And how covetous he was, these ex[amples] may serve to approve. Dr Godwin, now Bishop of Hereford, wri[teth] that when Dr Morton was Archbishop of Canterbury, 20 he exacted and extorted a much greater sum of money from the clergy of his dioces[e] than was ever before taken or extorted in that diocese. And moreover, he for his private commodity (which he chiefly sought) and for that purpose to bring certain leames to his own grounds about Wisbech, so weakened and shallo[wed] the fair River of Nine (which was before 25 navigable and of much good public use) as that it hath since served to little good use. [He was also the deviser] and persuader of so great and so grievous a tax to be laid and levied upon the people as that it made th[em to rise in arms and rebellion.]

His pride and his ambition appear plainly in his affectation of the highest 30 titles, in his aspiring to the dignities and highest offices and great honour, as namely of the Chancellor of England, of the first archbishop of England, and of a cardinal. And this his pride was also observed by his servant More, and thus taxed by him. Bishop Morton's pride abused his wisdom, and it s[erved] his turn to his own deliverance and proper advancement and to the 35 destruction [o]f the Duke of Buckingham. And his affection of the cardinal's hat and to be highest chief person in this kingdom be notable [tokens of his pride.]

I will not cloy and annoy this place with too much such noisome and fastigious matter; I will reserve the rest for other places. But by these it may 40 sufficiently be seen how little credit there is to be given to his report and censu*re*. But by these it may sufficiently be seen how unworthy and how unfit he *w*as not only to give counsel to so good a prince as King Henry VII, .but also to have the power to direct *and* [g]uide and rule him in anything.

And I say that the king his master was a good and also a wise prin*ce,* 45 [and] he was so reputed of many men. And I will hold him to be so, the rather also because that the best pri*nce or* [pri]ncess which ever reigned in this land was said to be so like to this king [her gr]andfather, as well in wit and in disposition as also in the favour and lineaments of body, as that [she was the lively and] perfect image of him. And now to return where we 50

St Thomas in *Liber*
Secundus∗∗ 4 art. 20

86

[Francis Godwin in
**Catalogue Episco-
porum**]

[John Stow]

[Queen Elizabeth]

began, that how far off soever the [earl was from the titles and rights] of the
crown when he first entered into his ambitious p*ractices of the crown* and of
the sovereignty, yet I will avow and maintain [that after he was anointed
and crowned king, he was the] *assur*ed and true proprietary of all the [rights
5 and titles which carried the crown and kingdom, and whereof they
depended.

[He got also the title of York by the marriage of the Lady Elizabeth]
Plantagenet, eldest daughter of King Edward IV, and who was prince or
head of the royal family of York and the first or chief Plantagenet. And the
10 title of Lancaster instantly, and others, fell and escheated to the Earl of
Richmond so soon as he was king, and the which before was in controversy
and **in nubibus,** or in abeyance (as our lawyers say). For no man being a
subject, how capital and chief a judge soever, and how great power of
judicature soever he had, might presume to give a definitive sentence in any
15 ambiguous and obscure cause or act of the king which was doubtful or
uncertain. But the king himself only must give judgement in such cases.
And this is an ancient and an authentic paragraph in the laws of England, as
the very grave and learned judge Henry Bracton affirmeth and thus
reporteth it: **De chartis regis et de factis regum non possunt Justitiarii**
20 **disputare, nec si disputatio oriatur possunt eam interpretari: sed in dubiis**
et obscuris et ubi aliqua dictio contineat duos intellectus domini regis erit
expectanda interpretatio et voluntas, etc.

[Bracton, Lib. 2,
Cap. 16]

And the reason hereof is given in th[e] books of the civil and imperial
laws, and peremptorily, viz.: **Quia de principali iudicio non est**
25 **disputandum.** And thus, and for these causes, that question and
controversy whether these Beauforts or Somersets and their descendants
were of the House of Lancaster and capable of the crown or no, it could not
be decided nor determined until there w[ere] a judge who was also a king,
and King of England. And Henry VII was both chief judge and also
30 sov[ereign]lord and king of this land. And thereby he had full powe[r] and
authority to determine this or any other ambiguous and doubtful [cause,]
and by the virtue and power thereof, he adjudged and decreed to himself
that the title of Lancaster, with all the royal a[ppurtenances] belonging *to it*
was his own and proper title. And accordingly he took the said title to
35 himself, and the Pope confir[med it as] due and proper to him (and as you
shall see anon). And then the writers of the stories said (as well English a[s
French]), and m[ight truly] say that this King Henry VII was **de la ligne de**
L[ancastre,] **et caput gentis regalis, et princeps** [familiae Lancastrensis.

[And the Chancellor Morton termed the marriage of this king and the
40 Lady Elizabeth (and not improperly, but very fitly) the union of York and
Lancaster. This was an eulogy very honourable and acceptable to the king,
at the least in the beginning of] / his reign. But afterwards (as I have
observed) he had no great good liking of them, and which is more, he
had none, or very small affiance in those his titles now lately acquired of
45 York and Lancaster, and much less of Somerset. He seemed tacitly to waive
and (to wit) to quit them. For after that he had gotten the crown in the field
and in victorious battle, he affected, and chiefly, so as it were, only the title
of his sword. And he claimed the kingdom to be his by conquest and **de jure**
belli. Because he would have this told, there were at his coronation
50 proclamations made with these titles: **Henricus rex Angliae, jure divino,**

King Henry VII
affected only [the]
title [de] jur[e] b[elli]

jure humano, et jure belli, etc.

But the noble barons liked not this title **de jure belli,** nor would they allow it. But the king maintained and avowed that he might justly assume and bear it, and as a title and style due to h*im* [as] a conqueror, because he entered this land with hostile and foreign armies and fought for the crow[n] 5 and won it. To this, the barons answered roundly and soundly that he was beholding to them for h[is] landing safely and for his victory, and that he could never have had that commodity of fair and prosperous descending upon the coasts of England, and much less to have marched in[to the] land and to have struck so much as one stroke for the crown and conquest of this 10 re[alm without their and] permission.

For it was clear that without the love and the help of the English nobles and people he had no hope [nor strength] but in his French soldiers; and they were not so many as the least legion of the Romans. By the tesimony of the grave and honest French writers th[emselves, they] were **les plus** 15 **méchants,** and no better than rogues and truhanes; that is, base men [and] men of no courage, and without sense of faith and of honour. And so that if ever they had la[nded, th]ey should have been so entertained by the valiant English as that within one hour *they s*hould all have been cut into pieces and never more have seen the sun. And besides this, the King Richard and the 20 ba[rons] *and* people would have conceived so mortal an hatred against the invader of this [kingdom] that they would never have left him nor the pursuit of him u[ntil they] had seen or wrought the death and destruction of him as of a most notorious traitor.

Wherefore the barons humbly prayed his grac[e to] consider these matters 25 and to give to the noble barons and to the valiant loving people [their du]e, and duly and justly to ascribe his good success and his achieving of the crown to their *loyal* forces and not to the French ragamuffins nor to his Welsh sword, for by them *he s*hould never have been able to have won one foot of land in this kingdom. And th[at t]hence he attained to the crown by 30 the favour and power of the noble and common English: he migh*t not be* said a conqueror of these people who entertained him with courtesy and safeguarded and *sustain*ed him with their forces and only put the crown upon his head.

Moreover, the barons a[ssevered] that this King Henry was no conqueror; 35 his achievement could not be called a conquest [or pu]rchase of the sword. Besides, they added that the names both of conqueror and of co[nquest were] very harsh and hateful words to all the English, and reputed as barbarous and heathenish and tyra[nnical titles.] And by good reason, for the work and end of them is to make all the people of the land sla[ves, to] 40 possess all their goods and fortunes at their pleasures, and in brief to do [Seneca] anything; as the wise man said, **Quidquid victor audet, aut victus timet.** And hereof the examples of the conquering [Va]ndals, Longobards, Saxons, and Normans in Italy and Spain, in England, and lately the Spaniards in America, and many other cruel lords, estated only by their 45 u[njust] *s*words, are not only very many, but also most hateful and detestable for their tyranny. *And for these* causes the barons would not endure the title **de jure belli.**

[An]no Domini   [But the king changed not] his mind, and therefore he made means to the
1486   Pope to obtain of him [the ti]tle of Lancaster. But the king did not seek the 50

titles d[irectly and desertly] *in his motion* and suit to the Pope, [but closely
and cunningly. For the outside of his embassage was only for his marriage,
fearing that therein he had committed incest, as he pretended, because the
queen his wife was his kinswoman,] / **et quarto consanguinitatis, et forsan**
5 **affinitatis gradibus.** Pope Innocentius VIII granted this suit to the king in
the first year of his reign. And afterwards, but on what occasion I know
not, the king renewed this suit to Pope Alexander VI, who confirmed and
ratified this pardon and dispensation made by his predecessor in the
fourth year of the reign of this King Henry VII.
10   And it is observable that the Pope taketh not upon him herein to confer
or to give any new titles to the king, but neither did [the] king pray the Pope
by his letters to give to him these two titles, but his ambassador had that
chiefly in his instructions. Therefore the Pope seemeth only to make a
rehearsal of those titles as due and proper to him before. And so by the
15 means of this device, the titles **de jure belli** and **de Lancastria** were not as
any matters or proper subject of the Bull, but rather in respect of the desire
which the Pope had to show the love and honour which he bore to the king,
that he was pleased, **ex proprio et mero motu et certa [sc]ientia suis** to make
an honourable memorial of all the royal and majestical titles which
20 belonged to the king by right, and they are the more stately ornaments and
precious embroideries of those his [gr]acious letters of apostolical
indulgence granted / for the dispensation of the said marriage. And in this
style and in these words they are co[nveyed]:
   Hic rex Angliae de domo Lancastriae originem trahens, et qui notorio
25 **jure et indubitato proximo successionis titulo et praelatoru.n et procerum**
Angliae electione et concessione, etc. Ac etiam de jure belli est rex Angliae.
Afterward, for the more certain clearing, [repairing,] and curing of all flaws
and defects of titles, the Pope addeth this gracious clause: **Supplemusque**
omnes et singulos defectu[s,] tam juris quam facti, si qui intervenerint in
30 **regno dic[to.]** And then and there in the end this charter or Bull is entitle[d,
and not in the front,] **Pagina confirmationis nostrae, approbationis,**
pronunci[a]tionis, constitutionis, declarationis, suppletionis, monitionis,
requisitionis, prohibitionis, benedictionis, inhibitionis, et excommuni-
cationis, et anathematiza[tio]nis in quoscumque qui praesumpserint
35 **infringere, ve[l] ausu temerario contravenire his litteris Apos[tolicis].** For all
this must be thought and held to be don[e] **auctoritate Apostolica:** by the
authority of the apostles St Peter and St Paul.
   And thus you s[hall] also see how the king received of the Pope *the*
confirmation of these two noble titles, **de domo Lancastriae, [et de] jure**
40 **belli,** [u]nasked, as it seemeth. For there appearet[h not any particular and
express] suit made for them by the king, yet it [is very probable it was his
suit underhand, because the] other things [are but slight and of necessity,
nor obnoxious to any danger, when those two titles were the things he most
aimed at.]
45   This king was not satisfied with those two titles, notwithstanding the
Pope's allowance and granting and authorizing of them, more than he was
with his title of York and of Lancaster, as he discovered (and not
obscurely) when he made very earnest request to all the estates of the
kingdom assembled in the first court of Parliament which was summoned
50 and held by him to give him an estate hereditary of the crown and kingdom

89v
This Bull is in the
hands of Sir Robert
Cotton, and which I
have seen.
90
[An]no Domini 1490

[The Pope's charter]
for [the title of
Lancas]ter [and **de**
jure belli;] and [for
the dispensing of the
king's incestuou]s
[marri]age

89v

91

of England with all the appurtenances, and to entail them to him and to the heirs of his body. And this great request and suit, and that suit of inestimable value, was granted unto him by the said high court of Parliament. And I will exhibit a copy of this gift as of a gift of a new title, and of the Act of Parliament conferring and confirming the same, when I 5 come to relate and to rehearse the most noble and royal titles of our Sovereign Lord the King of Great Britain now reigning and flourishing.

And it were no hard piece of work to divine what the mislike of this King Henry VII was to the titles of York, of Lancaster, and of Beaufort or Somerset, and haply there is some discovery of them here already. But I 10 must not confound this story with historologies, but rather, as we say in the proverb, with putting the cart before the horse preposterously and reporting matters out of their time and place. And I confess that this might be objected *justly*, were it not that I have no purpose to write the whole [st]ory of King Henry VII, but some parts thereof, and as they belong to this task. 15 And therefore I must of necessity insert [su]ch matters of his story into this discourse as are proper *and* behoveful thereunto, and without the which the Reader shall want [kno]wledge of sundry things which much concern the credit, [honour,] and actions of this story of King Richard.

But now I *turn my* style again to the story of that King Richard, and 20 according to the order [and affairs of] *these* times, I will proceed therein. And therefore now it must be considered that *there* be near ten months passed since the Duke of Buckingham was suppressed, and since the Earl of Richmond was chased from Poole with the storm. And there we have left him all this while. And in the meantime I have reported what things 25 of historical argument happened in this interim, and such as I have thought worth the writing, and with some arguments and discourses hereupon; and where they failed, I have entertained the time with other discourses, and not improper to the story of King Richard, and as I before promised.   30

And now I return to the affairs of that king. And whereas it must be supposed that and understood that King Richard had intelligenc[e] that the Earl of Richmond was very busy and very diligent in France in making of his warlike preparations for his second invasion and second enterprise upon Eng*land*. And the king being careful to defend himself and to preserve his 35 kingdom from invasion and from spoils and from bloody tumults and from such mischiefs and miseries as conspiracies and seditions and rebellion and war bring with them, wheref*ore* he caus[ed] a general levy of soldiers to be mad[e,] and armour and munition and other necessary things for th*e* war to be prepared and provided. And he gave order to have the havens and 40 frontier places and towns to be reinforced and well guarded. And he had soon set all things in g*ood* readiness and in good abundance and in very serviceable good estate, saving only the faith and true hearts of a gr*eat* part of his subjects, as well nobles as *commons,* and this was his only want and defect. But *that was* a secret and hidden and [unsuspected] *defect, and* 45 [could not provide against the evil of their hate and malice.]

And I must not omit to tell here how that the Earl of Richmond found it a more difficult work to obtain aid and succour in France now than he did before, and that by reason that all the labour and all the adventure of his first invasion and enterprise were lost and utterly frustrate, and his 50

91v
The [second] inva-
sion [of the] Earl
of Richmond

adventurers and favourers not only much damaged, but also disc*ouraged*.
For by the manner of his return into France, he distasted much his old and
noble friend the Duke of Brittany. For the duke took it ill that he went to
the French king and into France, albeit the earl could not otherwise do. For
5 when he was driven from Poole, he was also driven upon the coast of
Normandy. And being there, he came into the road at Dieppe, and there
landed to refresh himself and his company. And from there he went to
Rouen. And being then near to Paris, he thought it behoved him to see the
king and to have some speech with him about his design and to pray his
10 *assistance.*

And he came in very honourable and noble port, for (if Philip Commynes
saith truly) that he was followed then with five hundred Englishmen, and
he was entertained by the French king with much honourable courtesy. And
he gave good audience to the earl, and who soon propounded the cause of
15 his coming and his suit to the king. And the king liked well his
enterprise, but he was loath to be party therein, because he was in good love
and league with the King *of* England, and also because he was loath to
dispatch any [g]reat sums of money as were required in such a cause. *And*
the king desired the earl to give him leave [to] pause and to consider and
20 deliberat*e* of the matter.

And in the meantime, the earl (and as I related before) [behav]ed himself
so well in the court of France as that [he con]ciliated the love and favour of
the greatest persons, *gentlemen* and ladies. And amongst other, he became
[very gracious] with the princely Lady [Anne de France, eldest sister to]
25 King Charles VIII, and wife of Pierre de B[ourbon, Lord of Beaujeu, after
Duke of Bourbon. But because it was] / his most stately seat and his most
honourable signory, he would be called Monsieur de Beaujeu, and the
duchess his wife was called Madame de Beaujeu. And this great *lady had so
great* power over the king her brother in his minority as that her authority
30 was greater than that of Lewis, [Duke of Orleans,] chief [prince of the
blood; in envy or mis]like [whereof this duke took arm]s [and raised a civil
war] in [France, as John Tillet] and [others write.]

And this most noble lady so much favoured the Earl of Richmond as that
she ceased not to solicit and importune the king her brother, Charles VIII,
35 until such time as he promised to give good assistance to the earl for the
invading of England and for the recovery of the title and right and
possession, *s*ceptre and diadem of his English progenitors, and for the
seizing upon his royal patrimony and princely inheritance, and when the
king forthwith commanded that there should be a good sum of money
40 delivered to the e[arl, and] that there should forces be levied for this
journey. And the forces were levied in Normandy, and to the number of
3000 men. And they were odd fellows. For Philip Commynes saith that they
were **trois mille hommes, les plus méchants que l'on pût trouver.**

And whilst these forces were making ready, the earl, being desirous and
45 careful to procure all the aid and help that he could, he resolved to go to his
old noble friend the Duke of Brittany and to pray his assistance in this
enterprise once again. And the duke hearkened favoura[bly] unto his suit
and was minded to grant it. But when he propounded it to his council, his
treasurer and chief counsellor, Peter de Landois, disliked the notion and
50 dissuaded the duke from yielding thereunto. And for the reasons hereof, he

92v

[Commynes,] p. 536

told the duke that this enterprise, if it succeeded well, would prove very evil and unhappy to the duke.

'For', quoth he, 'the earl hath now obtained the favour and the assistance of Charles, the King of France, and he will now hold him to be his best friend and ascribe all his good fortune unto him. And so you shall lose the 5 earl and his love and confederation when he is king, and he will take part with the King of France against you if any jar[s] and wars should happen, and which the King Charles wisheth, because he hath a long time longed to possess this country and duchy of B[rittany,] and the which he cannot gain so long as [you] continue in the league and amity with the King of 10 Eng[land.] But when that is broken, and the league and amity contracted firmly bet*ween* the king*s of* [France and England, how easy is it for the King of France to invade and swallow up both you and your dukedom?]

93   'Wherefore it shall be much more safe and more profitable to hold the earl fast whilst you have him here in your hands, for so you shall be assured 15 to hold the King of England your fast and faithful friend. And if you will after deliver him to the King of England, you may set his ransom at what rate or price you will. For the king will think no sum too great for such a [purchase.] And so you may replenish your coffers with good store of treasure, and whereof there is now great want'.   20

Thus Monsieur Landois spake and delivered his opinion like a wise and an honest man. Albeit he loved the earl well, yet he well understood that he was bound to prefer the love and the good and safety of his master *to* those of any other man. And this counsel much prevailed with the duke, and it made him to alter his purpose. And he forthwith resolved to put a guard 25 upon the earl and to keep *him* as his prisoner again.

But now, worthy Reader, mark now how still Fortune is propitious to her favourite *Earl* of Richmond. For whether it were by the secret advertisement and warning of some dear friend of his of the duke's council, or whether *it* were suggested to him by his good angel, sure it is that the earl 30 came to knowledge, and by unknown means, or vehement suspicion of this treacherous plot of the duke before it could be put in operation. For it was not deter[mined] and resolved until it was night. And the execution was deferred until the morning, and that then there should be a guard set upon him. But in the meantime, and before midnight, the earl had prepared 35 good means to fly, and he being accompanied with twelve gallant gentlemen, his followers and friends, and all well mounted upon good and swift horses, and he departed from Vannes and rode with such speed as that the earl was got out of Brittany and come into Anjou (a town of the French king's) before it was known to the duke that the earl was gone forth of his lodging. 40

94   From Anjou he went to the French court at Paris, and there [he] was very welcome again, and still he thought and studied how he / might advance his cause and strengthen himself. And after that he obtained help [from the French kin]g, he thought it would also be very behoveful for him to use some mean[s to get the] Earl of Oxford out of prison of the Castle of 45 Hammes in Fr[ance, whither he was co]mmitted long before by King Edward IV. And herein also he [followed the means and counsel of the Bishop] Morton, who had good quarter with the Earl of [Oxford and sometimes visited h]im [and acquainted him with the] plot of the Earl [of Richmond] *to*
93v   *set him at* / liberty — because he was a great earl and a valiant gentleman 50

and a man of much power and very wise. And besides that, he hated King
Edward IV and his children and also King Richard and all the House of
York, and most mortally, and therefore *he would* be a sure and politic
friend *when* he raised a force, if he could be drawn by the earl's means to
5 like of his action of aspiring to the crown.

And hereupon the Earl of Richmond rode to Hammes, and then under
the charge and government of Sir James Blount, and who entertained the
earl with much honour and extraordinary and good respect. And the earl
told him that he desired to see the Earl of Oxford. And forthwith, Sir James
10 conducted him to the earl's lodging, and the Earl of Richmond propounded
his enterprise to the Earl of Oxford, and he liked it well and promised to
give him all the help he could. And Oxford, having great [confidence] in the
love and faith of the Captain of Calais, discovered the plot of Richmond to
him, and he liked it so well that he turned traitor instantly and alterned to
15 the Earl of Richmond. And the Earl of Oxford and James Blount went to
Paris back again to the Earl of Richmond.

And by this time all his military provisions were ready. And whilst he
was in the French [court,] he had a kind message from the Duke of Brittany,
and with offer of auxiliary forces, the which the earl most gratefully
20 accepted and prayed they might be sent to Harfleur, where his ships lay, and
whither all his solders were to march, and whither all his necessaries and all
his men and habiliments and instruments of *war were* to be conveyed. And
in the end of July, 1485, he took his leave of the King of France and of his
most noble and most favourable co*nfederate,* Madame de Beaujeu, and
25 promising all humble and mos*t* faithful and thankful remembrance of the
great *love* and graces of the king her brother and of her, and then departed
from Paris and went into Normandy to the [port of] Ha[r]fleur, and where
he met with 2000 Bret[ons sent thither by the duke] most honourably.

But b[efore he came to Harfleur, he made some stay at Rouen, receiving
30 advertisement] / which much troubled him and greatly distempered him,   **95**
and that was that the Lady Elizabeth, the eldest daughter of King Edward,
should forthwith be married to King Richard; and to the end to seek by all
means to prevent this match, he made the more haste to land in England,
hoping that by the means and skill and arts and practice of his friends, that
35 treaty of marriage should be frustrated. Upon this marriage depended all
the chief hope of the earl, and which of necessity must be effected, or else
that his fairest and haply his best colour for title would fade and fail him.
Yet if that should happen, he had so ready and so present a wit, and that he
w*as* so good and provident (as aforesaid) as that he was upon any sudden
40 chance instantly provided with counsels and resolutions for all fortunes.
And thereupon he straight resolved that if he missed the marriage of the
Lady Elizabeth, he would marry her sister the Lady Cecily.

But ere he could do anything in these matters, the other plot and hope
was also checked and crossed. For in the next packet which [c]ame out of
45 England to him he was certified that the Lady [Ce]cily was newly married.
But yet so quick and ready was his conceit *and c*ounsel and his resolution
that by and by after the receiving of that advertisement, he left the purpose
of that treaty, and he conferred a*bout it with* himself and his most wise and
noble friends which were with him in Brittany ([th]ey were for the most
50 part Welshmen). And one of them told that he knew *where* there was a very

[Polydore Vergil]

good wife for him, and with whom he should [no]t only receive a rich and large, bountiful portion, but also great *cel*ebrity of noble*s,* and with much esteemed allies and friends; and that this was a daughter of the foresaid Sir William Herbert, who was [a] gentleman of a noble family and had much noble alliance, and was a [chi]ef man in authority and power in the south 5 parts of Wales (and as hath *been* before declared, **Liber I**), and whose elder daughter was not long [before] married to the Earl of Northumberland.

The Earl of Pembroke in[stan]tly embraced this motion and this alliance and sent to the Earl of [North]umberland, his new and secret friend, to solicit and to mediate this *alliance* with the younger sister of his wife the 10 countess. And he required and *urged* him to be very careful and very earnest in this nuptial negotiation. *And the* Earl of Richmond made full accompt to be assured of the barons *and* of the best and greatest part of Wales, and easily by their means *to bear the ti*tle and possession of the principality of Wales. And th*is* [had been] a great fortune and an high advancement to a 15 [banished poor earl.

95v

[And] the better to confirm him in the hope and in the *expectation thereof,* [Dr Morgan,] a grave man [and a good] / politician advertised the Earl of Richmond that all the nobility and the people of Wales were exceedingly well affected to him and were all at his devotion and service. And therefore 20 the doctor advised the earl, albeit he knew nothing of the earl's purpose to marry in Wales, yet for other good causes he counselled and advised the earl that he should descend in some part of Wales, and nowhere else, and he would land secretly. And thereupon the news was very acceptable and welcome to the earl, and whereas he had before been doubtful where to 25 land, now he resolved to land in Wales.

And forthwith he put all necessary things aboard his ships, and he embarked his troops of soldiers at the port of Harfleur, and in the month of July, and then he weighed anchor and set sails. And he had a merry wind and a fair passage, and *with* which in seven days he arrived safely at Milford 30 Haven in Pembrokeshire, his nat[ive] country. And there he was with all joy and courtesies and caresses received of his kinsfolks and friends and countrymen. And after he had reposed and ref[reshed] himself [and] his army a little while in that harbour, he marched to a [port] called Haverford-west, and where he was also very well entertai[ned.] For he was now come 35 amongst his British or Welsh kinsfolks. And they bade him *welcome, and very* kindly and very heartily welcome, and they did not use him and caress *him* favourably and h[onourably] only as their friend and countryman and kinsman, but also [as] a prince descended from the ancient kings and princes of Wal[es.] 40

96*

And whilst he was in Wales, Sir Rice ap Thomas, Sir Walter Herbert, Sir John Savage, Sir Gilbert Talbot, who disloyally drew his young nephew, the Earl of Salop, into this rebellion to the Earl of Richmond, brought or sent their forces and power to him, and in good plenty. And in brief, many Welsh and false knights and esquires and many perfidious and rebellious 45 Englishmen of all qualities and inhabitants of the countries thereabout and near Wales came well armed and well resolved to fight for the earl and to make him king.

And the earl marched to Shrewsbury, where he found all pressed and ready at his service and commandment. And from thence he went to 50

Lichfield and had purpose to go to London if the [king had not stopped his way.] By that time, Sir Gi[l]bert Talbot came with the forces of the Ea]rl of Salop, his nephew, to the earl, and anon [the] most ingrate and of all other the most perfidious baron of all, the [Lord] Stanley, and his brother Sir
5 William, and the Earl of Oxford, and *many* other had brought and joined their forces with the army *of* the earl. And then Sir Walter Hungerford and Sir Thomas [Bour]chier and divers other treacherously forsook the king and fled to *his* greatest enemy, the Earl of Richmond.

[Philip de Commynes saith that the Lord Stanley brought 26,000 men to the Earl of Richmond, his son-ally, but our stories say but 5,000 at the most.]

[T]he king, at that time when the earl landed and whilst he marched
10 through Wales, lay [at] Nottingham, and he had spies upon the earl. And he presume*d* [he had a great] and a mighty army ready to encounter him. For the Earl of Northumberland and the Lord St[anley promised] to come to him [with all their powers, but unfaithfully] failed and forsook him. But there were many other valiant and most noble lords and knights, and which
15 stood faithfully *by him,* as namely [John, Du]ke of Norfolk, Marshal of England, the Earl [of] Surrey, the Earl of Westmorland, and the Viscount [Lo]vell and others, etc.

The king came to Leicester, and the next day [bein]g Sunday, he rode out of the town in the evening *very* gallantly, wearing the royal crown upon his
20 head, [and] accompanied with the said great lords aforesaid and with many other loyal barons and valiant and brave *knight*s and gentlemen (for all had not bowed their knees *against him*) nor any loyal and true subject, as I may boldly and truly say. For all they which [came] with arms against the anointed and sacred king, and with purpose to depose *and be*reave him of
25 the crown and of his life, who was [their so]vereign and liege lord and their lawful [anointed king,] were all rebels, and monstrous great *ones*.

Leices[trum inquit Rex] **Ricardus,** [cum maxima pom]pa, port[ans diadema in] capite. [Chronicle] Croyla[ndensis.]

For such bearers of arms [are not] to be called enemies, for that is too good a word for them, [as proper to the foreign adversary.] If the subjec*ts* [conspire against their sovereign and take arms against him, they ought to
30 be called perduells, traitors, and rebels, and their wars] / and conflicts not to be termed wars, but seditious tumults and felonious outrages and rebellion[s,] and traitorous acts, and as the divine Plato said in the like case: **Bellum quod Graeci Graecis inferunt non est bellum sed seditio.** And the blood which they shed and the slaughters which they make
35 in their seditions and rebellions are not to be said to be the good fortune of war and the honour of the victors, but the wilful murder and homicides perpetrated by traitorous parricides and by cruel assassins and unnatural murderers. For they kill their own kinsfolks, their own princes, and their own brothers, and their own friends and countrymen, and the lawful
40 magistrates whom they ought to reverence and to preserve. And that these cruel and barbarously unnatural acts [are] **de Criminae Laesae Majestatis omnis, tam divinae quam humanae:** crimes of all treasons, as well against God as against men and against the king.

The diffe[rence between] enemies and rebels
96v

[B]ellum subditorum non est bellum sed [sedi]tio.

And this point of law and this doctrine politic would have been made
45 manifest if watchful and circumspect prudence had so ordered and provided, *so that* all majesty had been drawn and stretched out, *and all* lawful arms and power of justice *had been* in readiness in those remote countries when these seditious persons arriv[ed] and when they marched toward their rendezvous, and that they had assaulted and charged those
50 per*duells with force,* and lawful and more mighty arms, and had duly

97

suppressed them and had then apprehended their chief commanders into the
presence of Justice. Then you should *have seen* her, or in her place her
lieutenants, the learned and reverent *judges* of this kingdom, tell the
proudest of them that they were felons, murderers, *and* rebels. And then it
would, and also plainly, have appeared who these men were, and what th*ey* 5
were, who was their captain and what his title was, and they would have
been taught that **Arma quibus lex non utitur, [legem] impugnant, et sicarii
et latrones dicuntur, qui arma lege [non praeci]piente tractant,** as a good
and a grave man hath truly pronounced.

[Joannes Sarisberien-
sis in **Policratico**
Lib. VI]

But these troops of rebels were so much increased and grown that they 10
were able to make their own way in despite of law *and of* royal faith and of
justice. And in this proud and rebellious manner *they* passed boldly and
safely to their rendezvous in Leicestershire. And there all the*se traitors* were
joined and united in one army, and all took part with the Earl of *Richmond*.
And they yielded themselves and their arms and their faiths (if they had *any*) 15
unto him and to his service and to the advancement of him and his cause.
And they *met* their true and lawful sovereign there; they presumed to *give*
[battle] to him.

And so (happily or unhappily) it fell out that [fortune] favoured them
upon that day of battle. Therefore, they were afte[r re]puted and renowned 20
for brave captains and valiant, and therefore wo[rthy] / and happy
conquerors. And some of them were honoured [with the] dignities and titles
of barons and of earls. And some were made knights, and s*ome were* made
bishops and archbishops, and others were made [great officers of the
kingdom.] And success did honour and bless the enterpr[ise. And as it is 25
well observed by a wise man,] / **Hon[esta quae]dam scelera successus facit.**
And a[gain, **Prosperum ac fe]lix scelus virtus vocatu[r.]**

98

→96v

99*
[Seneca in **Hippolito**]
[**Idem** in **Hercule
Furente**]

[But when fortune is adverse to those gallants that they] / be overcome
and taken, then they are the most wretched and most base, the most
reprobate persons in the world, etc. Examples hereof we have infinite, both 30
ancient and modern, as namely the Titans, Absalom, Eribastus, and
Catilina, Spartacus, M. Cethegus, the Gracchi, Belisarius, Cario, etc., and
m*any more.* And here at home, the fame and shame of the reason and fall of
Sir John Oldcastle, Wyatt, Owen Glendower, and of the late earls of
Westmorland and of Desmond, and many more, are m*entioned in our* 35
stories.

But to leave these examples and come to the relation of the affairs of
those armies, now that these two armies, i.e., the army of the king and the
army of the rebel Lancastrians, were to come to Redmore Heath and in the
view the one of the other, and were approaching and disposed themselves to 40
fight. And in the morning early, before the battle, there was some inference
and consultation held in the tent of the king with those noble and principal
gentlemen whom he best trusted. And it was there reported and affirmed
that there was many of those principal men, and in whom the king was
much affied, who were secretly fled to the earl and had forsaken the king, 45
and would fail him when their faith came to trial and in the chief business;
and those men following the example of Bourchier and of Savage and of
other who had a little before revolted *from* the king. And some of them
turned rebels even in the instant whilst the king armed himself and was
ready to fight.   50

And it was also then and there discovered plainly that the Earl [of]
Northumberland was turned Lancastrian, albeit he had faithfully *promis*ed
to assist and def*end the* king, and not without good cause, for the king had
a long time [be]en unto him a very kind and good noble friend in his private
5 life, and since, very gracious to him. And therefore he affied much in his
fidelity and forces. But yet for all this, he fa*iled him,* and he *sec*retly and
suddenly revolted to the earl's party, and therefore in the conflict he stood
aloof as neutral.

And moreover, in the said consultation it was then also *r*emembered and
10 urged that whereas the Lord Stanley, whom *t*he king very much loved and
had much advanced and made him Constable of England, and who
faithfully had promised to [bri]ng all his friends and forces to the king and
to make [the] king more confident in him, had left his son [Geo]rge Stanley
prisoner or in hostage with the king; yet [not]withstanding this, *he* left the
15 king most *treacherously* [by the persu]asions and [subt]le seductions of his
wife, the earl's mother. And this he proved true, for *he* [brough]t a great
army to the earl, and the which consisted [of] 26 thousand men (if Philip de
Commynes be not mistaken, for our own stories have but 5[000); and
indeed it was a very great defection. For all the lords and all the people]
20 were alienated from him, fled, and revolted as suddenly as they came
swearing to him when they made him king, such was their perfidious
inconstancy. And this happened by the few subtle and malicious
persuasions and arts of Morton and of some few other the chief plotters of
the rebellion.
25   And those are these doubts and mischiefs and treasons were declared and
debated now; but it was too late. And therefore there remained none other
matter for consultation or for counsel, but only to persuade the king to save
himself suddenly by flight and to retire himself with all speed to some safe
and strong and remote place, and but for a little while. For they told and
30 assured him that if the camp of the enemies broke up and were once
dissolved, which could not continue long, [i]t would never be reassembled
nor brought together again. And they (*and* so the better to persuade and to
encourage him to resolve to fly) had provided ready at the door of the
general's tent a fair and a very swift and strong horse. And they offered and
35 presented this horse to the king, and they desired and pray him earnestly to
mount that good horse and to be gone with all speed. For they said that now
otherwise the inevitable dangers and evil were so near as in a moment it
would be too late to depart.

But this counsel w*as* very unpleasing and very distasteful to the king, for
40 he scorned very much to [fly.] And the*n* his noble friends sought to terrify
him and with these threats and frights of strange porte[nts and] prodigies
which were seen and were for tokens of his great calamities *which would f*all
upon him if he would not, whilst opportunity served, avoid them. And then
also some *of* them repeated the rhyming prediction which was given to the
45 Duke [of] Norfolk, and although it seemed trivial, yet it was very true and
proph[etical:]

       Jack of Norfolk, be not too bold,
       For Dickon thy master is bought and sold.

And in brief, they told the king plainly and often that he was betrayed by
50 som[e of] his chief friends, who were newly gone to the Lancastrians, and

101

had carried the g[reat] strength and power of his army with them. Wherefore again and again, and very earnes[tly,] they prayed him and urged him to be gone and instantly to take the commodity of that s[wift horse,] and if he thought best, to go into the north parts, where he had most friends and the *chief* persons and the most places at his devotion, and to　5 remain there upon his gua[rd] but for a short time. For they told and assured him that the army of the enemy *could not* long continue, and their

102

victuals and money would soon be spent and *cut off,* / and by his better and more sharp sword.

But the king was so resolute, or rather so wilful and so obstinate, and　10 even fatally, as that none of these counsels, nor persuasions, nor provident care, nor warnings, nor terrors, nor prodigies, nor prophecies, nor any vehement intimations of the great dangers and mischiefs present and imminent, could prevail with the king or induce him to put on a mind or purpose so base as to run away or to seek safety by his fligh*t,* and by such　15 distance and absence to be secured until that violen*t* tempest of the rebellious furors was overblown and passed. But this prince was so jealous of his honour and of the reputa[tion] of his valour, and so much scorned and abhorred the imputation *and* taint of cowardice and of fear, as that he resolved to adventure his fort[unes] *and* his life and his crown and all rather　20 than by flight to save himself *or* to shun and avoid that present and dangerous conflict or battle with his traitorous enemies. [And,] as it were, in defiance of fate and of fortune, he pronounced *and* protested solemnly and peremptorily that whatsoever should [be]tide him, he was constantly purposed to stay and to try and *a*bide the worst, so long as his life and his　25 forces and his sword would maintain his resolution.

And this might seem to be a wi[lful and] desperate speech if he had not afterward by a particular action made demonstration of the hope — and of the great hope — which he had of victory and of good success in the battle of that day, and that he spake not these words aforesaid in despair either of　30 his good fortune or *of* his good sword. And he built his hope upon this platform [or] plot, and the which, although it was very dangerous and difficult, yet it was bravely and valiantly and most nobly projected and also attempted, [which] was this: this brave prince, because he knew well that the Earl of Richmond [was] ambitious and appetent of renown and worldly　35 glory; and that he *knew* also that he had small skill in military arts and in val*orous exer*cise and *prac*tice of arms; and that he was far inferior to him therein as in courage and contempt of peril; therefore the *king* [devised,] in the manner and lieu of a strategem and of a peculiar and strange *device* [that as soon] as both the armies were appr[oached and ready to charge] the one　40 the other, [he would] put [himself before the troops and make such signals as are usual for inviting the earl (being the Captain General of his forces)]

102v

to come forth and to enter into single combat with him, etc., thus so to bring the earl to fight hand to hand with him, and nothing doubting of the victory, because he knew the earl's chivalry to be much inferior to his.　　　45

[Why King Richard wore the crown at Bosworth]

And the king, because he would be the better known, would when he made the challenge he had the royal crown of England upon his helmet, and that was the fairest and most *a*ssured mark of a king which could be. And this was one of the causes why [King] Richard wore the crown in the day of the battle at Bosworth, but not the only cause, nor that which is brought　50

and rendered b[y] Polydore Vergil: to wit, that King Richard wore the crown *upon* that day because he made account that that day should [ei]ther give end to his life and reign, or else beginning to his better reign. But this cannot be the reason thereof, and by reason that the king wore the royal
5 ensign upon his head in the town of Leicester three days before. And he wore it when he departed from that town upon the Sunday before, and when he rode in great royal pomp and in martial magnificence toward Bosworth. Now these were no days of the trial of his fortune by battle. But doubtless the king chiefly wore [the] crown upon his head that all men
10 might see and consider there the most notable foul fault of disloyalty; for the crown was a certain token of the royal majesty and of the sovereignty *of* him which weareth it. And that albeit the rebels had made and nominated another king, there attended upon h*im, it was plain* that he had no crown nor might wear one, and so consequently he was no *king.* But that he
15 himself which wore the crown and possessed it was the only and the true and lawful king, and that therefore all [true] and faithful subjects ought to obey and to follow and to serve him and [de]fend him according to the divine laws and for the obligation of their allegiance.

And thus much for his wearing of the crown. And to proceed with the
20 matter of the combat: the king (according to this foresaid plot and purpose) as soon as the armies were confronted and preparing to fight, came forth, and with suc*h* signs of challenge to combat as aforesaid, summoned the earl to that single fight. And the ear[l] seemed gladly to accept the challenge, and pricked his [horse for]ward. And he came a good round pace, and very
25 g[allantly and brav]ely, as if he had a full purpose to [fight, which is testified by a good author: **Comes Richmontiae directe super regem Ricardum processit.**] / But this career was but dissembled, and rather done for a train to draw on the king into his deadly snares, or else for that he liked not the furious approach of the ki[ng.] For suddenly the earl stopped,
30 and withal he cunningly (and as mannerly as he could) he retired, and Mars became basely retr[ograde;] and he recovered by this means the vanguard of his battle. But King Richard pursued him so hastily and fiercely.

And the earl for his more safety put himself by the standard, and being the place of the most strength and security of the army. And thither also the
35 king followed him and *made* his way through his enemy's troops with his sword, and cam[e] to the standard, and there with his own hands slew the stand[ard] bearer, Sir William Brandon, father of Charles Brandon, [after]ward Duke of Suffolk. And he made accompt to have next despatched the earl. But the earl's men interposed themselves and
40 [preserved him. Amongst them was] Sir John Cheyney sometimes Master of King Edward's Horses. But the King Richard struck him [from his horse to] the earth.

And anon the king was environed with such multitudes [of] his rebellious enemies, and who all charged their weapons upon him. And they mangled
45 and gored him extremely, and ga*ve* to him many cruel wounds. And they slew him upon the p[lain. And] thus Richard failed of his stratagem, devised for this desperat[e plunge.] And the *re*ason was because it was his ill hap to meet with an [e]nemy or antagonist who loved no combats, nor would adven[ture his] person alone and hand to hand with his adversary. For if he
50 had *so* done, then without doubt Richard, being so far superior *t*o Henry in

[Chronicle Croyland]

103

the skill of arms and in chivalry, and also *in* courage and in hardiness, would have slain him in the combat, and not only so freed himself from his seditious practices, but also have brought an end to all other tumults [and] traitorous practices against himself.

And therefore the king's device *and* resolution in so desperate a case was 5 commendable and politic and wise and very *hero*ical. For if that had well succeeded, he had made an end of all such quarre*ls, and* he should have enjoyed all peace and prosperity. For there was no ambitious person besid*es* who would trouble the king or the state as a proud affectator *of the crown*. Neither was there any man else whom the barons *and the people* loved as 10 that they would adventure the*ir allegiance and their live*s for him. And so all seditions, / conflicts, and troubles had been at an end.

But **non sic visum est superis,** and the king had ill fortune in his enterprise. And ill fortune is accounted a vice in military adventures.For in the wars, the fortune and success and event commend or condemn the *coun*sel 15 and the actor and the actions. And for this cause this king is reputed to be vicious and namely to be rash and to be obstinate and to be furious [and ov]erweening his own strength and courage, and of which *fa*ults more shall be said anon.

[But] to return to the matter of the battle and to conclude it. Both the 20 battles at the instant joined, and their armies courageously en[countered.] And there was a cruel fight and much bloodshed on both sides. But the party of the earl was much stronger and more numerous, and therefore they prevailed and had the victory. And thus not only the king was lost and slain, but also very many of his most noble and most loyal servants and subjects 25 were sorely wounded or slain outright in the field, or else, being taken, some of them were pu[t] into prisons. And as far as the battle was fought, th*e* Earl of Richmond was victor.

The crown which King Richard wore in the field was brought to the Earl of Richmond, and the Lord [Sta]nley, his father-allié, put it upon his 30 head, [and] he was then forthwith hailed and styled Henry VII, King of England, etc. And this [was by the divine ordinance,] as the Prior of Croyland hath observed; and thus he writeth: **Ad postremum gloriosa victoria [Comiti] Richmondiae iam soli Regi una cum pretio[sissi]ma corona quam Ricardus Rex antea gest[avit] caelitus data est.** And so this gift 35 of the crown and [his patern]al name Theodore may seem to be fatal and divinely due unto him, the on[e and the other be]ing θεοῦ δῶρον, that is, the gift of God.

[And th]us Henry, Earl of Richmond, son of Edmund ap Meredith [ap Tudor, alias] of Hadham, Earl of Richmond, and Mar[garet, daugh]ter and 40 heir of John Beaufort, Duke [of Somerset, ob]tained to the crown of England [and the roy]al fortunes [of Richard, which he might have kept and enjoyed if] / life had been ordained for him, and if he had not omitted some few good and needful businesses and committed some errors in that catastrophe of his reign. And his fault of omission (and a chief fault and 45 error, and touched and observed before) was that he dealt not with the Marquess Dorset nor with the Earl of Devon, nor with his brother the Bishop of Exeter, nor with the Bishop of Ely, nor with the Lord Stanley and the rest of the chief conspirators and traitors who were in his power and a long time unarmed, as he did with the duke of Buckingham or with the Lord 50

103v

105*
Henry [of Richmond] crown[ed in the] fie[ld]

God gave [the crown] to Tedor, and so it [was] θεοῦ δῶρον *or Theo*dore: the gift [of God] to this earl so sur[named] Theodore.

105v*
[Omissions and commissions of King Richard]

Hastings, as I urged in the former book. For if he had cut off their heads or but bestowed them in sure prisons, he had prevented their rebellions and his own overthrow and saved his own life and his crown and the s*ate*, and in this manner, he having provided for his safety had done well, and that
5 which was fit and convenient to be d*one* by a just and provident and a happy prince (**ut supra**, and as I said before). And this for the fault of omission.

And now for those of *com*mission, the which he committed upon the day of bat*tle*, and the faults which were his scorn and contempt of his [ene]my:
10 his furious and rash pursuit of revenge, his surquidry and overweening of his own p[ower] and valour, the which are all unlucky and fa[tal] vices and haunt those men still and closely, **qui ferociter [ac] praepropere omnia agentes contemnendis quam ca[ven]dis hostibus sunt meliores,** as Cornelius Tacitus, a grave man, hath well observed, and therewithal *soundly* taxeth
15 sharply and shortly those faults of haste or rashness and of contempt. **For** the fault of temerit[y] or rashness alone had been too much. For it is both foolish and unlucky:**Temeritas praeterquam quod st[ulta] est etiam infelix.** And therefore they are very carefully so shunned by a good captain. For as Augustus Ca[esar] observed, **Nihil minus perfecto duci quam [festi]natio et**
20 **temeritas convenit.** For he which is [rash] and hasty in the affairs of war is apt [to fall] into the danger of all traps of treacheries *and en*gines. And by the testimony of the wise [and well-]experienced Polybius, **Temerit[as et impietas prae]ter rationem ad om[nes insidias et escas obnoxia est.]**

[The fault of contempt aforesaid is in the same way of perdition. This was
25 well known] / and reproved and taxed by Great Alexander in those his words, **Nil tuto in hoste despicitur; quem spreveris valentiorem negligentia facis.** And the Christian philosopher had learned, **nihil est in bello perniciosius quam hostem quantumvis imbecillum contemnere.** And this contempt and scorn is always accomplished with an overweening and
30 pride of a man's own wit and power. And it is also a presage and foretoken of his ruin and overthrow, and even by the testimony of the Holy Ghost: **Comminutionem praecedit superbia, et ruinam elatio spiritus.** And Strigelius, glosing upon this text, saith, **Superbiam comitatur error in consiliis, errorem infelicitas.**
35 The errors and the pains of this pride and contempt are prettily figured in the apologue of the Eag*le,* a proud and a scornful creature, and of the despised and poor and abject Scarabeius, or hornet. And thus the mythologers take it: the Eagle, holding the Scarab to be a base and contemptible *in*sect and of no power nor credit, used her proudly and
40 *dis*dainfully, and did also to her some wrong. The Scarab *thereupon* took this so ill as that she resolved to be revenged of *the* Eagle, and for the taking of this revenge she attended the time convenient, and that was when the Eagle did sit and lay her eggs. And when this time came, the Scarab *also* watched the time when the Eagle would go out of *her* nest to prey and solace
45 herself *after* her custom and kind. A*nd* the times being come and fitly offering occasion of the *ta*king her revenge, the hornet climbed up into the E*a*gle's nest and presently threw out the eggs down *to* the ground and broke them all to pieces. And then *she* sought out the Eagle's medicinal and precious *jewel, the* Aetites, or hatching stone, and she cast that away.
50 *And* thus this contemptible and vile animal took her *reve*nge upon the

[Contempt]

[Tacitus] **Historia,**
[**Lib.** 4]

[Rashness]
[Liviu]s, **Lib. 22**

[Suetonius] in
Augustus

[Polybius, **Lib.** 3]

106*
Curtius, **Lib. 5**
Erasmus in **Epistolis**

Proverbs, **Cap.** 16

proud and scornful and mighty Eagle, the king *of* birds and the chief
esquire of the God Jupiter. This *is only* a fable, and the moral is easy to be
conceived by the *Read*er. And shortly, it is a good warning for the *strong*
and potent persons not to contemn nor scorn *their rivals*, how mean or how
weak soever they *appear*.   5

106v*

I have praised the resolution of King Richard which he made to single out
the Earl of Richmond and to fight with him hand to hand, and called it a
gallant and heroical and most noble resolution. And that it may be objected
that I scoff at it afterwards and have reproved and taxed him for the
attempt and act or enterprise (and I confess that I have said th*is, and both* 10
*appro*ved him and condemned him), and the practice and execution of that
re*proof* may be thought a levity in me; but yet I am not contrary to myself,
but I still do and will still maintain the praise of his courage and resolution
in that attempt, for I hold it *noble*. But I mislike his fortune and his
judgement that he so unhappily made choice of a man which loved [no 15
combats.] But otherwise I hold it not only noble and heroical, but also very
proper to princes and *to this* prince, and even kind and also natural to this
king, and to seek such encounters.

For I find in our stories that the royal Plantagenets have very often
demanded and offered single combat to kings and princes being personally 20
in their armies, and in the absence of the sovereigns, to their chieftains or
Captains General. As, *for* example, King William Conqueror challenged the
combat of King Harold, and others did the *same*. [And] before, there was a
combat fought betwixt King Edmund Ironside and Cnutus, the Danish king,
for the [whole] k[ingdom] of [England.] And the kings Richard I and 25
Edward I in Palestine against *the Turks* [ch]allenged the combat with some
pagan princes. And King Edward III and Henry V sought and demanded
the like combat with the kings of France.

[The challenge of
James V, King of
Scots, to Thomas,
Duke of Norfolk]

And in the last age, the most valiant prince, James V, King of Scotland,
desired to fight in person with the Captain General of the King of England, 30
namely, Thomas, Lord Howard, Duke of Norfolk. And he gladly accepted
the challenge. But the king required that the count[ry] or the lands which
were then in controversy might be the [stake, and] to be **brabium victoris**
(the prize of the victor), and which the gener[al could not grant,] because
those lands were the inheritance of the king his master and not his, and 35
therefore he had no right nor power to *make* those lands the wager and
prize, as King James required. But the duke offered to pawn and to
adventure better lands of his own upon the [combat.] But that offer was not
accepted, and so the combat failed.

[But indeed the better end of those challenges and combats,] *and* their 40
good judgement, proceedeth from the divine virtue, mercy, and piety. For
the qua[rrel taketh end, and by that pious] and most noble [single adventure
all] the innocent [blood of] both the [armies] is saved and [preserved from]
shedding. And these provocations are also frequently occurrent in [the]
ancient foreign stories and in the Latin and Greek and French and Italian 45
and Spanish poesies. And it is reported in them, and with many good
words, that the kings and the generals have very often fought hand to hand
in their battles.

Valiant and adventurous princes and great captains held it to be a great
honour and most proper to them t*o be* matched and paired in arms with 50

their equals and peers — that is, chieftains and chieftains, marshals with
marshals, and dukes with dukes, and colonels *with* colonels, etc. And so
kings desire to be encountered *with people* of their own singular and
supereminent deg*ree and* like sovereign quality. For kings are p*eers of* none
5 else, as our grave Bracton h*ath related. Thus also the Great Alexander did
insinuate* / and acknowledge, being at the famous Olympic **agones** or
games, where he, being asked if he would contend in any of those noble and
festival and ludicral conflicts and heroical exercises, he answered that he
would gladly make one if there were any kings which would be his
10 **antagonistes** and contend with him. But there were no kings — that is, no
peers for the King Alexander.

    Neither did this our King Richard meet with any of his peers nor with
any of the heroical progeny of the foresaid antique princes, nor yet with any
Plantagenets at Bosworth. For if he had there accepted, he should have sped
15 better, or not so ill, for they would have come forth from their troops and
willingly and fairly h[ave] encountered singly, after the manner of other
brave and courageous princes *with their* honourable and courteous enemies,
and sought only honour and victory. And their manner was *to temper* their
enmity and ill affections with noble caresses and honourable usage. And the
20 example of this sat*isfied* men of invincible courage and most adventurous
upon all danger. And this is very memorable in that royal family: that there
was never any tainted of cowardice.

    But this manner of princes to combat and fight in their own persons is
discontinued and lost long since, and they are now so f*ar* from hazarding
25 their persons in singular fight as that they [t]hink not themselves safe
anywhere in the army, no, not under the standard nor in the tents and
trenches, nor in the midst of the main battle, but only at home and in their
castles and palace or *court*.

    And there is a late writer who ascribeth the beginning of this abstinence
30 from arms and absence from the army of the great princes to Philip II, King
of Spain. But he is therein deceived, for I say that I know the contrary and
can refell that report by the testimony of most ancient stories of the kings of
Syria and of Persia: to wit, that many of those kings did abstain from the
wars and from the camp, as you may read in Herodotu[s, in Diodorus, in
35 Trog]us Pom[peius, and the like. And I have also observed in t]he Roman
stories written by Suetonius, Dion, Plutarch, Tacitus, and others, that
Augustus Caesar, **post adeptum [e]t firmatum imperium domise continuit,
et bella [g]essit, proelia confecit, provincias invisit, rebelles con[t]udit, et
gentes barbaras subegit per proconsules prae[to]res, per legatos,** etc.
40   And if King Richard had considered *that* the Earl of Richmond was wise
and politic and [most apt] to follow great and safe examples, he would have
had [little] or no hope that this earl his adversary would *ever* come to
handstrokes with him. But notwithstand*ing, King* Richard being now grown
desperate / *trusted* in the joining of the battle, and whereof he had little
45 cause to hope by *reason that* the forces of the adverse side were much
greater and many more in number *than his own,* as hath been declared
before. Yet he had and might have good hope [to overcome] the earl in
single combat if he could have drawn him to have *fought with him in* person
therein. For doubtless King Richard was the better horseman *and the better*
50 soldier, and had much more skill and more courage and valour than the

107

The va ****
ch ****

P[rinces go not to
the] c[amp]

104

earl, and [as much] advantage of the earl in the monomachy as the earl
had of him [in his multi]tudes of troops. And therefore in all reason,
Richard was the *indisputab*le victor in the combat, and so consequently of
all his forces in the adverse host.

But yet suppose that he might *have received* deadly wounds in that single   5
conflict, and at that instant when *he struck* and slew his enemy, and that
they were both with mutual wounds *destroyed* (*and tha*t hath happened).
Yet it would much have comforted and cont*ented him at the end* of his life
that he had overthrown and destroyed his mortal *enemy: Solamen* **miseris
socium est habuisse malorum**, as it was well sung of one. And by another, 10
and as well said, **munu** ********************.*And in the ma*nner of these
old heroic and vindicative spirits, he would have comfort *of his victory* and
honour and joy of his vengeance, and said with them, and with good
contentment, and even with exultation, and in th*ese words:*

numquam omnes hodie moriemur inulti.   15

Vergil

For men of so great and high courage esteemed the revenge of injuries
and the rep*roof of dishonour* above life and all other worldly goods and
blessings. And for these causes *the* king thirsted so vehemently after his
revenge, and in the seeking thereof he dealt in *thi*s manner as is aforesaid,

107ᵛ*

and so proudly and scornfully, / and thus desperately and most unhappily 20
adventured hi*s* fortunes and his life and his crown and set them at a low rate
for the reparation of his honour and good fame, much wounded and
scandalized by his enemy, and for a revenge and punishment of him who
had conspired his death and sought by all means to destroy him and his
house.   25

But otherwise and at other times, this noble prince committe*d* not these
errors. These his faults, rashness and contempt and overweening of his
forces, were new faults in him, for in his former times, after the heat of his
youth was p*ast and* he came to know a*nd* to understand the business of the
world, he would do nothing either in civil or military affairs without good 30
advisement and ripe deliberation, and he would wait and attend the best
advantages and fairest opportunities.

But these new faults of this prince were ill-abod*ing* as they were new. And
they were always fatal errors and unlucky faults, and sinister prognosti-
cations and foretokens of calamities and of great evil to come, *and as it is* 35
observed by the learned, as well theologians as hu*ma*nists, that when God is
minded to scourge a state or king, a prince or any other great person, he
taketh his understandi*ng* and discretion and counsel from him, or so
darkenet[h and] obscureth those best and intellective facu[lties that he] can
make no good nor [proper use of them, and so, when his divine will is 40

108*

purposed to change the families of kings, and as the potter in Jeremy to
break one] / jar and to make another, then also he taketh the counsel and
understanding from the man whom he purposeth to throw down, and he

[Hinc dici potest Rex
a deo status]

followeth false counsels and errors, as the apostle discovereth: **Deus
tradidit illum in reprobum sensum.**   45

And this was also observed by the wise heathens, and thus, for example,
by one of them. First,

Lycurgus poeta

Iratus ad poenam si quis trahit deus,
Auferre mentem talibus primum solet,
Caliginemque offundit ut suas ruant   50

In clades, sibi quas noxiis
Averterunt ultro consiliis suis.
And another of them saith shortly and fully in the purpose:
Quos perdere instituit Jupiter,
5   **illos dementat.**
And thus hereof very divinely writeth another heathen man: **Mentem**
hominibus nonnumquam obscurat supera illa mens quam cuiusque
fórtunam mutare constituit, consilia eius corrumpit.
But we will cease to meddle further with these high and mystical
10 judgements, and leave them with reverence to the secret and infinite and
unsearchable wisdom of God. And we will proceed with the rest of the
tragical story [o]f this unfortunate king, and whom punishments and
miseries and wrongs and apprehensions left not in his death nor in his grave,
and whereof I will bring some instances here, and for the clearer
15 demonstration hereof.
First then, albeit he was slain and cruelly murdered, and *t*he quarrels and
wars at end, and the Earl of Richmond king and quietly possessed of the
crown and of all the royal *f*ortunes of King Richard, yet then, and after all
this, there *w*ere raised and maintained false slanders against *him* and against
20 his true and faithful friends and constant *f*ollowers. And (which was worse)
his [crue]l enemies made such haste to exercise their endless malice as that
he was no sooner slain [but they fall upon his body,] being before all
mangled and gashed with many *fatal w*ounds and all dyed in his blood, and
they stripped [his royal corse quite] naked, and then imitating the vultures
25 [or wolves, tore and rent his flesh and carcase. Some trailed it on the
ground, others pulled him by the beard and hairs and spurned and kicked him.
       [Occidit in bello miseranda caede Ricardus,   [Dr John Herd in
       Crinibus attractus dum saeviit hostis amarus, etc.]   **History Anglica**]
Those and such other be the words of his lamentable and miserable story,   **108v**
30 and then the carnifices, having not yet satisfied their inhumane eyes nor
their malicious hearts with these cruelties and with the so miserable   [Exer]cises *of cruelty*
spectacles, they laid this prince's dead body upon a jade, as the butcher   [upon the body of
layeth a flayed calf when he carrieth him to the market, and so basely and   King Richard]
reproachfully conveyed his body to Leicester. And in one word, they used
35 this sacred cor*s*e of a king so unreverently, so inhumanely, and so
barbarously as is almost incredible. Neither shall I need to aggravate this so
foul and so monstrous [a]n outrage and injury, and the which I may call an
impious and sacrilegious injury, being done to the body of a sacred person
and of an anointed king (as I said before), because it is so notoriously
40 known in all parts, and so far forth as that it sticketh as a stigmatical brand
of perpetual reproach and infamy to the cruel and barbarous actors and
authors thereof, and much to *their shame*.
But how in a contrary wise a [strange prince, William the Conqueror, to
his eternal honour, dea]lt with the body of King Harold, an usurper and his
45 perfidious enemy, this *example* shows: and that he severely punished the
barbarous [soldier which hacked the thigh of the dead king, and then with
all courtesy caused the body to be delivered to his mother to be honourably
buried as it should please her, which funeral was solemnly celebrated in his
own monastery at Waltham, as Henry Huntingdon and Matthew Paris
50 affirm.]

And at the same time also (and herebefore remembered), and upon cold blood and after the battle, many valiant and faithful subjects of King Richard were put to death at Leicester and elsewhere. And it was not raged enough yet, nor yet revenge nor vengeance enough was not yet taken, according to the minds and malice of his enemies. For in November 5 following, there was a Parliament held, wherein the said King Richard was attainted [of a stran]ge crime, a crime which a king cannot commit against his subject, and name*ly* this king was attainted (and very strangely and injuriously) of High Treason, together with the other subjects. And they

were men of great worth, and many of the*m* noblemen and nobly 10 descended; and their titles in the story show them to be signal persons and faithful liegemen, for they are there called and entitled chief aiders and assistants of King Richard at the Battle of Bosworth:

As nam[ely] Sir John Howard, Duke of Norfolk and High Ma[rshal] and High Admiral of England (**ut supra**). And h*e* was also a most wise and a 15 valiant and loyal knight, and of whom there is much honourable mention in th[e] stories of Philip de Commynes and of Enguerr[ant] de Monstrelet, and

109

in many author[s, as well] / foreign as domestical. And whereas some say that this Duke John retired himself from the court during the reign of King Richard, they err much therein, for it is certain that he was continually with 20 this king, and ever very near unto him and in great credit with him, and seldom from the king but when he was employed in some great affairs of

Sir Thomas More

state. And Sir Thomas More confuteth their opinion plainly, for he affirmeth that the duke was one of the privyest to this prince's counsels and to his doings, even until his death.   25

And Sir Thomas Howard, Earl of Surrey, and son and heir apparent of this duke, and a son worthy [so noble a father,] was al*so* in great favour and credit with King Richard. And he was a faithful and useful servant unto him. And he sped thereafter, for he was *with* the rest of King Richard's loyal servants attainted of High Treason [at] the foresaid Parliament. And 30 as in like manner were Sir Francis Lovell, Viscount Lovell; Sir Walter Devereux, Lord Ferrers of Chartley; Sir [John] de la Zouche; Sir Robert Harington, and James Harington; Richard Charleton; Richard Ratcliffe; William Berkeley; William Catesby; [Thomas Broughton]; John Buck; Humphrey Stafford; Thomas Stafford; Robert Middleto[n]; Robert 35 Brakenbury; and John Kendall, Secretary to King Rich*ard*; and Walter Hopton; Geoffrey Saintgermain; Roger Wake; Thomas Pilkingto[n]; William Sapcote; and William Brampton; and some heralds at arms and divers knights and gentlemen were then attainted of High Treason for the defending of their liege lord and sovereign.   40

And it was enacted by Parliament that they should all stand disabled and forejudged of all manner of honour, estate, dignity, and preeminence, and should forfeit to the new king all their castles, manors, lordships, hundreds, franchises, liberties, advousons, privileges, nominations, presentations, tenements, rents, suits, reversions, portions, annuities, pensions, rights, 45 hereditaments, goods, chattels, and debts. These be the words of the said Act of Parliament, and these very severe, and if **ius,** then **ius summum,** and in all extremity.

And I would have been glad to have *include*d the noble name of Percy in this roll, and the which I have *observed* in many such rolls and records. And 50

here it had been recorded if the [Earl of Nor]thumberland had been a true
and grateful man. For *he had done good* service to King Richard, and he
was much favoured, *as I sai*d before. And he came to Redmore He*ath, as
the* / Prior of Croyland hath informed me, and you shall be partaker of   109v
5 mine intelligence. And thus he writeth: **In eo loco ubi comes Northumbriae
cum satis decenti ingentique milite stabat, nihil adversi, neque datis neque
susceptis belli ictibus cernebatur.**

And here I cannot tell how his wisdom and judgement may be
commended. For this his manner of standing still and neutrally could not be
10 well taken of either of the generals, for the state of the victory stood in such
ambiguity and doubt. For as he had falsely forsaken the one, and he seemed
careless of helping and assisting the other, but yet he handled *the* matter so
well as that he soon got in good favour and credit with King Henry VII.
And he was serviceable and very officious to the king. But it succeeded ill.
15 For he, to please and gratify the king, undertook to levy a hard and grievous
tax upon the people of his country. They *t*ook such offence and indignation
thereat, and grew into such hatred of him as that they (the *common people*)
met him in great troups at a place near to York called Cocklodge, and set
upon him, and slew him there with some other of his friends.
20   But to return to the mention and memory of the faithful (but
unfortunate) followers and friends of King Richard, and of whom many
were slain in the battle and some fled, some were put to death. Yet they were
all condemned in Parliament of High Treason, **ut supra.** The foresaid mos[t]   [The Duke of Nor-
valiant Sir John Howard, Duke of Norfolk, was slain in the battle, and (as   folk slain by the Earl
25 it was thought) by John, Earl of Oxford. And the author of the story of   of Oxford]
Croyland seemeth to confirm this opinion for thus he writeth: **Comes
Oxoniae valentissimus miles in eam alam, ubi dux Norfolci[ae] constitutus
erat in agro /de Redmore/ tam Gallicorum tam Anglicorum militum
comitatu stipatus tetendit,** etc.
30   And there were then slain of King Richard's part the Lord Ferrers, Sir
Richard Ratcliffe, Sir William Conyers, Sir Richard Clarendon, Sir Robert
Brakenbury, and divers valiant and faithfu*l persons.* But Sir William
Catesby and Sir John Buck and some other knights and men of *honour and*
of good quality and of more stirring spirits, and the more witty and politic
35 men, and not well affected to *the* conqueror, as it was suspected, were
beheaded at Leicester two days after the battle. And that was upon St
Bartholemew's D[ay.] And it was another Bartelmy such as was in France in
our time, when the great and cruel massacre of the Protestants was acted,
and all such cruel and barbarous slaughters are now thereof St Barthelemies,
40 and Bartelmies, [simply, in a perpetual] stigma of that butchery.

And there were some which escaped that dismal day and *hid* themselves   110
until the storm of the bloody and cruel rage was overpassed. And here,
before I go any farther, I must answer an objection which will be made by
some against my saying that Thomas, Earl of Surrey was one of those which   [The Earl of Surrey
45 escaped out of the battle and saved his life by flight, because they hold an   escaped at Bosworth]
opinion (or error, as I think) that this earl submitted himself to the new king
at Bosworth immediately after the overthrow. But this must not be believed
of men of jud[ge]ment and who understand the state of those businesses.

For this [is] certain, that the Earl of Richmond resolved most constantly
50 and most cruelly to cut off all those noblemen and wor*thy* and wise men

which had faithfully loved and served King Rich[ard, holding] them to be
men most dangerous for his estate and to his safe possession of the crown.
And therefore they were most feared and most hated of him. And [after] the
Roman manner, he secretly proscribed them. And *these men* were *the* Duke
of Norfolk, Thomas, Earl of Surrey, Francis, Viscount Lovell, Wal*ter*   5
Ferrers of Chartley, Sir John de la Zouche, and Sir Humphrey *and* Sir
Robert Stafford, brothers, Sir Robert and Sir James Har*ington,* Sir
Thomas Broughton, Sir Richard Charleton, Sir Richard *Ratcliffe,* Sir
Walter Conyers, Sir William Catesby, Sir John Buck, *William Berkeley,* Sir
Robert Middleton, Sir Walter Hopton, Sir Robert Brak*enbury,* Sir Richard 10
Watkins, Sir Geoffrey Saintgermain, Sir Ro*ger Wake,* the Secretary
Kendall, Thomas Pilkington, William Sapcote, *William Brampton,* Andrew
Ratt, and some others whose names are partly in the roll[s] kept in the
Chapel of the Convertites in Chancery Lane, and partly were omitted by the
scribes.   15
    And so many of these as could be taken or were not slain in the battle
were beheaded the next day at Leicester most cruelly and most unjustly.
And those of this list which fled and escaped that present scourge and
violent and bloody fury of the execu*tion* escaped *and s*urvived, as namely
the Viscount Lovell, and the two Staffords, and Sir T*homas Broughton,*   20
and the said Thomas Howard, Earl of Surrey, and who, of all the rest, *if he*
had been taken in battle, was so hateful and so much feared of *the Earl of*
Richmond as that all the world could not have saved [his life], *and he must*
*have joined those valian*t brave prisoners who were executed at Leicester
with all speed: **Quia** ***********************. [And therefore let] no 25
man be so void of reason and sense to [think that he was taken or
submitte]d himself at Bosworth. But [he did that some months after, at a
happier time, which I can prove by the testimony] / of an ancient and wise
and veritable gentleman who was brought up from a child by this most
noble Earl Thomas, and was ever with him until his old age, and was well   30
acquainted with all his actions and his fortunes. Wherefore it must be
understood both for [the] truth and for the just causes aforesaid that this
earl fled from the [f]ield, and opportunely.
    But he could not post nor fly so fast nor [f]ar as the rest, because he was
sorely hurt and wounded in the fight. [But] he came by night to the house of 35
a gentleman not far from Nottingham who [much loved] the earl and his
father the duke and his noble family most dearly and faithfully. [There] he
lay in all safety and secrecy until his wounds were cured. [And in] the
meantime, that terrible Parliament held in November, and the attainder of
all the *friend*s of King Richard, was ended, and all the punishments to the   40
king's con*t*entment executed. And then, and soon after, followed a gracious
[par]don of all the offenders and partakers in that cause and quarrel *of* King
Richard. And now hereupon this earl, having good hope and not [on]ly of
pardon (as the rest) but also of the recovery of the favour of the *new* king,
and the rather because he knew that his offence in *t*he true and just   45
understanding thereof was a small offence, or none at all, but rather an act
of loyalty — wherefore he now was resolute to discover himself and to go
[to] the king, and in all humility to present and to submit himself to his
grace for / favour and pardon.
    The king's choler was not yet allayed, nor his displeasure and indignation 50

110v
[Robert] Buck, the
[grandfa]ther [of
this Sir George Buc]k

111

as yet passed over and worn out. But now he frowned and cast a stern look upon the [ea]rl, and uttered some sharp and rough words to him, and threatened to *cha*stise him severely for his bearing arms against him at Bos*wor*th. *And* the king commanded the earl to be arrested, to be carried to
5 the Tower of London, and there to be imprisoned during the king's pleasure, or *rather during* his displeasure. And this displeasure dured and continued by the space and *time* of four years or thereabouts, from the first of th[is king unto the fourth year.

[The third year, the kin]g came to the Tower to meet Queen Elizabeth
10 there, and to whom he was shortly to be married. And anon he called for the Earl of Surrey, and being *then in the Tower, and the* king *see*med still to be angry with him. And he challenged him upon his [o]ld quarrel and charged him with his partaking with the late [u]surper and tyrant (for so he termed King Richard). But the [ear]l, being a man of good courage and wise
15 and withal temperate, re[p]lied to the king (and yet in very humble and reverent manner) that he hoped that his highness would [not] always be displeased with him for an offence which [was of] that kind as that not only he, but also many thousand [good subj]ects took it to be no offence, but contrariwise, rather an action and an [effect of their] liege duties, and a just
20 accomplishment of the obligation [and al]legiance to their king and sovereign. And therefore he humbly *prayed his Majesty to remit his* displeasure and to receive him to [his better opinion.

[The king (as suddenly moved with this reply) sternly demands if he would excuse his fault, or how he could expect his grace, having served an
25 usurper and an unlawful king against him. The earl,] *in the* / like discreet   **111v**
and reverent manner as before, replied and said, 'Sire, I beseech your Grace to consider that the prince whom I followed was as solemnly and lawfully and with all the general suffrage and with universal applause crowned *king of this* realm. And the ceremony was performed by all the great officers and
30 peers of the realm, [both ecclesiasti]cal and lay. And he was my good and gracious master, and I held myself bound by the laws of God and nature and of this kingdom to obey and serve him faithfully. And I did never hold it my part or duty, nor fit for any good subject, to dispute or sift or question the title of the king his liege lord to the crown, but contrariwise to
35 defend him and his crown with all his best means and fortunes and forces, and with the adventure and expense of my dearest blood, [and] saw no reason in honour nor in justice to be of any other opinion. Wherefore I confess I held him to be the true and lawful king and to wear the crown rightfully and lawfully. And I was then and ever shall be of the mind to
40 serve and to love him with my heart who shall upon so good and honourable terms attain to the crown and wear it as he did. And I will live and die with him and in the defence of that cro[wn] wherever I shall find it, yea if it were set upon a stake', etc.

Thus the earl. And the king gave goo[d] ear unto his speech and marked it
45 well, and also liked it, and better than he discovered at the instant. And soon after, *he be*came instantly gracious to the earl and pardoned his offence or error. *And he was* content now to acknowledge that the earl's answer was not only plain *but* discreet and very reasonable, and that he verily believed that the earl would be a very good and true and faithful servant to
50 him who now had that imper*ial* crown of England, and would ever, as he

said, keep it by God's grace. [This was the king's third y]ear. And in the
beginning of the next, viz., **anno regni** 4, he set the earl at liberty and gave
him good access to royal presence, and well favoured him. And ere long he
made the earl one of his privy counse[l,] and he made him lieutenant or
governor of the north parts very soon after. And when there were wars to be 5
made against the King of Scotland, he m[ade] the Earl of Surrey general of
the army. Then (being captain and general) he overthrew the Scots.

But th[is was not when he took the king] at Flodden Field, for that was in
the time of Henry VIII, and who at the earl's return received him very
honourably and grac*iously,* and in reward of his many good services made 10
him High Treasurer and High Marshal of Engla[nd.] Also, Henry VII
restored him to his father's dukedom, being the inheritance of his
gr[andmother] Mowbray. And in brief, both these kings, the father and the
son, held him in great estimation and honour, and whereof he was very
[worthy.] For he was so truly noble and so valiant and provident as that he 15
crowned his actions with prosperous success and with immortal and
glorious memory. For v*erily,* fortune seemed to go hand in hand with him,
and **paribus pa***ribus***,** as the *Romans said.*

[Wherein] he resembled his most famous and very ancient progenitor
Heward[us,] / of whom it was doubted **utrum felicior an fortior esset,** so 20
fortunate and so heroical a knight he was. And sithence I have made this
mention of this noble Hewardus, and also entitled him the progenitor and
great ancestor of this great duke and of the noble Howards now flourishing,
I will make it known unto the generous Reader what and who this
Hewardus was, and that with as much brevity as I can. And not to the end 25
to add any more greatness to the House of Howard — for that were
needless, in regard of their very m[any noble extracti]ons and propagations
from the most noble families, and namely the Mowbrays of Warren, of
d'Albeny, of Marshall, of Segraves, and with the princely Plantagenet of
Brotherton, of Bigot, and with noble houses of Fitzalan, of Maltravers, of 30
Buckingham, of Oxford, of Dacres; and besides, th[eir infinite alliances] and
this cognation with all the most ancient noble families of the kingdom; and
in rea*son* of their many hard and high and most famous exploits and
achievements and great goo[d service] done to the king and to the kingdom.
And for these causes, their honour is so great and so well kn*own* as needeth 35
not my blazon.

Wherefore I have no [other scope] in this story of Hewardus but to
restore them whom I take to b[e] their proper [and original ancestor, as
farforth as I shall be able. And as I have endeav*oured to do so for this
family,* I shall be the rather pardoned because I have done the like honour 40
and service to many other the most noble families *of this country* in my
Commentaries in Librum Domus Dei and in this story. / And I will follow
Henry Húntingdon; Roger Hoveden; Matthew Paris; Matthew Florilegus;
Anonymous, the writer of the ledger book [of the] monastery of Ely;
Thomas Walsingham; and chiefly Ing[ulfus,] the Abbot of Croyland, who 45
lived in his time and in his c[ountry, therefore] might best know him.

This Hewardus was the son of Leofric, a very noble, magnificent lord.
And he was Lord of Burne in Lincolnshire, and of the c[ountry thereunto
adjacent. And his moth]er was the Lady Ediva, descended from the great
Oslac, a duke o[f the Easterlings in King Edgar's time. And I] find that 50
there was a noble kinsman of his called [Heward.] This Heward was a tall

112

Ingulfus

113

[Liber Eliensis]

man and of goodly personage and of great strength and very valiant, and
nimium bellicosus: much or too m[uch] affe[cted to] military affairs. And
to satisf*y* his desires, his natural inclination to martial enterprises, he
se[rved in] the wars in Northumberland and in Cornwall and in Ireland.
5 And when they were done, he went into the Lower Germany, and there he
showed so great courage and valour as that he w[as] not only much
esteemed there, but also much admired and reputed the *flower of honour.*
And be[ing] in Flanders, and there being a time of cessation from arms, he
fell in love with a fair lady called Turfrida, the daughter of a nobleman of
10 Flanders. And he ma[rried her,] *and* they lived some years there together.

And whilst he was in these countries, Leofric his father died, and about
that time William, Duke of Normandy, entered and conquered this
kingdom. And Heward here being advertised that the conqueror had seized
upon his lands and country and patrimony (and the which was in Holland and
15 in the Marshland) and given them to the French count, the new Earl [of
Holland,] Ivo Talbois, and that this count had handled very rudely the lady
his mother, and thrust her out of her proper possessions, and also out of her
dower, Heward hasted into England and came into Lincolnshire. And he
raised forces, and incontinently. And he went toward the new Earl of
20 Holland, and he fought with him and overthrew him and took him prisoner,
and held him in despite of the Conqueror until the earl had made
satisfactory recompense for the wrongs which he had done in Heward's
country, and that with a great sum of money.

[After that,] many barons spiritual and temporal and other good English,
25 [bein]g chased out of their countries, were glad to fly to [the Isle of Ely,] as
the place of most safety. They sent [to Heward] to come and take the charge
[of all their forces and be their general.] *And he* [condescended, fought for
them, and defended them. After, he built a castle there, called a long time
after 'Heward's Castle'.] / As that he continued in the isle, the king was not   113v
30 able to take this isle, nor to subdue the barons, nor so much as offend the
barons therein by all his forces. But in th[e meantime] the country of
Heward was invaded and infested of the Normans, whereupon he left the
Isle of Ely and returned home to defend his own country. And he so stoutly,
also so politicly and victoriously demeaned himself there as that he did not
35 only recover his own lands and large patrimony; but also he [brought] the
Conqueror to such terms as that he was content to [receive him to his
favour, which he enjoyed, and died] in good grace with him, [and] was
buried in the Abbey of Croyland.

And thus much for Heward. And now, as concerning his issue by his wife
40 Turfrida. [Albeit there] is no mention made of any but of one daughter,
named [also] Turfrida, who was married unto a nobleman called [Hugo]
Evermua, Lord of Deeping, yet there be divers reasons to in[duce many to]
*have certifi*ed that Heward had other children as well, if it be considered
[how] strong and how lusty and how able a body he had. And also because
45 there were [divers worthy persons which] bore his surname in that country a
long time after him until the time [they left] that [country] to [inhabit their
better heritage of acquists in other places.] *And* therefore it is very probable
that he had one natural [son a]t the least, and bearing his own name of
Howard, and that next to [his noble father,] *he* was the author [o]f this
50 noble house of the Howards.

And let it not be thought any disparagement for a noble family to be raised from a [na]tural issue, considering that there have been and are infinite number of noble and princely families which are derived and propagated from bastards or natural sons. As for example, Aeneas and Romulus, the found[ers] of the best Roman families, were bastards, and 5 Plutarch writeth that Theseus and Themistocles were bastards, and others say as much of Hercules and of many other noble and heroical persons. [The King of Spain descended from] Henry de Trastamara, base son of Alfonsus, the Justicer King of Castile. And some write that the ro[yal Stewarts of Scotland descend from a base son of Fleance.] And who hath 10 not and doth not honour the princely race of William the Conqueror, who was the bastard son of Robert, the Duke of Normandy? And [there was never] a more noble nor a more valiant nor a more heroical man than Robert, Earl of Gloucester, bas[e son of King Henry I.] And the Earls of Warren descended from Hamelin, a base son of Geoffrey Plantagenet, Earl 15 of Anjou. And the noble Herberts are said to descend from a base son of King [Henry I.] And the earls and dukes of Somerset (which followed the Red Rose) were the offspring of the Beauforts, natura[l] sons of John of Gaunt. And I could come nearer to these tim[es, if I should no]t offend, but these examples may suffice to take away t[he jealousy] or imputation of 20 blemish or dishonour from a bastardish or illegitimate original. [And this one example is above all, to wi]t, that Jesus Christ, the greatest and most noble king, was content to descend from Ph[ares, a bastard.]

And now to show some other reasons why I hold these nob[le Howards] to be descended from Hewardus, or Herewardus (for [so some writers] call 25 him — but Ingulfus, who best [knew him, calleth him always Hewardus). Both these names may signify in the Saxon or Old Dutch language a chief captain of an army, whom the Romans called Imperator.] / And that the titles and names of great offices have given surnames to many noble families, we have many examples, and particularly the Visconti of Milan, 30 the Chamberlains of Normandy, the Stewards of Scotland, the Butlers of Ireland, and divers others who had their surnames from the offices of their ancestors or fathers.

And this is rather a good argument, and not only for their taking of this surname of Howard, but also [for the origin of that family] fro[m] 35 Hewardus. For besides that (and before noted), to wit that the Ho[wards for many years and some] ages from the time of Howard dwelt in those countries of this heroical Hewardus, [as in] Holland and Marshland. And they continued there until they, acquiring more pleasan[t] possessions in Norfolk and in Suffolk by the marriages [of] the daughters and heirs of 40 Fitton, of Tendring, o[f] Mowbray, of Tilney, etc., and then they left their old sea[t] of Howard in Holland and Marshland and came into Norfolk and into Suffolk and were lords sometimes of Sunninghill near Windsor. But their fairest patri[mony was in Norfolk and Suffolk.] And they have also borne this surname ever since, or with small interruption, [the old surname 45 dis]continued, and have been lords and owners of some lands which belonged to the s[ame Hewardus.]

And I am of opinion if his arms could be found in any [charter, deed,] or monument of stone, metal, wood, or glass, and in all which there is n[o] doubt that his arms and gentilitious ensigns were imprint[ed or engraven] 50

[Homer, Livy]

114

119

and to be seen if they were well and diligently sought, I say I make no dou*bt that the* arms of Heward and of the Howards would be found to be al[l one, and then they must needs be reconciled.] Then also there would be no question of his being the ancestor of the nob*le Howards.* For it is a certain
5 and infallible principle not only in armory *but* in the imperial laws that **identitas armorum et cognominis praesum[it iden]titatem familiae**

And thus I have delivered mine opinion for the origin of the noble Howards or Hawards — for so they are for the most part written in stories, and He[reward] and Heward in charters and records, and which I have seen
10 in the [cabinet of my noble good lord, my lord [William Howard.] / And if   **114**
this be but a conjecture, yet conjectures made upon probable arguments and upon goo*d evidences and good* reasons usually pass for testimonies, as it is in the old leonine verse: **Qui bene coniectat, vates hic optimus extat.**
And besides, I doubt not that our better learned heralds and diligent
15 antiquaries (and whom it properly concerneth) can confirm all this which I have said with author*ity, and there be some of* them who agree with me and maintain this my assertion to be right.

And now to say something of the succession [and continuance] of this noble family of the Howards. It is most certainly and authentically to be
20 proved that whilst they lived and dwelt in [th]ose frontier countries of Lincolnshire and of Norfolk (namely in *Holla*nd and Marshland), there were of them very worthy and signal and [honour]able persons. And amongst them in the time of King Edward I, [Sir William Howard,] *a good*ly and learned and honourable gentleman, was Chief Justice. And he
25 [was grandfather to Sir John Howard, who] was Admiral of the North Fleet in th[e naval wars of King Edward III. His son Sir Robert Howard married the daughter of the Lo]/rd Scales.

Sir John Howard (who lived in the time of King Henry VI [and] died   **117v**
anno 16, Henry VI) had two wives: Margaret, daughter and [heir] of Sir
30 John Plaiz, a knight of a noble family. And by her he had [Eliza]beth, an only daughter, and married to John de Vere, Earl of Oxford. *And to* him she brought a goodly part of the lands of Howard. And her [heirs were] married to Latimer and to Winkfield, very fruitful [families.]

The second wife of this Sir John Howard was the [daught]er of Sir
35 William Tendring of Stoke Neyland in Suffolk, [by whom) he had his eldest son, Sir Robert Howard, who married [Margaret] Mowbray, daughter of a cadet of the house of Mowbray, and who became coheir with her sister, the La[dy Berkeley, to Thomas Mowbray, Duke of Nor]folk, dead in Venice and left his son John Howard [heir to H]oward and to Mowbray. And John
40 Howard, the son of [John Howard, was] created Duke of Norfolk by King Richard III in the right of his mother Mowbray. *And* [he] married the daughter of the Lord Moleyns, and by her *he* [had] Thomas Howard, the first Howard Earl of Surrey. *And* [this] is he who survived the dangers and calamities of the Battle [of B]osworth and became afterward Duke of
45 Norfolk and a *most* honourable and powerful peer of this realm, and from whom [all] the noble Howards now living are descended, and who, *as I* noted before, have matched with all the greatest and most *noble* families of this kingdom.

And it is also most memorable [that] this most noble house of the
50 Howards hath been so [hap]pily and so honourably fruitful as that it hath

furnished [this] kingdom with four dukes and many earls and viscounts [and] barons, and with three High Treasurers, and with [six] High or Great Marshals of England, and with ten High [o]r Great Admirals, and with some honourable **Custodes** of the King's Privy Seal, and with sundry honourable Chamberlains of the King's House.   5

126
And here I may be called to account what au*thors* I have followed in this story of the noble Howards (besides the vulgar chroni*clers and the monk of Croy*land: in some things Philip Commynes, Inguer de Monstre*let, and other* French writers. I have also followed the memorial*s set* up by the friars or monks of the monastery of Thet*ford* to the tomb of this great and first 10 Thomas Ho*ward, Duke* of Norfolk. And other things I have declared from *the* report of my grandfather, who was brought up *by the* first Thomas, Duke of Norfolk and was with him *in all* his expeditions, and after his death held the *same* estimation with the duke his son.

118v
[Sir Charles Howard]
And of this / most noble family there is yet one old and very heroical 15 Howard living, [who ha]th with great honour and with great good fortune borne and ad*orne*d the high offices of Great or High Constable and of Lord Lieutenant [of Eng]land, and of Lord High Steward or Great Seneschal of the kingdom, *of* [High] Marshal and of High Admiral of England, and of Lord Chief Justicer [in eyre] of the better part of this kingdom. Besides 20 that, he hath been Lord [Chambe]rlain of the royal house, and he hath also been very singularly happy in his *marti*al expeditions. And for example, he was famously and admirably victorious in the sundry marine battles and conflicts which were fought between him [and all] the naval powers of the King of Spain and of the Pope and of the princes [of I]taly, **Anno Domini** 25 1588. And he was also as fortunate in the siege and sack of [Cadiz, An]no **Domini** 1596. In these he had good success, *and* in other noble enterprises. And I speak not this by hearsay, but **ex certa scie[ntia, et visu pro]prio**: for I was both a spectator and an actor in them. And he is now the *ol*dest captain and the most ancient counsellor of estate in Euro*pe*.   30

120
And this is Sir Charles Howard of Effingham, Earl of Nottingham and High Admiral of England, and the most worth*y* grandchild of that most magnificent and most valorous Thomas, Lord Howard, Duke of Norfolk, and the which duke, for his better distinction and for his perpetual honour,

[Camden in Octa-dinis]
is styled **Triumphator Scotorum** and of whom I can never speak honourably 35 enough, and not only for his *v*ery many most noble acts and public honours, but also for his care in mine own particular obligation. Nor shall I ever be able to make sufficient testimony of my thankfulness for his great favours and many benefits bestowed upon mine ancestors and kinsfolks. And especially for the charitable and pious care which he had of the poor 40 distressed orphans of Sir John Buck, my great grandfather, who by the fatal day of Bosworth lost not only his life, but also his fortunes and means, and the livelihood of home and est*ates,* and w*hich* was then in Yorkshire for the most part, where his ancestors had li*v*ed wor*s*hipfully and opulently even from the time of *King John.*   45

Egerton 162v-163
[And since I have made this grateful digression, let me crave the Reader's favourable opinion if I stray a little further to show some reason why that most honourable peer made such favourable declarations of his favour to that unfortunate Buck and to his children, nor let my pious remembrance of him and of his obscured family seem ostentation or vainglory, since in other 50

histories and by others he is mentioned to be an intelligent, valiant, and
faithful man, much favoured by the king his master and in good credit with
him, bearing an ancient and hereditary love to the princely House of York,
was also well descended and allied to many worthy ancient and noble
5 families, by which means he came to be known to these noble Howards and
much esteemed by them.

[And because I must add proofs to what I have said, I will begin with the   [Camden in **Octa-**
testimony of the most learned Mr Camden Clarensius in his immortal   **dinis**]
Britannia, who deriveth this Sir John Buck from] / Sir Walter de Buck, a   **121**
10 gentleman of Brabant and of Fland[ers.] And he and his ancestor had that
surname of antiquity from the Castle de Buck in [Lisle, a] city and frontier
town in Flanders, where [the ancient] earls were accustomed much to
re[side.] And the ruins of the Castle de Buck were remaining in the time of   [Lodovic Guic-
Lodovic Guiccia[rdini. For] he saith that he saw [the] carcase of that *castle.*   ciardin in **Paesi**
15   And this Walter Buck was a cadet of the House of Flander[s and was]   **Bassi**]
employed by the prince then Duke of Brabant and Earl o[f Flanders] and
sent to King John with auxiliary troops of soldiers. And Roger Wendover
sai[th that this Walter Buck, and Gerard de Soceinni and] Godescalcus
venerunt in Angliam cum tribus legionibus Flandrensium et Breban-
20 **[tinorum militum,** etc.] And here he did good and valiant service to [the
king,] as many of our historians report, as namely M. Paris, M.
[Westminster,] Radulphus de Coggeshall, Thomas Walsingham, and others.
And the king bountifully reward*ed* him for his good service against his
rebel*lious subjects:* he gave lands to him in Yorkshire and in Northamp-
25 tonshire.

And [he] found in Yorkshire (where he made his seat and abode) an
ancient family of the surname of Buck, of Bucton in [the] Wapentake of   [The ancientry of
Buccross. And it seemed that that family had been *there* long, for the name   Buck]
is a Saxon or Dutch word and signifi[eth] a beech tree or a beechwood. And
30 Walter contracted friendship and amity with this Yorkshire gentleman of
his name, and also alliance. For he m*arried* Ralph de Buck, his eldest son,
to the daughter and heir of Gocelin[us] de Buck, who was grandchild to
Radulfus de Buck, and who / was a part-founder and a benefactor to the
Abbey of Bridlington, as I have seen written in the charter of King Henry I,   **122**
35 made for the foundation of that monastery.

And from this Sir [W]alter de Buck descended John Buck, knight, who
married [a Strelley, and was so constant in his love that although] she died
in his best age, yet he vowed never more to marry, and became a Knight of
the Rhodes. And [his] arms are yet to be seen in the ruins of the [Hosp]ital
40 of St John's near Smithfield and in the Church of All Ha[llows] in the
[upper end of Lombard Street,] which was repaired and enlarged with [the
stones brought] from that demolished [canopy. He lived **sub rege Edwardo,**
filio Regis Henrici, as I have seen by the date of his deed in Herthill, **anno** 1,
Edward I - **anno 22,** Edward I.
45   [And from this Knight of the Rhodes descended Sir John Buck, who for
his] / too much forwardness and hardiness in th*e assaulting and* the charging   **123**
a fleet of Spaniards without the leave [of] his Commander in Chief, the Earl
of Arundel, Lord Admiral, he was com[mitt]ed to the Tower, And this is
testified in the records of the [Tower,] **anno** 13, Richard II. Laurence Buck,
50 his [son, followe]d Edward Plantagenet, Duke of York, [and was a]t the

Battle of Agincourt with him, and *where* [this] duke was slain.

And John Buck, knight, [the son of this] Laurence, married a daughter and heir [of the noble] house of Staveley, and out of which house the barons [Parrs of Ke]ndal and Ross, and Queen Catharine, the last wife of [Henry] VIII, and the Lord Parr, Marquess of Northampton, and the [most noble] 5 Herberts, Earls of Pembroke and of Montgomery, [are desce]nded. And those more ancient Bucks resided for [the mos]t part at West Stanton and at Herthill in [Yorks]hire. And they took wives in divers worthy and ancient [families] of these parts, as namely of Strelley, or Stirley, of Woodhall, [of Th]orp, of Tilney (then of Lincolnshire), and of Saville, *and* [by] whom we 10 have much noble and worthy kindred. *Yet the*re be but few of them that claim any kindred of us. *And tha*t showeth that we flourish not nor are rich, *and* as it is in the Greek Comic:

τῶν εὐτυχούντων πάντες εἰσὶ συγγενεῖς.

fortunatorum omnes sunt cognati.   15

But this is by the way. And I will only add that that [m]atch with Saville was the last marriage of mine ancestors [i]n Yorkshire. For John Buck, that unfortunate man, who, following constan[tly the House of] York, was sore hurt and wounded at the battle of Barnet. But he received a gr[eater] blow and a deadlier wound, and that was for his service at Bosworth, / *as I ha*ve 20 intimated before, and for the which his head was cut off [a]t Leicester. And this John Buck married Margaret, the daughter of [H]enry Saville, and by whom he had [Ro]bert Buck, my grandfather, and most of his children, who were brought up into the south parts by [the] noble charity of the second Howard Duke of Norfolk, and where ever since we [have] remained under 25 the comfortable and honourable wings [of the] most noble and magnificent Howards [and their p]osters. For these children of Sir John Buck *were left* young and in poor and miserable estate by [reason] of the confiscation of all the goods and lands of [their un]happy father by Act of Parliament, **anno 1,** Henry VII, **ut supra.** / So that he might well say, as Iolaus said of 30 Hera[clides' orphans,] **Ego illos filios servavi, et sub alis texi:**

These bairns I fostered and fed
And over them my wings I spread.

But this noble duke did not only tender them in [their childhood,] but also provided well for them afterward and [bestowed the two] daughters in 35 marriage, the one with the heir [of Bure, the] other with the heir of Fitzlewis, both of very worthy families. And from these matches div[ers honourable and] noble persons descended. The sons were one [a soldier, the] other a courtier, and the third a priest. A[fterward, the duke] placed Robert Buck, the eldest son, at Melford [Hall in Suffolk, a] rich and 40 pleasant seat, and by his favour he [married into the] families of Higham and of Cotton, as also did [the Blounts of] Elwaston, the Talbots of Grafton, from whom the [barons of Mountjoy] and the earl of Shrewsbury now *living is* [descended.] The duke also bestowed in marriage one of the d[aughters of this Buck with Frederick Tilney of Shelley Ha[ll in Suffolk,] a 45 gentleman of a very ancient house, and h[is nearest kinsman by the duchess his mother's side.

[And I] have made a brief memorial of some of [my poor ancest]ors, and reason and duty also require *that I* should honour them from whom I have my being and my *source and* my pat[rimony and] mine interest in the 50

[And these Bucks] were all [soldiers, and so] were the rest [succeeding] *these*, for Robert [Buck, the son] of this unhappy [John Buck, fo]l-lowed Th[omas, Duke of Norfolk,] and was with [him at the Battle] of Flodden. [And Robert Buck, my father, served King Henry VIII at the

123v

siege of Boulogne, and the Duke of Somerset, Lieuten-ant General of King Edward VI, at the Battle of Mussel-burgh in Scotland. **Et nos militavimus et bella vidimus** G.B.]

126

[Euripides in tragedy **Heraclides**]

123v

quality / gentle or noble (for all is one.) And this was wel[l and worthily   **125**
acknowledged by the great consula]r philosopher: **Parentes carissimos**   [Cicero]
habere debemus, quod ab iis vita, patrimonium, libertas, civitas tradita est.
And certes I think there is no gentleman (if he be not stupid or degenerate)
5 but will take delight, also comfort, in the commemoration of the virtues and
wor*ks* of their forefathers, and in the reporting or hearing of the
commendations of those good men who brought or added honour or
dignities or all to their families.
    And this is not without warran[t,] for we have an express charge given to
10 us from the most mighty *Judge and* from the best Lawmaker, and from the
most severe exacter *of penalties and* of amends for the breach of His laws,
that we must h[onour our f]athers and our mothers. And this is not to be
understood only of [our parents **superstites** and living here with us, but of
our forefathers also — that is, beyond our great-grandfather (for we have no
15 proper word for them above that degree but 'antecessors', **vulgo**
'ancestors', whom the Romans] called **maiores)** and of all our progenitors
who departed [sooner or later] *from* this world and are (as we hope) in
Paradise and **in region*e* vivorum.**
    [For] the words **pater** and **mater** (as also **parens** and **parentes**) extend
20 [very la]rgely, and reach even up to the highest ancestor. And the ancient
Roman ju[riscon]sults deliver for an axiom in their law that **appellatione**
parentum [om]nes in infinitum maiores utriusque sexus significantur. And
this word **[pa]rentes** extendeth yet further, for it comprehendeth all our
kinsfolk [and] all the cousins of our blood and lineage. And it is used in that
25 sens[e by] Aelius Lampridus and by Julius Capitolinus and by other the best
[wr]iters of the times of the declined empire, and as Isaac Casaubonus ha[th
well] observed in his annotations upon these imperial historians.
    Moreover, the [Itali]ans and the Spaniards and the Frenchmen, whose
languages be for the [most part] **Romanzi** (that is, mongrel Latin and
30 broken and corrupted R[oman] language) use **parenti, parentes,** and **parens**
for all their [kinsf]olks and gentilitious cousins. But we Englishmen (being
[more pre]cise, and also more judicious) follow the more ancient and the
more [eloqu]ent and more classic Latin writers and hold 'parent' strictly [to
the] simple signification of **pater** and **mater,** and of the present and
35 immediate [parents.] But the using of the word **parentes,** as these [imperial]
historians, and as the Italians, Spaniards, and Frenchme[n use it, serveth]
better for our purpose here. And I could be [content also to imitate] the
pious gentlemen [of Italy, Spain, and France in their religious and charitable
endeavours to advance the joys and happiness] / of their parents defunct.
40 And if I thought that any such good offices of charity and of devotion
would do to those my **parentes** and forefathers any good, I would do them.
But if it be in vain and a vanity so to do, yet it is the more venial vanity
because it is an harmless and charitable and a gentle and a general vanity.
And whether we will or no, we must all be content to say and to confess,
45 **semel insanivimus omnes.**   Vergil in **Aegl** ***
    *T*his cannot be but acceptable to all these generous persons who are *of*
noble mind. And I would have those singular opiniasts which allow not
these things, nor anything but *relations of the living and in deri*sion call
these pious recordations the Legend of Lares and romances of shadows
50 firs[t] to consider that the **genii** of men and the **umbrae** or ghosts of men

deceased are as much on the other side delighted to behold and to speak
with their friends yet **superstites,** and with their kinsfolk and children and
progeny remaining upon the earth.

Circumstant animae dextra levaque frequentes:
nec venisse semel satis est, iuvat usque morari, etc.   5

This was the observation of that **pius** Aeneas when he went *to the* Elysian
paradise and land of ghosts to speak with his good *father* Anchises, and
who received him with great joy and gladness. [And] he was much delighted
to talk with his son Aeneas, and told him fine tales and notable prophecies
and good matters of stor*ies* because he would detain him in Elys*ium as* long 10
as he could. And as the same author (viz., the divine *Vergil*) reporteth,
Aeneas joyed as much to see his father's ghost and *have* speech and
conference with him. And he was so desirous to *hold and* (as it were) to
possess his father, as that he offered sundry t*imes to* take Anchises by the
hand and desired that they join their right hands together. And he desired 15
also to em*brace* and to accoll his father Anchises, and as in these words *he*
plainly declared:

Da iungere dextram,
da, genitor, teque amplexu ne subtrahe nostro.

126**   And with this I will end this second book, the nex[t] task being to refell 20
the slanders of King Richard, w[hich are] so many and so gross and false as
I have not read [or heard] of any prince so impudently and foully injured —
indeed [beyond] all comparison. And therefore I hope it will not displease
[the] noble, pious, and just disposition if the next book purge [him] from
the malice and venom of railing pasquil[lants and] libellers.   25

Explicit liber secundu[s]

THE THIRD BOOK
OF THE HISTORY OF KING RICHARD THE THIRD

The Contents of this Third Book

The accusations and slanders of King Richard exam[ined, answered,] and refelled.

The malice of Dr Morton and of his [servant Sir]Thomas More against King Richard.

5 Their style and strange [arts of defaming him,] *and* their idle and frivolous exceptions and gross and foolish cavils taken against [King Richard for his] gestures, looks, teeth, birth, deformity, and his virtues depraved [and concluded.]

[Utopia.]

10 The deaths of King Henry VI and of his son Edward, Prince [of] Wales, and the actors therein.

How great the offence of killing of a king [is.]

Truly valiant men [hate] treacheries and treacherous and cowardly slaughters.

15 King Richard not deformed.

The sl[anders] of Clarence translated maliciously to King Richard.

The cause of Clar[ence's] execution.

How the sons of King Edward IV came to the[ir] deaths, and that thereof King Richard not guilty.

20 The story of Perkin Warbeck.

He is compared with Don Sebastian, King of Portugal.

Who are **Biothanati.**

Counterfeit princes detected.

False friends.

25 Young Princes mar[vellously] preserved by Divine Providence.

Many strong arguments and testim[onies] for the assertion that Perkin Warbeck was Richard, Du[ke] of York.

His honourable entertainment with foreign people.

Vox [populi,] vox Dei.

30 Reasons why it is not credible that King Richard made away his two nephews.

Morton and More seem to excuse King Richard of their deaths.

The force of confession.

The cruelty of those of the faction of Somerset [o]r Lancaster.

35 Perkin imprisoned, tortured, and forced to accus[e and] belie himself.

The evil of torture.

The guilt of [at]tempting to escape out of prison.

What an escape is.

Heroum filii noxae.

40 The Earl of Oxford's persecutions of Perkin, and his [end.]

The base son of King Richard III, Captain of Calais, [secretly made] away.

The son of the Duke of Clarence put [to death for nothing.]

The [power of Furies,] De[mones, and Genii Apollonii Maiestas: **Quid tibi non vis, alteri ne feceris.]**

THE THIRD BOOK
OF THE HISTORY OF KING RICHARD III

I intimated in the former books that some [politic] and malicious clerks, hating King Richard and seek[ing] to be gracious with his enemies, employed their w[its] and their pens to make King Richard odious and abhorre[d] and his memory infamous forever. That for this purpose they devised and divulged many scandalous reports, and made false accusations 5 of him. And they made libels and railing p[am]phlets of him. And if haply they met with any of his [faults] (as they might doubtless, for there was never any man without fa[ults]), then, although these faults were small, and such unto which, or the like, even good men were obnoxious, they devise[d how they might] aug*ment* and amplify and aggravate them. 10

And so vehement and [constant] they were in their malicious prosecution thereof, as that they did [not] only much defame and belie him in his lifetime, but so farforth as lay in them, they persecuted even his shad[ow and] his ghost, and they scandalized extremely the memory of his fame and name. / And they would not suffer him to rest in the general place of rest, 15 and where all men rest and are at quiet — to wit, in his grave and sepulchre — but they molested and troubled his *mortal remains and exposed* them unto the wind and to the weather so that they did not on[ly,] according to the old proverb, and impiously, **Cum larvis luctari**; they st*rove* and they contended with his ghost and his immortal part, but also with his carcase and with [his 20 ashes,] *and* barbarously, so that it cannot be said in the case of the king as it was wont,

129*

Erasmus [i]n **Chiliad.**

[O]vid. D[e Po]nt., Lib. 3

T[erentius in Adelphi]

Pascitur in vivis livor, post fata quiescit,
Tunc suus ex merito quemquem tuetur honos.

But for these wrongs the times were most in fault, for then it w[as not] 25 only tolerable and allowable to make and to publish such scandalous and infamous writings of him, but also it was meritorious and guerdonable. And on the contrary side to write well and honourably of him was an offence. And these men had learned the rule of the comical [P]arasite and observed it: **Obsequium amicos, veritas odium [p]arit.** 30

And this malignant planet reigned a long time here. And it began *to give* [influence.] Name*ly, and* now in a few words to particularize these writers and to make them known: Dr Morton, that politician, as before, and often, remembered. For he was the chief *instigator* and *prime* sub*mover* of a*ll these* trea*sonous* de*tractions* and the ringleader of these detractors and 35 vi*tilitigators of King Richard. For he did not only bear malice and hatred to the princely family of York generally, [but m]ore particularly and more vehemently and more mortally toward King [R]ichard than to any other of

them, as well because King Richard removed this prelate from the co[unsel Libe[l of Dr Morton]
table] *because of his* false heart, as also because this king [imprisoned] *this*
*d*octor and Thomas Nandick of Cambridge, a notorious necromancer, and King Ri[chard had
with other such to be attainted by Parliament of treacherous [p]ractices and cause] to suspect
5 of sorcery and of such peccadillos of the reprobate Portuguese as were [and punish sor]cery
[ne]xt in rank to **No creer en Dios.**

For *t*his doctor, when the time served him to be revenged, took the
advantage of times, and the which was iniquous, *and he* had it most proper
and opportune for this revenge. And as is before intima*ted, he* was a good
10 clerk and learned, and made his pen the weapon and instru[ment] of his
malice and of his rancour and of his hatred. And for this purpose, he made
a book [in Latin] of King Richard and reported h*is acts, and* chargeth him
with many foul crimes, *and* aggravateth them. And on the other side, *he*
extenua*teth* or suppresseth *a*ll his virtues and good parts.

15   And *this book of Dr* / Morton came after to the hands of Mr More, who   **129v**
had been the servant of Morton, and a man much renowned for his [This book was lately
knowledge in poetry and in other good arts. But when he was young, and in the hands of Mr
servant to Dr Morton, and also be*ing* a clerk to one of the sheriffs of Roper of Eltham, as
London, and being then a man of small reputation, yet the[n] he was Sir Edward Hoby,
20 ambitious and desirous of preferment and of honour (as all the ingenious who saw it, told me.]
and best wits will for the most part), *and it well appea*red for a man
of so mean fortune to have an aspiring mind and ambit[ion.] And for
that purpose he must be provided with a good and fit viaticum of things.
And he employed his wit and his best means and arts, and amongst them
25 assentation and slander were of chief use.

And moreover, he was in two sciences or professions more dexterous and
more skilful and more delighted than many other witty men, *to* wit, in the
studies of the law and of the art of poetry. And by these two arts or
professions he might be holpen much in writing fables or in doing of
30 injuries. For lawyers have a privilege to tell false tales, or, in the plain
English, to be for advantage. And I find such fortunes and false arts in one [Amongst the dia-
of the translations of Mr More thus warranted: **Ii qui cum usus postulat, et** logues of Lucian, Sir
ad rem conducere vident, si mentiantur venia, immo laude plerique digni Thomas More made
sunt. And much more is to this purpose in those his transl*ations.* And poe*ts* choice for h]is [trans-
35 as well as painters have **quidlibet audendi aequam potestatem.** And that Sir la]tion [of seven]
Thomas More was a good poet and much delighted with poetry and with only, [whereof three
quaint inventions, his many poems and epigrams yet extant testify; besi[des] were The Cyn]ic,
the many petty comedies and interludes which he made and oftentimes [The Art of Necrom-
acted in person with the rest of the actors (as his loving and familiar friend ancy, and] this [of
40 Erasmus reporteth). And to these, hi*s* practices fantastical and his **Utopia** **Philopseudes,** or
may be added. Lover of Lies.]

And this Mr More, having been a servant of Morton, and which is more,
an understanding servant, knew that it was a chief duty of a servant **iurare** [Juvenal]
in verba magistri, ut supra. And therefore he had a care to *make* good and
45 to confirm what his master had forged or hewed in his spiteful and
slanderous anvil. And accordingly, he translated and inter*p*reted and glosed
and altered his mas[ter's] book at his pleasure, and then he publish*ed* it.

And here that saying of King Dariu[s,] which after became a proverb,
hath place and use: **[Hoc] calceamentum confuit Histiaeus, in[duit autem** [Herodotus]
50 **Aristagor]as.** So Dr Morton, [acting the part of Histiaeus, made the book,

130   and Mr More, like Aristagoras, set it forth,] / and added some things unto it.

And he had a purpose to write the whole story of King Richard III (as he himself intimateth in the title of his book), but it seemeth by his cold proceeding that he grew out of liking of that melancholic and uncharitable 5 work and weary of that base and detracting and scandalous style, and proper to the cynic or barking philosophers, who like cu*rs growl and snarl* and *detract and slander their betters.* And in truth it was more kind to such a maledicent mome as the deformed Thersites, who, as Homer writeth, was of such a railing disposition, and so immeasurably as that he reproached 10 and reviled at kings and princes. And for these causes it is likely that Sir Thomas More left the story imperfect and defective, for otherwise he had time enough to have finished it. For he lived twenty-two [yea]rs after he undertook this work, and for the most part at his pleasure, [and] prosperously. For he began this work **Anno Domini** 1513, when he [was] 15 Under-Sheriff, or clerk to one of the sheriffs of London, [and] in 1535, he died as he had lived, that is mocking and scoffing, [as Richard] Grafton reporteth.

But yet he was much favoured *of* fame and of the partial affection of men as that his vices were not only concealed and smothered, but also have 20 greater [commendation] ascribed to him than there w*as* just cause. And for example, Mr M*ore was* [reputed a] great learned man, and also (and which

131   is much greater praise) that he was [a very holy man.] *But there is* / no just cause for either of these praises. For albeit it is [tr]ue that he well understood the Latin and Greek [la]nguages — [which was than held great 25 learn]ing — but that was not enough to give to him the style of a great clerk. [Bu]t contrariwise, he was held to be a man of small [lear]ning by the profoundly learned men and by the great clerks, insomuch as he was

[Brixius **Antimoro**]   censured by Germanus [B]rixius to be no better than **ineruditus** (that is, [unlearned]).   30

[As] concerning his holiness, there were then many men more [ho]ly and more godly than he, and who never had the style *of* holy and of singularly godly men. And of the matter *there* writeth a plain man but a learned man, and one [that would flatter] nobody, and who better knew Sir Thomas

[Johannes Baleus,   More than these who since and [now have as]cribed so much learning and 35
De Scriptoribus Bri-   holiness to him:
tanniae, Century 8
cap. 69]   **[Hoc nos] probe novimus, qui eramus eidem Thomae [Moro viciniores,]**
130v   **quod pontificum et Pharisaeorum crudelitati [ex avaritia turpiter subser]-**
         viens, omni tyranno truculentior feroc[iebat.] / Immo insaniebat in eos qui
         aut Papae primatum, aut purgatorium, aut mortuorum invocationes, aut 40
         imaginum cultus, aut simile quidam diabolicarum imposturarum negabant,
         a vivifica (licet) Dei veritat*e* edocti. Consentire porro noluit hic Harpagus,
         ut rex Christianus in suo regno primus esset: nec quod ei liceret cum Davide,
         Solomone, Josaphate, Ezechia et Josia, sacerdotes et Levitas, reiecta
         Romanensium Nembrothorum tyrannide, in proprio ord[i]nare dominio, 45
         etc.

And doubtless this author had a*n* ill opinion of Sir Thomas More. For besides this his censure of *him,* he giveth to him the sole attribute and titles

132   of **te[nebrio, of] veritatis Evangeliae per/versissimus osor,** and of **obstinatus Calophanta, [of im]pudens Christi adversarius.** And then, 50

[s]peaking of the end of Sir Thomas More, saith that **decollatus fuit in turre Londinensi, 6 die Julii, Anno Domini 1535. Capite ad magnum Lond[ini] pontem (ut proditoribus fieri solet) stipiti imposito, et nihilominus a papistis pro novo martyre colitur.** And thus he became a martyr, and this is
5 his legend, according to Mr Baleus.

But there were other causes of his condemnation to death, as you shall see and know, and by his own testimony, having, as the p*rosecution declared*, judged himself by his own mouth. / For when he stood at the bar, **134** arraigned and to be tried for his offences, he confessed that there had been
10 some exceptions taken at him because he seemed to uphold and maintain the Pope's supremacy in England. And that he said that he could not see **quomodo laicas, vel secularis homo poss[it vel] debeat esse caput status spiritualis aut ecclesiastici.** [But] he insinuated that this opinion was taken hold of and urged for a colour to supplant and to subvert him. And he
15 affirmed that the chief ca[use] of the king's displeasure against him, and the greatest cause of *the* troubles and calamities whereunto he was fallen, was h[is with]standing the divorce between the king and Queen Cath[arine] of Castile, his wife, and his marriage with that most noble and fair Lady Anne Boleyn, Marquise of Pem[broke.]
20 And his own words spoken to the judges, according as they were taken and set down by hi[s dear] friend George Courinus in a short discourse [Courinus] which he wrote [of Sir] Thomas [More's] death, are these: **Non me fugit quamobrem [a] vobis condemnatus sim (videlicet) ob id, quod numquam volu[erim] assentire in negotium novi matrimonii regis.** And
25 these words were uttered by Sir Thomas More after the sentence of his condemnation was pronounced, and that is a time when no evasions nor any subterfuges would be of any worth or benefit, and therefore they proceeded from his heart and conscience. And before this, he wrote a long [letter to Mr Secretary Cromwell, which I have seen, wherein he protesteth]
30 that he is not against the king, either for his second marriage nor for the church's primacy, but wish[eth good success to the king and those affairs, etc. Which words we]ll considered, it will plainly discover that Sir Thomas More, Lord Chancellor of England, was not so faithful and so stout a champ[ion] for the Pope and his sovereignty as many Romanists and his
35 partial friends suppose.

Neither was he so good a Christian as they think he was. For I have seen [In scriniis Domini amongst the multitude of writings concerning the strange conferences, R. Cotton] counsels, and deliberations and resolutions had about the alteration of the religion and for the suppressing of all monasteries and religious houses, and
40 too many churches, that he [made no opposition to] that sacrilegious plot and gave also his consent to the suppression and destruction thereof, and the which profane and barbarous work [the] king had never done nor put in practice if the Pope and his agents and his [instru]ments had not withstood that his second marriage — [which] error and insolency they have all since
45 repented them, *but* too late. And of both these faults or crimes or *sacrileges* [the Lord Chan]cellor More was guilty, and so farforth as that he could [not defend his connivance] and consent [with any] arguments of wit or of policy.

But it was a happy turn for this kingdom that he was so by [j]ustice at that **134v**
50 time taken away. For if he had lived and flourished and enjoyed his former

credit and authority, England had been defrauded and deprived of the best queen that was, the sacred and worthily eternized Lady Elizabeth, late Queen of England. For she was a kingly queen, and a masculine dame. And she *was* wise and learned and temperate and chaste and frugal, and yet liberal and rich, and in a *manner* far exceeding these much renowned 5 Amazons, Thalestria, *Pen*thesilea, Antianira, Hippolyta, and the rest, and also those *im*perial and monarchizing ladies Semiramis, Thomyris, and *Artemis*ia, as that they were but May-ladies and maidens in comparison of her.

For she was ever dreadful to her foes, and always vict*orious* against her 10 enemies, and a true **parens patriae** at home and everywhere and at all times. And she was *a m*artial and true heroical **virago,** which better deserved the honourable title of **mater castrorum** [tha]n Victoria Augusta did, and yet by the testimony of Trebellius, she was a wise and valorous and excellent woman. But *yet* I say still that Queen Elizabeth surpassed them all. And in a 15 word, *she* was the phoenix of her sex. And the variety of her noble acts and of her many arduous achievements and of her victories and of her *wise* counsels and of her prudent policies is so great and so manifold and so exce[llent] with virtuous and good and pleasing matter as that the poets and romancers shall have no need to study for any new devices or delightful and 20 artificial inventions to set them forth or to embellish the*ir* poesies of her, because this bringeth matter enough, and abundant of that kind.

But this place and the time will not serve to tell the least of her high praises and rare merits. And therefore I think it better to say little or nothing than not that which shall be worthy of her. And as for her early and 25 cruel adversary [before she was in] **rerum natura,** Mr More, I have made bold to discover him and to pay him in his own coin and to paint him in his own colours. But yet I have not finished his character, but I will make it complete ere I finish this work. And in the meantime, if the Reader desire to know any more of this ungentle knight, I refer him to the ecclesiastical 30 history of Mr John Foxe in the reign of King Henry VIII, and where you shall see him graphically described, and what a **morosus morus** he was.

And I will leave his description and ret[urn] to his book, or to that his historical fragment, and wherein he took much pains to write the faults and false accusations and the evil fortunes of King Richard, and it was base and 35 a bad subject and an incivil and inhuman ar*gument*. But yet his labours were well accept*ed*, especially in that time w*hen it was written,* and was more safe/to rail at King Richard than to tell his virtues and to *praise him* **(ut supra).** Therefore his writings were received plausibly and held as canonical and authentic, and not only by the readers of that time. But also 40 annalists and chroniclers of this la[nd] *succe*eded him, or at the least of the weaker and more shallow sort, and who **(tamquam ignavum et servum pecus)** have followed him step by step and word by word, not having the judgement nor discret[ion to] consider his affections, nor his drifts, nor his arts, nor his placentine manners, nor his ends, nor to examine [the truth of] *the* relations 45 which he maketh, nor to search out the truth of his writings.

[But] yet I must confess that there may some excuse be made for these more simple scribblers or romancers, [if i]t be considered that the authors of that story, namely Morton and More, [were reputed] men not only of great learning and of much experience, and also of muc*h understanding* in civil 50

and public affairs, and both men of great credit and authority in this realm *and* kingdom. And by these means, if they had been men free from malice on the one s*ide and ambition on the other, they* must have committed the accidents of these times and the *truth of events* and all historical matters
5 growing in those times to writing, *especially those which pertained to* / King Richard and to the whole princely family of York, as I intimated be*fore,* partly for their own aim and worldly ends, and for the respect of their preferment and advancement (being men very *am*bitious and skilful and desirous to insinuate themselves into the favour of gr*eat* ones of that state
10 and to please the time, and to either of which King Richard was hateful.

And *by these* means, and by flattery and obsequious ob*serv*ation of humours and of affections, they gathered credit and promotion, *and in this busi*ness they turned their style upon King Richard and much wronged him, smothered and concealed his virtues *and the good* acts on the *one s*ide, and
15 they aggravated and exaggerated his vices and offences maliciously and in all extremity, and these on the better side, and to curry the more favour, *and* extolled the acts of Richard's flourishing foes and magnified them much above the cause and above their deser*t*. And to my seeming ****************, *s*peaking of certain sycophants, saith that they **Id obser-**
20 **vantes conspiratione concordi, ut fingere*nt* vere supprimerent Caesarem,** as these men dealt with King Richard.

And in this base kind, some tr[ivial] and clawing pamphleteers and some historical parasites ha*ve* dealt with the famous and most magnificent and very royal p[relate] (if prelates may be said to have the epithets of royal) and
25 namely Thomas Wo[lsey,] Cardinal and Archbishop of York, who bore the mind of a grea*t* king, and he was a man without peer in his time. Yet they wronged him, for *they maliciou*sly extenuated his virtues and derogated from hi*s good parts,* and have depraved or suppressed m[any] excellent things in him. And they have detracted from the honou[rable] and immortal
30 merit of many good and glorious and sumptuous works, and instead thereof, they have imputed to him many vic[es] and excesses whereof he was not guilty, and they have laid many crimes upon him which he never committed. And thus much in that high and *critical vein.*

And now I will return to the writers of the story of King Richard; and
35 wh[o] so many of them have followed the foresaid Morton and Mor[e,] although haply they were honest men, yet because they were [of] small learning and of lesser judgement, and some of th*em* so simple and so credulous as th*at they* could swallow any gudgeon and never examine the [style or faith] of those aforesaid authors nor bring th[em to the touchstone
40 of verity;] *but* / contrarily, they would believe anything and take any counterfeit and false coin of those crafty mintmasters for pure and current money.

And I advertise this by way of caution, because they which read their books should be wel*l advised to consider* and examine what they read, and
45 make trial of such doubtful things are as written before they give credit unto them. And here also I signify to the*m of* those injurious writers, that by their leaves or without their leaves *I will reveal the* frauds of their faults, and I will lay op*en* their sland*erous* reports, and I will reprehend them and tax them for *their slanders;* and their false accusations and scandals and
50 calumnies sha*ll receive* no better entertainment at mine hands than they

deserve. And they must be content to *suffer the* same whip wherewith they
have scourged others, and much better persons. And they must think and
know that this *is a* just doom, and of the credit of an oracle, and recorded

[Iliad, XX]

by *the* ancient and most wise Homer: **Quale verbum dixisti, tale etiam
audies.** It is just and due that they hear ill which speak ill, and [therefore it 5
must be said] to Sir Thomas More or to any of his followers, as the old

[Terentius in
Phormio]
137*

Comedian said, **Quod ab ipso allatum est, id sibi [relatum esse putet.]**

And men have / received and followed and passed for authentic many
gross fables, and such other vain matters as all the world knoweth. And

The *****

although Raphael Holinshed, Edward Hall, Richard Grafton, John Stow 10
were honest men, yet they have incurred these faults, for they have followed
the said Dr Morton and Mr More, and they have, without choice,
transcribed the wh*ole* reports and speeches of these Antirichards into their
stories and romances. And Polydore also so farforth may be numbered with
them as he followeth Dr Morton's pamphlet. And in brief, the historians, 15
chroniclers, and romancers writing these matters are but the tru*m*peters and
echoes of Morton and More.

Therefore, the Read[er] must read their writings warily, and consider
what men th*ey be. For it* is a hard thing to find that prince's story truly and
faithfully written, who was so hateful to the writers th*en; for when they* 20
w*r*ote they might write no better. And therefore, *t*hese reasons being
considered, their writings must be *re*garded and the authors censured
accordingly. And neither they nor their **manes** must not *be* offended if their
false accusations and crimina*t*ions be laid upon here, and if their *s*landers
and their railing discourses be reproved, and if they be taxed for their ill 25
writings and find their scandals *an*d malicious style to be retorted upon
themselves.

136

And now that these preparatives and advertisements be made for th[e
facilitating of my] way to the answering and refelling and confuting of the
said scandals and criminatio[ns, I will come to the su]bstance and the matter 30
of them by sundry instances, and exhibit [them faithfully] *to* the Reader,
and with the answers thereunto. And I doubt not but that we shall discover
strange and uncouth notions, and foul tokens of malevolence and of envy
particularly in the enemies of King Richard, and re*veal such* conceits of
railing and of malice, and such as very seldom or never fell unto the style or 35
pen of *any dis*creet and ingenious or wise or indifferent or charitable writer.

For these [men by their malicious] alchemy will transmute virtues into
vices. *And when it* so falleth necessarily into their discourse and pens they
must make mention of King Richard's good parts and virtues, then their
manner is either slightly and [scornfully] *to* overpass them, or else to 40

137v*

extenuate them and to pervert and t*o* / deprave them and to make gross and
scandalous construction of any virtue or good part of his, and if they write
of his faults and vices, they will aggravate them and make them more
grievous and more heinous than they were, and suppose *every mole*hill to be
a mountain.   45

And as concerning this, their first manner of their strange kind of
cavilling and depraving of the come*ly and* good parts which was in the king,
you shall see some examples in their words, and truly transcribed hither. It
must be then understood that whereas, then, this king was ever and
generally esteemed to be very courteous and affable, and that much to his 50

honour, so far as these cavil[lers] could not deny it, but were forced to confess it. But they *maliciously* cracked the credit of that good eulogy and crashed it all to nought with this spiteful glose: viz., that his *courtesy was faul*ty and was a dissembling device to get the favours of men.

5   When also they were driven to confe[ss] that he was liberal and had a mind to give boun[ti]fully, they perversely interpret this a subtle practice with large gifts and prodigality t[o] buy friendship. And he concealed his knowledge of his wrongs and slanders and bore them with patience and silence: they censured him for a secret and deep dissem[bling.] And as for his

10 friendship and love, although there was never any m[an loved his friend] better nor more faithfully, yet they make it of no worth, or nought, for they say that to both fri[end] and foe he was much indifferent. And moreover, that he was held and reputed to be merciful and ready to forgive such as offended him, and in the high kinds of *offences,* and such offences as that

15 of Fogg the attorney, who, not*with*standing he had made a libel of the king and count[er]feited his hand and seal, yet the king mercifully pardoned him and divers other the like. But these *cavillers* and hard and injurious censors term this clem*ency* and mercy to be a deceitfu[l clemency,] and to have been exercised and exhibited, and cunningly, to win [upon the good wills of the

20 people.]

    And they made other gross and ridiculous depravations [against his election. Though it was performed with all general good liking and suffrage, yet they shame not to say it was wrought] / by packing and practice, and slanderously and ridiculously they term it a mockish election.

25 And many such malicious mockeries and apish and ridiculous depravations and perverse constructions they make of things which were in him good, and the which good men would convert to his praise and honour. But the scandals of this kind, as they are very frequently obvious in the writings of those and of such like malicious men, so are they of all other scan*dals* the

30 most injurious and the most malicious. For by the very breath and poisoned speech of such perverse and envious persons, all the good works, and all the good words, and all the good gifts and good parts and vir*tues not only of King Richard but* also of any good man may be traduced and depraved, and all good things may receive false interpretations and foul

35 constructions as of vices and of crimes. And all the good which is said or done by a man, yea, a good man, shall be censured to be *d*one out of dissimulation and hypocrisy.

    But [th]ese detractors are not satisfied with these kind of [ca]vils, for they rest not thus, but they taint and carp at and [re]proach this prince in a

40 more subtle and more [cap]tious kind, and they find such strange faults in him as [e]ven Momus himself (the prince of carping and of railing *r*eprehensions) would not have found and noted them. As for *e*xample, these men make the casting of his eyes, *and* the motions of his fingers, and the manner of his pace and of his gait and his gesture and his other natural

45 actions to be faults. I confess with Cicero that **status in[cessus, sessio accubitio,] vultus [oculi, manum motio,** have] a certain decorum belonging to them, but he maketh it no vice to err in them, nor that any error committed in them w[ere a vice] or a sin. [But it must be so] defined by the laws of [Utopia.]

50   [They can search yet nearer his soul, finding] *great* faults and heinous

[The virtues of King Richard maliciously censured to be vices]

138 *

A [strange kind of] cr[imination]

[Cicero, **De Officiis,** Lib. 1]

crimes to the dreams and visions *and* nocturnal phantasms of the prince, and hold them as not only fearful and pernicious [an]d terrible, but also as precious and prodigious things. And yet I make no doubt *but* that they themselves, as well as I, find *that* *o*ther men, and good and virtuous persons, have had troublesome *and* terrible dreams and strange, frightful 5 visions. Wherefore *doubt*less all these objections and exceptions are but frivolous *and* malicious curiosities, and mere ridiculous cavillers, and [not] worth the answering. Neither had I meddled with them, but that it was and is fit that *these* sundry varieties of the malice of these men should *be remember*ed in everything and in every kind, that as *well the inj*ustice and 10 falsity as the grossness and ridiculousness *might bett*er appear, and that it might also *become apparent how that o*ther princes hath been *wronged*.

138v*   *These* [calumniators and detractors,] if this prince had prevailed at Bosworth and flourished, would have highly extolled him and his virtues, and rather like to chemical imposters, have pretended to augment their 15 golden value of his virtues and to multiply their precious essence with their glos*sing and* cogging *and* parasitism. And on the other side they would have concealed or extenuated his vices, his errors, and faults. But such have been the practices of these men against this king after that great storm of calamities and adversities fell upon him, as that *they* either smothered and 20 suppressed his virtues and good deeds and good parts, or else they extenuated and depraved them, and as I have often already intimated, and I may do again, for such re*quire many* confident affirmations. And in those adverse times of this king, they *c*ould find nothing to talk nor to write of him but vices *and* faults, and they were studious to make their lucubration of 25 that argument and to amplify and to aggravate his *faults, how trivial* and how light soever. Some, and almost all of these his faults were feigne*d* and falsely imputed to him.

But this is no new case, nor his case alone. Virtue in adversity hath ever been not onl*y* wrong*ed, but also* accursed and oppressed, as very gravely 30 hath been observed by the divine Philo, and*w*in these few words: **Res praeclarae calumniis et rebus adversis solent obscurari et op[primi.]** And as the noble and pious Trojan told Achilles, it wa[s] very easy to detract much

[Homer, **Iliad XX**]   and rail without measu*re*, and **et navem centirerem conviciis onerari:** (to lade a sh[ip] of a great burden with reproaches.

And of this kind of contumelies also, and those practised upon King Rich*ard,* I will bring some instances. As namely, these curious spy-fa[ults] impute as a great fault and a prodigious evil to King Richard that he was born with some teeth in his *mouth* — though I do not think that this prelate

[King Richard not monstrous]   or the lawyer ever spake with the duchess his mother or her midwife about 40 this matter. And therefore I may doubt whether they had any certain intelligence here[of,] or whether they feigned it. But yet if it be a true tale, I am indifferent and I care not, for it importeth nothing. For there is no reason wh[y] those early or natalitious teeth should be turned t[o] his reproach, considering that there have been man[y] noble and good men who 45

[Pliny, Livy, Valerius   have had teeth imputed as a fault [to] them. And namely Manius Curius
Maximus, Plutarch]   (surnamed there[upon] Dentatus); and Gnaeus Papyrius Carbo, [King of the Epirots, a prince much renowned in the old stories for his prowess,

139*   victories, and virtues; and Monodas, son of] / Prusias, King of Bithinia, were born with an entire semicircular bone in their mouths instead of teeth. 50

And these early teeth were never objected to these men or to any other as matter of vice or crime.

Then the pains which the duchess mother of this king felt in her travail of bringing him forth are ascribed by these cavillers to the wickedness and 5 frowardness of this prince. And yet her pains were not extreme and intolerable, for then they would have killed her. Because *a*ccording to the principle of the best Stoic, Seneca, **quod ferri potest leve est, quod non ferri breve est.** But her pains and pangs were sufferable, for she overcame them and lived almost fifty years after his birth — when the pains of many 10 childbearing ladies and of other women have been so extreme as that they have been mortal, and yet the children were never condemned as guilty of [murder,] but hel*d* for innocents.

Julia, the daughter of Julius Caesar, and wife of the Great Pompey, and Tulliosa, the [d]ear daughter of Marcus Cicero and wife of Dolabella, [and] 15 Junia Claudilla, the empress, and wife of Caius Caligula, [di]ed all of the difficulties and extreme pains of [the]ir childbearing and travails. And here in England, [Qu]een Elizabeth, the wife of Henry VII, died in childbed. And since that, Queen Jane, the *g*ood mother of our most towardly and hopeful prince, Edward VI, died in travail of his birth. And many 20 [th]ousand women more have done the like, and yet their deaths, and much le[ss their pains,] were never laid nor im[puted to] the children born so painfully and so fatally.

The next objection and exception which they take at King *R*ichard, and which is of more regard than these before *r*emembered, but yet not to be 25 made nor to be regarded by wise and *l*earned and discreet persons, and that is the note of his deformity. For [they] / impute that to him as a great *and* heinous crime. But because there be two kind of deformities, the one *of the* body and the other of the mind, and therefore distinction here were necessary, *t*hus, the deformities of the one are vicious and criminal, but *not* 30 of the other. For the deformities of the mind, as namely heresy, sacrilege, *l*echery, and the other such are sins and great crimes and faults of an heinous *nature, and* most foul and most ugly deformities. But these calumniators have *not made* this distinction, for they disertly inveigh against the bodily deformities of King Richard, and when they *bring* 35 *for*ward deformities and crimes, they name them plainly and in their proper terms.

But the case is not clear, for it is controverted whether the prin*c*e *was* *d*eformed of body or no. And some say peremptorily that he was *not deform*ed. One of these is the honest John Stow, who could not flatter and 40 *speak dishonest*ly, and who was a man very diligent and much inquisitive to un*cover* all things concerning the affairs or words or persons of princes. And he was very curious in [his] description of their forms, their favours, and of all *the line*aments of their bodies. And he by all his labour and search could not find any not[es of such] deformities in *the person* of king 45 Richard, albeit he had made great inquisition to know the *certa*inty thereof, as he himself told me. And further, he said that he had spoken with old and grave men who had often seen King Richard, *and th*at they affirmed that he was not deformed, but of person *and bo*dily shape comely enough, but they said that he was very low of stat*ure*. 50 *And th*is is also the same deformity and no other which other men have

[The Duchess of York died about the 11th of Henry VII at Berkhamsted, and was buried at Fotheringhay. John Stow.]

King R[ichard not] deform[ed]

140

observed in the p[rince,] amongst them Archibald Quhitlaw, the
ambassador of the King of [Sco]tland unto the King Richard, who said in his
description of this king that he had **corpus [exigu]um.** And to my seeming,
Philip de Commynes and the Prior of [Croy]land, who had seen and known
this prince and king, seem to clear [him im]plicitly of this note of deformity.   5
For in their many mentions and [dis]courses of him, they never directly nor
indirectly nor covertly nor aptly ever insinuate any deformity of body in
him, and the which they would not have concealed if any such thing had
been. And this same Mr Stow told me also [that John] Rous, who knew

139v

King Richard and wrote much of him and well described him, / noteth not 10
any deformity in him nor a*ny* fault in his lineaments. And I myself have
seen sundry picture[s of this king, but could never] discover any deformity
in them. I have observed his warlike face, or crabbed [visage, as Sir
Thomas More termeth it.]

And also maketh much against this objection that this Richard, of all the 15

[Rotuli in Anno 2,
Richard II]

ch[ildren] of the Duke of York, is said to be the most like [in] stature and in
favour and in shape to his father; albeit the duke his father were not tall, yet
he [was] of good and comely feature. Moreover, it cannot be [thought] that
Dr Shaw would openly in the pu[lpit at St Paul's Cross,] when King Richard
was [Protector and there present with many hundreds of people who had 20
before seen the king and knew him well and might then take their full view

142

of him and amend] / their knowledge — I say it cannot be that this divine
doctor would have made this fair description, and not only of the mind of
this prince but also of his person, if he had been a man deformed.

And these be his words: **The Lord Protector is a very noble prince, and** 25
the special pattern of knightly prowess. And he as well in all princely
behaviour, as in the lineaments and in favo[ur] of his visage, representeth
the very face of the noble duke his father. [This is] the father's own figure,
this is his own countenance, the very sure [and] undoubted image and the
plain express likeness of that noble Duke of York. Thus Dr Shaw in his 30
sermon at St Paul's Cross. And he was Dean of St Paul's, and a [grave] and
a lear[ned man.]

141
[Sir] Thomas [Mo]re
a[pud Hardyng] *and*
Graf[ton]

Sir Thomas More himself, speaking of the supposed def[or]mities of King
Richard, doth not affirm that certainly he was deformed, but that he rather
took it to be but a false [s]peech. For he saith that King Richard was 35
deformed, as th[e] fame ran, and as men of hatred to him reputed or
im*puted.* And thus **habemus rerum confitentem.** So that I rather think th*at*
[this] adversary of King Richard, after his usual manner of translat[ing] *the*
faults and vices of other men to the prince (and as it shall plainly app*ear by*
his manner hereafter) hath here transferred a deformity of hi[s o]wn to King 40
Richard. And that is where he reporteth that King Rich*ard h*ad one shoulder
higher than another; and falsely as it hath appeared [by] the former
testimonies and arguments. But it is certain that Mr [Mo]re had this
deformity. For it is plainly affirmed *of M*r More *by* his friend who wrote the
life of this Mr More in Latin and was as much *in* his favour as he could, that 45
Sir Thomas More had one shoulder higher th[an the other.] So that to
conclude, I see no cause, the arguments *and* proofs and testimonies of King
Richard's clearness from deformities being so f*ar* manifes*t,* [why there
s]hould any apology be made for him in that behalf.

But suppose and admit that this prince were deformed of body. [Yet] this 50

is no discreet nor just objection, nor hath any analogy with piety or humanity, but it savoureth strongly *and manifes*tly of cavil and of malice, and partly of superstition, and of trivial vulgar fancies and false *crimin*ations. For without doubt, a man deformed of body may,
5 not*withstanding* that, be wise and valiant and learned and liberal and bountiful *and magnificen*t and temperate and religious and pious, and be in every good part *sufficient* and absolute, as all men know.

And if examples thereof be *required, Epic*tetes / was reputed and adjudged the most wise of all Greece, yet he was a man in face and in bodily
10 lineaments vicious and deformed. And although Sergius Galba was ill-faced and ill-favoured and crookbacked, yet he was so wise and so valiant a man and so expert *and* excellent a captain as that the Romans, even those of the greatest *j*u*d*gement and of the greatest authority, preferred him in the election of their new emperor before all the fair and handsome and
15 personable *gen*tlemen of the whole empire. And these men, whatsoever their *outwar*d appearance was, yet they were well known to *have* had beautiful insides. And these be the true and necessary beauties, [as] sins and vices be the worst deformities of the internal parts.

142v
[Socrates, Aesopus, Epictetus, Galba, a great and excellent captain of the Romans]

And to come nearer home, there have been here in this land, as well in the
20 present age as in the more ancient times, men deformed in bodies and ill-favoured in visage. But those vices of nature were no blemishes unto them, because they were of those kind of deformed who (as I said even *now*) were wise and valiant, magnificent and magnanimous and virtuous and liberal and learned and pious and religious men, etc., and in so good and
25 great measure as that few or none of the most f*air* and goodly and comely personages might be compared to them for their virtues and rare gifts of mind. And whatsome*ver* the outward appearance of such men was, yet all w*ise* and discreet persons, knowing that some men, albeit deformed in body, and yet that they had good internal bea*u*ties and virtuous minds, hold
30 them worthy to be esteemed and honoured.

But not to spend any time more in the answer and confutation of so idle and foolish and ridiculous objection or imputation as this, I dare boldly say and *affirm as the* final conclusion of this argument or disputation that without a*ny* doubt men of deformed bodies may h*av*e very beautiful minds,
35 and may have lesser and fewer vices than the fair and *com*ely persons./And therefore defor*mit*ies of the body, where the mind is fair and beau*tif*ul, ought not to be objected, and much less upbraided, nor held as things of shame *or* offence and as crimes.

143*

But we will leave these mali*cious slanders and th*ose slight and peevish
40 cavils, for they are but *tri*vial and ridiculous calumnies of envious detractors and of idle sycophants, and are here at the ful*l confuted.* Now we will go to the great and more heinous offences *wh*erewith the adversaries *of* King Richard charged him.

The first of King Richard's great and more heinous crimes is said to be
45 the murder of King Henry VI. And he were very much to be condemned if it could be proved against him. For this prince was not only a good prince, but also a sacred and an anointed person — that is, so much privileged and, as [the learne]d say, so sacrosanct, and as no man by the express and strict interdict of Almighty God might lay violent hands upon him, or so much as
50 u̶nreverently or rudely to touch him, and much less to kill him. Wherefore

144
[Whether King Rich-ard were guilty of the death of King Henry VI or not]

the murder of a king anointed is so foul and so extremely atrocious a crime
as that *the* perpetrator is worthy of the most sharp and most shameful
punishments which may be devised.

And this King Henry, although he were of an usurper's line, yet he was
so virtuous, so pious, and so religious a man as that he was s*tyled* and   5
entitled by the*s*e grave and good men which knew him, **Sanctus rex,**
[sanctus] Henricus, et rex sanctissimus, etc. Of this prince Richard thought
well, and was never said to bear any evil affection towards him, and *as* [the]
adversaries of King Richard (though obscurely) insinuate, as none of them
imputeth the plotting and contriving of this murder to [him,] but disertly   10
and only to the King Edward.

But I must c*onfess that* some of his accusers say that the said king his
brother persuad*ed and* commanded this his brother the Duke of
Gloucester to execute the said murd[er.] But the request or tax and work be
so foul and so bas*e* as that it is not credible that they were even moved or   15
p[ropounded] to the Prince Richard. For first there is not any honourable
and truly n[oble and] *valorou/*s person (and such as King Edward was),
who would require so vile, so dishonoura*ble* [and hate]ful a piece of work to
be done by a prince and by his own brother. And next it is not to be
belie[ved that] the duke his brother, being a man of most honourable and   20
noble and pious disposition, w[ould endu]re to hear such a villainous and
nefarious motion made to him, and much less entertain th*e motion* thereof.
For such foul murders and treacherous assassinates be no offices nor
act*ions fo*r any heroical and honest and truly noble persons. Wherefore
Quintus Curtius reporteth *that the* murder of the noble Clitus was held the   25
more heinous and more odious because th*e king* was the executioner and did
the office of a hangman and of a villain: **Detestabile carnificis ministerium**
occupaverat rex. For it is the **mestier** and the proper office of a ruffian and
villain and of an **assassino,** as the Italians call them, to murder men cruelly
and barb*arously and to* kill them secretly and treacherously.   30

And Sir Thomas More himself is of opinion that King Edward would
appoint th[at butcherly office rather to any other than] to his brother. Thus
More. But he useth so much to speak ironically and in jest as that it is hard
to *impute so* foul and so base and treacherous a design to a prince and to a
man of equal blood and royal [lin]eage to himself, if it be considered that   35
the king had plenty and great ch[oice] *for* [such] employments, and who had
been bred in his long and cruel civil war[s,] *and who would* make no
conscience of shedding any human blood, and were to b*e led by the reward*
and good look of the king, and who, as they knew, also was *tender of the*
honour of himself / and his dearest brother.   40

Besides, there is no man of any brave, noble courage and of the true and
right noble and generous spirit, and truly valiant, or if he have any religion,
who will ever plot or conspire, and much less act the secret and treacherous
murder of any man, and above all other men, of a king anointed of God.
And to this purpose also make these *strong and* inseparable principles in   45
philosophy and in nature and in humanity, viz., πἄνδεινον φονικόν
omne timendum est cruentum. Or, as some say, **Omnis tim*ens* est homicida:**
that is, every coward is bloody and *cruel; and* **omnis vir fortis odit insidiosas**
homicidias et caedes insidiosas: that every truly valiant man hateth to shed
blood secretly and by treachery *a*nd treason.   50

[Polydore Vergil]

145

146*

****su-
****k.
**** chther
**** Axio*mat.*
Polit.

And there is no writer, either friend or foe of King Richa*rd,* *w*ho doth not confess and testify that he was a most valiant and *most* courageous prince, and one that feared nothing. And therefore he was obnoxious to treacherous effects *and* base practices of cowards. And besides all this, this
5 duke is not *charged* [direc]tly by any creditable writer of that time to have committed *that act.* Ne[ither is it discovered by th]em who murdered King Henry VI. Because, [being the actor is so] concealed, it were no hard matter to acquit also King Edward, *who was as* noble and as magnanimous and as heroical *and judicia*l as any hath been a long time.
10   But I fear it *wi*ll be harder to acquit him than the duke his *br*other. And the Prior of Croyland maketh it the more suspiciou[s, because he] giveth the [ti]tle of **tyrannus,** i.e. tyrant, to him who was [the] actor in this murder of King Henry. And the proper in*terpretation* of **tyrannus** is **rex, id est** 'king'. And whoever is **rex** is **tyrannus,** [according] to the genuine and ancient
15 signification of **tyrannus.** For anciently and properly amongst the Gr[eeks, τύ]ραννος was used for a king simply, were [he] good or bad. And when this murder was committed, [R]ichard was Duke of Gloucester, *a su*bject and not a king. And there was not any king then in England *but* these kings Henry VI and Edward IV.
20   *But I sha*ll argue this question no further, but I will bring some authorities and only offer the words of the authors to the consideration of the judicious Reader and leave the [gloss to him:] **Hoc tempore inventum est** [Chronicle Croyland] **corpus [Regis Henrici Sexti] exanime in turre Londiniarum. [Parcat Deus et spatium] paenitentiae, ei donet [quicumque sacrilegas manus in Christum**
25 **domini ausus immittere, unde et agens Tyranni et patiens gloriosi martiris titulum mereatur.** Thus he, and this is] / that maketh against King Edward.   146v
    And that this *is* but a doubtful and but a suspicious accusation, and it may be answered and refelled by good authority. There be some grave men of opinion that this King Henry was not slain nor murdered, but that he
30 died of natural sickness and of extreme infirmity of body. And certainly he was a weak man, and sick in body and also in mind. And at the least seven years before his death, **Rex Henricus 6 ab annis iam multis ex accidente sibi   Idem** Croyland **aegritudine quandam animi incurrerat infirmitatem, et sic aeger corpore et impos mentis permansit diutius.** And then this infirm state of his body being
35 consid[ered,] it is very p[robable] that he died of infirmity and [g]riefs, and lesser cause of sorrow than he had might soon and easily shorten the life of him and of a stronger man than he. But certes his griefs and cares were great, and extreme*ly* great, and not tolerable, especially to so weak a heart and so weak a mind and so weak a body as h*is* were.
40   For the great grief and care which he took *for* the loss of his crown and of his liberty (he be[ing] then a prisoner); and of all his friends, and for[ces] which were then overthrown in the Battle of Te[wkes]bury; and above all evils, the greatest evil happened unto him, for th*at was* where his only and most dear son, [the] prince, was murdered, and which was a killing c[are]
45 alone. And therefore it is very probable that *he* [under] these many and very heavy occasions of grief came to his death, and not by the sword and by violence. And this opinion and report is also received and alleged by a learned and discreet gentlem[an] who wrote in this age of this matter, and in these words: **This accusation (of the murder of K[ing] Henry VI) hath no   [Anonymous MS.]**
50 **other proof but the malicio[us] affirmation of one man. For many other**

[Rex Henry] VI in
custodia [ut alii refe]-
runt gladio, [ut alii
m]aerore deperiit.
[Johannes Meyerus,]
Annal. Flandr.
[Lib. 17]

men more truly did suppose that he died of mer[e] grief and of melancholy
when he heard th[e] overthrow of his cause and of his friends and of the
slaughter of the prince his son. [Thus he.] And Johannes Meyerus, a good
historian, saith that it was reported King Henry VI died [of grief and
thought.] And doubtless from that one man whom the English gentleman 5
meaneth, the which one was the malicious Morton, the **malus genius** of
Richard, all the other [succeeding] writers have sucked this slanderous *tale
of the* death of King Henry VI.

[The slaughter of the
prince, son of Henry
VI]

148*

Concerning this slaughter [of the prince, the only son of this King Henry
VI] here menti[oned, it is noted his death is not affected out of pretended 10
malice or premeditated treachery; and so it cannot be called wilful]
murder, because his slaughter *was* [casual] and sudden, and occasioned at
the instant [by his] own fault and by his insolence and [proud speech. For]
when the king demanded of him why he invaded his kingdom and for what
cause he raised tumults and bore arms against him in the field, the prince 15
proudly answered that he did that which he ought and might do, and tha*t* he
took arms for the defence and preservation of the right of the crown and of
the kingdom belonging rightfully to the king his father an[d] to his heirs.

[Holinshed in
Henry VI]

The king, being much moved a[nd] put into a choler and wrath with this
peremptory and proud [an]swer, replied and said to the prince that he *never* 20
had any right to the crown, and that the *prince* lied. And the king might well
so say, because [th]e crown was entailed to his father, Richard, [Du]ke of
York, and to his heirs by Act of Parliament, [aft]er the death or deposing or
resignation of King [Hen]ry VI. Besides that, King Henry IV, grandfather
to King Henry VI, was but [an usurper.] But the prince still maintained his 25
[asse]rtion boldly and stoutly, and whereat the king, *being* moved, struck
the prince with his fist (*and he*, as some say, was armed with a gauntlet of
[i]ron). And then instantly the noblemen attending *upon* the king — and by

[Polydore Vergil,
Lib. 24]

name, George, Duke of Clarence, the Marquess of Dorset, and the Lord
Hastings [and] others — drew their swords and instantly struck [the] 30
prince and killed him.

147

And whereas it is said by the [adversaries] of the Duke of *Gloucester* [that
only he] slew this prince with his sword, the contrary hereof is true. For I
have read [in] a faithful manuscript chronicle written of those /[tim]es that
the Duke of Gloucester only, of all those great persons, stood still and drew 35

[Chronicis in quarto
MS. apud Dom.
Rob. Cotton]

[not] his sword. And for this his forbearance there may divers good reasons
be [give]n. And first that it grew out of the mere conscience of honour and
out of this *heroi*cal and truly noble detestation of base murders. And
secondly because there [was] no need of any more swords, there being too
many already drawn. For where *there* was need of his sword to defend the 40

Anna u[xor Ed]wardi,
f[ilii Regis] Hen. VI
[capta] est cum [mar-
ito.] Johannes
M[eierus in Annal.]
Fl[andr. Lib. 17]

king his brother, there was no man's sword [more] ready. And chiefly, he
abstained to be a fellow homicide in this *act in* regard of this prince's wife,
who (as Johannes Meyerus saith) was in [the room with him, and] was near
akin to the Duchess of York, his mother, and whom also *he loved* very
[affe]ctionately, though secretly. But he professed to love the prince, and 45
her for his sake only, like a lover *of chivalry, and he* spoke as he soon after
showed, for he married this widow.

*And besid*es all these reasons, a charitable man would rather think *that*
[this noble duke] had forborne to be a partisan in that *he* [bore such a sense
of noble actions in his bosom;] which maketh somewhat more to the 50

purpose *when* [that misliking the obscure and mean burial] of the corpse of
King [Henry VI, this prince's father, he caused his corpse to be taken from
Chertsey and to be honourably conveyed to the royal and stately chapel of
Windsor, ordained for kings. And therefore with these reasons our charity
5 may excuse and acquit him of] *the* / slaughter *of this* King *Henry* VI and of
his son.

   And now we will exa*mine another* crime of King Richard *III.* Sir Thomas
More writeth [that some] suspected that duke to be a pr[acticer] and
[procurer of th]e death and *of the* execution of his b[rothe]r, the Duke of
10 Clarence. But yet notwithstanding this su[spicion,] this author [confesseth]
that it was commonly said [that] Richard [opposed hi]mself against those so
unnatural proceedings of [th]e king, and resisted them both privately and
openly. But I will make it better appear and more p[lain]ly by and by that
Richard was not any whit guilty thereof. For the [truth is] it was a doom
15 whereof the king had [immov]ably a[nd] inexorably resolved, and that the
execution of the [punishment was justly and] necessarily [inflict]ed [upon]
the Duke of Clarence. For as I declared in the tenth chapter of the third
book of my **Baron** and here in this story, *the* Duke of Clarence
had committed many and great tre[asons,] and by his much ingratitude and
20 continual perfidiousness had so ex[tremely] provoked the wrath and hatred
and indignation of [the] king his *brother* against him as that no man had
hope to gain any [grace] for him. Neither durst any of his friends move th[e]
king for it nor speak for him. And this did the [king] afterwards
acknowledge, and with much discontent, when his wrath was over, and had
25 remorse of his brother's blood. And then h*e repented,* and he was grieved
that nobody would make s*o bold* to save the duke his brother's life. And he
declared his grief in these few words: **O infelicem frat[rem,] pro cuius salute
nemo homo rogavit.**

   These word*s* are reported by Polydore, but not rightly understood by
30 him, [as] you shall see by the sequel by and by. And *you shall* see these
foresaid railers detected of another false a[ccusa]tion. And I think best first
to relate that, and this *it is.* They affi[rm] that Richard, Duke of Gloucester
raised a sland[erous] report of the birth of the king his brother and [gave] it
out that he was not the son of Richard, D[uke of] York, but of another man
35 who had secret familiarity with the Lady Cecily, th*e Duchess of York,* his
mother (and whom hereby *she bore a* son) and the*se corrupt chroniclers so
affirm,* [making this slander one special matter of Dr Shaw's sermon, that
he should say in the pulpit that King Edward was a bastard, and that the
duchess his mother had wanton familiarity with a certain gentleman.
40   [There is none but will say this loose and foul language deserved] *to* / be
blamed, and the rather because it is certain that *he ha*d not any inf*ormation*
from the Lord Protector for that speech nor for some other. But he
exceed*ed* his commission and spake according to his own conceit, and
according to such false intelligence as he had, and as I will prove. And for
45 example, this d*octor* in that sermon called the gentlewoman to whom it was
said that King Ed[ward] was betrothed before his marriage with Lady Gray
by the name of Elizabeth Lucy; whereas it is certain that her name was
Elean[or Butler,] alias Talbot, and so called by King Richard, and so
written in the record[s and] all authentic writings. And whereof more in the
50 fourth book.

   148v

[Richard not guilty
of the death of the
Duke of Clarence]

[Polydore Vergil]

Polydore [Vergi]l

[Errors of Dr Shaw]

149

[That the Duke of
Gloucester raised not
the slander of his
mother's whoredom
nor his brother's
bastardy.]

That King Richard willed not this preacher to say that his brother King
Edward was a bastard, there be many good and irrefutable reasons, and
besides, testimonies of great credit. And first it may be thoug[ht King
Ri]chard was not so gross and so blockish and insensible as to lay an
[imputation of] whoredom upon his mother, and a virtuous and honourable   5
[lady,] about the begetting of the king his brother, because it laid also an
asper[sion of] shame and of bastardy upon himself. For if his mother did
offend [in] the getting of one child, she might as well be dishonest and
offen[d in] like manner in the begetting of the rest. And besides, it is a good
pre*sum*ption that this prince raised not this defamation upon his mother,   10
and in the most scan*dalous and* injurious and unnatural kind, because he
was never noted to be *used or* accustomed to speak foul and reproachful
words of any man, *and* much less of ladies, and therefore in no wise to
slander and defame his *own* mother, and so great and noble a lady.

And if these arguments will not *serve* to acquit King Richard of the   15
raising of this slander (albeit they be *very* strong and efficacious), yet I shall
make it out of doubt by credible *testimonies.* It is affirmed by Sir Thomas
More and by Richard Grafton and by Mr [Ha]ll that King Richard was
much displeased with Dr Shaw when he heard *tha*t he had laid so foul a blot
and stain upon the honour of his most *dear* and virtuous mother. And this   20
was also affirmed by the Duke of Buckingham [in] his speech with the Lord
Mayor of London, and the which was in these words: *he said* that Dr Shaw
had committed a foul fault and had incurred the [great d]ispleasure of the
noble Protector for speaking so dishonourably and *slander*ously of the
duchess his mother in the pulpit at St Paul's Cross; [and that] he was able to 25
say upon his own knowledge he had done [wrong to] the Protector therein,
in regard that it was certain that [the Protecto]r reverently, and as nature
required, bore a true and [filial love] to the duchess his mother.

And lastly, and which chiefly *puts all doubt from the* question, it was
proved and it is test[ified upon record that George, Duke of Clarence, who   30
bore extreme hatred and malice to the king his brother, raised this slander,
not Richard. For he, most of all men, loved and honoured his brother King

150*

Richard, *Duke of
Gloucester,* his love
for his brother
Edward

Edward,]/and *he fai*thfully adhered always to him and took his part against
all his *enemies* (as I have said before), and still followed and *accom*panied
him in all fortunes, good and bad, and as well *in exi*le and in foreign   35
countries as at home, and in the war *as* in *p*eace. And when the Duke of
Clarence, the other *brother* of the king, and the Marquess Dorset, his
wife's son, *and his* much professed friend and best servant, the *mighty* Earl
of Warwick, and when almost all his friends *deserted him,* yet Richard of
Gloucester never forsook *him, and did* partake with the fortunes of this   40
king, *and what*soever they were.

[Lib. MS in quarto
apud D. Rob.
Cotton]
150v
Anno 10 Edward IV

Chroni*cle* Croyland

And in their most calamities, and when [King Henry VI had overthrown
King Edward in a battle, recovered the kingdom, and made King Edward
to be proclaimed an usurper, yet Richard stuck still unto him, and so far as
that he was] *exiled /* and proclaimed traitor for him. And when the Queen   45
Margaret besieged the city of Gloucester with the king's power of Henry VI
her husband, the [citizen]s defied the queen and resisted her army and told
her that it was the Duke [of] Gloucester's town, who was with the king and
for the king, and [they] would hold it for him, and most *peremptorily* and
briefly.   50

And certainly he was very just and faithful and constant to his friends; and of his faithful *service* and firm loyalty a gentle overture in his poesy or motto, and which was *this*: **Loyaulte me lie,** and the which I have seen written [w]ith his own hand, and subscribed Richard Glouceste[r'.] *A*nd to
5 be brief, it is manifest that he ever kept good *q*uarter with his brother King Edward and was al*ways in* amity and friendship with him, and *always* very obsequious to him. Therefore I say and conclude that Duke Richard co*uld* not and would not be the author of these foul scan*dals* against *his mother.* [Loyalty bindeth me]

[But if you] will hear the truth, then I must tell you that these scandals of
10 whoredom [were] devised and broached by the Duke of Cla[rence,] who a long time bore a hollow heart toward the [king.] And there were many jars and piques between [the] king and him. And certainly Clarence gave to the k[ing] just cause to hate him very much. For Clarence loved the king's enemi*es* better than the king, and cared not how little *he* was with the king
15 or to his court: **Visus est Dux Clarentiae magis ac magis a regis praesentia se subtrahere, in consilio vix verbum proferre, neq[ue] libenter bibere aut manducare in domo regis.**

After this the Duke of Clarence confederated [with] the Earl of Warwick his father **allié,** and then the k[ing's] false vassal. And they went into
20 Fr[ance,] and there solicited the French king for forces [to] be brought into England against the king. [And he and] the earl brought them in and brought them against [the] king, and fought with the king his brother and [overthrew] him, and then so fiercely pursued his victory [that] the king was fain to fly out of the land, *as I* related in the thirteenth chapter of the Third
25 Book of the **Baron.** [Father **allié,**] quod vulgo [et corrupte 'f]ather-in-law'] dicitur

And seeking and studyin[g how] he might utterly supplant and r*emove* [the king his brother,] / Clarence had falsely and untruly published that the K[ing] Edward was a bastard, and not legitimate to reign, and that he himself was therefore the true and lawful heir of the kingdom, and that the
30 regality and the crown of England belonged only to him and to his heirs. And these be the very words of the record. And now we see plainly who raised that slander of the bastardy of King Edward and the whoredom of his mother, and how slanderously and injuriously Dr Morton and his followers deal, which ascribe it to King Richard, and falsely. And by the premises also
35 it is manifest that the king had just and very important cause to rid Clarenc[e] out of the way and to be inexorable in the suit for his [par]don **(ut supra).**

151*

[In Parliament, **anno** 17 Edward IV, John Stow **vidit et legit**]

And here was a bitter proof of [the] old proverb, to wit, **fratrum inter se irae acer[bissi]mae sunt.** For all the favour which Clarence could at [his en]d
40 obtain was to choose what death he would die. [And h]e, loving malmsey, desired (as Jean de Serres reporteth) to be choked with it. [Thus you may see] that the Duke of Gloucester was not guilty of the death of the Duke of *Clarence,* [but] it pro*ceeded from* [the king's] *deep* and imp[lacable] displ[easure] conceiv*ed of his brother* for [his malice and treasons that cut
45 him off.] *And* the king *had so great fear* of him [that he never thought] himself [secure until he] was dea[d. Witness Polydore] Vergil: **[Edwardus rex,] post morte*m* [fratris se a] cunctis t[imeri animad]vertit, et i[pse iam timebat] neminem,** et*c.* [Erasmus, **Chiliad.**]

[Jean de Serres, **Invent.**]

*And n*ow I will take another accusation to task, and *which was a* very
50 heinous crime in itself. But for aught [I] can see, it is rather suspicious and

ambiguous [than c]lear and proved against King Richard III. But [be it] as it
may be, I will set down truly what [I fin]d written of it and in good authors
and in good books *and as w*ell printed as written. [And I will give the
accusers free liberty to] *a*ccuse and to indict him and to give all the evidence
which they can give against *him,* [and where their] memories fail in any of   5
these things, I will help them to make the supply. In this fair manner they
shall be dealt with here.

Who [made away]
the sons [of] Edward
[IV]

The case is the conspiracy and treasonable slaughter or murder of the two
young princes, the sons of King Edward, *n*amely Edward V, the king in
hope, and Richard [of S]hrewsbury, Duke of York and Norfolk, his 10
younger brother. *And King Richard is* accused and condemned for the
death and murder of them. *And in* this manner and form the accusation is
made, and *name*ly, *his* accusers say that King Richard, being desirous to rid
his two nephew out of the world, first employed [a tr]usty servant, John
Green, to Sir Robert Bra[kenbury,] the Lieutenant Constable of the 15
Tower, [about the] *e*ffecting and executing of this murder; and by reason
that that plot took no effect, because Brakenb*ury misliked of* [it,] the
Protector [suborned four] desperate and reprobate villains, and [John
Dig]hton, Miles Forrest, James Tyrell, [and William Slater, to undertake it.]
And [the] accusers affirm boldly that these **sicarios** [did,] *and* [the] manner 20
thereof was [by smothering the noble children in their beds, which done,
they made a deep hole in the ground at the foot of the stairs of their lodging,

151v

and there] *the/*y buried them, and very secretly, and laid a heap of stones
upon the grave after the ancient manner of **tumulus testis** mentioned in the

Genesis **Cap.** *35*

burial of Rachel, but not to that fair and famous end.   25

Thus the murder is reported by some of the accusers, but some others
vary from them and say that these young princes were embarked [in] a ship
at Tower wharf, and that they were conveyed from hence into the seas, and
so cast into the deeps and drowned. But some others say that [they] were not
drowned, but were set safe on shore beyond the seas.   30

Here it is manifest that these accusers (like to the false *ju*dges in their
accusation of Susanna) differ much in their tales, and in very many and
material points. And these differences or contradictions shake the credit of
the whole accusation and make it very suspicious and uncertain, and so
farforth as that no just and learned and religious judge would condemn 35
[any upon such false suggestions and contradictions.] For here the one
accuser giveth the lie to [the] other, and to my seeming also it is likely so to
fall ou*t in* the end that they must be content to share the lie *among* them.

152

For it will by arguments and by authorities *be* demonstrated here that
neither both these p*rinces* were buried in the Tower, / nor both conveyed 40
into foreign countries by sea. And then it must needs follow that they could
not b*oth be smothered* and buried in the Tower and also be cast into the
seas. And here it is worthy [the noting how] *these methods* and forms are
opposite and, as it were, **ex diametro,** the one repugnant to the [other,] *and
as our author for*getteth, **argumentum bicorne,** and a dangerous dilemma, 45
and needeth a *good so*phister to solve it and also to salve it. For indeed it is
against the art *of sophistry* and logic. For the professors thereof hold
peremptorily that two *con*traries in one subject may not stand, because
there is but one *truth.* And yet there be many contraries in this report.

For some say tha*t they* were shipped alive and conveyed over the seas: **In** 50

vulgus [fama] valuit filios Edwardi regis aliquo terrarum partem migress[e, atque] ita superstites esse. Thus Polydore. Dr Morton and Sir Thomas More agree in [one] place with this place of Polydore. The man (they say) commonly call[ed Perkin] Warbeck was as well with the princes as with the
5 peo[ple, English] and foreign, held to be the younger son of King Edward IV, and a[gain they say] that the deaths of the young King Edward and of his brother Richard h[ad come so] far in question as that some are yet in doubt whether they [were destroyed] in the days of King Richard or no. Here you see that it w[as held and believed that] th[ey] were living after the
10 death of King Richard. And then those ta*les of their* burying and drowning must needs be lies.

　　And as the act [of their death is thus] uncertainly disputed, so the manner of it is also controv[erted. For Sir Thomas] / More affirmeth, as before related, that they [were smothered] in their beds and in their sleep. But
15 Polydore saith [peremptorily] it was never known of what kind of death these two *princes* died. And another author, an ancient and a reverend man, *the Prior of* Croyland, agreeth with him and thus writeth: **[Vulgatum est] regis Edwardi pueros concessisse in fata, sed q[uo genere] interitus ignoratur.**
20 　　And one reason thereof may be be*cause that* they who held Perkin Warbeck and / Richard, Duke of York to be one, give another a[ccount] and of the manner thereof, for they say that he was [hanged] after King Richard's death, and at Tyburn, **anno 15**, Henry [VII. Again,] if it had been certain and undoubted that these four assassi[ns] had murdered these two
25 young princes, then it had bee[n] known certainly the place and the time and the manner of *their death, by* the due examination of those villains who were al*ive* [long after this] murder was said to be done by them, and went up and [down freely and] securely everywhere and every day. And therefore there can be n[o excuse] for this neglect of the examination of them, and
30 much less [for the suffer]ing such fellows to go unpunished and to live at liberty. *And I urge* the Reader to mark and well consider this, for this manner of dealing *hath* much to make for the clearing of King Richard from having suborne*d* **sicarios** to murder his foresaid nephews. And whereof more shall *be* said anon.
35 　　And as for the burying of their bodies in the To[wer,] if that be brought in question, certes then the affirmative w[ould] be much more hard to be proved than the negative or contrary. For this is clearly true, that there was much and diligent search made for their bodies in the Tower. And all these places were opene[d] and digged where it was said or supposed their bodies
40 were laid. But they could never be found by any search. And then it was said that a certain priest took up these bodies and buried them in another and so secret a plac[e] *that* it could never be found out. And hereunto, and with decorum, and for the more credit of this ass[ertion, they might have ad]ded that this burial by the priest was made **sub sigillo confessionis,** and which
45 may not [be] revealed.

　　But Sir Thomas More and the rest, seeing the absurdities and contrarieties of these op[inions,] and as a man puzzled and distracted with the variety and uncertainty of them, concludeth *that* the said princely bodies were cast <u>God wot where</u>, and in another place he saith [that it] <u>could never</u>
50 <u>come to light what became of the bodies of these two princes.</u> And

[Polydore V]ergil, [Lib. 26]
[Dr M]orton; [Sir Thomas] More

152v

[Prio]r [of Croylan]d

153

154
[More, Holinshed, Grafton, Hall, Stow]

Holin[shed] and Hall and Grafton and the rest confess that the very truth hereof was never known.

And [questionless the] princes were not buried in the Tower nor drowned in the seas. Wherefore there must some [better] enquiry and some better search be made for the discovery of this dark mystery. And for [the body of 5 one of them and the finding it,] / there is good hope and possibility. For it hath been averred and testified by sundry grave and discreet and credible men, and such as knew the young [Duke of] York, that he was preserved and saved and conveyed secretly into a foreign [c]ounty, and was alive many years after the time of [this] imaginary murder, and as it shall be largely and 10 with good argument *and* testimonies declared and demonstrated ere long.

And rath*er first* I will speak a word or twain of his elder [brother, and] *make* [the] best [enq]uiry and the best conjectures that we can to know what became of him. [It is first said the Lord Protector before his coronation] *had them mur/*dered, and cruelly and treacherously, in the Tower. But this 15 report *is* [false.] For there may certain proofs be made that not *only* the younger brother, but also that Edward, the elder brother, *was* living in the month of February following the death [of the king thei]r father, and which was ten months after. For [King Edward died in April] before. [And this] is plain in the records of the Parliament of **anno** 1 of [Richard III,] where 20 there is mention made of this prince, and as then living. [And Sir Thomas More] *in one* place confesseth that they were living long after that time aforesaid. [But I think the elder] brother Edward died [of sick]ness and of infirmity (for he was weak and very sickly, as also w[as his br]other, and as the queen their mother intimated in her speech to the [Card]inal 25 Bourchier). And their sisters also were but of a weak constitution, as their short live[s showed.]

And it is likely also that he died in the To[wer, and some] men in these days are the rather brought to think that this young king died [in] the Tower because there were certain bones, like to the bones of a chi[ld, fo]und lately 30 in a high and desolate turret in the Tower. And they suppose that *these* bones were the bones of one of these young princes. But others are of opinion *tha*t this was the carcase and bones of an ape which was kept in the [To]wer and that in his old age he either chose that place to die in, or else h*ad c*lambered up thither, according to the light and idle manner of those 35 wanton animals, and after, being desirous to go down, and looking downward, and seeing th[e] way to be very steep and deep and the precipice to be very terrible to behold he durst n[ot] adventure to descend, but for fear he stayed and starved there. Although this ape were soon missed and being sought for, yet he could not be found, by reason that that turret being 40 reckoned but as a wast and damned place for the height and uneasy access thereunto; nobody in many years went up to it.

But it is all one for this question and disputation wh[ether] that was the carcase of an ape or of a child, and whether this young pr[ince] died in the Tower or no. But wheresoever he died, I verily think that he died of a 45 natural sickn[ess] and of infirmity. And that is as probable as the death of his cousin germ[ane,] Edward, Prince of Wales, son and heir of King Richard, and who was sai[d] to die of a natural infirmity.

And there be many causes and reasons why they should both die of one kind of death and at one time. For they were like and very even parallels 50

153

153v

almost in all things, as *that they w*ere both of one composition, both of one
age, and b*oth alike in* bodily constitution and in one like corporal
h[abitude. And to make this parity the more complete and general, they
were both of one forename and surname, of one quality and fortune, and]
5 *there is little doubt* / but that they were (or might very probably be) both of
the [same] studies, of the same affections, of the same passions, and of
the like common distemperatures, and so consequently subject to the like
and [to the same infirmities.] And to these may also be added equal and
common constellations and [the same] compatient and commorient fates
10 and times. And then there is [reason] and natural cause that they should
both die of the like disease[s and na]tural **infirmities.**

   And then they could not be said to be βιο[θάνατοι] — that is, men
taken away by violence, secret or overt. [I say] *this* because the adversaries
of King Richard will needs have *it* [suspected] that this *Edward,* the eldest son
15 of King Edward IV, died a violent death, *and b*ecause also it may be as well
suspected that the other prince Edward, son of King Richard, and being in
the like danger of secret vi[olence] and for the same cause as his cousin was,
died of violence.

   I will say therefore th*ese things and* will still b*e of the* opinion that the
20 deaths of them both were alike, and that the same dis*ease* or destiny
predominated over the lives of both. But then it never may be granted that
King Richard made away the one of these princes, because one of them was
his only and most dear son, and all the hope of his succession and of his
future being. Neither may I be brought to belive that King Richard would
25 treacherously make away Edward, the other prince, who was his nephew,
and whom he did not only love most dearly, but also gladly took him for his
king and sovereign lo[rd,] and observed and served him with all reverence
and obsequious duties, *and* as I have fully demonstrated in the former
books. Besides that, he being king and by just and true title, and so taken of
30 all his subjects, and that on the other this his nephew and his brother were
reputed illegitimate, and so declared and pronounced by the spiritual
forecourts and by the high court of Parliament, he had no cause to doubt or
fear that the lif*e* of his nephews, being bastards, could do him any hurt or
any ways endanger his estate and title.

35   For we see by infinit[e] examples and continual experience that there is no
danger nor / evil dreaded nor doubted in the claim of any of the bastards of
[sovereign princes.] And for the more credit of this assertion, let any m*an*
[peruse the historie]s and chronicles of France, and he shall not find any
re[lation of any attempt or] enterprise made by any royal [bastards upon the
40 crown and kingdom.] Neither shall he [find any such thing] in [the histories
of Spain, the ambit of one only royal bastard excepted: Don Enriq, Earl
of Trastamara, who was drawn into that action by the violent rages of the
people and by the persuasions of the revolted estates of Castile to put down
a monster of sovereignty, the hateful tyrant Don Pedro el Cruel.

45   [Neither have I read of any bastards of the kings of England who have
made any public sign of their aspiring. And therefore Henry II was secure
of Robert, Earl of Glou]/cester, base son to King Henry [I. And we find not
that] King Richard I ever suspected his base brothe[r, Geoffrey
Plan]tagenet, of any affectation of royal state. And the like [may] be said of
50 the security of the three kings of the House of Lancaster, and albeit their

156

160

157

158

father and forefather, John of Gaunt, / Duke of Lancaster, left many base
children, and gallant and [aspiring enough,] the Beauforts or Somersets,
and those very fertile and faithful. Th[ese kings never suspected] or feared
any treacherous and proud aspiring in any of these bastards or of their
noble posters. [Neither] Henry VII nor Henry VIII ever suspected [Arthur   5
Plantagenet] *of such ambi*tions and so highly aspiring practice. And why
then should this [Richard III, who] was as wise and as courageous and as
secure and as c[onfident] *and as* kind and as pious as any of the kings his
pr[ogenitors, be] *more* [afraid of] *bastards* than they (I speak as they were
then taken and adjudged), or be more c[ruel and bloody-minded than they,   10
having then no cause to fear]? And that those tw*o princes* should be
destroyed by him for fear, and by him who s*aved this kingdom with his
sword!*

This is somewhat for King Richard, and very considerable. But there be
ma[ny] arguments and reasons besides, and which is more, many and *various* 15
testimonies and authorities that this king made not away his nephews. And
amongst *these arguments,* and a good one, and affirmed by Sir Thomas More
[and others, our] best chroniclers: to wit, that it was doubtful whether these
tw[o] brothers were taken away in King Richard's time or no. And again that
[one of them] was living many years after the death of King Richard. [And   20
what can be said] more for the acquitting of King Richard?

And I like better this opinion, because it maketh mention of [the
sur]vivance but of one of them. Neither do the best [stories] make mention
of the transportation of more than one of th[em into] Flanders. Neither had
they reason so to do otherwise, for surely the [elder] brother died before,   25
and in manner as hath been before decla*red and* discussed even now. And it
shall be sufficient for the clea[ring] of King Richard of this conspiracy and
treachery if one of them su[r]vived him more or less time. And now we will
see *how* that may be proved and sufficiently warranted. And because it will
be the more apparent and conspicuous in the true and simple relation of the 30
story of this one brother, and the rather because every story is full of
repor[ts] of him and few or none of his brother, albeit that some write th*at*

[Holinshed,   [the]y were both secretly taken out of the Tower and both set a*float in* [a
Polydore]   ship] and conveyed together over the seas. But because I [find no mention]
                 of the being of the elder brother in Flanders, but [very frequent mention of 35
                 the younger] brother's being there and of his other adventures and travails,
                 I will let th[e elder brother, Edward, rest, and speak of his] brother's
                 [transport]ation and [the rest of his actions and life.

[And because the question may be who sent him away, I will first resolve
that. We must know then this prudent and honourable care of sending away   40

158v   this younger brother is ascribed to that worth]/y and faithful knight Sir
                 Robert Brakenbury, Lieutenant of the *Tower.* [Others] say it was the
                 good device of the queen his mother. And it may be [well ascribed to her.]
                 And there is no doubt but that there were other grave and well-[affected
                 friends, as shall appear, and not obscurely. And it is the more credible the 45
                 qu]een was a dealer therein, because in the story of Sir Thomas More [it is
                 affirmed] she was before suspected to have in purpose to take her son *out of
                 the* sanctuary at Westminster and to send him out of the land. [It is also
                 intima]ted there and in the other stories that this plot of the conveying [out

o]f the realm was objected to the queen by some of the lords. [And the]
Cardinal Bourchier, Archbishop of Canterbury, told the *queen* [the] chief
reason why the Lord Protector and the other nobles were so [earnest to
have] young Richard sent to his brother, being then in the Tower, was
5 because [they had a strong] suspicion and fear that she would send him out
of the realm.

And no*w by these* premises it hath been made plain enough that the
younger son of King *Edward* was conveyed into a foreign land by sea, and
that foreign country was Flanders, as all the sto[ries testify,] *and* that he was
10 recommended by those his most dear and careful [friends to] the safe and
courteous and secret custody of an honest and worthy gentléman [of
Warbeck,] a town in Flanders, and where this Richard had good education.
And he was still, and a long [time, kept close,] first because these friends
durst not trust the king his uncle with that counsel and cau*se,* [nor let him
15 know] where his nephew Richard was. And there may the more credit [be
given to] that report of these matters because it agreeth well with that which
was made thereof [by Duke Richard,] or Perkin Warbeck himself (for so
now he was called or [nicknamed) unto the] most noble and prudent prince,
James IV, King of Scotland. And the which [was th]at he, after the death of [Grafton]
20 his brother, was preserved by the favour of God and by the means of a good
man, and so good and charitable a man as Josada, who saved the little
prince Joas from the bloody practice of Queen Athalia. *And he* said then
that for his more safety he was sent out of England into *Flanders, and took
ship* into a foreign country, etc. Thus he.
25 And thus obscurely and [un]known this young duke lived until King
Richard was dead. And then the Earl of [Rich]mond being come to England
and being a great enemy to the House of York, [the young duke was st]ill
kept unknown. But then *some* careful friends of Duke Richard, for the more
safety of him, thought best to put him into the *stu*dy and tutelage of Charles,
30 Duke of Burgundy, and of the Lady Margaret, the duchess, aunt [to this
prince,] and a kind lady. And these his friends took the example hereof
from the Duchess of Yor[k, who, upo]n like fears on the one side and upon
like hopes of security on the *other,* [sent her two] younger sons, George
and Richard, to the same du[chess, and her own daughter,] their good and
35 most loving sister, as hath been b*efore related.*

[The duchess] *was* [very gracious *and* **********nt of this young duke,
[to let] *him* [have all princely and virtuous education in Tournay, in
Antwerp,] / and after in the court of the Duke of Burgundy, as he had [been   **161**
in Warbeck, etc.,] and [the greater] care taken of his safety because the
40 Duchess of Burgu[ndy] was as jealous of King Henry VII as the queen
widow [was of King] Richard III. And she heard that king had ma[ny ears]
and had many and long and strong hands, and could find out such as they
would and reach them anywhere. Besides, she knew the king's ha[tred] of
the House of York to be such as that he would use any means to have and to
45 possess this young [duke.] Therefore she would not yet have the name and
the quality of [the young] prince to be known, as well for the reasons
aforesaid as / because he was not yet of years and of strength and of   **162**
knowledge ripe enough to undertake the enterprise for the recovery or
gaining of a [kingdom,] *and* the crown and kingdom of England. And
50 besides that, the times and opportunities for such were not yet ready nor

prop[itious for such] business.

It must *be* expected that there should be tumults and mutinies and seditions and also rebellious factions in England, and whereof their king was great and pregnant, because the government of the realm of *England was very* grievous to the subjects by reason of his covetousness and of his 5 actions and of some acts of cruelty and tyranny. And for the which grievances it was not long ere there were sundry rebellions in the north and in the west count[ries or other parts of the kingdom. And not long after also (which ma]de well for these purposes), great unkindness and enmities *fell* betwixt King Henry VII and Charles, the French king, by the fault of 10 our king. For he so far provoked the French [king that he passed] into [France with a great army,] *and* he besieged Boulogne by land and by sea. And the quarrel (and as I noted [before) made well for this purpose and was of good] use for the plots of the Duchess of Burgundy and for the advance[ment of the D]uke of York, as you shall better understand anon.   15

And in the meantime, the duchess was very careful that her princely nephew *should* have education. And to the end that he might know and be acqua[inted too with foreig]n princes and with their courts and governments, she sent him into France and unto [Portug]al and unto other places, and where he was honourably entertained, and like a prince. [And in 20 the] meantime, the English noblemen and gentlemen which were privy to the conveyance of the Prince Richard (as I intimated before), and who knew where he lurked or lay close, [finding good] opportunity to help him to his right sent Sir Rob[ert Clifford and Sir William Barley] into Flanders to the Duke of York to [give him a visit and acquaint him what] potent [friends he 25 had ready to assist and aid him. For there had been some counterfeits, which

162v   by private encouragement had taken upon t]/hem to be Edward, Earl of Warwick and Richard, Duke of York. *And they instructed* those gentle knights their messengers in that charge to [examine those secret] marks of this Richard and to look diligently that he *was not* an imposter and a 30 counterfeit. And this was a fit charge to those gentlemen, for they knew the young duke even from [his cra]dle.

And they went to him and viewed and considered him well and warily, and they had secret markings. *And* they found that by his face and countenance and other [lineaments,] and by all tokens before known to 35 them that he was [the young]er son of King Edward. And they observed a princely [grace and] behaviour in him, and which *was* a good token of his princely birth. And he could readily account very *accurately for* [many thin]gs he had heard or seen whilst he was in England, and some [things that had been done and spoken very] privately. And besides this he spake 40 English very perfectly, [and be]tter than Dutch or Wallonish. And hereupon Sir Robert [Cli]fford and the rest were so confident in their certain plain discovery and knowledge of the young prince as that they wrote to the Lord Fitzwalter and to Sir Simon Montfort and other the better and more faithful friends of the duke they were not *in doubt* [in their opinion] *of his being a* 45 *gentleman, and his being* in good health and a princely spirit. And his most noble behaviour, and such as became the son of a king, bewrayed well that he was no counterfeit. And that besides all this, he had all the marks and tokens of the young Duke of York, and was certainly the second son of King Edward. This they affirmed **ex certa scientia et supra vi[sum corporis.]** 50

But now it happened that one of the said counterfeits began to be stirring, and it happened there was a bruit that some noblemen and other principal persons, well affected to Edward, Earl of Warwick and in hope to get him out of the Tower, and in purpose to make him king, and who, as it seemed
5 had no certain intelligence of the state and condition of Richard, Duke of York, and therefore they, desiring to set up the Earl of Warwick *by and* by, they got / a handsome young fellow and like to the said earl, and whose name was Lambert Simnel of Lancashire. And he was bred in the University of Oxford and was instructed in the royal genealogy. And he was taught to
10 say th[at] he was the son of the Duke of Clarence, an*d* other particularities of that kind fit for him *to* know. And he was maintained and abetted [by the] Viscount Lovell and by the Earl [of Lincoln, Sir] Thomas Broughton, [and Sir Simon Priest, etc., and was presented to the Duke and Duchess of Burgundy, who honourably entertained him.] *And he was entreated* / and
15 much made of, and as the son of the Duke of Cla*rence.*

    And in Flanders, he drew to him Martin Swartz, [a great] captain, to assist him. And he came with forces into Ireland, where he was received [as the] Earl of Warwick and as a prince of Englan[d.] From thence he came into England and was [well] received here of many. But this deceit was soon
20 discovered, [and in excuse thereof it was] said that [the intent] of those lords was but to use this Lam*bert* as the [counterfeit] of the Earl of Warwick and for colour of their [practice] whilst they could get the said Earl Edward of Warwick out of the Tower and ma[ke] him king (as their purpose was, and as I noted before). And this Lamb*ert* was soon found to be a
25 counterfeit. And all this while Richard, Duke of York, lurked *in hiding.*

    And it is a very easy thing to discover an imposter of that kind, and such a counterfeit prince as this Lambert was, as by many examples it is manifest: although he deceive many men, yet there be some who know him so well that will not be delu*ded,* as there was a Ψeudo-Agrippa in the time of
30 Tiberius, who was soon found to be Clemens, the servant of Agrippa, and very like to Agrippa. And there was a Ψeudo-Nero in Otho's time, whom some took to be Nero revived, [but] he was also soon unmasked. And [Velleius Paterculus telleth us of a certain ambitious counterfeit in Macedonia who called himself Philip and would be reputed the next heir of
35 the crown, but was discovered and nicknamed Ψeudo-Philippus]. And in the reign of Commodus there was one pretended to be Sextus Condianus, the son of Maximius. And many such impostures are obvious in old stories, and they were still easily detected and convicted and in sharp manner, according to their demerits. And many such counterfeit princes and per*sons*
40 [ha]ve been discovered here in this our kingdom, and the reports whereof are everywhere obvious in our stories and chronicles. And by reason of th*ese examples, there was much doub*t and jealousy had of this Richard (alias Perkin) and of his fame and of the truth of his *birth and report* thereof when he first came to be heard of.

45   I will intermit therefore a while the continuate narration of his acts and story until I have made [a brief digression] in answer to these jealousies and suspicions which were had of him. [For] those jealousies and doubts, as afterward it was found, proceeded not from the detection [of any] frauds or dissimulations of Richard, but from the late abuse and impostures of this
50 said Lambert and of the shoemaker's son, who both *passed* for the Earl of

163*

164*

[Dion, Tacitus, Sue-
tonius]
[Counterfeit
princes]

[It is written by some
of the old historians
that King Harold
was not slain at the
Battle of Hastings by
the Conqueror,] but
h[e survived and
went to Jerusa]lem,
165
[etc. But it not
importeth whe]ther
[he were the true
Harold or] Ψeu[do-
Harold, because he
never] cam[e to claim
anything in] *this*
kingd[om.]

Warwick, son of the Duke of Clarence. And the people had thus been before illuded and abused by th[ose Ψeudo-Clarences,] so that they feared that everyone th*at* [assumed the name of greatness *was a* counterfeit. [In regard whereof, many shrunk in their opinion of this Perkin, or Richard, and many others, suspecting their belief] *who had* / considered better of this 5 matter and taken good and full *note of* him, well informed themselves of his true condition and estate. Then the[y were very careful,] and curiously they looked upon him. And after that the *more they searched and the*y pried into him, the more certain they grew and the better, the more they were per[suaded] that he was the second son of King Edward IV. And this 10 knowledge ripely and *timely* came, for **Tarda solet magnis rebus inesse fides.**

There were some men of harder belief, and *so jeal*ous as that *they* [o]bjected first that it was not possible that this [young duke] should be conveyed out of the Tower, nor next that he could not be so secretly 15 preserved anywhere. This objection was held by the wiser to be very weak and of *little credit,* and by many reasons and examples. And it only *betrayeth* and showeth little reading and knowledge in histories. And at the observation of *the clai*mant thus argued and pleaded: there be, said they, *examples* in the ancient histories, both Greek and Latin, many reports and 20 many relations of many nob[le] children, the deaths and destruction of whom hav*e* been plotted and determined by tyrants and by other cruel persons and thought to have been accomplished, and yet those child*ren* have escaped those [deaths] and bloody plots and have been secretly and safely preserved, a[s Livy and Diodorus witness in some, and others in many,] 25 *by the grat*eful providence of good men. And many of them have been preserved by the divine ordinanc*e.*

As for example, Herodotus and Trogus write that King Astyages most unnaturally purposed and resolved to destroy his young n*ephew and* gave charge to Harpagus, his noble servant, to slay this innocent infant Cyrus. 30 But *he, abhorring* this act, conveyed the child away, and he was secretly preserved, and so safely as that he came afterward to *be a* grandfather and to be king of the Medians and of the Persians. Likewise, King Amulius in Italy willed that Romulus and Remus (being then infants) should be made aw*ay.* But the compassionate Faustulus saved them and brought them up 35 unknown. In like manner the death of the famous and great Queen Semiramis, when sh*e* was a child, was decreed. But yet she was *pre*served in a secret and remote place until that tyrannou*s king was dead. And in* the Holy Scripture it is recorded that Joas was saved from slaughter by the good *Josada and preserved* six years, *and Joa*s became *king six* years *after* this 40 ex*perience, according to Holy Scripture.* But of all the examples of this kind, *the story* of Moses is the most signal and the most strange and the most authen*tic,* for as it is recorded in the Book of God. And there it is *recorded that* he being an infant was desperately and cruelly e*xposed to* the mercy of the unmerciful elem*ents* and to the most dangerous water, the 45 River of Nilus.

[And this Perkin himself, in his own behalf, when such objections were made against him, did allege to James, King of Scotland, the history of Joas mentioned in the Book of Kings, and that most signal one of Moses, by which it is made possible for this] / child Richard, the young Duke of 50

164v

Ovid in **Epistul.** 16

[Noble children destinated to be slain divinely preserved]

166

York, to escape his *death,* being practised and destinate by man, and to be *pre*served safely and secretly in a remote place. This noble child so escaped, and so was kept and *preserved* [beyond the] seas, and in the towns of Warbeck, of Tour[nay,] Antwerp, and elsewhere, and until there was a fit
5 time for his revealing and for the making of h*is identity and* his quality and his titles known, and according to the *considerati*ons and reasons before delivered.

And although he *was* an unknown and concealed person, yet he was honoura[bly] kept and entertained, and by the said duchess his aunt, [sister
10 germane] to his father, King Edward IV. And which lady, being wise, after good deliberation and consideration had of *the c*ertain quality and condition of the young lord, and well assured that he was the second son of the king her brother, she entertained him as a prince and as her nephew. And he was not only honourably entert*ained* by her, but also by all the chief
15 nobility of those parts, and much honoured by them, and in testimony of the good and certain opinion they had of being a son of England and an heir of the House of York, they gave, or rather rendered to him the noble and gentilitious ensign and title of La Rose Blanche: the White Rose, being [the] proper and ancient device of the House of York. And in *reg*ard of his
20 princely condition, there was a guard *of honou*r, a gallant guard of soldiers and armed men [to a]ttend and to defend him. And he was much esteemed and favoured [by] *other* princes, as namely by the Archduke Maximilian, King [of the Roma]ns, and by Philip his son, Duke of Burgundy, and [by Charles, the] French king, and by the kings of Portugal *and Scotland* and
25 [by the nobles] of Ireland, and by other many *noble princes.* / And they promised to give good assistance in his enterprise.

But as soon as King Henry heard these news and well apprehended the dang[er,] he [bestir]*red* himself so dexterously and so diligently, and he was so vigilant and so provident as that he found means to alter and to check
30 and finally to *quench the* good affection and gracious inclination of the foreign princes and lords towards this young duke, and to make them to ab*andon him.* And first, and to *thi*s end, he sent Dr William Warham (after Archibishop of Canterbury) [and] Sir Edward Poynings, a grave and worthy knight, to [the] said princes and lords of Burgundy, etc., and to
35 inform them that *they were misin*formed and were abused. For the king affirmed peremp[torily] that [he w]hom they took to be the son of King Edward [was merely a counterfeit and the son] of a Fleming and of a base fellow, and the[refore requests they would no further countenance him nor so much wrong their wisdoms and nobleness to give him any hope of
40 succour.] *And they received this* / message so well as that they obtained of [Philip,] Duke of Burgundy (for Maximilian his father was before returned into Austria), that Perkin should have no grace *nor succour* nor help in his dominions by any of his [subjects.] But he excepted the widow Duchess of Burgundy, the [aunt of Richard,] and whom as he had no power to
45 command, because she had all [jus]tice and consideration in those great and large signories whereof her dowry was composed. And the duke's [Council also] assured the king's ambassadors that no lords in their provinces should [as]sist Perkin nor any of his complices, for the [honour and] love which the duke and they bore to the King of England, and for the desire which the
50 duke their *mast*er had to be in peace and amity with the King of England,

169

[The practices of Henry VII with the Duke of Burgundy]

169v

*and concluded a*new the ancient and reciprocal league which had been between England and Burgundy. [T]hus the king supplanted Richard of York in the countries *under authority of the D*uke of Burgundy.

But I can say little of the hope of help which he *was promis*ed by his voyage into Portugal, where albeit he was well and honourably received, yet 5 by reason of the far distance of the country it ma*y be guess*ed that he built little upon the aid of the King of Portugal. But he re*turn*ed, for he understood that he had many great friends in England and also in Ireland, and that they desired much to see him and to have him to be their king. And

168

hereupon he sailed with a pretty fleet into Ireland, / and there he [w]as very 10 welcome therefore, and received as the younger son of King Edward IV. [Some of the] Geraldines and other great lords in Ireland purposed to make him their king. But [whilst] this matter was there treated, King Henry sent Dr Henry Dean, Abbot of Llanthony, and a w[ise, able] man, into Ireland.

[The means used by Henry VII to prevent the practice of Perkin in Ireland]

And he made him Chancellor of Ireland, and he sent also with him the 15 foresaid Sir Edward Po[ynings,] *and he* gave them so good instructions as that anon the reb*els persuaded* Perkin he could do no good with the Irish. And he resolved to return home.

169v

But in th*e mean*time, whilst he was in Ireland, he was informed and assured that King James of Scotla[nd] / wished well unto him and had a 20 good opinion of his cause, and would help him to his right by all means. This news was most welc*ome* to Perkin, and he forthwith went into Scotland, and he found his entertainment there answerable to the adver*sity* which he had before. For the king did not only receive him honourably, but

[This lady was so ra]ely [fair and so lovely that King Henry VII wondered at her beauty and was enamoured of h]er, and so [sent her to

170

London to be safely kept till his return out of the West Countries where he was then and first saw her. Richard Grafton]

also yielded to him his title and style of Duke of York, and promised to give 25 him strong footing in England. And he called him cousin, and to make him yet *more* akin or nearer allied to him, he bestowed in marriage upon him the most noble and fair lady Catharine Gordon, his ne[ar] kinswoman, and daughter of Alexander, Earl [of] Huntley. And further also, he forthwith raised forces to hel*p him* to recover his right in Engla*nd.* 30

[When King Henry heard this, he was more perplexed than before, knowing King James to be a wise and a valiant] / prince, and that he would not easily be gu*lled or* abused by any counterfeits or imposters. And [true it is] that King James was very precise and curious in the discerning of *impostures and* would not accept Perk*in* [till] he was clearly ascertained that 35 he was the true son [of Edward IV.] *And he became a* friend unto him, and the rather also because there was then *some contention,* and between King Henry and King J*ames, and who bore* him little good will; by reason whereof, King James was *the enemy of King Henry,* and therefore would be apt *to give* grace and aid to Perkin. All this was well understood. But yet he 40 was *so circumspect* and so provident as that he thought that there might practice be brought to pass to bring King James out of his good opinion *and* liking of [Perkin, and alienate him, as] he had done with other princes in the same cause.

[The practice of Henry VII with the King of Scots and of Castile, to get or supplant Perkin]

And for this cause he wrote to the King James, and he persuaded and 45 informed him th*at he should* abandon his enemy, who was a counterfeit, etc., and that *he* would requite the king's courtesy and favour in anything he could, and he also made great offers of rich rewards. But all could not prevail with King James, for besides that he stood *in* [ill affection to Henry VII,] he would n[ot] dishonourably leave and abandon a distressed prince 50

flying to him for succour, and much less delive[r him] to King Henry, being
Perkin's mortal enemy, and to be slain and destroyed by h*im*.

This answer was very unpleasant and distasteful to King Henry. But he,
being a man that could suddenly apprehend all occasions and all
5 adva[ntages,] and could readily find means of help and remedy for his evils,
called to mind that there was great love and friendship betwixt King James
and Ferdinand, King of Castile, and who was a prince worthy to be beloved
and honoured, for he was one of the most worthy princes then living. And
as it also happened then (and happily) there was good intelligence and amity
10 betwixt King Henry and King Ferdinand, insomuch as there was a motion
or treaty of marriage to be made betwixt Arthur, the Prince of Wales, and
Catharine, daughter of the King Ferdinand. And it [wa]s mutually well liked
and embraced.

Therefore, King Henry [des]patched in post a wise and worthy gentleman
15 toward [Casti]le, and gave him instructions (besides his letters) to advert*ise*
the King of Castile of that which had passed between [the King of Scot]land
and him, and how unkindly King James answered *him*, [and so to urge]
Ferdinand to use his power and credit [with King James] *to* del[ive]r Perkin
to him or *dismiss him*. [King Ferdinand undertakes this, sends Don Pedro   [Don Pedro Ayala]
20 Ayala, not one Peter Hiales nor Peter Hailes, as our vulgar stories have,] / *an*   **170v**
obscure man, but a signal gentleman [of a ver]y noble house, and a wise and
learned man, [as he well declare]d himself to be in this employment; *for he*
*so w*ell acquitted himself therein as that he obtained [of King J]ames his
faithful promise forthwith to dismiss [Perkin] *and* quite to leave him to
25 himself and to his fortunes. [But] *he* would by no means deliver him to the
King of England. For he held that were barbarously and impiously to
violate the law of hospitality and to betray his friend and his noble guest to
his *certain de*struction. And yet this king, according to his promise,
[comma]nded Perkin to depart out of his country. And [thu]s again King
30 Henry overreached Perkin with his arts and *his* policy, and **virtute vel dolo,**
supplanted him everywhere.

And now Perkin was driven of force to return into Ireland for his
convenient repassage unto his friends. And being arrived there, he was
again well entertained as a prince of England. And whilst he was in Ireland
35 and practising for the domin*ion,* Charles, the French king, sent to him two
gentlemen, Loys de Lucques and Estienne Friant, earnestly to request   Ha[ll] in H[enry VII]
Perkin to come into France to him, as to one who was and would be his
best friend, and that he would take his part and assist him to recover the
kingdom of England, his inheritance. And this offer was made then
40 unfeignedly and from his heart. And the reason was because the King of
England and he were fallen out (as I declared before), *and there was* great
feud. And the King of England threatened to invade France with a mighty
army, and [both of them prep]ared forces to fight.

And Perkin hasted into France, and the king received him with great
45 honour, and as a great prince, and appointed a guard to attend upon
him, the captain whereof was Monsieur Congresalle. And this was another
thorn in King Henry's eye. And on better advisement, fearing that he
should take more hurt than good by force, therefore he began to think of
accord and peace, and made his desire thereof and also very fair conditions
50 to be propounded to the French king, who soon and willingly hearkened

thereunto. And there was friendship made and a league concluded *bet*wixt these kings.

And anon the French king looked stra*ngely upon* Perkin, and was alienated suddenly from him. And Perkin, not liking that, [suspecting King Charles might upon some capitulation of the new league deliver him to the   5 King of England, therefore he secretly made from Paris to his aunt of Burgundy again, to whom he was as before very welcome. She encouraged

171

him afresh to pursue his design.] / And although Perkin was thus dishonourably left and forsa[ken,] *and although he might* have been much discouraged and dejected, but yet all his spirits nor all *his daring was not* 10 *quenched,* presuming that he had many and good and great friends in h*is party,* and who favoured his right and title and wished him *well* and would afford their best means for the accomplishment *of his designs.*

[And he makes another voyage] into Ireland, but albeit and as in like manner the Irishmen had promised to him [all assistance,] *by the king's* 15 means they fell from him and failed him. I have d*isclosed that* they were so hardly and secretly curbed by the care and wisdom of [the king's officers.] And then from Ireland he sailed into England, and he *landed* [at Bodmin] in Cornwall. And the Cornishmen and other western men [received him very] gladly and honourably and were willing and ready to assist him. And th*ey* 20 *proclaimed* him King of England and of France, etc., and by the title of King of England, etc., as he was before proclaimed in the [north parts o]f England and by the counsel and countenance of the King of Sc[otland.

[And now] Perkin marched into Devonshire, and he came to Exeter and [lay siege to it,] *and not*withstanding so many great foreign and domestical 25 friends had forsak*en him,* he had above five thousand men in his train and army. But yet the king's army was at hand and much stronger. And not to be cha*rged,* he was fo[rced to leave the] siege and to seek to save himself. And now those few followers which were left, seeing his weakness of forces

172

and fearing the great and many mischiefs, and *seeing* / the great forces of 30 [t]he king which were approached unto them, they fled from Perkin. And he being thus abandoned resolved instantly to save [h]imself by flight, and being well mounted and accompanied with [some forty or fifty] gallant and resolute gentlemen, he posted toward the Abbey of [Be]aulieu in Hampshire and he arrived safely there. And he [en]tered the monastery and took the 35 sanctuary and claimed the holy privilege *and pro*tection of the place. And the king's forces pursuing him [foun]d where he was, and came to the Abbey and would have *taken* Perkin away perforce. But the abbot and the religious [persons] would by no means endure that there should be any violent and impious *threat* to be offered [against their holy privilege.] 40 Whereof the king being advertised sent his messenger*s with* [proffers of favour] and mercy to Perkin, and to promise to him [such hon]ours and dignities [and revenues as should be grateful to him. Upon which fair conditions and protestations Perkin yields himself up.]

175v

*And the king k*ept him in the court as a noble person and used him very 45 bount[ifully.] But his kindness lasted not long. For [the king's jealousy

[Perkin's entertain-
ment in the court]

tor]mented him much, as that afterwhile he abated his favour [and bounty toward him] *then* and there, and whereby he was restrained of much of that liberty *which he had at* his first coming. Whereupon he grew malcontent and *despairing* of his safety. And thereupon soon after, he passing [by the 50

monastery] at Sheen, he entered it suddenly and gave his guard the slip, [claiming the privilege of] that holy house, and the which was granted to him. And so he was then rid of his keepers and of his fea*rs. When the king* heard this, he sent again messengers and mediators to *go and* persuade him to
5 return to the court, and with great and large [promi]ses of honours and of advancement, as before. But Perkin [durst] not trust the king, because he had broken such promises before.

And then the king dealt with the [pri]or to deliver Perkin to him. But he was a good and pitiful man and would not yield to deli*ver his* prisoner or
10 guest unless the king would promise to [use] him favourably. And the king made faithful promise *to do this,* and Perkin was again delivered to him. But as soon as he had him in his hands, he sent *him* to the Tower, and where he was hardly used, and much *lament*ed therewith the care and misery of his imprisonment *and* grief, and insomuch as he would curse his princely *state*
15 *with* groans and oftentimes deep sighs, and *w*ould desire and wish that he rather had been the son of a peasant than of a king or of any Plantagenet. And indeed everyone could tell he fared t[he] worse for his name, for it was observed then there were three m[en] who were most feared of the king, therefore most hated by him: Edward Plantagenet, Earl of Warwick,
20 Perkin Warbeck (alias Rich[ard] Plantagenet), and Edmund de la Pole, son of King Edward's sis[ter,] all of the family of York. But the king feared Perkin much [more] than the other twain, being of a more ambitious and active spir[it] and more sensible of his wrongs than they. Therefore he took mu*ch* more care and employed more counsel and treasure in the seeking
25 [and] suppressing him, and answerably aggravated his miseries and dis[graces,] which now began to exceed. For now he was not only sharply rest[rained] in the Tower, but the fame was that the question, or **Gehenne,** was given him. Sometimes he was taken forth of the Tower and [carried in the] most ignominious manner abroad and set in a pillory, [otherwise in]
30 the stocks. / But he was not yet *arrived* at the worst of his entertainment in the Tower, for anon some wise and eloquent and treacherous orators were sent to him to persuade him to [submi]t himself to the king and to crave his pardon and to confess his fault and to renounce his blood and his birth and his title and to take the name of Perkin Warbeck, that of a poor Dutchman,
35 upon him, and they *m*ight the more colourably do it, because he was brought up in the Lower Germany. But he utterly refused to slander or to belie himself, and in no case to abuse and to defa*ce his* lineage.

But when the king saw that he could not be [wrought] to this recantation by fair means nor by any cunning persua*sion or a*ny flattering devices, then
40 his durance was made much more hard, [and now he was] lodged and more hardly and poorly fed and worse clad, [until at length] he [by mi]series and by torments and other [extremities was forced to say anything and content to unsay what the king would have him.] / And then (after that he was taken from the *Tower and* by these cruel m*ethods tortured, he* made a
45 recantation and a renunciation and of his princely name of Plan*tagenet,* [and] *of his* parentage, and of his title to the *crown, and* he confessed and professed himself to be but a mean *and base* son of Warbeck and some *lowborn woman.* And he *confessed* himself to be very base and mean, as you may see at large in the chron*icles of* Grafton and of Edward Hall, etc.
50 And he was constrained to sign this confession, and this being done, he

173**

175v

176

was brought by the officers unto the more public places of London and West[minster,] *and as before* related, there he was used like a base malefactor, and he was se*nt* to the pillory; and now he was prepared and accommodated to speak anything basely. And then he was commanded to read *and to* pronounce with a loud voice the writing cont*aining the* foresaid   5
recantation and renunciation. And he obeyed and rea*d it,* as that *he persuaded* the multitude to think he was so mean and so base a man as he professed.

*And it sou*nded so basely and so vilely in the ears of the people standing about him and giving cre*dence to th*at vile and base matter which was 10
delivered by him and of himself, as it had *been* [current.] *And* immediately **varium et mutabile vulgus** changed their opinion of Perkin and of his princely birth and quality and said that now *he w*as *ignoble* in that he was but a counterfeit *a*nd an imposter and a base and ignoble fellow and a fore*igner and a* poor Fleming. *Nor was it* suspected, or at the least at that 15
time or a good while after, that this was a forced and c*o*unterfeit confession drawn from him by threats and by terrors and torture; for that *many of* them which had heard thereof had not the wit and reason *to c*onceive and to

[The force and mis-   consider that racks and torments [will] make a man say anything, and **belie**
chief of torture]   himself, a*nd* [falsely accus]e any other man (although he be a good *and just* 20
176v   *man*). *And in* testimony hereof there be many exa[mples of m]en who
[Of tortures I have   in [torture have not only] *been brought* / to accuse *their* fellow thieves, but
written at large in the   [other, and falsely.
13th Book of my   [Seneca telleth of a man who, being suspected of theft, was enforced by
Baron Cap. 16]   torture to confess the theft and his fellow thieves. But having none, he 25
                             a]ccused the good and just Cato, to the end to avoid the tortures. [Which is
                             worse, it] maketh men not only to slander other men, but also by false oaths
                             to blaspheme Almighty God. Wherefore, [St Augustine] enveigheth sharply
                             against this cruel [use of torture,] and amongst many other faults which he
                             findeth [in it, this is] one: **Tortus si diutius nolit sustinere tor[menta, quod** 30
August*ine,* **De Civita-** **n]on commisit, se commississe dicit.** And this the pri*soner does* because he
te **Dei, Lib.** 19   may the sooner come to exchange those [torments with] death, and the
                             which is much less painful and less grievous.
                                And by *these* **Gehennes** and cruel means of expression of confession, *this*
                             *Rich*ard (alias Perkin), not able to endure the question, confessed and 35
                             professed anything [which] was required of him and slandered and belied
                             hims[elf and hi]s princely parentage, and the which to do, although *it wa*s a
                             great fault, yet it was the more excusable and *v*enial in him because he was
                             young and ignorant [and could not yet] be confirmed in any brave and firm
                             resolutions of princely ambit and of religion, and the worse also by reason 40
                             of his long imprisonment and great t[rouble,] besides that he had no friends
                             to advise and to counsel him, nor so much as in charity to comfort him. But
                             he was a miserable and desperate and a forlorn man, and feared so to be
                             forever. And at th*is point* hereunto, I may add that if learned and grave
                             men, and me[n of gra]ce, [ha]ving large and great talents of spirit and of 45
                             science, have for fear of such pu[nish]ment denied some chief points of
                             Christian faith and have been accused fo[r the torture sake] (and whereof
                             there is testimony in the ecclesiastical stories) then may th[is] young and
                             unlearned man Perkin be allowed and excused in tortures to renounce
                             earthly and worldly things.   50

But because *the means* and effects of torture are always evil, therefore
not *only* the doctors of the civil law, but also of theolog[y,] / and the best of   177
them, condemn and abhor tortures. And they have good warrant, and
drawn [from the ex]ample of our Lord Jesus Christ, who, notwithstanding
5 that he certainly knew the *care of his* celestial father to be infinite, and his
faith and his love toward him most constant and *firm, yet* in the extremity
of his tortures and torment charged his father im*plicity with* ******p and
with inconstancy, and, as it were, dishonourable revolt.

[There is yet a]nother mischief of torture, and it is **Arc[anum Gehenne,** a   [The French call tor-
10 secret of torture, or of hell. That is when the prison]er's body by extreme   ture **la Gehenne**]
torment [is brought into any mortal state or symptom of death, or made
incurable and deadly. Then to avoid the imputation of murder, the prisoner
by a short and private process is condemned of some capital crime and
presently executed whilst there is yet some life in him. And to that censure
15 Perkin at last came.] *This* / ignominious degradation, and (as it were) the   178
utter *denial of all honour* and dignities, wrought such effects in the commo*n*
people that in a moment they reputed him to be a counterfeit. And yet this
was not sufficient to satisfy *the king,* nor to secure and void *him* of
jealo*usy,* nor anything else but the shedding of his life and his blood, and
20 the dea[th] of Perkin. And that could not be brought to *bear* by course of
law nor by the hand of [justice,] because Perkin had not been attainte[d
nor] condemned of any capital crime. [But] after that scruple or obstacle
had been a little considered, th[ere] was soon found out a way to take that
away [and ma]tter enough to make him guilty of a capital offence.
25   And for this purpose it was devised and resolved that there should a
practice of escape be offered to him. And be[c]ause the case of Edward
Plantagenet, Earl of Warwick, was the like unto this, as well because he was
not attainted of any cri*me as that* his death was as much desired as that of
Perkin, and that his guilt was as little or less, [therefore he must also desire]
30 to escape. There wanted nothing of their slaughter but matters of capital
guilt. Therefore, these false friends and treacherous instruments were now
sent and willed to propound the same practice of escape to the said Perkin
and the Earl of Warwick. [And some say] the innocent Earl of War[wick at
his] arraignment was charged with the persuading of his cousin Perkin to
35 make an escape. *And he was an* innocent young man and gladly hearkened
to that [mo]tion and plot of their escape, prizing liberty above all things, and
ex*pecte*d nothing but death or miserable captivity continual and most
woeful.
     And [soon after], both these young men, and cousins, and *innocent, as*
40 *the* world thought, were accused [as guilty of practice and conspiracy] to
steal out of the Tow[er, and were for the same arraigned and condemned to
die, but great difference put in their process and execution. For the Earl of
Warwick was] / tried by his noble peers, and he had th[e suppliance of a   179
noble] and an honourable place, to wit, in the [Tower of London.] But
45 Perkin (alias Richard) was tried [by a common jury, who] are men many   [York and Warwick
times of little honesty. *And* [his punishment] *was that* which they call a   parallels]
dog's destiny (that *is, hanging.*) And he suffered it in the most infamous
pla[ce, Tyburn.] *And the* extremity of his punishment answered well with
the hatred which was borne to him. And he was in this base and vile manner
50 proceeded *against so it might* be thought that he was a base fellow, and *as if*

the name or nickname of Perkin Warbeck [was] supposed to have utterly
disnobled him and (as [it were]) divested him of all noble blood and of titles
of honour. But it serve[d best for a cloak] against that purple shower which
fell at the fall of this miserable prince.

But yet [methinks] in consideration that the capital crimes of young 5
Clarence and of Richard [were alike and] the same, and their quality of
much equality, it ha[d been more] honourable to have made them both to
pass the same fi[lle] *and* justicing sword. But I rather think that the [Earl of
Warwick] had been brought to as shameful a death as Perkin, if the [wit and
malice of the cruel Car]dinal could by any trick or device have brought him 10
to be reputed a counterfeit and a base *person*. [But all men knew] *this earl*
was no counterfeit, no more than was King Richard nor his son nor the de la
Poles. Yet *their fates were all* alike, and all passed one purgatory. And
therefore it was all one to be fi*ctitious* or a true prince. And this Edward of
Warwick was not only a tr[ue] prince of the royal blood of England, but he 15
was also an honest man, *free from a*ll evil desires and evil practice. Yet he
was restrained [of his liberty,] and [for the] most part of his life a prisoner,
from the time of the attainder of his father until he [suffered.] And he was as
inno*cent* as the lamb which was wont to be sacrificed. And this was after
they had [survived King Richard] their uncle [about fifteen years.] And *the* 20
survival of one of them was a sure and a happy means to clear the king
from the slander of this murder.

And these were the ends of these two noble plants of the roya*l* Genest,
and of the House of York. And they may well be said to be parallels, but
not after the manner of Mr T.G., but after Plutarch's manner. For they 25
were bo*th eq*ual in blood and in time, and partakers of the same and of
the like ill for*tunes* and like calamities. And they were both held in jealousy
for one strange *reason,* and both arraigned and both condemned and both
put to death *for a crime* which is disputable and *held by some to be no fault*
at all. 30

[Now let us bring their fault (if it were one) to the test and better opinion
of the more grave and learned ju]/dges of the best *laws,* and whereby we
shall come to know certainly [of wha]t kind their fault *is* called in our law.
[And first] I will advertise that I have observed that some hold an escape to
be but an [error, a natural dislike of bondage, or a forfeit] of simplicity. 35
And they hold also that it proceedeth from a [natural and very toler]able
desire of liberty. And these opinions may [also] be good and right, and at
the least in the cause [of these two p]rinces, and they may also the better be
received and enter*tained* [if it be we]ll considered and weighed that this plot
of [these two] cousins for escape was not projected by themselves, but it was 40
cunningly and treacherously [propounded] by proper instruments of such
frauds and deceits unto them (being silly and simple and inexperienced
*young me*n), and to the end to entangle them in the snares *of* [some c]apital
offence, and so consequently of death, and of [which kin]d of offences they
stood clear before, or not accused, and were not obnoxious *to the penalties* 45
of them, by reason that they had never been [in]dicted nor attainted of any
capital crime. *And the r*eason thereof must be because they were guiltless *or*
*in*nocent persons, as all men would think.

And I confess that here I say very much more than I would have said if
the most p*rofound judges and o*ther our historians had not said as much. 50

For they all agree in opinion *and they* say and affirm that the king / could
not take away [the lives] of Perkin Warbeck nor of the Earl of [Warwick]
until the practice of their escape wa[s laid to] *their charge,* and that they
were also found guilty ther[eof] and condemned for it. **Ergo,** then they were
5 [not traitors] before, neither was Perkin a counterfeit now to be thought,
but [a prince of the] blood and claiming the crown. Otherwise, as he was
Perkin of Flanders and a base fellow, *he* was a most culpable [and]
notorious traitor, and there needed no e*xcuse* to be sought to put him to
death, because trea*son is of* all the greatest offence. But surely if he were
10 [not a traitor, it was] as great as tyranny to make of an innocent man and of
a g[uiltless] captive a traitor or a felon, and that by trains and [acts to] *make
him* guilty and attainted of a crime which was not any offence or cri*me or
semblance* of a crime.

For a man without offence *may* desire and seek freedom and de*sire to be*
15 out of bondage and out of the miserable and hate*ful* state of captivity. And [Escape, what]
an innocent and a tru[e man] may purpose and intend that act of es[cape,
also] commit it, and yet be still an honest man and a faithful subject and a
true ma*n* to God *and* to his country. For nature and reason teach an[d]
allow all men to eschew injuries and oppression a[nd] to avoid and also to
20 hate captivity and servitude, and to love and seek liberty and security above
all other *things.* Bes[ides,] this practice of these young men to escape
[was] found (as Polydore well observed) **crimen alie[num]** and not **crimen
proprium.** And then how much [greater was the wrong] and cruelty to
chastise, and much more to take [away their lives] *for the of*fence of
25 another man.

But [however i]/t may be laid upon them, yet it was nothing [but a desire
of] liberty and of deliverance out of the hard captivity [in which they were
*restrain*ed for small or no offence. The civil law holdeth a suspicion [of
flight or escape to be no crime: su]**spicio fugae, quia non solet detrimentum**
30 **Reipub***licae* **adferre, non censetur crimen.** [So Ulpian. And by the laws of
England, if a prisoner] do escape who is not imprisoned for felony nor for
[treason,] but for some other less fault, and which is called trespass, then
according to the old [law of England,] Escape **non adiudicabitur versus eum** [Justice Stanford in
qui [commissus e]st prisone pro transgressione: i.e. escape shall not be **Pleas de la Corone,**
35 adjudged for felony or other crime in one who is committed for a tres[pass. **Lib.** 1, **Cap.** 26, 27]
For the offence of escape is made in] common law to be of the same guilt
and nature [with] the crime whereof the prisoner is attainted *and judged*
guilty. For certainly neither Edward, Earl of Warwick, and Richard (alias
Perkin) [were attainted] for any felony or treason or other capital offence
40 committed by *them and la*wfully proved against them.

And therefore the desire to e*scape* is no offence, and according to that,
the French word **eschapper** *is interprete*d 'to be free', and the Frenchmen
translate **eschappé** into Latin, **salvus.** For a man, especially an innocent
man, and guiltless *of* felony or treason, to seek to be at liberty and to be
45 safe, and *for deliv*ery of bonds and the fear of an unjust death is a very
small and a very venial *offence,* and much more if it be **crimen alienum.** But
be whose or what it will, it was but t*his natural desire for liberty.* And
therefore it was not the law, but the will — and the wicked will — of the
princes' enemies which cut off their l*ives.* Pleading for those two young men
50 will now do them no good, and therefore I will say no more but **requiescat**

in pace. as also their persecutors *may say.*

As soon as these noble Richard and Edward were cut off, some of those treacherous varlets which were the instruments *for* betraying and drawing

184   them into this snare *or* n[et,] as [W]/alter Blewyt and Thomas Astwood, servants to the L[ieuten]ant of the Tower, were sent soon after them in post 5 to Elysium by the w*ay* of Tyburn, beca[use] they should tell no tales.

And thus much for the his[toric]al relation of the life, adventures, actions, and *attempt*s of Richard, the younger Duke of York. And for the true

185   *report thereof*/there cannot be produced greater testimonies than these faithfu*l* [witnesses] of all conditions and estates. And they all maintained at 10 the last g[asp that Perkin was the true Duke of York,] and whose testimonies shall follow by and by.

Before *that, however,* [give me but leave on the way] to answer a calumny brought against this duke who was called in scorn Perkin Warbeck. [A new writer] affirmeth that this Prince Richard was a counterfeit and an 15 imposter. And therefore he would have it thought he knew much, and especially matters of [histories] as of other countries and nations, and would not have *himself thought ignorant* of any of them. And yet he shows himself pl*ainly ignorant in* stories, as well of Don Sebastian of Portugal as this of Perkin Warbeck, and that in a pamphlet or b*ook* to have discovered 20 his knowledge of the story of this p*rince*. The title· and the subject thereof is **The History of P[erkin Warbeck.]**

In this book he spendeth all his skill and wits and his labour [to prove him] *to* be a counterfeit prince, and to make him as a parallel in adv[erse fortune and supposed base quality] to this great Don Sebastian, late King of 25 Portugal, whom also he terms [an imposter. And to arrive] to this extraordinary knowledge, he would have us think that he took much pains in perusing and sifting [of authors; and indeed I think he did sift them.]

[Whether Don Sebastian of Portugal were a counterfeit or no] And yet I will not deny but that these two may be *compared* as well for their fortunes as also for their true and proper qua[lities.] They were both the 30 sons of kings, and both unhappy and miserable *men,* [but] no counterfeits — and as it hath well appeared here already for the *one, and* Perkin, and as it shall appear reasonably well for the other by and by, and by the leave of th*is* gentleman, and who will find that he understood not rightly either the story or the prince.   35

But as concerning his ignorance in the case of Don Sebastian, [it may be tolerated,] because the Spaniards, when he was in Spain, disguised the certain rep*ort* and concealed the truth thereof from him; for they are close and wary and [most politic,] and will give many gudgeons to tramontane travellers. Bu*t there is no* excuse to be made for this ignorance, being a 40 professor of such knowledge of the public and common stories o*f this* country. At the least for *a* professor to profess such ignorance therein *is* a gross and a silly blindness, and worse than **caecutire in sole,** as the p*roverb is.*

But mark the strange power of verity, and ever to be reverenced. For she 45 from this wi*tness* hath drawn, and, as it were, extorted such a confession of the right of this p*rince that ma*tter could not be more thereof, nor more could not be said of them who have earnestly ass*isted him* and most endeavoured to deliver him from the scandals put upon him. For he saith that Richard, Duke of York, and Perkin Warbeck were both one man. 50

And because you shall see that I do to him no wrong, *h*ear his own words;   **186**
and these they be: **Whether I name** *Peter, or Perkin,* **or Warbeck, or Prince**
Richard, or Richard, Duke *of York,* **or King Richard the Fourth, all is one**
man, and all had *one end.* Thus he, and thus (and unwillingly, as it seemeth)
5 he confes*seth and consorte*th with and agrees with the advocates for the
right of Duke Richard, and he is on our side most *when* he pretendeth to be
against us.

*In t*he comparing Perkin and Don Sebastian together, he argueth and
censureth and he conclu*deth* both counterfeits. Yet I doubt not but to give
10 him such better [reaso]ns of Don Sebastian as that he shall also change his
opinion in that matter and conclude the contr*ary of* him after the manner
which he said of Perkin, viz., that whether *he saith Don Seba*stian the
counterfeit or Don Sebastian late king, all is one. And because this may
seem to be a digression, and will then require to be sh*own to be one* of the
15 many reasons and arguments which I have for this prince, [I will urge some
reasons] such as I think may serve sufficiently *at* the least to prove that Don
Sebastian was [no Ψeudo-Sebastian, nor a false kin]g.

It must then be prem[ised that Don Sebastian, King of Portugal,] / was   **186v**
overthrown in a very fierce and bloody battle [in the fields of Alcaz]ar by
20 the King of Morocco, and where it was thought that he was [slain. But] he
escaped the fatal edge of the sword and fled [secretly, travestite, or
disguised.] And travelling in that manner through many [parts of Afr]ica
and of Asia, *he* spent therein by the space almost of thirty years, and in the
which he suffered much care and lived in captivity and in muc*h* [misery. But
25 a]t the last, by the favour of God, he escaped and came [into Europe, with]
purpose to have gone into Portugal and to have taken again his kingdom.

And as he passed on his way, *he* [came] to Venice, and there he
discovered himself and craved a[id of the Venetian] state to assist him for
the recovery of his kingdom and the crown of Portugal. And the Venetian
30 state entertained him w*ell and honourab*ly, and as a prince distressed, and
gave him good words. But they durst not give h[im] *any* aid or lend any
forces for fear of giving offence to the King of [Spain.] But yet the chief
senators, and a great many of the wisest, and gentlemen of the signory,
made no doubt of his truth and of his title. And amo[ngst them] Signor
35 Lorenzo Justiniano, a gentleman of the senatorius order, and [a very] wise
and grave gentleman, was appointed by the state of Venice to [be a]
commissioner with other worthy and wise gentlemen to hear and to examine
th[e cause] of Don Sebastian. And they took much pains for the searching
and finding *out* the truth of this cause. And the Signor Justiniano, being   [Hic legatus haec
40 here [not] long since Ambassador Ligier for the Signory of Venice a*verred*   domino Baroni Dar-
and protested solemnly that he and all the other honourable and grave   ceii retulit]
[commissioners] were clear and very confident that this Sebastian (whom G.
saith was a counterfeit) was certainly, and without all qu[estion he was] *the*
true Don Sebastian, late King of Portugal. But not[withstanding] all this
45 their knowledge, yet, and as I said even now, the Venetians durst not,
because of the King of Spain, lend any succours.

And then he p*urposed to* try some other great lords and princes of Italy,
and he solicited them, but they all *for the same* cause as aforesaid estranged
them/selves from him and withheld their helping hands. Whereupon   **187**
50 Sebastian was counselled to leave Italy and go into [Fr]ance, in regard there

was a king who favoured right and feared *no*body. And he took Florence in his way, and entered the city disguised [in] the habit of a friar. But yet by some who were set as spies at Venice by Ferdinando, the Grand [Duke of Tuscany, to follow] and to observe him, he was discovered and made known to Ferdinando, this Grand Duke, who, to curry [favo]ur with the   5 King of Spain, Philip II, and for some other weighty, commo[dious,] *and formida*ble [consi]derations, delivered Sebastian to the governor of [Orbatella,] a Spanish port in Tuscany, and he sent him by sea to the [Count de] Lemos, Viceroy of Naples, and from thence he was con[veyed into Spain.] And there for a while his entertainment was [no better than in 10 the galleys. And what othe]r entertainment he had I know not, [but the fame went certainly that he was secretly] made away since Philip III [was king.

187v   [But the said Viceroy of Naples confessed to a friend of his that he verily believed] / his said prisoner was the true Sebastian, [King of Portugal, and] 15 was induced to be of the opinion by [the strange testimonies and many] strange and peculiar marks which [some honou]rable Portugueses — and the which were all *well acquainted with him — did find* [about the body of] this Sebastian. And this also is a good argument: *that* [the French king,] Henry IV, was by good information persuaded that this was the true King 20

[Henry IV]   Sebastian. For when [the news was] *brou*ght to him that the Duke of Florence had sent [this Sebastian to] the King of Spain, he was much moved and troubled and offended, *and he c*alled for the queen and told her what an ill deed [her uncle] had done, and used these very words: **Votre oncle a [fait u]n acte forte indigne de sa personne.**   25

189   [And much more] / might be said in the behalf of this Don Sebastian if the place w*ould permit.* [But this] may serve for sufficient intelligence and instructions for the gent*leman to* recant his errors, which made him injuriously to call Don Sebastian *and* Perkin Warbeck imposters and counterfeits, lest these and such errors be *the work of* a counterfeit 30 historian. And the causes neither of the one nor of *the other are* to be liked any whit the worse for erroneous or hard and rash censure *in his work*, as I noted before.

And thus do men experienced in the affairs of state and of policy who think their titles and claim to be s*light*ed because that they were slightly or 35 inconstantly or perfidiously used by some princes of *better claim;* that the end and scope of all which these princes do is their own good, and to serve their *own* turns. And it is a very rare thing to find in any story the example of a [prince bei]ng seized and possessed of any signory or principality, how

188   unlawfully or how wrongfully [soever,] who hath res/igned or rendered 40 them or any of them willingly and quietly to the true heir *and owne*r and *the* right proprietary thereof. And the reason is because that for the covetousness and the oppres*sion* of usurpers and of raptors and of tyrants, and their extreme thirst after the p*ossession*s and sovereignties and signories of other men are as insatiable *as* hell, and the which (as they say) will never 45 be filled nor satisfied. And the*ir* greediness is fed with a violent and fanatical imagination that the *confines* and limits of their signories and principalities are never large enough ext*ended* so long as their neighbours have any land. And such were th*ey* who were Giants — that is, men mighty and impious, such as would do any*thing*. *And such ambi*tious men desire to 50

extend the bounds of their domin*ions,* and for the force and reputation of
great martial men and of conquerors. And that which these men *seek is
solely their own gain.*

But it is a much more dishonourable act in a prince *to seize by* force or by   **190**
5 fraud the signories or territories or principa*lities from his cousins* or
brothers or fathers and parents or *children, men stronger than* all heirs, but
weaker than those Giants, and whom the laws of nature and *of nations
exhort* to defend and to protect, as they are *the rightful* possessions and
hereditary signories *of these men.* And such disseisins are mere avarice and
10 of extreme injury, and **latronum praed**a*e,* and are no*t only illegal* acts, but
also impious and damnable *sins.*

And of such kind of men there be many *examples,* as well divine as
profane, and none mo*re famous than* that of King Herodes, who, albeit he
kn*ew the* blessed saviour and eternal and universal lord w*as the true* and
15 most rightful and lawful heir of the kingdo*m of the Jews,* and the which
right was publicly *under* his hand, yet that subtle and false and covetous fox
the usurper was so far from restoring that kingdom to the true p*roprietary,*
Jesus Christ, as that he sought and desired much rather to see him *perish
and* to be cruelly and shamefully crucified. And by this e*xample,* we see that
20 the vassal renounced and disseised his liege. And it was a great treason.

But yet *in* the world it is thought to be a much more heinous crime *for* the
son to disseise his father and hold and usurp his signories and kingdom.
And yet in this land it hath been seen that the so[n] hath taken the kingdom
from his father and would not render [it again] to him, but rather sought to
25 bring his father to his end. The *signal* persons were Kings Edward II and   [Edward II **et**
Edward III, and much after the same manner, Henry, Duke of Lancaster   Edward III]
(after he had gotten the kingdom wrongfully) held it by force and by tort,
and would not resig[n it] to the true heir thereof, namely to King Richard
II, nor after his death to the Earl of March, although he knew [t]hese men
30 to be no counterfeits nor imposters.

Neither was Edward, Earl of [W]arwick a counterfeit, but an undoubted
Plantagenet and an heir [of] the House of York without all question. Yet
King Henry VII would not *give up* the royal throne nor resign the sceptre
unto him. But / I wish that there had *been done no* more than the detaining   **192v**
35 of his royal heritage from him. *And* [all the injury] *which* were done him is
not by the unjust disposition of the king, but [by the cruel] and evil counsel
of his Cardinal favourite, and who *wanted the* blood of the young earl
spilled, and then finding and seeing that [he could not prevail] with the king
to have his way by law, yet he brought it to pass by another Machiavellian
40 advice which he gave [to Ferdinand, King of Ca]stile, and the which was
that he should not yield to con[clude the treaty of the mar]riage between
Prince Arthur and his daughter [until] this earl and also Perkin were [taken
away.] King Ferdinando followed his advice and advised and admonished
the *king* for his own safety and security, as also for the more assured *safety*
45 [of his son] and of his wife and of their issue, that these dangerous
[impediments mi]ght be removed out of the way and out of the world. And
this suit [took hol]d, and they were both dispatched and put to death, and
were *removed that* all might sing his **nunc dimittis.** For he desired to see the
ruin and utter destruction of the House of York. *And he* died soon after
50 execution of these two young princ*es.*

*I m*ight add hereunto for further example of the resolute and *obstinate and envious* withholding of lands and signories and principalities by *foreign* princes from the true heirs and rightful lords and owners thereof, as namely the French kings, who certainly knew that *the king*s of England were and are the true heirs and just lords of Nor*mandy, of* Aquitaine, of Poitou, etc.   5 Yet they would never restore these lands and provinces to our kings.

Moreover, he who [hath r]ead the book of Sir Edward Hoby entitled **La Anatomia de [Espagna,** and] some foreign writers, hath seen and understood that the kings of Spain unjustly detain [sundry] signories and principalities from the true and lawful heirs and just prop*rietaries* thereof. 10 And many more such examples of such wrongful rapines and tyrannical usu*rpers* might be brought here, but I like not to lay any imputations *of scandal* or infamy upon princes. And besides, such relations are occ*ursive everywhere* to the studious in ancient and modern stories. Wherefore I *keep silence* for all that I have read and heard of many oppressed prin*ces who* 15 demanded and claimed signories and principalit*ies from their true* heirs and proprietaries, but I *could relate much more.*

And therefore I dare not give any *com*fort to Don Sebastian. And in [brief, it is not possible] to persuade a king or prince who *is possessed* of any principality or signory, and althoug*h without* justice, to believe or to 20 confess that another *is the* true lord and proprietary thereof and [hath a better] title or better right than he. And that is *a* maxim of nature and of *nations,* that possession or seisin of land is be*tter than any* titles. But if the wrong done by another such usurping *or* disseising lord be put to this former usurper and *detainer* and false possessor (and the possessor **male** 25 **fidei,** as the [Imperial] jurisconsults will term him), then he will not st*ick* to say that such an usurping and rapinous prince d[oth] wrong, and that he unjustly occupieth and possesseth th*e* lands of another man. And hereof we have seen *some* examples in the very case and story of Perkin herebefore related.   30

But enough of this matter. And now we will [ex]hibit the catalogue of witnesses or martyrs before promised. / And although the arguments and the *testimo*nies here already brought be *enough* for the proof and warrant of his *being* the son of King Edward, and there needeth no mor*e,* and yet, because *there be* plenty of proofs, and that according to the *ancient* 35 principle, **abundans cautela non *nocet***; *I* will add hereunto the names and testi*monies of* men, some noble and very signal person[s, and] worthy and honest and well-understanding, *and who* maintained this duke's birth and title very st*rongly.* And some of them confirmed their testimonies *with t*heir bloods and lives given in witness of their *kno*wledge and belief in the 40 premises. And they shall be as **testes** and witnesses *summoned.*

And I have made mention before of the testimony of Sir Robert Clifford, a knight of [a] noble house, namely of the barons Cliffords. I will [proceed with that whic]h is the more remarkable here in him because he was of a family *whic*h had long hated the family of York, *ever* since the Battle of 45 Wakefield, and when and where [they] resolved upon such deadly enmity against that princely house *t*hat they vowed never to be reconciled nor satisfied *so* long as anyone of that family was remaining alive. But it happened happily that this un[charit]able vow was broken,´ and the Cliffords became again [followe]rs of the House of York, and this **Robert** 50

193

194

[More, Holinshed,
Stow, Gainsford]

Clifford [serving] King Edward very near, and in good credit, [and] *su*ch as
he had good and certain means to know [the king's son]s and to have special
marks of them. *And he stated* as is aforesaid and certified that Perkin was
[certainly the younger son] of King Edward IV, **ut supra,** and [though there
5 was much wrought to change him in this opinion and alienate him from the
prince, yet his knowledge stood upon such certainty that he confir]/med the   194v
opinions and beliefs of many *who had been willing to recei*ve him and to
learn by all *those many wise and sig*nal persons, and who for the most part
[served] *the king and knew* the younger son of King Edward IV *and* were
10 privy to the conveyance away *from England.*
    And a chief among these *was the* Baron Fitzwalter, who maintained this   More, Holinshed,
[Perkin the] true Duke of York most constantly, and even [unto death.]   Stow, Grafton, Hall,
Likewise, Sir William Stanley was a*n a*ffecter of this Duke of York, albeit   Gainsford
he was Lord [Chamberla]in to the King Henry VII and in great favour with
15 him. And he *so mu*ch loved this king being Earl of Richmond that h*e
for*sook his good and gracious lord and sovereign King Richard and
preferred the advancement of the earl to the crown before his faith and
allegiance to the king his master. And he died in the maintenance of the
right of Richard, Duke of York. Likewise, Sir George Neville, brother to
20 the Earl of Westmorland, and Sir Simon Montfort and many other were
confident and avowed th*at* Perkin was Richard, Duke of York. So did Sir
William Da[ubeney,] father to the Lord Daubeney; Sir Thomas Thwaites;
Sir Robert Radcl[iffe] of the house of the Baron Fitzwalter; Sir John
Taylor; Sir Thomas Challo[ner;] Thomas Bagnol; and many other
25 gentlemen of quality and of good credit. And all these maintained that   [Idem auctores]
Perkin was the son of King Edward IV. There were also sundry prelates and
priests, very learned and grave, and who had been chaplains to the king his
father, or otherwise occasioned [to] attend in the court, as namely Dr
Rocheford, Dr Poynes, Dr Su[tton,] Dr Worsley, Dean of St Paul's, and
30 Dr Leyburn and Dr Lessey, and many o[ther] learned professors of divinity,
and intelligent clerks who would [not] endure to hear that he who was called
Perkin was a count*erfeit,* but that he was Richard, Duke of York.
    And some of the nob[les] and more signal persons before named, viz., the
Lord Fitzwalter, the noble progenitor of the earls of Sussex, and Sir William
35 Stanley, Lord Chamberlai*n, and* [Sir Si]/mon de Montfort, and Sir   196
[William] Daubeney and others could not be brought, [neither by] fair
offers or with sharp cruel words or threats, to *change* [their] opinions and to
recant t*heir beliefs,* [but in the affirmation thereof, as martyrs of state,
confirmed their testimonies and liege faith with their bloods. In the same
40 faith, the king's Serjeant Ferior, for the knowledge he had of Richard (alias
Perkin), leaving the king's service, was executed as a traitor. Likewise, one
Edwards, who had served this duke Richard and afterward the queen, his
sister, in the place of a yeoman, was cut in pieces for the same cause, as also
was Corbet, Sir Quentin Betts, and Gage, gentlemen of good worth. And
45 two hundred more at least were put to death in sundry cities and towns,
particularly in Kent, Essex, Suffolk, Norfolk, and about London for their
confidence and opinion in this prince.
    [And there were some great men, though they made no profession of their
opinions and certain knowledge of this prince, yet they could whisper it one
50 to another, which likewise in general words passed by all our better writers.]

198
[Holinshed, Grafton,
Hall, Stow]

And in brief, he was held *in all* places to be the Duke of York and the son
of [King] Edward, and as Holinshed and Grafton and *Hall and* Stow write.
Not only the meaner sort of *the* people of England, but also the nobles
b*elieved* all that was said of him, although he were called Perkin'Warbeck.
But if you suspect any favourable or partial dealing in these author*s* before 5
cited (and for the which I know no reason, *for they were* not anything
beholding to this young prince) you shall hear the same testimony and to the
same effect given by the enemies both of King Richard [and of this Duke]
Richard, and the which, doubtless, verity drew and ex*tor*ted from them.
And that is Sir Thomas Mo[re aft]er Dr Morton, and thus he writeth: 10

[John Morton,
Thomas More]
197

**[The man commonl]y called Perkin [Warbeck was as well with the princes
as with the people held to be the younger son of King Edward IV.** And
Richard Grafton affirme]/th this. In Flanders, saith he, [and most of all,
here in] England, it was received [for an undoubted truth,] not only of the
people but also of [the nobles, that Per]kin was the son of King Edward IV. 15
[And they all swore and] affirmed this to be true. Thus this hones*t author.*

[Mr William
Camden]

[I have also heard a] very grave and well-learned and well-experienced
[writer say] there were many wise and grave and great persons [of good
intelligen]ce who lived in that time and near unto it, and who affirmed
[confidently this] Perkin was the second son of King Edward, *and that not* 20

199

only the nobility / but also that the people took Perkin for the certain Duke
of *York,* and so consequently for the next and true heir of the crown.
   And *this is firm testi*mony and proof that King Richard killed not both
the brothers, *since one was alive* long after he was dead. And he had no
[reason to kill the one and spa]re the other, being both of equal blood and 25
titles. [Neither indeed was there ever any proofs made by testimony,

200

argument, / by presumption, nor by reason of honour or of poli[cy that he
was or could be] the perpetrator of this crime. But there *were* [many to the]
contr[ary,] and arguments and testimonies brought here to prove that *he*
loved those his nephews very dearly; and that he was full of their health and 30
welfare and prosperity; and that he *cared for* them and kept them in safety
so long as he could preserve *their* safety and life; and that he served the
young king very obsequi*ously* and reverently and loyally; and that he was
very loving and kind to the *sisters* of the young king, albeit they were to
succeed their brother*s in the* inheritance of the kingdom before him (if 35
they were legitimate).
   And he kept not only *alive his* nephew, the Earl of Warwick, Edward
Plantagenet, son of his elder brother George, Duke of Clarence, but also in
safety and in pleasure, and was pleased that he should live in a stately and
delightful house of his own. But if this Prince Richard had been ambitious 40
and treacherous, he would rather have made that earl away, because his title
was to take place before his own title, if his blood and title had not been
corrupted and attainted by his father's attainder for treason.
   In regard thereof, this good King Richard, when his own and only dear
son died (and very immaturely), he then forthwith caused his other nephew, 45
John de la Pole, eldest son of the [Du]ke of Suffolk and of the duchess his
sister, and then the next lawful [hei]r of the crown, to be proclaimed heir
apparent (as hath *been* aforesaid, **Liber** I). And all this well showeth and
testifieth that *the* king loved his princely kinsfolks and favoured the true
and just and next title to the [crow]n in whomsoever it was.   50

But other men regarded [not] these rights so much, as the unhappy sequel showed, for they which *were* princes of the blood royal and the nearest to the crown [were soon]er or later rid out of the world, and violently. And [it is most probable that] they which were the plotters and practicers of [the
5 death of the princes of] the House of York before made away were [as likely to dispatch the] rest afterward. And these evil *actions,* [without any great straining, might be imputed to the Lancastrian faction, instigated by the counsel and malice of that mortal enemy to the House of York, the Cardinal.

10 [For the clear proof hereof, the] *execu*/tion of King Richard and of his son were *contrived by him, and not only of* his son, but also of the *Earl of Warwick* and of the rest of the princes *of the House of York. And what was prac*tised and acted herein may be imputed to these *ill-affected Lancastrians* [and to Morto]n. And there was necessity, though an impious necessity,
15 that the Lancastrians must act this.] For unless all those princes of [York, especially the males, were taken away, no other] titular lords or pretenders could be kings of this *land by any* colour of right nor by any other [means, unless he] *could* have married a daughter, and the eldest daughter, of [King Edward IV.

20 [And although] the deaths, and also the manners and kinds of the making away of the sons of King Edward are held by our writers [uncertain and obs]cure, yet it is manifest [at least for the general m]anner of their deaths. It may be affirmed that they were made away either by [the public or] by the private sword. And by the public sword, that is [the sword of
25 justice and o]f battle or war, King Richard and the children of the Duke of [Clarence and the Duke] of Suffolk were dispatched. And to these some add [Perkin Warbeck.] And by the private sword (that is by secret [slaughters and close treachery,] which the Romans called **insidiae** and **dolus,** by smothering, by strangling, by poison, by sorcery, and the like) [so
30 passed] the eldest sons of King Edward and of King Richard and also [King Edward] himself, if he died of poison, as some credible authors [say;] *and that will be else*where argued here.

And that this private and treacherous sword was exercised [a]gainst this family of York, there is not only conjecture for it, but good [testimony,]
35 and also records. For I have read in an old manuscript book [it] was held for certain that Dr Morton and a certain countess, [conspirin]g the deaths of the sons of King Edward and some other, resolved that *these treach*eries should be executed by poison and by sorcery. And in the Parliament [of **anno** 1] Richard III, there were taken and accused of sorcery and such
40 [other devilish] practices, Dr Lewis, Dr Morton, William Knevet of Buckingham, [the Countess of Richmond, and Thomas Nandick of Cambridge, conjurer, and others.

[There] was then also an earl accused of this crime of sorcery and other such hellish [and devi]lish arts. And I call them devilish arts because they
45 were devised and always practised by the devil and his ministers and instruments. And I make no doubt but that whosoever they *were* which gave counsel to shed the innocent blood of our English Abel, Edw*ard Planta*genet, Earl of Warwick, had their instructions from some infernal spirits, and th*at the* devil dealt with them, or they with the devil. And this
50 is canonical. F*or it is revealed by* the Holy Ghost that the devil is a

201v

Public sword,
private swor[d]

Sorcery and [the acts
of treachery]

murderer, and the murderers' fa*ther; and they obey* him and observe him, even as the dutiful child obeyeth his natural fath*er. And the* father doth not only will and command his child*ren* ******************************
****

203

imperii infernalis, and the which many t*imes are* so sore as that they may 5 not be tou*ched; yet I would* touch them, but yet tenderly and softl*y.* And *I would not have* ventured had I not been bound by my solemn profession and in the *name of honour* to maintain the truth, and as well for the *regard which* I bear to all truth, as also for the special love and *duty which I bear* to the House of York, and the *which persuades* me to tell the truth for them and to 10 do *them justice.*

And for this cause, I have laboured to purge and clean*se King Richard* in sundry foul crimes laid to his charge, but falsely, *and as* hath been made apparent here before. And especially my care hath *been to* redeem him from that most infamous and ugly scandal of the murder *of his* princely nephews, 15 and for all the which crimes he hath been *a*ttainted, and ever without proofs and lawf*ul eviden*ce, and ever unheard. And therefore there may doubt be justly *cast upon* the justice of those processes.

And whereas *he is* accused and charged with the murder *of his* nephews, and falsely (as it hath been prov*ed*), *I* marvel why that they, holding 20 Richard to be so politic and so pr[ovident] *and wis*e as they acknowledge him to be, should not suggest and add tha*t he was t*he murderer of his nieces, the sisters of these princes. For as it was to no purpose *to* make away the one brother and not the other, so it would not serve his turn [to rid] away the brothers if he spared the sisters. Wherefore certainly it behoved 25 *him* to have made away / all the other female child*ren of Edward* IV,

202*

because the women of the blood [royal of England] are also capable of the crown [and have their] turn royal before any collateral [males.]

[Reasons why King
Richard would not
destroy his nephews]
He must also have destroyed the ch[ildren of his elder] brother George, Duke of Clarence, [Edward] Plantagenet, Earl of Warwick, and [the Lady 30 Marga]ret his sister, after Countess of Salisb[ury, for they,] without their father's attainder and the [corruption] of their blood thereby, the which might easi[ly have been salved] by Parliament — for the lords pitied them, as also did the *people, who* respected no*t their* defects much — and that being then obtained, then those children of the *Duke of* Clarence had 35 priority of blood, and a preced[ence] and preeminence of right and title to the crown before the said Richard the Protector.

And moreover, [I would know the reason] why King Richard might not endure the lives of [h]is nephews, being held to be illegitimate and so adjudged by [Parliament,] as well [as] the kings Henry VII and Henry 40 VIII endured Arthur [P]lantagenet, the bastard of the same King Edward (and before noted), their **natales** and cases being alike *in* manner, *as I* intimated before. But more probably it might be supposed *the work of Henry VII* and of the cruel Cardinal: he who put to death the said innocent Edward, Earl of *W*arwick (not having committed any crime against the king 45 or the people) did also by the same counsel, and of the same **malus genius,** take away the title of the foresaid Richard, Duke of York, and both for an imaginary fault, **et falso damnati crimine mortis** (at the least if Perkin and Richard of York were *one,* and as all the world thought and said.)

And Sir Thomas More or Dr Morton or both (who shamed to *s*peak 50

anything in favour of King Richard) yet they *c*onfess (being doubtless
enforced and adjured by verity) that there was no *c*ertainty of the deaths of
the two brothers, nor of the *circumstanc*es thereof, nor that they were killed
in the reign *of* King Richard III, and in these words. And although I have
5 cited *this before,* I will again, *for it is true that* **repetere frequen***ter* **pulchra,**
and that such repetitions press and require more earnestly the credit *of the*
Reader: **The deaths** and final infortunes of the young King Edward *and his*
brother have come so far in question that *some remai***n yet in doubt whether**
they were destroyed *in the days of* **King Richard or no.** Thus they say, *and*
10 *it must be believed* as well because they lived in those times as because they
speak *ex propria scientia.*

But against *this they speak* / in another place, and contrary to their   202v*
former *saying. And thus we find* them often contrary to themselves. And
*this deprives them of their reputa*tion, or in any man *the imp*utation of a
15 veritable writer. *And it must* proceed not only from their *malice, but* also
from ill memory, and whereunto all these *writers are obno*xious who are
delighted with telling *falsehoods and* in reporting of leasings and fables.
And *a wise p*hilosopher adviseth such men to have *a ca*re to preserve and to   Aristotle
strengthen their memo*ries. And he* holdeth peremptorily that **oportet**
20 **mendacem esse memorem.**

*And the*se authors, Morton and More, write in one *place th*e contrary to
that which they said in another. *For they sa*y in one place, as I have cited it
before, that it was held in doubt whe*ther they were murdered. But the*y say
afterward that Tyrell and Dighton, being examined, confessed plainly and
25 certainly the murder of the two princely brothers, the sons of King Edward
IV, and all the man[ner] of it. These be contrarieties. And by these
con*tra*rieties their speech falleth into another argument bicorne or
crocodilites, a*nd* bringeth much disadvantage to their cause and scandal to
their greatest friends. In this their revealing of the[se men,] there is secretly
30 and implicitly intimated their fault was not then to be [punished,] and as it
will appear plainly if it be cons[idered.] And it is clear that the confession
of·a man is the greatest evide[nce] and testimony which can be given against
him, for th*at* he judgeth and condemneth himself. And there*fore* this axiom
of the law, viz., **Confessi pro damnatus habentur.** And it is a strong axiom in
35 the civil law, and as *well* in other laws.

And then in regard that the confession of [those was such as that] it might
not be disclosed nor the crime called in question and to justice, but left
unpunished (as the said authors confess), then it was but a counterfeit
confession. And these writers there had in mine opinion [done] better to
40 have concealed the report of that confession than to have revealed and   [Other grea]t ones
published it, for thereby they raise suspicion [of the] falsity thereof, or else   [privy to the] deaths
of consciousness and of privity of some gr[eat] ones (and before insinuated,   [of the princes, espe-
and chiefly Cardinal Morton) in lying, and an imputation of injustice a*nd*   cially of King
connivance upon the chief presidents of j*u*dgement and upon the rest of the   Edward's sons]
45 honourable justi*ce*s.

Here I may note also that this fault and error of these writers is the *result*
of their own ill will to which they give the chiefest and cunningest scope,
or of some sinister stratagem *of their patrons.* For if it were true that Tyrell   205
and [Dighton, Forrest and Slater] confessed the murder and the act and
50 [manner, and King Richard being dead, who was said to suborn and protect

them] during his life, as it might be thought, and no longer, for *after his death he could not, then* [necessarily, and especially in] so heinous and so bloody a crime *and* [an act of so high a nature, of due] course of law and justice, the punishment [should have been] extremely inflicted by his successors and the rather *because we must else suppose that they were* 5 murdered *after* Richard's death. But being for some [strange causes deferred, and after a while omitted and pardoned,] it may be [thought such] strange clemency and impunity [proceeded from some] singular and high indulgence, and from some good will and favour borne by the great *ones* towards the person*s who confessed* and were accused or accusable by the 10 confessants afore*said.* By this me*ans,* for the great favour borne to them, might the capital magistrate or prince *not* have brought in question, and much less to have the persons chastis*ed* condignly for this offence.

Or else it will be thought that the report and dispersion by secret fame and rumours of these examina[tions and] confessions about the murder of the 15 two young princes were but buzzes and quaint devices and counterfeit *practices* to amu[se the] people and to entertain them with the expectation of some jus[tice] to be done after in convenient time upon the guilty and grievous offenders therein. But this justice was deferred so long as that the tr*aitors lived.*   20

But this is to be understood after the death of King Richard. For all that [was done before was th]at he was made the only author and contriver of that horrible crime, and the rest of the sicaries were in peace and safety and

205v   at liberty. *And it is not a new /* policy to make an innocent *man* culpable, but it is an old and stale *stratagem* and court juggling. And amongst other, I 25 have *good example* thereof in the story of Great Alexander. There was in the court of this king [a great] man, and so great in favour and honour of the [nobles and] of the people as that the king grew jealous [and fearful of his] *reputation* and his greatness and his popularity. And he would *study how to* put him down, or at the least to much abate his *great*ness and his 30 credit, and, if it were possible, to bring him [to] contempt, into utter disgrace.

But he could find no col[our nor] fit means for the effecting hereof, because that *great* man was in great favour with the people, and he was so honourable and so virtuous as that there was no crime noted in him. And 35 therefore the king's jealous[y] and fear troubled and perplexed him the more. And he, being des*irous* to be holpen by some advice herein, imparted his care and [unbosoms himself to the] counse[l and care of his] most crafty and trusty counsellor, who was calle*d* Medius, and of his country, as I think. And he asked him [to] advise and how he could devise to abate the 40 greatness of that great man and bring him into disesteem and to make him contemptible and hated of the people, in respect that he was so good and so virtuous a p*erson.*

'O sire', quoth Medius, 'let not that trouble you. This is easy enough to be done, and by this means: we will have him to be accus[ed] of some 45 grievous crime (though falsely), and we will find means to have him to be pronounced and declared culpable and guilty of that feigned crime. And it shall be so formally and firmly done as that the infamous note and the b[rand] of that scandal or crime shall ever remain upon hi[m'.] And he uttered that sentence in these terms, though diverse, but th[e same in effect]: 50

.medea[tur] **licet vulneri qui morsus aut dolatus [est, reman]ebit tamen
cicatrix.**

And it is very true and [approved by an ancien]t Christian [poet thus:

Paulum distare videtur   [Ausonius]

5   **suspectus vereque reus:**

The guilty and the suspected innocent
In man's opinion are little different.]

And there is nothing worse, *nor* [a more dangerous destiny,] nor a more   **206**
fatal to greatness *in a* prince than to be brought *into the* [contempt] of
10 the people. For, according to [the doctrine of the great] master of policy,
odium et contemptus be the two evils [which overthrow] kings and   Aristotle in **Politics**
kingdoms. And they proceed, the one, to wit, cont[empt, proceeding from
vanity and dissoluteness] of the prince; and the other [from this opinion]
which the people have *of* those and of his other vices and tyranny. And then
15 he must neither reign nor live any longer, but must instantly perish. For as   [Ennius **apud** Cicer-
the old and wise Ennius said, and which sentence is attes*ted* to the credit of onem, **Offic., Lib.** 2]
an oracle with the most wise Cicero, **Quem oderunt perisse expetunt.**   [**Perisse prisce**
                                                                                 pro perire]
And to conclude this disputation, all this was practised by the
Lancastrians and executed upon the fortune, fame, and sacred person of
20 King Richard. And it may here out of the proceedings in [t]his cause against
this prince be gathered that he was not held by the good men and best and
wisest to be guilty of this bloody crime, nor that the same cunning **translatio
criminis** could not take any hold of him in their judgement nor in equity of
wisdom and of [r]eason. But rather, and according to these judgements, this
25 translation reflected and returned upon these magistrates who suffered the
confessed cri*mi*nals to pass with impunity. And surely that layeth a scandal
upon them, and it tacitly accuseth *them* of some secret guiltiness, **ut supra.**
For otherwise, *the rulers* and chief magistrates neither tolerate nor acquit
nor *pardon* such heinous offences.

30   Neither is it probable [that] the Earl of Richmond, when he was
possessed [of this kingdom (for he was a wise and] religious prince), [and
all] justice in his hand and in his [power, was of opinion that King Richard   **206v**
was guilty of the murder or subornation of these felons]/ to perpetrate that
treason, [nor yet that he thoug]ht [them] the actors and executioners *of the*
35 murder of the two sons of King Edward IV (and as it hath been before
urged), because those men were not apprehended *and brought* to justice,
nor yet so much as restrai*ned of their li*berties. But contrariwise, they were
suffered to go up and down and at their pleasure and in peace *with
imp*unity, until they came to die their own na[tur]al death. And this is
40 affirmed by Sir Thomas More and *by* Raphael Holinshed and by John
Stow and others. But Tyrell may be excepted in one respect, because he died
not his natural death but a violent death. But yet that was not inflicted upon
him for the murder of the two young princes, but for other treason long
afterward committed by him, and against King Henry himself. Moreover,
45 John Green, who was said to be a party in the practice of this foul treason
against the young prin*ces,* was never called in question.

But to conclude, if all the accusations against these cutthroats had been
known true and plain without sophistication, and to have been taken **bona
fide,** then doubtless the king himself (who was reputed a good and godly
50 and a wise prince) would have had that due care to have done right to justice

and to honour and to the laws divine and human, as that he would have
provided and commanded that men gui*lty* of so horrible crimes should have
had not only *the* puni*shment* which the law ordinarily ordaineth and
usually inf*licteth* upon traitors, but also he would have caused *exqui*site
torments to have been added to their executions, and given in the most   5
public and frequent place of their *performance,* that their terrible sufferings
might be *the more grievous to them*selves and terrible [to the people and to
the times.]

207

   And / plainly there was *no reason why* King Richard should take away
the lives of *his two nephews, since they were allowed* to be bastards, and   10
then and before that King Richard was avowed generally to be the true and
lawful heir, and as hath before been often and at larg*e related. And he had*
much more reason to preserve them, being so near kinsmen.
   But I cannot say so much in the behalf of any [of the Lancastrian faction,
for there] was a necessity for them, if they would [have a king of that   15
family] (as the Cardinal and some others did) to take those princes aforesaid
away, as so t*o destroy not only* King [Richard] *and* [his son,] but also all the
legitimate issue of Lan[caster; for all those were before any of the house of
Beauf[ort in the true order of the succession in the kingdom. And they
stood in the *way, as* did the lawful progeny of Brotherton, of Woodst[ock,   20
of both the] Clarences, of Gloucester. But they feared few or n[one of
those] titular lords, for they were modest men and affected n*ot the*
[sovereignty,] but were content with their own private and safe [fate and
feudal estates.
   [Bu]t all was one with the *amb*itious and malicious Lancastrians, and   25
whose malice *was* so vehement that they regarded no title, how juster or
better soever. For besides the death of King Edward IV and his two sons,
of King Richard and his son, the Prince of Wales, there was afterward, and
as occasion served, the Earl of Warwick, the Duke of Suffolk, and others,
both male and female, of that princely family laid in their urns. And it must   30
be so, else there could be no place upon the royal throne for the Beauforts
and Somersets, their turn, if any, being last, the kings of Portugal and of
Castile and others being before them, if not excluded by Act of Parliament.]

208

   *And Richard was accounted a go*od and *faithful man all* his life, and was
reputed *a* virtuous prince and a *wise, and his law and govern*ment were of   35
the best and without *stain.* Hereunto, he was most unhappily and *falsely
slandered* by disloyal practice. Why th*en do they say* that he was only a
wicked man and a p*arricide a s*hort time and (as it were the moment of his
corona*tion and* inauguration? But that cannot be, neither, for *his nephews*
were both living after his coronation and after his pro*gress to the* north, and   40
also after his Parliament which he had after *his* progress. And it is clearly
and certainly to be proved that the prin*ces* lived *during* his reign and royal
government. And the most chron*iclers and histori*ans write that very
many men confidently affirm *that these* two princely brothers were alive
many years after th*e death of King* Richard.   45
   Why then, it is not likely that *he* killed or murdered his nephews in his
lifetime, but that he committ*ed that murder* after that he hims*elf was
deceased* and dead and laid in his grave to rest. And this tale *is as likely* and
as credible as that which is told in the anthology of a certain stepmother
being dead and entombed slew *as many of her* stepchildren as touched or   50

approached her tom*b*. But this is an invention of a poet and may be allow*ed*. *But* I hope our adversaries and anti-Richards, though *they be insolent* and impudent, yet they will not so grossly *abuse* their writings and their names with such false and absurd fictions, and so to make King
5 Richard an assassin after *his death*. Well then; the case *proves* plainly that there is no time of Richard*'s life when he s*hould kill his nephews, and that after that he coul*d not*.

Now I will add to the tragedy *of these* Plantagenets *one act more, and of the* Earl of Oxford, and worthy to be well regar*ded* [for example's sake,]
10 besides that here it also may make [somewhat for the cause] and for the innocency of the two young men, *Edward, Earl of Warwick, and Richard, Duke of York. And* this it is. [T]he Earl of Oxford, Sir John de Vere, w*ho was m*uch affected and devoted to this King Henry VII, *as w*e have seen here by some good instances, was a great ene[my to] this Richard, alias Perkin,
15 and I think the only [en]emy which he had of the greater nobility. And wheth[er his] evil will grew out of incredulity, or were it out of malice, *or becau*se he hated King Edward and all the House of *Y*ork; or else because he applied himself very obsequiously [to o]bserve and to humour the king then reigning in everything — but [I] cannot determine whether of these. But this
20 is certain, [th]at he was so vehement a persecutor of Perkin as that he and t[he Cardinal were] said to be the chief persuaders and procurers of *the* more hasty dispatching of Perkin out of the way *and* of his destruction. And this earl also [pronounced the] cruel [sentence against the] Earl of Warwick, son of the Duke of Clarence (for he was High Judge or Constable
25 in that a*c*tion), [whose dealing thus in those matters] *was much* misliked.

And this dealing with them being reported, and near to Heveningham Castle, [t]he chief seat of the earl, it came to the ears of an [old] hermit who lived in the woods near to Heveningham [*Cas*]tle, and who was held to be a
30 very good and devout [and] holy man. And this man as soon as he heard this *new*s was much troubled and grieved afterward, because he much [loved the ancient and noble family of Oxenford. And in] much anguish of spirit, he said the earl and his house would repent and rue this [guilt] and bloody pursuit of these innocent princes. And for the events of [which
35 prophecy,] this hath been observed, viz.: that not [long after, the earl] was arrested for a small offence, [and so small that no man thought] that a man of [his merit and credit with the king could be called in question. He was fined also £30,000, the which in those days was a kingly sum. After this he lived many years in great discontent, and died without issue or any child
40 la]/wfully begotten him.

And in much [shorter time than his] life's time, that great and stately [earldom of Oxenford, with the] very opulent and princely patri[mony, was dissipated] and wasted, and it was very suddenly *and swiftly u*sed and consumed, and **como sal en agua,** [as the Spaniar]ds say in the refrain. But
45 not by the fault *of the earl t*hen lord thereof, but rather by the fate of the *divine or*dinance. For certainly the earl was *a dev*out and a magnificent and a very learned and religious [nobleman,] and so worthy in every way, as I have heard some grave and [di]screet and honourable persons (who knew this earl from his *y*outh and could very well judge of the hopefulness and
50 the *spring*times of young men) say and affirm that he was much more like to

209*

[The Earl of Oxen-ford persecutor of Perkin]

[This Earl John died **anno** 4, Henry VIII, 1512]

[**Dominus de Arun., viva voce**]

210

raise and to acquire and to establish a new earldom than to decay *and* waste
and lose an old earldom. And in a word, he was a *Vere* in deed as in name,
vere nobilis. For he was *verily* and truly noble and a most noble Vere.

And I spea*k that* which I know, for he vouchsafed me his familiar
a*cquaintance.* And whereas I call his earldom a stately [earldom] / and a   5
princely patrimony, I do *so after the te*stimony of that aforesaid most noble
and late Earl of Oxford, who, being pleased to do me the honour to come to
my lodging at Hampton Co*urt*, there he told me that after he was come to
the possession [of it,] there were certain rich and *prosperous men* who
desired to farm a part of his earldom, who offered to pay him yearly the   10
sum of [twelve] thousand pounds, and to leave to his use and [occupation
all] castles and manor houses and wont*ed places* of residences of the ancient
earls, with *all* the parks and woods or forests. And all the *de*mesne lands
thereunto adjacent and appertaining *to* this surplusage might doubtless be
of mor*e w*orth, being brought to a yearly value or *re*venue, than are sundry   15
earldoms in this age.

An*d* this earldom was wasted and almost all dilapidated and spoiled, and
the castles and manors pulled do[wn,] and the chapel wherein this Earl John
de Vere was entombed and where all the sepulchres and goodly monuments
of his ancestors were erecte*d were* all defaced and demolished and razed to   20
the ground, and the bones of the ancient earls w*ere* left under the open air
and in the fields, and all [which happened] within less than threescore years
after the death of the said Earl John.

It *is a warning not to lift* a finger in the shedding of innocent blood, nor
to wrong nor to oppress, much less to destroy princes nor the children of   25
prince*s* and of heroical persons. And thereof we are wa*rned* to take heed by
an ancient oracle or sacred proverb *in* this heroical hemistich:

$$\text{Ἀνδρῶν ἡρώων πήματα τέκνα}$$

Heroum proles est perniciosa vivorum.
That is to say, children of heroical *lineage,* of princes or (as we say) those of   30
the *blood royal,* are dangerous and mischievous th*ings when* they be
outraged.

It happened about the same time that these unhappy gentlemen [su]ffered
there was a base son of King Richard III [ma]de away, and secretly, having
been kept long before [in] prison. And the occasion whereof (as it seemeth)   35
wa*s* [to] prevent a practice of certain Irishmen of the wes[t an]d south parts
of Ireland who sought and atte[mpted] to get him into their hands, and with
a purpose to [ma]ke him their chief or prince, for they would *have been* glad
of any noble gentleman of the house of York, wer[e he legitimate or
natural, for] the love which they bore to Richard, Duke of York, *w*ho was   40
sometimes their very honourable and good [an]d magnificent governor or
viceroy **(id est,** king's deputy).

And thus much b[riefly of that.] *N*ext, I will only endeavour to resolve a
doubtful question which is or might be demanded or enquired what the
reason should be why the king deferred [so] long the death and execution of   45
those Plantagenets [an]d took so long deliberation about that matter,
considering *th*at he was resolved to do it, and that there was no *ma*n could
impeach him nor withstand the act. For there was there not any man who
had po*wer, or who*m he had cause to fear, because he was a sovereign and

209v

[The mathematicians
that calculated the
nativity of this Earl
Edward told the earl
his father that the
earldom would fall in
the son's time]

212*
[Grafton et Chronic.
MS. **in quarto apud**
Mr Robert Cotton]

[Bastard of King
Richard]

[Thomas Gainsford]

[Why the public] jus-
[tice] de[ferred the
death of these men]

not a subject, nor *obnoxiou*s to any human power or authority. Therefore these doubts *and dang*ers and difficulties which were (if any were) *must doubt*less be understood to be scruples of *conscience* and conflicts of the mind, the which are of all oth*er scruples the most troub*lesome and full of
5 cares and of vexation, *and so power*ful as that they will curb the *highest* disdains by *the force of their truth and are obno/*xious to any human power and higher authority.

There be some reasons brought by some men why the king deferred *the* execution of Perkin so long, but they are not all worth the reciting. But [the]
10 chiefest of them is (viz.) that because Perkin was an alien and born out of the *king*'s dominions, and in the allegiance of a foreign prince, that therefore he could not be condemned nor executed for felony nor for treason by our la[ws.] But this is a fiction and an idle evasion. For we have many examples in our stories wherein we find that the natural subjects of
15 the kings of France and of Scotland and of the princes of Germany and of Italy and of the kings of Spain and of Portugal have had judgement and execution by our laws for felonies and for treasons: as namely, [Peter de Gaveston, a Fren]chman, and Sir Andrew Harclay, a Scot, and now lately Dr Lopez, a Portug[uese. T]herefore certainly there was no cause nor
20 worldly nor civil respect why King Henry should so long, [so doubtfully, and, as it were, timorously,] defer the arraignments and executions of these men.

[Then it must be some other cause, and not most unlikely some inward awe and secret and concealed scruples] *of the king. /* They are also so   **211v**
25 forcible and powerful as that they *can* resist and check and cross and crush the designs and plots *and* practices of the greatest men, of the most mighty *men* in the world. And the heathen people called *th*ese scruples Eumenides   **[Daemones, Genii]** and Erinyes, which as they said and believed haunted and frighted *and* terrified those men who had devised and [practised some] murder or other   **212v**
30 most wicked [act.] *And he*reupon it was that the poet said well, **[Pati-** Claudian **turque tuos mens sancta] manes.**

And they also [assign to every man his pr]otecting spirit, whom [the Greeks called **Daemo]nes,** and Latins **Genios,** And *they affirm that some*times when the genius of him against [whom the mis]chief is plotted is
35 more strong and more [active than the] genius of that man who is the plotter and prac*tiser,* the practice hardly or never prevaileth. And [for example,] *when the* feud and irreconcileable enmity was between Octavianus [Caesar and Marcus Antoni]us, and that Antony could not prevail by any practice or in an[y] a[ttempt against Oct]avian, he consulted with soothsayers who
40 told him that the reason thereof [was] that the ge[nius of O]ctavian was too mighty and too strong for his genius, and that it held his geni[us in awe.]

And good authors likewise write that the great philosopher [Apollo]nius had such a secret protection, and so strong as that alb[eit] Domitian the Emperor, hating him much, would fain have taken [his life from him, yet he
45 had not the power to do it;] and Suid[as] addeth that this philosopher in the   **[Philostratus in** confidence of this his protec*tive* genius, when he departed from this   **Vita Apollonii]** emperor, uttered this verse:

οὐ μέν με κτενέεις, ἐπεὶ οὔτοι μόρσιμός εἰμι.

Me non occides, quia fataliter protectus sum.

And this is that which Flavius Vopiscus called **maiestatem Apollonii,** as I [guess.]

The professors of Christian and the best religion agree with these heathen in the effects of such secret and sacred protectors, but not in the cause of them, for those whom the heathen theologers called Δαίμονες, **Daemons,** 5 and **Genios,** the Christian theologers called angels and *archangels, and* so like, and that there be of them good and bad. And they also hold and teach, and that by the best warrant, *that* Almighty God giveth charge to his angels to guard and protect the *good* and godly persons in all places and in all needs, and to defend them from their enemies and from the practices and snares of 10 Satan. And they hold also that the eternal God hath given such power *to his* angels as the heathens believed that the Eumenides or F*ates* and the **mali genii** had, and that he useth their ministry for *chastizing* the wicked and ungodly persons and for the affrighting and tormenting of the minds and consciences of the re*probates, and to* hold them in such imperious awe as 15

213   that *they refrain from evil deeds. For otherwise* / by the craft of Satan's *spirit his* malice secretly breaketh through ************* and worketh mischief against that *reprobate,* and also useth his devilish mischief to *make him cease to be* in awe of any other angels or divine powers and *cast* away all fears of God and of divine justice as vain, *and as a* miserable captive to 20 proceed with his impious design and *will. And by* these means this evil angel bringeth his misera*ble* client *from that which* bringeth all security and good success and happi*ness and* fear of God, and which preserveth a man from sin and *from evi*l acts. For that fear is a curious and a severe censor of all crimes *for the* faithful and pious to know: that it is **horrendum incidere in** 25 **manus Dei,** and that **Deus est terribilis.** But to the ungod*ly and* the reprobate, this fear is unknown or at the least of no account, although there be *no other fe*ar profitable or of any worth or good use, for (as it wa*s di*vinely said by a holy man) **Nullus est dolor utilis nisi pe***ccati,* **nullus metus nisi Dei.** But the wicked ar*e subject to an un*happy fear and entertain other 30 fears — desperate fears and base, vain and idle fears — *and as* the prophet said, **Timent ubi non est timor,** and they fear to *cross* and *to o*ffend the Devil and loss of his favour, and therefore to preserve that their b*ondage they do* his unjust and hellish hests and his wicked will *and pr*actise and execute these wicked things and impieties whereunto *the Devil* hath tempted 35 and drawn them in longer or in shorter time.

[But] those philosophical and theological arguments may seem [to b]e parerga or not grateful to some, and therefore I will leave them, returning to my *main* argument, and that was the purgation of King Richard of the

214   crimes and of th/e other scandalous matters imputed to him, and chiefly for 40 the deaths of his *n*ephews, and for the which much hath already been said, and enough. And therefore at length upon the allegate and probate matters passed, it may be concluded that King Richard was no more guilty of their deaths than he *was o*f those of his two brothers, King Edward and Clarence, nor of his own legiti*mate and* base sons. And he had been sure enough to 45 have been made the plotter and author of the deaths of the children of the Duke of Clar[ence, the Earl Edward,] *and* the Countess Margaret, and of Edmund de la Pole, and of the oth[ers,] notwithstanding the falsehood thereof, *ha*d not the parachronism have been to[o gross, he being dead before.   50

[But] as the good antiquary and diligent searcher [of] *kno*wledge of the   **215v**
obscure and *hi*dden things appertaining to our story, and by name Mr John
[Stow,] when I pressed much to know and *under*stand the certainty of this
murder of the *sons* of King Edward IV and what he [thought] of it, and
5 what proofs thereof he had found in his [various and m]anifold readings,
his answer was this, and as peremptory as sho*rt,* that it was never [pr]oved
by any true evidence nor by credible testimony, nor by [prob]able
suspicions, nor so much as by the oaths [o]f the knights of the post, nor yet
by any fine fiction or ar*gument* or poetry, that King Richard killed his
10 nephews or was guilty of the practice thereof.

And whereas Mr Stow addeth fiction and poetry to the proofs, he alluded
(as I conceivéd) to the poetical disposition of Sir Thomas More, because he
was a poet and wrote *a poetical book*, to wit, **Utopia** is a fable. And whereby
it seemeth that he could *better indite and that he* had more felicity and
15 facility in fictio*ns and in counterfei*t histories and fables than in historical
narratives and true *re*lations (**ut supra**). And he first published this *story of*
this murder. / [And Sir Thomas More, being puzzled with his equivo-   **Egerton 237v-238v**
cations, and that it never could come to light what became of the bodies
of these two princes — Grafton, Hall, Holinshed, and Stow agreeing
20 in this report that the very truth hereof was utterly unknown. And they say
well, for it is not possible it could never be known that they could be both
murdered in the Tower and buried there, or both have sunk in the deeps if it
be considered one of them survived until the fourteenth or fifteenth year of
King Henry VII. Therefore their contradiction is, as the comedian said,
25   **Quod dictum est indictum est,**   [Terentius in
                   Quod modo erat ratum, irritum est.   Phormio]
[Besides, if Perkin were not the second son of King Edward, he must be
nothing. For the Flemish, French, and Wallons acknowledge no such noble
young man to have been bred in Warbeck or in Tournay, but make
30 honourable mention of a young son of the King of England who was
brought to the Duchess of Burgundy, his aunt, being then in Flanders, and
how he was in France and in other kingdoms.

[We will therefore close this book with his own affirmation and
protestation to King James of Scotland, to whom he avowed that he was
35 conveyed, being young, into a strange and foreign country and preserved
secretly by the Divine Providence, as young Joas was.

                              [Explicit Liber III]

THE FOURTH BO[OK
OF THE HISTORY] OF KING RI[CHARD THE THIRD]

The Contents

[THE FOURTH] BOOK
OF THE *HISTORY* OF KING RICHARD III

216v

[It hath been declared] at large and often before that the [title King] Richard had to the crown accrued and [fell to him by the illegiti]mate birth, or bastardy, of the children [of King Edwa]rd IV, and by the attainder of the [Duke of C]larence, and which was accompanied with the corruption of
5 his blood and [forf]eiture of his title in him and in his heirs, [of which there] was no question. But of the forfeiture and [dis]heritage of the sons of King Edward IV, th[ere hath b]een much question, and the true ca[use thereof hath no]t nor cannot be well known without th*e* [true] report made of the sundry loves, wooing[s, especially con]tracts and marriages of the king their
10 father.

Therefore, I must crave leave to unfold and to relate these. I shall not need [to intimate how amorous] *he* was, and wanton, for that is well known. Yet it shall not be amiss [to say something] *here,* and how that he had many m[istresses,] or **amasias,** and who were kept in severa[l] houses
15 and very honourably entertained, after the [manner] of the seraglios of the great [Turks.] And amongst these dainty and dear damoiselles and loose and b*eautiful ladies,* the [most fa]mous were Catharine de Claringdon, Elizabe[th Wayte] (alias Lucy), Joanne Shore, the foresaid La[dy Eleanor] Talbot, and others.

[How extreme his desires were, y]ou [may see in the speec]h [of the] Duke of [Buckingham] set [down by Sir] Thomas More

20 And it is worth the remembering amon[gst such matters as these that there] was another fair woman very dear unto him, and *whom he* [suspected] to be false, and therefore the king caused her to be *chastened,* and he gave her warning of his suspicion *of* her error by a quaint device. And for this purpose *he had* [a symbolical figure] made, much after the
25 manner [of the trivial ierogliffs used in France and called **rebus de Picardy,** *and pro/*vided a fair and rich jewel as a love token, and therein the device or **rebus** was a falcon encom[passed] with a fetterlock. And the mott hereof was **[au fa]ulcon serrure.** And what the meaning hereof [was I] will forbear to tell in plain terms, for offending modest ears. But I will [intimate
30 the dev]ice lieth in the ambiguity and double sense of falcon, which, being wh[ole, signifieth the hawk c]alled a falcon. But the word being divided into two words hath an [obscene] signification; [and by this means] 'falcon' [becometh] aequ[ivole.] And the king afterward liked this device of the *falcon and fetter*lock so well as that he caused it to be [carved and painted in
35 many] of his royal works, and yet to be seen, [at Fotheringhay and elsewhere.

[But though the king's jealousy was thus particular to her, his affection was as general to others, being a frank gamester, and one that would cast at

217

218ᵛ*

all fairly set. Yet above all for a ti]me, *he* loved the Lady [Eleanor Talbot,]
a very fair and noble lady, [daughter of John Talbot,] Earl of Shrewsbury;
and [her mother was] the Lady Catharine Stafford, [daughter of

[Philip Commynes in
Lud. XI, **Cap. 112**
et 132]

Hum]phrey Stafford, Duke of Buckingham. [And this Lady E]leanor was
the widow of Thomas, [Lord Butler,] Baron of Sudeley. And the king's   5
[affection] *was so strong, and* he was so fervent and vehemen[t, and also at]
that time so honest toward her as th[at he mad]e choice of her for his wife.
And he was *firmly and* [sole]mnly contracted and also married to [her by] a
reverend prelate, namely Dr Thomas [Stillington, Bishop of B]ath, a grave
and learned man and a counsellor of state, and much favour[ed] by the   10
king, and often employed in great affairs (as I have partly int*imated*
before). And this matter is witnessed by our Eng[lish] stories, and also by
the honourable and veritable [histo]rian Philip de Commynes, and in these
word[s:]

L'Évêque de Bath (lequel avait été conseiller du Roi Edouard)   15
disait que ledit Roi avait [promis] foi de mariage à une dame d'Angleterre,
et qu'il avait nommée, et que le Roi avait fait la p[romesse] entre les mains
du dit Évêque: et dit a[ussi] cet Évêque qu'il avait après épou[sé] et [n'y
avait q]ue lui et eux deux. That is summarily in English thus: The Bishop of
Bath, a Privy Counsellor of [King] Edward, said that the king had plighted   20
[his] faith to marry a lady of England, w[hom] the bishop named /viz., the
Lady Ele[anor] Talbot /, and that this contract was made [in the] hands of
the bishop. And he said that afte[rward] he married them, and no persons
being presen[t but] they twain and he. And he said also th*at* [the king]
charged him very strictly that he shou*ld not* reveal this secret marriage to   25
any man [living.] And this contract and marriage are related in the Act [of
Parliament] aforesaid, and where it is di[sertly called a former marriage.
And the king had a child by this lady.

[But too soon growing out of liking of her, he entertained others into the

219*

bosom of his pleasure.] / And not long after, the [fame filled] the court of a   30
very fair and [excellent lady living] in the court of France with th[e Queen
Charlotte, wife] of King Lewis XI and s[ister to this lady, whose] name was
Bona. And she was the d[aughter of Lewis, Duke] of Savoy. And the king,
being very *affectionate,* also so covetous of fair women, fell [straight in
love] with the fame of this Lady Bona and w[as so strangely and suddenly   35
engaged in the report of her beauty that he was] desirous to have her to his
wife. And [he dispatch]ed an ambassador speedily into Fran[ce to treat
about this] business. And he committed the treaty a[bout this allian]ce to

[The great Earl of
Warwick]

the great and renowned earl, and t*o* h[is best] friend and most faithful
subject, namely Ric[hard N]eville, Earl of Warwick and of Salisbury, an[d   40
Captain of Calais, who, wi]th much good·liking and a*ll* alacrity, undertook
this *wooing business and went into France in very [honoura]ble and
magnificent manner. And there he propounded *the k*ing's suit to the
French king and to the queen, as [the] fittest mediators in this behalf. And
he [presen]ted the most loving and honourable offer of the king and *his l*ove   45
and affection and devotion to the Lady [Bona.] And to be brief, this earl
ambassador [express]ed himself so wisely and so honourably and so
[magn]ificently in this negotiation as that he brought [it to] the wished
effect, and that he did effect with the more faci[lity] *because* he *was* a man
of great estimation for his valour and [wisdo]m and other heroical virtues,   50

as well in France as [in all] parts of Europe. And having happily
accomplished *this nupt*ial expedition, he took his leave of the [king an]d
queen and of the lady bride and the rest of France and came *home again a
pro*ud man, thinking that he should be very [welcom]e home *to* the king,
5 having so well and so speedily *done for the ki*ng the great business wherein
he was *employed*.
  But when he came to the court, he [found an alterat]ion of the affections
and also [the countenance of the king.] And the reason was *that* [the king
had suddenly wooed and wedded another lady, the Lady Elizabeth Gray,
10 relict of Sir John Gray, daughter of Sir Richard Woodville and of
Jacquetta, sometime Duchess of Bedford and daughter of the Earl of St
Pol. The] / late husband of this Lady [Gray was a knight of Gr]ooby, but he
became a ve[ry vehement Lancastrian,] falsely revolting from the House [of
York, and therefore] was hateful to those of that family,. also to the] Earl of
15 Warwick as to the other fo[llowers thereof. He] was slain at the Battle of
[Barnet. And of] this lady and of her husband, Philip de [Commynes
writeth] some words which I shall not or will [not under]stand. I will set
down here [the sentence] and leave the interpretation of it to [the more]
skilful Reader. These be the words: **[Et depu]is ledit Roi Edouard épousa la
20 fi[lle d']un Chevalier d'Angleterre, femme ve[uve,] qui avait deux fils et
aussi pour amourettes.**
  [But] neither the despised state of widowhood of this lady nor [the
meanness] of her quality and conditions, nor the [earnest] dissuasions of the
duchess mother of th*is king* [and] best friends could make him withdraw his
25 af[fection] from her, so exceedingly and so deeply he was s[urprised] with
her beauties. But yet if he could ha[ve enjoyed] her sweet embraces
otherwise, he woul*d* [not] have married her. But she was so wit*ty and* so
wise a gentlewoman, and had so good c[ounsel] given by the well-
experienced lady, [the] duchess her mother, as that she withstood *the* king's
30 temptations and lustful batteries as a*n* immovable rock, or as an
unassault*able* or impregnable citadel. And she vowed *and* protested that she
would never yield to [any] dishonourable parley or unchaste motion,
although it stood upo*n the* safety of her life.
  Then the king told *her* that he perceived that she would not *resist* whilst
35 they were married; and then she [implored] and humbly prayed his grace
not to thin[k her so] exorbitantly and so vainly am[bitious as] *that* she
would [wish herself a queen or to have the hope and presumption to be
anything higher than what she was, his poor and humble vassal.] *And on
the* other / side, she said that she *was not of so* dishonest and so foul a mind
40 [as to violate] her chastity or lose her hono*ur* [or be the] mistress of the
greatest king.
  And then the king (when he [perceived there was no other remedy)] told
her that he was willing [to marry] her, and notwithstanding his inequali[ty.
For] *he* esteemed her love and her beauties and [her virtues] so rare and so
45 precious as that in reg*ard of these he thou*ght her in birth and in fortunes
and *in powers as no*ble and as worthy and as great *as th*e greatest king in
Christendom. *And he* [d]id not long deliberate of the tying of th*e
matri*monial knot, nor deferred the accomplish*ment* any longer than there
was necessity; but *so* suddenly and hastily (and haply with more haste *than*
50 good speed) he was married unto her without *the c*harity of any counsellor,

The [Lady Bona] was
af[terwards mar]ried
to [Don Galeazo]
Sforza, Duke of
[Milan.] El. Reu-
suer[q]
219v*

[Philip de Com-
mynes, **Cap.** 112]

220*

kinsman, baron, *or any* friend whatsoever.

And there was so much haste made *that* the much approved ceremony of
the banns' [asking] was pretermitted, and such was the want [of reve]rend
bishops then as that he was fain to [take an] ordinary priest to marry him.
And that was *done* in a chamber instead of a church, and in [a lod]ge or 5
forest-house instead of a palace, and nobody present but the duchess and
her company, *and tha*t few of them. And where he first saw *this fa*ir widow,
and by chance, there at the next [interv]iew he married her, and by ill chance
and *unhappi*ly, and much to his dishonour and disparagement, [and as]
much to the offence and dislike of the barons *of the* kingdom, and who 10
took double offence at *this marri*age. The one offence was because he
matched so *unworthily* and so unequally to his estate, and *also that* he
married without privity of them *and without obtaining their* [con]sent, and
the which they assevered [the king ought to have done, by their ancient and
privileged honours. But it much exasperated their dislikes when they 15
considered the great inequality between her conditio]/n and the regal
condition [and the Imperial Maje]sty of England, as also *that she was the
wid*ow — that is, the reliquies and *the leavings* [of another ma]n, and that
of a poor knight *and of a* false and mortal enemy.

But yet [above all, the Earl of Warwi]ck was much more offended, and 20
by *much mo*re scandalized than all the other *barons, and besi*des that he was
as farforth wronged *in the common* case of the noble barons as any *of
them,* he besides held himself much *disgra*ced in France for the matter of
the king's light and loose dealing with the Lad[y Bo]na and her princely
friends, and to whom *and to* her friends the earl had engaged his *honour* for 25
the king's due performance of the espous*al, and* he had mediated and
laboured at his great *trouble* and great charge and brought to fair eff[ect.]
Also of such covenants as being authorized by t[he king's] commission he
had made and undertaken *the* foresaid treaty of the marriage with the said
L*ady* Bona of Savoy, and the which he had so lately *done* in his embassage 30
in France. And he was als*o* aggrieved and troubled with the affront and
s[corn] offered to the French princes by this levity [and] rashness of the
king, and whereof he kn[ew] that the French king and the queen and t*he*
other princely friends of the fair virgin *and* noble espouse would be very
sensible [and] apt by occasion to revenge it.   35

And for these *slights* and disgracious usage, the Earl of Wa[rwick]
forsook the king and renounced *his* love and allegiance unto him and would
nev*er more* come to him, but soon after took arms against him. And of this
hasty and so much d*istasted* match and marriage, and of the offences th*at
followed,* and of the many evils thereof ensuing, [you shall hear] the grave 40
and judicious historian P[olydore] make report and also censure:

[Rex Edwardus, mutato consilio de ducende in uxorem Bona, filia Ducis
Sabandiae, Elizabetham, viduam Johannis Gray militis, in matrimonium
duxit, et de eo matrimonio mulieris humilitatem, non modo necessarios
principes, verum etiam Ricardum Widdeuillum,] / patrem mulieris celat; qua 45
[causa cognita cuncti pro]tinus mirari, principes [fremere passimque voces
emittere] indignationis, et regem no[n ex sua dignitate fecisse,] easque
nuptias ei crimini [dare, et dedecori] assignare, quod caeco amore n[on
ratione ductus esset,] sed inde initium profectum est [simultatis ortae inter]
regem Edwardum et Ricardum co[mitem Warwici,] etc.   50

Thus Polydore the Italian. But [if you will not] give credit unto him (for indeed ma[ny are jealous of him,] and yet in my opinion not for any *or many* just causes), then you shall hear a[n Eng]lishman and a prelate, and living [in those tim]es report the same matter, and in this manner:

5 **[Edward]us rex fretus propria electione [cuius]dam militis relictam nomine Elizabeth, [inconsu]ltis regni proceribus clandestino sibi desti[navi]t matrimonio: postea ipsam in reginam co[ronar]i fecit. Quod quidem regni optimates aegre [tuler]unt, quia de tam mediocri stirpe feminam procre]atam ad regni consortium secum praepropere [sublim]aret.**

[Kings must not marry the daughters of their vassals]

10   And thus you see how this lustful [king] lost his honour and his reputation and very many *and* very great and best friends by this mean and *base* marriage, and he had much trouble afterwards; [ye]t he escaped well that he had no more real and present [feeling] of the error and ill of this his strange marriage. And *this* king was the first king of England who [ever]

15 debased himself and so disparaged his royal [blood] and sovereign majesty in the alliance and mixture *of it* with *a* private and mean family and with *the da*ughter of his vassal, and she also a poor *widow,* and of a man who hated the king and his *family,* **ut supra.** Therefore, all circumstances consi*dered, this* marriage was a dishonourable and a rash *contract* and a perilous act.

20   I have read [in the story of Arag]on of a king who was not only *dishonoured but also* [deposed] for marrying of the daughter [of his] subject. And King Edward fared not much better, for soon after, he was deprived of this kingdom and expulsed. But being a man that in his troubles was industrious and diligent, of invincible courage, he happily recovered]

25 the kingdom again; but [never the honour and friends] and reputation which he lost, [which he might have prevented, and all th]e miseries and calamities which [overtook him in h]is issue and in his friends.

But if he would have been ruled [by the duchess his] mother, he had prevented all *these miseries and* calamities. For she, having secret

30 advertisement of] this love of the king to Lady Gray, *as I said b*efore, and having much misliking of *it, persuad*ed him from it, and she bestowed all the *fine tou*ches and all the art which she had, *and she* used also her authority of a mother to [dehort hi]m from that lust and to leave the said Lady [Gray, and] to return again to the Lady Eleanor Tal[bot, his] former

35 love and wife, or at least his contra[cted] *s*pouse. And further, and most earnestly, she *exhorted* and charged him upon her blessing and upon h*is love* to God and to Christian religion to finish and [consummate] with public ceremonies of matrimony that his contra*ct w*ith the Lady Elizabeth Talbot, alias Butle*r.*

40   And because the arguing and discoursing and disputing of this que*stion* concerning the king's marriage aforesaid between the duch*ess his* mother and him is very witty and *wis*e and full of weighty *argu*ments, I think it good to transcribe it hither, and as I have gathered *it* [out] of the stories and chronicles of Sir Thomas More and of the rest of our English [writers.] And

45 I will follow them faithfully so long as they err not in the ma*tt*er nor write false and incongruous English.

First then *I will relate, as I have* done here before, that the ki*n*g's mother, bein[g much troubled with] his purpose and resolution to mar*ry the Lady Gray,* [with a strong hope to dissuade him, came to him thus:

50   '[My liege lord and my dear son, it is very commonly reported you are

221v

222

[The speech of the
Duchess of York to
King Edward IV]

223

purposed to marry the Lady Gray, a widow and a mean gentlewoman, which you cannot but conceive will redound to your disparagement and dishonour. All the wise, great, and noblest persons of your kingdom think it far more to the advantage of your honour, profit, and safety to seek the alliance of a noble progeny, and rather in] / a foreign country than in your 5 own realm, [as well in regard] *that* thereupon dependeth great strength to your estate [and] great possibility of increase of your possessions, as also [if well considered,] *that* [you may] not safely marry any other than the Lady Bona, the Earl of Warwick having proceeded in the motion [so far, w]ho (as it is likely) will not take it well if all his [troublesome and costly 10 n]egotiation should be in such wise frustrate, and his appointments [deluded.]

*M*oreover, she told him that it was not princely for a king to m[arry his ow]n subject, at the least no great and important occasion lea[ding him the]reunto, nor possessions, or other commodities depending thereup[on. 15 B]ut it would be in the same kind as if a rich man should [marry his] maid, and only for a little wanton dotage upon her person, [in which kin]d of marriages many men commend more the maid's fortune [t]han the master's discretion. And yet for all that, there was more honesty in such a marriage than there was honour in the marriage which you affect and seek, for so 20 much as there is not great difference between a rich merchant and his own maid as is between the king and the widow Gray. And in whose person albeit there be nothing to be misliked, yet there is nothing [s]o excellent in her but that it may be found in divers other women, yes, much better than she, and more meetly and more agreeable to your state — and those also 25 virgins, and who are of a much more honourable [estimation] *and* estate and condition than widows.

'Wherefore the only widowhood [o]f Elizabeth Gray (though she were in all other things convenient *and fit* for you) yet that alone should suffice fully', in the opinion of *his* lady mother, 'to make you to refrain and 30 abstain from that *match,* especially you being a king, and because it is an unfitting *matter and a* great blemish and a high disparagement to the sacred ma[jesty of a prince (who] ought as nigh to approach the priesthood [in pureness and cleanness as he do]th in dignity). And that is not [to be defiled with bigamy in his first marriage'. 35

[Thus far the king could have attention to hear the duchess, but being extremely far g]/one in love, or rather *in lust,* [he] was resolute to marry her, [and to that purpose framed his answer] *unto the duc*hess his mother, partly in [earnest and partly in play,] as one that wist and well *knew that* [he was out of the check and rule of a mother.] And albeit he would have been 40

[The answer of King
Edward IV to the
Duchess of York, his
mother]

*glad of her satis*faction and contentment, yet he was *fixed in his own* mind to proceed in these espousals and *took she it well or otherwise.* Yet reverently and in good *part he* [thus replied] to his mother's speech, and as followeth:

'[Madam,] although marriage, being a spiritual thing, [ought rather to be 45 m]ade according to the will and ordinance of [Almighty God, whe]re He by his grace inclineth either parties to [love mutually] and virtuously (and as I trust and hope that God doth [work in our] cause), and not for the regard of any temporal a[dvantage, ye]t natheless, this marriage, as it seemeth to me, and bein[g consi]dered even after the worldly accompt, is not unprofitable, 50 nor [I re]ckon not the amity and alliance of any earthly nati[on or foreign pr]ince so necessary for me as the friendship and love of mine [own subjects,] and who, as I hope, will bear to me so much the [more l]ove and favour because I disdain not to marry with a w[oman of my ow]n land.

5   'And yet if foreign alliance were thought so requ[isite, I cou]ld find the means to enter therein much better by other [of my] kin, and where all parties would be content, than to ma[rry myself] to one whom I should haply never love, and for the possi[bility of] more possessions lose the fruit and pleasure of this which I ha[ve alr]eady. For small pleasure taketh a man
10 of all that ever he [hath] beside if he be wived against his appetite. And I doubt not but there be (as you, Madam, say) other women which be in every [point] comparable to the Lady Gray. And therefore I let not other [men] to wed them. No more, then, is it reason that any man mislike *for me to* marry where it liketh me.
15   'And I doubt not that my cous[in of] Warwick neither loveth me so little as to grudge at that [which I] love, nor is so unreasonable to look that I in choice of a [wife shou]ld rather be ruled by his eye than by mine own. For th[at were] as though I were a ward, and were bound to ma[rry by the appointment] of a guardian. But I would not be *bound* [with] *such* [servile
20 and hard condition] as that I should [not be king.

'[As for the possibility you urge of more inheritance by new affinity in strange lands, that is not always certain. But contrariwise,] / that is often the occasion [of more trouble than profit. Besides, we] have already a title and sei[sin so good and great as may suffice] to be gotten and to be kept [by
25 one man and in one man's days.]

'And whereas you object [that the Lady Gray hath been a wife and is now a widow, and hath] already children, why, by God['s blessed Lady, I that am a bachelor] have some children too, and so for [our better comfort] *each of us* hath a proof that neither of us is [like to be barren. And I trust in] God
30 that she shall bring forth [a young prince, and your pretty son,] who shall be pleasing and acceptable to [you.

'[For the bigamy] which is objected, let the bishop hardly lay it [in my way when I come t]o take orders of priesthood. For I con[fess I understand] bigamy is forbidden to a priest, but I never wi[st it yet] was forbidden to a
35 prince. And therefore, good Madam, I [pray you be c]ontent, and not to trouble yourself nor me any furth[er.]' And here the king ended his speech and answer to the duchess.

But she was nothing content nor satisfied. And therefore [she must urge] one point and one objection more, and which she thought to be the *greatest*
40 of all other. And that was his contract with Dame Elizabeth [Lucy, and his having had a child by he]r. So, as the duchess said, he was bound in discharge of her conscience to cha[rge him with t]hat act, and by means whereof he was her husband before [God.] And Mr More and Grafton and Stow and the rest say that the king denied that contract or betrothing
45 to Mistress Lucy. And the foresaid authors may and ought to retract that which they hav[e written therein.] For the truth is he was never contra[cted to] her, but he loved her well, and she was his witty concubine, *for she* was a wanton wench, and willing and ready to yield herself to [the] king and to his pleasures without any conditions or capitulations. And she herself never
50 said *that* the king was betrothed unto her, but only that he would speak

224

[very] kind and sweet language unto her. And who knoweth not that **credula**
res a[mor est.] And it is also true that the king [had] a child by her, and that
child was the bastard Arthur, and [called c]ommonly (but unduly) Arthur
Plantagenet. And he was afterward [made Viscou]nt Lisle by Henry VIII.

But in this relation the [historians] have much and foully erred. *For they* 5
have not only corrupted the story, b[ut have injured the Duchess] of York
*and mu*ch detracted from he[r judgement and knowledge in those matters
and from the tenor of her former speech. For they make her to charge the
king that he was contracted to Elizabeth Lucy, who was of birth and quality
much meaner than the Lady Gray, whom she conceived so basely of, as her 10
speech implies. For Elizabeth Lucy was the dau]/ghter of one Wayte of
South[ampton, a mean gentleman, if he w]ere one. And she was the wife [of
one Lucy, as mean a man as Wayte. And it is true that the [king kept her as
his concub]ine, and she was one of these *who were known by* peculiar
epithets. And this Mistress Lucy was *his witty concubine,* for difference 15
called by the *king. And* she was the mother of the bastard Arturus. [For]
the confession which the said writers [say she made and] protestation that
she was never [assured] *to the king,* [they impor]t nothing, and therefore [I]
doubt that they were ever exacted [from her.]

But if you will truly understand th[e story and salve the errors] of the said 20
writers, then you must know [for certain that the lady to whom King
Edward was first betr[othed and also married] (**ut supra,** as it was affirmed,
and whereof more anon) was [the Lady Eleanor] Talbot. And she was the
daughter of a great pe[er of this realm, a man of most noble and illustrious
fam]ily, and of the rank and quality of princes (*for the hera*lds say that earls 25
be princes). And her father was [the Earl of] Shrewsbury, and a man very
highly honoured and of great authority. And she is also called in authentic
writ[ings the Lady] Butler, and that was because she was then the widow
[of] Lord Butler, Baron of Sudeley, and as hath been here before declared.
And she was a very fai[r and vir]tuous lady. And the king was much in 30
love with her, but h[e could] not prevail in his wanton and luxurious
attempts until he promised her [marriage, and] was not [only contrac]ted to
her, but also married (and the which shall be ·better demonstr*ated*) [and]
had a child by her.

And this is that noble lady (and not Elizabeth Lucy) to whom the duches*s* 35
said the king was contracted, and for the which she so wisely and so
*e*ar*nestly* [presse]d *and ex*horted and urged her son to take and to hold and
to avow the said Lady Talb*ot hi*s true and lawful wife, and none other. And
here to note, **obiter,** this [king's breach with] this lady was the cause that the
subtle widow would not for any promises or solemn p[rotestations from 40
him yield] of her dainty person to his burning appetite and venerous
amplexes until he had married her, [for she had learned **credulitas damno**
solet esse puellis. And therefore,] neither good counsel nor motherly
authority nor religion nor threatened *war* and imminent dangers could
dissuade or deter him from his purpose*:* his affections or lust were so 45
excessively fervent and so vehement and so violent that there was *no reme*dy
but he must needs wed and bed, and in all haste, the said Lady Gray, and
that in so sudde*n and strange* and disparageous and clandestine and obscure
manner as aforesaid.

And when that news was told to the Lady [Eleanor But]ler, she was 50

[Ovid]

[Elizabeth Lucy]

224v

[Lady Eleanor
Talbot]

[Ovid]

greatly grieved, and she lived a melancholic and heavy and solitary life ever
aft[er, and how sh]e died is not certainly known, but it is out of doubt that
the king [killed her no]t with kindness. But he exceeded in all manner of
kindness and of care*ful love* to [his new] wife and queen, the Lady Gray.
5 And many years following, he fully satisfied and satiated him*self with the*
[joys and pl]easures which he conceived to be in her, and he bega*t* [many
children] *upon her.*
   And yet afterward that precontract stuck in his cons[cience after a time
and much perplexed him, labouring by all occasions to suppress it. And it
10 so much and nearly touched him that he held them not his friends nor good
subjects which mentioned it. And this was the cause of his displeasure
against his ancient chaplain Dr] / Stillington, Bishop of Bath, a[lthough he   225
did but what he was bound to do] in conscience before God and by his [duty
to the kingdom.]
15   *But* [it is not known] *to every*body how and to whom he first discovered
this m[arriage, nor everywhere] *set* down, but this is the opinion thereof
which some men hold of the matter, and this it is. That after the Lady
[Eleanor, being much] troubled in her mind with this wrong and d[ishonour
done her by the king, he]r heart was so full of the grief *that she was rea*dy to
20 burst, and that she could no longer conceal *it,* she revealed her marriage [to
a lady] who was her sister, or, as some say, her [mother, the Countess of
Shrew]sbury, or to both. And her mother told it to the earl her husband
herewith. *And* [he acquaints it to his noblest] and wisest and nearest friends.
And they were all much offended and scand*alized with this* affront and
25 wrong.
   And because they would be better *and more firmly* resolved herein, they
thought it fit to talk with Dr [Stillington, who] *knew the truth of the* matter,
and they so did. And he confessed and affirmed that the king and th[e Lady
Elea]nor were contracted and married by him. And hereupon [they] *said* to
30 the bishop that, he being a man of holy orders and [a bishop,] also a privy
counsellor to the king, it behoved him in [his duty to God and to the king to
admonish the king of this fault and to advise him better to considerati[on of
the wr]ong which he had done to the Lady Eleanor and to her [noble]
lineage and family, and to take some course to salve it and to redress and
35 make satisfac[tion.]
   The bishop liked w[ell the proposition, but durst not deal with the king]
in this matter and manner, but yet he promised that he w[ould use some
means whereby it might] be imparted to the king. And then he acquainted
the Duke of [Gloucester] therewith, [who was most inward and gra]cious
40 with the king of all other. And hereof thus writeth Philip de [Commynes:]   [Philip de
Cet l'Évêque de Bath mit en avant à [ce Duc d]e Cloucester que ledit Roi   Commynes]
Edouard était fort amoureux [d'une] dame d'Angleterre et lui promit de
l'epouser, pourvu [qu'il couch]ât avec elle. Elle s'y consentit et dit cet
Evêque [qu'il les] avait épousés, et n'y avait que lui et eux deux, ut supra.
45   [And the Duke] of Gloucester dealt with the king about this business, but
he could do no good. [For all the effect] hereof was nought, and that was
that the king grew exceedingly wroth [with the Bishop of] Bath for revealing
this marriage, and checked and rated *the bishop,* and bitterly, and charged
him that he had betrayed [his children,] *and said that* he would make him
50 repent his treac*hery, and* [put him from] the coun[s]el [table and

225v

[1620]

[How King Edward died]
226
[Polydore, **Lib.** 24]

[**Lib.** 4 en Hist. de Bretagne]
227
[Monstrelet, pt 3 **de se Chronique**]

228

229

commit]*ted* [him to] *pri*/son, where he lay a long time [in much sorrow] and misery, and at the *last* [the king made him glad to] redeem these bonds of imprisonment *for his* garrulity at a heavy fine. And this [is testified by] Francis Godwin, now Bishop of Hereford, [in his **Catalogus**] **Episcoporum.** And hereof also this *same* noble Frenchman, Philip [de Commynes, thus 5 writeth:] **Le roi Edouard désappointa l'[Évêque, et le] tint en prison, et le rançonna d'une bonne [somme d'ar]gent.** But this was injustice, for the bishop [not deserving to] be punished in this case because he was [bound i]n conscience to reveal this former marriag[e.]

Not long after, King Edward died, and it was [held] doubtful upon what 10 disease or evil he came to *it.* / Polydore Vergil saith he died of a disease u[tterly] unknown to all the physicians, which showeth some that there was some *foul play,* and that may be understood to be either poison or sorcery. Who were the dealers in th[ese arts I have show]ed before. And the author of the History of Brittany [in] plain terms saith that the king was killed by 15 poison, as the report in France was: **Aucuns disaient que le [Roi] d'Angleterre avait été empoisonné [au mois d'avril en l'an 1483.]**

And Enguerant de Monstrelet [writeth that some said] / he died of an apoplexy, and that some other said that he was poisoned in wine of ·Creu w[hich King Lewis XI sent him.] And Philip de Commynes seemeth to be 20 of the same opinion, for he saith that [**Aucuns**] **disent que le roi Edouard mourut d'un catarrhe:** some say [that King] Edward died of a catarrh. For so they say in France when a grea[t man] is made away by poison. And of such a venomous catarrh died the young King Edward [VI.] And in this sense the French king Henry III *died of a* catarrh. And I came to understand 25 it upon this occasion: it *fell th*en unhappily that when I was in France and in the *court, there was* news brought that the Lady Mary Queen *of Scots* was beheaded in England, and at *the arrival of this news they said that she had died of a catarrh.*

[But at whose hand King Edward IV had his is not told. This is certain: he 30 was generally beloved of all his subjects, e]/xcepting [those of the Lancastrian faction, who in their hearts ha]ted him and wished his death and the short *lives of* [all the Pl]antagenets, and especially those of the royal family of [York.] *And they* made quick and round riddance ere it was long time. *And* the King Edward acted the first part of this truculent tragedy, 35 and *then* his sons stayed not long after him in this world. And King Richard and his son bled out m*ore in the next a*cts, and they were succeeded in that bloody protasis by Edward Plantagenet, *Earl of* Warwick, and by Perkin Warbeck and by the Countess of Salisbury, by the de la Poles and others. And the daughters of King Edward were but short live*d. And it* was a long 40 tragedy, for it was in acting forty years at the leas*t. And it* was well performed, for there were none then left which had any parts to play *on that* dismal stage. But these be harsh and distasteful matters, and *I* will speak no more of them, but I will proceed.

[As soon as] King Edward was dead, the silence broke. And now there 45 was not only [general muttering] of the king's marriage, but also loud and common and public inveighing [against it.] And now all tongues were loose and at liberty, and pardons were hoped [for all offences.] And then the general voice / and common opinion was that this ma[rriage was] *contracted invali*dly and that the children were illegitim[ate (in plainer 50

terms,] that they were bastards). And Dr [Morton affirmeth the] Duke of
Buckingham and other noble [lords saw and read certain] authentic
instruments made and signed by [learned doctors] and proctors and notaries
with the depositions of [sundry] credible persons, importing and testifying
5 that th[e children] of King Edward IV were bastards. Moreover, [the city] of
London was possessed with this base opinion, and the *p*reachers also, and
namely Dr Shaw and Friar Pynk [and others] declared in their pulpits and
prounounced them illegitimate, and that they were **spuria vitulamina** —
bastard [branches — and might take no r]oot. And likewise the people of
10 the north parts *made* known that they held these children *to be ba*stards in
their supplicatory scroll, [before m]entioned. And finally the court of
Parliament declared, *pronoun*ced, adjudged and decreed both the marriage
and the children to be unlawful, as I have related, and at large, before.

[But there] was a means and an opportunity, and [which lasted] some
15 years, and if it had then and timely been *taken,* whereby King Edward might
have salved [that fault] and might have anteverted and made [frustrate a]ll
future claims and repaired and *salved all flaw*s and defects of titles and have
avoided all quarrels and [questions which after arose upon] the foresaid
precontract. [He might] also have taken away and cleared [the error and
20 inconvenience of the postcontract and later marriage, from whence grew
the imputation of bastards to his children, and so have avoided all ensuing
mischiefs and calamities.

[For if first he had procured a divorce of the first contract or marria]/ge
with the Lady Eleanor fro[m the Pope, who was then held] to have all the
25 power of [heaven and earth] *and to be* able to confirm or ensure and to
d*ivorce or unbind.* [Or if after] the second marriage, and while he *was king,*
which was the best part of fourteen years, he had either [by his own
prov]ident care and due consideration, or by the good counsel [of his best
friends] and counsellors craved [the Pope's] pardon for his breach of the
30 pre[contract with] the Lady Eleanor Talbot, and next his Ap[ostolical B]ull
of dispensation for his postcontract (or m[atrimony] superinducted, as they
call it) — and which suits mig[ht] have been obtained at Rome for money.

And the*reafter,* these suits being obtained, to have summoned a
[Parliament,] and therein to have desired and required the Th[ree Estates]
35 of the kingdom to have ratified and confirmed [the Bulls] containing the
pardon and disp*ensation or* approbation of the said marriage with the
Lad[y Gray,] and the legitimation of his children. And *after these things*
were obtained of Parliament, to accept and *declare* and pronounce and
establish those things *as* [lawful] by Act of Parliament according to the
40 indulge[nce] *of the* Pope (which was then held a most sacred and [inviolable]
thing). And lastly to have declared and prono[unced] and decreed in
Parliament that the said childr[en of this] king, being thus now made
legitimate, were [ca]pable of all honours and dignities and of a[ll estates,]
public and private, whereof the king was [possessed] and seized, or which
45 were anyways appertaining and proper to [the king] of England and of
France.

I say if he had done thus, [he had] *accommo*dated and compassed all
errors and defects and had prevented all the succeeding dangers of claims
and practices and had forestalled and *secured that then* no claims nor titles
50 of any ambitious, presumptuous and inju*rious upstart could be of* any force

[Dr Morton, Sir
Thomas More, Graf-
ton, Holinshed,
Stow]

230*
How King Edward
might have pr[even-
ted] all the afte[r
evils]

230v

or regard; and all might have been obtained and *performed* by the king living, he having then so great *authority and* power in this kingdom, and so good *favour* with the popes. [And this course was by another opportunely thought on.

[But it may be thought the judgement of God, hanging over the king's 5 head for his many and great offences, captivated and took his understanding and provident care from him. For his sins were not only his adulteries and fornications, those in the height and excess, but he was burthened with the crying sin of bloodshed. Yet Polydore Vergil imputeth his greatest guilt to the violating his faith and solemn vow to God and to the 10 holy clergy when he was suffered to enter York upon condition he should demand nor seek anything but his dukedom of York. And these indeed are the just causes of God's punishments against men. And many times He is pleased to leave them so blinded and secure in their sensualities and sins that they have no sense or power to see or prevent the mischiefs that stand at 15 their doors.]

231

And whereby the children of King Edw*ard were* pronounced illegitimate and made incapable *of the crown*, which, or the like Parliamentary power, also *could* have made them legitimate (as I *intima*ted). And these great and high and difficult wor[ks are indeed] *the provi*nce of the great and transcen- 20 dent p*ower of Par*liament. And those courts are well worthy to have *such cred*it and authority if they be assembled and used [and held] as they ought to be. For the court of *Parliament* is or should be a general assembly of all the most [noble] *and m*ost honourable and most just, the most godly and the *most* [rel]igious persons of the kingdom, as well laical as [eccle]siastical. 25 And by the many good and wholesome laws *which were* made in that Parliament of **anno** 1 **Rege Ricardi,** the second marriage of King Edward was adjudged [unlaw]ful. And the aims of that Parliament were for the most part repealed and abrogated [afterward.] And yet it appeareth plainly en[ough that t]he general judges and the lawmakers of that Parliament were 30 [wise] *and* just and good and godly men, and that their laws were good and jus[t,] and therefore whatsoever [was adjud]ged and decreed then by them was to be received as *just and* authentic and inviolable, how roughly soever it was afterward h[andled.]

And in the case of [the disa]bling of the sons of King Edward, there is 35 least cause [to suspect] them because the cause was so new and plain and so notoriously [known th]at no man might be ignorant therein. [Therefore to hav]e given any other judgement in that cause [but according] to the evidence and proofs, it might justly have been censured an ac[t of error and ignorance, or partiality and inju]stice. If it be objected that [the case was 40 o]bscure and doubtful, [that cannot be. For the Estates had all substantial and ready means to inform themselves] of the truth, and whereby they [might be satisfied and cleared of all doubts. For all the witnesses and

233v

dealers in that cause, and such per]/sons as were privy and [acquainted with] *those* businesses were then living, [and they must and would] have 45 truly and certainly informed the court of Parliament] *and* delivered to them the state *of the matter there*unto lawfully required and called and sworn *to it.*

[For the special and reverend] care which the court of Parliament hath [is the advancing of justice] and truth. [And therefore] all subjects by nature or 50

gr[ace are bou]nd by the duty of their allegiance to give rev*erend* credit to
Parliaments and to believe in their a[uthority] and power as the ancient
pagans did in ora[cles.] *And* further also, we must confidently hold and
belie[ve] the [high] and transcendent quality and virtue of tha[t court] to be
5 such as the Papists held the power o[f the] Pope: that is, to have all power
and [authority,] and that they can do anything [but err.]   234

But this must be understood of the courts of Parliame*nt* *a*ssembled and
holden by such wise and good and just and godly men as aforesaid. For if
th*e* court be pestered with ignorant, corrupt, unjust, and irreligious
10 persons, then it is **thronus anomiae et consilia impiorum** and *la* **chapelle de**
mal conseil, and the tribunal of tyranny and consistory of corruption. And
the laws which are then made are naught, and taint, and not to be kept nor
observed. And in *such* cases if the next or another court of Parliament,
good and godly men shall decree to revoke and to annul the evil and unust
15 laws made by such unjust and unworthy men, their proceedings and acts are
good, just, honourable, and pious. Otherwise, and generally, to repeal and
abrogate the acts of a good Parl*iament is a* violent and a giantlike and an
unjust work, and *it is gener*ally taxed, **Clavum clavo pellere**. And no   Erasmus, **Proverbs**
question, to repeal or abrogate a good and just law made in Parliament is a
20 wrong and scandal to that general counsel and to the universal wisdom,
providence, justice, and piety of the kingdom, which at the best is but an
intestine war of civil dissention.

[And there be examples of such] / Parliaments here in Eng[land,   235
wherein many acts firmly made] were repealed and rescind[ed,] *and*
25 [sometimes the whole Parliament] abrogated. But these tr*ibunals and*
manner of proceedings were but in time of the greater [seditions and
factious tumults,] and in the times of the civil or un[natural wars, when]
injustice and wrong and oppression overra*n* [all.] *And* [some] of these
irregular and evil gr*oups have nicknam*es as stigmas left upon them, [as the
30 Parlia]ment of Wonders, the Black Parlia[ment, the Bloody Parliam]ent,
etc. And none was worthier of an evil name than that Parliament [which
condem]ned to confiscation and destruction a gr[eat] many [churches and
re]ligious houses erected and dedicated to the service of God.

And so great were the evils and mischief th*ey pronounc*ed and decreed as
35 it may well be doubted whether *the Holy* Ghost were in the midst of that
synod or court or no. *And it* is great presumption that the deviser and giver
of ancient and most pernicious *c*ounsel, viz., Satan, was there. For he hath
also his synods, and he requireth his or*ators to* persuade *the* spoil and the
destruction of all the houses of God and of his *ministers. And* he hateth
40 piety, faith, and charity and verity, and would fain *abolis*h them. But God
giveth such an invincible strength *to verit*y above the rest as that she is
champion able enough to defen*d them, and she* overcometh Satan in the
end with all his hosts of lies and of sin. *And truthfulnes*s hath only thes*e*
great and all victorious eulogies, viz.: **Magna et prae omnibus fortior, super**
45 **omnibus** *est* **Veritas. Magna est Veritas, et praevalet.** *And also,* *********d   235v
veritatis iudica*ndi.* But these judgements be but opinions *fit only for*   Cicero
consilia impiorum et thronus iniquitatis. And I have already spoken
abundantly and generally of *this matter in the* *******Book of my **Baron.**

Therefore I will speak *briefly, and as I reck*on is fit and proper to the
50 place and *give examples of Parliaments* of that kind. And amongst them *I*

*will say some*thing of the Parliament holden **ann**[o 1 Henry VII, wherein the]re be Acts enough to frustrate and to enervate [and dissolve] and abrogate itself, as by examples and parag[raphs of that] Parliament I will plainly demonstrate and prove *beyo*nd affection. First then, whereas there is an Act for [attaint]ing the true and lawful king of this land, namely, 5 R[ichard] III, of High Treason, and that for his bearing of arms ag[ainst the Earl of] Richmond, fal*sely in r*ebellion proceeding from Milford Haven into Leicestershire, entitled the Sovereign Lord. For when he came on land to fight [the] battle, he was then no king nor sovereign, which can *any way be* proved. But the truth is, the earl was then in the time aforesa*id,* or oug[ht to 10 have been,] a vassal and a liege subject of King Richard, the true [king] and only sovereign lord of the realm and of the people *as long* as he lived.

Therefore it is plain that in this paragraph there be th[rice] *monstrous* gross faults and falsehoods. For first it is certain that Richard was [during his reign] a sove[reign: therefore] he was no subject. Secondly, there was no 15 enemy in the field [who was] then a sovereign, but all were vassals of the crown and King of England. And to conclude upon these two *first* arguments, Richard, being a king and a sovereign, and no subject, could [not] be adjudged a traitor, nor justly and lawfully be attainted of [High Treason,] because there was no man in those armies but he was the humble 20 and loyal vassal of him, the said King Richard. And *this is to turn* all things topsy-turvey and very preposterously, to set f*irst the subject above the sove*reign and the malefactor above the magistrate. In one word it is to revere *the* subject and the disloyal and rebelling and seditious *traitor when* he committeth the **crimen** of **laesae m***ai***estatis** *and violates the sacred* 25 *maj*esty of the k*ing*.

236

However, / as I *intimated, King Richard was attainted,* with all the rest of the true and c[onstant subjects of the king that bare arms] in the field and battle [at Bosworth] *and risked* their fortunes and their per*sons to defend* their sovereign lord, and of *right as they were* bound to do. All these men 30 *were for this* service done to their sovereign accus*ed of* High Treason, and their goods and lands confis[cate.] And this must needs be a great *scandal* in this Parliament.

One Thomas Nan[dick, a necromancer, havin]g been with other his consorts justly condemnned to di[e for necr]omancy and sorcery, was in this 35 Parliament [pardoned the horrible things] which he had committed by his art. But it seemeth that [he had not then left the] *practice of sorcer*y and of conjurations (or rather adjurations), because he [hath in that Act of Parliament still the style of] conjurer, viz.: Thomas Nandick of Cambrid[ge, Conjurer and Necromancer, which h]ad been a fitter title for 40 his gibbet than for his pardon, and to be sent and dispatched by the post of Newgate, albeit he ha[d not by his sorcery or] enchantments hurt or destroyed any human and Christian creature, but [for his abjura]tion of Almighty God. And the opinion of a great and a lear[ned and religious doctor, **Magos et] incantores** (saith he) **hominum genus dignum quod vel ob** 45 **[solam Dei O.M. abjurationem] capitali supplicio afficiatur.** And other such matters t[here be in that Parliament] which detract and derogate much from their credit and authority thereof. But I will *hold* my promise.

And now I will return to King Richard and bestow some *time in the* 237* *defend/*ing and clearing of him of one offence more, [or rathe]r of an error, 50

for it was no worse at the worst (although made a very heinous crime). And
that was also about *a m*arriage matter. For his adversaries devise and derive
this new crime [from] the treaty which King Richard had about the marriage
[of the] Lady Elizabeth Plantagenet, his niece, and whereof [I ma]de some
5 mention in the beginning. And his old adversaries *bla*me this king very
much for this suit or attempt thereof, *and they* censure it to be a thing not
only most detestable *but also mu*ch more cruel and abominable to be put in
execution. *And they* add hereunto that all men, and the maiden *mo*st of all,
detested this unlawful copulation; *and that* he made away the queen his wife
10 to [make way for this marr]iage; and that he propounde[d not this treaty of
marriage until the queen his wife was dead.

[That there was such a motion for the marriage of this lady to this king is
true, and which is more, and most,] / certain it [was entertained] a good
while and well liked by the k[ing and his friends, also by the Lady Elizabeth
15 and the] queen her mother. And indeed, [the treaty of this] match was so
acceptable [unto the queen, concern]ing very much comfort and [happiness
therein, that] she presently sent into France [to her son, the Marquess of
D]orset (who was there with [the Earl of Richmond, prac]tising treason with
him against [the king), and requires] him earnestly to leave that earl and his
20 treacher*ous* prac*tices* [and come] home, and she assured him that he should
be wel[come to the king] *and be pardone*d by him, and also advanced so
great*ly that his* fortunes should be much mended.

And in further token of [her liking to] th[is match, she sent the Lady
Eliza]beth her daughter to the court to attend upon the quee[n, that she
25 might be,] and by that means, more in the eye and in the heart of King
Richard. And at Christmas follow[ing, the Queen Blanche, for the better]
colour for the sending of her eldest daughter to the court, she *also* [se]nt her
other four daughters to the court, and where they we[re all re]ceived with
the most honourable courtesies and the best welcome that could be given,
30 [and with] great feast and revelling during all the Chris[tmas,] the which the
king then kept in Westminster Hall. [And t]he queen regnant entertained
also the young ladies with all h*er* courtesies and gracious caresses, and
espec[ially] the Lady Elizabeth, whom she used with so much famili[arity]
and kindness as if she had been her own sister, and ca*used* her to wear robes
35 and apparel and attire of the same *pattern* and the same colour and of the
same fashions which she herse*lf wore*.

But the queen had small joy and little pleasure in these festiv[al and]
pompous times, because she was sick and was much in langour and
[sorrow] for the death of the prince, her dear and only son, and the which
40 *grieved her sorely*. But albeit this counterfeit wooing of the king was kept
very close, yet the curious and w*aver*ing enemies of the king, and who were
devoted to the Ea[rl of] Richmond, began to suspect that the king had a
purpose *to* marry the Lady Elizabeth and so to prevent and to bereave the
earl *not* only of her marriage, but also of his best and chiefest ho[pe,] *which*
45 was to attain the crown by her title. And therefore these [mal]*con*tent and
seditious lords and other murmured and [muttered] very much and very
broadly against the motion and suspic*ion* of this marriage of the Lady
Elizabeth with the *King Richard*. Thereupon the treaty of this marriage was
carrie[d more closely] and more coldly also on the king's part.
50 And in [April follow]ing, the young Prince of Wales, son *of King*

[The treaty of mar-
riage between King
Richard and his
niece, the Lady
Elizabeth Plantage-
net]

[Dr Morton, Sir
Thomas More, and
their followers]

237v

238*

Richard, died, *as ha*th been before related, as also *hath the effect of it.* [All
this while, neither the queen widow nor her daughter were altered or
estranged, but continued constant in their desire and expectation] *and*
pursuit of this marriag[e. Only there was objection made by the ladies
against the] king for having a w[ife, as though she living, he could not   5
marry another] at once, not considering [it was usual not only with kings]
but also with private me[n to put away one wife and] take another, and not
only for ad[ultery and treason] *but for* other lighter crimes, as, for example,

[J]ustus [V]ulteius
[in] **Jurispru[den]-**
tia Rom.

[the Romans might repud]iate their wives for conversing [with men which
were not of] their kindred, or for g[oing to see play]s and to behold 10
Circensian spectacles where their [husbands] *were* [not with them,] or if the
wife were an unquiet [woman, or curst of her tongue,] *or,* as we say, an
arrant shrew, her husband might *properly put her away.*

And King [Henry VIII put away two] wives, Queen Catharine of Castile
and Qu[een Anne of Clev]e, for none of these crimes, but one becau[se she 15
was] *too ugly* and too old and not pleasing to him, and the other [because
she] was not fruitful or not wanton enough. And som[etimes men] have put
away their wives because they were sluts [or] *had* unsavoury and
unwholesome breaths, or else for some infec[tious disea]se. Yet none of
these repudiators took away the lives of their wives, nor needed *to do so,* 20
because it was lawful for both of them to marry when they wou[ld. And] the
Pope Clement VII so ratified the divorce of King [Henr]y VIII against
Catharine of Castile, as he defied all laws, [div]ine as human, which should
contradict and impugn his power and dispe]nsation, and in these words:

[**Bulla** Pope Clemen-
tis VIII, **apud D.**
Robert Cotton]

Non obstante iure divino [nec] humano, nec quibuscumque constitutioni- 25
bus repugnatibus [aut in] contrarium editis.

[And t]his manner of putting away of wives which their husbands [like]
not was very ancient and in common use amongst *the* Israelites and the Jews
and the select people of *God. An*d there is a law of divorces and of
repudiations *compos*ed by Moses. And there was also a formal bill or [libel 30

[Osiander in **Annota-**
tions in IV Ebr.,
Harmonius
Evangelic.]

m]ade for the separation and divorcing of the man and [wife,] and it was in
this tenor, as Andreas Osiander, a learned man, [wh]o thus translated it out
of Hebrew into Latin affirmeth, *and the which, b*ecause it is rare and proper
to this argument, I have *transcribed it* hither, and thus it is:

[Die] tertia Hebdomadis 29 die mensis [Octobris, anno ab orbe 35
condito, 43]49 .... Ego Joa[chim cognominatus N. filius Nathanis, qui
consisto hodie in urbe N. in regno N. te, N. uxorem meam cognominatam
N. filliam N. quae fuisti uxor mea antehac, nunc demisi et liberavi et
repudiavi te tibi, ut sis tui iuris, et domina animae tuae, et ad abeundum ut
ducaris abs quolibet viro quem volueris, et ne vir quisquam prohibeat quo 40

238v

minus sis in manu tua ex hoc di]/e et in aeternum. Et [ecce permissa es
unicuique viro. Et hic esto t]ibi a me datus libellus [repudii, et epistola
dimissoria et instr]umentum libertatis, iuxta [legem Moses et Israelis.

[But to pro]ceed and to relate the answer which was [made in the name of
the king to the Lady Elizabeth,] *to* wit, concerning the life or death of the 45
Queen Anne. And the *queen'*s life, which was very near at an end, would be
no impediment of any [long continuance, she being a very weak] woman
and in a consumption and [past hope of recovery,] *t*hat according to the
opinion of her physicians, she could not live much [past the middle of
Februar]y next following. And they guessed *not* [much amiss, for the] 50

queen died in the next month, viz., M[arch. But when the mid]st and more
days of February were gone, [the Lady Eli]zabeth, being very desirous to be
marri*ed, and growing n*ot only impatient of delays, but also suspicious of
the [success,] wrote a letter to *Sir John* Howard, Duke of Norfolk,
5 intimating first therein that [he was the] one in whom she most [affied,]
because she knew the king her father much lov[ed him,] and that he was a
very faithful servant unto him and to [the king his brother then reign]ing,
and very loving and serviceable to King Edward's children.

*Fir*st she thanked him for his many c·urtesies and friendly [offices, an]d
10 then she prayed him as before to be a mediator for her in the cause of [the
marriage] to the k[i]ng, who, as she wrote, was her only joy and maker in
[this] world, and that she was his in heart and in thoughts, in [body,] and in
all. And then she intimated that the better half of Fe[bruary] was past, and
that she feared the queen would nev[er die.] And all these be her own words,
15 written with her own hand, and this is the sum of [her] letter, whereof I have
seen the autograph or original d[raft] under her [own] hand, and by the
special and honourable favour of the mos[t noble] and first count of the
realm, and the chief of his family, Sir Thomas Howard, and Baron
Howard, etc., Earl of Arundel and of Surrey, and the immediate and lineal
20 [heir]/of this Sir John Howard, Baron Howard, Mowbray, and Duke of
Norfolk, etc. And albeit he be young and in his flourishing age, yet for his
courage and much knowledge and ripe judgement, he is capable of any
hard employment, and ready to undertake and to embrace any *noble
acti*ons. And he keepeth that princely letter in his rich and magnificent
25 cabinet, among precious jewels and rare monuments.

And by this letter it may [be] observed that this young lady was inexpert
in worldly affairs, and hereby igno[rant that a man] having a wife living
might marry another and suffer her to live. *But she* understood and wrote
like to herself, that is to say like to a *young* maiden, and as having heard
30 nothing of repudiations and *divorces, s*he seemeth to say as the young and
fa*ir ones think.* / But I have here sh*own that she could have been* married to
the king and the que*en have remained alive if he had wished* and had any
hearty desire to proceed or purpose *to marry her.* [But the truth is, the king]
had no mind nor inten[t in his heart to make her his wife from] the
35 beginning, but in policy he entertained [this treaty,] and as it plainly
appeared afterward, when the queen his wife was dead,] and that he had
then all fit op[portunity] *and* commodi*ty* [to marry her, no let nor
impediment being, but so strong in absolute power] that it was not in the
power of *any man to* [debar] that alliance.

40 Yet he took her *not, although he professed intent* to marry her, but for
the said other causes. And *he* made open protestation in the Great [Hall at
St John's near] Smithfield before all the Knights of Ma[lta and a great
asse]mblance of noblemen and of gentlemen, [the Lord Mayo]r and
aldermen also, and many citizens being [likewise pre]sent, that he had no
45 purpose nor desire nor intent [to marry the] Lady Elizabeth. And he
protested, **Quod ea res,** [viz., volu]**ntas contrahendi matrimonium cum
consanguin[ea germ]ana sua, numquam ei venerat in mentem.** For [so it is
testi]fied by the Prior of Croyland.

But it may not be [deni]ed but that he made love to this lady and
50 pretended [to marr]y her, and obtained both the good will of the lady [and]

[The credit of the
Duke of Norfolk
with King Richard
and with the Lady
Elizabeth, and her
letter to him]

239
[The cabinet of the
Earl of Arundel,
now Earl of Surrey
too]

240*

[Chronic. Croylan.]

of the queen her mother, as hath been before showed. But this love was made [in] policy and cunningly, and that was to draw her to him that thereby he migh*t* [divert her affection] from the Earl of [Richm]ond (**ut supra**), to whom Morton and the seditious barons had promised *her,* and upon which marriage and by the title thereof dependin*g, the* earl's hope of 5 the crown also and chiefly depended. And th*us saith* [a good auth]or: [**Non a]liter videbat Ricardus Rex regnum sibi confirmari neque spem competitoris sui auferri posse, nisi in matrimonio [cum dic]ta Elizabetha contrahendo,/vel simulando/.**

And as I verily believe *and appreh*end, the king had no other end in 10 wooing of the Lady *Eliza*beth but to prevent the earl and to frustrate [those hopes of] his fortunes which he had by her — so I think verily — nor that the king *had this s*ame will or purpose by treachery to make a[way] the queen his wife. And I am the rather of this opinion, and have before proved, that he ever hated base and secret acts *and treac*hery, and besides 15 that he was always so [affectionate and kind that] he was rather ta*ken to be* [uxorious than otherwise, and at her death expressed it in his heavy mourning, causing very magnificent exequies to be prepared for her, interring her **non cum minore honore quam reginam decuit,** as the Prior of Croyland testifieth.]   20

Now for the opinion of his / adversaries, viz., that *the Lady Elizabeth detested* this unlawful copulation, [that you may see appears a false suggestion, the contrary being proved by] her own letter, before cited. And *this affirm*ation, to say that this marriage was a [detestable and cruel thing, is a vain and ignorant affirmation] because she was so near akin to him, 25 whereas [m]arriages between uncles and [nieces have been very frequent and allow]ed in other countries, and by the Church. And in our [times, the daughter and heir] of the Duke of Infantasgo in [Spain was married to his brother, Don Alonso de Mendoza. [And more recently the Earl] of Miranda married his brot[her's daughter. In the] house of Austria, marriages of [this 30 kind have been] rife and usual and thought [lawful and] honourable when the Pope hath dispensed [with them. For] they say in Spain, **Que el padre san[to quiere, Dios l]oquiere.**

And now lastly I will say one word *concerning* the queen, wife of King Richard, although it be almost *the last.* And whereas it is affirmed also by 35 the adversarie*s that* King Richard made away his wife to marry this *Lady* Elizabeth Plantagenet, I have demonstrated already this also to be as fal*se by arguments* and proofs. I desire therefore the worthy Reader to review and consider what *I have said before.* But the king cleared himself of the imputation of seeking of that marr*iage by swearing on his hono*ur (which is 40 a great oath) and by his neglect when his w[ife was] dead and he free, and that then her life could be *no* hindrance to his second marriage, yet he pursued *not this* cause, nor had any desire to marry her. And thirdly, this is a good *i*mputation or accusation, to wit, all his accusers charge him not with the practice of the death of *the* queen his wife directly and disertly, but 45 doubtfully and in this [manner]: **the [queen] (howsoever it fortuned) departed out of this life the 16th of March in the Lent season.** And this rather maketh to clear him of these a*ccusations than accuseth him.*

But albeit he were a good and loving husband to his wife, yet I say *not* that he always lived continently and with[out wrong] to her bed, because I 50

[Chronic. Croyland]

[The queen died the 16th March, 1484]

[Prior Croyland]

240v*

[Sir Thomas More; Holinshed]

find that he had some [bastards,] and two of them I have mentioned before, here *in this work.* [Yet] haply he had them in his youth, and before his m[arriage, and then the] fault was the less.

And thus much for the many injurious censures and sha*meful slanders*
5 made of King Richard by his quadrupla[tors,] and whose brains doubtless were very fertile of inventions and very ingenious in such *false and evil* slanders and foul *detractions, and which* should *not be believed.* [So that all King Richard's guilt is but suspicion. And suspicion is] / in la[w no more guilt or culpableness than imagination] or the *accusations whi*ch are weak
10 be*cause they are* false. *And they are not to be belie*ved, nor *are they credited by the learne*d judges, because *they have not been pr*oved to them certain by idoneou*s* proofs.

241

[For] suspicion, although it many tim[es lay a great blame] upon a man ([for men hold him to be guilty] whom they suspect to be guilty, althou[gh
15 the suspicion be false and] injurious), but it is not held in the law to be a crime: **and** [in regard] that suspicion supposeth many tim[es] *men* [to be g]uilty and culpable of crimes whereof they are n[ot. So that an innoce]nt may as easily be condemned as a malefactor, [being an evil grow]n from the error of men. Wherefore mere suspicion of itself bring[eth no sentence
20 against any man by the laws natural or moral, civil, or divine.] And therefore the wise and just judges and magistrates requ*ire strong* evidence of the accuser, or else they pronounce the *accuser guilty of* condemnation, and the execution of the same punishm*ent is decreed against him for being an* accuser and not being furnished, which is due by law to him who is guilty
25 of the offence or crime which is laid by the *accuser to the* innocent man's charge.

[Suspicio est opinio male ex levibus signis. S. Thomas Aquinas. Suspicio est actus, per quem indubitationem trahimur. Prateius.]

And after this manner proceed the *learned* judges of the imperial and civil laws, and by good right, *accor*ding to that wise sentence of the old Mimographus, **Suspicio [grave est homin]ibus malum.** And therefore the
30 divine Chrysostom admonisheth [that **Suspicio t]ollenda est, non inferenda.** And he tacitly giveth another reason [in another] place where he saith that [a] good man hardly suspecteth [another man to be] evil, and an evil man scarcely ever supposeth any man [to be good. He fur]ther amplifieth and exemplifieth this argument: an adulterer **(sai[th he)** or fornicator thinketh
35 o]ther men to be such as he is. And the proud man thinketh *that all men are proud,* and the murderer thinketh that all men [are murderers.

[And born under the like influence were they that] raised this suspici[on upon King Richard. But it had been more credit to have observed the rules and counsel of this divine epigram:
40   **Culpare in quoquam, quae non sunt nota malignum est,**   [Anthologia Sacra]
             Praesertim si quae cognita sint bona sunt.
             Non pateant faciles duris rumorib]/us aure[s;   241v
             Quae nescire iuvat credere n]on libe[at;
             Linquantur secreta deo cui] quicquid [apertum est;
45   **Inspicit et nullis] indiget indicibus.**
And this is the sense in English:
             [Accuse no] man of faults to thee unknown,
             And much less him from whom good fruits h[ave grown.]
             Lend not thine ears to scandalous repo[rts.]
50   Believe not that which known nought t[hee imports.]

Leave secret things to God, who knows [all hearts,]
And hath no need of the promoter's arts.

But to be short, I confess that the best were never to be suspe[cted of any crime:] **Felicior innocentia est citra suspicionem,** as Sen[eca said well.] And as Julius Caesar, who had many excellent observations, was [wont to say,]   5
that **Vir bonus [tam suspicione] quam crimine carere oportet:** that a good man must be as [well without] suspicion as without crime. But yet let no [man] presume of his righteousness and of his integrity and of his innocency but that h[e may *be* suspected of some crime, and by some malicious or env[ious] *persons, and conde*mned for it, although he never committed it. 10
For such per[sons, like to the **polypus,**] will take any colour and make any show of crime serve their [turn.]

But it shall be well for a Christian man, and it shall savour of more charity (and which is *grateful* to Almighty God, who only knoweth the secret soul*s of men, not to credit the* suspicion of his neighbour, nor to 15
suppose and report none other men *guilty of* crimes according to their opinion or ill affection, and whereof they *have no knowledge.* For suspicion is for the most part an erroneous and an injurious and an unchari*table opinion, and oftenti*mes it wrongeth and condemneth an innoce*nt man and even after death when he cannot be woun*ded any more.   20

[Suetonius]

THE [FIFTH BOOK]
OF THE HISTORY [OF KING] RICHARD III

The Argument

Herein is discussed what a [tyrant is,] and how a tyrant and King Richard
   diff[er.]
[The destruction of the Plantagenets.]
[The daughter]s of King Edward, how bestowed.
5 Death of the queen their mo[ther.]
The sundry virtues of this King Richard III.
[The eulogy of the three brothers, King Edward IV,] George, and Richard
   III.
The magnificent, public, and charitable b[uildings] and other good works
10   of King Richard [III; his good laws and other good works.]
That to die in the [wars is no dishonour, but an] honour.
The age of King Richard III.
Artes r[egiae, crimen regale.]
His comparison with other kings accounted good, but worse than he.
15 All the Pla*ntagenets put to death by his successors.*
[The] character of King James; his gracious demeanour t[owards his
   cousins.]
[A character and eulogy of King Richard] III.
The title of the Norman race and of [York] defended.
20 The sundry titles of King James.
The wedding ring of England, **lapis regno fatali[s.]**
King Richard's sepulchre and epitaph.
The author's scope, peroration, **et votum.**

THE FIFTH BOOK

243*

That I have examined and sifted and tried and found guilty and fal*se the accusers of King Richard will be now apparent. And the greatest of them was Sir Thomas More, whose chief studies were philosophy and law.* / But yet besides *these studies and* delights and other and studious *activities,* he was much transp*orted by, and much* addicted to poetry, *as I intimated* 5 before. And it appeareth *so by this* pamphlet, for many of these accusa*tions* are but fables and fictions and poetical in*ventions. B*esides, he had much intelligence with the *kingdom* of Utopia, and perhaps many of those imaginary *accusations were* advertisements from that strange and uncouth land, *or* some of them might be suggested to him in his dream*s and* visions 10 by his worser genius. But I doubt that those *excus*es will neither salve his credit nor make amends to *the* extremely wronged and slandered King Richard. *And* yet this good knight hath so many good friends as well *abroa*d as at home, as that they will excuse him for any *faults* and cover the multitude of them with their love and *partia*lity. 15

What a ty[rant is]

But I like the plain and honest dealing of *John S*tow better, who affirmeth confidently that those greatest *crime*s, as namely the slaughter of his nephews, etc., were *never* proved against him, neither by witness and lawful evidence *nor* so much as by the oaths of the knights of the post.

Now that I *have refuted* the particular and special and more spite*ful* 20 *scan*dals and accusations of King Richard, I *will say* some things in the interpretation and declamation of a vocable or term of *s*candal cast upon him, and which comprehendeth all scandals *and accusation*s and all impieties whatsoever. And that is the word 'tyrant', or an evil king. **Tyrannus est qui**

[Aristotle in Ethics]
[Idem]
[Proverbs, Cap.19]
243v

[suis propriis commodis stud]et et publicis adversatur. [And again, 25 **Tyrannus est qui dominatu crudeliter abutitur.** [And the Holy Ghost resembleth a tyrant to a roaring lion, bent upon spoil and bloody cruelty. A tyrant is by another wise man] *liken/*ed to ✳✳✳✳✳✳✳✳✳ and by *P*lato termed a wolf, *and by another to* a dragon who becometh [not a dragon until he hath eaten] and devoured many ser[pents, of which conceits t]his epigram was 30 framed, and wittily:

> **[Post plures colu]ber serpentes Draco fit esos,**
> **[Gustata hum]ana fitque homo carne lupus.**
> [The dragon which doth many serpents eat
>   Becomes a dragon of huge shape and strength. 35
> And so the man which makes man's flesh his meat
>   Transformed is unto a wolf at length.]

*And so much for these re*semblances. For the tyrant *lives on hu*man blood.

And another wise sa[ying of a philoso]pher dissenteth not far from hence, *who, when he was as*ked what beast was of all the most perni[cious] *and* heinous, he answered that of all tame beasts [the flatt]erer or parasite was the most hurtful, and of [all wil]d beasts, the tyrant was the most cruel and
5 pernicious. *For the* tyrant forbeareth not for any respect, nor maketh a *gentle* conscience to do any ill, but he is delighted in oppressi[ons,] *in* wrongs, in exactions, in robberies, in sacrileges, in [bloodshed,] in murder, in adultery, in incest, in rapes, in r[iot,] in gluttony, in prodigality and lavishness, and in a[ll manner] of excesses. These be his arts of reigning, and
10 these [be his] virtues. For as for the true virtues and the pro*fessors* thereof, he hateth them.

[Philosophus Anony-mus apud Plutar-chum]

    Invident [tyranni] claris, fortesque trucidant, as saith one. And another saith, **Tyr[annus miserum vetat perire, faelicem iubet.** And he exalt*eth* and advanceth the persons most contaminate therewith. *And* it was truly said of
15 the famous orator of Athens, **[Libe]ralitas tyranni nihil aliud est quam translatio pe[cuniarum] a iustis dominis ad alienos idque indignos.**

[Lucan]
[Seneca, **Hercule Furente**]
[Demosthenes]

    And the tyrant's t[hirst] *for* gold, and his covetousness, is so great and so *unquenchable,* and all for the serving of his inordinate lusts and prodigal humours, *and it is* so extreme; and for his foolish and monstrous largitions
20 and inordinate lusts and those of his truhanes and parasites, bestowed upon *spoil*ers which are so excessively costly and wasteful as *to consume all his substance.*

    [**Non Tartesiacis illum satiaret harenis tempestas pretiosa Tagi, non stagna rubentis aurea Pactoli; totumque exhauserit Hermum, ardebit maiore siti,**
25 etc.

[Claudian in **Ruffino**]

      [Quidquid conspicuum pulchrumque est aequore toto, Res fisci est, etc.]

[Juvenal, Satire IV]

    And in brief, a tyrant *is one who embraces both with* heart and wit o*ppression and avarice.* [And] this [may serve] here for the descrip*tion and*
30 *qualification* of tyranny, and the which *I have made* to the end that it may be the *pattern of such actions* and by the comparing of them *with the actions* of this King Richard (and the which shall here follow), *it shall be m*anifest that he was very *susceptible to the virtues and not* obnoxious to the vices. And I *doubt he can in any wis*e justly be called a tyran*t; for he* had
35 many virtues and qualities, and he was *noble and generous, w*hich I will declare more at large, and offer *evidence thereof, after* that I have compared some of the acts of a tyrant *and the acts of* King Richard together, of the same subject, but contrary in their *effects.*

244*

    First then, whereas the [tyra]nt imposeth many and grievous taxes and
40 tribu*tes upon h*is subjects, this King Richard took away such grie[vances.] And *there had been enac*ted by Act of Parliament a hateful tax, but disguised with the [name of] 'benevolence'. *And he relea*sed his subjects of the burden thereof, and forebore a*lso to levy any* new tax or charge upon them. *S*econdly, tyrants do not only pill and poll their people *and ta*ke their goods
45 from them, but also they spoil and [rob] churches and churchme[n and take from them holy things *d*edicated to God. But King Richard contrariwise [did m]any good things as well for the good of the people and for the public *bene*fit, as also for the promoting and advancing of the [servic]e of God and for the maintenance of his ministers the [churc]hmen, as shall be more
50 particularly demonstrated in the *list of his achievements.* And this showed

[King Richard no tyrant]
[In Parliament **anno** 1 Richard III]
[The Duke of Buck-ingham said that the name of 'benevol-ence' as it was taken in the time of King Edward IV signified that every man should pay not what he of his own good

will list, but what the
king of his] g[ood
will list to take. Duke
Buckingham **apud**
Thomas More.]
[Sir Thomas More]

244v

245

[King James]

[Comes Arundel,
viva voce]

that he was a bountiful and a pious prince. [B]ut **Tyrannum pium esse non est facile,** as Sophocles [well obs]erved. Nor may he be happy or blessed, for the oracle pronounced **portae feli[citatis] ad tyran[nidem clausae.]**

Item: Tyrants be cruel and bloody. But [this king,] even by the testimony of his enemies, was very [merciful] and mild. For they say that he was of 5 himself [very gentle] — these be their own words. Therefore, where *there are* [tyrannica]l acts objected to him, they must be under*stood to be* [done by other m]en or by their practices and [ill persuasions, or else before he was king. And what he did then was not or could not be properly called tyranny.

[And amongst those acts] done by him whilst [he was king,] *there are many* 10 *not tyrannical when considered* properly. The beheading [of Henry Stafford, Duke of Buckingham,] is held to be one, and [the chiefest. Yet that act, the cau]se and just motives of the duke's cutting *off* [being considered, it cannot be censu]red tyranny, but due and [necessary justice. For if the king had] not put down that duke, [the duke would have put] *him* 15 down, and he would have usurped [the throne royal] and seized upon the principate, if his p*ower and force could* have reached so far, and if w*ith arms he could have achieved the* sovereignty. And I have also *recounted* what and how gr*eat his offen*ces were, and deserving justly to *be punished by this hon*est and most mild and gracious king. 20

I have s*een accounts wherei*n King Richard is reported to have used [tyranny] against his nephew Edward, Earl of Warw[ick,] *son* to George, Duke of Clarence. It is true that [he sent him] to Sheriff Hutton, a goodly and pleasant house of h[is own in] Yorkshire, and where this young lord had libert[y, large diet,] air, pleasure enough, and lived in safety there. 25 Therefore, if that [were imprisonment,] it [were **prison] curtois,** as J. Froissart says. But yet this must be no les[s than] tyranny, according to the judgement and style and charity of Sir Thomas More. *But* Henry VII, as soon as he had got the crown at Bosworth, instantly sent for t[his young prince,] and afterward cut off this prince's head, and for *nothing,* as you 30 have heard before. But Sir Thomas More could no*t say th/*at this was an act of tyranny in that prince.

But let h*is acco*mplices make as light of it as they will, yet I dare boldly *say th*ere is a prince within the British world who would not have done *the* like cruel act to have gained thereby the whole empire and mona*rchy* of 35 Europe. And I have reason to be of this opinion, and first because I know [he hath protested against that particular act and held it] in detestation. And secondly because the time by experience hath made it known that he destroyeth no regal titul[ars,] albeit there were some noble person[s in] one of the kingdoms who pretended title to the crown thereof by *right,* being 40 descended from some kings of that country, yet this most magnanimous and gracious and pious prince was so far fr[om] seeking the destruction of any such aspirer, or so mu[ch as the] restraining them, as that he suffered them to live at [liberty] and to possess and enjoy quietly all their honours and p[ossessions] in safety and in peace. And the king might safely a*llow* 45 *them with* security, for he knew that his title [was good, and so strong that he needed] *not* [fear] *a*ny m[éaner titles.

[Yet now his title and right is better than it was, for he is the true and next heir of King Edward III, of all his crowns and kingdoms; so hath he also a title to the crown of Scotland by him, and even that old title of the Balliols. 50

For Edward Balliol, King of Scotland, surrendered all his right and title to
King Edward III)/ in Roxburgh: **Ed[wardus Balliol, Rex] Scotiae [regnum et
coronam Scotiae] transtulit in [Edwardum Regem Angliae litteris suis
patentibus] et authenticis inde confec[tis anno regni sui 33, anno Domini**
5 **1356.]** And thus King Edward III, besides [his most ancient titles from King
Arthur and from] some of the Sax-Angle kings, hi[s title **de jure belli et de
jure gladiis** came also by transaction] and [by purchase] (for he paid a great
sum of m[oney to the said King Edward Balliol) and by] lawful surrender,
to be the more abso[lute and rightful King of Scotland than before.] *And*
10 *this prince* and king, my master, possesseth *by right* the many and all the
royal titles of *all the per*sons descended from the princes of Scotland.

246
Thomas [Walsi]ng-
ham

And when I consider his majesty's justice, so *full of clemency* and
magnanimity, it maketh me to be of opin*ion that if the* young Clarence,
Edward Plantagenet, had been his *subject*, being as he was a man peaceable
15 and loyal, that *the* king would not only have pardoned and redeemed his
life, and *removed* the duke his father's fault and attainder, but also would
have restored *to him* the dukedom of Clarence and his other paternal
signories and *honours.*

[But to] return to King Richard and to answer some more of the
20 objections *made a*gainst him, and who is reputed a tyrant for punishing of
[Jane S]hore, a common and notorious adulteress. And as the Duke of
[Buckingh]am, who knew her very well, censured her, a vile and an
*abomina*ble strumpet. And she deserved so justly to be punished, *and* the
punishment which was inflicted upon her was rather [favour]able than
25 severe, and savoured more of clemency than of rigour [or t]yranny. For by
the sacred and most authentic law, such offen*ders* were to be punished with
death. And in this punishment the king showed not obscurely that *he hate*d
and abhorred whoredom and adultery, and whereof also he [made an]other
famous overture when he declared by public [proclamatio]n the foul
30 incontinency and palliardise of Thomas Gray, Marquess of Dorset, [in these
w]ords: **Thomas Gray, late Marquess of Dorset, [not fearing G]od nor
regarding the peril of his soul, hath devoured and [deflower]ed many
maidens, widows, and wives, and holding t[he unshameful and mis-
chievous] w[oma]n, Shore's wife, in adultery.**

[Jane Shore]

35 [Then the death, the execution of William Colingbourne is censured
another tyranny, because (as some trivial romancers chant) he was hanged
for making a satirical or railing rhyme, when the truth is he was arraigned]
for some treasons or *libels* [and] condemned of High [Treason, as it may be
yet seen in the record.] And so then this execu[tion was an act of justice, not
40 of] tyranny.

248

[A]nonymus [Juris
pe]ritus in [Ap]ologia
*th*is Richard III.

[Moreover, **Tyrannus est res inimica civibus,**] / **legibus contraria,** as
De[mosthenes well observed. But King] Richard was very loving [and
gracious to his people, and caref]ul to have the laws duly [observed. And his
ma]king many very good laws [was no small argument of that and his love
45 to] law and to justice, and whereof m*ore will be said anon.*

246v

[I*t*, is oberved too that tyrants contemn good counsel and advice] / but
rather con*sult only their own wills.* [For they] *have too* good an opinion of
[their own wisdoms, and] *are* [obstinate to d]etermine all matters by
themselves [without co]nsultation or taking advice. [And these philautists
50 are] called by the Greeks ἰδιοβουλεῦται: self-counsellors. And they say

247v

[Axiomata Politica
cap. 219]

that they are **natura [plerumque occ]ulti et insidiosi, et arte et astu ea tegere [et dissimul]are conantur quae agunt, non communic[antes] quicquid de suis consiliis aut rebus cum aliis, [nec a]b aliis consilium petentes, neque admittentes, sed [tant]um sua consilia sequuntur.** And herein [they err] much. This sentence well showeth, and which is equal to an oracle: 5 **Opti[mus v]ir eget consilio.** And in brief, this other is an axiom of [a] grave and great Christian clerk: **Nullo consilio qui[cquam m]agnae rei aggredi tyrannicum est.**

And now to show that [King] Richard was not obnoxious to this fault, but contrariwise, *he* would do nothing of importance without advice and 10 counse[l of] the wisest and most noble and most expert counsellors. And if in [m]atters of consultation he had declared and delivered his opinion and his judgement as it were resolutely and confidentl[y,] yet then his manner was (as even his adversaries confess) to say in the end and conclusion of his speech, 'My lords, this is my mind, but if any of you know or perceive 15 anything else to be better, I shall be ready to change mine opinion, for I am not wedded to mine own will'.

Now lastly, largition and excessive expenses and prodiga*lity* [have been] thought vices proper to tyrants, and the rather be[cause those tyrants] of the Roman Empire (and whose excesses were so extr[eme that they were call]ed 20 **m[o]nstra et prodigia et l[ues] imperii, pes[tes reipublici,** etc.) were observed to be great prodigals and acolasts in all excess, as Caligula, Nero, Vitellius, Domitian, Commodus, Alagabalus, Caracalla, etc. But King Richard was held to be as frugal as might stand with the honour of a prince.] / And lastly, and in a word, this king wa*s not giv*en to prodigality, nor to 25 palliardise, nor to riots, nor to gluttony, [which be] vices following many tyrants. But he was mo[derate a]nd temperate in all his actions and in all his appetite[s, whic]h is by his enemies confessed, and therefore it needeth [no] *more g*losses.

And thus ye see by that these many acts and notions of *tyra*nt and of 30 tyranny that both the one and the other were unjustly imputed *to* King Richard, because they are not to be found in him. *B*ut I think it had been better for him that he had [been] a tyrant for a while and to have used some tyranny or cruelty for a *while,* [for that had been the preserv]ing of his life and of his kingdom in the other *while. But he did not so because of his* 35 *dis*like of tyranny and his little skill therein, and so little as that knowing no*t even so much* as a stage player: for he can put on the tyrant suddenly and act that part cunningly. *A*nd certainly the ignorance of King Richard in the tyrant's part, or his neglect the*rein to act it accor*dingly in due and needful and fit times, was the *cause of* his ruin and utter overthrow. For if he had 40 *been a tyr*ant or could have played the tyrant when *he ought,* [Bishop Mo]rton, the Marquess of Dorset, and the Earl of Devon and his [brother the bishop,] the Lord Talbot and the Lord Stanley [and his brother] Sir William Stanley, with his wife [the Countess of Ri]chmond, and Hungerford and Giles [Daubeney, Reyno]ld Bray and Parson Urswick, 45 [Dr Lewis and the rest, had met their dooms ere their practices had took head, he having sufficient notice and intelligence of all their plots and agitations;] *and had he dealt with them as with the* / Duke of Buckingham, *he would have been secure, a*nd the success thereof *in their removal* might for many years have so *assured him as to give him as much* happiness as any 50 other *prince. But his cl*emency bred his bane, [not his cr]uelty or tyranny, for that at *least* [had been] his best safeguard and protection.

But this King Richard is also from this violent in*terlude shown to be* a wise prince, and namely for *the love he showed his* people *and the care he*
5 *took to man*age all his studies for the ad*vancement of* some fit and prosperous estate of the king*dom and the peo*ple, and to order his reign and government, which *was all his care,* after the *rebellion, with* clemency and with equity, and to make his *magnanimity and justice* examples to others. And he was resolved to love and honour the clergy and *to revere the* holy
10 church. And when he had made all the good to appear by long e*ffort, he* supposed and presumed th*at their hatred, by h*is good life and good endeavours would abate and q*ualify* the malice of his enemies and reconcile and d*eliver* them and their love to him. And he had good reason to presume and *expect that it would.* But the malice and *long enmity* of the factious and
15 seditious persons *was* grown so great *and to* such extremity, and the traitors so obstinately resolved to r*evolt,* and *neither goo*d example nor good deserts nor fear nor force might prevail nor pres*erve him from t*hese plots.

And although this general revolt and rebellion was sudden, the king was not altogether secur*e in his* cause, nor negligent and careless [of the] manner
20 to encounter and to prevent these mischiefs [and] treasons when hatched. Nor had the conspirators so farf*orth suc*ceeded nor so prevailed if Sir Ralph Ashton had [diligently] and faithfully discharged the trust and service committed to him when the king made him Vice-Constabl[e of England] by *Vice-*Constabular letters patents and gave to him the authority [and power] of the office of the *office*
25 High Constable of Engla[nd, or rather] more and greater, and he gave him full [power] *and* authority to attach any person suspect[ed or guilty] of [Rotul. in domo Con- treason, and to examine him *and* imprison and proceed to justice at his versorum, anno 1 discretion. But it appeareth not that Sir Ralph made proper use of his] Richard III] commission, or did [any service according] to his charge. Fo[r all the 249*
30 conspirators] *went up and* down freely and [enjoyed themselves and liberty] until they joined [with the Earl of Richmond,] *and they* had such success and victory as hath *been recounted here before, and* as all the world knoweth an*d acknowledgeth to be true.*

The virtues and properties of a good king are wisdom, justice, fortitude, [King Richard's
35 bounty, [magnificence,] temperance, and piety. And I do[ubt not] to find virtues] here that these royal virtues, and proper to *sovereignty, were in the heart* and mind of this *defamed* King Richard, and by him put in practice and in execution in the *government of his kingdom.* But also that they were fairly *applied, and there is no doub*t that he was endowed with wisdom and
40 *prude*nce and skill, especially in those arts which he more properly professed, the *conduct and dealing* in politic affairs, that mad*e itself* *mani*fest in the judgement and pr[udence] in the wise and provident managing and ord*ering* not only of his own private affairs, but [als]o in the administration and government of [the p]ublic business and affairs of state,
45 and in the m[ilitary] *counse*l when he was a subject, as afterward when he was a *sovereign* and a king. And I shall not need to demons*trate* this assertion with testimonies and autho*rities,* because his adversaries and calumniators [confes]s that he was a very wise and a prudent and [politi]c [Justice Shelly com- and an heroical prince. mendeth the laws of
50 And moreover, this wisdom, together with his justice, appeared very King Richard III to

Cardinal Wolsey.
Vide John Stow, in
Henry VIII, p. 882.]

plainly and beautifully in the good] laws which he caused to be made and *in
their number* and quality. He made so many as ever *did any king* whose
reign was so short. And *this* [hath been acknowledg]ed and also honourably
[predicated by our reverend and most learned professors of the laws. For his
farther knowledge and love of justice there can be no fairer argument than] 5

249v
Chron[icle] MS. [in
quarto] apud R.
Cotton

his desire and [custom to sit in court of justice] and to hear the [causes of
his subjects with an] *in*different ear, and [distributing justice] *equally* to all
men. And when [he made his progress in]to Yorkshire, and being
[informed there were some] extortioners and other foul and notorious
[offenders apprehended and] not tried, he caused *the punishment* due by 10
law to be inflic*ted on them.* Before this, he gave strict [charge and
command]ment to the judges and justicers and [to all officer]s of justice, as
well of the greater a*s of the lesser* nobility, to do justice to all men
indifferen*tly in the* circuits and in their courts and counties, and in every
place of jurisdiction and through t*he* re*a*lm.   15

And as concerning his clemency and his gentlene*ss and* mercy I have
spoken already, and some things *have I said of his* piety, and more anon.

The fortitude and magnanimity of this prince, [though] he was but of
small and low body, yet they were [so great] and so famous as they need no
testimony and [precony.] *The princi*pal reason hereof was *that* he was from 20
his youth bred in arms and in [martial] actions, and (as I have related
before) he was a*n* actor in many conflicts and in many battles, as in the
battles of Barnet, of Exham, of Donca[ster,] the second of St Albans, of
Tewkesbury, etc. And h*e so* valiantly and so skilfully bore himself in a*ll these
martial* and warlike affairs as that he won the *honour* and high reputation 25
of an excellent soldier and of a *valiant cap*tain. And being made General of
the king's [armies into] Scotland, he prevailed happily in this e[xpedition,]
and particularly, recovered that famous [and strong] frontier town of
Berwick, th*e* [which King Henry VI] had so [weakly let go. And in this you
shall hear the eulogy of his adversary, one that was loath to speak much in 30
his favour, yet occasion forced him to speak his knowledge, though coldly

251*

and sparingly, who of his valour,] / magn[animity, and bounty] *thus* writeth:
**King Richar[d was no ill captain in the war.] He had sundry victories [and
sometimes overthrows, but] never by his own default, [for want of hardiness**

[Dr Mo]rton
[Sir Thomas M]ore

or poli]tic order. [Whereunto he addeth, concerning his bounty,] **Free [was** 35
he called of dispense, and libera]l somewhat above his [power. These be the
words o]f More and Morton, f[or their books are all one

[In Parliament anno
1 [Richard III]

[To which I w]ill add one more such eulogy or testi*mony*, [above all] for
credit and authority, and [recorded in Act of Parliament, and it was addressed
to him [in the name of] the whole high court of Parliament, in these words: 40
**We consider your great wit, pruden[ce, justic]e, and courage, and we know
by experience th[e memora]ble and laudable acts done by you in divers
[battles] for the salvation and defence of the realm.**

[Her]e followeth another memorable and general testimony of the su*ndry*
endowments and virtues of this prince, and it is the more to be [regard]ed 45
because it was made and propounded by one which had known [him from]
his youth and had held much and long familiarity [with him, which was] the
foresaid Duke of Buckingham, who, after that Richard was made king and
that this duke was become ill affected and malcontent [for his] repulses
which he suffered in his suits (as declared), yet notwithstanding he 50
acknowledged and confessed to Bishop Morton in private speeches between

them that he thought King Richard from his first knowledge even until that
time a man clear without dissimulation, tractable and without injury, and
that for these [respects, and love] of King Richard's good disposition, he was
[very desirous to] advance him, and laboured earnestly to make him
5 [protector. The]se be the words of Dr Morton, and [reported by Sir Thomas
More. T]herefore, whatsoe[ver the duke said after in reproach of the king,
it may justly be thought to proceed from spleen and malice.

[And there is to this another commendation added, and that is of his
eloquence and pithy, witty, pleasing] speech and the which, [though it be no
10 royal virtue, yet it is an] ornament to [the greatest] princes, [and a gift]
commendable and [gracious in any. You] / shall hear this eulogy of their eloquence delivered by [the Prior of Croyland, who, rep]eating the debating of
a [controversy bet]ween the two brothe[rs, George, Duke of Clarence, and
this] Richard, Duke of Glo[ucester] *in the* [council] *cha*mber before the king
15 th[eir brother, sitting] then in his chair of estate. *Thus he saith of* the
eloquent and grave arguing *of* these two brothers: **[Pos]t suscitatas inter
duces fratres discordias, [tot u]trimque rationes acutissime allegatae sunt in
prae[sentia r]egis (sedentis pro tribunali in Camera Consilii) [quod] omnes
circumstantes, etiam periti legum eam [rationis] abundantiam ipsis
20 principibus in suis prop[riis causis] adesse mirabantur,** etc. And this author,
then speaking of the excellent wit an[d] of the rare gifts of all the three
brothe[rs,] maketh this honourable precony th[ereof:] **Hi tres germani, rex
et duo duces, tam ex[cellenti] ingenio valebant, ut si discordare non
vo[luissent] funiculus ille triplex difficillime rumpere[tur.]**
25 And now I will derive some testimonies of th[is king's] virtues from his
good works and from his *honourable* and charitable and magnificent and
profitable and piou*s and* religious works and monuments. And as for
[example]:

This King Richard founded a collegiat[e church of] priests at Middleham
30 in Yorkshire.

Item: He founded another college of p[riests in London in] Tower Street,
near [to the church called Our Lady of Barking.]

Item: [He built a goodly church or chapel in Towton in Yorkshire, a
monument of his thankfulness to Almighty God for the happy and great
35 victory the king his brother had upon the partisans of the family] / of
Lancaster and [the son of Henry VI, who] before slew Ric[hard, Duke of
York, king designate and] father of the two k[ings] *Edward IV and Richard
III.*

Item: King Richard *III* [founded a college in York,] convenient for the
40 enterta[inment of a hundred priests.]

Item: [For] the good and benefi[t of the people of Oxfordshire and the]
places adjacent, he [deforested a great part of the fo]rest of Wychwood and
[other vast woods between] Woodstock and Bristow.

Item: [He] built the high stone tower at W[estminster, and it i]s a work of
45 good use yet to this day. [And when he] had repaired and fortified the
Castle of Carlisle, he fou[nded and built the Castle of Penrith in
Cumberland.]

Item: [He] manumissed many bondmen.

Item: [Fo]r the better encouragement of the Aesterling [Haunces,] and
50 because their trade was beneficial and [profita]ble to this kingdom, he

[Morton, More, **apud**]
John Stow, p. 77[4]

[**Eloquentia principi-
bus maximo orna-
mento.** Cicero **De
Finibus, Lib.** 4]
251v*

[The praise of the
three princely
brothers]

[The good works of
King Richard]

[John Stow, **Annal.**]

252*

[Poly]dore [**Lib.**25]

[King Richard loved
not Wychwood for
his brother's un-
happy marriage]

granted to them som[e good pr]ivileges (as Polydore Vergil writeth.)

[In Rotul. in Domo
Conversorum, anno
1 R III]

Item: [H]e also first founded the College and Society of [Hera]lds, and made them a corporation, and as the words in the ch[arter are, he ordained it **ut sint in perpetuum corpus corporatum in re et nomine, habeantur successionem perpetuam,** etc. In which all men may see] a good and 5 commendable testimony of his love to [honour] and of his noble care, and for the conservation *of the m*onuments of nobility and of chivalry and of honour [and gentry.] And this college is of good and honourable and very necessary use for the continuance and preservation of *the ensi*gns and arms of nobility, and of all generous *and gentle persons,* and well-deserving and 10 ennobled for their virtue. And this king established *this* [cor]poration by his royal charter and placed the heralds [in an anci]ent fair house which was called York Inn, some[times] after commonly called Coleharbour, and situate upon the Thames. [And he orda]ined and established four Kings at Arms, and by these names and titles: [John Writh, Garter; Thomas 15 Holme, C]larensius; John Moore, Norway; and Richard Champney, Gloucester. And for Wa[les I have the charter wherewith the k]ing created first [Rich]ard Champney, Esquire, King at [Arms by the title and name of Gloucester, dated in the mon]th of March, when the charter [of the foundation was granted.   20

[And he further established that these four Kings of Arms and the rest of the heralds, who are in the charter called **Heraldi et Prosecutores, sive Pursueandi,** should lodge, live, and common together in that house] *with* [the rolls, monuments, and writings appertaining to the art of heraldry] *and*

252v*

of armory. And *he gave* [also certain lands and t]enements for the 25 perpetual maintaining of a chap]lain or chantry priest [to say and sing divine serv]ice every day [and to pray for the] *prosper*ity of the king and [queen and] *for the p*rince their son, and *for* [their souls when t]hey were dead. La[stly, he gave sundry] good privileges an[d immunities to the said] corporation and coll*ege, and this s*ame charter [was] kept continually in the 30 office of the h*eralds* [unt]il within these few years. But now it is no *longer*

[Mr] *Ralph* [Brooke,
York Herald at
Arms]

there, but I know where it is and I have seen it. And the lack of it [importeth nothing, being] the duplicate of it is in records [in the archives] and [the Convert] House, now called the Rolls. And this charter was confirmed [by the Parliament and dated **ii die Martii,**] **anno regni primo, apud** 35 **Westminster.** Barowe. [And underneath was written, **Per breve de privato sigillo, de datu praedicta auctoritate Parliamenti.**]

And moreo[ver,] *King* Richard III built or repaired some parts [of the] Tower of London toward the Thames, and in memory *and* token thereof there be yet his arms, impal[ed with] those of the queen, standing upon the 40 ar[ch adjo]ining to the sluice gate.

Lastly, this king began many other good wor[ks] *which* miscarried by his untimely death, as Polydore Ve*rgil* [thus] witnesseth: **Ricardus tertius multa opera p[ublica] et privata inchoavit, quae, immatura mo[rte prae]reptus, non perfecit.** And these good, magnific*ent works* be not the [acts] of the 45 minds of tyrants nor of any wicked princes, *but of virtuous* and religious princes, as all indifferent and sensible men will judge and confess. [And Polydore] Vergil (being neither of the House [of York] nor of Lancaster, but only an honest man) write[th in the] same book much in the commendation of his [piety and] of his charitable disposition, and 50

whereunto for brevity I [refer the readers and put it to their indifferent judgements.] I would desire these men which give to this King Richard III the *name of tyrant to judge* [how many good kings have exceeded him in such good, charitable, and magnificent deeds in their much longer and
5 prosperous time of government, being in quiet possession, too, of their crowns and kingdoms.]

And though I have given testimony / and proof of the *virtue and piety* of this prince, yet th*ere is* [one thing more,] the which I may not om*it* [of him, promised before,] *and the good* will therein showed c*andour and truth and*
10 *is* a corollary of the honour[s and commendation made by a stranger, and one that had] sometimes more caus[e to dislik]e him than to lo[ve him; for King Richard, not long] before, and oftentimes, had [stuck upon his friends and made] spoils in his country. [Therefore, it can be thought no flattery or partiality in him] *that he* hath spok*en and sai*d favourably of this kingdom,
15 but *true report*.

And the man by nation was a Scot, and *he spoke truly* and out of his good knowledge, and for the *Scots were* thought not apt to give to Englishmen more *prai*se than was due. This man also was a wise man and well [experien]ced and acquainted with the affairs of state of [divers] countries,
20 and knew the princes and chief persons [in them,] by reason he had been employed to foreign prince[s] *in serving* his master, James IV, King of Scotland. [And] *he* [knew] King Richard well, and the Duke of [York, hi]s father, and was with him in Ireland when [he was] Lieutenant of that kingdom. And above this, *he was* a priest and a spiritual man: that is a
25 special *professor of* truth. And he was of the king's Privy [Counci]l and Chief Secretary, and one of the [honourab]le commissioners which were sent by King James *of Scot*land into England to King Richard [III to t]reat of the making and concluding of a [p]eace and of making and contracting [a mar]riage betwixt James the prince, eldest [son o]f the king, and the Lady
30 Anne, daughter [of John de] la Pole, Duke of Suffolk, as hath been *related*.

[An]d this worthy prelate, and by name [Archibald Quh]itlaw, being to make the oration [for the] more solemn proposition of the[ir legation before the king, and publicly, amongst other things, his illustrations gave much to the praise of military art and chivalry, still reflecting the period of that
35 praise and honour to the king.] *And the speeches of the Archbishop are* good and exact *and made by a* worthy and *pious man. And I* / *have thought* good *to collect these, and* also *the* speeches of the king *in reply to this oration,* and to present them *to the judgement of the R*eader. And here these follow:

40   [Serenissime Princeps: Una me res consolat]ur, et iuvat
            tua scilicet in [omni virtutis genere celeberrim]a fama per
            omnem orbis terraru[m ambitum disseminata,] tuae etiam
            innatae benignitatis c[arissima prae]stansque humanitas,
            tua mansuetudo, libera[litas, fides, su]mma iustitia,
45   incredibilis animi magnitudo, tua [non humana sed]
            paene divina sapientia, quibus te non modo s[ingulis]
            facilem verum vulgo et popularibus affabilem pr[aebes,
            et] quibus virtutibus, altaque prudentia, cuncta et
            pron[unciata] et dicta in meliora commutas.
50   Serenissimus Princeps, Rex Scotorum, dominus me[us,

253*

253v*

[Pacem et uxore nep-
tem Regis petiti]

qui te] alto amore prosequitur et desiderat, tuam
ami[citiam et affinitatem affectat super captum [cogita-
tionis] meae. Si quid a me erratum erit, tuis id divinis
vir[tutibus,] quibus commercium cum caelestibus
numinibus et [societatem,] contraxeris, tribuendum   5
putato. Faciem tuam summo imperio et principatu

[Ricardo fu]it [stat-
ura parva]

dig[nam inspicio,] quam moralis et heroica virtus
illustrat: de [te dici] praedicerique potest quod Thebanum
principi [inclutissi]mo Statius poeta his verbis attribuit:
　　Numquam tantum animum natura minori   10
　　corpore, nec tantas nisa est includere vir[es.]
Maior in exiguo regnabat corpore virtu[s.]
　　In te enim sunt rei militaris virtus, peritia [felicitas et]
auctoritas, quae omnia in optimo exercitu[s principe
Cicero] requirit. In te, Serenissime P[rinceps, praeclari   15
regis,] et imperatori praecepta ita concurrunt, ut nihil ad
tuam bellicam aut domesticam virtutem cuiusquam
oratoris verbis apponi possit. Tu igitur, Serenissime
Domine et Princeps, de ineunda inter te et nostrum
principem caritate et amicitia sic age, ut Angli et Scoti dilec   20
tionis respectu nullum penitus discrimen habeatur, sed in

254*

unum amoris et benevolentiae vinculum] / videantur esse
conn[exi. Sic innumerabiles commoditates ex tui et] nostri
populi dilect[ionis unione dulci, connubio, matrimonio,
et] affinitate, consurg[ent.]   25
　　In freta dum fluvii cu[rrent dum montibus imbres,]
　　sint arati convexa, polus [dum sidera pascet,
　　dum iug]a montis aper fl[uvios dum piscis amabit,
　　dumque] Thymo pascentur [apes dum rore cicadae,
　　semper ho]nos nomenque tuum laud[esque manebunt.]   30
　　[Thus t]his grave and learned and ing[enious Scottishman] *has given*
noble testimonies of the good parts *of King* Richard, and to the shame and
reproach of *all those* men which contrariwise have raised so *many scandals*
and reproachful tales and taxes o*f him. And these* have not been satisfied to
traduce and depra*ve the a*ctions of his life, but have also found a *way* how 35
to put in practice and to exercise their *malice* upon him after his death, as I
partly showed before, *and which I shall a* little amplify here. For these
spiteful persons, and in the same kind *and manner,* retrieved another crime

[To be slain in the
wars is no evil or un-
happy death]

and the *punishm*ent thereof in his death and after his death. *And that is*
when they make the catastrophe or last [tragical] act of his life, and the 40
manner of his cruel slaughter *to be a m*anifest declaration of the divine
wrath, enkindled [for] his offences and tyrannies and against his sins, and
to be as a present purgatory *or incor*poral chastisement for them. And
therefore, they inchantally infer that in due *recompense* of those his
manifold and excessive *crimes,* God brought him to that just, miserable, 45
and *tragical* end at Bosworth.
　　These speeches and *censures, a*lthough they be sharp and peremptory *and
un*christianlike, yet they might be tolerated *in certain per*sons, viz., in
superstitious clerks and [in women,] *and such as there* be who are enemies
to [fighting and bloodshed.] But if the malice of [Bishop Morton and 50

Chancellor More (although they were men of the long robe) had not much
blinded their knowledge in these affairs, considering with whom they
conversed] / and where they [most lived, they could not have been
ign]orant that for a martial and heroical person to die] in a battle and [war,
5 and fighting valiantly for his country] and for his life and [friends was
always held] to be a glorious bidding [farewell to the world.

[And what simple man knowe]th not that infinite [numbers of virtuous
and most noble] *and* very honourable [captains have been slain] in the wars?
And in brief, Lampridus [affirmed that all the best men have died by violent
10 deaths. And no prince nor other heroical] person could adventure his *life* [in
a better] quarrel than King Richard did, *who undertook* to fight for his
crown and kingd[om and all] his happy worldly fortunes and al*l his
subjects.* [He was also,] according to the charge of his high **justitiaria,** and
his office and sovereign ob[ligation, t]o take vengeance upon murderers and
15 rebels and trai[tors,] *who* are hateful to God and to all good men.

[Optimos quosque
violenta morte con-
sumptos esse osten-
dit. Lampridus in
Alexandro Sev.]

Wherefore there must some better consideratio[n] *be made* of the cause
of the prince's slaughter and bloody death, for *he may* not be said to have
been punished as a tyra*nt, for he* was no tyrant, as I demonstrated bef*ore,*
but a good king, and did no act of a ty*rant all* the time of his reign. Neither
20 may it be said that he *was dishonoured by* the battle, because that is an
honourable death, **ut supra.** And it [hath] been seen very often in this world
that [God hath taken] away good and godly and just princes in the field and
[elsewhere] for *the transgressions* and iniquities of the people, and whom
God *deems* in His divine judgement to be utterly unwor*thy of a* good and
25 virtuous king. And being minded to punish them, *he* suffereth them *to fall*
into the hands of a prince who will mo*rtify and* punish them, and scourge
them with rods for their wickedness and for their ingrate*fulness.*

And hereof we have many examples, as *well in* Holy Scripture as also in
sundry te*stimonies,* as namely of King Josiah, and great and *horrible crimes*
30 of Ti*berius the* Emperor. And here in England, ********************* .

[Therefore I see no reason why the cause of King Richard's death should
not be favourably interpreted, or at the least held in an indifferent scale
until it be safe to enquire further after it. And he that owes him no malice
(all things considered with charity and justice) will confess] *that he* / was a
35 good king and *that he died in a* just quarrel, and in the *Battle of Bos*wo*rth,*
22 August, **Anno Domini** *1485,* [when he] had reigned two years and five
m[onths, account]ing his protectorship, which is a king*ship,* [abou]t the
thirty-seventh year of his age, and he *might have live*d as many more years
by the course *of nat*ure, and haply for the great good of the *kingdom,* if it
40 had stood with divine providence.

255*

[Las]tly, I will crave leave to tell them who [cen]sure the lives of men by
the manners of *their* [dea]th that many of the enemies of King [Richar]d
had worse deaths, having their [throat]s cut by the reprobate and most vile
crea*ture,* the hangman, as namely the Duke of *Bucking*ham, Sir William
45 Stanley, and Sir *Thomas* More himself, and many others. [And th]ere is no
man who in *him* hath any Christian [charity] or but a reasonable pittance or
portion [of humani]ty who will judge a man's life by his [death,
con]sidering that very many good and [holy men,] even the best men, have
suffered the *most* [shameful] deaths. Witness the most *virtuous man* that
50 ever was, our blessed *Saviour, who suffered crucifixion.*

254v*

255v*

[And although this prince was not so superlative to assume the name of holy or best, you see him a wise, magnificent,] / and a valiant man, *and a* [just,] bountiful, [and temperate;] *and* an eloquent *and magnanimous and* pious prince; and *a benefactor to the holy* church and to this *realm.* [Yet] for all this, it ha[th] been his [fortun]e to be aspersed and fouled *and* to fall 5 into this *malice of those who have* been ill-affected *towards him* and who have be*en ready* to plunge and *vilify* his fame and good name and *noble* memory in their blackest and Stygi*an* *r*eproaches and calumnies, and in th*is* *mali*gn and injurious kind they have r*ailed* more vehemently and more dispitefully *against* *t*his king than against any other, albeit [many] of those 10 kings were not endowed w*ith* good parts and with so many virtues as he, *but* rather and contrariwise were more vic*ious and* more blameworthy than he, and com[mitted more public] evil and more crimes than he; and th*is* *is* manifest and well proved, and wherea*s* [his] crimes are for the most part but suspected, *but* never proved and made known, as I *have* intimated and 15 approved in several passages of this *work* and confuted the accusations.

256*

And the gre[atest] fault whereof he is suspected or conv*icted* and presumptively accused / is for [the re]moving the Prince Edward out of his way. And yet that fault hath be[en] *freely* and usually committed by many other prin*ces,* [and yet] they are thought brave and magn*animous and* 20 glorious princes. For the [ambitious great ones who desire sovereignty and affect empire, having means and power to advance] *and to ac*/complish and attain to th[eir designs] *spare not* brother nor sister no[r nephew] *nor* [niece,] nor any person if he ha*th a kingdom* before him or else after the *kingdom is in* his possession. And in this *regard ambition impels* them to 25 *repudiate* faith and *justice for the possession of a* kingdom.

And *they have a* [rule for i]t, and this it is:

[Euripides in Phoenisses]

[Εἴπερ γὰρ] ἀδικεῖν χρή, τυραν[νίδος πέρι Κάλλιστον] ἀδικεῖν, τὸ ἀλλὰ εὐσ[εβεῖν χρεών.]

Th]us verbatim in Latin: 30
[si iniu]ste agere oportet, pro tyrannide (aut re[gno) pulch]errimum est iniuste agere, in aliis pietatem [colere] expedit. [But Juliu]s Caesar, having long in purpose to make use [of this doctr]ine, translated it better to his

[Cicero, Lib.3, **De Officiis, et** Suetonius in Julio]

purpose, and in this manner, as Cicero relates: **[Si viola]ndum est ius, regnandi gratia [violan]dum est; aliis rebus pietatem colas.** And thus in 35 English:

[If right fo]r aught may ere be violate,
[It must] be only for a sovereign state.
[And Antonius Car]acalla alleged this text for the justifying [the killing] of Geta, his brother and his colleague and partner of [empire with him.] 40

Euripides is the most ancient recorder of this sentence, but the [au]thor is more ancient than Euripides, or than he [whom he maketh to spea]k this speech, namely Eteocles, and is [even as an]cient as Lucifer. But this ambitious Eteocles, [affecting] the kingdom of Thebes, usurped this sentence [and put it] in practice, and as many other aspirers have [done.] 45 *A*nd the said Julius Caesar had it often in his [mouth, and] gave such authority to it as both his acts [and also Cicer]o and Suetonius witness. And he held *murder in such c*ase but one and a chief of these arts which are called

[Vide Lib. 1]

artes imperandi or **artes regiae.** [And if it be an offence,] it is a princely

offence. It is **crimen sacrum [vel crimen regale,** or **crimen] sacri
ambitio.** And it is so highly privile[ged that it is not punishable by] human
laws, at the [least if that imperial axiom be infallible: **Princeps est solutus**   [Ulpian]
legibus — which some great clerks approve, or else the reign of princes is
5 miserable, as it was told to King Atreus: **Ubicumque tantum honesta**   [Seneca in **Thyeste**]
dominanti licent, precario regnatur. And Polyneices, the brother of
Eteocles, was of the same religion, for he said a kingdom could not be
bought at too high a rate; that he would give the lives of his best friends
and] / burn his nearest kinsfolks, [his wife and all his riches for a kingdom.]   256v*
10   And besides the *case of these Thebans and of* Julius Caesar, *there might*   [Imperium quolibet
many other examples of this proud principle afore*mentioned be added* out   pretio emptum vili
of foreign stories [Greek and Latin] *and others*, frequent mention of [such   tamen constat. Poly-
offences] *and of such* causes and motives as before *were seen in these*   neices apud Euri-
examples, and here *also we find* unjust as*saults upon the* rightful heirs, but   pidem in Thebaide.]
15 [by men who had better wits, higher] courages, prouder hearts, and sha[rper
swords than those princes which] had the true and bes[t titles.] *And they*
*appli*ed their haughty and *proud hearts to all* perils and obtained the
garland, a*nd they usurp*ed the kingdom or principality *which they had*
*conquer*ed and had won by force or fraud. And they and their post[ers]
20 reigned *over their* princely purchases, and happily, and they have been
accounted [lawful and] worthy princes.
    But I will leave these fo[reign and] exotic precedents, and I will bring
d[omestical] examples, and those of English princes (because the prese[nt
cause and question] *requires them*) and who, h[aving no] better titles than
25 their swords and their ambition ga*ve them* have imitated these foreign
princes in their affectation of sovereignty and of *ambi*tion, and with as
good success as they.
    And I will begin with King Henry [I,] the good clerk and learned prince,   [King Henry I]
but a*s* [covetous] and as ambitious as any ignorant *and unlearned* and bad
30 *commoner, though* of good letters. And he was not content to usurp here in
[this kingdom] of England the right and privilege of the *inheritance* and of
the primogeniture of his eldest brother, [Robert Courtheuse, but also by
force took the D[uchy] of Normandy from him, and to make his [injuries]
the more complete and his crime m*ore* [monstrous,] he put his brother in the
35 Castle of G[loucester and] kept him there in hard and cruel durance, and
put out his eyes, [and with his tyrannies] wearied and tired and [consumed
him till he died most miserably.
    [King John is likewise by the general voice charged with the murder of   [King John]
Arthur Plantagenet, the son of his eldest brother, and so the next prince, in
40 right of blood, to succeed King Richard I,] *and* / so got wrongfully the   257*
possessi*on of the crown.*
    Item: It is written [that King Edward] III was not only pri[vy and   [King Edward III]
consenting to the deposing] of the king his fathe[r, a king anointed, but
also] to his massacre. And because [Edmund Plantagenet, Earl of Kent,
45 Protector, and his uncle, moved him to restore the crown to his] father,
King Edward [II, he called him traitor and cut off his head at Winchester.
    [Now King Henry IV caused Richard II,] his king, another anointed
[king, to be cruelly] butchered at Pom[fret; and this was] **scelera sceleribus**   [Seneca, De
tueri.   Clementia]
50   [King] Edward IV is accuse[d of the murder and death of the king St

Harry, and of the Princ]e of Wales, his son, **ut supra.**

*And in order the*reof King Henry VII is next, and he m[ust have a] place in this catalogue, alth[ough] a very good king. But he was not innocent [nor guilt]less of that **crimen sacrum vel regale,** which adventureth to *destroy princes with better titles.* For he, as you [hear]d before, cut off the head of 5 Edward [Plantagenet, Earl of Warwick, an innocent: **Edwardum filium ducis Cl[arensi purum et insontem] in [suam et suorum securi]ta[tem capite plexit.**] H[e was the] son and heir [of the D]uke of Clarence, and then the chief of the House of [York (un]less Perkin Warbeck may be taken [for Richard,] Duke of York, as he must.) And then he must be the *first prince* 10 of the blood royal of England, and *heir ap*parent of the crown. But all is one. For by the malice of the [Cardinal instigating the king, they were both dispatch]ed, as hath been before declared. And it hath been all one with them whether they [had been] both counterfeits and impos[ters or true princes] of the blood royal. For princes acknowledge no man to have a better 15 title than [their own,] if they be in poss[ession. And I] do verily believe that if this King [Henry VII had confessed or] certainly known that Perkin had *been* [the second] son of King Edward IV (as he [knew hims]elf to be the grandchild of that [famous Owen] Tudor) yet he would not have [resigne]d the crown and sceptre, [so dear and sweet an enchantment is in the name, 20 much more in the possession of empire. But he left not thus, nor was secure of his estate whilst he lived, therefore proceeded to subtle and sharp forms of policy to establish his own and prevent] *the urging by others* / of all claims, bec*ause his own was weak.*

[Amongst other, his practice] with Philip of Aust[ria, Duke of Burgundy, 25 King of Castile and of A]ragon is very mem[orable. This Prince Philip was by cross fortune] put into the king's hands *who* [out of Flanders took shipping at sluis,] purposed *and* resolted to go [into Spain with the queen his wife. And passing by the coasts] of England, he w[as by a tempest forced, for his safety, to put into] the port of Weym[outh in Dorsetshire. 30 And the queen being ill and distempere]d much with the stor]m, he was compelled to make some stay] *at* Weymouth for the refreshing *of his company.*

[In the meantime,] Sir John Carew and Sir Thomas [Trenchard, principal men and magist]rates of those parts, gave advertisement to the king *of the* 35 *arrival of the s*aid duke and of the queen his wife in th*e port of Weymouth.* The king was glad of this news, and he straight pu[rposed to make good us]e of this their misadventure, and he forthwith sent to those [knights] *and commanded* them first to give all honourable entertainment to the du*ke and his wife* and to all his train, and next that they should not suffer [them 40 depart] until he had seen and saluted them.

The duke, as soon [as his queen *w*as well and all his company well refreshed, thanked these knights [for the honourable] courtesies which they had done to him, and told them that he *would set* sail and be going on his journey into Spain. And he bid them *farewell.* [But] they earnestly desired 45 him to stay, bec*a*use they were advised *by* [the king] *t*hat he greatly desired to see him and the queen. This motion [was distasteful] to the duke, and he pressed much to depart with their favour, but [there was no] remedy but he must stay, and also ride to Windsor, where the [king would me]et him and bid him most heartily and royally welcome.   50

[King Edward IV]
[King Henry VIII]

[Gul. Camden in
Britan. et Cornav.]

258

[Grafton, Holinshed]

[Historia de Curita
et Garibus]

And thither th[e duke went,] much against his will (for this entreaty was somewhat imperious) [and there] *the king* received him and the queen in all magnificent and princely manner. *And* [the king propou]nded a suit to the duke, and that was that he would deliver [into his hands] Edmund de la
5 Pole, a pretender of title to the crown of England, [and] disloyal to him, and who was then lurking in the duke's [dominions.] This suit seemed strange and unreasonable to the duke, and therefore *he would fain be requesting* the king not to desire such a dishonourable thing of him. And the *deed was not only a base* and a reproachful thing for him to do, but also a
10 dero[gation from all princely] prerogative and privilege of his sovereignty, whereby he as other [princes had power to receive and] to protect such distressed noble persons [as did appeal to their] faith and [tui]tion, and that to perform his requ*irement* was [to violate **ius gentium et sacro sanctam hospitii fidem.** For to deliver any oppressed by fortune, malice, or envy,
15 and flying under another prince's wings for favour and protection, was to betray them into the hands of their enemies and utter ruin.]

*And the king so wrought that thus shoul*d be betrayed the noble   258v
gentleman Edmund de la Pole and that in this ma*nner* his patron and defender should *be the oc*casion and instrument *of his death. And* the duke
20 pleaded for his *safety and his life. But this* was all in vain, for no argu*ment was o*f any weight. *But fo*rthwith *he must deliver up* Edmund de la Po*le, or he must stay here* still. When the duke s*aw* [the obstinate resolution of the king,] *and discov*ered in what danger *he was and into what* [extreme disadvantag]es *he* was fallen, he told the king th*at* [if he would accept and
25 perform some] honourable [condi]tions which he would offer, that then h[e would take order to send] *Edmund* de la Pole hence to him into England. And the [conditions were that the] king should not use the young gentleman rigorously, *and that he was no*t to lay any punishment upon him, and in no case to p[ut him to dea]th. The king promised solemnly, and bound himself
30 in a[ll the s]trait bonds of honour and of religion to observe those con*ditions and* covenants aforesaid.

And the duke sent this noble and unhappy de la Pole [into England,] and the king received him and committed him to the Tower. But when he lay a-dying, he finely frustrated his prom*ise* to the Duke of Burgundy by a kind
35 of sophistical equivocation: for his part, he would keep his promise and not put Edmund de la Pole to death, [but by a mental reservation desti]nated de la Pole to death. And that was when he was dead, the prince his son and heir should cut off the head of th*is* [young man.] *And o*f this business and butchery he gave charge to the said prince, and the prince fulfilled his
40 fath[er's charge so soon as] he was king. But this could not be without taint of dishonour and of perfidious*ness in the* king the father, nor of tyranny in the king the son.

The son held himself both ac[quitted and also] warranted by the example of King Solomon, the son [of] David, who was made the instrument of such
45 a subtle and perfidious s[laughter.] And David also helped himself by the   259
virtue of equivoca[tion, which ought not to be follo]/wed by any Christian prince. For this was a sin, and [sins are to be] shunned and not to be imitated.

[But let us] look a little further into the miserable estate of those *of* [the
50 family d]e la Pole, descended from the royal Plantagenets of [York.] *And* (as

259v

[Grafton]

[Polydore, **Lib.**4]

[Although the Lady
Anne and the Lady
Catharine were well
married, that may
not be alleged here,
for they were be-
stowed in the time of
Richard III, the one
to the Lord Howard,
after the Duke of
Norfolk, the other to
the Earl of Devon.
Robert Glover.]

[Grafton, Gainsford]

[Thomas Gainsford]

[Joel, **Cap.** I]

260

[**Dominus** Johannes,
Baron Lumley, **viva
voce**]

it seemeth) this Prince Henry VII was not willingly and malicious*ly, as it* were, [their **malus genius,**] as it may appear by this example. The eldest brother of these de la Poles, [John de la Pole, heir to the Duke of Suffolk, and the h]ead of this noble family, was slain cas[ually in the Battle of Stoke, being fought for this king. This is he who, being nearest kinsman to King 5 Richard III, was proclaimed heir apparent. And the sister of these princely de la Poles, the Lady Catharine, was kept close prison]/er in [the Tower until grief and sorrow set both her soul and body at liberty.

[Nor is it much from this purpose to note that] the chief Plantagenets, [namely, the children of King Edward IV, were littl]e regarded or favoured 10 th[en. For the Lady] Bridget was thrust into [a nunnery at Dartford, chiefly, as it was] thought, because she might [live sterile and die without issue. Th]e Lady Cecily was [worse] bestowed, for she was [married to a base fellow,] that so her iss[ue might be ignoble and contemptible, and her] wrong therein [was the greater, in regard she might have been matched 15 according to her] degree and quality. And [the King of Scotland] *sought her to be the* wife of the Prince James, his [son. The French king Lewis also demande]d her for the spouse of the Dauph[in, Charles of France.

[It was observed too] that this king was but an unkind and s[evere husband to the Lady El]izabeth, the queen his wife. And they all had b[ut 20 short lives. It is] reported in our stories that he picked a quarrel [with the Queen Dow]ager, his mother-alliée, for an old and a venial er[ror,] and because she delivered her son Richard to the Lord Pro[tector. And for t]his there was a sentence of confiscation of all her goods, [chattels, and revenues,] and she was confined as a prisoner to Berm[ondsey Abbey,] and 25 where she lived, and not long, but very sorrowfully, and *full* of care and grief.

And the bastard of Gloucester was sud[denly and secretly] made away about the time that Perkin and young Clar[ence suffered.]

And therefore, to my seeing, it was well observed and s*aid* [by a lear]ned 30 gentleman, and yet living, that it was a fatal time to them, for it rid them *and deprived* them of their liberties and also of their fortunes and of the*ir lives.* And this prince showed himself to be of the House [of Lancaster] in nothing so much as in his hatred and cruel dealing *with the members* of the House of York and with their kinsfolks and best friends. And when he was 35 gone and had bidden farewell to the [glories of this] world and to the policies and practices thereof, and so could *unburden his* heart, then came his heir and supplied his room and office. And th[en **Residuum lo]custae bruchus comedit, et residuum br[uchi comedit rubigo.** For he utterly] con*founded and* [made an end of the remainder of the House of York, and 40 besides the putting] / to death of the for[esaid Edmund de la Pole, he caused] the Lady Margaret [Plantagenet, Countess of Salisbury, and the daughter] and heir of th*e* [Duke of Clarence to be attainted of treason] by Act of P[arliament, and contrary to justice to be condemned unheard.] *And she* was dragged [to the block very barba]rously, and being th*en* [above 45 three-score years in age, **anno** 33 Henry VIII.

[And] Sir Henry Pole, her [eldest son, was also soon after] put to death. And her [son Reynold Pole was attainted o]f treason with her, but no m*ore harm befell him, beca*use, as it seemeth, it was *forbidden of God, and* Divine Providence so safeguarded him [that he was] conveyed secretly and 50 suddenly out of the king[dom, and wen]t [highly renowned for his le]arning and for his piety and for his other truly noble and *truly* [Christian] virtues. But all they could not have saved his life *if he had* not fled hence.

5   **Item:** Richard Pole, anoth[er son of] this Countess of Salisbury, was fain to fly [and live a]s a banished man in foreign countries, and with good [reputati]on until he was slain at the Battle of Pavia. *And by that* honourable dispatch he escaped the English hangman's ha*nds.* [And this was the last act of the] catastrophe of the violent and turbulent trag[edy of

10   York.]
     And to conclude, these great wrongs and bloody prose*cutions* were not crimes of suspicion only, as these *of King* Richard's were. But these cruel acts were and are most *widely* known, and were very manifest and clear. And **velit quod non fuit dictum, et scriptum calum*niæ* gratia et privileg*ii*.**

15   *But we* must be wary and sparing in the relation of matters of this kind, because they are not everywhere agreeable and current and plausible generally, as also because I had no purpo*se to condemn* the faults of any princes.   Neither have I so done but where the defence of *King Richard and* the necessity of the cause drew me into it and extracted such a style and

20   *relation of the* crimes of *princes who destroyed those with better titles than themselves.*
     [Nor is it strange, nor by me only noted, that] / King Henry VII [had his] faults as well as oth[er princes.] Yet I aver still *that he was a* [good] *and a* wise and a provident and a [religious prince,] and further also that he was

25   the restorer of the ancient lin[e of the British] kings to their reign and kingdom, *and that he* was the nephew of King Henry [VI] by his grandmother, Queen Catharine, [widow of] King Henry V, and mother of King He[nry VI and of his brother uterine, Edmu]nd Tudor, Earl of Richmond, the father of this King Henry VII. [And so he] was nephew also

30   to Charles VII, King [of France,] and that by the Pope's grant and prerogative royal, he was an [offspring of] the House of Lancaster. And besides, I [will ever] say (and to his greatest honour) that h[e was the most] happy grandfather of as noble, as [wise, virtuous, h]/appy and as victorious a queen as ever lived and reigned in the [world.]

35   And lastly, and to declare myself more plainly, I [do not mislike] his having of the crown and his possession of the kingdom, as I have said before that it was foretold by a *divine* prophet that the Earl of Richmond should be a king. And I hold also that he was ordained from above to *be the* sovereign of this land. But (and as I said, **Liber** II) I utterly mislike *that he*

40   *would not* tarry the Lord's leisure and receive a kingdom *in His time;* and that would have been *time enough.*
     [To hasten, then, to the conclusion, I will only by the way, for my promise's sake, say something in answer to the imputation of some defect or break in the titles of the Normans and the princes] / of York, a[lthough

45   there is no need in that] behalf; and *yet there has* been some d[efect supposed and insinuated covertly] by our vulgar [historians] (as I *said before*). And [I will in brief deliver mine] opinion thereof.
     And the*refore,* [first it must] be supposed that if there happened *a weakness and a blemish* by the err[or of the marriage of King Ed]ward,

50   whereby that title was held to be impaired, [that w]eakness and that blemish

262v

263

264*

[The sundry titles of King James to the crown of England]

had no force nor faith but for *a short time, and it* was made good and sound again as soon as K[ing Richard bega]n to reign. And afterward it was so well [cured and] reinforced by the most mighty power of sundry Parliam[ents that it was] made as strong and firm as ever it was. And the [holy aids of the dis]pensations and confirmations apostolical [of those t]imes were sacred 5 and very authentic, and so that by these *it was* fully restored, and reinforced even, and borne of *King Henry even as not havi*ng been broken by mischance and cunning, *and by th*e setters' hands hath been made as **** *and as strong and* as sound — yea, and more strong and more sound than it was before. 10

And besides, and if need were w[ithout that], this *mighty* prince now happily and gloriously [reigning h]ath of other titles and rights rich [varieties and] more than **funiculus triplex,** and some [more ancient] *a*nd some more authentic and more just, and therefore mor[e assured and secure and] more prosperous hopes *tha*n that Norman title for which was a violent 15 acquis[t] *and c*ruel *pu*rchase made by blood, and [so consequently n]one of the best, as it was well conceived [by that great Mac]edon when he said, **[Non est diuturna possessio] in quam gladio inducimur.**

[Neither would it avail in this behalf to cite or avouch the donation of this kingdom which the Confessor is said to have made to William the 20 Conqueror, being to no purpose, because that great gift or legacy was disclaimed and disavowed by the barons of this land and found to be void and of no force. But yet time, now, and prescription have also made that title good and authentic, for prescription hath power to ratify and confirm not only the titles of princes, but also of private men. 25

[Yet as I said even now, our sovereign hath better] / and [more noble titles. For first, he is immediate,] true, and sol[e lawful heir of King Egbert, who] first gave the name [of England to this land and] was absolute lord of it. [And from him, by the] *great* and glorious kings Edgar, E[dmund, Athelstan, Alfred,] and many other rightfully good kings, as well [Saxons 30 and An]gles as Anglo-Saxons, the right and title [of this king]dom was duly descended and devolved to Edmund Ironside, Kin[g of England,] who was father to the most noble Cliton, [Edward surnamed] Exul, whose fair daughter and heir, [and a holy lady,] the Princess Margaret of England, [was married] to Malcolm Canmore, King of Scotla[nd, from] which 35 ancient, princely, and blessed allia[nce the king] our sovereign lord is certainly and [directly descended,] and is their true and only heir to their right[s and] t[itles, which were without flaw.]

Likewise, the most ancient and famous [title and right] of the antique kings of Britain are in King Jam*es,* [being the] next heir to our late British 40 king [Henry Tudor,] whose genealogy I have seen derived [from the ancient] king of Britain, Coëlus and from Cad*wallader, the* last king of Britain, and from diverse [other British] princes. And this Henry Tudor, or t[he Seventh,] would have all the titles of this king[dom confirmed to him by the strongest and greatest [authority, procured] to have them decreed to him 45 and to his issue and settled *and* [established in himself] and in his royal issue and his posterities forever by [Act] of Parliament, and in [this] man[ner and words:

[To the pleasure of Almighty God, and for the wealth and prosperity and surety of this realm of England, to the singular comfort of all the subjects 50

[Alexander **apud** Curtius, **Lib.**8]

[Prescription]

264v

[Clito: prince of the blood]

Egerton 305v–307v

of the same, and in avoiding of all ambiguities and questions, be it
ordained, established, and enacted, by the authority of this present
Parliament, that the inheritance of the crown of the realm of England and
also of France, with all the preeminences and dignities royal to the same
5 appertaining, and all other signories to the king belonging beyond the seas,
with the appurtenances thereunto in any wise due or appertaining, to be,
rest, remain, and abide in the most royal person of our Sovereign Lord King
Henry VII and in the heirs of his body lawfully begotten or coming
perpetually with the Grace of God, and so to endure, and in none other.
10 [Thus this Act, which is also another title of our king, heir to Henry VII.
And this Act was renewed firmly and fully established for our sovereign
lord King James, **anno regni primo.** But yet King Henry VII, not contented
with all these titles, obtained of the Pope another title, **jure belli (ut supra.)**
And so this great king had all the titles and rights which ever were
15 appertaining to this kingdom and to the empire of Britain. For as we see
here, he hath not only the titles of the ancient kings of Britain, of the Saxon
and Anglo-Saxon kings and of the Norman race, but also the titles and
rights of the royal families of York and Lancaster and of Wales, etc.
    [He hath in possession also those singular and particular monuments of
20 empire and reign, by some called **fata regni,** and **instrumenta et monumenta**
regno et imperio destinata. The one of these being the ring of the holy King
Edward, the son of King Ethelred, which was consecrate and extraordinarily blessed by St John Baptist in Palestine, and sent back to the king,
as old writers affirm. Which ring hath been carefully and religiously kept in
25 the Abbey of Westminster, being, as they say, the ring which the
Archbishop of Canterbury is accustomed at the inauguration and
consecration of the kings to put upon their finger, called, in our stories, the
wedding ring of England.
    [The other monument of British empire is the marble stone whereupon
30 Jacob laid his head when he had those celestial and mystical visions
mentioned in Holy Writ, which stone was brought out of Palestine into
Ireland, and from thence carried into Scotland by King Kenneth, after
translated to the city of Scone, and used for the chair wherein the kings sat
at their coronation. And out of Scotland it was brought by Edward I into
35 England, which is witnessed by the best historians of Scotland and England:
    Cathedram marmoream regibus Scotorum fatalem (in qua insidentes
Scotorum reges coronari consuerant).
    [Rex Edwardus primus e Scona Londinum transtulit, in Westmonasterio,
ubi hodie visitur, deposuit.
40 [It is set and borne in a chair of wood and for a perpetual honour. This is
written upon a table hanging in the chapel at Westminster:
        Si quid habeat veri vel chronica cana fides ve,
        Clauditur hac Cathedra nobilis ille lapis;
        Ad caput eximius Jacob, quondam Patriarcha,
45   **Quem posuit cernens numina mirapoli,**
        Quem tulit ex Scotis Edwardus primus, etc.
    [And George Buchanas saith that the people are persuaded that in this
stone, which he calleth **lapidem marmoream rudem,** the fate of the kingdom
is contained, and that **fatum regni** is thus understood, viz., that what king
50 of Scotland soever is lord of that stone and sovereignly possessed thereof

[Anno 1, Henry VII
in Parliament in
November]

[The wedding ring of
England]
[Edmerus Alvredus
d'Rivallis]

[Hector Boethius,
Lib.14, et George
Buchan]*an*

[Guil. Camden]

[In hoc lapide fatum
regni Scotiae con-
tinetur. George Bu-
chanan]

shall be king and reign in that country where he findeth that stone, which is told in a prophetical distich:

[Scotus: rex Scotus, ut Anglus, Gallus, Hispanus Dominus, etc. Pro Rex Angliae, Galliae, Hispaniae, etc.]

[Ni fallat fatum Scotus quocunque locatum
Inveniet lapidem regnare tenetur ibidem.

[Which prophecy was accomplished in King James, when he came first 5
into England. For his titles were not only **funiculus triplex (qui difficile rumpitur),** but also **funiculus multiplex, qui numquam rumpitur.** And this large and spacious divinely established reign from him shall be, according to the saying of the heavenly messenger, **regnum perpetuum et cuius non est finis.** Amen.] 10

Why King Richard lost the kingdom:

265

**** *tha*t im*peria*l *justice a*nd exer*cise performed by* God, wh*en presump*tive men th*rough abusing* of his justi*ce caused him* to put down *their impious power* which hath high offen*ces done unto Him, and hath* still 15 gone on in their wicked *ways. And for* example, the crown of Israel was taken *from Solomon for hi*s disobedience and for the favour borne by *him* to idolators, and the kingdom was transla*ted to another* family. And as the wise men directly said, **Regnum a gente in gentem transfertur propter iniustitias** *et iniurias et* **dolos,** etc.: God translateth a kingdom *from one* 20 *nati*on to another nation, and from one family to *another fami*ly, and from one people to another people fit for *rule over them* and at such time as He is resolved to be revenged thereof **(ut supra).**

And this was the cause (as Gildas the wise Briton *saith) that* the Saxons and other barbarians *were commanded* by God to conquer and to destroy the 25 *native Bri*tons. And afterward, when the Saxons, and *in the dark*ling age of their monarchy, *were* as foully polluted with all sin as the old Britons were, and worse, then and thereby *they provoked* the wrath and vengeance of God to come with *more force an*d more fury against them. And Henry *Huntingdon sai*th that God gave the English nation *to be conquered an*d to 30 be spoiled and to be destroyed by the *French* nation for their manifold and

[Malmesbury, De Gestis Anglorum]

enor*mous cruel*ty. And in testimony hereof, [W]illiam Malmesbury writeth [it was declared in the time of] Edward the Confessor, and pronounced [as by a voice from Heaven,] that neither the princes, [nobles, prelates, priests, nor people of England were the ministers or servants of God, but of the 35 devil. And therefore King William I, though in his pride and jollity he would pretend he came to the kingdom by right of title and blood and by heritage and gift of the King Confessor, and power of the sword, yet when he came to shake hands with death and was **articulis morti,** he disclaimed

265v

t]/he titles [and disliked that] of the swor[d, confessing it was] *by* [the 40 **providence** of God] **and by the** means [of his favour only,] saying, **Non**

[Liber Abbat St Stephani]

e[nim tantum decus (viz.) regni Angliae heredita]rio iure possed[i, sed diro conflictu, et multa effu]sione humani cru[oris, etc. Diadema regale,] quod nullus predecessorum [meorum gestavit] adeptus sum, quod divina sol[ummodo gratia mihi] non ius hereditarium contulit. 45

An*d this* [was well said, f]or doubtless God sent him hither for two [causes: the] one, to be a scourge to the sinful Saxons and to e[xtirpate

[The causes of alterations of kingdoms]

the*m]* and their generations, and the other cause *was* [God's] gracious purpose to advance this prince [to the crown of England] and to plant his

family and nation in th[is kingdom.] These two be the chief ends of the
alteration [of estates] and of the translation of kingdoms which t[he learned
observe.]
   And to be brief, Polydore (who was a g[ood divine)] in this present case
5 of the rejected and [detected children] of King Edward bringeth the same
r[easons and] causes aforesaid, and thus he delivereth: **[Illud] fortasse istis
duobus innocentibus puer[is contigit,] quod Edwardus eorum pater
neglect[ae religionis] crimen subiisset per sanctissimum insiu[randum
violatum] qui ad portas urbis Eboraci aliud [mente aliud] verbis promissum**
10 **fecit et postea [per Ducis Clarentiae] fratris necem, /et regis Henrici, et fi[lii
eius caedes, et pro] violatione sponsalium cum Domina Alien[ora, etc./
magna] se suosque apud Deum poena obligass[et.**
   [And here these words **apud Deum** — that is 'with Go]d' — give fit
occasion and good reason to make [the true and better interpretation of the
15 letter 'G', which was so terrible to King Edward by reason of the prophecy
that 'G' should be the destruction of the kingdom. For by this it may appear
it was not meant (as some men sillily expound) by 'George', much less
'Gloucester'. But doubtless that fatal and terrible letter 'G' was to be
understood of God, and for and of his divine vengeance.
20 [And now we are come to the last act of this tragical story to see the place
where, after all the malicious eyes were satiated in beholding those
barbarous cruelties done unto the body of this dead prince, they gave his
royal corpse a bed of earth, which was done by commandment and order of
King Henry VII, and honourably in the chief church in Leicester, called St
25 Mary's, belonging to the order and society of the Greyfriars. And the king
also, soon after, caused a fair tomb of mingled colour, marble adorned with
his image, to be erected upon the monument. There was also an epitaph
made for him, whereof I have seen the copy in a recorded manuscript book,
chained to a table in a chamber in the Guildhall of London, which here (the
30 faults and corruptions being amended) followeth, together with the title
thereunto prefixed as I found it:

Egerton 308-309v (margin, line 20)

**[Epitaphum Regis Ricardi Tertii, Sepulti apud
Leicestriam, iussu et sumptibus Sancti
Regis Henrici Septimi**

35   **Hic ego quem vario tellus sub marmore claudit
        Tertius a iusta voce Ricardus eram,
      Tutor eram patriae patruus pro iure nepotis,
        Dirupta tenui regna Britanna fide
      Sexaginta dies binis dumtaxat ademptis**   [(A)Annos 2 et 52 dies]
40   **Aestatesque tuli tunc mea sceptra duas.
      Fortiter in bello certans desertus ab Anglis.
        Rex Henrice tibi Septime succubui.
      At sumptu pius ipse tuo sic ossa decoras
        Regem olimque facis regis honore coli.**
45   **Quattuor exceptis iam tantum quinque bis annis**   [(B) Anno Domini
        Acta trecenta quidem lustra salutis erant,   1484]
      Anteque septembris undena luce Kalendas   [(C) 1 die 22 Augusti]

Reddideram rubrae iura petita rosae.
At mea, quisquis eris, propter commissa precare,
Sit minor ut precibus poena levat tuis.

Deo O.M. Trino
et Uni sit laus   5
et Gloria aeterne
Amen.

[Epigramma in tres Ricardos Angliae Reges,
ex vet. lib. MS. transcriptum:

Tres sunt Ricardi quorum fortuna erat aequa,   10
In tribus ast aliis sua cuius propria sors est,
Nam concors horum finis sine posteritate,
Corporis atque rapax vitae modus, et violentus
Interitus fuerat, sed maior gloria primi,
Proelia quod terra sancta gerit, et redeuntem,   15
Tela Balistarum feriunt apud extera regna.
Alter depositus regno quum carcere clausus
Mensibus extiterat certis, fame velle perire
Elegit potius quam famae probra videre.
Tertius exhausto satis amplo divitiarum   20
Edwardi cumulo proscribens auxiliares.
Henrici partes post annos denique binos,
Suscepti regni bello confectus eisdem,
Mundanam vitam tum perdidit atque coronam,
Anno milleno, centum quater, octavageno;   25
Adiunctis quinque et cum lux sextillis adesset,
Undena duplex, dentes apri stupuerunt,
Et vindex albae Rosa rubra refloret in orbe.]

TEXTUAL NOTES

Abbreviations used in these notes:

T   Cotton Tiberius E. X
T*   scribal hand in T
Ted   George Buck, Esq.'s emendations in T
E   Egerton 2216
M   Malone 1
F   Fisher MS., University of Toronto
A   Additional 27422
P   printed edition, 1646
***   lacuna in MS.
[ ]   crossed out portions in MS.
\/   addition above the line in MS.
{ }   one word written on top of another in MS.

Where a reading is not followed by indication of a source, the emendation has been mine.

Where the reading in T is clear and indisputable, there has been no purpose in giving the copies' variants. When dealing with the copies' variants, I have listed them by order of composition, and when more than one copy shows the same reading, the spelling I have given in these notes is of the earliest composed.

Numbers heading notes refer to page and line numbers in the text.

1 T contains no title page. This is a draft used for the back of an insertion in *Comm.*

3-5 All non-conjectural emendations are from M, the only copy representing any part of this section.

17/43-18/37 This material, of which there is no representation in T, would have been approximately equivalent to one normal leaf in that MS. I have therefore assumed that a leaf is missing from T at this point and have filled the gap from E.

20/3rd mar. n. Howard] Haward EMFAP.

23/15 of them] of him T.

23/23 of honour and of piety] of pietye, and of honour E.

24/30 the people] that the people T / [that] the people Ted.

26/40 politicians] crossed out in T, and revision above the line is lost / politicians EMF.

27/34 acknowledge] crossed out in T, probably in error. No equivalent in copies.

27/36 Catesby] crossed out in T, probably replaced in lost section / Catesby EMFAP.

28/21 servant] word unclear; may be 'second'.

28/34 as pertain] ***taine Ted.

29/20 were] not in T but should have been added as part of above-line revision in Buck's 'erasure hand'.

31/4 had drawn] had not drawn T.

31/24-25 most true and certain heir] most & true & certayn heyr T / most [&] true & certayn heyr Ted.

32/2nd mar. n. 1340] 1440 EMFP.

35/23-24 afresh troubled with this news] This newes gaue freshe, and newe trouble E.

36/6 bishop's] Bishop T.

37/26-39/23 A leaf is evidently missing from T here and has been supplied from E.

38/4 and he esteemed] being [And hee] esteemed E / and hee esteemed MF.

38/22 his brother] hi{^m_s} brother E / him MF.

38/42 filium] filiam EMF.

39/4 to him] [to hym] E / *omit* MF.

42/7-42 This section is in a very chaotic state of partial revision, and I have revived some crossed out words and deleted some not crossed out to render it coherent and intelligible.

42/18 repositum] repostiu*m* T (Buck seems to have meant to cross the 't' in a hurried revision and accidentally crossed the 'i', smearing the word as well.

42/38 reprehended] seemed to reprehend TedEMF.

43/23 The sentence beginning here is preceded in T by '\scrupules/ vaynly suspicious termed' whose purport is lost to us since the Editor has made drastic revisions to this part of T, crossing out the second half of f. 32^V and the first three quarters of f. 33 when writing a new version in the margin.

46/3 regimine] Regimen EMFAP.

46/5 Marmoream] P / Marmoreu*m* EMFA.

46/15 ut] P / Et EMFA.

46/2nd mar. n. Dobuni] Dolucu E / Dolucuus M / dobic*us* F.

48/26 and most extraordinary rich and gallant] [and most extraordinary rich, and gallant] \in/ [and bra] \that dayes brauery/ E / in that dayes brauery MF / of that dayes Bravery AP.

53/21 of her] of his T / of [his] \her/ E / of her MF.

55/49 viceconstabularium] vice viceconstabularium T (not Buck's hand).

56/5 seu] se TEMF.

57/18 agreement] MF / line omitted E.

59/28 Bohun] MFAP / Bohum E.

61/25 to assist him] [to assist hym]; the like E / the like MF.

61/26 as] at T.

61/26-63/4 This section is confused, difficult to read, and in a state of incomplete revision. I have made minor deletions of uncrossed out words and reintroduced crossed out words.

65/9-10 E actually says 'the sodainesse, and strangenes, there of, strooke such a terro*r*, and fright, into the souldjers'. Since T has 'fright' earlier in the sentence, it would be redundant to repeat E's altered word order. Hence I have deleted 'and fright' in the passage taken from E here.

69/16 Hereupon he] Hereupon which he T.

76/22 quelle] qui EMFAP; concession] P / contessois E / concesso{^i_r}s M / concessors F / concessores A.

77/1st mar. n. This note I have taken from an earlier version of this page, f. 69^V.

78/3rd mar. n. Dr Stephen Gardiner] MFAP / Dr. Hen: Gardiner E.

79/26 spuriorum] P / spurios EMFA.

79/mar. n. patrui] patrai EMF.

81/2nd mar. n. MFAP / *omit* E.

82/49 pille] pilla EMFA / pile P.

83/28-39 This passage is confused, damaged, and crossed out, probably by George Buck, Esq. The author is not in the habit of deleting passages derogatory to Henry VII, and when he repeats this information in Book V (text, p. ***) he refers to having already spoken of it in Book II. George Buck, Esq., on the other hand, is in the habit of crossing out material derogatory to Henry VII, and either he crossed it out for this reason or the author crossed it out intending to rewrite or transfer it (a mark shaped like a theta suggests a possible intention to transfer it).

85/9 perȯ ch'. The 'per' is actually on f. 83, which was originally pasted at the bottom of f. 82.

86/9 and 1st mar. n. The words 'peccatum mortale' and the marginal note are taken from f. 86, of which f. 85 has rewritten a portion.

86/38 pride] MF / price E.

87/40 and not improperly] [and] not improperly E / not improperly MF / and not improperlie AP.

90/22 that there be near] that be near T / there bee neere Ted.

91/40 the earl] [the Earle] \him/ E / him MF.

94/43 brought or sent] and brought or sent T.

95/2nd mar. n. Chronicle] A / Chronije E / Chronice M / Croni F (page has been trimmed) / Chron. P.

95/4th mar. n. Copies include a note before this one: 'Arma subditorum rebellorum non bellum sed seditio'. It is probably an accidental duplication, derived from an attempt to improve the sense, of which no trace appears in T.

99/27 processit] MF / possessit E.

99/27-28 but dissembled . . . train] but a dissembled . . . train T / but a dissembled, [& rather don for a] trayn Ted.

100/11 that] yt that T.

101/23 escas] estas EM / astus F.

101/27 facis] EMF / facias T*.

101/28 imbecillum] MF / in becillum T*E.

102/6-103/6 This scribal folio is extremely confused with authorial revisions.

102/42 taketh end] Judging from the crossings out and substitutions in E, there was great difficulty in reading T at this point. This is possibly a misreading. 'Quarrel' was first written as 'Generall' in E, possibly a correct reading: 'ffor the [Generall] \Quarrell/ taketh end, [taketh And] \and/'.

103/16 encountered singly] encountered him singly T.

103/38 contudit] M / conludit E / condudit F.

104/36 humanists] Ha∗∗mists T* / Hamanists EF / Hamamists M.

104/2nd mar. n. status] M / *omit* E / datus F.

105/2 Averterunt] averserunt T*.

105/25-26 It is clear from the partial revisions by the Ed. in T that he intended to turn all the verbs into the present tense. He has succeeded only in producing a mixture of tenses ('stripped', 'tear', 'rent', 'pulls', 'spurns', 'kicks'). I have followed the structure dictated by T in giving all these verbs in the past tense.

108/25 And] [And] E *omit* MF / And AP.

110/48 Ediva] Edina TEMFP.

111/42 Evermua] Enermua TEMFP.

113/6 identitatem] Identatem E / Identotem MF.

113/10-27 Certain short sections of this folio have been crossed out by the author. They are reinstated here, following the practice in EMF, because the construction requires them.

114/6-14 This paragraph fits nowhere else in the text. This folio is in the hand of George Buck, Esq. and probably rewrites an authorial draft now lost.

114/45 King John] These words are retrieved from an earlier draft of this page, f. 118^V.

114/46-115/9 Evidently a short section is missing from T here. I have supplied the gap from E.

115/14 Guicciardini] Guiccardjne E / Gui{cc tr}ardine M / Guirrardine F / Guicciardine P.

115/2nd mar. n. Guicciardini] Guicardjn E / Guicardni M / Guirrardin F / Guicci. P.

115/3rd mar. n. MFP / *omit* E.

115/41 Lombard] Lumbard TEMFP.

116/14 συγγενεῖϛ] συγγενεϛ T.

116/1st mar. n. Thomas, Duke] Tho: 1: Du: EMF (probably misreading for the 's' of 'Thos.').

116/1st mar. n. at the Battle of Musselburgh] MF / & ye Batell of Musselborough E; militavimus] F / melitauimus EM; vidimus] videmus EMF.

116/30-47 This page is in the hand of George Buck, Esq., probably a rewriting of an authorial draft now lost.

116/44 the Earl of Shrewsbury now living] [thus bee the erle of erles] and the late erle of Shrewsbury nowe l∗∗∗∗∗ E. George Buck, Esq. in writing this folio revises as he goes along and in so doing seems to be altering the sense of the author's original. I have emended the passage so that it accords with what appears to have been the author's intention: to refer to a contemporary earl of Shrewsbury. George Buck, Esq., tends to alter references to persons living in the author's time.

117/15 but] MP / *omit* EF; antecessors] Antocesors EMF / Antecessours P.

119/44 alteri ne feceris] P / alteri [non] feceris E / alteri feceris MF.

121/4th mar. n. Philopseudes] Philopseude EMF.

123/21 Courinus] EMFP / Corvinus T. The author has marked this name with a cross, probably pointing to a marginal note giving the correct spelling.

123/1st mar. n. MFP / *omit* E.

124/14 Trebellius] Tebellius T.

125/20 Caesarem] Caesaris T.

125/40-126/1 This portion is crossed out in T, certainly by George Buck, Esq., though some lighter strokes below his crossings out might indicate authorial deletion as well. The material is in some respects duplicated on the scribal f. 137, and possibly the author decided to discard this version of it. The copies have rejected f. 137ᵛ and used only f. 136. Because of the uncertainty and because the material is not necessarily exclusive but can be seen as reinforcing, I have retained both folios in full.

127/45-49 This sentence is a late addition by the author in T which continues down the margin of the page saying 'never ha***** very of******* moreover'. It is impossible to fit these fragments into the reconstruction.

127/46 accubitio] accubatio EMF / occubatio P.

128/47-49 In T this section, at the bottom of a page, is badly burnt and reads 'and Cn. Papyrius Carbo, two most *********** most honorable Romans, \& who/ were bornne ******************s the vertuous and *********'. This is too seriously damaged to be reconstructed, and a corresponding passage from E has been substituted which seems to represent a later authorial version, since it contains more additional factual information than George Buck, Esq. is in the habit of adding.

129/1st mar. n. Fotheringhay] Fotheringham EMF / Totheringham P.

130/16-17 All copies have here a marginal note, 'Rotuli in anno 2. Richard 2' which, since it makes no sense, I have deleted, assuming it to be an error in placement by George Buck, Esq. or his scribe.

130/28 This is] M / whoe is EF. M's version is closer to More.

130/ 2nd mar. n. Hardyng and Grafton] Hardington EMF / Harlington P. In the process of copying, the scribe has evidently left out the first part of the name that follows 'Hardyng'.

131/18 This sentence is followed in T by the passage below, p. 131, ll. 34-35 ('men of . . . comely persons'), which I have transferred from this place to that for the sake of organization. Buck never completed his revision: having apparently concluded his argument here, he decides to continue it, making the conclusion — which he has failed to delete — inappropriate at this point. He has then failed to finish organizing the conclusion at the later, appropriate point.

131/34-35 See note 131/18, above. The conclusion has been shifted here from that point to replace a partly obliterated and incompletely composed similar statement appearing here.

132/46 πάνδεινον] πανδειλον T.

133/16 τύραννος] MF/ τοραννος E.

133/25 martiris FP / marticis EM; titulum] P / titul{ᵘₐ}m E / titulam MF; mereatur] mereantur EMFP.

135/3 Chertsey] FP / Chelsey E / [Cherley] \Chertsey/ M.

137/1st mar. n. me] men EMFP.

137/48 timebat] MFP / tinebat E.

139/16 an] his T.

139/39 were] wher T.

139/49-50 Underlining occurs in T but not in the copies.

141/3 parity] perity E / [perily] parralell M / perilly F.

145/33 Velleius] Valleius E / vallerus M / Valerius FP.

146/28 Trogus] Trogas T*.

148/4-5 This passage is in a confused state of partial revision.

148/2nd mar. n. Richard Grafton] Robt: Grafton E / Rob: Grafton M / Ro: Grafton F.

149/2 Perkin's] Perkin T.

149/25 But] FP / [but] \yet/ E / yet MF

151/17-30 This folio is in the hand of George Buck, Esq. All of it may be the Editor's reworking of what still appears in T, but in case some of it represents authorial work now lost I have included that part of it not represented elsewhere so explicitly.

152/1st mar. n. of torture] MFP / or torture E.

153/25-38 T is very confused here from incomplete revision and crossing out by author and Editor. I have made some minor changes through deletion of uncrossed out material, reinstatement of crossed out material, and rearrangement of word order.

155/33 Escape EMF / escapa T / Escapae P.

155/2nd mar. n. 26.27] M / 29.26 E / 26.29 F.

157/mar. n. Darceii] Darey EF / [Darey] Darcy M.

161/50 in general words passed] [in generall words passed] is confessed E / in generall words is confessed MP / in generall words [passed,] is confessed F.

166/1-6 This section is badly damaged and the version in EMF paraphrases and alters word order. In restoring it I have had to guess at the order the author intended.

166/6 after] Ted.

167/1st mar. n. Ausonius] MF / Ausonus E.

167/4 videtur] videntur EMFP.

167/5 reus] reas EMF / rei P.

169/38 the which] [the] which E / which MF.

169/3rd mar. n. Dominus de Arun.] Dominus Dr. Aran. E / Dominus Dr Arun: M / Dominus D^r A^{nnn} F / Dominus de Arundell P.

169/41 his] MFP / this E.

171/36 At this point the hand changes from scribal to authorial.

171/49 κτενέεις] κτανεεις T; μόρσιμος] μορισμος T.

173, f. 215^v The first part of this folio is in a state of incomplete revision and cannot be reconstructed. Hence I have had to omit it. It reads:

> *******e paynes, and Care to demonstrate his yong **********cause it was so lowe ********** but otherwis ********d as little labour and care in the refelling & an*********f the rest, as well for the reasons before declared as also becaus the greate accusation*n* *********nne lawfull & good euidence prooved; but its concern ****************ed & ***roached by ye Calumnie or slander of them who haply were guilty of ******** and afterward it was *************d broached and nourished by lyeing fame & by the mal********ue; and other ******* faction or the Credulous people: But certanne grounde or proofe therof was *********

173/25 indictum] P / indicte EMF.

173/26 irritum] P / irratum EMF

175/18 Waite] Wyat EMF / Wiatt P.

176/12 English] M / Englished E / Engl^{sh} F.

176/41 all alacrity] a allacritie T*.

177/44 her virtues] MF / hertues E.

178/2nd mar. n. ils] P / vls EMF.

178/42 ducende] ducenda EMFP.

180/12 deluded] The copies' wording is clearly a revision, repeating some of the wording that survives in T. Since this whole section is very close to More's wording, I have taken this emendation from More (p. 62).

180/36 have attention to hear] [haue] \with/ attention [to] heare E / with attention hear MFP.

180/38 his] MF / this E.

184/7 rançonna] rangona E / ran{^n_g}ona M / rangon*n*a F / Ranson P.

186/5-34 There is evidently a fragmental page missing from T here. I have supplied the gap from E.

187/2 and to believe] MF / *omit* E.

187/15 men] [men] vniust & vnworthy law T.

188/10-11 ought to have been] MF / (line omitted) E.

188/40 which] FP / [which] that E / [that] w*h*ich M.

189/1st mar. n. Plantagenet] MFP / *omit* E.

189/29 honourable] EMFP / honourably T.

190/41 ex] ea EMF / ito P.

190/42 repudii P / repudis EMF; dimissoria] MP / dimistoria E / demissoria F.

192/19 minore] immorte EMFP; reginam] P / Regmani EF / regimani M; decuit] deciat EMF / dicunt P.

193/1st mar. n. S] B. EMFP.

193/41 bona] P / boreas E / borea MF.

193/43 nescire] P / nescere EMF.

193/44 cui] qui EFP / que M.

194/2 promoter's P / promooters T / dilators EM / Promotors (with 'dilators' as a marginal gloss) F.

196/35-38 This translation may have appeared in the burnt away margin of T; there is no place for it in the body of the text. Since there is no trace of it remaining in T, it is impossible to say whether it is the work of the author or the Editor. It is a form Buck uses elsewhere in his short translations, and its simplicity and unpretentiousness point to him rather than to the Editor.

197/1st mar. n. Philosophus] Philosoph*um* EMF.

197/16 pecuniarum] P / pecunierum EMF.

197/23 Tartesiacis] Tertessiaris EF / Tartessiaris MP.

197/27 Res fisci est, etc.] P / Res fisci est et terrebrion*um* &c. EMF.

199/42-45 Emendations here have been taken from M, since M and F do not alter the construction of the original, whereas E does.

199/49 philautists] Philantists EMF.

201/31-33 The transitional section in T at this point is too badly burnt away to be reconstructed and has been crossed out, apparently by the author, who seems never to have written a substitute for it. The Editor substitutes in the copies a transition of his own.

202/20 precony] MFP / praecoy.

203/1st mar. n. Morton] MFP / Mooton E.

203/17 allegatae] P / allogatae T* / allogate EMF.

203/36 son] sonnes EMFP.

204/5 perpetuam] perpetuum EMF.

204/2nd mar. n. Ralph] Robert EMF.

204/36 Barowe] Barone EM / Baron F.

205/47 praebes] P / praebos E / probo M / prabo F.

206/1 prosequitur] P / prosequart T* / prosequart EMF; et desiderat] te desiderat T*EMFP.

206/8 dici] P / deci EMF.

206/19 nostrum] FP / nostram EM.

206/20 amicitia] MFP / amicta E.

206/21 respectu] P / respectis EMF; nullum] P / nullam EMF.

206/22 unum] P / unam EMF; benevolentiae] P / benevolentia EMF.

206/26 fluvii] P / flauij T*EMF.

206/28 amabit] P / amubit EMF.

206/30 manebunt] P / manebant EM / munebant F.

207/ mar. n. consumptos] P / consumptus EMF; ostendit] affaris E / affarit M / afferit F / affirmat P.

207, f. 255 The first few lines of this folio are too badly damaged to be reconstructed or placed in the existing context: 'et multiplicuntur ✱✱✱✱✱✱✱✱ no reason but th✱✱✱✱✱✱✱ might be more fauor✱✱✱✱✱✱✱✱✱✱✱ful and in suspense ✱✱✱✱✱✱✱✱✱✱ neither is it safe to en✱✱✱✱✱✱✱✱✱✱✱ God ✱✱✱✱ forbidden vs to ✱✱✱✱✱✱✱✱✱✱✱✱✱ matters whereof ✱✱✱✱✱✱✱bly it only to himself ✱✱✱✱✱✱✱✱✱✱'.

207/36 1485] 1493 EMFP.

208/33 colere] colore EMF.

209/6 precario] precacirio E / precaririo MF.

210/7 insontem] infontem EMF / infantem P.

210/14 had been] MF / had bee E.

210/25 Austria] Austriche EMFP.

210/34 Trenchard] P / Treachard EMF.

211/13 sanctam] sanctum EMF.

212/11 Dartford] P / Datford EMF.

212/42 the] then EMFP.

212/47 soon after put to death] MF / put to death soone after E.

213/32 I will ever say] [I will euer saye] it must ever bee acknowledged E / it must ever be acknowledged MF.

213/33 happy] [happie] \fortunate/ E / fortunate MF.

213/40 receive] receiveth T. I cannot reconstruct the passage so as to make this form fit it. The whole section is in a state of partial revision, badly burnt, and crossed out by G.B., Esq.

214/22-23 void and] MF / [void and] E / void P.

214/30 Athelstan] P / Athelston EMF.

214/49-215/9 A leaf is evidently missing from T at this point.

215/4th mar. n. Lib. 14] MF / lib 4 EP.

216/44 diro] dico EMF; multa] multam EMF.

217/20-218 This section is missing in T.

217/20 And now we are come] MF / [And nowe] wee are \nowe/ come E.

217/39 iusta] FP / iustae EM.

217/46 decoras] diceras EF / decoras M / dicaras P.

218/15 terra sancta] terrae sanctae EMF / terrarum P.

218/25 milleno] P / millerio EMF.

GENERAL NOTES

When referring to Buck's sources I have where possible used the edition, sometimes the copy, that Buck used. Where this could not be determined, I have used either an edition to which Buck could have had easy access or, when one exists, a good modern edition or reprint.

It must be understood throughout that Buck does not quote exactly from the sources cited. His tendency is to paraphrase. I have not given the original version in every case where deviation occurs but have done so where the alterations are either very drastic or materially affect the sense.

1. The first quotation, a translation of Plato, *De Legibus*, V, 730, is correctly documented. The second I have been unable to locate in St Ambrose's *De Officiis Ministrorum*, though certain passages resemble it.

3/1-6. Born in 1585, Thomas Howard was educated at Westminster and at Trinity, Cambridge. He was created a Knight of the Garter in 1611 and a member of the Privy Council in 1616, and in 1621 officially made Earl Marshal, after acting for some years in the post in commission with others. He died in 1646. A scholar and avid antiquarian collector, he possessed some family papers and relics. He numbered among his friends Cotton, Camden, Spelman, and Selden. He was interested in acting and performed in court masques. He and Buck shared a passion for ancestry: 'In his will, he desired that a history might be written of his "noble auncesters, whereby their good memory may be preserved, and those that shall succeede may bee invited to bee virtuous, or at least ashamed to bee vitious" ' (Mary F.S. Hervey, *The Life . . . of Thomas Howard Earl of Arundel*, Cambridge, 1921, p. 137). Lord Maltravers was not his title, but that of his eldest son. Buck was listing it among all the other Howard family titles.

3/14. Buck is probably referring here to Cornwallis, cited again on pp. 133f and 199. Later versions of this work conclude 'yet for all this knowe I hold this but as a Paradoxe' (p. 32). For discussion of this defence and Buck's indebtedness to it, see above, pp. ciii-cvi

3/mar n. I have been unable to trace this quotation or to locate an author named Johannes Veteranus.

3/25-29. Richard III created John Howard first Duke of Norfolk and his son

Thomas Earl of Surrey a few days before his coronation, in which Norfolk bore the crown and Surrey the sword of state. Norfolk was granted the offices of Earl Marshal and High Steward of England, the former, the traditional Mowbray office, in right of his Mowbray mother. He was King's Justicer and Commissioner of Array in East Anglia. One of the chief commanders, as was his son Surrey, in the Battle of Bosworth, he died fighting for Richard, despite the famous warning pinned to his tent (see text, p. 97). Surrey became a military hero under Henry VII and Henry VIII without compromising his loyalty to Richard III, as both Camden (*Remaines,* p. 283) and Buck (text, p. 109) tell us.

3/34-36. Buck discourses further on the history of the Howard family, text, pp. 110-114.

4/9-13. In text, pp. 114 and 116, Buck acknowledges his gratitude to the Howards for their aid to his ancestors, as he had in *Comm.,* f. 453.

4/29. Buck uses 'story' throughout this work in the sense of 'history'. For a discussion of Buck's historiographical methods, see above, *passim,* especially pp. cii-cxxx.

4/47-49. Buck is probably referring to Grafton. The controversy between Grafton and Stow, discussed in Charles Lethbridge Kingsford's Introduction to Stow's *Survey of London* (Oxford, 1908), I, and in F.J. Levy, *Tudor Historical Thought* (San Marino, 1967), p.188, was based to a great extent on Stow's objections to Grafton's lack of documentation. For a discussion of the technical ideals of the antiquaries in Buck's time, see above, Introduction, pp. xl-xlix.

4/50 - 5/4. For a discussion of popular literature see above, pp. cxxii-cxxiv. Levy, p. 211, says that abridgements of the chronicles were made for the poorer people by men of little learning.

5/5-7. Cicero, *In Verrinem* II, 3. 209.

5/18-19. Vergil, Eclogue VI, 3-4.

5/21. Buck refers to James I.

6/5. For a discussion of Buck's *Baron,* a work no longer extant, see above, pp. 34-37 and cxxxii. The tendency of some of Buck's digressions to grow to proportions exceeding the work intended to contain them can be seen in the extensiveness of his digression on Perkin Warbeck in Book III of the *History.*

6/14-15. Yarnold in Egerton 2218, f. 50 identifies the 'worshipful shallow magistrate' as Thomas Gainsford, author of *The True and Wonderful History of Perkin Warbeck.* However, since Gainsford's active life was spent in Ireland, and Buck's references to him in other places are not so discourteous, this is not plausible. I cannot identify the person Buck means.

6/1st mar. n. Hermannus Vulteius, *Jurisprudentia Romana* (Marpurgus, 1602), I, xiii, 64.

6/39. For Morton's possible contribution to Ricardian historiography, see above, pp. ciii-cvi; also Kincaid and Ramsden, Introduction to Cornwallis. The 'apes' are those historians who incorporate More's history into their own: Grafton, Stow, Hall, and Holinshed.

7/1-2. II Corinthians, 5:10.

7/8-9. I can locate no specific source for this axiom.

7/11-12. Plato, *Philebus,* 59e-60a; *Gorgias,* 498e; *Laws,* 754c and 956e.

7/22-25. This could again refer to Grafton.

7/26-28. Authors commonly made lists of their sources at the beginnings or ends of their works. Hall and Holinshed list theirs at the beginning, and there is some marginal documentation in Holinshed. Grafton does not document at all. Stow lists his sources at the beginning and documents fairly thoroughly in the margins, though not as thoroughly as Buck does.

7/35-36. See above, pp. xl-xlix for discussion of antiquaries. William Camden, educated at Winchester and Oxford and for some time schoolmaster at Westminster, became Clarenceux Herald in 1597. He was an indefatigable and highly respected antiquary, travelling to make collections for his *Britannia,* first published in 1586, and his *Remaines,* first published in 1605. He possessed, through purchase, some of Leland's and Stow's collections of manuscript material, including historical observations, records, and chronicles. Ralph Brook, York Herald, was a vehement critic of Camden's *Britannia.* Probably his animosity arose in part from Camden's appointment above him as well as from Camden's errors in genealogical matters. Brook's criticism had the effect of forcing Camden to closer examination and documentation of sources. It is interesting that both these men were willing to assist Buck in his research, and that he was able to ignore their differences of opinion and consider them both his friends. He cites them both in the *Commentary* also.

Sir Robert Cotton, a former pupil of Camden's, whose library inherited both a great portion of Camden's collection and the original manuscript of Buck's *History,* was the greatest collector of his time. As will be seen often in the course of these notes and Buck's own marginal notes, Buck made considerable use of Cotton's extensive manuscript collections.

7/42. Desiderius Erasmus, *Adagiorum Chiliades* (Basle, 1536), p. 557.

8/12. For dating of this work, see above, p. cxxxi.

BOOK 1

9. Buck follows his outline quite closely in Book I. He deviates only in that though Richard's lineage and family are discussed first, his 'birth, education, and tirociny' are not considered until after 'The antiquity of surnames'; 'The quality and title of the Beauforts . . .' are discussed not here but in Book II; 'King Richard demandeth a tribute of France' follows 'His careful and godly charge . . . for the administration of Justice'; and the two topics 'He holdeth a parliament . . .' and 'Morton . . . attainted of treason . . . and the king is declared . . . heir to the crown' are reversed.

10/3. Richard, Duke of York's father was Richard, Earl of Cambridge, second son of Edmund of Langley, Duke of York, whose eldest son, Edward, had inherited the title. Richard, Earl of Cambridge, was executed for conspiracy against Henry V before his embarkation for France. Edward, Duke of York, died at Agincourt, leaving his nephew heir to the title. He was therefore the third, not fourth Duke of York.

10/4-5. Richard, Duke of York, was proclaimed Heir Apparent to the throne on 31 October 1460, in recognition of the Yorkist claim's superiority over the Lancastrian. Henry VI's son Edward was to be passed over.

10/31 - 11/17. For a previous example in Buck's work of his admiration for Henry II, see above, pp. xxiv-xxv, in the discussion of *Daphnis*. There also he speaks of the extent of Henry's empire, quoting at length from Du Haillan, Newburgh, Giraldus, and Salisbury, and referring also to De la Hay, Fabyan, Stow, and Camden.

11/1-2. Camden, *Britannia* (1607), p. 119:

> Dux primus est post Principem dignitatis titulus. Hoc pri-
> mùm nomen erat officij, & non honoris. Circa Ælij Veri
> tempora qui limitibus praeerant, Duces sunt primum dicti,
> eratque hic gradus Constantini aetate Comitibus inferior.
> Deleto Romano imperio hic titulus etiam vt officij nomen
> remansit, quique apud nos in antiquis chartis Saxonico
> seculo tanto numero *Duces* dicuntur, Anglica lingua tan-
> tùm *Ealdormen* vocabantur, ijdēmque qui *Duces* etiam
> *Comites* sunt appellati, vt Guilielmum illum Angliae Vic-
> torem quem plerique omnes *Normanniae Ducem* dicunt,
> Guil. Malmesburiensis *Normanniae Comitatem* vocat. Sed
> cùm Ducem, tùm Comitem nomen fuisse officij . . . .

Camden then quotes a charter listing 'Comitatus and Ducatus' as equivalents. In Hearne, I, 177-86, are several discourses on the etymology, dignity, and antiquity of dukes in England. All mention the interchangeable use of the terms 'Dux' and 'Comes' in the time of Edward the Confessor and William I.

11/2nd mar. n. Buck evidently means this documentation to apply to the whole of his information on Henry II, not simply to the title 'Regum Britanniae Maximus', which in *Daphnis* (sigs. C and C2) he twice documents explicitly as coming from Salisbury. Giraldus Cambrensis, *Topographia Hibernica,* in *Opera,* ed. James F. Dimock, R.S. 21 (London, 1861-91), V, 189ff gives these limits to Henry's empire, but not this particular epithet, though his praise is lavish. John of Salisbury, *Poly-craticus,* ed. Clemens C.I. Webb (Oxford, 1909), II, 49, 614b, calls Henry 'rex optimus apud Britannias' and 'maximus regum Britanniae' (II, 424, 822a). William of Newburgh, *Historia Regum Anglicarum* in *Chronicles of the Reigns of Stephen, Henry II, and Richard I,* ed. Richard Howlett, R.S. 82 (London, 1884-5), I, 278, says, 'inclitus ille rex Henricus, inter reges orbis terrarum nominatissimus, et nulli eorum vel amplitudine opum, vel felicitate successuum paulo ante secundus'.

11/25 - 16/11. The origin of the name 'Plantagenet' is still uncertain, but there is agreement that it was the personal nickname of Geoffrey of Anjou, father of Henry II, though he never used it officially. How he acquired it is disputable, and there are several traditions to account for it: his love of hunting in the broom, his wearing a sprig of it in his cap, his applying it to himself for penance, and the existence in Anjou and Maine of place names incorporating the plant's name (*DNB*, 'Plantagenet'). The name was not used after Geoffrey until Richard, Duke of York adopted it as a surname:

> Après lui le surnom disparaît. Henri II est appele 'fitz
> Empress'. Aucun membre de la famille ne porta plus ce
> nom-même au XIIIe siecle, quand la mode fut aux sobri-
> quets,–jusqu'à Richard d'York qui, en 1460, voulut, par ce
> nom, marquer la superiorité de sa maison sur celle des
> Lancastre.
>
> (Josèphe Cartrou, *L'Anjou de 1109 à 1151,* Paris,
>   n.d., p. 84)

GEC favours the traditional assumption that Geoffrey's nickname was derived from his habit of wearing a sprig of broom in his cap (XI, Appendix G, 140), giving 1448 as the date of Richard, Duke of York's adopting it and noting that it has only recently been observed that none of Geoffrey's earlier descendants bore it (I, 183n). Camden in *Remaines* makes Geoffrey the bearer of the sobriquet 'Plantagenet' and goes on to say, 'wheras these names were neuer taken vp by the sonne, I know not why any should thinke *Plantagenet* to be the surname of the royall house of *England,* albeit in late years many haue so accounted it' (pp. 107f).

11/31-32. For discussion of Buck's *Commentary,* see above, pp. xxix-xxxiv.

11/40-41. Sir William Dethick succeeded his father, Sir Gilbert, in this office. He was a member of the original Society of Antiquaries, who often held meetings at his house (Van Norden, p. 306). He became involved in an internal squabble within the College of Arms which has biased our evidence of his character and attainments and makes it difficult to assess them. In 1606, he was brought before the Earl Marshal's court for abuse of his office through embezzling books and falsifying pedigrees. This case seems to have arisen from the interest of Sir William Segar in obtaining Dethick's office and from the king's wish to confer it on Segar, previously Norroy Herald. Records of the proceedings exist in B.L. MSS. Additional 25247, ff. 291^v-296; Harl. 1453, ff. 31^v-71; and Cotton Vespasian C. XIV, f. 96. According to Dethick's own explanation in Cotton Vesp. C.XIV, f. 96, the accusations were stirred up by his jealous associates who had themselves removed and hidden the books.

Wagner's description of the College of Arms at the end of the sixteenth and beginning of the seventeenth century (*The Records and Collections of the College of Arms,* London, 1952, pp. 9-13) accounts to some extent for the internal disputes and accusations. The library was built up gradually and passed on by heralds to their successors. Some books were privately owned, some belonged to the College, and for some the ownership was uncertain. In 1568 the Earl Marshal, Thomas Howard, Duke of Norfolk, established the rules for the College, including incorporation of the library. Further reform came in 1597 when Camden was made Clarenceux. Wagner thinks the accusations against Dethick probably manifested resistance against the Earl Marshal's imposition of rules and the heralds' insistence on continuing to regard as private property what had to belong to the College for it to function effectively as a corporation. Brook, provoked by the promotion of Camden, seems to have added fuel to the fire with 'A Catalogue of a fewe Arms and Crestes as hath byn given by William Derick [*sic*] . . . with some note of other his abuses maynteyned and lyked of by some his followers new elected Officers of Armes which haue byn Brokers for the same' (B.L. MS. Harl. 1453, f. 31ᵛ).

Buck's description of Dethick does not accord with the accusations of dishonest and incompetent practice and unpleasant behaviour. In any case, Dethick seems to have retained a library of some sort, perhaps partly furnished from the collection left him by his father, who instituted the College's library. That Buck praises his library is not evidence of his embezzling from the College, for the private collecting activities of his contemporary antiquaries were considerable. However, the ethics of collecting to which these men adhered were not always strictly scrupulous by our standards.

12/5. Jean Nicot, *Thresor de la Langue* (Paris, 1606), p. 602): 'Toutesfois le sotbriquet (comme le vocable de foy le monstre) est vne adiection populaire au nom d'aucun, faicte par accident, & tendant à gosserie'.

12/10-23. A similar collection of surnames with their etymologies appears in Camden, *Remaines,* pp. 115-21 and 149-51. Camden on p. 107 comments upon sobriquets which do *not* pass to the bearer's descendants.

12/2nd mar. n. Roger de Hoveden, *Chronica,* ed. William Stubbs, R.S. 51 (London, 1869-9), II, 300f. 'Rievall' refers to Ailredus, Abbot of Rievaulx, who wrote an historical work of which there are several manuscript copies in the Cotton collection. In the volume Buck used (Julius A. XI), it was bound with a history of Henry II's reign by an unnamed Benedictine abbot, and it is this history, not Ailred's, that Buck cites. He confused the two because the Benedictine's history, beginning f. 29, follows, both in the volume and chronologically, directly after Ailred's. The hand, to an eye not carefully trained in palaeography, appears the same, and only close examination reveals that these are two separate works. The Benedictine history is edited by William Stubbs as *The Chronicle of the Reigns of Henry II and Richard I,* 2 vols., R.S. 49 (London, 1867). There are several mentions in it of the projected crusade: Henry in 1172 when formally absolving himself of Becket's murder swears to go on a pilgrimage to Jerusalem the following summer (I, 32).

13/29 - 13/48. Claude Paradin, *Alliances Genealogiques des Rois et Princes de Gaule* ([Geneva], 1606), p. 176: Fulke had his stepson (not nephew) Drogo drowned in a bath by his nurse and usurped his inheritance in Brittany. To avoid the weight of guilt in old age,

> S'en alla donques en Ierusalem, suyui de deux seruiteurs:
> &, y entrant, s'accoustra en criminel, &, comme vn con-
> damné, se mit vne corde au col, &, se faisant trainer par
> l'un de ses gents, se faisoit aussi (ce pendant) fouetter par
> l'autre sans cesse auec des verges: & ainsi, arriuant au lieu
> de S. Sepulchre, se print à crier, disant: Recoy, mon Dieu
> & Seigneur, ton miserable Fouques fugitif & parjure.

Bernard de Girard, Seigneur du Haillan, *L'Histoire de France* ([Paris], 1577), p. 342, whom Paradin uses as a source, copying from him the quotation cited above, says it was not known what crimes Fulke had committed. Paradin himself does not mention his defrauding a church. It is Du Haillan who notes that Fulke lived afterwards in the regard of all men (p. 342). More recently, Chartrou says of this episode that Fulke 'par maniere de pénitence, se faisait flageller nu dans les rues de

Jérusalem, qu'il dût d'être désigné par Louis VI aux envoyés de Baudouin de Jérusalem' (p. 78). Fulke seems to have been, like Geoffrey Plantagenet, a colourful and charismatic figure. Joseph Calmette, *Le Moyen Age* (Paris, 1948), p. 164 calls him 'le premier des grandes comtes'.

13/33-34. Du Haillan, p. 552, says mistakenly that he was the son of Geoffrey Martel, who was in fact his son. Grisegonelle was the third count of Anjou (see Marchegay and Salmon, *Chroniques des Comtes d'Anjou*, Paris, 1871, p. lxvii).

13/34-36. Geoffrey 'Plantagenet' was the fifth count of Anjou after Fulke, but removed from him by only four generations (Paradin, pp. 176-88).

14/1st mar. n. Zosimus, *Historia Nova*, II, xxix.

15/27. For 'the hieroglypical learning', see below, note 175/24-33.

15/30. Vergil, *Georgics*, II, 434.

15/2nd mar. n. Leonard Fuchs, *De Historia Stirpium Commentarij Insignis* (London, 1551), p. 218: 'Genistram autem vocant haud dubiè quod modo flexillis ad nexus sit: vel, vt alijs placet, quia genibus medeatur dolentibus'.

15/39. It is evidently from Fuchs that Buck derives this quotation, which comes from Pliny, *Naturalis Historia*, XXIV, xl, since the spelling follows Fuchs' version (p. 219): 'Genista tusa cum ax ungia, genua dolentia sanat'. Buck has substituted 'etc'. for 'ax ungia' (Pliny gives it as one word), presumably because he did not understand it. It means axle grease.

15/40-41. Fuchs, p. 219, comments on the purgative value of the plant.

16/5. Strabo, *Geography*, XVI, ii, 36.

16/2nd mar. n. Du Haillan, p. 553: 'Ce qui fait que plusieurs croient, que pour ceste grand & humble reparation, Dieu voulut que son peche fut entierement celé'. He says that Fulke's descendants were kings of Jerusalem and England. Buck adds France, Ireland, and Scotland.

16/31-48. Robert Glover, Somerset Herald, one of the original members of the Society of Antiquaries, was highly regarded by both Buck and Camden. *The Catalogue of Honour* is a genealogical work which begins with a discussion of ranks and ceremonies in England and continues to show the genealogy of all the noble families in England. It was compiled and published after Glover's death by his nephew, Thomas Milles, with the help of Camden and Cotton. There were editions in 1610 and 1616, the latter using Croyland as a source. In discussing creations to various orders of the nobility and to offices, Glover reproduces original documents, a practice Buck follows in reproducing the order of creation for Vice Constable (text, p. 55f).

The name Plantagenet appears occasionally in Glover. It does not appear in Jean du Tillet, *Recueil des Roys de France* (Paris, 1602), or in Du Haillan, or in Jean de la Haye, *Les Memoires et Recherches de France, et de la Gaulle Acquitanique* (Paris, 1581). Paradin (p. 28) mentions the name Geoffrey Plantagenet. Camden's only references occur in *Britannia*, p. 217 and *Remaines*, pp. 107f. The latter states that there is no reason to consider it a royal surname. This collection of references illustrates the type of inaccurate recollection of which Buck was sometimes guilty when relying entirely on memory. Glover is the only one which completely suits his description.

16/49-17/1. Camden, *Remaines,* p. 107.

17/13-14. According to Paradin (p. 168), the counts of Anjou were descended from Robert, Prince of Saxony, who in 870 was created the first count of Anjou.

17/20. Ovid, *Metamorphoses,* XIII, 147.

17/22-23. Richard was born at Fotheringhay (William Worcester, *Annales Rerum Anglicarum in Letters and Papers Illustrative of the Wars of the English in France,* ed. Joseph Stevenson, R.S. 22 (London, 1864), II, ii, [771]. The suggestion of Berkhamsted comes from Stow, p. 766: 'King Richard the third, borne at Fodringhay: some say at Barckhamstede'.

17/25-27. Richard III was born in 1452, Edward IV in 1442. There were twelve children, nine surviving infancy, seven born between Edward and Richard. This information comes from William Worcester, who gives name, date, and place of birth for the Duke of York's children. The name of the one child he neglects to mention is listed in a contemporary rhyme quoted by Augustine Vincent in *A Discoverie of Errours in the . . . Catalogue of the Nobility* (London, 1622), pp. 622f.

17/28. Edward IV died at 40, not 41.

17/34. Richard was not brought up at Middleham until after his father's death when he resided there as a ward of the Earl of Warwick in the early 1460's.

17/37. The battle of Wakefield occurred in 1460, not 1461.

17/44-45. Clarence and Gloucester were welcomed by Duke Philip of Burgundy, father of Charles the Bold. In 1467, after his father's death, Charles married Richard's older sister Margaret, not his aunt. Buck seems to be confusing this occasion with Richard's second exile in Burgundy, in company with his brother King Edward, who in 1470 was driven from his country by Warwick and Clarence. In text, p. 143 Buck mentions that Margaret of Burgundy gave Perkin Warbeck as warm a welcome as she had given Clarence and Gloucester many years earlier. There, however, he seems at least to realize that Margaret was Richard's sister and Perkin's nominal aunt. The error of assuming Margaret was aunt rather than sister to Edward IV and his brothers appears also in Shakespeare's 3 *Henry VI,* II, ii, 144.

18/8-16. George and Richard were made Knights of the Bath 27 June 1461 and created respectively Duke of Clarence (28 June) and Duke of Gloucester (1 November), then Knights of the Garter. The earldom of Richmond was originally granted to Richard but transferred to Clarence. Richard was made Admiral, 1461; Constable of England and Chief Justice of North and South Wales, 1469 and 1470; Warden of the West Marches, 1470; Great Chamberlain, 1471 (surrendered to Clarence in 1472 and reappointed in 1478). Carlisle was not at this time an earldom, but in 1483, as a reward for his actions against the Scots and to assist him in protecting the border, Richard was granted 'the Castell, Cite, Towne and Lordshipp of Carlile, and the Feeferme of the same' for terme of life and successively thereafter to his heirs (*Rot. Parl.,* VI, 204).

18/15. See text, p. 20, 5th mar. n. for documentation of this manuscript.

18/19-24. Buck is in error. Clarence and Isabel were married, contrary to the king's consent, in Calais in 1469, during the rising of Clarence and Warwick against Edward

IV. Richard and Anne were married in 1472, after Warwick's death.

18/28. Halsted, I, 231, calls Buck's remark that Anne was 'the better woman' a 'quaint expression' suggesting 'superiority, either in mind or person'. It is obviously nothing of the kind but refers to her social position as widow of the Prince of Wales.

18/30-31. There is no evidence that Richard loved Anne, but none that he did not, except for the tales introduced into the Tudor histories that he planned to poison her to marry Elizabeth of York (see text, pp. 73 and 192). All three brothers showed inclination to marry within the kingdom, and Edward, at least, married for love. Anne and Richard probably grew up together while Richard was training in Warwick's household. Although Polydore (p. 557) claims that Richard killed her with cruelty by forsaking her bed in her last illness, by complaining of her barrenness, by rumouring her death, it seems unavoidable that he should have felt duty bound to avoid contagion when so urged by her doctors (Croyland, p. 572). He may have made known his fears of her death and have spoken to members of his Council (Polydore, p.557, says he confided in Rotherham) about her barrenness, since these matters concerned the safety of throne and kingdom.

Richard did stand to gain from the marriage, becoming joint heir to Warwick. We cannot know how much interest in gain swayed his choice. And as T.B. Pugh points out ('The Marcher Lords of Glamorgan and Morgannwg, 1317-1485', *Glamorgan County History*, III, Cardiff, 1971, p. 200), Anne too had reason to be motivated by self-interest in that Richard was the only potential husband powerful enough to enforce against Clarence her claims to her inheritance. The marriage took place without waiting for a Papal dispensation or for final arbitration of the lands.

18/32. For the creation of Richard's son as Prince of Wales, see text, pp. 48 and 51.

18/34-45. For the character and actions of the Duke of Clarence, see below, notes 135/7 and 136/48.

18/36-37. Stow (p. 716) was the first to discover and print the record of Clarence's indictment, in which he is accused of stating that Edward IV was illegitimate. He documents this information from 'Tower Records'. The accusation is given in *Rot. Parl.*, VI, 193-5.

19/16-18. The first Battle of St Albans took place in 1455, the second in 1461, Blore Heath in 1459, and Mortimer's Cross in 1461. Richard was too young to have fought in any of these, and during the last was in Utrecht with his mother. Bearing a commission of array, he conducted forces to join the king at Pontefract in 1464 (Kendall, *Richard III*, p. 56), but the Battle of Hexham in the same year was fought by Lord Montagu's forces. Near Doncaster in 1470, Edward IV and his supporters, Richard among them, were routed and fled thence to Holland. At this time Clarence was supporting Warwick and Henry VI. At Tewkesbury in 1471, Richard commanded the vanguard, particularly distinguishing himself. Shakespeare also makes Richard fight at Mortimer's Cross as well as at Barnet and Tewkesbury.

19/27 - 20/12. In *Comm.*, Buck gives Camden and Glover as his sources regarding Fauconberg. Here he seems to be using Polydore, pp. 530f, or the English historians who translate him. The chroniclers' accounts are variable and inaccurate. Warwick placed his cousin Fauconberg in command of a fleet to guard the Channel against

Edward IV's adherents. However, according to Hall and Grafton, he fell into poverty after Warwick's death and 'he robbed both on the sea & the lande, aswel his enemyes as also his frendes' (Hall, p. 302), then gathered a force against London, ostensibly to release Henry VI, but actually to rob and spoil. Stow (pp. 707f) adds that the Bastard withdrew to Sandwich after being beaten off by the Londoners and there sued for pardon, which Richard was sent to bestow, but later he was taken by Richard at Southampton and beheaded at Middleham. Paston Letters give the date of execution as 27 Sept. 1471 (I, 443).

Holinshed's account (pp. 321ff), based on the *Historie of the Arrivall of Edward IV* (ed. John Bruce, Cam. Soc. 1st ser. 1, London, 1838), pp. 33-8, is the most detailed. The dates of Fauconberg's movements are confirmed by J.R. Scott in 'Letters Respecting Fauconberge's Kentish Rising in 1471', *Archaeologia Cantiana* XI (1877), 359-64, on the basis of original letters: he wrote to the Council (8 May) asking permission to land, supposing Warwick and the Prince of Wales still alive. The Council refused, telling him of Edward IV's victory. He attacked the Kentish coast on 12 May. Edward sent men against him. From 16 to 18 May, Fauconberg lurked near London, fleeing when he heard of Edward's approach. He was captured by Richard on 23 May. His fate between the time of his capture in May and his death in September is uncertain. Cora L. Scofield, *The Life and Reign of Edward the Fourth* (London, 1967), II, 1f, says that he was released for service with Gloucester in Scotland but fled and was recaptured and put to death by Gloucester at Middleham (p. 20), his head being sent to London, as the Paston extract indicates.

20/15-16. Richard was Warden of the West Marches. Although it has been claimed that he also held 'supervisory authority over Northumberland's wardenship of the East and Middle Marches' (Kendall, p. 151), Charles Ross, *Edward IV* (London, 1974), pp. 199ff, shows that this was not the case until Richard was made Lieutenant of the North during war with Scotland in 1482.

20/16-17. See note 18/8-16 above for discussion of this appointment. The earldom of Carlisle did not come into being until the seventeenth century, and that Buck's friend Lord William Howard of Naworth, who was to be the founder of the line of earls of Carlisle, had his seat there was probably the cause of Buck's eagerness to find a precedent in Richard. Buck qualifies this appointment below, ll. 38-43.

20/18. Strictly, Yorkshire cannot be called Richard's native place, since he was born in Fotheringhay Castle, Northants. However, he almost certainly spent a period of his childhood there, from about 1461 to 1465, under Warwick's tutelage at Middleham Castle.

20/22. Ovid, *Ex Ponto,* I, iii, 35-36. All editions read 'ducit' where Buck has 'mulcet'.

20/35. Camden, p. 639, in 'Cumberland'.

20/35-37. William Hutchinson in *The History of the County of Cumberland* (Carlisle, 1794), I, 317, says that Richard resided at Penrith for the purpose of setting up opposition to the Scots. While there he built new towers and strengthened the whole structure.

20/3rd mar. n. William Howard of Naworth, born in 1563, was an uncle of Thomas

Arundel, to whom Buck's *History* is dedicated. He was, according to Hervey, p. 138, known for his upright character and intellectual interests. An antiquary, he numbered Cotton, Camden, and Spelman among his friends. In **Comm.** Buck often cites him as a *viva voce* source and refers to documents in his collection.

20/39-42. See note 18/8-16 above.

20/5th mar. n. This manuscript, to which Buck makes six references in the *History*, is no longer extant. In the early Cotton catalogues are listed several chronicle histories which can no longer be traced and therefore probably perished in the fire of 1731. For further discussion of this manuscript, see Introduction, pp. xlvii-xlviii and pp. cxii-cxiii.

20/45-46. For the cooperation between Richard and Northumberland as rulers of the North during Edward IV's lifetime see Ross, pp. 199-230.

20/49-50. There is no evidence that Richard desired greater power before the death of Edward IV. After Clarence's death, says Dominic Mancini, *The Usurpation of Richard the Third*, trans. and ed. C.A.J. Armstrong, 2nd ed. (Oxford, 1969), pp. 62-64,

> Ex eo perraro in regiam veniebaι. In provincia sua se continebat. Suos officiis et justicia sibi devincire studebat. Alienos clara fama morum et studiorum suorum ad sui amorem non mediocriter alliciebat. In militia ita clarus erat, ut quicquid arduum et cum periculo pro regno gerendum esset, eius consilio et ductui committeretur. Iis artibus Ricardus populorum benivolentiam sibi quesivit: et regine invidiam, a qua procul vivebat, vitavit.

20/50 - 21/1. For a detailed account of Richard's Northern government see F.W. Brooks, *The Council of the North*, rev. ed. (London, 1966), and Ross, pp. 199-203. The day to day relations of the Council of York with Richard can be seen in Robert Davies' *Extracts from the Municipal Records of the City of York* (London, 1843). Local loyalty to Richard went so deep that the Council recorded profound grief at his death (Davies, p. 218). Davies also records (p. 242) a dispute in 1491 when an insult to Richard by one Northerner to another was met with a threat of violence. Several references in *Letters and Papers, Foreign and Domestic, of the Reign of Henry VIII*, ed. J.S. Brewer, 2nd ed. (London, 1920) show that the efficacy of Richard's Northern government was still held up as a model in Henry VIII's time (I, pt. ii, nos. 2382 and 2913). But the view of Richard as a brilliant administrator has been challenged recently by Pugh, p. 202.

21/13-16. Polydore, p. 538, states that Edward IV's grievance against the Scots was a raid on his territories, despite the truce between the two countries. Buck seems to have misunderstood his source or to have treated it too curiously, for Polydore had said just previous to this that it was King Louis of France who refused to pay tribute, and that this breach of promise led King James, an ally of France, to break his treaty with England.

21/21-26. Albany went to France in 1479 and returned in 1482 in response to Edward's solicitations. Edward was to promote Albany as claimant to the throne in return for securing Berwick and breaking off Scots alliances with France (Ross, p. 287).

21/32-33. Polydore, p. 538, 'Hoc feliciter expedito negotio . . . .'

21/34 - 22/34. Buck has confused the account of this campaign by indicating that the castle of Berwick fell with the town. There were two excursions made to Berwick, the town falling in the first, the castle in the second, with Richard's journey to Edinburgh intervening. The order of events, according to Hall, pp. 331-6, is thus: on their entrance into Scotland, the army marched on Berwick. The town surrendered, but the castle held out, so Richard left Lord Stanley to besiege it while he himself proceeded to Edinburgh. Persuaded by the Duke of Albany, who had defected to his brother, to spare that city, he proclaimed that the King of Scots was to keep covenant with King Edward and make recompense for the Scottish raids. King James asked for peace, but refused the Castle of Berwick. After negotiations, James yielded, and Richard returned to Berwick to complete the siege of the castle, which fell. A detailed account of the campaign is given by Scofield, II, 302-49 and Ross, pp. 287ff.

21/46-47. Sir Edward Woodville was not Lord Rivers; it was Queen Elizabeth's other brother, Anthony Woodville, who held this title.

22/10-11. Croyland, pp. 562f: 'Nam sine ulla resistentia cum universo exercitu veniens usque *Edinburgam,* ditissimum oppidum dimittens incolume, rediit per *Berwicum:* villa namque ipsa in primo patriae introitu capta fuit: ac castrum quod diutius tenuit, tandem non sine caede & sanguine in *Anglicorum* potestatem venit'.

22/11-12. Hall, p. 336: 'kyng Edward . . . muche commended bothe his valiaunt manhode, and also his prudent pollicie . . . .' Croyland's seems a more mingled tribute: 'Doluit Rex *Edwardus* frivolum tantarum exitum expensarum; tametsi dolorem ipsum tantisper alleviaverit recuperatio *Berwici* supradicti' (p. 563).

22/32-34. Richard III's peace with Scotland was concluded in 1484. See text, pp. 57f and 205.

22/38-40. Polydore, p. 538; Holinshed, pp. 350-4; Hall, pp. 330-6; Stow, pp. 719f; Grafton, pp. 71-7.

23/11-16. There is considerable documentation for these letters sent to Richard from London after the death of Edward IV. Polydore, pp. 539f, says that Hastings sent to Richard in Yorkshire to tell him of the king's death and his appointed guardianship of Edward's sons and wife, and to urge him to come to London, 'ad rerum omnium curam suscipiendam'. Mancini, pp. 70-2, says the report was that Hastings wrote to Richard because of his affinity with him and hatred for the Queen Mother's party. Croyland (p. 565) makes it appear that Hastings would have been likely to contact Richard, for it was he who persuaded the Council to limit the new king's escort.

The final will of Edward IV does not survive. But we know one was made because its executors differ from those designated in the will of 1475, which does survive (it is transcribed in *Excerpta Historica,* London, 1831, pp. 366-79). Among other differences, the Woodvilles are excluded as executors of the second will. Croyland says (p. 564) that Edward on his deathbed added codicils to his will. If the Chronicler were sufficiently close to Edward IV's counsels to know what codicils were made on his deathbed, he might be relied upon had he stated that Edward in his will had named Richard Protector. However, he does not mention the Protectorship in connection with Richard until Richard had arrived in London and had the office conferred upon him by the Council. As a member of the Council, the chronicler probably felt that this was the highest authority for confirmation of the office, and thus his not mentioning the disposition of the Protectorship in the will does not exclude the possibility of Richard's being named therein. All other authorities agree in stating that Richard was appointed Protector by Edward IV (Polydore, p. 539; Mancini, p. 70; John Rous *Historia Regum Angliae,* 2nd ed., Oxford 1745, p. 213; Bernard André, *Historia Regis Henrici Septimi,* in *Memorials of King Henry the Seventh,* ed. Gairdner, R.S. 10, London, 1858, p. 23). Mancini qualifies his statement with 'ut ferunt', which may refer to the appointment in the will rather than to the appointment itself. Edward IV had the precedent of Henry V, who appointed his brother Humphrey, Duke of Gloucester, for making an appointment to the protectorship in his will. Gairdner, p. 44, considers the appointment probable and suggests that the king's brothers had been excluded from the early will because there was dissention between them over the Warwick estates. By the time the second will was presumably made, Clarence was dead, the queen's family patently unpopular, and Edward probably considered Richard the man 'most likely to be able to keep the peace between two opposite factions'.

23/16-17. Polydore, p. 539.

23/22-26. Davies indicates, pp. 143f, note, that there is no evidence of this visit by Richard to York. Croyland mentions it, however (p. 565), and says Richard made all the nobility of the North parts take an oath of fealty there to Edward V.

23/41 - 24/5. Those Tudor chroniclers who follow More's pathetic account of the Duke of York's removal from sanctuary ascribe it entirely to Richard's desire to have both boys in his power so that he could usurp the throne without leaving the Woodville party a prop for their hopes and machinations. Their retaining the Duke of York had, according to More, this specific aim: Rotherham in delivering the Great Seal to Elizabeth Woodville informed her that 'if thei crowne any other kinge then your sonne, whome they nowe haue with them, we shal on the morowe crowne his brother whome you haue here with you' (More, p. 22). Also there was a plot afoot to send the daughters of Edward IV abroad (Croyland, p. 567). In securing the Duke of York and surrounding the sanctuary with armed men to prevent escape, Richard crushed the Woodvilles' last hope. Charles T. Wood, 'The Deposition of Edward V', *Traditio,* XXXI (1975), 262f, emphasizes the impossibility of conducting a coronation when division threatened, with the king's mother and brother (the next heir) still in sanctuary. The Council certainly acquiesced to Richard's plea for York's release by means of a threat of arms (Mancini, p. 89, More, p. 27). It should be noted that the duke's removal from sanctuary occurred on 16 June, after the execution of Hastings (13 June), not before.

24/9-10. The Tower was not at that time exclusively a prison, but a royal palace as well. The repository of royal treasure, it was the strongest and safest place in the kingdom. Edward IV used it as a palace, and it was the customary lodging for kings before their coronation. According to Croyland, p. 566, the Council agreed to Edward's removal to the Tower as a place where he would be less restricted.

24/25-26. Commynes, II, 305.

24/26-28. More's testimony, p. 24, is that 'the Duke of Gloucester bare him in open sighte so reuerentelye to the Prince, with all semblaunce of lowlinesse'.

24/38-40. Croyland, p. 565.

24/42 - 25/11. See text, pp. 39-45 for an extended version of this solicitation, for which Buck's source is More.

25/50 - 27/14. Edward IV died leaving factions behind him. His failure to secure the succession led to upheaval on his death (see Ross, pp. 424ff). That the heir was a child meant that control was open to the party which could wield greatest power. Feeling against the Woodvilles was such that 'the old nobility' were anxious to prevent their gaining greater influence over Edward V.

Croyland and Mancini, the only contemporary sources on the events of Richard's takeover, agree substantially about the details leading to it. More, who may have derived information from Morton, confirms these details, though it is difficult to separate his facts from his irony. It appears that the Council which met immediately on Edward IV's death debated whether Richard should, according to his brother's will, govern alone, or whether there should be a council at the head of the government with Richard as chief advisor. The latter decision prevailed and was reported to Richard by Hastings (Mancini, p. 70). This placed Richard in an uncomfortable position, with the precedent of Duke Humphrey of Gloucester, designated Protector by Henry V's will, restricted by Parliament to a function under a council, and ultimately murdered. Richard wrote urging the Council to dispose the government according to his brother's will, giving him the Protectorship (Mancini, p. 73). Some thought the coronation should not be scheduled until Richard's arrival; others, like Dorset, thought, 'Nos tanti sumus momenti, ut etiam sine patruo possimus hec statuere, et statuta perficere' (Mancini, p. 74). The date for the coronation was fixed and the king told to arrive three days before it, presumably to forestall any move by Richard.

Then began a race toward London. Richard wrote to Rivers, in whose charge the boy was, to arrange a meeting so that they could enter London together. But though he met Rivers, the king's party had gone on. Richard caught up with it at Stony Stratford. Buckingham, meanwhile, had joined him with forces. Rivers, Gray, and other members of the party surrounding the king were arrested. The Woodville contingent in London prepared armed resistance to protect themselves and take the young king from Richard, but general feeling that it was just for the king to remain with Richard caused Elizabeth Woodville to withdraw to sanctuary (Mancini, p. 78). Dorset and Edward Woodville fled, and it was rumoured that they had plotted Richard's death (Rous, p. 213). Dorset had the royal treasure, and he and Edward Woodville, who had been under orders from Edward IV to make naval preparations against France, were fitting out a fleet.

According to Polydore, p. 541, Richard told the council that Rivers had hindered him in his legitimate attempt to secure the king, whom his brother had left in his care. Arms found or planted in the Woodville baggage were produced as evidence that they intended an ambush. Rivers fell prey to political jealousies: he was a rival of Hastings for the captaincy of Calais and of Buckingham for the Vice-Regency of Wales (John Gough Nichols, Introduction to *Grants, etc. from the Crown during the Reign of Edward the Fifth*, Cam. Soc., 1st ser. 60, London, 1854, p. xxiv). He had the power to govern the prince's household, command his retinue, remove his person, and levy Welsh forces in his name. And he had proved an inveterate political plotter, as E.W. Ives, 'Andrew Dymmock and the Papers of Anthony, Earl Rivers, 1482-1483', *BIHR*, XLI (1968), 216-29 demonstrates. On 24 June, Rivers and Gray were executed under form of law, Northumberland presiding (Rous, p. 213).

26/2nd mar. n. The title given the work here indicates that Buck is referring to its representation in one of the chronicles which have chapters divided under regnal names (Hall, Grafton, Stow, or Holinshed). All these authors copy More *verbatim*. What More says (p.14) is that the queen surrounded the prince with her own kin, 'whereby her bloode mighte of youth be rooted in the princes fauor'. Richard objects that it was 'vnto vs no litle ieopardy, to suffer our wel proued euil willers, to grow in ouergret authoritie with the prince in youth, namely which is lighte of beliefe and sone perswaded'. And if the Woodvilles bring the prince to London with great force they will antagonize the old nobility, 'And thus should all the realme fall on a rore' (p. 16).

26/27-32. More, pp. 10-11 says that there was dissention between the queen's kindred and Lord Hastings (not between the queen's kindred and the king's blood), which Edward IV tried to reconcile on his deathbed. However, More does have Richard suggest the Woodvilles' hand in removing Clarence: 'Why not as easily as they haue done some other alreadye, as neere of his royal bloode as we' (p.15).

26/47-48. More, p.19, 'they sayde that the Lorde Marques hadde entered into the Tower of London, and thence taken out the kinges Treasor, and sent menne to the sea. All whiche thinge these Dukes wiste well were done for good purposes and necessari by the whole counsaile at London . . . .' Mancini, p. 80, reports a division of the late king's treasure among the Queen Mother, Dorset, and Sir Edward Wood-ville. Armstrong, p.119f, considers this evidence against the Woodvilles, though he feels that Edward Woodville's putting to sea was a legitimate measure dictated by the preparations for war with France at the time of Edward IV's death.

26/49 - 27/1. More, p. 24:

> such of the Dukes seruantes as rode with the cartes of theyr
> stuffe that were taken (amonge whiche stuffe no meruayle
> thoughe somme were harneys . . .) they shewed vnto the
> people al the waye as they wente: loe here bee the barelles
> of harneys that this traitours had priuelye conuayd in theyr
> carryage to destroye all the noble lordes with all.

27/15 - 28/12. More is Buck's source for Hastings' death, the events surrounding which are obscure. As an enemy of the Woodvilles, Hastings allied himself on Edward IV's death with the party which opposed them, that of Richard and Buckingham. Under Edward IV his influence had been immense. But Richard shifted the centre of power, and rewards went to rising men such as Norfolk and Buckingham. Perhaps Hastings, once head of 'the dominant household clique' (E.F. Jacob, *The. Fifteenth Century*, Oxford, 1961, p. 581), felt himself slighted and his power curtailed. B.P. Wolffe, 'When and Why Did Hastings Lose His Head?', *EHR,*LXXXIX (1974), 842f suggests an alternative motive: that Hastings opposed Richard's plans to extend his protectorship beyond the coronation. Whether what Hastings opposed was a scheme of Richard's to retain this formidable power (Wood, p. 256, suggests he intended to do so by indefinitely postponing the coronation) or to deprive Edward V of the kingship is not known. In any case, Hastings, Rotherham, Morton and possibly Stanley — prominent members of Edward IV's council — formed an intermediate party with the young prince as their rallying point. According to Polydore, pp. 540f, Hastings called this party together, with the intention of liberating the prince from Richard's control. Some, says Polydore, favoured violent action, but others felt there was no need. Since control of the prince was the object, it probably necessitated communicating with the Woodville party, and the agent of this communication seems to have been Dorset's mistress, Jane Shore — possibly Hastings' mistress as well — whom Richard let off with a public penance for adultery. Wood, (p. 267) suggests that she helped Hastings to communicate with Dorset, not with Elizabeth Woodville. Thus there seems clearly to have been organized opposition led by Hastings, some of whose members favoured violent means of putting an end to Richard's power.

Hastings had to be executed peremptorily because he was an immensely powerful man with many retainers who could be summoned to take his part (see William Huse Dunham, Jr., *Lord Hastings' Indentured Retainers, 1461-1483,* Transactions of the Conn. Academy of Arts and Sciences, 39, New Haven, 1955). He was powerful also in his association with France, from which he received a huge pension, and he had already threatened to oppose the Woodvilles by retiring to Calais, where he could set up an independent naval station, if they insisted on bringing Edward V to London with too large a force (Croyland, pp. 564f).

For recent arguments about the date of Hastings' death see the four articles by Alison Hanham and B.P. Wolffe in *EHR,* LXXXVII, LXXXIX, XC and XCI and the very useful one by J.A.F. Thomson, 'Richard III and Lord Hastings', *BIHR,* XLXXXVIII (1975), 22-30.

27/22 - 27. More, p. 46, 'And vndoubtedly the protectour loued him wel, & loth was to haue loste him, sauing for fere lest his life shoulde haue quailed their purpose'. He means this ironically.

27/36 - 28/1. According to More, Richard's informant against Hastings was William Catesby, who sat on both his and Hastings' councils. That Catesby stood to gain by Hastings' death may have biased his reports (see J.S. Roskell, 'William Catesby, Counsellor to Richard III', *Bulletin of the John Rylands Library,* XLII (1959), 145-74.

28/13-16. The defence on grounds of reasons of state Buck probably drew from the whole tenour of Cornwallis' essay, which instead of clearing Richard of the crimes attributed to him grants their existence but finds a roundabout way of justifying them. Cornwallis uses this defence in exculpating Richard when he speaks of the murder of the Princes: 'sutch is the difference, betwene the thought*es*, the actions, the dispositions of Princes, and Subiect*es*, that I houlde no Subiecte sufficiantly Iudiciall to Censure them: theire Courses soe vnlike, that what is meete and expedient in a Prince in a lower fortune is vtterly vnmeete, vnexpedient' (p. 19).

28/17. Ogygus, according to the *Oxford Classical Dictionary*, 2nd ed. (Oxford, 1970), p. 748, was 'a primeval king . . . . The first Deluge was in his time'. Buck is saying 'since the flood'. Camden also uses the expression.

28/24-25. Seneca, *Thyestes*, 222-224:

> coniugem stupro abstulit
> regnumque furto; specimen antiquum imperi
> fraude est adeptus.

28/27-28. Seneca, *Thyestes*, 312-13. Buck has given the line division incorrectly.

28/5th mar. n. *Axiomata Politica* seems no longer extant. It was originally part of Cotton's collection, and was evidently a compendium of political maxims. Buck quotes from it once in the *Commentary*. For further discussion, see above, p. cxiii.

28/40-50. Aristotle, *Politics*, III, viii, 5.

29/24-44. The idea that Richard should be taxed for not killing those he should have destroyed instead of for those he did kill is derived from Cornwallis, who cites his lenity to the Countess of Richmond and to Stanley, pp. 26-8:

> for though he Cutt of the head of a mighty Conspirator
> [Buckingham], yet he suffred the Conspiracye to take soe
> deepe Roote, that, in the end it cutt of his glorey, and ouer
> shaddowed his greatness . . . . would a cruell bloodthirsty
> Prince haue done so . . . . what Prince could haue done
> lesse. nay what Kinge would not haue done more, since
> both the effecte, and the precedent ffeare, are both such
> inward tormenters, as hard it is to determine w*h*ich is
> moste greeuious, so opposite, soe contrarye to the nature
> of a prince: beinge borne not to feare, but to be ffeared;
> that it is most naturall, *and* moste iuste to remoue sutch a
> teror.

29/29-36. Dr John Morton, Bishop of Ely, according to his pupil More (pp. 90-3), roused Buckingham to rebellion against Richard, then fled to Flanders to aid Henry Tudor. Richard had committed Morton to Buckingham's custody after arresting him at the famous Tower council. He granted him a general pardon in December, 1484 (Harl. 433, f.89). **Christopher Urswick,** an agent of Morton's who bore his messages to Henry Tudor, became chaplain to Henry VII and was probably one of More's informants for his *History* (Sylvester, Introduction to More, p. lxvii). **Peter Courtenay,** Bishop of Exeter, and his brother **Edward, Earl of Devon,** after the failure of Buckingham's rebellion fled to Brittany and joined with Richmond. They were thereupon attainted by Richard. Elizabeth Woodville's son, the **Marquess of Dorset,** who had taken sanctuary after the failure of the Woodville cause, then escaped and gone into hiding, also joined in plotting for Buckingham's rebellion and fled to

Brittany after its failure. He was associated with the Courtenays in the attainder, but after Richard had persuaded Elizabeth Woodville to come out of sanctuary late in 1484, she wrote to Dorset urging him to return to England and make peace with Richard. He was discovered by Henry's men and forced or persuaded to go back to the Tudor party. Nevertheless, Richard seems to have trusted in Dorset's good faith, for he omitted his name from his June proclamation against the rebels, though he had previously included it. Perhaps he had reason for this trust, for the Marquess was imprisoned briefly by Henry VII on that monarch's accession. The **Earl of Oxford** was an ancient enemy of the House of York, rebelling first against Edward IV, then against Richard III. He aided the rebellion of Warwick and Clarence, taking part in the Battle of Barnet, from which he fled. Taken by Edward in 1473, he was imprisoned in the Castle of Hammes, Richard III made generous provision for his wife (Harl. 433, f.53^v). Oxford, having won over his custodian, **Sir James Blount,** escaped from Hammes to join Henry Tudor's expedition and become commander of a huge army against Richard at Bosworth. **Walter Hungerford** was attainted for his part in Buckingham's rebellion, but was pardoned by Richard, only to join Henry Tudor at Bosworth. **Sir John Fortescue** was Porter of the Town of Calais and assisted Blount in releasing the Earl of Oxford. Interestingly enough, he had accompanied Oxford and Blount on 6 July 1483, on a commission to the French king for the purpose of renewing the treaty between England and France (*Foedera,* XII, 195f). On 20 September 1485 Henry VII granted Fortescue the office of Chief Butler of England (*Pat. Rolls,* 1485-1494, p.8). **Sir Thomas Bourchier** left Brakenbury's contingent along with Hungerford to join the Tudor band at Bosworth. **Sir John Savage, Sir Brian Sanford,** and **Sir Simon Digby** defected from Richard the night before the battle (Polydore, p.562). **Dr John Morgan** and **Rice ap Thomas** held positions in Wales, the latter being a prominent military leader. They secretly entered Henry's service and assisted Henry on his landing in Wales. The desertion of **Sir Gilbert Talbot** and his nephew the **Earl of Shrewsbury** was, Kendall suggests (p. 414), for personal causes: Shrewsbury was married to Hastings' daughter, and Lady Eleanor Butler, whose shame Richard had proclaimed, was his kinswoman. Kendall, p. 569n, mentions Shrewsbury's presence on Richard's side at Bosworth, documented from Harl. 452, and his capture afterwards by Henry, but considers the evidence of his adherence to Richard insufficient for including him among Richard's followers. **Reginald Bray** was an instrument of the Countess of Richmond, employed in carrying messages for her, and acting as her agent in organizing the Kentish leaders associated with Buckingham's rebellion. He was pardoned by Richard for his actions in Buckingham's rebellion, but continued secretly to assist Richmond. **Dr Lewis** was a physician in the entourage of the Countess of Richmond employed in carrying messages between her and Elizabeth Woodville. By **Poins,** Buck may refer to Sir Robert Poins, knighted in the field by Henry VII, a member of Henry VII's council and of Henry's forces at Taunton against Perkin Warbeck. But seeing this name and that of the much more prominent Sir Edward Poynings in the chronicles, he might have confused the two. Poynings escaped to Brittany after Buckingham's rebellion and aided Henry Tudor abroad. Stow (p. 785) notes that knights made by Henry in the field included **Sir John Mortimer** along with Sir Robert Poins. By 'young **Stanley**', Buck means either Sir William Stanley, or George, Lord Strange, son of Lord Thomas Stanley. The former was directly responsible for Richard's death at Bosworth, holding apparently neutral until the last moment. Having thrown in his lot with Richmond, though nominally loyal to Richard, he was, like his brother, a timeserver, waiting to see how the battle went before acting. When Richard broke away from his host to attempt a daring onslaught upon Henry and those immediately surrounding him, he rode across Sir William's flank. Sir William then cut the king off from his army and descended upon him and his small band. Lord Strange was held by Richard during the preparations for the battle as hostage for his father's loyalty. Lord Stanley continually refused Richard's orders to join him in the battle, and Richard declared Strange's life forfeit, but the sentence was delayed until after the battle, and Strange survived to become the subject of Henry Tudor, as did his father and uncle.

Most of the supporters in this list of Buck's can be found in *Pat. Rolls* as recipients of grants and offices under Henry VII.

30/23-27. Morton, when he saw that Buckingham's rebellion was doomed to failure, after stopping briefly at Ely fled not to France but to Flanders and from there communicated with Henry Tudor, forwarding his aims.

31/9-38. Buck mainly follows Polydore, who probably derived the information from Henry himself, in this account of Henry's early years, as do the other Tudor chroniclers and modern historians (Scofield, II, 19 and 172f and Chrimes, pp. 15ff).

Buck has either been careless with his sources or confused by them, or both. Some alterations seem accidental, others designed for effect. He distorts the facts regarding Pembroke's efforts to rescue Richmond: Richmond was in Pembroke, not Raglan Castle, and Pembroke was coming from Tewkesbury, though he had previously been in France. Sir William Herbert had died in 1469. Buck deviates from Polydore to return to his old authority Glover (see below, note 32/2nd mar. n.) in the motivation he gives Duke Francis for retaining the earls and places Edward IV's first embassy somewhat later than Francis' private decision to keep them under guard. He adds an extra embassy from Edward by splitting in two parts the one which followed the French peace. The confusion probably arose from Stillington's being mentioned by the chroniclers (Hall, p. 332, Grafton, Stow, and Holinshed) but not by Polydore. Buck gives the date of the Stillington embassy as 1480, however (text, p. 35), the chroniclers as 10 Edward IV (1476). Buck's descriptions of events and motivations are more detailed than Polydore's, and he increases the dramatic effect by reversing the roles of Richmond, Landois, and Chenlet (not 'Chandait', as Buck has it, perhaps confusing him with Philibert de Chandée, who later commanded Henry's Norman recruits) and inventing a scene of direct discourse. He has compressed into one negotiation Hutton's embassy before Richmond's first invasion, which was rejected, and the second embassy, after Richmond's return to Brittany, which was accepted, though Richmond escaped.

31/15-18. This is actually Grafton's statement in his continuation to *The Chronicle of John Hardyng,* ed. Henry Ellis (London, 1812), p. 463.

31/33-40. Henry was four years old when he was committed to the custody of Lord

Herbert. He was born in January 1457, and captured by Herbert in September 1461.

31/34-37. Commynes, II, 233, 'lequel m'a autresfoiz compté, peu avant qu'il partist de ce royaulme, que, depuis l'aage de cinq ans, il avoit esté gardé comme fugitif ou en prison'.

31/42-43 and 32/1st mar. n. This is an example of incorrect recollection. Stow merely says (p. 707) in an entry under the year 1471, that Pembroke and Richmond fled to Brittany.

32/34-37. Alain Bouchard, *Les Grandes Cronicques de Bretaigne* (n.p. [1517] — publication date given in Buck's hand), f. cxcix. The copy Buck annotated has an 'X' in the margin at this point. That the quotation suffers virtually no alteration except in spelling probably indicates that Buck was copying directly from the book as he wrote at least an early draft.

32/3rd mar. n. According to Glover, p. 609, John the Valiant, Duke of Brittany and Earl of Montfort and Richmond was the last to have held both titles. He lived from 1339 to 1399 (GEC, X, 822) and left no issue.

33/32-33. Commynes, II, 234.

33/ 26-29. Johannes Meyer, *Annales Flandriae in Annales, sive Historiae Rerum Belgicarum* (Frankfurt, 1580), Ch. 17, p. 418. Buck's references to Meyer vary the Christian name from Johannes to Jacobus. At this point the Editor misread 'Meyerus' as 'Neyerus', and it appears thus in all the manuscript copies and the printed edition.

33/48. The word 'politician' was frequently used in a derogatory sense during the late sixteenth and early seventeenth centuries. For example, in *1 Henry IV*, Hotspur's 'I am whipped and scourged with rods, / Nettled and stung with pismires, when I hear / Of this vile politician Bolingbroke' (I, iii).

34/7-10. Ennius, in Cicero, *De Officiis*, II, vii, 'Quem metuunt oderunt; quem quisque odit perisse expetit'.

35/7-14. Since Polydore gives no dates, it is impossible to say exactly when Edward's overtures were made.

35/1st mar. n. The justification for this statement is probably the passage quoted in text, p. 32 from Bouchard, f. cxcix.

37/35-36. Commynes, II, 233 says fifteen years, not twelve: 'Ce conte de Richemont avoit esté quinze ans ou environ prisonnier en Bretaigne'.

37/39. Lucan, *De Bello Civile*, III, 448.

38/1st mar. n. The reference is evidently to Seleucus I. Confusion may have resulted from the fact that this ruler was killed by Ptolemy 'Ceraunus', so called from the Greek for thunderbolt (Trogus Pompeius, XVII). The second epithet Lucretius applied to Scipio, *De Rerum Natura*, III, 1034: 'Scipiadas, belli fulmen, Carthaginis horror'.

38/16-17. Henry the Saint is Henry VI, for whose canonization Henry VII applied (Polydore, p. 532). The prophecy appears in Polydore, p. 522: 'Iste nempe iste est, cui nos ac nostri aduersarij rerum possessione cedemus'.

38 - 46. The recent articles by Wolffe and Wood have stressed that knowledge of later events must not make us too ready, as were the Tudor historians, to see in the events preceding the deposition a carefully planned scheme by Richard to take the throne: self protection and desire to extend his protectorship after the coronation were his first considerations. But that he should eventually seek the throne was logical, since, although there was in the fourteenth and fifteenth centuries 'a strong predilection' for primogeniture,

> usurpation by the strongest and ablest male member of the larger royal family became almost the norm. From 1399 special 'inauguration ceremonies', by which the king performed every kind of royal act prior to his coronation, were designed to convert usurpation into a valid authority. The office of king was a very exacting one. Its holder had to be physically tough, able to win battles and campaigns, with a commanding presence and integrity; able to inspire loyalty, service and confidence.
>
> (B.P. Wolffe, *Yorkist and Early Tudor Government,*
> London, 1960, p. 6)

Because no law governed succession, the strongest claimant could make his own case. Richard's case relied on bastardizing the heirs by primogeniture to maintain the Yorkist platform of legitimism by which his father had claimed the throne. He also had his election by the Three Estates ratified by Parliament, making his title thus doubly sure according to public authority (Chrimes, *English Constitutional Ideas in the Fifteenth Century*, Cambridge, 1936, *passim*; Wood, *passim*).

The formal steps Richard took in his accession closely followed his brother's precedent, according to Armstrong, 'Inauguration Ceremonies of the Yorkist Kings and Their Title to the Throne', *Transactions of the Royal Historical Society*, 4th ser., XXX (1948), 51-73: the popular petition, the formal protest by the inaugurated king, the political sermon at Paul's Cross, followed by the people's assent to his accession, the act of sitting in the King's Bench, addressing the judges, and making a symbolic gesture of pardon all followed his brother's pattern. Wood stresses the importance to Richard's claim of the ratification by Parliament (pp. 276ff).

38/42. Genesis 21:10.

38/5th mar. n. Buck's disclaimer of responsibility resembles Cornwallis' conclusion (see above, note 3/14). It is interesting that at this late date Buck should feel compelled to protect himself against the charge of attacking the Tudors, but since James was descended from Edward IV's daughter, the allegation of illegitimacy could not be expected to please him. For Buck's general attitudes toward James and toward the Tudors, see above, pp. cxxvi-cxxviii.

38/47 - 39/6. For the statement regarding the general consent to Richard's title, Buck is relying entirely on the *Titulus Regius* (*Rot. Parl.*, VI, 240-2), which he takes at face value, and on his reading of More, which disregards the irony of that author. Richard was popular in the North, but in London there seems not to have been strong feeling in his favour. That this was partially the result of antagonism of South against North one can sense from Croyland's anti-Northern bias. The special circumstances which exacerbated this traditional antagonism in Richard's particular case are studied by A.J. Pollard, 'The Tyranny of Richard III', *Journal of Medieval History,* III (1977), 147-165. How far acquiescence to his claims was influenced by the presence of forces assembling in London we can only guess.

39/21-22. Richard's descent into the Great Chamber is an addition of Buck's. More, whose account he follows in this scene, has Richard listen to Buckingham's address from a balcony of Baynard's Castle. Buck obviously has his own dramatic image, for he sees Richard sitting down when he enters the chamber, and then standing to reply to the address, after which he sits down.

39 - 45. This account is taken, with some liberties, from More, pp. 73-80; Holinshed, pp. 390-6; Grafton, pp. 107-12; Stow, pp. 758-65; and Hall, pp. 369-74. The reference to Morton as the first of the chroniclers follows the assumption, discussed above pp. ciii-civ and cxxi that Morton was the original author of a pamphlet which formed the basis of More's work.

39/37 - 40/40. This speech is actually an abbreviated version of Buckingham's speech to the Mayor and citizens, More pp. 72-4. More merely reports the petition to Richard without using direct discourse (p.78).

39/4th mar.n. The *Titulus Regius* and Croyland, p. 567, give Eleanor Butler as the woman to whom Edward was contracted. More and the historians who reproduce his account of Edward's marriage call the woman to whom he was allegedly precontracted Elizabeth Lucy, one of Edward's mistresses and probably the mother of his illegitimate son Arthur Plantagenet. The change of name may be one of Henry's efforts, like his destruction of the *Titulus Regius,* to obscure what actually happened. But for his historians to say that a precontract with Elizabeth Lucy actually occurred would have made Arthur Plantagenet ostensibly legitimate heir to the throne (A.F. Pollard, 'Sir Thomas More's "Richard III" ', *History,* XVII, 1933, 320). Instead, More, or his sources, invent an inquisition, for which no evidence exists, in which Elizabeth Lucy denies that she was ever contracted to Edward (More, p. 66). The whole affair is minimized, made to seem a desperate measure by the king's mother to stop the Woodville match. Her argument was that Edward was Elizabeth Lucy's husband before God because he had got her with child (pp. 64f):

> By reson of which wordes, such obstacle was made in the mater, that either ye Bishoppes durst not, or the king would not, procede to the solempnisacion of this weding, til these same wer clerely purged, & the trouth wel & openly testified. Wherupon dame Elysabeth Lucy was sent for. And albeit y^t she was by ye kinges mother & many other put in good comfort, to affirme that she was ensured vnto ye king: yet when she was solempnely sworne to say the trouth, she confessed that they were neuer ensured.

Thus two purposes were served: the precontract basis of Richard's claim, the existence of which, though not the details, were doubtless remembered by many, was shown to be trivial and without foundation; and Arthur Plantagenet was soundly proven illegitimate, without claim to the throne. That More and his followers knew this information to be false is unlikely. The Parliament Rolls did not become available for inspection until the 1580's, and so it was not until then that the error could be seen and corrected.

41/14-15. More, p. 78, 'he loked very strangely therat'.

41/17 - 42/1. This speech is constructed, using much of More's phraseology, from More's report of Richard's reply (pp. 78f), which is indirect discourse.

43/9-44. This second attempt is Buck's own addition, as is the Lord Mayor's speech. Buck's final speech of Buckingham is expanded from More's report, and in it he deviates farther from More's wording than he has in the previous portions of the account.

43/50 - 44/3. More, p. 79: 'These wordes muche moued the protectoure, whiche els as euery manne may witte, would neuer of likelyhoode haue inclyned therunto'. More's intention is ironic. Richard's protestations were, as More has the populace assume, a matter of form. His father's formal protestations when granted the Protectorship under Henry VI may be seen in *Rot. Parl.*, V, 242 and 286.

44/9. The reference to the Earl of Richmond is Buck's own interpretation of More's words, p. 79: 'If he woulde geue them a resolute aunswere to the contrarye, whyche they woulde bee lothe to heare, than muste they needes seke and shold not faile to fynd some other noble manne that woulde'.

44/17 - 45/4. This speech is very much expanded and inflated in style from the speech More gives to Richard, pp. 79f.

44/49 - 45/2. If Richard had lived long enough it is possible he would have renewed the war against France. He stood out strongly against his brother Edward in the latter's decision to accept a peace and take his army home in 1475. In using the war with France as part of his platform, he would have been following the precedent of his father, who adopted the name 'Plantagenet' on the surrender of Maine and Anjou as a sign of Yorkist defence of France. Montague Rhodes James, *A Descriptive Catalogue of the Manuscripts in the Library of Lambeth Palace* (Cambridge, 1930-2), no. 506, registers a book, William Worcester's *Collections on Normandy*, which includes a prefatory letter addressed by Worcester's son to Edward IV. However, it appears to have been originally addressed to Richard III and the name altered by erasure. It mentions the king's (presumably Richard's) intention to war with France. Queen Isabella wrote to Richard on his accession to propose alliance with him against France, but although he responded with friendship and renewal of alliance, he did not mention France (*Letters and Papers Illustrative of the Reigns of Richard III. and Henry VII.,* ed. James Gairdner, R.S. 24, London, 1861-3, I, 31-51).

45/19-20. Richard's claim was ratified in Parliament on 23 January *(Rot. Parl.,* VI, pp. 240-2). This is one of several examples of Buck's upholding the authority of Parliament, an important contemporary question. See above, p. cxxv. Wood, like Buck more than three hundred years before him, stresses the importance of the proceedings surrounding Richard's accession in exalting Parliamentary authority (*passim*). He and Dunham, in 'The Right to Rule England', *American Historical Review*, LXXXI (1976), 758, go so far as to say, 'No king of England did so much — on paper — as did Richard III to raise parliament's position in the frame of government': his need to have his election ratified in Parliament showed that its 'authority now derived from that of the kingdom; and hence that in politics, if not in law, that body had become transcendent' (p. 761).

45/26-30. This suggestion of a petition sent from the North originates with Croyland. See note 46/3-16. The extant evidence of Richard's dealings with the North is in the form of urgent letters, one on 10 June to the City of York (Davies, p. 148-50) and one on 11 June to his kinsman Lord Neville (*Paston Letters*, ed. James Gairdner, Edinburgh, 1910, III, 306, no. 874) asking for immediate assistance of as many men in arms as can be sent. He gives as his motive for these requests the plots of 'the Quiene, hir blode adherenttes and affinitie, which have extended, and daly doith intend, to murder and utterly distroy us & our cousyn the duc of Bukkyngham, and the old royall blode of this realme' (Davies, p. 149). Whether these requests were really made in fear of a suddenly discovered Woodville-Hastings plot or merely contrived to look as if they were is uncertain. Certainly Richard's life was in danger from the Woodville faction. Possibly his real purpose in summoning the troops was to ensure order during his takeover, toward which end he wished to intimidate the London populace and Council by show of force. According to Croyland, p. 566, this is the impression he created.

45/40-46 and mar. n. For a similar disclaimer by the author, see text, p. 38, 5th mar. note. Cornwallis feels a similar fear in setting forth so unpopular an opinion and one which challenges the claim of the ruling house: '. . . I neuer had taken sutch paines to defend his Innocency, nor in some Iudgementes to Indainger my owne' (p. 29).

45/47 - 46/1. That Richard took possession of the marble seat in Westminster Hall on 26 June is attested by Croyland, p. 566, More, p. 82, and confirmed by a document of 28 June in Harl. 433, f. 238 (see below, note 46/3-16). The calculation that this was six or seven days after he was proclaimed stems from Grafton (p. 113),who says Richard began his reign on 19 June and was 'proclaymed king openly by sounde of trompet the next day folowing'. Since this seat was the official chair of the king in his role as dispenser of justice, it was probably at this time that Richard, as More relates (p. 81), lectured his officers of justice on administration of the law and pardoned John Fogg.

46/3-16. Croyland, p. 566f:

> *Richardus* Protector vicesimo sexto die praefati mensis *Junii* Regimine Regni sub titulo Regii nominis sibi vendicavit; seque eodem die apud magnam aulam *Westmonasterii* in cathedram marmoream ibi intrusit. Color autem introitus & captae possessionis hujusmodi is erat. Ostendebatur per modum supplicationis in quodam rotulo pergameni, quod filii Regis *Edwardi* erant Bastardi . . . . Quocirca supplicabatur ei in fine ejusdem rotuli, ex parte dominorum & communitatis Regni, ut jus suum in se assumeret. Divulgatum enim tunc erat, quod rotulus iste in partibus Borealibus, unde tantus populus *Londonias* venire debet, conceptus fuit, cum tamen qui fuit unicus tantae seditionis & infamiae auctor continue apud *Londonias* constitutus, à nemine ignorabatur.

Because we no longer have the manuscript Buck used, we cannot tell to what extent the differences between his and the above version are the result of differences between manuscripts and to what extent they represent intentional changes on his part in order to reduce derogatory implications for Richard. His addition of 'et tum mox omnibus proceribus tam laicis quam ecclesiasticis et ceteris assidentibus et astantibus' is too long to be accounted for by deliberate rewriting and may have been in a manuscript he used. There is evidence of its accuracy in Harl. 433, f. 238 (quoted in *Letters and Papers,* ed. Gairdner, I, 12), which calls the attention of the king's officers in Calais to the accession of Richard:

> whose sure and true title is evidently shewed and declared in a bill of peticion which the lordes spirituelx and temporelx and the commons of this land solemplye porrected unto the kinges highnes at London, the xxvj^ti day of Juyn. Where-upon the kinges said highnes, notably assisted by welle nere alle the lordes spirituelle and temporelle of this roy-aume, went the same day unto his palais of Westminster, and ther in suche roialle honorable appareilled within the gret halle ther, toke possession and declared his mynde that same day he wold begyn to reigne upon his people . . . .

46/42-43. Howard was knighted at Towton, 29 March 1461, by Edward IV and made Knight of the Garter 24 April 1471. Writs of Edward IV from 1470 to 1482 refer to him as '*Johanni Howard de Howard, Militi,* and *Johanni Howard, Chivaler,* whereby he is held to have become LORD HOWARD' (GEC, IX, 611).

46/47-48. Buck refers to Thomas of Brotherton (b. 1300), fifth son of Edward I. He was not the first earl of Norfolk who was also Marshal.

46/49. The barony of Breus or Brewes really became extinct in 1399. It was associated with the dukes of Norfolk in the marriage of Thomas of Brotherton to the sister of Thomas, Lord Brewes, and the subsequent marriage of this Lord Brewes to the widow of Thomas of Brotherton's son Edward.

46/50 - 47/2. I have not located this precise copy of this warrant. For notice of other copies, see below, note 57/27-30.

47/6-7. Kendall, p. 551n, has compiled evidence to show that Stanley was released almost immediately. It is possible that he was never formally arrested or perhaps only briefly kept under observation. Richard allowed Stanley to carry the mace of High Constable at his coronation and conferred this office on him at the death of Bucking-ham. He made him Knight of the Garter. No evidence of his holding the office of High Steward in Richard's household survives except in Grafton's account (p. 116). This is the office Stanley had held under Edward IV, and Richard probably restored it to him along with his place in Council.

47/10-11. This reference is not in More. Buck has failed to note where the More section copied *verbatim* into the chronicles ends. Grafton, p. 116, is the source for the statement that Surrey executed the office of Constable at the coronation.

47/12-13. Stanley's appointment to the Constableship for life at the annual fee of £100 is given in *Pat. Rolls* (1476-85),p. 367, 18 Nov. 1483.

47/15-18. Rotherham was arrested, along with Morton and Hastings and possibly Stanley, at the Tower Council on 13 June. His collusion with the Woodvilles is beyond question, and his offence, admitted by all authorities, considerable. He had, in the panic following the arrest of Rivers and Gray, handed over the Great Seal to Elizabeth Woodville, but, regretting the rashness of his action, retrieved it (More, p. 22). He was Archbishop of York, not of Canterbury. He was restored to his place in Council after his release, but not to his position as Chancellor, which was given to Dr John Russell, Bishop of Lincoln (More, p. 25, Mancini, p. 84).

47/19. The 'old Order' is that of the Garter, established under Edward III. The 'new Order' is that of the Bath, which took on its name and procedure at the coronation of Henry IV.

47/23-33. All existing representations of this list, printed or in manuscript, are in the order Buck follows. B.L. MS. Harl. 1386, ff. 16-16^v and 2115, f. 124 (the latter is printed in *Excerpta Historica*, London, 1831, p. 384), as well as College of Arms I. 18 seem to be copies of the manuscript source, probably once in the College of Arms, from which Grafton took his account of Richard's coronation.

Henry Neville: the son and heir to the Lord Abergavenny was George Neville. The name is given in Grafton, p. 113 and Holinshed, p. 398, and the manuscripts listed above as Sir Henry 'Aburgauennie', 'Burgany' or 'Burgaveny'. Buck's form may indicate that he used another manuscript in addition to the chronicles. **Henry Baynton:** this name is given in Grafton, p. 113 as 'Banington'; in Holinshed, p. 398 and in Harl. 1386 as 'Babington'; and in Harl. 2115 and Coll. Arms I. 18 as 'barington'. **Breus of Clifton** (corrected to 'Jarvis' in Additional and 'Gervoise' in the printed edition): all printed sources except Grafton give this name as 'Gervais of Clifton', Harl. 1386 gives 'Gervis', but it is difficult to read, and Harl. 2115 and Coll. Arms I. 18 give 'denys', which is equally difficult to read. **Thomas of Vernon:** printed sources give this as 'Vrmon', Harl. 1386 as 'Vrmonde' and Harl. 2115 and Coll. Arms I. 18 as 'Ormond'. Buck first wrote 'Vermon', probably trying to make sense of 'Vrmon', and replaced it, through inaccurate guesswork, with 'Vernon'.

47/47-49. Richard became king in the 22nd, not the 25th year of Louis XI, who succeeded in 1461. The dates 19 and 20 June, given by Grafton, are incorrect. See note 58/32-33.

48/1st mar. n. More mentions the coronation, p. 82, but gives no detail. Buck follows Grafton, pp. 113-16 in very close paraphrase. The first appearance of this description was on pp. 516-18 of Grafton's continuation to Hardyng, and it is the source of all the chroniclers' accounts of the coronation. Hall, pp. 375-6 follows Grafton. Polydore, p. 546, who is normally Grafton's main source where More is not, gives no detail. Croyland, p. 566, gives no detail, stating only that Richard took the chair in Westminster on 26 June and was crowned on 6 July. Holinshed, pp. 397-400, follows Grafton's account with a few omissions which Buck does not share. Stow's account, pp. 766f, ends after the description of the events of 4 July. Buck's deviations from Grafton are minor: Grafton says the queen sat on the left hand of the

table, not necessarily on the left hand of the king; and Buck's Archbishop Cardinal'
is merely 'the Byshop' in Grafton (p. 116). Of those attending on the king at the
coronation, Grafton (pp. 113-15) gives a complete list. Their number, which Buck
rounds off to eighty, is seventy-seven.

48/ 2nd mar. n. There is no such reference in Enguerran de Monstrelet, *Chroniques*
(Paris, 1595). Buck several times makes the mistake of citing references to Howard
in Monstrelet. There is a reference in Commynes, II, 241.

48/10-11. According to Davies, p. 281, Edward was created Prince of Wales on 28
June. According to GEC, III, 441, this creation occurred on 24 August, the investiture
on 8 September.

48/11-16. Buck was correct above, p. 46 when he gave the date of these investitures
as 28 June. This incorrect dating comes from Grafton, p. 113.

48/18-20. See notes 47/6-7 and 47/15-18.

50/25-34. There seem to have been two separate occasions on which Richard gave
a memorable address about law: first on 26 June when he addressed the judges in the
Great Hall at the Palace of Westminster; second, after his coronation, when
'to suche as wente home he gaue straighte charge and commaundemente to see
their countrees well ordred, and that no wrong nor extorcion shoulde be doen to his
subiectes' (Hall, p. 376). The proclamation against Buckingham of 23 October 1483
(*Foedera*, XII, 204) gives more detail of Richard's judicial policy during and soon
after his coronation:

> the King . . . rememberyng his solempne Profession which
> he made at the tyme of his Coronation to Mercy and
> Justice, and folowyng the same in dede; first beganne at
> Mercy in yevyng unto all maner Personnes his Full and
> Generall Pardon, trustyng therby to have caused all his
> Subgettes to have be surely Determyned unto hym accord-
> ing to the Duety of their Ligeance; and eftson his Grace, in
> his owne Person, as is well knowen, hath dressed himselfe
> to divers Parties of this Reame for the indifferent Admyny-
> stracion of Justice to every Person, havyng full Confidence
> and Trust that all Oppressours and Extortioners of his
> Subjectes, orible Adultres and Bawdes, provokyng the high
> Indignation and Displeasure of God, shuld have be re-
> consiled and reduced to the wey of Trouth and Vertue,
> with the abiding in good Disposition.

50/mar. n. This is not in More. It appears in Hall, p. 376 and Holinshed, p. 400.
Spiritual lords and religious worship are not mentioned.

50/45 - 51/6. This poem is extant in manuscript, with the author's corrections, in
B.L. MS. Cotton Julius C. II, ff. 97-263: 'Historia Anglicana Heroico Carmine con-
scripta authore Joanne Herdo medicinae doctore'. It was no doubt part of Cotton's
library when Buck used it. This section appears on f. 182 at the beginning of 'Historia
Richardi tertij'. The first line Buck gives does not exist in the original, but only a
suggestion of it in the words 'In solioque sedet'. In 1.7, the original has 'Sed' where
Buck's Editor gives 'Et', and the words 'a vobis' are substituted by Buck for

something completely illegible in the original. Buck evidently copied the passage with the work in front of him, since he follows it so closely.

51/7 - 52/3. Davies, p. 160n has traced Richard's progress on evidence derived from Harl. 433: Windsor, Reading (23 July), Oxford (including Woodstock), Gloucester, Tewkesbury (4 August), Worcester, Warwick (8 August), Coventry, Leicester, Nottingham (20-23 August), Doncaster, Pontefract, York. Rous says the progress was accompanied 'clamore populi' (p. 216), and Dr Langton, Bishop of St David's, who accompanied Richard on his progress said,

> He contents the people wher he goys best that ever did
> prince; for many a poor man that hath suffred wrong many
> days have be relevyd and helpyd by hym and his commands
> in his progresse. And in many grete citeis and townis wer
> grete summis of mony gif hym which he hath refusyd. On
> my trouth I lykyd never the condicions of ony prince so wel
> as his: God hathe sent hym to us for the wele of us al.
>
> (*Christ Church Letters,* ed. J.B. Sheppard, Cam.
> Soc., 2nd Ser. 19, London, 1877, p. 46.)

51/12-13. The fresh air and green woods and red and fallow deer are an example of seventeenth century embellishment. They have no origin in Buck's sources.

51/15-16. On 22 July, the founder of Magdalen College, William Wayneflete, Bishop of Winchester, came to receive King Richard. On 24 July he was received by the Chancellor, Regents, and Founder and brought in procession to Magdalen, where he spent the night. On 25 July there were two disputations presented before the king, in which Grocyn was one of the participants, and he rewarded the disputants (William Dunn Macray, *A Register of the Members of St Mary Magdalen College, Oxford,* London, 1894-1915, n.s. I, 11-12).

51/17-21. This information about Gloucester comes from the *Arrivall,* p. 26f by way of Holinshed, p. 317. Queen Margaret's forces, on the way to Gloucester, were prevented from entering by Edward IV's messengers. The story is repeated, text, p. 136.

51/26-30. This ceremony was, according to the chronicles and to Rous (p. 217) not a second coronation, but rather the investiture of Richard's son as Prince of Wales amid great splendour and acclamation. Only Croyland (p. 567) speaks of it as a second coronation. Davies (p. 287) points out that neither in Rotherham's papers in the York episcopal registry nor in the archives of the corporation of York can be found any reference to a second coronation, as there surely would have been had one occurred. All chronicle accounts derive from Polydore, pp. 546ff.

51/31-34. Croyland, p. 567. Considerably paraphrased for brevity and clarity.

51/38-40. Davies, pp. 163f, records a direction from John Kendall to the council of York to receive the king with pageants, and on 28 August it it recorded that 'it was agreid that the Creid play shall be playd afore o*u*r suffreyn lord the Kyng of Sunday next cu*m*yng, apon the cost of the most onest men of e*v*ery *p*arish in thys Cite' (pp. 171f). Hall records that 'the citezens receyued hym with great pompe and triumphe, according to ye qualities of their educacion and quantitie of there substaunce and habilitie, and made diuers daies playes and page*a*ntes in token of ioy and solace' (p. 380). This is not in More but derives from Polydore, p. 546: 'aliquot dies gaudium publice celebrarunt'.

51/40-41. John of Gloucester was not created Captain of Calais until 11 March 1485 (*Foedera*, XII, 265f). Buck's source for the error of placing the creation at York during the progress is Fabyan, p. 670 (Buck's 'As some say' refers to this source). For the error in the name of the boy no source can be traced. Fabyan gives no name, and Buck probably guessed that he was named for his father. It appears nowhere else that Buck knows of the second illegitimate son, whose romantic story of uncertain credibility is told in Francis Peck, *Desiderata Curiosa* (London, 1732), II, 13-15.

51/45-48. Fabyan, p. 670: Richard 'in shorte processe folowynge [the coronation], rode nothwarde to pacyfie that countre, and to redresse certayne riottes there lately done'. The executions of rebels are mentioned in Stow, p. 767, Hall, p. 376, and Holinshed, p. 400.

51/50. Vergil, *Aeneid* XI, 97-98: 'salve aeternum mihi . . ./ aeternumque vale'.

52/4-39. Buck's information on Richard's dealings with the French king comes from Commynes, II, 305, who states that Richard wanted Louis' friendship and probably the continuance of the pension, 'mais le roy ne voulut respondre à ses lettres ne oyr le messaige et l'estima très cruel et mauvais . . . .' Hall, who follows Commynes here, may have been Buck's immediate source. He says (p. 376f) that soon after Richard's coronation,

> he sent a solempne Ambassade to Lewes the Frenche kynge, to conclude a league and amitie with hym, trustynge to obtayne the tribute whiche kynge Edwarde his brother had before out of Fraunce, but the Frenche kyng so abhorred hym and his crueltie, that he would neither se nor heare his Ambassadors, and so in vayne they returned.

The communication between the two kings took place not after but before and during Richard's progress. The existing documents contradict Commynes' assertions about Louis' refusal to communicate with Richard. *Foedera*, XII, 195f, reproduces a commission of 16 July for renewing the treaty. In Harl. 433, f. 236^v, there is a brief letter from Louis, dated 21 July, acknowledging the favourable reception of Richard's letters and his news (presumably of his assuming the crown) and desiring his friendship. Richard replied on 18 August from Leicester that he intended to keep the truce concluded by his brother with Louis for the stipulated term. However, he mentions that his merchants have been harassed by Frenchmen and asks what Louis plans to do about this (Harl. 433, f. 237). Two days later, on 20 August, from Nottingham, Richard writes again to Louis about the conveyance of Burgundian wines for himself and his queen (Harl. 433, f. 237^v). These three letters are printed in *Letters and Papers*, I, 25 and 34-6. No communications directly regarding the tribute seem to have occurred. Louis died on 30 August. On 11 and 21 March 1484 (*Foedera*, XII, 221 and 223f), Richard sent a commission for renewal of the treaty to Charles VIII, and on 13 Sept. (*Foedera*, XII, 234f) he granted a safe conduct to messengers from Charles. No other communications are preserved.

52/9-10. Commynes, II, 303-4, 'et se doubtoit bien d'avoir perdu sa pension que le roy luy donnoit, ou tribut que l'appelloyent les Angloys . . . .' Also, II, 231, 'luy fut rompue la pension qu'il prenoit de nous qu'il appelloit tribut; mais ce n'estoit ne l'ung ne l'autre . . . .'

52/1st mar. n. Jean du Tillet, *Recueil des Roys du France* (Paris, 1602), *Traictez*, p. 248 (this book is divided into two parts separately numbered, 'Recueil des Traictez d'Entre les Roys de France et d'Angleterre' and 'Recueil des Roys de France, Leurs Couronne et Maison', henceforth distinguished as *Traictez* and *Roys*): 'septante-cinq mille escus, vallans chacun escu trente-trois sols, que ledit Roy Louys promit payer audit Roy Edouart pour les frais de son armée'. This was evidently a lump sum, the annual pension being referred to as 'pension annuelle de cinquante mille escus . . . .' B.L. MS. Add. 6297, ff. 108^v-109^v, is a copy of a letter, dated 29 August 1475, in which the French king promises to pay an annual rent to Edward IV of '50 Thousand Scutes of Gold every Scute being of the Value of three & thirty great Blancs', half at Michaelmas, half at Easter.

52/25. Meyer, p. 418, 'Constitutum Anglo tributum annuum pro iure Aquitaniae quinquaginta milia coronatorum. Data illi ã Gallo LXXV. milia prae manu'.

52/27-30. Ibid., 'Constituta nonnullis magnatibus Anglicis annua vectigalia multi auri'.

52/30-34. Rotherham was Bishop of Lincoln before his translation to the arch-bishopric of York. It is interesting that of this list so many ultimately betrayed Richard: Dorset, Hastings, Rotherham, Cheyney. Perhaps in their connection with France lies a partial explanation of their betrayal. It was noted previously that Blount, Fortescue, and Talbot, who became traitors at Bosworth, were also sent at one time as ambassadors to France (see above, note 29/29-36). It was primarily through the wooing of the French king that Warwick was led to break faith with Edward IV, who favoured a Burgundian over a French alliance. Cornwallis, with the anti-French prejudice of his time, thinks that Hastings' connections with France made him untrustworthy: 'could Hastinges be inocent whom Philippe Comminns reporteth to be a Pentioner of the ffrench king Lewis the 11th the onlye subtile Prince of that time & he of all others that moste affected Tirranie, and was naturally the mortall and most vndermininge enimie of this kingdom' (p. 10).

52/34-35. 'Mr Challoner' is a misreading or mishearing by Commynes for Thomas St Leger.

52/40-42. All Monstrelet says is 'passerent la mer d'Anglettere pour venir en France par deuers le Roy, le Seigneur Hauart, vn Prothonotaire, & outres Ambassadeurs Anglois, pour le fait de l'entretenement de la trefue d'être le Roy, & le Roy d'Angleterre' (*Nouvelles Chroniques,* f. 71).

52/44-46. John Howard's installation as a baron and Knight of the Bath are not recorded in extant documents. See above, note 46/42-43.

52/4th mar. n. Du Tillet, *Traictez*, p. 248: Howard and Cheyney stayed as hostages until Edward returned home with most of his army.

52/46-50. Commynes, II, Bks. IV-VI, *passim*, writes of Howard's prominent part in arranging this peace. The amount is noted in Vol. II, p. 242. J.R. Lander, 'Council,

Administration and Councillors, 1461-1485', *BIHR*, XXXII (1959), 161 observes, 'The fact that a newly created peer (Howard) and a mere knight [Montgomery] got more than a bishop-chancellor and the chamberlain [Hastings] twice as much, seems to lend credibility to these figures as an index of Louis' estimate of their influence with the king'.

52/50 - 53/1. Bouchard, f. cxcix: 'le conte de Vuaruich qui tant auoit au roy de france couste a entretrenir'. Buck has placed an 'X' opposite this information in his own copy.

53/5-6. See above, text, p. 44, 11. 49-50.

53/14-16. See above, note 52/4-39.

53/17-23. See Harl. 433, f. 308ᵛ (printed in *Original Letters Illustrative of English History,* ed. Henry Ellis, 2nd ser., London, 1827, I, 149f) for Richard's promise to Elizabeth Woodville, made in a public ceremony on 1 March 1484, that her daughters should be assured of their lives, protection, freedom, and provision for marriage to gentlemen, and granting her an annuity for life. On the basis, evidently, of her trust in Richard's good faith, Elizabeth sent for her son Dorset, urging him to return and make peace with Richard. That the daughters were well treated seems attested by the fact that according to Croyland, p. 572, Elizabeth, the eldest, was given apparel similar to the queen's at the Christmas celebrations of 1484. Elizabeth Woodville seems not to have been easily won, for Croyland, p. 570, says that she gave in only after frequent intercession and terrible threats.

53/25. The information on the magnificence of Richard's Christmas celebrations in 1484 is derived from Croyland, p. 571f.

53/28-30. See text, Book V, pp. 197 and 203f.

53/42-43. *Rot. Parl.,* VI, 240-2 mentions this as a petition of the Three Estates, not of the Northern people. Buck is relying on Croyland's statement (p. 567) that the petition was rumoured to have been concocted in the North.

53/48 - 54/3. See note 45/19-20.

54/4-25. During Edward IV's reign, the earldom of Richmond was in gift of the crown and was given first to Richard, then to George, Duke of Clarence, then restored to Richard after Clarence's death. Henry had an hereditary claim to it from his father, Edmund Tudor, to whom it had been granted in 1452 by his half-brother, Henry VI, but he was deprived of it by Edward IV. Mention was made in this Parliament of Richmond's conspiracy. However, as is stated in *Rot. Parl.,*VI, 245, he was in Brittany, not in France, at the time. No mention is made of his Lancastrian claim or marriage plans. The Pope had no power to confer or confirm titles.

54/31-41. *Rot. Parl.,*VI, 244-49 lists these, among others, as being attainted for treason in Buckingham's rebellion. Morton, Knevet, John Rush, and 'Thomas Nandik late of Cambridge, Nigromansier' are said to have conspired with Buckingham at Brecknock on 18 October and persuaded Henry and Jasper Tudor to bring a foreign army and navy to attack England, landing at Plymouth on 29 October. Risings in Kent, 18-25 October, are mentioned, in connection with which most of the other participants were attainted. In *Pat. Rolls* we find every one of these rewarded by Henry VII, who reversed their attainders in his first Parliament (see note 188/34-

40, below). Agnes Ethel Conway, 'The Maidstone Sector of Buckingham's Rebellion', *Archaeologia Cantiana*, XXXVII (1925), 97-119, studies the Kentish participants in Buckingham's rebellion. The Woodville seat was at Maidstone, and 'the outstanding rebels were relations or connections by marriage of the Woodvilles, the Hautes, and the Guildfords. Some others seem to have been friends of Bishop Morton . . .' (p. 106). **John Guildford** was a friend of Rivers. He was sent to Newgate for one month. **Sir Thomas Lewkenor,** father or uncle of the Thomas Lewkenor who was made Knight of the Bath at Richard's coronation and who remained faithful to Richard, was pardoned. **Thomas Fiennes of Hurstmonceux** was pardoned. **Nicholas Gainsford,** who already had a history of rebellion under Edward IV, was pardoned. That **Sir George Brown**, husband of **Edward Poynings'** mother, was executed indicates that he was probably the leader of this sector. **Sir John Fogg,** husband of Alice Haute, a cousin of Elizabeth Woodville, was pardoned. **Darrell** was nephew to Guildford. **William Clifford** is unidentified but is possibly one of the Cliffords related by marriage to Guildford.

54/33-34. 'Thomas Morton' is obviously an error for 'John Morton'. Buck was probably thinking of More.

54/45-48. *Rot. Parl.,* VI, 241ff.

54/50 - 55/11. If the *Titulus Regius* incorporated in *Rot. Parl.* is intended to represent the petition presented to Richard before his accession, it merely proves that the Princes were living at the time Richard was formally petitioned to be king, and not that they were still living at the time of the Parliament. Those present at the Parliament evidently had no reliable knowledge of whether they were at that time alive or dead, since no contemporary source mentions anything but rumours of their death. As for Buck's statement that their lives could not prejudice him, this is an argument which has from Buck's time to the present day been naively put forward by Richard's defenders. It is clear from the circumstances surrounding Buckingham's rebellion that the Princes' lives, despite their disability, were still a threat to Richard's security. Croyland, pp. 567f, indicates that the Princes' freedom served as an excuse for the uprising, and the rumour of their deaths was perhaps used as colour for the rebellion. Under these circumstances it was far from true that their lives posed no threat to Richard. As long as they could serve as a rallying point for conspiracy, they threatened his security. This was not a novel problem in cases where one king had deposed another. Henry IV found it necessary after imprisoning Richard II to have him put to death because of plots, uprisings, and pretenders. Edward IV, after the Bastard of Fauconberg's uprising, saw the death of Henry VI as unavoidable. Henry VII, pursued by pretender after pretender, disposed of Clarence's son Warwick on a flimsy charge. This is not proof, of course, that Richard did murder the Princes, but the argument that he had no reason to wish for their removal ignores the facts of the case and the insecurity of kingship in this period.

55/14-15. Text, pp. 74-82 and 141f.

55/29-30. Buck's source for the oath sworn to support Richard's son is Croyland, pp. 570f. There was no legal practice governing succession, and Richard, like Henry IV and Edward IV before him, was making special provision to try to ensure the crown to his own issue.

55/36 - 56/36. J.G. Bellamy, 'Justice under the Yorkist Kings', *American Journal of Legal History*, IX (1965), 141: 'It was the practice in the Yorkist period for the king to appoint a constable whenever a rebellion was thought to be imminent. His special function was to administer summary justice on those traitors who had been taken in arms'. This office has particular interest for Buck, whose sole surviving contribution to the collection of documents which represent subjects considered by the Society of Antiquaries concerns the office of Constable (see above, p. xxxvii). The patent of creation suggests by its wording ('pro ille vice tantum') that it was intended as a temporary appointment, necessitated by the fact that Buckingham, who was High Constable, was the major rebel. Ashton therefore was called upon to preside at Buckingham's trial and sentence him. After Buckingham's execution, Stanley was appointed High Constable. There is no evidence of Ashton's inefficiency. On 29 April 1485 he was reappointed Vice Constable, 'De Fidelitate, Circumspectione, & Industria . . .' (*Foedera*, XII, 268).

55/47 - 55/21. Given in *Foedera*, XII, 205. Buck's reference in the margin is correct, and the lack of deviation except in occasional accidentals from the version given in the *Foedera* suggests that the copy was made directly from the document with particular care. The italic script in which it appears may suggest that someone copied it for Buck and he inserted it directly without recopying. The italic could have been his own, though it appears nowhere else in the work. The one omission, the word 'Domino' in the first line after 'suo', and one addition, the words 'anno regni primo' in the last line are suggestive of Buck's own habits.

56/43 - 57/10. (All information in this note is from *Pat. Rolls* unless otherwise indicated.) The Constableship was granted to Buckingham on 15 July 1483. Lord Howard was created Marshal 28 June 1483 and the office made hereditary. He was created Admiral of England, Ireland, and Aquitaine on 25 July. The Lord Chancellor was **John Russell**, Bishop of Lincoln, but no record of his creation can be found, though he is often mentioned in that capacity. Francis, Viscount Lovell, was King's Chamberlain (i.e., Chamberlain of the King's Household). **Sir John Wood** was progressing toward his office through the reigns of Edward IV, when he was Under Treasurer of England, and Edward V, when he was Treasurer of the Exchequer, to which office Richard III reappointed him. Evidently he died, for on 6 December 1484, **John Touchet,** Lord Audeley was named Treasurer. From numerous references in Harl. 433, we know that Russell, as Chancellor, possessed the Great Seal. This office is mentioned in *Foedera*, XII, 203. On 22 September 1483, **Thomas Barowe** was appointed Keeper of the Rolls. There is no evidence that Henry VII kept him on in this office. **John Kendall** is frequently mentioned in *Pat. Rolls* and in Davies as the king's Secretary, but the appointment is not recorded. In March 1484, **William Hopton** is mentioned as deceased, without any indication of his office. He is referred to as Treasurer in Grafton's coronation record (p. 116). Buck gives Percy's name incorrectly, following Grafton (Ibid.). The Controller was **Robert Percy**, who was, along with Lovell, one of Richard's boyhood companions at Middleham. His appointment is not recorded, but he is mentioned in *Pat. Rolls* as Controller of the

Household. There is no mention to be found of **John Buck's** office. That he held a post in Richard's household is suggested by his position directly after John Kendall in the list of Henry VII's Bosworth attainders (*Rot. Parl.*, VI, 276). See above, pp. xiii and cvii-cviii for discussion of Buck's research methods on this point. There is a reference of 16 July 1483 to **John Gunthorp**, 'whom the king appointed keeper of the privy seal . . . on 27 June last'. **William Hussey**, or Huse, Chief Justice of the King's Bench under Edward IV and Edward V, was confirmed by Richard on 26 June 1483. **Thomas Tremayle** (not Tremain, as Buck has it), **Roger Townsend**, and **John Vavasour** also began their careers as Sergeants at Law under Edward IV. They received their grants of office from Richard III on 27 June 1483. **Morgan Kidwelly** was appointed Attorney General by Edward V, and the appointment was renewed by Richard. For the appointment of **John of Gloucester** as Captain of Calais, see above, note 51/40-41. A number of these officers were kept on by Henry VII: Tremayle, Vavasour, and Townsend became justices; Hussey, Russell (as Custodian of the Privy Seal), and Audeley; Percy was pardoned; Barowe was pardoned and given a prebendary; Gunthorpe is mentioned only as 'clerk'; and **Thomas Fitzwilliam** became Mayor of London. No appointments for him are listed, since his offices were bestowed locally, not royally.

57/11-16. *Foedera*, XII, 248-50.

57/19-22. The negotiations with France appear in *Foedera*, XII, 195f. The only negotiations between Richard and Denmark occur in connection with the treaty with Scotland mentioned directly below. Hall, p. 400 gives as Article XIII of that treaty an agreement that the allies of each party should be entitled to be included in the league. Charles VIII of France, and John, King of Denmark and Norway, are listed as the special confederates of the Scots. The treaty is printed in one of its original Latin forms in *Foedera*, XII, 235-43. Buck may be referring to this treaty when speaking of Richard's relations with Denmark, or he may be referring in error to the negotiations of 1476 when the King of Denmark sent an embassy asking for a new treaty and redress for grievances from Edward IV (*Foedera*, XII, 27 and 29f).

57/27-30 and 5th mar. n. In this treaty (*Foedera*, XIII, 234-43) 'Argyle' is given throughout as 'Ergile'. One of the commissioners, Laurence, Lord Oliphant, has been omitted by Buck. It is clear from the form of Buck's representation that in listing the items and ambassadors involved in this treaty, Buck did not use the manuscript printed by Hall in English and later in the *Foedera* in Latin, but probably B.L. Cotton Caligula B.V, ff. 151-2, in which similar mistakes are made: the name of Colin, Earl of Argyle, is given as 'Coly Erle of Erguile', William, Earl of Nottingham's name as 'John', and places for the Christian names of Strange and Powys are left blank. Strange's name is George, Lord Powys' John.

57/31-41. For Quhitlaw's address, see text, pp. 205f.

58/13-15. GEC, XII, pt. i, 453, seems confused on this issue. It mentions no daughter to John de la Pole, but says in a note to the paragraph on Richard's nephew Edmund de la Pole, who was born in 1472 and consequently could not have had a marriageable daughter by the time of this embassy, 'His only daughter Elizabeth (not

Anne, as usually stated . . .) was professed as a nun in the Convent of the Minoresses without Aldgate, July 1510'. *Foedera,* XII, 233 refers to Anne, daughter of John, Duke of Suffolk. Glover, p. 539, lists under John de la Pole, Earl of Suffolk, and Elizabeth, daughter of Richard, Duke of York, '*Anne,* a Nunne at *Syon*'.

58/24-25. *Foedera,* XII, 255 and 260ff.

58/28-31. Commynes, II, 305 suggests that Richard's communication with Louis was for the purpose of exacting tribute, but there is no evidence of this in the messages themselves (see note 52/4-39, above). Richard attempted to establish a truce with France in 1484 after Charles VIII's accession, but without success.

58/32-33. Text, pp. 189-192.

58/43-46. Text, pp. 203f.

59/13-15. Matthew 21:9 and John 19:6 and 15.

59/21 - 60/14. Buck gives this account also in *Comm.*, ff. 128f, citing Glover as his main source. In the earlier work he is slightly more detailed, since genealogy is his subject there. Richard did not deny the Hereford lands to Buckingham, but granted them provisionally on the assumption that Parliament would confirm the grant (Harl. 433, ff. 107^v-108). Buckingham's power was already immense, similar to that Richard held in the North after the Scottish campaign. He had the supervision and array of Shropshire, Hereford, Somerset, Dorset, and Wiltshire, was Chief Justice, Chamberlain, Supervisor, and Governor of the whole of Wales, and Constable, Steward, and Receiver of several important Welsh castles and lordships with power to appoint officers therein. His rebellion, therefore, cannot be attributed to dissatisfaction at not being granted lands and power — this is a fiction derived from More and Polydore — but more likely to his possessing too much already.

Richard's supposed retort to Buckingham when he asked for the restoration of the lands is from Polydore, p. 549: 'Num Henrice dux, uis tibi id ius Henrici quarti uindicare, quo ille perperam regn*um* occuparet, atqu*e* ita ad illud uiam patefacere?'

60/20-22. More (p. 44) is the originator of the story that Richard and Buckingham had formed an agreement, on the latter's promising to aid Richard's elevation to the throne, that Buckingham's daughter would marry Richard's son. It recalls the agreement between Queen Margaret and Warwick that the Kingmaker's daughter was to marry the heir to the throne as a reward for the restoration of Henry VI.

60 - 64. Buck is combining with some difficulty the conversations between Morton and Buckingham as reported by More and by Hall. More breaks off, and Hall (pp. 383-90), continuing this conversation, is obviously inventing to fill a gap. More for his part of the conversation might have had the direct authority of Morton, and he is probably right in attributing the duke's rebellion to Morton's persuasion, at least in part. Buck observes this in his notes to his copy of Godwin: in the margin of the entry for Morton, p. 117, he says 'Morton made this duke a traytor & other good men he did to harm Witness S. Tho Mor'. Buck has somewhat confused Hall's account, which allows for little wavering on Buckingham's part. The alterations may result from clumsiness in combining the More and Hall sections, but more likely they are intended to show Morton more clearly as the instigator, corrupter, and manipulator. And Buck may also have been attempting to add tension and vividness by portraying

Buckingham's changes of emotion.

61/2nd mar. n. More, p. 91, says Morton devised this marriage and does not mention the agency of Elizabeth Woodville.

63/1st mar. n. This sounds Senecan but does not appear in either *Declamations* or *De Clementia*.

63/48 - 64/35. Kendall, pp. 314f, notes that the story of Buckingham's meeting with the Countess of Richmond is improbable: she was probably in London busy with her own plots while Buckingham left Richard at Gloucester and went to Brecon. Bridgenorth, where they were supposed to have met, was northwest of Buckingham's route. However, Conway, p. 103, notes that the countess had a residence near Brecknock.

64/1st mar. n. Glover lists Margaret, Countess of Richmond, on p. 399 and Buckingham's mother on p. 401. Their fathers were evidently brothers, though Glover confuses this issue by calling Edmund, Duke of Somerset nephew instead of grandson to John of Gaunt.

64/38-39. Buck means Sir Thomas Bourchier.

64/49 - 65/1. *Paston Letters,* II, 442f, no.799 is a letter from Norfolk to Paston on 10 October urging him to come with men at arms to London, since the Kentishmen are in arms and plan to rob the city. Richard heard of the insurrection two days later at Lincoln. A letter of 13 October 1483 from Richard to the Council of Southampton shows the nature of his preparation. He states that Buckingham has turned traitor 'and entendith thutter distruccion of us, you, and alle othre our trewe suggiettes that have taken oure part . . . .' He urges them 'that with as many as ye may reise and make in defensible array on horsback ye do sende to be with us at our Citie of Coventre the xxij day of this present moneth withouten faile . . .' (*The Manuscripts of the Corporations of Southampton and King's Lynn,* Historical MSS Commission, 11th Report, Appendix, pt. iii, 1887, p. 103). On 18 October, Edward Plumpton writes to Sir Robert Plumpton:

> People in this country be so trobled, in such comandment as they have in the Kynges name and otherwyse, marvellously, that they know not what to doe. My lord Strayng goeth forth from Lathum upon munday next with x m. men . . . . The Duke of Buck: has so mony men, as yt is sayd here, that he is able to goe where he wyll; but I trust he shalbe right withstanded and all his mallice: and els were great pytty. Messengers commyth dayly, both from the Kings grace and the Duke, into this country.

> (*Plumpton Correspondence,* ed. Thomas Stapleton,
> Cam. Soc., 1st ser. no. 4, London, 1839, pp. 44f.)

65/2nd mar. n. Polydore, p. 552. The reference to Lib. 25 is correct.

65/3rd mar. n. The source of this misinformation is Hall, p. 395, whose whole account is a blatant fabrication for the purpose of creating a crude moral exemplum. Banister's Christian name, given by Hall as Humphrey (this error originated with Polydore, p. 552) was actually Ralph. The subsequent fate of his family is outlined as follows: his first son went mad, his daughter contracted leprosy, his second son became deformed, his third son was drowned, and he himself was tried for murder in old age. After this follows the statement about his reward from Richard:

> And as for his thousand pound kyng Richard gaue him not one farthing, saiyng that he which would be vntrew to so good a master would be false to al other, howbeit some saie y^t he had a smal office or a ferme to stoppe his mouthe with al.

Actually, both Harl. 433 (f. 133) and *Pat. Rolls,* p. 482 (15 August 1484) record grants to Ralph Banister for help in taking the rebels. Fabyan (p. 670) and the Great Chronicle (pp. 234f) give no Christian name for Banister, and in addition to the £1000 reward they mention an alternative reward of land worth £100 annually to the person who brought in Buckingham and to his heirs perpetually.

65/29. Buckingham's execution occurred the first year of King Richard, 2 November 1483.

65/33-35. More, pp. 90-93. For notice of the flight of the conspirators in Buckingham's rebellion, see above, note 29/29-36.

BOOK II

66-67. Buck follows his outline somewhat less closely than he does for Book I, and he is more digressive within certain areas. 'The Prince Edward and Queen Anne die . . .' follows 'The Earl of Richmond . . . came first to Poole . . . and secondly to Milford . . .'. 'The nobility of King Henry VII' is in the right place, but 'He affied not much in the titles of York and Lancaster' is not discussed until after 'The prerogative of the king in judgements and controversies', then it is followed by 'His aptness for diverse wives'. 'The titles of King Henry VII' and 'Kings go not now to the wars' are reversed. 'His goodness to the children orphans of Sir John Buck' precedes 'Walter de Buck and his progeny'.

68/7. Euripides, *Heraclides,* 866.

68/11. Valerius Maximus, VII, i, introduction.

68/12-13. This sentence is a close paraphrase of Hesiod, *Works and Days,* l. 825.

68/34-37. Polydore and the English chroniclers do not make one of the two invasions by Henry Tudor. Only Fabyan (p. 672) may be said to have done so, for he mentions only the second invasion. Stow (p. 779) mentions the first, but does not allow that Richmond's party landed in England, saying they sailed away without setting foot on land when, after their ships had been scattered by storm, they saw the army on shore. Polydore (p. 553), Grafton, and Holinshed say that the storm occurred before Richmond sent his scouts ashore, and when their report made him suspect a ruse he set sail. He stopped in Normandy, planning to proceed to Brittany, and while there sent ambassadors asking safe conduct of Charles VIII, who sent money as well.

69/8. There is no evidence that Stanley was implicated in Buckingham's rebellion or involved with Richmond's schemes this early, though there is the possibility that he was secretly involved through his wife, the Countess of Richmond.

69/40-42. Commynes, II, 306: Henry was 'riens estimé, sauf que sa personne estoit et est honneste'.

69/42-43. Vergil, *Aeneid* V, 344.

70/21-23. Bouchard, f. ccviii.

70/24. 'British' in this context means 'Breton'.

70/32-45. This information is from Polydore, p. 553.

71/24-27. The accounts given by Polydore, p. 551, and his followers say that when Richard heard of the invasion he was unprepared and did not know where to meet the enemy. His plan was to pretend he had heard nothing until he had raised an army. Nothing is said of a 'secret friend', who seems to be Buck's invention and is reminiscent of the secret friend of Dorset whom Buck mentions above, text, p. 27. For neither is there evidence in Buck's sources, but in both cases it is a likely assumption.

72/20-23. More says nothing about Henry VII except that Morton arranged for his support by Buckingham and his marriage with Elizabeth of York (p. 91). Buck follows Polydore, pp. 548-53 very closely in this section. The invasions are mentioned by Commynes, I, 54; Grafton, pp. 128-57; Stow, pp. 775-9 and 783-8; Hall, pp. 383-98 and 402-21; Holinshed, pp. 410-79; and Du Tillet, *Traictez*, p. 251.

73/12-15. The prince died 31 March 1484, probably at Middleham or Sheriff Hutton. A tomb traditionally supposed to be his may be seen at Sheriff Hutton.

73/18-19. Croyland, p. 571, 'Vidisses . . . patrem & matrem . . . prae subitis doloribus pene insanire'.

73/26-27. Seneca, *De Consolatione ad Marciam*, XIV, 3, '. . . tam cito dolorem vicit quam omnia solebat'.

73/29-30. Croyland, p. 571.

73/31-35. Queen Anne died 16 March 1485, nearly a year after the death of her son, following a long illness.

74/3 - 8. There is no reliable evidence of Richard's ever having officially nominated an heir. All sources except Rous say that Lincoln was nominated. Rous (p. 218) notes that Warwick was proclaimed heir 'in curia regali' after the death of Richard's son and was served after the king and queen at table, but that afterwards Lincoln was preferred. Kendall notes that after a four month delay following his wife's death, Richard appointed Lincoln Lieutenant of Ireland, the usual post for the heir apparent of the House of York (p. 349). Lincoln was also made head of the Council of the North (Brooks, pp. 11f; Kendall, p. 377). Warwick's youth, even assuming the reversal of his attainder, would have been a risk to Richard in establishing a strong succession. John de la Pole, Earl of Lincoln, was his sister's son, but a man of proven ability. Richard, recalling the chaotic situation in which he found himself on the death of his brother, is not likely to have preferred a child.

74/42. Salisbury, *Letters*, ed. W.J. Millor and H.E. Butler, revised by C.N.L. Brooke (London, 1955), I, 230: 'liberi qui ex dampnato et illicito coitu . . . sunt, ab omni prorsus haereditatis beneficio excluduntur, eosque nec iura ciuilia nec leges agnoscunt, canonumque adeo improbat vigor . . . .'

75/8-16. The surname Beaufort was derived from Gaunt's castle of that name in

Champagne (GEC, XII, i, 39n). The illegitimate children to whom he gave this name were not actually born there. The name was not discarded by John, Duke of Somerset, but persisted until the natural son of Henry Beaufort, Duke of Somerset, who became Earl of Worcester under Henry VIII, took Somerset as a surname (see text, p. 78).

75/1st mar. n.   Thomas Walsingham, *Historia Anglicana,* ed. Henry Thomas Riley, R.S. 28 (London, 1863-64), II, 219.

75/19-21. John of Gaunt had three years more to live. He married Katharine Swynford in 1396 and died in 1399.

75/2nd mar. n. For this charter see text, pp. 79f.

75/31-36. See above, note 16/31-48 for 'Plantagenet'.

75/36-41. Members of the royal house belonging to these families are given the surname Plantagenet by Glover, *passim.*

75/42-43. John of Gaunt's daughter Philippa married King John of Portugal in 1387.

75/4th mar. n. For Buck's accounts of the Cadiz expedition, see Stow (1601), sigs. Pppp3-Pppp8 and Bod. MS. Eng, lett. b. 27, ff. 106-9.

76/7-8. Henry Fitzroy, Duke of Richmond, was the natural son of Henry VIII. William de Longuespée was the natural son of Henry II. Sir Roger Clarendon was reputedly the natural son of the Black Prince.

76/20-23. Du Tillet, *Roys,* p. 207. This is nearly an exact quotation.

76/26-45. Hamelin Plantagenet, illegitimate son of Henry II's father Geoffrey of Anjou, married Isabel, daughter of William de Warenne, third Earl of Surrey, and in her right succeeded to the title as fifth Earl of Surrey. Camden in 'Surrey', p. 217:

> verûm vltimus solam filiam suscepit, quae primò Guiliel-
> mum Stephani Regis filium, & postea Hamelinum Gal-
> fredi *Plantageneti* Comitis Andegauensis nothum, maritos
> eodem titulo adornauit. Priore autem marito sine prole
> defuncto, Hamelinus Guilielmum Surriae Comitem ex ea
> genuit, cuius posteri ascito *Warrennorum* nomine, eundem
> titulum gesserunt . . . .

Arthur Agard in his discourse for the Society of Antiquaries, 'Of the Antiquity of Arms in England', 2 November 1598, gives a different explanation from Buck's of Hamelin's bearing his wife's name (Hearne, *Curious Discourses,* I, 175):

> And of what great accompte, the same Normans and
> other Angevyns made of theyre armes of antiquytie ap-
> peareth in a role of the pedegre of the howse of earle
> Warren, which is in the Q. Majesty's threasaurye, wherein
> it is said that Hamelinus, brother to kinge H. 2^d. after he
> had maryed Isabell, the daughter and onely heyre of the
> sayd howse of Warren, *assumpsit arma Uxoris suae, et
> arma patris sui dimisit & heredes sui post ipsum,* esteminge
> yt greatter honor to carye the auncyent armes of his wiffes
> auncestors, then his fathers, which was a straunger.

Buck is under the delusion which he exhibits above, text, pp. 11-16, that Plantagenet was 'the royal surname' before Richard, Duke of York's time. It was not a surname at all but a nickname. That a bastard's son should prefer his mother's native surname, when he acquired with it an earldom, to his grandfather's foreign nickname is not remarkable.

76/34-35. These two John de Warrens became earls of Surrey in 1240 and 1304.

76/46-47. Arthur Plantagenet, Viscount Lisle, was the illegitimate son of Edward IV, probably by Elizabeth Lucy. Since 'Plantagenet' as a royal surname had originated with his grandfather, Richard, Duke of York, and another family, associating itself with the House of Lancaster and never having borne this surname, now held the throne, it was quite suitable for a bastard to bear it.

77/1st mar. n. Psalms, 136:9.

77/2nd mar. n. Thomas Gainsford, *The Trve and Wonderfull History of Perkin Warbeck* (London, 1618), p. 111, 'For it was a dangerous time for any Plantaginet to liue in . . . .'

77/11-15. Camden's genealogical collections in B.L. MS. Cotton Julius F. XI indicate that Hamelin's grandson was styled 'Joannes Plantagenett' (f.42). During the genealogy craze under Elizabeth there was considerable heraldic fabrication arising either from false evidence or from family tradition's being the only available evidence (Wagner, p. 16). Forged documents in Latin, Old English, and Old French were readily accepted by the heralds (J. Horace Round, *Family Origins*, London, 1930, p.5), since the sciences of palaeography and philology were not well developed, and possibly the heralds shared actively in the fabrication of these documents. According to Michael MacLagan ('Genealogy and Heraldry in the Sixteenth and Seventeenth Centuries', *English Historical Scholarship,* p. 42), there were layman 'herald painters' who sold fabricated arms and pedigrees.

77/15-21. Hamelin's arms, according to English heraldry, appear in the sixth quarter of the coat of arms which formed part of the accusation against the poet Earl of Surrey, executed in 1547, as drawn by Dethick in B.L. MS. Harl. 1453, f. 69. They contain the arms of Anjou, the gold fleurs-de-lis borne by the later earls. The ancient Angevin earls (pre-fourteenth century) bore, as Buck says, a scarboucle.

77/33-35. In the Public Record Office Museum (Museum Catalogue, No. 8, P.R.O. register no. E42/244) can be seen a seal of John de Warenne, Earl of Surrey and Strathern, from the year 1346. Though worn and broken, it seems to show a military scarf tied at the base of the shield.

78/2nd mar. n. Although this is a *viva voce* reference, it is confirmed in Sir Edward Coke's published work. See *The First Part of the Institutes of the Laws of England,* ed. Francis Hargrave and Charles Butler (London, 1794), III. References to bastardy occur in Book II, sec. 188, n. 189 and Book III, sec. 400, n. 180. The latter says 'the pope cannot legitimate in temporals'.

78/3rd mar. n. Buck mentions these two cases in the *Commentary* as well. For Gardiner he derives his information from Glover and Godwin, saying that he was the son of Lionel Woodville, Bishop of Salisbury, who married his mistress to a gardener in his employ (*Comm.*, f. 83ᵛ). Of Egerton he says, '& what hath it prejudiced Tho. Egerton . . . in his preferment to be a bastard? he having attayned to the first place of . . . honor in this kingdome, & to bee made a pere of the realm?' (*Comm.*, f. 18ᵛ). Stephen Gardiner (1483-1555) was Bishop of Winchester and became Lord Chancellor in 1553. The story that he was the Bishop of Salisbury's illegitimate son seems discredited by lack of reference to it by enemies during his lifetime and first appears in the early seventeenth century (*DNB*). Sir Thomas Egerton (1540?-1617) was Lord Keeper and Master of the Rolls under Elizabeth, nominated Baron Ellesmere and Lord Chancellor in 1603. He had a substantial library and was a friend of Buck, whom he assisted in the lawsuit over the Tilney inheritance (see above, p. xiv), in gratitude for which Buck sent him an inscribed copy of *Daphnis* (see Eccles, pp. 455f).

79/1-3. Somerset did not follow Edward IV very long. A Lancastrian leader, he surrendered to and was pardoned by Edward in 1463 but deserted him later in the same year. He was defeated, captured, and beheaded at Hexham in 1464.

79/9-24. *Rot. Parl.*, III, 343 (20 Richard II).

79/26 - 80/10. *Foedera*, VII, 849f and *Rot. Parl.*, III, 343 (a grant of 20 Richard II, 1397). There is only very slight alteration by Buck of this document, mainly in the form of minor omissions and reversals of word order. The name 'Beaufort' appears in the document only as Joan's surname.

80/9-10. 'Nono die Februarii', says *Foedera*. The year was 1397.

80/23-33. Buck's copy evidently did not contain the interlineation 'excepta dignitate regali' which had been inserted in Richard II's grant in a later hand and was incorporated in Henry IV's 1407 confirmation and exemplification of this charter (see *Excerpta Historica*, pp. 152f). Although *Excerpta Historica* mentions that Henry IV could not legally interpolate a Parliamentary statute, Kendall says that 'Whether, in the light of present-day constitutional studies, he had the right so to alter an act of Parliament matters little; most people of the fifteenth century took it for granted that the legitimating patent barred the Beauforts from the throne' (p. 185), and Mortimer Levine, 'Richard III — Usurper or Lawful King?' *Speculum*, XXXIV (1959), 391n, says,

> Though J.D. Mackie (*The Early Tudors* [Oxford, 1952], p. 48, n.1) may be correct in maintaining that Henry's addition could not avail against the act confirming Richard's patent, it is questionable that Richard's legitimation could extend to the crown in the case of bastards born while their parents' lawful spouses were living.

Buck, who was not aware of or does not recognize the interpolation, makes this assumption.

80/46-48. Vulteius, I, xii, p. 62: 'Princeps est potestas summam in Republica autoritatem imperium obtinens, superioritatem vocant, frequentius majestatem'. This is the closest precept to this reference that I was able to locate in the work.

81/1st mar. n. *Rot. Parl.*, III, 574.

81/29-47. Francis Thynne, Lancaster Herald, in a discourse for the Society of

Antiquaries on 'The Duty and Office of an Herald of Arms' given in 1605, notes that by English law bastards cannot bear arms, because they cannot inherit, having no blood interest; for 'they are not any man's children, but *filii populi, & concepti ex prohibito coitu'*. The custom of nations, however, allows for a bastard who bears his father's name to carry his father's arms with a difference (Hearne's *Curious Discourses*, I, 140). The currency of the term 'filii terrae' is attested by Erasmus' listing it in *Chiliades*, p. 292.

82/2nd mar. n. Glover, p. 398.

82/3rd mar. n. See charter, text, pp. 79f.

82/4th mar. n. Polydore, p. 546. This chapter reference is correct.

82/15-18. Since Henry's title was slight, he reinforced it with mythical rights of inheritance. Welsh nationalism came to his aid with the prophecy of Cadwallader, last of the 'British kings', that the British would one day reign again in England. During the plans for Henry's conquest, Welsh bards spread prophecies of British supremacy and Richmond's future success (see Introduction to *The Poetical Works of Lewis Glyn Cothi*, Oxford, 1837, p. xxxiv), and urged the people to regain their rights under a saviour descended from Brut and Cadwallader (see W. Garmon Jones, 'Welsh Nationalism and Henry Tudor', *The Transactions of the Honourable Society of Cymmrodorion*, 1917-18, pp. 1-59). Associated with these prophecies and the revival at Henry's accession of the 'British History' was the cult of King Arthur. Henry included in his arms quarterings for Brut and Arthur as well as England and France and adopted the red dragon as his badge (see T.D. Kendrick, *British Antiquity*, London, 1950, p. 35). He arranged for his son to be born at Winchester and named him Arthur as if in fulfilment of this prophecy. Pageants associated the new prince with the legendary kings (see Thomas Sharp, *A Dissertation on the Pageants or Dramatic Mysteries Anciently Performed at Coventry*, Coventry, 1825, p. 155, and *The Great Chronicle of London*, ed. A.H. Thomas and I.D. Thornley, London, 1938, p. 298). The Welsh prophecies and Arthurianism seem to have waned when there was no longer great need for them (see Josephine Waters Bennett, *The Evolution of the 'Faerie Queene'*, Chicago, 1942, p. 68). Sydney Anglo claims that the emphasis on British descent was not much exploited after Henry's accession ('The *British History* in Early Tudor Propaganda', *Bulletin of the John Rylands Library*, XLIV, 1961, pp. 17-48) until Elizabethan nationalism revived the Arthur cult and inspired poets with the theme (see Charles Bowie Millican, *Spenser and the Table Round*, Cambridge, Mass., 1932).

82/35-44. Du Tillet, *Traictez*, p. 7.

82/49-50. Commynes, II, 306.

83/5-9. *Rot. Parl.*, V, 375-80.

83/45-46. 'Festina lente'.

83/mar. n. Suetonius, *Augustus*, XXV, in *Vita Caesarum*, 'Sat celeriter fieri quidquid fiat satis bene'.

84/8-9. Edmund Dudley and Sir Richard Empson were lawyers, members of Henry VII's council, and rigorous tax collectors for the king. Popular hatred forced Henry VIII on his accession to have them executed on a charge of treason. They are mentioned in Polydore (pp. 613 and 620-1) and all his English followers. There is no indication that they caused any difficulties for Richard III. Buck probably introduces them because they were particularly hated men who rose under Henry VII. For the others in this list, see above, note 29/29-36.

84/1st mar. n. This quotation I have been unable to find in either Pontus Heuterus, *Rerum Burgundicarum* (Antwerp, 1584), whose Book V covers Charles of Burgundy, or in Meyer, whose Book XVII deals with him.

84/2nd mar. n. I have been unable to locate this quotation or this work, though there are several collections by similar titles. The closest I can come to this quotation in one of them is 'Admitte consilium prudentis' in *Proverbiorum Arabicarum*, ed. Joseph Scaliger and Thomas Erpenius (Leiden, 1614), p. 78, no. 36.

84/34-35. More, p. 91, 'Thys man . . . hadde gotten by great experience . . . a depe insighte in politike worldli driftes'.

84/43-50. Herd, ff. 188^v-189. This is an exact copy.

85/1st mar. n. Ariosto, *Orlando Furioso*, XIX, i. There are a few alterations in Buck's copy: 'Nessun' for 'alcun non'; 'chi' (1. 4) for 'che', and 'amico' for 'Signor'. The first two are grammatical improvements. The last is an adaptation to Buck's sense. In Tib. he wrote 'signor' first, then crossed it out and substituted 'amico'.

85/17-24. Buck's translation bears no resemblance to Harington's, first published in 1591.

85/33-35. There is no evidence that Morton was tutor to Henry or chaplain to the Countess of Richmond. However, Buck has qualified this statement, saying it is something he has heard. Since the source is not named, as in cases of *viva voce* evidence he considers sufficiently creditable to be worthy of documentation, it assumes the status of rumour.

85/36-39. Morton became Archbishop of Canterbury in 1486, Lord Chancellor in 1487, and Cardinal in 1493.

85/46-48. II Corinthians, 5:10.

86/1st mar. n. Thomas Aquinas, *Summa Theologia*, pt. II^{a}II^{ae}, quest. XLII, art. 2. Buck's 'art. 20' is a slip for '2', perhaps because he misread his own notes. The section discusses this problem and comes to this conclusion.

86/2nd mar. n. On p. 117, Godwin says that Morton, with the Pope's authority, forced the clergy to contribute towards his translation and that 'of his owne Dioces onely (which is one of the least in England) he receaued 354 pound'. He does not say specifically that this was a greater sum than ever before exacted. And on p. 221 he says,

> At wisbich castell likewise all the building of brick was of his charge. As also ye leame that he caused to be made for more conuenient cariage to his towne, which they say serueth now to smale purpose, and many complaine that the course of the riuer Nine into the sea by Clowcrosse is very much hindred thereby.

Godwin became Bishop of Hereford in 1617.

86/3rd mar. n. Stow, pp. 801f.

86/33-38. More states, p. 91, that Morton held these offices, but does not consider them evidences of ambition: 'he . . . went to Rome neuer minding more to medle w^t the world til ye noble prince king Henry y^e .vii. gate him home again, made him archbishop of Canturburye & chaunceller of England wherunto ye Pope ioined thonor of Cardinal'. Of his pride More says precisely the opposite of what Buck reports: 'Whose wisedom abused his pride to his owne deliueraunce & the dukes destruccion' (p. 90).

87/1st mar. n. Henricus de Bracton, *De Legibus et Consuetudinibus Angliae,* ed. Sir Travers Twiss, R.S. 70,I (London, 1878), 268.

87/39-41. More has Morton originate the marriage between Richmond and Elizabeth (p. 91) but does not call it a union of York and Lancaster. Hall expands this remark, saying that Morton's service to Henry Tudor consisted in 'Fyrste deuisyng the mariage betwene the lady Elizabeth daughter to kynge Edwarde the fourth by the whiche his faithfull and true seruice declared to bothe his maisters at once, was an infinite benefite to the realme, by the coniunction of the bloudes of Lancaster and Yorke . . .' (pp. 382f). Buck in his copy of Godwin, p. 221, has made a marginal note opposite the remark that Morton promoted the match and union of the houses: 'of this Morton & of his coniunction vide Philip. Com.' Commynes says nothing about it, nor does Buck refer to him at this point in the *History*.

88/2-48. These remarks seem to be expanded from a statement in Croyland, p. 571:

> In hoc Parliamento confirmatum est Regnum domino Regi, tanquam sibi debitum non ex uno sed ex multis titulis, ut non tam sanguinis quam victoriae bellicae conquestusque jure rectissime populo *Anglicano* praesidere credatur. Fu-erunt qui consultius aestimabant, verba ejusmodi silentio potius quam edicto committi; eo potissime, quod in isto eodem Parliamento tractatum est, atque per Regem as-sensum, super matrimonio dominae *Elizabeth* primogenitae Regis *Edwardi*: in cujus persona visum omnibus erat posse suppleri, quicquid aliunde ipsi Regi deesse de titulo vide-batur.

88/15-16. See below, p. 91 for full quotation.

88/1st mar. n. Seneca, *Troades,* 586.

89/5-44. This Bull is printed in *Materials for a History of the Reign of Henry VII,* ed. William Campbell, R.S. 60 (London, 1873-7), I, 392-8. Text, p. 89, ll. 4-5 is an exact quotation. Text, p. 89, l.15 'submovendum contentionem . . . inter . . . praedecessores de Lancastria, de qua Henrice ipse rex, et Eboracensis . . .' (p. 392); text, p. 89, ll. 24-26 is derived from the following (p. 393):

> Henricus rex praefatus, quanquam non modo jure belli ac notorio et indubitato proximo successionis titulo, verum etiam omnium praelatorum, procerum, magnatum, no-bilium, totiusque ejusdem regni Angliae plebis electione et voto necnon decreto statuto et ordinatione ipsius Angliae

regni trium statuum in ipsorum conventu, Parliamento
nuncupato . . . .

Text, p. 88, ll. 28-30 and ll. 31-35 are only slightly paraphrased.

89/6-9. Pope Alexander's Bull of 1494, confirming Pope Innocent's of 1486,
appears in B.L. MS. Cotton Cleopatra E. III, f. 147, and was printed several times by
de Worde and Pynson. See *STC* 14097-9 and E. Gordon Duff, *Fifteenth Century
English Books* (Oxford, 1917), nos. 228-30. Duff assumes that the reissue was due
to the uprisings connected with Perkin Warbeck. It is perhaps this Bull rather than
Pope Innocent's to which the marginal note refers.

89/48 - 90/7. This hereditary title can be seen in *Rot. Parl.,*VI, 270, 1 Henry VII.
Buck quotes it, text, pp. 214-15.

90/31 - 94/8. For the outline of the story of Richmond's second invasion preparations Buck has followed Polydore, pp. 553-61, with information added from
Commynes and Tillet. He seems to have invented Landois' speeches.

91/11-12. Commynes, II, 234.

91/43. Commynes, II, 306.

91/48 - 92/40. Richard sent to the Duke of Brittany offering him the revenue of the
earldom of Richmond in return for the surrender of Henry (Jacob, p, 628). The
message was received during the duke's illness by Landois, whose interest was in
getting money and increasing his own influence. Henry was warned by Morton
through Urswick, who then went on to procure a safe conduct to France for Henry
and his followers (Polydore, p. 555). Negotiations between Richard and Brittany are
recorded in *Foedera*, XII, 226f and 229 and *Pat. Rolls* (1476-1485), pp. 517 and 547.

94/mar. n. Polydore, p. 559.

94/18. That Buck used Polydore as his source in this section we can tell from his
reference to Dr Morgan ('Johannes Morganus', Polydore, p. 560), whom his followers
turn into 'Morgan Kidwelly' (Hall, p. 410, Grafton, p. 147, Holinshed, p. 434).

94/19-48. For the important part played by the Welsh in Henry's rise to the throne,
see Howell T. Evans, *Wales and the Wars of the Roses,* Cambridge, 1915.

94/39-40. See note 82/15-18, above.

95/1st mar. n. Commynes, II, 306: 'se vint joindre son beau père le seigneur de
Stanlay avec bien XXV mil Angloys'. The sixteenth century editions of Commynes
all give the number as 26,000. Since Calmette does not note the discrepancy, the
number in his edition may be a misprint. Polydore, p. 563, and most of his followers
say Lord Stanley had a good company and Sir William Stanley 3,000 (Holinshed, p.
435, says almost 5,000). Ross conjectures (*The Wars of the Roses,* London, 1976, p.
139) that 20,000-25,000 men were involved in the battle on *both* sides.

95/12-13. Northumberland, whose power in the North was overshadowed only by
Richard's, had once before played the game of neutrality, not stirring to strike for
either Henry VI or Edward IV in 1471. Before Bosworth he failed to call the citizens
of York to arms, leaving this job to the city itself, so that he could command an army
composed primarily of forces personally loyal to him (Kendall, p. 420). According to

accounts from Hall (p. 419) onwards, he made no move during the battle and afterwards was captured but soon restored to favour. A recent article by Anthony Goodman and Angus Mackay, 'A Castilian Report on English Affairs, 1486', *EHR*, LXXXVIII (January, 1973), 92-9, throws new light on Northumberland's behaviour at Bosworth. According to a contemporary account by Mosén Diego de Valera, Northumberland committed himself to Henry before the battle but was afterwards arrested on information that he planned to replace Henry with Edward, Earl of Warwick, and imprisoned until Warwick was in custody. Valera, contrary to the common report of Northumberland's neutrality during the battle, says that he marched before Richard's vanguard, turned his back to Henry's, and began fighting along with it. But, Goodman and Mackay suggest, the chroniclers concealed his assistance because of Tudor reluctance to be indebted to Percy influence. It is perhaps significant in this context that all copies of Buck's work omit the reference to Northumberland which appears in the original (text, pp. 106f).

Stanley had a history of waiting to see which side was winning before joining battle. At Blore Heath in 1459, he was summoned several times, and when he came did not engage in the fighting. For this he was attainted by Henry VI. *Paston Letters*, II, 432f report that after the Welles uprising, Clarence and Warwick hoped for his aid. At the readeption, Stanley joined Henry VI, then reappeared at Edward's side after the latter had regained the throne. His behaviour while Richard and the Woodvilles were battling for control was so ambiguous that we are in doubt as to whether or not he was arrested at the Tower council. If so, he was very soon released. Before Bosworth, he was making promises to both Richard and Henry. He was also making excuses to both for not presenting his forces in overt support of either side. He waited until Norfolk had fallen and the king, detached from his army, was assaulting Henry's bodyguard and was then on hand to share the spoils of the Tudor victory.

95/2nd mar. n. Croyland, p. 573.

95/19-20 and 98/46 - 99/18. Armstrong, 'Inauguration Ceremonies', pp. 70f, discusses the revival by the Yorkist monarchs of a much earlier custom, crown wearing outside Parliament, a practice indulged in by Edward IV and Richard III when their authority was not in danger as well as when it was, 'to stabilize, by an appeal to the visual senses, social conditions which had become dangerously fluid . . . . At a crown-wearing the identity between the person and the office of the king could be intuitively perceived, because the formal and actual seat of authority was unmistakably apparent'.

95/33-34. Plato, *Republic*, V, xvi, C. Also quoted in Erasmus, *Inst. Principis Christ.*

96/1st mar. n. Salisbury, *Polycraticus*, '. . . in veterum scriptis sicarii dicuntur et latrones quicumque lege non praecipiente arma tractant. Arma namque, quibus lex non utitur, legem impugnant' (600b).

96/2nd mar. n. Seneca, *Hippolitus*, 598.

96/3rd mar. n. Seneca, *Hercules Furens*, 251-2.

96/34-35. Sir Thomas Wyatt the younger, son of the poet, led a Kentish rebellion against Queen Mary in 1554. He was beheaded, drawn, and quartered. **Sir John Oldcastle,** a Lollard conspirator against Henry V, was executed in 1417. **Owen Glendower** led the Welsh sector of rebellion against Henry IV. **Charles Neville, Earl**

of Westmorland, co-leader of a rebellion against Queen Elizabeth in favour of Mary, Queen of Scots, was attainted in 1571, and died in 1601. **Gerald Fitzjames, Earl of Desmond,** rebelled in Ireland against Elizabeth in 1579, was attainted in 1582, and slain in 1583.

96/47. Polydore, pp. 561f, and all his followers say that Sir Walter Hungerford and Sir Thomas Bourchier and others joined Henry Tudor between Lichfield and Tamworth, and in the evening of the same day, Sir John Savage, Sir Brian Sanford, Sir Simon Digby and others, having left Richard, came to him.

97/17-18. See above, note 95/1st mar. n.

97/25-38. This story was related first by Polydore (p. 564), cited as popular report, and copied by his followers. It is corroborated by Valera, who says that Salaçar, a Spaniard in Richard's service, urged Richard to seek personal safety. Richard refused, wishing to 'die like a king or win victory in this battle'. He then put on his crown and mail and fought with such strength and courage that those who were with him fought hard by his example (Goodman and Mackay, p. 92).

97/47-48. First reported by Hall, p. 419. This rhyme 'one wrote on his gate' to warn Norfolk to refrain from the field.

98/39-45 and 99/20-32. Polydore, p. 563, mentions a combat between Richard and Richmond in much more general terms than do his followers: 'Sensit contra se Henricus Ricardum ire, & quia omnis spes salutis in armis erat, ce certamini auidè offert. . . . Sustinuit tamen Henricus impetum diutius, quàm etiam eius milites putarent, qui uictoriam iam penè desperaba*n*t'. Hall (p. 418) turns this into a personal combat: 'Therle of Richmonde perceyued wel the king furiusly commyng toward him, and by cause the hole hope of his welth and purpose was to be determined by battaill, he gladly proferred to encountre with him body to body and man to man'.

99/1. Polydore, p. 564.

99/mar. n. Croyland, p. 574. This does not refer to single combat. Buck omits the words 'cum militibus suis' after 'Richmundiae'.

100/22-24. Richard's force appeared larger to begin with. Richmond had about 5,000 and Richard nominally about 12,000 men (D.T. Williams, *The Battle of Bosworth,* Leicester, 1973, p. 9). 3,000 of Richard's men were led by Northumberland, who either did not join in battle or fought actively for Henry. At Henry's disposal were the Stanleys, who had between them about 6,000 men (Kendall, pp. 435; Williams, p. 9). This, and the defection of the Welsh from Richard during the battle (see Introduction to Cothi, p. xxxvi) meant that Henry's forces ultimately outnumbered Richard's. Richard was destroyed by defection of Northumberland and the Stanleys, who had huge forces personally loyal to them. The Tudor historians stressed that Henry's army was small in comparison with Richard's (it was, if we count only the forces he brought to England), since if the number is small the victory seems more attributable to God's favour. 'Non in multitudine bellantium sed in Dei manu consistit victoria', says Bernard Andrē, *Vita Henrici VII* in *Memorials of Henry the Seventh,* ed. Gairdner, R.S. 10 (London, 1858), p. 27. Polydore (p. 563) and his followers set Henry's small army against Richard's great one. Hall (p. 418) has Henry say in his oration that God does not favour the multitude, and the smaller the force the greater the glory. Holinshed (p. 436) points out the superior numbers of Richard's army, noting that the victory is not always with the larger force. Buck either realized that treachery made Richard's force smaller than Richmond's in the long run or assumed that victory does naturally lie with the greater numbers and postulated from this that Henry's was the larger.

100/29-31. Polydore, p. 564, is the first to report that Lord Stanley crowned Henry in the field, and all his followers copy this report.

100/33-35. Croyland, p. 574.

101/2nd mar. n. Buck gives a paraphrase of Tacitus, *Historiae*, IV, lxxi: 'contemnendis quam cavendis hostibus melior, ferocia verborum militem incendebat . . . .

101/4th mar. n. Livy, *Ab Urbe Condita*, XXII, xxxviii, 12, 'temeritatem, praeterquam quod stulta sit, infelicem etiam ad id locorum fuisse'.

101/5th mar. n. Suetonius, *Augustus*, XXV.

101/6th mar. n. Translated from Polybius, *Historiae*, III, lxxxi, 9.

101/7th mar. n. Quintus Curtius, *Historiarum Alexandri Magni*, VI, iii, 11.

101/8th mar. n. I have been unable to trace this quotation.

101/9th mar. n. Proverbs 16:18.

101/33-34. This remark is not in Strigelius' gloss, *Salmonis Libri Tres*, n.p., 1565, which says 'Signum secuturae ruinae est insignis insolentia' (p. 78). I have not sought it in his other works.

101/36 - 102/2. This is an Aesopian fable, given in Erasmus, *Chiliades*, p. 777, under the title 'Scarabeus aquilam quaerit'.

102/29-39. The King of Scots requested a single combat with Surrey for the town of Berwick and the fishgarths on the Western Marches. Surrey replied that

> he thanked hys grace that he wolde put hym to so moche honour, that he being a kyng anointed wolde fighte hande to hande wyth so poore a man as he, howbeit he said, he wolde nat deceyve hys grace, for he seid though he wanne hym in batayle, he quas never the nerer to Berwicke nor to Fyshgarthis, for he had no suche commyssyon so to do.
>
> Surrey's epitaph in Thomas Martin, *The History of the Town of Thetford*, London, 1779, Appendix, p. 46).

The chroniclers repeat the story.

103/4-5. There are several references in Bracton to the concept of the king being without peer: Vol. I, p. 38, Vol. II, p. 172, Vol. V, p. 402, and Vol. VI, p. 248.

103/5-11. Plutarch, *Moralia*, 179 D.

103/36-39. Suetonius, *Augustus*, XX, says that Augustus conducted only two foreign wars in person, and his others were conducted by generals, though he was often present or nearby. Dion Cassius, *History of Rome*, LIII, 4. I can find no reference in Plutarch incorporating this information. Tacitus, *Annales*, I, ii, says something similar in sense but not in expression to the quotation that follows.

104/9-10. This quotation appears in Marlowe's *Doctor Faustus*, II, i as 'Solamen miseris socios habuisse doloris'. John D. Jump, editor of the Revels edition (London,

1962), pp. 27f, n. 42, says 'It occurs also in Greene's *Menaphon* . . . and other works of the period. Previous editors have found the same idea expressed by mediaeval authors . . . and have traced it back as far as Seneca, *De Consolatione ad Polybium*, xii, 2'.

104/1st mar. n. Vergil, *Aeneid*, II, 670.

104/41-42. Jeremiah, 18:3-4.

104/44-45. Romans, 1:28, slightly paraphrased.

104/3rd mar. n. Translation of Lycurgus, *Against Leocrates*. The verse breaks down in the third line, between which and the fourth Buck makes no division, and appears to end in two lines of inferior verse.

105/4-5. A translation of Euripides, Fragment inc. B. xxv.

105/6-8. I have been unable to trace this quotation.

105/22-25. Hall, p. 421, whose description is an elaboration of Fabyan's (p. 673), says

> his bodye was naked and despoyled to the skyne, and nothynge left aboue hym not so muche as a clowte to couer hys pryue members, and was trussed behynde a pursiuaunt of armes called blaunche senglier or whyte bore, lyke a hogge or a calfe, the hed and armes hangynge on the one syde of the horse, and the legges on the other syde, and all by spryncled with myre and bloude . . . .

Croyland says that Richard's body was treated with many indignities and 'non satis humaniter propter funem in collum adjectum usque ad *Leicestriam* deportato' (p. 575). Richard was not, of course, bearded: Buck's mental picture is conditioned by fashions of his own day.

105/1st mar. n. Herd, f. 186ᵛ.

105/43-50. Henry of Huntingdon, *The History of the English*, ed. Thomas Arnold, R.S. 74 (London, 1879). Though Huntingdon's history includes this period, he does not relate this detail. It is contained in Matthew Paris, *Chronica Majora*, ed. Henry Richards Luard, R.S. 57 (London, 1872-83), I, 542.

106/1-3, 107/32-36, and 108/16-17. Polydore and his followers speak of these executions after the battle, mentioning only Catesby by name. Since Buck mentions only Catesby and his own ancestor, it is clear that he had no source other than the chronicles and a family tradition regarding his great-grandfather. Polydore says, (p. 564), 'Biduo post Lecestriae Gulielmus Chatysby leguleius, cum paucis suis socijs, supplicio afficitur'.

106/5 - 108/15. The attainder of Richard's followers appears in *Rot. Parl.*, VI, 275-8. Buck's list agrees, with very little deviation. The Act of Attainder given in *Rot. Parl.* does not include Thomas Broughton, who was attainted later in connection with Lincoln's uprising (*Rot. Parl.*, VI, 397, 3 Hen. VII), or Sir William Conyers, or Thomas Stafford, who ought to have been included, since he is listed by Polydore (p. 564) and his followers as one of Richard's party who escaped after the battle (in Buck's second list, 'Robert' is probably an error for 'Thomas' Stafford). Only one Herald at Arms, Richard Watkins, is mentioned as such in *Rot. Parl.* Where in text,

p. 106, 1.45 Buck says 'suits', *Rot. Parl.* says 'Services'. Buck's wording here seems more likely: *Plumpton Correspondence,* Letter X of 13 December 1485 contains a similar list, also leaving out Conyers and Thomas Stafford. The attainders were passed, it says, 'Howbeit, ther was many gentlemen agaynst it, but it wold not be, for yt was the Kinges pleasure' (pp. 48f).

106/16-17. Commynes, Book IV, *passim.* Monstrelet gives one mention: see above, note 52/40-42.

106/18-23. The idea that Norfolk retired from court during Richard III's reign seems to have come from Surrey's epitaph: 'they both [Norfolk and Surrey] servyd . . . kynge Richard truly as hys subgettis duryng hys lyffe, lieng at home in their owne cowntrys, and kepyng honorabyl howses' (Martin, Appendix, p. 44). Tucker, pp. 44ff shows that the epitaph is misleading in suggesting that they stayed at home and that it ignores Richard's reliance upon them. Both were often with him, Surrey as Steward in constant attendance. Norfolk was Admiral of England, Ireland and Aquitaine and had power of array in thirteen shires. Their military, Parliamentary, and ambassadorial activities were numerous and important.

106/23-25. This statement is not in More as we now have his text, but seems to have been in an earlier draft which is represented in Grafton and Hall's inclusions of More's *History* in their works (see Sylvester, Appendix, in More, pp. 273f). Hall speaks of Thomas, son to the Lord Howard, 'whiche lord was one of the priueyest of the lord protectors counsaill and dooyng' (p. 361). Whereas the More passage seems to refer to Surrey, Buck takes it as referring to Norfolk.

107/4-7. Croyland, p. 574.

107/25-29. Croyland, p. 574. Buck has read 'magno' as 'in agro'.

107/43 - 110/1. Fabyan (p. 673) says that Surrey was taken in the field. Polydore (p. 564) and his followers state that Surrey submitted and was taken prisoner in the field and held a long time. Hall adds that he had submitted in the field and says that he was at last restored '& for his trueth and fidelity after promoted to high honors offices & dignites' (Hall, p. 419). A fuller account is given on Surrey's probably autobiographical epitaph (Martin, Appendix, pp. 44f): he went to Bosworth with Richard, was wounded and taken in the field and imprisoned in the Tower. During Lincoln's rebellion he refused the Lieutenant of the Tower's offer of the keys to liberate himself, saying that he would wait until the king who had committed him had released him, and

> after that for the true and feithful sevice that the seid kynge Henry herd of hym doon to hys other prince; and also that he sawe himself, he dide on Bosworth feld, and for the great prayse and truth that he herd of him whills he was prisoner, and that he wold nat, thoughe he had libertie, come oute of the tower at the erl of Lincolns feld, he toke hym out to hys presence, and to be about hys owne person . . . .

Buck is in the habit of supplying circumstantial detail to add narrative interest, so its presence cannot serve as evidence of this story's reliability. But because of his grandfather's reputedly intimate connection with Surrey, his account should not be dismissed. Either the story of the chroniclers and the memorial was invented to add greater glory to the Tudors or the story Buck heard was invented to add greater glory to the Howards. Surrey's attainder was removed in 1488 (*Rot. Parl.*, VI, 410f).

109/9-10. Henry married Elizabeth in 1486 and had her crowned in 1487.

109/26-43. Camden in *Remaines*, p. 283, gives the tale a pro-Parliamentary twist:

> When *Richard* the third was slaine at *Bosworth,* and with
> him *Iohn Howard* Duke of *Norffolke,* King *Henry* the
> seauenth demaunded of *Thomas Howard* Earle of *Surrey*
> the Dukes sonne and heire then taken prisoner, how he
> durst beare Armes in the behalfe of that tyranne *Richard.*
> He answered; *He was my crowned King, and if the Parla-*
> *mentary authority of England set the Crowne vpon a stocke,*
> *I will fight for that stocke. And as I fought then for him, I*
> *will fight for you, when you are established by the said*
> *authority.* And so hee did for his sonne King *Henry* the
> eight at *Floddon* field.

The source is given as 'Anonymous'. Whether Buck has used Camden here or Camden Buck, or both the same anonymous tradition is unknown.

110/10-11. Surrey was made High Treasurer in 1501 under Henry VII and restored to the dukedom of Norfolk under Henry VIII in 1514, not under Henry VII, as Buck says. Buck is correct in stating that he was made Earl Marshal under Henry VIII (1510).

110/20 - 113/39. The name is possibly Scandinavian, from an original 'Hereward', which has led to the genealogical conjecture current among heralds in Buck's time that the Howards were descended from Hereward the Wake. But more likely it comes from 'Heyward', a warden of barns (Brenan, I, 3f). William Dugdale is unable to trace the family beyond Edward I's time and mentions that some trace them to Hereward, but he cannot support this theory since Croyland mentions as Hereward's sole issue one daughter (*Baronage of England,* London, 1676, II, 265). Nor does Henry Howard of Corby (*Indications of Memorials*) try to trace them farther back.

Buck gives a similar account of the family's origins in *Comm.*, using all the sources he cites here except for Matthew of Westminster. For the more modern history he seems to have used the Rolls and the private collection of the Lord Admiral. *Comm.'s* account contains more direct quotation from Ingulph, whereas the *History* para-phrases the same material. *Comm.'s* information on Hereward is substantially the same, but Buck in that work is more explicit in attempting to derive the Howards from Hereward by logical proof: the Howards might have sprung 'from a Heward or Hereward in Marshland who liued about the tym of the Conq.' (*Comm.*, f. 18), since there was a Fulco *filius Hewardi* living under William II or Henry I, and this man's family possessed lands in Marshland very early. The same error in reading 'Edina' for 'Ediva' appears in *Comm.*, but there is no mention of her ill treatment or of Tailbois' ransom. The interchangeable spellings are documented in *Comm.* as they are here from papers in Lord William Howard's possession: 'my L.W. Howard of Naworth shewed me out of an ancient deed made by the sayd Hereward his ancestor, & who is called in one place Hereward & in another Heward . . .' (ff. 18f), and from records found by St Low Kniveton. For the interpretation of the name as 'leader of the army' he cites Camden's *Remaines*, and for recent history, Nicholas Charles' researches in the archives. He argues that bastard stock is not dishonourable, giving as examples William the Conqueror, King Arthur, the Bastard of Orleans, the Bastard of Burgundy, Alexander the Great (according to Plutarch), and Christ (*Comm.*, f.18ᵛ). Some of the recent details differ in the two accounts. Both confuse the John Howard who lived under Henry VI with his sons John and Robert who by predeceasing him made the John who was to become Duke of Norfolk heir to his grandfather, not his father. Because of the numerous tipped in pages in that section of *Comm.* which describes the origins and history of the Howards, it may be surmised that Buck was actively working on this genealogy quite late in the course of *Comm.*'s composition, around 1614. He had mentioned the Howards' derivation before that only once in *Daphnis* (sig. E3ᵛ) saying that they sprang from Edward I's son Thomas of Brotherton. By the time of writing the *History*, he has managed to sort out some of his evidence and fill in some gaps.

110/20. Croyland, p. 67.

110/42-46. Huntingdon, p. 205; Hoveden, I, 125f; Matthew Paris, II, 7; Matthew of Westminster, *Flores Historiarum*, ed. Luard, R.S. 95 (London, 1890), II, 5f; and Walsingham, *Ypodigma Neustriae*, ed. Riley, R.S. 28/7 (London, 1876), p. 72, all tell the same story of Hereward's defence of Ely. *Liber Eliensis*, ed. E.O. Blake, Cam. Soc., 3rd ser. 92 (London, 1962), pp. 173-92, of which there were manuscript copies in Cotton's library, gives a detailed description of Hereward's defence of Ely. But most of Buck's material seems to come from Croyland, pp. 67-71.

110/45-46. Croyland, p. 67: Hereward's father is described as a great benefactor of the monastery; his wife had died an inmate there four years before; his daughter still lived nearby and had just married Evermue, 'nostro monasterio multum familiar[us]'.

110/51 - 111/2. All sources stress Hereward's strength and vigour. Croyland (p. 67) says he was 'fortissimum rubore tunc adolescentem . . . procero quidem corpore, pulcherrimum ephebum, sed nimium belliscosum'.

111/13-18. Croyland (p. 70) says only that Hereward's lands were given to certain Normans. That this meant Tailbois is suggested by a later remark (p. 71) that Tailbois ruled all the surrounding country.

111/19-23. Croyland is not clear as to whether Hereward took Tailbois or Thorold, Abbot of Burgh (Peterborough) prisoner. Without much doubt, he means Thorold and Buck has misinterpreted. Also, Buck has confused Ingulph's sequence of events: first Hereward returned and drove out his mother's persecutors; nothing is said of taking the new earl prisoner, nor is the earl identified (p. 70). Next he defended Ely (p. 71), during the siege of which he defeated Tailbois (p. 125). Next Tailbois egged Thorold on against Hereward, who captured the abbot and released him for ransom.

111/24-29. This information is from Paris, II, 7.

111/40-41. Croyland, p. 67. See note 110/44-45, above.

112/mar. n. There is a general reference to Aeneas' birth in *Iliad* II, 819-21. In several places it is stated that he was son to Venus and Anchises, but legitimacy is not mentioned. Livy speaks of Romulus and Remus' birth, I, iv.

112/6-7. Plutarch, *Lives,* in 'Theseus', 3-4 and 'Themistocles' 1.

112/30-33. In *Comm.* (ff. 161ff) Buck gives more examples of surnames derived from offices.

113/6. I cannot locate the origin of this axiom.

113/13. I cannot find the origin of this verse.

113/34-41. This passage, in an incomplete state of revision, makes more sense if we read in 11.39-40, 'John Howard, the son of Robert Howard', which is what Buck meant to say. Robert Howard, the father of Richard III's John Howard, was the younger son of a John Howard who already had a son John by his first wife. Robert died in England, but his father John died in Jerusalem on a pilgrimage, and his elder brother John is said to have died on a pilgrimage as well (see Brenan, I, 10-12).

114/6-14. Commynes, II, 242 and Book IV, *passim.* Monstrelet gives only one mention: see above, note 52/40-42. The memorial on Surrey's tomb at Thetford is printed in Martin, Appendix, pp. 43-9.

114/26-30. See note 75/4th mar. n., above.

114/2nd mar. n. Camden in 'Iceni', not 'Ottadini', p. 352, tells how Henry VIII honoured Howard for the victory at Flodden, but this particular title is not mentioned. Buck makes a correct reference to 'Ottadini' in his next note.

114/37 - 116/47. For a discussion of Buck's ancestry as given in *History* and *Comm.,* see above, pp. xi-xiii.

115/1st mar. n. Camden in 'Ottadini', p. 668:

> in subsidium Regis Joannis Falcasius de *Brent,* & Walterus *Buc* adduxerunt, *Brent* homo efferatus tandem regno eiectus, *Buc* verò sedatior cùm strenuam operam regni nauasset, possessiones in agro Eboracensi & Northantonensi a Rege accepit, eiusque posteri ibidem floruerunt vsque ad Ioannem *Buc* proscriptum sub Henrico Septimo. Cuius pronepos est Georgius *Buc* . . . .

Camden may well have got this information from Buck.

115/2nd mar. n. Ludovico Guicciardini, *Descrittione di Tutti i Paesi Bassi* (Antwerp, 1581), p. 432: 'vi si veggono ancora le reliquie dell' antico castello di Buck, doue fu la prima dimora di quegli Signori, che alla guardi di Fiandra, per i Re Franzesi dimorauano'.

115/19-20. Roger de Wendover, *Flores Historiarum*, ed. Henry G. Hewlett, R.S. 84 (London, 1886-9), II, 147.

115/21-22. Paris II, 622, 636, and 645. Radulphus de Coggeshall, *Chronicon Anglicanum,* ed. Joseph Stevenson, R.S. 66 (London, 1875), pp. 177f. Matthew of Westminster, II, 155. Coggeshall's and Westminster's comments on Walter Buck are unfavourable and are given as evidence of King John's tyranny in hiring foreign mercenaries in 1215. Wendover's in a later passage than the one Buck cites, is not favourable either: 'Walterus Bucc cum Brebantiis suis, versus Hebereie Eliensem intrans insulam, ab omnibus ecclesiis in illa constitutis homines rapiens crudelissimo membrorum cruciatu ad gravissimam redemptionem coegit' (p. 171). Paris follows Wendover but emphasizes Walter Buck's atrocities. Walsingham does not speak of Walter Buck by name but briefly mentions the Flemish mercenaries (*Ypodigma*, p. 133).

115/33-35. This charter, B.L. MS. Cotton Augustus II, 56, is printed in Dugdale, *Monasticon Anglicanum* (London, 1830), VI, pt. i, pp. 285, no I. A charter of the Abbey's foundation dating from around 1130, it lists the contributions of the founders, among them 'Radulf*us* buhc. & Gozelin*us* fili*us* ei*us*' who gave four bovates of land each, the former in Grendale, the latter in Bucton. Buck mentions this charter in *Comm.*, noting that it is in Cotton's collection. There he follows it in describing Gocelinus as the son of Radulphus, rather than the grandson (*Comm*, f. 451ᵛ).

115/45-49. *Pat. Rolls.* (5 Nov. 1389), 146, 'Discharge of Richard, Earl of Arundel and Surrey, admiral of England' from a bond to keep safe Sir John Buke, 'a prisoner of war lately captured at sea' and not to ransom him without licence from the king or Council, on which assurance Buke was delivered from the Tower and was in Arundel's custody until his death in October 1389.

116/14. Menander, Γνῶμαι Μονόστιχοι, 748.

116/2nd mar. n. Euripides, *Heraclides*, 10-11.

116/43-44. George Talbot (1545-1630) became Earl of Shrewsbury in 1618.

117/1st mar. n. Cicero, *Oratio cum Senatui Gratias Egit,* I, 2.

117/20-22. *Digest,* II, iv, 4: 'parentum hic utriusque sexus accipe: sed an in infinitum, quaeritur. Quidam parentem usque ad tritavum appellari aiunt, superiores maiores dici'. Ulpian, *Edictum,* V.

117/24-27. *Historiae Augustae Scriptores,* ed. Isaac Casaubonus (Paris, 1603), p. 479. This annotation is actually made on a section by Trebellius.

117/2nd mar. n. This proverbial remark is not in Vergil.

118/4-5. Vergil, *Aeneid*, VI, 486-7.

118/18-19. Ibid., 11. 697-8.

BOOK III

119. The initial heading is really a general description of the whole of Book III, just as 'The story of Perkin Warbeck' is a general description of a major part of it. The rest are really subheadings under these two. Buck follows his outline well — except that 'King Richard not deformed' should follow '*Utopia*' — until he begins to discuss Perkin Warbeck, when his organization goes awry. All the topics listed are covered, but not in the order given, or sometimes more than once. Indeed, the repetition is so considerable that most of the Book's final third could be discarded without much loss.

119/39. See text, p. 170, l. 29 and note thereto for this quotation.

119/43-44. Matthew 7:12 and Luke 6:31.

120/17-22. Richard's body was carried naked and 'unreuerently' (Fabyan, p. 673) to the monastery of Greyfriars and, covered with a mean black cloth from the waist down, displayed for about three days, presumably on the day of battle and two days thereafter: Valera says three days (Goodman and Mackay, p. 92), Polydore, p. 565, says two — 'biduo post terra humat*ur*' — then 'with lytel reuerence buryed' (Fabyan, p. 673). Holinshed mentions that Henry had a tomb made in the church of Greyfriars with an effigy in alabaster, 'dooing that honour to his enimie, vpon a princelie regard and pitifull zeale, which king Richard (mooued of an hypocriticall shew of counterfeit pitie) did to king Henrie the sixt, whom he had first cruellie murthered' (p. 447). A reference in the section on Henry VII's privy purse expenses in *Excerpta Historica* confirms this by recording a disbursal in 1495 'To James Keyley for King Richard tombe, £10.1s' (p. 105). Kendall states that when Greyfriars was plundered during the dissolution of the monasteries, Richard's tomb was destroyed and his body thrown into the Soar' (p. 572).

120/1st mar. n. Erasmus, *Chiliades*, p. 81.

120/2nd mar. n. Ovid, *Amores*, I, xv, 39. Buck cites the wrong work. The several uses of 'livor' in *Ex Ponto,* III probably led his memory astray.

120/3rd mar. n. As in the previous reference, Buck's citation of the author is correct, but not of the work. The quotation is from Terence's *Andria,* I, 68.

120/22-26. This is the first statement of 'Ricardian historiography', the first recognition that the historical view of Richard was prejudiced by Tudor bias and the necessity for Tudor historians to foster it.

121 - 122. For a discussion of the More-Morton book, see above, pp. ciii-cvi.

121/15-22. More was a page in Morton's household about 1490-92. He was an Under-Sheriff between 1510 and 1518. He can hardly have been described as ambitious and seeking preferment at the age of twelve, when, in any case, his family was of sufficiently high standing to place him in the household of the Archbishop of Canterbury and Lord Chancellor. The office of Under-Sheriff was, R.W. Chambers tells us (*Thomas More,* London, 1935, p. 103) an important one, and More prospered in it. He was not lacking in professional preferment or unknown in humanist circles. The book was written when, Sylvester says, 'More was at the height of his powers' (in More, Introduction, p. lxxx) both in the legal profession and in literature.

For recent discussions of More's *History's* genre and purpose, see Sylvester, Introduction to More, pp. lxxx-civ; Kincaid, 'The Dramatic Structure of Sir Thomas More's *History of King Richard III*', *Studies in English Literature* XII (1972), 223-42; and Hanham, pp. 153-90.

121/3rd mar. n. See above, pp. ciii-civ.

121/4th mar. n. More, trans, Lucian 'Philopseudes', *The Translations of Lucian,* ed. Craig R. Thompson (New Haven, 1974), p. 45. More translated four, not seven dialogues. His attitude to this one, which he considers of moral value in ridiculing love of lying, can be seen in his dedicatory epistle, pp. 4-7.

121/35. I have been unable to locate a source for this remark, which sounds axiomatic.

121/38-40. Erasmus, *Opus Epistolarum Des. Erasmi Roterodami,* ed. P.S. Allen (Oxford, 1904-58), IV, 16, to Ulrich Hutten: 'Adolescens comoediolas et scripsit et egit'. Buck would have had access to this letter, appended as a 'Vita' of More to the 1563 edition of his *Latin Works.* There is a fuller account of More as improviser in William Roper, *The Lyfe of Sir Thomas Moore, Knighte,* ed. Elsie Vaughan

Hitchcock, EETS, orig. ser. 197 (London, 1935), p. 5.

121/5th mar. n. This is not Juvenal but Horace, *Epistulae,* I, i, 14.

121/47. More did not publish his history, which is unfinished. It was first published by his nephew William Rastell in 1557 and seems to have circulated little during his lifetime, for it is first heard of in 1538, after his death. Sylvester remarks that 'By failing to finish and to publish his work, More avoided the dilemma that plagued the humanist historians of Renaissance Italy, who had endeavored both to establish historical truth and to placate their patrons by a favorable account of their glorious ancestors' (p. cii).

121/6th mar. n. Herodotus, *Histories,* VI, i.

122 - 123. Unknown to himself, Buck is helping to disseminate slander against More which is comparable in origin and falsity to the slanders of Richard III which he is so ardent to dispel in the name of charity and justice. He was the victim of the current writing on More, as he objects that the chroniclers were victims of the current writing on Richard.

122/8. The word 'kind' is here used to mean 'natural'.

122/9-11. *Iliad,* II, 212-14.

122/15. See the section on dating the work in Sylvester, Introduction to More, pp. lxiii-liv.

122/16-18. Hall, pp. 817f reports More's jests on the scaffold with a tone of enmity and contempt. Grafton, p. 454, merely reports the anecdote with no critical tone.

122/1st mar. n. Germanus Brixius, *Antimorus* (Basle, 1519). This work and the aspersions it cast upon More's literary style were part of a literary quarrel which had developed from a political one between the two men. For an account of it see Chambers, pp. 190f. The poems that sparked and fed the controversy will be found in *The Latin Epigrams of Thomas More,* ed. Leicester Bradner and Charles Arthur Lynch (Chicago, 1953).

122/2nd mar. n. John Bale, *Scriptorum Illustrium Maioris Brytanniae* (Basle, [1557-9]), p. 655. Buck repeats, to some extent in paraphrase, almost the whole of Bale's account.

123/1st mar. n. G. Courinus Nucerinus in 'Epistola de Morte D. Thomae Mori', printed as a supplement in the *Latin Works* of More (Basle, 1563), pp. 511-30. Reynolds, pp. 2-8, says that Courinus was an amanuensis to Erasmus and probably not the author of the document. First published in 1535 with a different heading, it is the main source of information on More's trial and is known as 'The Paris News Letter'. Several manuscript copies exist in the Bibliothèque Nationale. Quite likely the original author was Philip Montanus, a friend and fellow scholar of Erasmus, who sent it to Erasmus, and Erasmus had it prepared for publication by Courinus. Buck's suggestion that Courinus was More's 'dear friend' was natural since he obviously assumed Courinus was the author.

123/28-31. The letter from More to Cromwell is in B.L. MS. Cotton Cleopatra E. VI, ff. 144-53. More states that he has kept aloof from arguments and meddling in both considerations as too high for his learning. He is sorry that the king 'shold reken in me eny maner of obstinate harte agaynst his pleasure in eny thing that ever I sayed or did concernyng his great mater of his mariage or concernyng the prymatie of the pope'. He had never in his writings or speeches 'advaunced greatly the popes authoritie', and he himself had had doubts on the question of whether the Pope's authority was divinely established until convinced by the king's own book and other learned works that he would be in peril of his soul if he did not believe this doctrine. As for the king's marriage, now that it is accomplished and Anne Boleyn anointed queen, he wishes them both 'long to lyve & well'. This letter was printed in More, *Workes* (London, 1557), pp. 1424-8. Buck could have seen it either there or in the Cotton manuscript. In the modern edition of More's letters, *The Correspondence of Sir Thomas More,* ed. Elizabeth Frances Rogers (Princeton, 1947), it appears on pp. 492-501.

123/36-41. There is no extant evidence in the present Cotton collection or elsewhere that More in any way assisted or assented to the suppression of monasteries.

124/13-15. Trebellius Pollio, *Triginta Tyranni,* XXXI, in *Hist. Aug. Scriptores.*

124/30-32. John Foxe, *The Ecclesiasticall Historie, Containing the Acts and Monuments of Martyrs* (London, 1583), II, 1008f and 1068f. Buck seems to have followed Foxe's attitude to More on various counts. For example, on p. 1008, Foxe refers whimsically to *Utopia* as if it were an actual place, 'from whence . . . can come no fittons but all fine Poetrie'. And again on pp. 1009 and 1013, he refers to More's 'licentiam poeticam'. On More's fanciful writings he bases the supposition that More must of necessity be considered dishonest: 'If M. More had neuer made fictions in hys writinges beside, or had neuer broken the head of veritie, in so many places of hys bookes as I could shewe hym, then might this argument goe for somewhat. . . . hee hath crackt his credite so often, and may alwayes be bankrout . . . ' (p. 1009). Concerning More's 'Holiness', Foxe notes 'a bitter persecuter he was of good men, and a wretched enemie against the truth of the Gospel', and that he 'wilfully stoode in the Popes quarell against his owne prince . . .' (p. 1069).

125/19-20. I have been unable to trace this quotation.

125/22-23. Polydore and Hall are vehemently hostile to Wolsey. Cavendish's life of Wolsey, written in 1554-8, not published until 1641 but circulated widely in manuscript and used by Stow, Holinshed, and Speed, is sympathetic and temperate. Written under Mary, it tries to correct what the author probably thought the result of Protestant propaganda in previous reigns and seems to intend direct contradiction of Hall (see Sylvester, Introduction to his edition of George Cavendish, *The Life and Death of Cardinal Wolsey,* EETS 243, London, 1959). Although Stow and Speed use Cavendish for information, their attitude remains essentially that of Hall, on whose account they primarily base their own. Holinshed is more sympathetic.

126/1st mar. n. Homer, *Iliad,* XX, 250.

126/2nd mar. n. Terence, *Phormio,* Prologue, 21.

126/10-17. All these authors have used More's narrative *verbatim* for their section on Edward V and the first part of Richard III's reign, interpolating only Grafton's description of Richard's coronation: Hall, pp. 342-79; Grafton, pp. 79-123; Stow, pp. 722-73; Holinshed, pp. 360-96 and 400f.

126/13. In coining the word 'Antirichards', Buck seems to be associating Richard with Christ, as he has done in his Biblical reference, text, p. 59. Rous, whom Buck seems not to have read, calls Richard an Antichrist (p. 218).

126/37-45. Cornwallis, p. 13: Richard's virtues 'through mallice are either not registered, or yf registred, they are detracted as yf all his vertues had a vicyous intent . . . .'

126/46 - 127/12. Cornwallis, p. 13: 'this worthey, this princely ornament, some Calumniators haue sought in him to deface, alledginge that his liberalitye to some proceeded from his extortion from others . . . .'

More, p. 8:

> Free was hee called of dyspence, and sommewhat aboue
> hys power liberall, with large giftes hee get him vnstedfaste
> frendeshippe, for whiche hee was fain to pil and spoyle in
> other places, and get him stedfast hatred. Hee was close
> and secrete, a deepe dissimuler, lowlye of counteynaunce,
> arrogant of heart, outwardly coumpinable where he in-
> wardely hated, not letting to kisse whome he thoughte to
> kyll: dispitious and cruell, not for euill will alway, but ofter
> for ambicion, and either for the suretie or encrease of his
> estate. Frende and foo was muche what indifferent, where
> his aduantage grew, he spared no mans deathe, whose life
> withstoode his purpose.

127/13-20. Cornwallis, p. 22:

> beinge desirous to reconcile him selfe to all sutch as held
> them selues offended (as before he had done with ffog a
> meane Attorney who had highly offended him) he
> laboured to winne the one sorte with benefit*es* & gift*es* and
> freely pardoned the others misbehauiours & offences: he
> had noe cause to feare fogg, therfore ffeare was not the
> cause, noe it was a worthie, a kingely, humilitye, that would
> rather abate his greatnesse then haue it Stained with the
> blood of soe meane a vassall for a crime comitted againste
> him selfe: yet was he guiltye of Counterfaitinge his roiall
> hande and signet & of a moste vntrue & infamous
> libell . . . .

More, pp. 81f:

> And fynally to thentent that no man shoulde hate hym for
> feare, and that his deceitful clemency mighte geat him the
> good wyll of the people, when he had declared the dys-
> comoditie of discorde, and the commodytes of concorde
> and vnitie, he made an open proclamacion, that he did put
> oute of his minde all enymities, and that he there did
> openly pardon all offences committed against him. And to
> the entente y^t he might shew a proofe thereof, he com-
> maunded that one Fogge whom he had long deadly hated,
> shold be brought than before him. Who being brought oute

> of the saintuary . . . in the sight of the people, he tooke him
> by the hand. Whiche thyng the common people reioysed at
> and praised, but wise men tooke it for a vanitye. In his
> returne homewarde, whom so euer he met he saluted. For
> a minde that knoweth it self giltye, is in a maner deiected to
> a seruile flattery.

Polydore ascribes Richard's generosity to a political move to win friends for his cause
and to his guilty conscience (p. 548).

127/24. More, p. 82: 'When he hadde begonne his reygne the twenty sixth daye of
Iune, after this mockishe eleccion, than was he Crowned the sixte day of Iuly'.

127/3rd mar. n. Cicero, *De Officiis,* I, xxxv, 128.

127/43-45. More (p. 87) with the marginal title, 'The out & inward troubles of
tyrauntes', says:

> . . . I haue heard by credible report of such as wer secrete
> w^t his chamberers, that after this abhominable deede
> done, he neuer hadde quiet in his minde, hee neuer thought
> himself sure. Where he went abrode, his eyen whirled
> about, his body priuily fenced, his hand euer on his dager,
> his countenance and maner like one alway ready to strike
> againe, he toke ill rest a nightes, lay long wakyng and
> musing, sore weried with care & watch, rather slumbred
> then slept, troubled wyth feareful dreames, sodainly
> sommetyme sterte vp, leape out of his bed & runne about
> the chamber.

Polydore (p. 565) mentions Richard's biting his lip and his habit of pulling his dagger
out of its sheath and putting it in again.

127/48-49. See note 124/30-32, above.

127/50 - 128/3. Croyland, p. 574 merely reports the dream as current rumour and
says that Richard regarded it as a presage. Polydore (p. 562), who is followed by
Hall, Grafton, and Holinshed, draws a moral from it:

> The fame went that he had the same night a dreadful & a
> terrible dreame, for it semed to hym beynge a slepe y^t he
> sawe diuerse ymages lyke terrible deuelles whiche pulled
> and haled hym, not sufferynge hym to take any quyet or
> rest. The which straunge vision not so sodeinly strake his
> heart with a sodeyne feare, but it stuffed his hed and
> troubled his mynde with many dreadfull and busy Imagina-
> cions. For incontynent after, his heart beynge almost
> damped, he prognosticated before the doubtful chaunce of
> the battaile to come, not vsynge the alacrite and myrth of
> mynde and of countenaunce as he was accustomed to do
> before he came toward the battaile. And least that it might
> be suspected that he was abasshed for feare of his enemyes,
> and for that cause looked so piteously, he recyted and
> declared to hys famylyer frendes in the morenynge hys
> wonderfull visyon and terrible dreame. But I thynke this

> was no dreame, but a punccion and pricke of his synfull
> conscience, for the conscience is so muche more charged
> and aggrauate as the offence is greater & more heynous in
> degre, whiche prycke of conscience allthough it strike not
> all waye, at the last daie of extreme life is wont to shewe
> and represent to vs our faultes and offences and the paynes
> and punishementes which hang ouer our heddes for the
> commyttyng of thesame.
>
> (Hall, p. 414)

Cornwallis presents a corrective (p. 29):

> It is affirmed that the night before the daie of battell, he
> dreamed a most dreadfull & horible dreame, which by our
> Chroniclers ys Interpreted to be a testemonie of his wicked
> and Tirranous life, did not Caesar before he attayned the
> Empire, dreame that he knew his owne mother Carnally.
> had not both Dion, & Brutus the figures of horible spirites
> represented vnto them the night before theire end? yet
> these weare accounted good men, and Louers and Pro-
> tectours of theire Country: and because Kinge Richard
> dreamed with some terrour, must his life of necessity be
> euell?

128/31-32. This idea is expressed in Philo, *On Abraham*, 264.

128/1st mar. n. *Iliad*, XX, 246-7.

128/38-41. Rous originated the story that Richard was born with teeth: 'exiens cum dentibus & capillis ad humeros' (p. 215), and More adopts it with a caveat (see below, quotation in note 129/3-5). Cornwallis, p. 3: 'His beinge toothed as soone as borne, me seemes rather a blessinge, then anie imputation, as beinge a prognosti-cation of his future worth, since it was an extraordinarie and noe vnproffitable marke, for nurses houlde the cominge out of Childrens teeth to be verie painefull'. It is a not uncommon medical phenomenon.

128/3rd mar. n. Pliny, *Natural History*, VII, xvi, 68f notes that Carbo and Curius were born with teeth, and the son of Prusius (not named) was born with a bone instead. Although Valerius Maximus, Livy, and Plutarch mention Curius, and Plutarch and Livy have references to Carbo as well, these anatomical details appear in none of them. Livy in Book XI gives Curius the epithet 'Dentatus'. L. Domitius Brusonius, *Rerum Memorabilium* (Frankfurt, 1600), III, ii, 290, says 'Prusia filius Prusiae Bythiniae regis, superiori ordine dentium vnum os aequaliter extentum habuit'.

129/3-5. Richard's mother's travail at his birth is another invention by Rous enlarged on by More. Both associate it with the teeth and hair story to suggest Richard's unnatural origin. Rous says Richard was two years in his mother's womb (p. 215). More notes (p. 7) that he was

> from afore his birth, euer frowarde. It is for trouth re-
> ported, that the Duches his mother had so muche a doe in
> her trauaile, that shee coulde not bee deliuered of hym

> vncutte: and that hee came into the worlde with the feete
> forwarde, as menne bee borne outwarde, and (as the fame
> runneth) also not vntothed, whither men of hatred reporte
> aboue the trouthe, or elles that nature chaunged her course
> in hys beginninge, which in the course of his lyfe many
> thinges vnnaturallye committed . . . .

Cornwallis, p. 3: 'why should not the same Axiome be a motiue to Cleare this
wronged Prince, whose Accusers lay to his Charge, the anguish his mother felt, when
he came in to the worlde, then which accusation what can be more friuolouse, it
beinge a punishment hereditarie to all woemen from the firste'.

129/7-8. Seneca, *Ad Lucilium Epistulae Morales,* XXIV, 14.

129/23 - 131/38. Cornwallis, pp. 3f:

> but he was Crookebacked, lame, ill fauored, I might impute
> that fault to Nature, but that I thinke it rather her bountie,
> for she beinge wholy intentiue to his minde neclected his
> forme, soe that shee infused a straight minde in a Crooked
> bodie, wherin she shewed her carefull prouidence, for
> often times the care to keepe those partes well formed,
> withdrawes mens mindes from better actions, and drownes
> them in effeminate Curiositye, his lamenes turned to his
> glorye, for with those vnperfect limmes, he performed
> actions moste perfectly valiant . . . .

130/9-11. Although Rous originates the story that Richard was born with teeth and
hair and had one shoulder higher than the other, there is no record of deformity
either in his *Historia* or in his drawing. It is undoubtedly true that Rous knew
Richard's appearance well (see T.D. Kendrick, *British Antiquity,* London, 1950, pp.
18f). In Buck's time the manuscript of Rous' *Historia* was in Cotton's collection, but
Buck does not seem to have read it.

130/13-14. More, p. 7, describes Richard as being 'hard fauoured of visage, and
suche as is in states called warlye, in other menne otherwise'.

130/25-30. This is from More, p. 67f, with the most minor alterations.

130/31-32. Dr Shaw, or Shaa, was not Dean but a canon of St Paul's, an office he
held from 1477 until his death in 1484 (A.B. Emden, *A Biographical Register of the
University of Cambridge to 1500,* Cambridge, 1963, p. 520).

130/mar. n. More, in Grafton's continuation of Hardyng, p. 469 and in Grafton, p.
81; '. . . whither menne of hatred reporte aboue the trouthe' (More, p. 7). This is
actually said in relation to the rumour that Richard was born with teeth. More does
not qualify his reference to Richard's deformity, saying that he was 'little of stature,
ill featured of limmes, croke backed, his left shoulder much higher then his right' (p.
7).

130/44-46. Erasmus, *Opus Epistolarum,* IV, 14: 'Dexter humerus paulo videtur
eminentior laeuo'.

131/21-38. See Appendix A, below.

131/44 - 134/8. All contemporary accounts of Henry VI's death either suggest that
he died of natural causes or that Edward IV was responsible, depending on whether

their bias is Yorkist or Lancastrian. Fauconberg's rising would have shown Edward
the danger of letting Henry VI remain alive, and his exhibiting the body confirms that
Henry's existence was a threat to him. He followed Henry IV, who had Richard II
put to death secretly and countered rumours that he was still alive by exhibiting the
body. Richard III followed Henry V, 'atoning' for his brother's crime as Henry V
'atoned' for his father's by giving the body a noble burial. Abroad there was no
question as to the murderer's identity. *CSP* (Milan) says quite bluntly, 'King Edward
has not chosen to have the custody of King Henry any longer . . . as he has caused
King Henry to be secretly assassinated in the Tower . . .' (p. 157).

Later the deed is attributed to Richard. The only contemporary corroboration
Tudor authors may claim for this attribution is the dubious account of John Warkworth
(*A Chronicle of the First Thirteen Years of the Reign of King Edward the Fourth,* ed.
J.O. Halliwell, Cam. Soc. 10, London, 1939, p. 21), which mentions that Richard,
among many others, had accompanied Edward to the Tower on the night Henry was
killed. No account mentions Richard's complicity as a fact: each includes some
qualifying remark. Rous seems to have originated the story, saying that Richard
killed Henry through intermediaries or, many believe, with his own hand (p. 215).
Commynes speaks uncertainly: 'si je n'ay ouy mentir, incontinent après ceste bataille
le duc de Clocestre, frère dudit Edouard, lequel depuis a esté roy Richard, tua de sa
main ou feït tuer en sa presence, en quelque lieu à part, ce bon homme le roy Henry'
(I, 215). Andrē remarks that Richard killed Henry, 'si vera est fama' (p. 19), but says
he was sent by Edward (p. 23). Fabyan and the Great Chronicle are equally
uncertain: 'Of ye deth of this prynce dyuerse tales were tolde: but the moost common
fame wente, that he was stykked with a dagger, by the handes of the duke of
Glouceter . . .' (Fabyan, p. 662). More and Polydore follow this pattern. More says
'He slewe with his owne handes king Henry the sixt, being prisoner in the Tower, as
menne constantly saye' (p. 8). Polydore's wording is 'Hunc, ut fama constans est,
Ricardus Glocestria dux gladio percussit, quo ita Edouardus rex eius frater omni
hostili metu liberaretur' (p. 532). The succeeding authors copy More and Polydore,
though Holinshed notices the writers who say the king died of melancholy (p. 324).
In Shakespeare, Richard's killing Henry VI becomes no longer a doubtful event, but
dramatic fact (3 *Henry VI*, V, vi).

A violent death was suggested by the apparent matting with blood of the little
remaining hair (W.H. St John Hope, 'The Discovery of the Remains of King Henry
VI in St. George's Chapel, Windsor Castle', *Archaeologia*, LXII (1911), 533-42.

132/1st mar. n. Polydore does not refer to Henry by these epithets but does call him
'uir bonus, gratus, pius, modestus, sapiens' and says that Henry VII 'eum inter diuos
referendum . . . curare coepit' (p. 532).

132/25-28. Curtius, VIII, ii, 2.

132/31-32. Richard slew King Henry 'without commaundemente or knowledge of
the king, whiche woulde vndoubtedly yf he had entended that thinge, haue appointed
that boocherly office, to some other then his owne borne brother' (p. 8).

132/46-49. I have been unable to trace these quotations.

133/11-13 and 22-26. Croyland, p. 556. H.T. Riley, translator of Ingulph's *Chron-*

icle of the Abbey of Croyland (London, 1854), p. 468, says, 'This appears to be a hint of Edward's complicity'. The chronicler had reason to conceal Edward's name since he was father to Henry VII's queen, but none to conceal any suggestion there might have been of Richard's complicity. His mentioning none suggests that there was none.

133/32-34. Croyland, p. 532, 2nd continuation, under 1461.

133/3rd mar. n. Cornwallis, pp. 6f:

> The death of Henry the sixt in the Tower can noe way belonge to him, since the same reason that cleareth his brother acquiteth him, he beinge able if desiringe his death to haue effected it by a more vnworthey hand: And in deede this accusac*i*on hath no other proffe, but a malicyous affyrmac*i*on, for many more truly did suppose that he dyed of meere melancholy & grief when he had hard of the ou*er*throw of his frend*es* & slaughter of his sonne.

By 'others', Cornwallis refers to the *Arrivall*, p. 38: 'not havyng afore that, knowledge of the saide matars, he toke it in so great despite, ire, and indignation, that, of pure displeasure, and melancoly, he dyed the .xxiij. day of the monithe of May'. This account appears to have been concocted for Yorkist benefit: Henry's death is post-dated so as not to coincide with Edward's presence in London. That the news of Tewkesbury should have taken nineteen days to reach Henry is not credible.

134/1st mar. n. Meyer, p. 403: 'Henricus Rex Londini in custodia, vt alij, vt moerore, vt alij Glocestrij gladio deperijt'. The reference to Book 17 is correct. Buck omits to mention Richard as owner of the sword that killed Henry.

134/5-8. This theory has been pursued more recently by Zeeveld and by Kincaid and Ramsden. More likely the reference is to More. See Alison Hanham, review of Kincaid and Ramsden, *The Ricardian*, IV (1978), 24.

134/9 - 135/6. No contemporary or near-contemporary suggests that Richard killed the Prince of Wales. Contemporary accounts agree that he was killed in battle (see Kendall, p. 528), and these leave no room for doubt. That Richard is now thought of as the sole 'murderer' is probably attributable to his confession in the wooing scene of Shakespeare's *Richard III* (I, ii). Since this is one of the most famous scenes in Shakespeare, one forgets 3 *Henry VI*, V, v, which shows the prince being stabbed by Edward, Clarence, and Gloucester, and *Richard III*, I, iv, where Clarence, describing his dream, says the prince's ghost accused him of stabbing him. But this is a late version of the story, which, like that of Henry VI's murder, was subject to many accretions.

Fabyan (p. 662) and the Great Chronicle (p. 218), state that the prince was taken after the battle and brought before King Edward, who questioned him, eliciting an unpalatable answer, upon which the king struck him with his gauntlet and the king's servants slew him. Polydore follows this version, substituting for the servants the names of Clarence, Gloucester, and Hastings (p. 530). Hall (p. 301) adds Dorset. More does not even mention this 'murder'.

134/3rd mar. n. Holinshed, p. 320: 'At which words king Edward said nothing'.

Polydore, Hall, and Grafton say the same.

134/4th mar. n. Polydore, p. 530. He does not mention Dorset as one of the slayers, as his successors do, but does mention Richard.

134/5th mar. n. See above, note 20/5th mar. n.

134/6th mar. n. Meyer, p. 403: 'Est qui Annam Principis vxorem vna cum marito captam tradit'. Neither this nor Buck's paraphrase of it actually says she was in the room at the time.

135/7 - 137/48. More is the first to suggest Richard's complicity in Clarence's death, though Rous (p. 215) and Polydore (p. 537),who, like all historians before Stow, were at a loss to account for it, mention that the 'G' prophecy came true in Richard's usurpation. Contemporary sources, foreign and native, say only that Edward had his brother put to death for treason, and this is confirmed by his indictment (*Rot. Parl.* VI, 193-5), first discovered by Stow and reported in the 1592 edition of his *Annales,* p. 708. Croyland's report, which reads like that of an eye-witness, makes plain that sentencing and execution were conducted by form of law. The execution was not public, but there seems to have been no expectation that it should be. Relations between Clarence and Edward had been so threatening for many years that it is a wonder the king did not dispose of his brother sooner. Clarence had fomented rebellions, contrived and fought with Edward's enemies, tried to make himself king, publicly impugned the king's justice, and spread rumours derogatory to Edward. See Ross, *Edward IV,* pp. 116-244 *passim* and 441f.

135/7-13. More, p. 8: 'Somme wise menne also weene, that his drifte couertly conuayde, lacked not in helping furth his brother of Clarence to his death: whiche hee resisted openly, howbeit somwhat (as menne demed) more faintly then he y^t wer hartely minded to his welth'. This opposition of Richard's is confirmed by Mancini, who ascribes it to inability to dissemble, as opposed to More's accusation of dissimulation (p. 62). In Harl. 433, f. 265^v is yet another implication that Richard was incensed at his brother's death and blamed the Woodvilles (quoted in Gairdner, ed., *Letters and Papers,* I, 68).

135/2nd mar. n. Polydore, p. 537 reports several causes of enmity between the brothers. But the remark opposite which this note appears is better illustrated by Croyland, p. 562: 'nemo arguit contra Ducem, nisi Rex; nemo respondit Regi, nisi Dux'.

135/3rd mar. n. Polydore, p. 537.

135/32 - 136/32. Armstrong says that 'One result of the xenophobia prevalent in England during the latter middle ages was that a member of the royal house born abroad was liable to be called a changeling or a bastard by his enemies' (in Mancini, p. 109). Lander observes that 'Accusations of bastardy were . . . part of the common stock of political smears in the fifteenth century and should not be taken too seriously' (p. 26n). Richard did not originate the story of Edward's bastardy. Warwick spread this rumour in France in 1469 (J. Calmette and G. Pērinelle, *Louis XI et l'Angleterre,* Paris, 1930, 'Pièces Justicatives', no. 30, pp. 306f). Commynes reports that Louis XI heard in his presence how in 1475 Charles of Burgundy called Edward 'Blayborgne, filz d'un archer' (II, 50). Clarence used Edward's supposed illegitimacy in his campaign for kingship ((*Rot. Parl.,*VI, 194). Edward's debasing marriage lent fuel to the story, for Mancini says the Duchess of York was so upset that she offered to submit to a public enquiry to prove Edward was illegitimate and hence not fit to reign (pp. 60-2). *Rot. Parl.*, VI, 241 in stating Richard's claim makes a point of his being born in England, 'by reson wherof . . . all the thre Estatis of the Lande have, more certayn knowlage of youre Byrth and Filiation'.

Gladys Jenkins, 'Ways and Means in Elizabethan Propaganda', *History,* new ser. XXVI (1941), 108, notes the importance of the pulpit as a means of communication and its use in politics. The Paul's Cross sermon 'was delivered every Sunday at the cross outside the cathedral, and to it came not only the ordinary citizens, but also the notables of the city and court'. Richard in his use of this sermon to set forth his right again followed the precedent of his brother Edward IV, who had had the Bishop of Exeter preach a sermon at Paul's Cross setting forth evidence for his title to the throne, then rode in procession to Westminster Hall where he took possession of the royal seat. Neither Croyland nor Rous mentions Shaa's sermon. Fabyan takes it as a matter of course in the succession of political events.

136/17-28. More, p. 73 does not say directly that Richard was displeased but rather has Buckingham refer to the illegitimacy by *praeteritio*:

> . . . other thinges, which the said worshipful doctor rather
> signified then fully explaned, & which thynges shal not be
> spoken by me as ye thing wherin euery man forbereth to
> say that he knoweth in auoidinge dyspleasure of my noble
> lord protectour, bearinge as nature requireth a filial reuer-
> ence to the duches his mother.

Hall, p. 371 and Grafton, p. 109 repeat More, as do Holinshed and Stow.

136/2nd mar. n. If this is the same work Buck refers to in other places in the *History* by this description, it seems no longer extant. Cornwallis says, 'in which his miserye who did more truely follow him? who more faithfully ayded him then his now disgraced brother' (p. 5).

136/45-50. See note 51/17-21, above.

137/3-4. Richard's signature, along with those of Edward V and Buckingham, and Richard's motto in his own hand above his name are in Cotton Vespasian F. XIII, f. 53. There is a photograph of the document in Kendall between pp. 304 and 305.

137/15-17. Croyland, p. 561.

137/3rd mar. n. Stow, p. 716. *Rot. Parl.,*VI, 194: 'uppon oon the falsest and moost unnaturall coloured pretense that man myght imagyne, falsely and untruely noysed, published and saide, that the Kyng oure Soveriegne Lorde was a Bastard, and not begottone to reigne uppon us'.

137/4th mar. n. Erasmus, *Chiliades,* p. 80.

137/5th mar. n. Jean de Serres, *Inventaire General de l'Histoire de France* (Paris, 1600), II, 215: 'Mais à la priere de leur commune mere, Edouard moderant la sentence, luy donna l'option de tel gêre de mort qu'il voudroit élire. & suiuant ce pouuoir, il voulut mourir dans vne pipe de maluaisie'. This is also reported in Commynes, I, 53 and Fabyan (p. 666) and the Great Chronicle (p. 226), and may well be true.

137/46-48. Polydore, p. 537.

138 - 173. See below, Appendix B for discussion of the Princes' death.

138/12-24. This story was originated by More and copied by Hall, Grafton, Stow and Holinshed.

138/2nd mar. n. Genesis, 35: 19-20.

138/27-30 and 139/1st mar. n. Polydore, p. 569 reports a rumour that they were sent abroad, John Rastell, *The Pastime of People* (London, 1811), p. 292 that they were thrown into the sea.

138/31-32. Apocrypha, story of Susannah, 'Daniel, 13'.

193/3-10. More, p. 82:

> Whose death and final infortune hathe natheles so far
> comen in question, that some remain yet in doubt, whither
> they wer in his dayes destroyde or no . . . . Perken Warbeck,
> by many folkes malice, and mooe folkes foly, so long space
> abusyng the worlde, was aswel with princes as ye porer
> people; reputed and taken for the yonger of those two . . . .

139/15-16. Polydore, p. 547: 'sed quo genere pueri affecti fuerint, non plane liquet'.

139/3rd mar.n. Croyland, p. 568. Although Strype (in Kennett, p. 525) and Myers (in Buck, reprint, p. vii) set great store by the omission of 'violenti' from this passage, all we can say is that the word is missing in the Editor's copies: in the original everything between 'sed q' and 'interitus' is burnt away, and there could conceivably have been room for the word there. Or the omission (which is not in any case crucial) could have resulted from assimilation to the similarly worded quotation from Polydore, p. 547, given above, note 139/15-16. One cannot ever make a case against Buck's accuracy on the basis of omissions from the copies. See above, pp. xcvii-xcviii.

139/26-28. More, p. 87: 'Dighton in dede yet walketh on a liue in good possibilitie to bee hanged ere he dye'.

139/4th mar. n. More, p. 86; Holinshed, p. 402; Grafton, p. 118; Hall, p. 378; Stow, p. 769.

139/46 - 140/2. More, p. 86: 'thei say that a prieste of syr Robert Brakenbury toke vp the bodyes again, and secretely entered them in such place, as by the occasion of his deathe, whiche onely knew it could neuer synce come to light. . . . theyr bodies cast god wote where'. This is echoed by Grafton, p. 118, Hall, p. 378, Holinshed, p. 402, and Stow, p. 769. The words emphasized here are underlined in the original MS.

140/16-21. See above, note 54/50 - 55/11 for discussion of Buck's argument that the Princes were living in February 1484.

140/24-27. More, p. 35.

140/26-27. The relatively early deaths of Edward IV's daughters may be attributable to tuberculosis, which was evidently the cause of Anne, Countess of Surrey's death and the death in childhood or infancy of all her children (Brenan, I, 122). Elizabeth, wife of Henry VII, was born in 1466 and died in 1503; Cecily, born in 1468, died in 1507; Margaret was born and died in 1472; Anne was born in 1475 and died in 1511; Catherine, born in 1479, died in 1511; Bridget, born in 1480, died in 1517; and Mary was born and died in 1482.

140/28-42. There have been many cases of bones dug up in the Tower and supposed to be the Princes'. The most famous were discovered by workmen in 1674 in a wooden box under the stairs outside the White Tower and buried in the Abbey — where they still reside — in 1678, under Charles II's assumption that they were those of the Princes. Between discovery and burial, the bones had been damaged, lost, given away, and replaced by animal bones, and as GEC points out (XII, pt. ii, Appendix J,. pp. 35-9), it is not at all certain that those found in 1674 were the same ones interred in the Abbey in 1678. An examination of them in 1933 (Lawrence E. Tanner and William Wright, 'Recent Investigations Regarding the Fate of the Princes in the Tower', *Archaeologia,* LXXXIV, 1935, 1-26) seemed to suggest that the bones could have been those of the Princes. The ages were judged to agree with those of the Princes, and a stain on one of the skulls suggested possible suffocation. But date of death and sex could not be determined.

Dr Richard Lyne-Pirkis in a talk before the Richard III Society in London, 1964, pointed out that in the light of more recent research we can no longer determine age from eruption of teeth, from the appearance of ossification centres, or from the joining of the epiphyses, which were the evidences on which the 1933 investigation entirely relied. His conclusions were that the bones belonged to children of different ages, perhaps roughly between seven or eight and fifteen or sixteen. He notes that the skull of the elder shows signs of osteomyelitis, a potentially fatal disease. Dr W.M. Krogman, quoted in Kendall, p. 577n, demolished the theory that the stain was caused by suffocation.

141/2-3. Edward V was born 2 or 3 November 1470, Richard III's son Edward in 1473.

141/29-34. See above, note 54/50 - 55/11 and below, Appendix B for discussion of what threat the Princes' existence posed to Richard.

141/49 - 142/5. Clearly there was some such fear, since someone did an inter-lineation in Richard II's order of legitimation indicating specifically that the Beauforts were not to be held capable of the crown (see note 80/23-33 above).

142/5-6. On the other hand, Henry VII may have put to death Richard's bastard son John of Gloucester, and if the mysterious 'Richard Plantagenet' (see note 192/49 - 193/3 below) was really Richard's son, he took great care to stay out of harm's way. Even if he were not, his story reflects a knowledge of the attitude toward kings' bastards.

142/17-20. More, p. 82, quoted above, note 139/3-10.

142/mar. n. Holinshed, p. 484; also Hall and Grafton. For Polydore, see above, note 139/15-16.

141/44 - 142/6. More has Buckingham say, 'is it not likelye ynoughe that she shall sende him [York] somme where out of the realme? Verely I looke for none other' (p. 29). Later he has the Archbishop say to the queen, 'So much drede hath my Lorde his vncle, for the tender loue he bereth him, lest your grace shold hap to send him awaye'

(p. 37). Croyland, p. 567, mentions a suggestion by the Woodville party that the Princes' sisters be shipped out of the country to be preserved in case anything happened to their brothers.

143/7-9. The idea of York's being sent into Flanders parallels a curious accusation in the indictment of the Duke of Clarence: that he tried to have a strange child brought to Warwick Castle and substituted for his son while he sent his son to Ireland or Flanders to serve as a figurehead in the raising of forces against Edward IV. If Perkin really was York sent abroad, this precedent might have given the idea to the person who sent him.

143/mar. n. Grafton, pp. 202f, copied from Hall, pp. 473f, and thence derived from Polydore, pp. 596f and embellished: the oration of Perkin to James IV of Scotland. The Biblical reference, from II Kings 11, is in the speech itself.

143/29-35. Charles, Duke of Burgundy died in 1477. Buck seems particularly vague in his information on the House of Burgundy, calling Margaret aunt to Richard and Clarence (see above, text, p. 17 and note thereto).

143/43-45. There exists a letter (Ex Orig. inter Chart. Antiq. et Miscellan. in Bibliothec. Lambethan., Vol. XII, quoted by Gairdner in *Memorials,* Appendix A, pp. 393-9) from Margaret of Burgundy to the Pope asking assistance in favour of Perkin against Henry Tudor, who holds the crown by right of conquest and pretends he is of the blood of Lancaster, knowing full well that he is illegitimate on both sides and that his nomination by the Three Estates in a Parliament called by himself is illegal. She states that he invaded and seized the kingdom just after the House of York had acquired safe possession of it. When Henry took the throne Margaret had other reasons for grievance, since her dowry had never been paid in full, and with Henry's accession the payments stopped.

144/11-15. Shortly after the siege of Boulogne in 1492, Perkin was received in France and Burgundy.

144/26-28. Lambert Simnel in 1487 pretended first to be Richard, Duke of York, but decided instead to impersonate Warwick, who was still alive in the Tower.

145/2-4. It is doubtful that Warwick was the man the rebels intended to crown. John de la Pole, Earl of Lincoln, who may have been Richard's chosen heir, was doubtless pressing his own claim, using Simnel as a stalking horse.

145/13. 'Sir Simon Priest' is an error for Sir Richard Simon, who was a priest. The mistake may have come from rapid reading by Buck, since Hall (p. 428), Grafton (p. 169), and Holinshed (p. 484) all speak of 'Sir Richard Simond priest' without any intervening punctuation, as if it were all one name. It may, of course, equally well be the mistake of George Buck, Esq. or his scribe.

145/13-14. There is no evidence that Simnel himself ever went to Burgundy. His nominal supporters, John, Earl of Lincoln and Francis, Viscount Lovell did so and were granted aid by Margaret, Duchess of Burgundy. Buck seems again to be assuming, erroneously, that Charles, Duke of Burgundy was still alive.

145/1st mar. n. Dion Cassius, LVII, 16.3; Tacitus, *Annales,* II, xxxix; and Suetonius, *Tiberius,* XXV all speak of 'pseudo Agrippa'. 'Pseudo Nero' is referred to only by Dion Cassius LXIII, 9 and LXVI, 19; and Sextus Condianus only by Dion Cassius,

LXXIII, 6.

145/33-35. Velleius Paterculus, *Historia Romana,* I, xi, 1.

145/50 - 146/1. The shoemaker's son who impersonated Warwick was Ralph Wilford. His parentage is given by Stow (p. 805), and Holinshed repeats it with reference to Stow (p. 523). Fabyan, p. 686, calls him 'sonne of a cordyner'.

146/1st mar. n. Ovid, *Epistulae Heroides,* XVI, 130.

146/19-26 and 34-36. Livy, I, iv (Romulus and Remus). Diodorus in fragmentary books VII (5.1) and VIII (3-6) refers to Romulus and Remus.

146/27-33. Herodotus, I, 108-13; Trogus Pompeius, *Historiae Philippicae,* I, fragment 24.

146/38-41. II Kings, 11. See above, note 143/mar. n.

146/49. There is no reference to Moses in Perkin's speech as the chroniclers record it.

147/17-19. Hall, p. 463. Frederic Madden, 'Documents Relating to Perkin Warbeck', *Archaeologia,* XXVII (1838), 176 says the conspirators planned to attach white roses to their garments if they succeeded (p. 176).

147/35-40. The message Henry's ambassadors gave was not a statement or proof of Perkin's real identity, but merely a statement that he was obviously an imposter because everyone knew Richard had killed his nephews, and to believe otherwise was the height of madness (Polydore, p. 591). Here Henry's historian speaks better for Perkin than does Buck, in giving Henry a very flimsy argument.

148/2nd mar. n. Grafton, p. 215, derived from Polydore, p. 606. Also in Hall and Holinshed.

149/19-20. Polydore, p. 603, gives 'Petrus Hyalas'; Hall, p. 482 and Grafton, p. 211, 'Peter Hyalas'; Stow, p. 803, 'Peter Helias'; Holinshed, p. 517, 'Peter Hialas'; and Gainsford, p. 88, 'Peter Hialos'.

149/2nd mar. n. According to Perkin's confession, given in Hall, p. 488f, and his followers, ambassadors named Loyte Lucas and Stephyn Fryan were sent from the French king to invite him to France. Frion — as his name is given in *Pat. Rolls* (1485-94), pp. 118 and 344 — was Henry's Clerk of the Signet and Secretary of the French Tongue from 1486 until 1491 at the latest.

149/44 - 150/2. This French visit actually occurred earlier. At this stage Perkin went directly from Ireland to Cornwall, where he was captured. His stay in France had occurred after his first visit to Ireland. After his expulsion from France because of the Treaty of Etaples, he returned to Flanders, then set out for Kent, Ireland again, and Scotland.

151/44 - 152/17. For comments on Perkin's confession, see below, Appendix C.

151/48-49. Grafton, p. 218; Hall, pp. 488f; also in Holinshed.

152/25-26. Seneca, *Controversiae,* X, 8.

152/3rd mar. n. Augustine, *De Civitate Dei,* XIX, vi, 'Si enim secundum istorum sapientiam elegerit ex hac vita fugere quam diutius illa sustinere tormenta: quod non commisit, commississe se dicit'.

153/4-8. Psalm 22, Matthew 27, and Mark 15.

154/12, 170/35, 172/45 and 212/28. See note 170/34-43. The son of Richard's referred to here is John of Gloucester.

154/23-24. Buck is recurring here to imagery on which he based his long poem *Daphnis.*

154/24-25. Gainsford parallels Simnel and Warbeck.

155/21-23. Polydore, p. 608, 'cùm nullo suo delicto supplicium quaerere posset, alieno ad id tractus est'.

155/33-34. I have not succeeded in locating this sentence in the *Institutes* or *Digest,* possibly for lack of a satisfactory index.

155/2nd mar. n. William Staundford, *Les Plees del Corone* (London, 1607), I, 27, 33ᵛ. Ch. 26 covers 'Escape Voluntary' and Ch. 27 'Negligent Escape'.

156/14-16. Gainsford, Preface, sig. B2.

156/19 - 158/32. Sebastian, King of Portugal, who reigned 1557-78, after his death in battle in somewhat confusing circumstances became the focus of a messianic-hero image associated with millenarian prophecies. There were four main pretenders to Sebastian's identity, the last of these being the one to which Buck refers:

> The last Sebastian appeared in 1598 in Venice, where there was a colony of adherents of Dom António and Portuguese Jews. He did not speak Portuguese — owing to a vow he had taken, he said. At the behest of the Spanish ambassador, he was arrested. Dom João de Castro, an opponent of Philip II, took up his case, and it was arranged to get him to Paris, but he was identified as a Calabrian, Marco Tullio Caltizzone, and condemned to the galleys for his imposture. Funds were collected to rescue him, and he was executed in 1603.
>
> (H.V. Livermore, *A New History of Portugal,*
>   2nd ed., London, 1976, p. 167)

156/43. Quintilian, *Institutio Oratoria,* I, ii, 19: 'caligat in sole'. Erasmus, *Chiliades,* p. 513 gives this quotation with the explanation, 'in re clarissima caecutire'.

157/1-4. Gainsford, p.60. In context, and taken with other similar remarks of Gainsford, this assumes an aspect of sarcasm rather than factual statement (p. 42: 'this misnamed *Richard*').

158/24-25. I cannot find the source of this quotation.

158/25-26. At this point the printed version of Buck's *History* inserts some supplementary material appearing in no other version, a letter from Dr Stephen de Sampugo to Joseph Texere giving evidence from Venice that Don Sebastian is not a counterfeit.

159/35-43. There is no reference in Buck's sources to Morton's complicity in the death of Warwick. Buck seems to be deflecting blame from Henry VII. Hall says 'The fame after hys death springe abroade, yᵗ Ferdinand kyng of Spayne woulde neuer make full conclusion of the matrimony to be had betwene prynce Arthur and the lady Katheryn hys daughter nor sende her into England aslong as this erle lyued' (p. 491) and is followed in this by Grafton and Holinshed. Warwick and Warbeck were executed in 1499, and Morton died in 1500, ten months later.

160/7-8. This book is no longer extant. It was probably in manuscript privately circulated among Hoby's friends, of whom Buck was one (see above, p. ciii-civ).

160/mar. n. This is not in More, Holinshed, Stow, or Gainsford. This oath is given only in Hall, p. 251.

160/50 - 161/1. There is no evidence of Sir Robert Clifford's following the House of York except for a very few minor grants to a Robert Clifford, Esq. under the Yorkist kings in *Pat. Rolls.* Buck presumably uses for his evidence the fact that Clifford is expected to have known the Duke of York well enough to identify him.

161/1st mar. n This does not appear in More. These followers are recorded, *passim,* in Holinshed, Grafton, Stow, and Hall, under 'Henry VII' and in Gainsford, *passim.*

161/13-18. Sir William Stanley was executed in 1495 for treason in complicity with Perkin Warbeck; Sir Robert Clifford, who informed against him and received a substantial reward from Henry for so doing, reported that Stanley had said that if Perkin really were the son of Edward IV he would not fight against him (Polydore, p. 593). For further information on Sir William Stanley, see above, note 29/29-36.

161/19-20. George Neville was not the brother of the Earl of Westmorland. He is cited in Hall, p. 463 as 'syr George Neuell bastard'. *Rot. Parl.,* VI, 504 records an Act of Attainder passed against 'George Neville, late of London Knight, otherwise called George Neville bastard, comonly called bastard sone to Sir Thomas Neville'.

161/24. Grafton, Hall, Holinshed, and Stow give 'Thomas Astwood' instead of 'Thomas Bagnol'. According to Stow, p. 799, Bagnall was executed the next year for an unstated offence. Hall, p. 467, Grafton, and Holinshed give 'Cressenor' and Stow, p. 798 gives 'Chressenor' where Buck has 'Challoner'. Probably 'Challoner' was a misreading of 'Chressenor', since at a glance long 's's might look like 'l's.

161/29. Gainsford, p. 49, spells the name Rochford. It is given as Richeford in the chroniclers.

161/44. Buck evidently got these names from Gainsford, p. 62, wnere '*Moumford, Corbet, Whight, Bets, Quintine,* or *Geuge*' are listed, and George Buck Esq. and his scribe probably garbled them further in copying. The chroniclers give them rather differently: for example, Hall gives 'Mountforde, Corbet white belt, quyntine or otherwyse Genyn'. p. 472. Interestingly enough, More refers to them in *The Debellacion of Salem and Bizance,* 1553 (in *Workes, 1557,* p. 990, sig. R3^v) as an example of felons put to death for treason without indictment and calls them 'captaine Quintyn, captein Genyn, Corbet & Belke'. I can find no other record of these men, nor can I locate Buck's source for Serjeant Ferior and the yeoman Edwards, which may have been confused by misreadings or incorrect copyings by George Buck, Esq. and his scribe. Buck seems to have misunderstood the statement about the executions: there were, Hall states, 160 prisoners taken, but only the five captains noted above were put to death. Hall says later that 200 of Perkin's soldiers were slain at Exeter (p. 484).

162/1st mar. n. Holinshed, p. 505; Grafton, p. 193; Hall, p. 464; Stow, p. 797.

162/2nd mar. n. More, p. 82, quoted above, note 139/3-10.

162/13-15. Grafton, p. 193.

162/3rd mar. n. Camden, *Britannia,* p. 148. This reference speaks only of the siege of Exeter, does not say who was convinced by Perkin, and calls him a base pretender.

However, Buck's use of the word 'heard' here suggests this is a *viva voce* reference, and that Camden's opinions were changing or, like Stow's, differed from those he had published.

162/44-48. For Richard's naming John de la Pole his successor, see above, note 74/3-8.

163/35-38. I have been unable to trace this manuscript. The countess referred to is undoubtedly the Countess of Richmond.

164/38-40. See above, note 54/50 - 55/11 and below, Appendix B.

164/48. *Aeneid,* VI, 430.

165/7-9. See above, note 139/3-10.

165/1st mar. n. I have been unable to find this reference in Aristotle. However, Quintilian quotes it as an already well known saying: 'verumque est illud, quod vulgo dicitur, mendacem memorem esse oportere' (*Institutiones,* IV, ii, 91).

166/25 - 167/2. Plutarch, *Moralia,* 65D. Buck has invented the detail of the conversation.

167/1st mar. n. Ausonius, II, iii ('Oratio'), 11. 63-4. The line division is correct and corruptions which crept in obviously scribal.

166/2nd mar. n. Aristotle, *Politics,* V, 1311a.

167/3rd mar. n. Cicero, *De Officiis,* II, vii. This quotation is given above, text, p. 34, as well. Buck has made a translation which he crossed out first in pencil then in ink: 'Men wish to see the finall fate / of him, whome they doo looth, & hate' (Tib. f. 206).

167/36-40. More, p. 87: 'Miles Forest at sainct Martens pecemele rotted away. Dighton in dede yet walketh on a liue in good possibilitie to bee hanged ere he dye. But sir Iames Tirel dyed at Tower hill, beheaded for treason.'. Holinshed, p. 402; Stow, p. 770; also in Hall and Grafton.

169/23-25. Warwick was tried before Oxford as High Constable of England (Hall, p. 491 and followers). There is no other suggestion of Oxford's persecuting Warwick or Warbeck.

169/3rd mar. n. The informant is the Earl of Arundel to whom Buck dedicates the work.

170/29. Erasmus, *Chiliades,*p. 208 gives the Greek version and translates it 'Heroum filij noxae'.

170/34-43. It is unfortunate that Buck's main source for John of Gloucester's execution is lost. The only other intimation we have of Henry's treatment of John is in the chronicles, where Perkin in his confession reports that the Irish with threats tried to induce him to pretend to be Warwick, but when he refused said he was a bastard son of Richard III, which he denied. 'And after this they called me duke of Yorke, second sonne of Kynge Edward y^e. iiij. because king Rychardes bastard sonne was in ye handes of the king of England'. On the other hand, perhaps John managed to escape the net after all, since *Pat. Rolls* (1494-1509), pp. 447f, records a pardon on 27 November 1505 to the Mayor of the Staple of Calais and to a long list of merchants of the same, among whom 'John Gloucestre' is one.

170/41-43. Richard, Duke of York, father to Edward IV and Richard III, was

Lieutenant of Ireland 1447-53.

170/2nd mar. n. There is no such reference in Grafton.

170/4th mar. n. Gainsford, p. 108. Perkin's confession mentions that the Irish welcomed him first as the Duke of Warwick, then as Richard's bastard son, who was in Henry VII's keeping at the time. Other chroniclers do not mention Richard's bastard son here.

171/2nd mar. n. This quotation, lacking a dactylic foot before *manes,* is not in Claudian. I have been unable to locate it.

171/36-41. Plutarch, *Lives,* 'Antony', 33.

171/3rd mar. n. Philostratus, *Vita Apollonii,* VIII, viii. The verse quoted is from Philostratus, not Suidas.

171/45-50. Suidas, *Lexicon,* in his entry for Apollonius, refers to Philostratus' account but does not quote this verse from it.

172/1. Flavius Vopiscus, *Divus Aurelianus,* XXIV, 7, in *Hist. Aug. Scrip.*

172/25-26. Hebrews, 10:31.

172/26. There are several Biblical quotations to this effect.

172/29-30. I have not located this quotation. Margins are completely burnt away here, along with all references, and there is no representation in the copies.

172/32. Psalms, 52:6, 'illic trepidaverunt timore, ubi non erat timor'.

173/17-19. See note 139/46 - 140/2.

173/mar. n. Terence, *Phormio,* 951.

173/33-36. This is the gist of Perkin's statements about himself as given in Polydore, pp. 596f and Hall, pp. 473f. There is no evidence that a report of a speech by Perkin to the king of Scots ever existed, but there does exist a copy of a proclamation made while Perkin was with King James (Harl. 283, copied from an original once extant in the Cotton collection; it is printed by James Spedding in Francis Bacon, *Works* (London, 1858), VI, Appendix II, pp. 252-5). This does say that Perkin escaped from the Tower and was conveyed abroad where he remained a number of years but mentions no attempt by Richard against his life, as Hall and his followers do.

BOOK IV

174. Buck has followed this outline rather closely. Two items are out of place: 'Kings must not marry . . . without consent of the barons' (a topic barely touched on) should follow 'His wooing the Lady Eleanor . . . and his marriage with her'. 'King Edward's death' should follow 'Dr Stillington . . . imprisoned'. 'The mortality of Plantagenets' is not dealt with in this book at all, and the three final headings are discussed near the beginning of Book III.

175/mar. n. More, p. 72:

> For no woman was there any where yong or olde, riche or
> pore, whom he set his eie vpon, in whome he any thinge
> lyked either person or fauour, speche, pace, or coun-
> tenance, but w^tout any fere of god, or respect of his

honour, murmure or grudge o^f ye worlde, he would im-
portunely pursue hys appetite, and haue her, to the gret
destruccion of many a good woman.

175/14. 'Amasia' is a post-classical word, normally found in the masculine.

175/24-33. My guess is that the key to this double-entendre might be in the
separation of 'faucon' into the words 'faux con'. 'Serrure' is a lock. The
fetterlock was a traditional badge of the House of York (see Madden, 'Political
Poems of the Reigns of Henry VI and Edward IV', *Archaeologia*, XXIX (1842),
332). Kendall (p. 28) mentions the towers of Fotheringhay rising in the shape of a
fetterlock. Camden, *Remaines*, p. 215, notes that Edmund of Langley

> bare also for an Impresse a Faulcon in a fetter-locke,
> implying that he was locked vp from all hope and possi-
> bility of the Kingdome, when his brethren beganne to aspire
> thereunto. Whereupon he asked on a time his sonnes when
> he sawe them, beholding this deuice set vp in a window,
> what was the Latine for a fetter-locke: Whereat when the
> yong gentlemen studied, the father said, Well, if you can-
> not tell me, I will tell you, *Hic, haec, hoc, taceatis*, as
> aduising them to be silent & quiet, and therewithall said,
> *Yet God knoweth what may come to passe hereafter.* This
> his great Grandchilde, King *Edward* the fourth reported
> when hee commaunded that his yonger sonne *Richard*
> Duke of *Yorke*, should vse this deuice with the fetter-locke
> opened, as *Roger Wall* an Herald of that time reporteth.

Buck several times mentions these 'speaking pictures' in *The Third Universitie* using
interchangeably the works 'Ierogliffe', 'Hieroglyphick', and 'Rebus'. Camden,
Remaines, p. 164, notes that the idea came from France and they are called 'painted
Poesies. For whereas a Poesie is a speaking picture, and a picture a speechlesse
Poesie, they which lackt wit to expresse their conceit in speech, did vse to depaint it
out . . . in pictures, which they called *Rebus* . . . .' Sir James Ley's discourse on 'Motts'
in Hearne's *Curious Discourses*, I, 123, says that their purpose is 'First, in a word to
contain a world. Secondly, when thereby a dumb beast, or bird, or dead creature
doth, as it were, speak, and bewray his own primary quality. Thirdly, when the
simple cannot understand it, and yet the wise cannot but understand it'.

176/1-28. We have no way of knowing whether or not a trothplight between
Edward IV and Eleanor Butler ever took place. All we have is the *Titulus Regius*, a
document in *Rot. Parl.* (VI, 241) setting forth Richard's title to the throne, using as
part of its evidence Edward's contract with Lady Eleanor before he married
Elizabeth Woodville:

> at the tyme of contract of the same pretensed Mariage, and
> bifore the longe tyme after, the seid king Edward was and
> stode maryed and trouth plight to oone Dame Elianor
> Butteler, Doughter of the old Earl of Shrewsbury, with
> whom the same King Edward had made a precontracte of

> Matrimonie, longe tyme bifore he made the said pretensed
> Mariage with the said Elizabeth Grey . . . .

The validity of the later marriage was rejected on the basis of the precontract and because of its impropriety both in the wife's status and the form of the ceremony.

The circumstances seem to have been that (1) Richard was a powerful magnate with military support; (2) the claimants to the throne were children, and the Woodvilles rivalled the Protector for the power behind the throne in a struggle which had already led to violence; (3) no law existed governing succession, though right of primogeniture, taken from land law, was the course expected; (4) to maintain the Yorkist policy of legitimism, Richard had to declare the children's illegitimacy (Chrimes, *Eng. Const. Ideas*, p. 32). As noted previously (above, note 135/32-136/32), the aspersion of bastardy was the most common method of discrediting claimants to the throne.

The flexibility, uncertainty, and ambiguity inherent in the customs, both legal and ecclesiastical, of marriage and trothplight made the excuse of illegitimacy easy to promulgate. F.R.H. Du Boulay notes that marriage

> could, in the eyes of the Church, be validly performed in complete privacy but . . . without witnesses, could be denied later by one or both parties who might want to . . . contract other marriages. Church pronouncements were constantly read out from pulpits against clandestine marriages which in this way could so easily lead on to adulteries and the procreation of illegitimate children in a society where divorce in the modern sense of the term was regarded as impossible and children could not be legitimized by the subsequent marriage of their parents.
> (*An Age of Ambition: English Society in the Late
> Middle Ages,* London, 1970, p. 99.)

The Council, not being an ecclesiastical court, hesitated to pass judgement on the marriage's validity but did so because of the influence of Richard's supporters (Croyland, p. 570).

It is, Levine suggests (pp. 400-1), possible that Edward's notorious relationship with Elizabeth Lucy gave rise to the precontract story, but the name of another lady had to be substituted, since Elizabeth Lucy's children would become legitimate heirs if she were upheld as Edward's lawful wife. Gairdner points out that the facts stated about the lady named as Edward's betrothed would have had to be well enough known to make the allegation believable (p. 91). She was probably daughter to John Talbot, Earl of Shrewsbury, who died in 1460 and whose widow died in 1473. The John Talbot Buck mentions did not marry until 1467 (GEC, XI, 706) and thus could not have been father to Edward IV's mistress. GEC calls her sister to Sir John Talbot (XII, pt. i, 422), presumably the John Talbot Buck mentions. It is not impossible that she was daughter to the famous John Talbot, Earl of Shrewsbury, who was married for the second time in 1425 to the daughter of Richard Beauchamp, Earl of Warwick. He died in 1454 and his wife in 1467. Eleanor married Thomas Boteler at some time after 1450, was predeceased by her husband, and died in 1468 (*Pat. Rolls,* 1467-77, p. 133).

176/1st mar. n. Commynes, II, 323 and 305.

176/8-19. Commynes, II, 305: 'ung evesque de Bas . . . qui autresfoys avoit eu grand credit avec ledict roy Edouard . . . disoit que ledit roy Edouard avoit promys foy de mariage à une dame d'Angleterre (qu'il nommoit) . . . et en avoit faict la promesse en la main dudict evesque' (the Paris ed. of 1576 says 'entre les mains', f. 307). Buck has combined this with an earlier passage: 'Et dist cest evesque qu'il les avoit espoused, et n'y avoit que luy et eulx deux' (II, 232), which he later quotes in its context, text, p. 183. Only Commynes tells us that Stillington was responsible for revealing the secret to Richard. There is no proof of Buck's suggestion that Stillington's imprisonment under Edward IV was connected with his revealing the precontract (see below, note 183/45 - 184/9). But he is a not unlikely person to have revealed or invented it. Edward IV had imprisoned him and deprived him of office. He hated the Woodvilles. And being instrumental in the power shift, he might well hope for reward from Richard. Henry VII on his accession instantly imprisoned him.

176/9-12. See above, text, p. 35.

176/28. Hugh Ross Williamson, 'George, Duke of Clarence', *History Today,* XVI (1966), 819, says that Edward IV had a son, Edward de Wigmore, by Eleanor Butler, but he derives this information from a family tradition, not from a reliable source (*The Butt of Malmsey,* London, 1967, p. 90).

177/1st mar. n. *El Reusuerq* seems no longer extant. Buck uses it once in *Comm.* as well.

177/8 - 178/8. On text, pp. 177-78, Buck follows More's account of the marriage (p. 61). The lodge or forest-house is added by Buck, who has a tendency to visualize scenes. He is elaborating on Fabyan (p. 654), who says Edward pretended to go hunting when he went to marry Elizabeth, and that only the bridegroom, the bride, her mother, the priest, two gentlemen, 'and a yong man to helpe the preest synge' were present. The story of his having seen her first in the place where he married her comes from Hall, p. 264 (it is repeated by Grafton and Holinshed): while hunting in the Forest of Wychwood Edward stopped at her family's manor at Grafton and soon after married her there, 'where he first phantasied her visage'. For the marriage and its repercussions, see Ross, pp. 85-93.

177/2nd mar. n. Commynes, II, 232.

178/2-7. Buck follows here very closely the wording of the *Titulus Regius (Rot. Parl.,* VI, 241): 'the said pretensed Mariage was made privaly and secretly, without Edition of Banns, in a private Chamber, a prophane place, and not openly in the face of the Church, aftre the Lawe of Godds Churche, but contrarie thereunto . . . .'

178/9-19. Edward concealed the marriage, which took place 1 May 1464, until 29 Sept., when negotiations for the French alliance forced him to reveal it (Fabyan, p. 654; and *The Historical Collections of a Citizen of London* ['Gregory's Chronicle'], ed. James Gairdner, London, 1876, Cam. Soc. 2nd ser. 17, pp. 226f). All sources report that the nobility were angry as a result (Croyland, p. 539; Fabyan, p. 654; Mancini, pp. 60ff).

178/20-38. At the basis of the breach between Edward IV and Warwick seems to have been their difference over the question of alliance with France or Burgundy. 'Hearne's Fragment' (*A Remarkable Fragment of an Old . . . Chronicle . . . of the Affairs of Edward the Fourth . . .* in Thomas Sprott, *Chronica,* ed. Hearne, Oxford, 1719), p. 299, says that Warwick's councils with the French king aroused his greed. Croyland (p. 551) goes to some lengths to say that he considered the previous continuator wrong in attributing the breach to Edward's marriage and puts the blame on the marriage of his sister Margaret to Burgundy.

178/2nd mar. n. Du Tillet, *Traictez,* p. 246. Word order is altered somewhat for compression and clarity.

178/3rd mar. n. Polydore, pp. 513f. The reference to Book 24 is correct. This is a paraphrase of the sense of the passage.

179/5-9. Croyland, p. 539, second continuation.

179/22-25. In 1470, Warwick and Clarence with French assistance drove Edward from the kingdom and restored Henry VI. The next year Edward killed Warwick at Barnet, defeated Henry's forces at Tewkesbury, and resumed the throne.

179/28 - 180/12. That Edward's mother opposed the marriage is reported widely. More and the chroniclers who follow him allege the impediment with which she charged him to be Elizabeth Lucy, and there is agreement that her objections involved a charge of illegitimacy or bigamy (More's word without our modern meaning; it refers only to Elizabeth's having been married before). See note 135/32 - 136/32, above.

179/38. Buck has accidentally given 'Elizabeth' for 'Eleanor'.

179/28 - 180/36. This is largely indirect discourse in More (pp. 62-3) and has been turned into speeches by Buck, who has added some expansion and repetition, though More's organization and the skeleton of his wording remain. More does not shift into direct discourse until 'And I doubt not' (p. 181, 1.15). Buck makes almost no changes. It is interesting to see what he considers 'False and incongrous English'. P. 180, 1.47, 'love mutually and virtuously' is 'loue together' in More; p. 180, 1.50, 'and being considered even after the worldly accompt', is in More 'euen worldly considred'; p. 181, ll. 3-4 'love and favour' is in More 'herty fauor'.

181/43-45. More, p. 64f. It is Elizabeth Lucy, not Edward, who is asked to and does deny the marriage. Hall, p. 367, Grafton, p. 105, and Stow, p. 756.

181/47 - 182/1 and 182/14-16. More, p. 56: 'The king would say that he had .iii. concubines, which in three diuers properties diuersly exceled. One the meriest, an other the wiliest, the thirde the holiest harlot in his realme, as one whom no man could get out of ye church lightly to any place, but it wer to his bed'. More identifies Jane Shore as the 'meriest'. He does not mention one called the 'wittiest', but the appellation would seem to agree with his description of Jane Shore: 'a proper wit had she, & could both rede wel & write, mery in company, redy & quick of aunswer, neither mute nor ful of bable, sometime taunting w^{t}out displesure & not w^{t}out disport'. Buck's description of Elizabeth Lucy agrees in all other respects with More's (pp. 64f).

182/1st mar. n. Ovid, *Epistulae Heroides,* VI, 21.

182/2-13. Arthur Plantagenet was created Viscount Lisle in 1523. Scofield (II, 161) states that Elizabeth Lucy was probably the mother of Edward's illegitimate daughter Elizabeth as well. However, GEC, VIII, 63 says that the mother of Arthur Plantagenet is unknown, some saying she was Elizabeth Lucy, some Jane Shore, some Elizabeth Waite, 'He himself being at first known as *Arthur Waite*'. In 1538/39 a John Wayte leased manors to his kinsman Arthur Plantagenet (GEC, VIII, p. 63n). According to Buck, Elizabeth Lucy's maiden name was Wayte.

182/5-35. Not until Speed wrote was it realized that Eleanor Butler was the woman to whom Edward was reputedly contracted: '*Eleanor Butler, as we find it recorded vpon the Parliament Role, was contracted vnto King Edward:* but how true considering the occasion, the time of the Act, we must leave for others to iudge . . .' (*The Historie of Great Britaine*, London, 1623, p. 691).

182/4th mar. n. Ovid, *Epistulae Heroides*, XVII, 41.

183/36-44. I have been unable to find a source for this story. Buck or a *vive voce* informant (Stow?) may have pieced together a plausible sequence of events from the few known facts, or Buck may have derived this version from a work no longer extant. On the other hand, he may be indulging his taste for elaborating dramatic scenes from a meagre suggestion.

183/45 - 184/9. There is no evidence of the bishop's revealing the marriage before Edward IV's death or that his imprisonment sprang from knowledge of it. Coming so soon after Clarence's execution, it more likely arose from suspicion of aiding or associating with Clarence. Had Clarence known of the precontract, he would not have failed to publish it. In his general pardon on 20 June 1478 is a 'Declaration that Robert, bishop of Bath and Wells, has been faithful to the king and done nothing contrary to his oath of fealty, as he had shown before the king and certain lords' (*Pat. Rolls*, 1476-85, p. 102). Scofield (II, 312) notes that the story of Stillington's efforts on Lady Eleanor's behalf are not credible because Commynes 'gives his readers distinctly to understand that the story of Edward's pre-contract . . . was not told to Gloucester until after Edward's death'.

183/mar. n. Commynes, II, 305.

184/3-4. Godwin, p. 307, actually says Stillington 'died a prisoner in the Castle of Windsor, whether he was committed for foure yeeres before his death (for what cause I know not) in the moneth of October 1487'. The Godwin reference is to imprisonment, not redemption from imprisonment, and the imprisonment to which it refers is much later than that under Edward.

184/5-7. Commynes, II, 305.

184/10-19. Mancini, p. 58, says Edward IV's death was caused by depression over the French hostility, aggravated by a stomach chill caught while he was in a boat watching his party fishing. Armstrong considers this account not improbable and summarizes the accounts of the king's death, noting that its causes were not mentioned in English sources until the sixteenth century; 'but by this date sudden death in noble or princely families usually aroused . . . suspicion' of poison (in Mancini, notes, p. 107).

184/3rd mar. n. Polydore, p. 539. The reference to Book 24 is correct.

184/4th mar. n. Bouchard, f. ccvi: 'En lan dessusdit lxxxii. en apuril, le roy dangleterre fut frappe dune appoplexie: dont mourut soubdainenment sansparler. Acuns disoyent que il auoit este empoysonne'.

184/5th mar. n. Monstrelet, 'Nouvelles Chroniques', f. 76ᵛ, 'le Roy Edouard d'Anglettere, mourut audit Royaume d'vne apoplexie qui le print. Autres dient qu'il fut empoisonne en beuuant de bon vin du creu de Chaluau, que le Roy luy auoit donnē'. Buck has mistaken 'creu' for a place.

184/20-72. Commynes, II, 304, 'il tomba malade et bien tost après mourut, aucuns dient d'ung quaterre'.

185/1st mar. n. This reference is not in More. It is in Hall, p. 387, Grafton, p. 126, Holinshed, p. 409, and Stow, p. 775, in a section invented by Hall, immediately following More's narrative.

185/7. By Friar Pynk Buck means Friar Penketh (More, pp. 58f). The chronicles sometimes give his name as Pynk.

185/9-11. The petition incorporated in the *Titulus Regius* is not from the North parts but from the Three Estates. Buck misreads Croyland, p. 567 (quoted in note 46/3-16, above).

186/3-4. Henry VIII.

186/9-12. Polydore, pp. 524 and 547 attributes the death of the Princes to this sin of their father.

187/10-11. This resembles Psalm 1, which, in the Vulgate, begins as follows: 'Beatus vir qui non abiit in consilio impiorum, et in via peccatorum non stetit, et in cathedra derisorum non sedit'.

187/18. III Esdras, 4:41, Apocrypha: 'Magna veritas et praevalet'.

187/45-46. Cicero, *Tusculian Disputations,* V, xxiv, 68, in speaking of qualities necessary for a man who wished to discern the truth: 'in quo inest omnis cum subtilitas disserendi tum veritas iudicandi'.

188/34-40. *Rot. Parl.,* VI, 273f. Pembroke, Morton, Knevet, 'Thomas Vandyke [*sic*] late of Cambridge, Nigromancer', Lewkenor, John and Richard Guildford, Fogg, Poynings, Haute, Fiennes, Gainsford, the bishops of Salisbury and Exeter, and many more had their attainders reversed.

188/45-46. 'O.M.' means 'Optimi Maximi'. I have been unable to locate this quotation.

189/2nd mar. n. This is not in More. It is in Polydore, p. 557f; Hall, p. 389; Grafton, p. 144; Stow, p. 782; and Holinshed, p. 431.

189/3-4. We cannot know how serious were Richard's reputed plans to marry his niece. Croyland indicates that it was a fully formed scheme which he was forced through opposition of his own party to abandon, making public denial of such an intention; though, says the Chronicler, many of the Council knew this to be false (p. 572). As Jacob says, 'it is difficult to see how he could have been justified in marrying a lady who had been declared illegitimate' (p. 637), but there is at least a plausible reason for his allowing to spread a rumour that he intended to do so. Henry Tudor was planning to draw to himself Edward IV's former supporters by marrying Elizabeth and was discomfited at hearing the rumour that Richard's wife was dead and he planned to marry his niece (Polydore, p. 559). Richard could ill afford to risk letting Elizabeth marry someone else, knowing that she was a potential figurehead for rebellion, despite the declaration of illegitimacy, which the winner could cancel, as Henry did. Nor, with Henry's pretensions so heavily relying on this hope, was it safe for Richard to leave her unmarried. Thus, though it is doubtful that he did contemplate so inconvenient a marriage, the rumour was convenient to him. Buck's interpretation of it as 'counterfeit wooing' is probably correct. After the marriage scheme was publicly denied, it seems that Richard made other plans for both himself and Elizabeth. There is a good argument from existing records that he sent an embassy to Portugal to arrange the marriage of himself with Princess Joana and Elizabeth with Don Manuel, Duke of Beja (Domingos Maurício Gomes dos Santos, *O Mosteiro de Jesus de Aveiro,* Lisbon, 1963, pp. 92ff; I am grateful to Drª Joana Vaz and Møns. Aníbal Ramos for calling my attention to this information).

189/8-9. Polydore reports in manuscript, though not in print, that Elizabeth said she would prefer to suffer the torments of St Catherine for love of Christ than to marry an enemy of her family (*The Anglica Historia of Polydore Vergil,* ed. and trans. Denys Hay, Cam. Soc. 74, London, 1950, p. 3). This could be interpreted as a reference to Richard but seems much more likely to refer to Henry, who was an enemy of the House of York, and perhaps the awareness that this interpretation could be placed on it determined Polydore against printing it. It is Hall (p. 157), copied by the chroniclers who followed him, who gave the projected contract the colouring Buck notes, saying that Richard

> compased all the meanes and waies yᵗ he coulde inuent how to stuprate, and carnally to know his owne nece vnder the pretence of a cloked matrimony . . . . At whiche most importunate and detestable concupiscence, the common people . . . grudged and maligned . . . . But God of his only goodnes preserued yᵉ Christen mynde of that verteous and immaculate virgin, and from their flagicious and facinerous act*es*, did graciously protect and defend.

189/9-11. Catesby and Ratcliffe in their opposition to Richard's marrying Elizabeth may have originated the rumour that he murdered his wife. They threatened to raise a northern rebellion by attributing to him his wife's death to gratify an incestuous lust (Croyland, p. 572). Rous is the first to mention it in print (p. 215), and the Great Chronicle (p. 234) and Commynes (II, 235) also report it. Polydore, who is followed by Hall, Grafton, Stow, and Holinshed says Richard killed her with sorrow or poison, his cruelty consisting in his forbearing to lie with her, his complaints of her barrenness, his spreading rumours of her death (p. 557). Hall stresses the likelihood of poison (p. 407), while Stow omits it. Croyland says, after mentioning the similar dresses worn by the queen and Elizabeth, that there was talk and speculation (p. 572):

> dictumque à multis est, ipsum Regem aut expectata morte Reginae, aut per divortium, cujus faciendi sufficientes causas se habuisse arbitratus est [her barrenness], matri-

> monio cum dicta *Elizabeth* contrahendo mentem omnibus
> modis applicare. Non aliter videbat Regnum sibi confir-
> mari, neque spem competitoris sui auferri posse.
>   Paucis enim post hoc elapsis diebus, Regina vehemen-
> tissime aegrotare coepit, cujus languor ideo magis atque
> magis excrevisse censebatur, quod Rex ipse thori sui con-
> sortium omnino aspernabatur.

There is no suggestion here of murder but of a long illness: the queen's death was anticipated as early as Christmas, she worsened a few days after, and her death occurred in mid-March 1485. The expectation of her death is confirmed by the letter from Elizabeth of York in February, of which Buck gives the substance (text, p. 191).

189/14-29. There is no indication that Elizabeth Woodville favoured a match between Richard and Elizabeth. All we know is that she was persuaded to send her five daughters out of sanctuary to court in response to Richard's promise that they should be protected, married well, and treated as his kinswomen (Harl. 433, f. 308f), and that she sent for her son Dorset. Richard's entreating the Woodvilles to come out of sanctuary need not be construed as generosity, for the former queen had been intriguing with Henry Tudor and promised him her eldest daughter. It was thus in Richard's interest to have the Woodvilles under his control. It could not have been a promise of her daughter's marriage to Richard which made her yield, since she did so in March 1484, at least a month before Richard's son died and a year before his wife's death. Croyland says that she yielded only after entreaties and threats. Buck, assuming that Richard's nieces did not come to court until Christmas, is erecting a theory based on the queen's expected demise at that time.

189/26. 'Queen Blanche' is an error for 'Queen Elizabeth', probably one of absent-mindedness. Buck (if indeed the error is his and not the Editor's) may have been thinking of John of Gaunt's wife.

189/34-36. The reason for the similar dresses being worn by Anne and Elizabeth is not known. Croyland does not say Anne presented Elizabeth with garments similar to her own, but that similar garments were presented to them both: 'vanisque mutatoriis vestium *Annae* Reginae atque Dominae *Elizabeth* . . . eisdem colore & forma distributis' (p. 572). There is not necessarily a suggestion that Richard did the presenting or a clear connection between this similarity of dress and the suspicion that Richard planned to marry Elizabeth, though because one statement follows the other they can be interpreted as connected. Possibly the remark about the apparel derives solely from the author's concern with the attention to worldliness, expense, and fashion.

190/1st mar. n. Vulteius, I, xxi. The name 'Justus' is incorrect. Hermannus Vulteius had a contemporary named Justus, but his works were not on legal subjects.

190/6-43. The discussion of divorce in this connection originates with Cornwallis: 'but how absurd ys yt to ymagynne that the king contryved her death, when yf he had pleased during her lyfe to marry elsewhere . . . he might and woulde haue used a more honorable and safe meanes by a dyvorce . . . .' He gives as example Louis XII of France who was granted a divorce because of his wife's barrenness: 'might not king Richard haue donne the like? for he had the like cause . . .' (p. 21).

190/9-13. Valerius Maximus, VI, iii, 9-12.

190/2nd mar. n. This Bull is in Cotton Vitellius B.X, ff. 109-112.

190/3rd mar. n. This appears in a book called *In Euangelium Secundum Matthaeum, Marcum, et Lucam* (Paris, 1553), printed and possibly compiled by Robert Stephens. At the end of it is printed Andreas Osiander's *Harmoniae Evangelicae Libri IIII,* but there is no indication that the earlier portions of the book, from which the quotation comes, are by Osiander too. It appears as an annotation to Matthew 5:31, on f. 20. Buck's quotation makes few changes other than deletions of subsidiary material.

191/1-25. See above, pp. xc-xciv and cxiv for discussion of this letter. It seems quite probable that the shaky position of the Woodvilles under Richard might have prompted their appeal to the nobleman whose influence with him was most powerful for assistance in a move which would restore them to the royal position they had lost and were at pains to recover. The intriguing nature of Elizabeth Woodville, seeing no hope at this time in the banished Richmond, could easily have turned to her daughter's marriage with Richard as the easiest expedient in gaining power for her family, and possibly young Elizabeth wrote the letter at her mother's prompting.

191/3rd mar. n. Croyland, p. 572: 'Denique dicto Regis proposito, suoque animo contrahendi cum consanguinea sua germana *Elizabeth* memorata, ad quosdam qui id non vellent, perlato, coactus est Rex convocato consilio sese multis verbis excusare, quod ea res nunquam venerat in mentem suam'.

192/1st mar. n. Ibid. Buck has indicated by the brackets in his manuscript that 'vel simulando' is his own addition.

192/3rd mar. n. Ibid.

192/4th mar. n. This reference is not in More. Holinshed (who copies Hall) says, pp. 430f, 'But howsoeuer that it fortuned, either by inward thought and pensiuenesse of hart, or by infection of poison (which is affirmed to be most likelie) within few daies after the queene departed out of this transitorie life . . . .' The reference to the Lent season is from Stow, p. 782.

192/49 - 193/3. Richard's bastards were John of Gloucester, who in childhood was made Captain of Calais by his father; Katharine Plantagenet who married William, Earl of Huntingdon in 1484 (Harl. 258, ff. 11^v-12 and *Pat. Rolls,* 1476-85, p. 538); and possibly the Richard Plantagenet who, according to Peck, II, 13-15, was told of his identity only on the eve of Bosworth and lived a long and quiet life as master mason in Eastwell, Kent. The little that is known of John and Katharine suggests they were born before Richard's marriage There are traditions of other illegitimate children.

193/28-29. Publilius Syrus, *Sententiae,* S. 46: 'Suspicio probatis tacita iniuria est'.

193/30. I have been unable to trace this quotation.

193/1st mar. n. Aquinas, *Summa Theologica,* pt. II^{a}II^{ae}, quest. LX, art. 3. Pardulphus Prateius, *Lexicon Juris* (Frankfurt, 1581), entry under 'Suspicio', p. 549.

193/2nd mar. n. I have been unable to trace this quotation or this work.

194/4. I have been unable to trace this quotation.

194/mar. n. Suetonius, *Divus Julius,* LXXIV.

194/11. Erasmus, *Chiliades,* p. 55, 'Polypi mentem obtine' (i.e., change colours).

BOOK V

195. There are a few matters out of order in this list of contents: the second, third, and fourth headings all follow 'All the Plantagenets put to death by his successors'. 'The character of King James' appears in the midst of the discussion regarding Richard's tyranny or lack of it, and 'The author's scope, peroration, *et votum*' is apparently Buck's diffuse summing up of Richard's case, pp. 410f. George Buck, Esq., unable to find a justification for this heading, deletes it in the manuscript copies, but in the printed version he has come to the conclusion that the heading referred to this information and has compressed it and brought it together in a single page, giving it the prominence of larger type at the end of the book, immediately preceding the two verses, and he has restored the subject heading to the list of Book V's contents.

196/16-19. This is evidently a *viva voce* reference: it exists in none of Stow's works.

196/2nd mar. n. Aristotle, *Ethics*, VIII, x, 2.

196/3rd mar. n. This is similar to a statement in *Ethics*, VIII, x, 3.

196/4th mar. n. Proverbs 19:12.

196/28-29. Plato, *Republic*, VIII, xvi, 566.

196/32-33. I have been unable to locate this reference. Cf. Erasmus *Institutio*.

197/1st mar n. Plutarch, *Moralia*. This remark occurs twice, and its originator is disputed. In 61, Bias is asked and replies to the question. In 147, the remark is ascribed to Pittacus. The printed edition gives the marginal reference as 'Bias apud Plut. Libell. de adulat. c. 37'.

197/2nd mar. n. This is not in Lucan. I have been unable to locate it.

197/3rd mar. n. Seneca, *Hercules Furens*, 513, paraphrased.

197/4th mar. n. I have been unable to locate this quotation in Demosthenes.

197/5th mar. n. Claudian, *In Rufinum*, I, 101-104, an exact quotation, but the editor's MSS. give it with corruptions and without line endings.

197/6th mar. n. Juvenal, Satire IV, 54-55, an exact quotation.

197/40-43. *The Statutes at Large* (London, 1770), II, 54, 23 Jan. 1484, Cap. II. This tax had been introduced by Edward IV.

197/8th mar. n. *Rot. Parl.* VI, 261.

197/9th mar. n. More, p. 70.

198/1-2. Sophocles, *Ajax*, 1350.

198/3. I cannot locate this reference.

198/5-6. More, p. 78. This is said in an ironic context.

198/11-20. Commynes, II, 233 lists the death of Buckingham among the cruelties leading to Richard's overthrow. Polydore, p. 553, Hall, Grafton, and Holinshed point out the irony of Buckingham's death in such a way as to make it appear to represent ingratitude in Richard: 'This death (as a reward) the duke of Buckyngham receaued at the handes of kyng Richard, whom he before in his affaires, purposes and enterprises had holde*n* [Grafton and Holinshed read 'holpen'] susteyned and set forward aboue all Godes forbode' (Hall, p. 395). Cornwallis, pp. 25f says,

was it a fault to punish his periurye, whoe had sworne true
alleageance, then the execution of Lawe is a sinne: if soe,
let transgressors be accounted inocent, and magistrates, &
Iudges, be accounted guiltye of transgression — but had
this bene the acction of some other Prince, it had bene
good, iust and necessarey, — but being his it is Censured
the Contrarey . . . .

198/21-28. Polydore, p. 565, and followers say that Richard kept Edward, Earl of
Warwick a prisoner in Sheriff Hutton during his reign. In fact Richard's older
nephew and heir, John de la Pole, resided there also, and both were prominent
members of the Council of the North. More does not mention Warwick's treatment
by Richard.

198/28-32. As soon as Henry secured the throne, he took Warwick from Sheriff
Hutton and imprisoned him in the Tower. Simnel's revolt forced Henry to show him in
public. Difficulties with pretenders and desire for alliance with the Spanish royal
house forced him to destroy Warwick at last. Polydore explains that Ferdinand
exacted Warwick's death, because he posed danger to the succession, as a condition
for the marriage of Catherine of Aragon with Prince Arthur. Henry executed
Warwick in November, 1499, on the pretext of conspiracy with Warbeck to escape.
The chroniclers favourable to the Tudors unanimously deplore this act of Henry's.

198/37-45. James did imprison for life his cousin Arabella Stuart who married
William Seymour, so that the pair, both of whom had a claim to the throne, would be
childless.

199/1st mar. n. Walsingham, *Hist. Angl.*, 1, p. 281.

199/19-25. Mistress Shore was arrested in connection with Hastings' and the
Woodvilles' plots against Richard and made to do public penance as a harlot. More
(p. 54) arouses sympathy for her by describing her beauty, dignity, and the pity of the
populace at her penance. According to the Great Chronicle (p. 233), she was
attached so that Hastings' goods could be accounted for. Richard's treatment of her
was far from harsh. He expressed willingness to allow her marriage to his solicitor,
Thomas Lynom (though he hoped the Bishop of Lincoln would dissuade Lynom) and
to have her released into her father's custody (Harl. 433, f. 340ᵛ).

199/21-23. This reference occurs in Buckingham's oration, More, p. 71, and is
obviously manufactured to suit character and occasion. Buck quotes it exactly.

199/31-34. Quoted without material alteration from *Foedera*, XII, 204, 'De Pro-
clamationibus faciendis pro Morum Reformatione'. The proclamation was issued
October 1483, in connection with Buckingham's rebellion.

199/35-40. Holinshed has copied the indictment against Colingbourne for treason,
p. 422f. He had been intriguing with Richmond since July 1484 and had published
writings to stir up the people against the king. The one rhyme of Colingbourne's
which comes down to us is 'The Rat, the Catte and Louell our dogge / Rule all
Englande vnder the hogge' (Hall, p. 398), referring to Ratcliffe, Catesby, Lovell,
and Richard. James H. Ramsay, *Lancaster and York* (Oxford, 1892), II, 528,
suggests that this was the revenge for Colingbourne's being deprived of his appoint-

ment as Richard's mother's officer in Wiltshire in favour of Lovell (Harl. 433, f. 2^v). Fabyan, p. 672, describes Colingbourne's arrest and execution as he does many minor cases of scandal, complete with grisly anecdote, yet clearly says that he was executed for treason as well as for a rhyme in derision of king and Council. The accusation regarding the rhyme completely obscured the accusation for treason. Harington, under the influence of *A Mirror for Magistrates,* uses Colingbourne as an example of evil fortunes befalling poets: 'one Colingbourne, that was hanged for a distichon of a Cat, a rat, and a dogge' (*Metamorphosis of Ajax,* p. 100). The information that Colingbourne was put to death for other treasons as well as for the rhyme was first given by Stow, p. 780.

199/3rd mar. n. See above, pp. ciii-cvi for discussion of this manuscript. Cornwallis, p. 22: 'how falsely doth our Chronicler seeke to Cleare Collingbourne whoe noe doubt was (as may app*ere* by his Inditem*ent*) executed for treason againste the state, not for that silly folish ridiculous libell'.

199/41-42. Demosthenes, 2nd Philippic, 25.

199/4th mar. n. See above, note 28/5th mar. n.

200/1st mar. n. See above, note 84/2nd mar. n.

200/2nd mar. n. I have been unable to locate this quotation.

200/3rd mar. n. More, p. 27. This is slightly but not materially paraphrased. More means it to be taken ironically in the context of his characterization of Richard.

200/4th mar. n. Suetonius, *Caligula,* XXXVII (the figure given is 270 million) and *Nero,* XXX.

200/18-28. See Armstrong, notes to Mancini, for an interesting theory about Richard's alleged expenditure: the division of Edward IV's treasure by the Woodvilles probably led to his impoverishment, generally attributed to his 'reckless purchase of friends' (p. 120).

200/21. I have been unable to locate this quotation.

200/23-24. Richard's enemies do confess his temperance but ascribe it to a sense of guilt and an attempt to win friends by deceit. See Polydore, p. 548 and Hall, p. 381.

201/21-29. See above, note 55/36 - 56/36.

201/50 - 202/1. For a discussion of Richard's legislation see H.G. Hanbury, 'The Legislation of Richard III', *American Journal of Legal History,* VI (1962), 95-113. Many of his enemies refer to his excellent legislation: Polydore, p. 548, Hall, pp. 380f, and Bacon, VI, 28.

202/1st mar. n. Stow, p. 882: 'although he did euill, yet in his time were many good acts made . . . .' Justice Shelley is identified there not by name but only as 'a counsellor'. Stow has taken the reference from Hall, p. 698.

202/2nd mar. n. I have been unable to locate this manuscript, which was probably burnt in the Cotton fire. Fabyan is the only other author to give this information: see above, note 51/45-48 mar. n.

202/23-24. See above, note 19/16-18.

202/26-29. See above, text, p. 22.

202/3rd mar. n. More, pp. 7f. This is a very close paraphrase:

None euill captaine was hee in the warre, as to whiche his disposicion was more metely then for peace. Sundrye victories hadde hee, and sommetime ouerthrowes, but neuer in defaulte as for his owne parsone, either of hardinesse or polytike order. Free was he called of dyspence, and sommewhat aboue hys power liberall.

202/4th mar. n. *Rot. Parl.*, VI, 241. 'Wee considre also, the greate Wytte, Prudence, Justice, Princely Courage, and the memorable and laudable Acts in diverse Batalls, whiche as we by experience knowe Ye heretofore have done, for the salvacion and defence of this same Reame . . . .'

203/1st mar. n. More says only that 'ye duke first began to praise & bost the king, & shewe how much profit ye realm shold take by his reign' (p. 92). Stow: '. . . whome I thought to bee as cleane without dissimulation, as tractable without iniurie, and so by my meanes hee was made Protector' (pp. 774f). This directly follows the More account in the continuation of the conversation invented by Hall. Buckingham, far from still thinking Richard honest, is in this speech expressing his disillusionment.

203/2nd mar. n. Cicero, *De Finibus*, IV, xxii, 61.

203/11-20. Croyland, p. 557.

203/20-24. Ibid.

203/25 - 204/45. Of Richard's achievements, Rous notes (p. 215) that he was to be praised for his building at Westminster, Nottingham, Warwick, York, Middleham, and many other places. He mentions the chantries at York, Middleham, and Barking, gifts to the commons of London, Gloucester, and Worcester, and endowment of Queens' College, Cambridge. Stow (p. 787f) says,

> He founded a colledge at Midelham beyond Yorke, and another at London beside the Tower, in a chappell called our Ladie of Barking: he also endowed the Queenes Colledge at Cambridge with fiue hundred markes of yeerelie rent. He deforested the great field of Wichewoode, betweene Woodstocke and Bristowe, which king *Edward* the fourth had incorporated before to the forrest, &c.

203/29-32. Stow, and Rous, p. 215. Also Stow, *Survey*, I, 131.

203/33-38. Richard's grant for the building of a chapel at Towton, 28 November 1483, is recorded in Harl. 433, ff. 38 and 124^v.

203/39-40. Rous (p. 215) and also Polydore: 'Instituit Eboraci collegium centum sacerdotum' (p. 548).

203/44-45. Stow, *Survey*, II, 122: Richard built the tower at Westminster 'a great height, and many faire lodgings in it, but left vnfinished . . . .'

203/45-46. Camden, p. 641 mentions Richard's work on Carlisle Castle. His badge can still be seen carved on a tower he built there.

203/46-47. Richard was not the founder or original builder of Penrith Castle, which was among the seats he acquired with the Warwick inheritance. It was founded in 1397 by William Strickland, later Bishop of Carlisle. Richard did considerable building there. The foundations of a stairway he added can still be seen.

203/48. This probably refers to Richard's bail bond law, listed as item 21 in *Rot. Parl.*,VI, 263 under the title, 'An Act for Bailing of Persons suspected of Felony'.

203/49 - 204/1. This reference is not in Polydore but in *Rot. Parl.*, VI, 238-40. It consists of a levy of tonnage and poundage to be applied to the safeguarding of the seas, but stipulates that this is not to be prejudicial to the Hanseatic merchants or to Spain.

204/1st mar. n. *Foedera*, XII, 215f, 2 March 1484.

204/1-37. Buck, *Third Universitie* (Oooo3^v) says 'I will not say that they were any collegiate societie here in England, vntill the time of King *Richard* the 3. but it is certaine that he by his charter made them a company and corporation, and setled the office in Cole-herbert'. As Constable of England while he was Duke of Gloucester, Richard 'had shared with the Marshal the supervision of the heralds' activities' (Wagner, p. 9). In B.L. MS. Cotton Tiberius E. VIII, ff. 158-159^v is a record of Richard's orders as Constable and Marshal for the officers of arms. Harleian 433, f. 39^v mentions the grant of incorporation from Richard to the heralds. Stow, *Survey*, I, 237, mentions the grant to the heralds of Cold Harbour.

204/13. Cold Harbour, Stow says in *Survey*, I, 236, was originally called Poultney's Inn.

204/29-30. Polydore, Bk. XXV, *passim*.

204/35-37. *Foedera*, XII, 216. The signature 'Barowe' is that of Sir Thomas Barowe, referred to as Master of the Rolls, text, p. 56f. Because all copies misread the name as 'Baron' or 'Barone', Yarnold (Egerton 2217, f. 134^v) mistook it as a reference to Buck's *Baron*.

204/38-41. Stow, *Survey*, I, 49, notes Richard's repair of the Tower.

204/43-45. Polydore, p. 548.

205/21-22. As on pp. 21-2, Buck erroneously refers to James III as James IV.

205/29-30. See above, n. 58/13-15.

205/30. Above, text, p. 57f.

205/40 - 206/30. Buck derived the text of this speech from B.L. MS. Cotton Vespasian C. XVI, ff. 75-9, headed 'Scotia Anno 2 Ricardi 1484 ∗∗∗tember "Oratio Scotorum ad regem Ric 3^{ii} per pace firmanda inter anglos & scotos" '. Buck's crosses may be seen in the margin on f. 35, where he begins quoting, and elsewhere. He omits some digressive material and makes infrequent minor transpositions, but there is no material alteration. His grammatical changes seem intended as improvements, but because the portions derived from Egerton are corrupt, it is difficult to make a definite pronouncement on this.

206/10-11. Statius, *Thebaid*, VI, 845-6: 'nisa' is substituted for 'ausa' in the original, a scribal error.

206/26-30. These lines are a mixture of *Aeneid* I, 607-9 (the first two and last line) and Eclogue V, 76-8 (the last three lines). The confusion has resulted from Vergil's duplicating his own line from Eclogue V in *Aeneid*, I, 609. Vergil reads 'umbrae' for 'imbres' and 'lustrabunt' for 'sint arati'. Vesp. C. XVI also reads 'Lustrabunt'.

207/mar. n. Aelius Lampridius, *Alexander Severus*, LXII in *Hist. Aug. Script.*

207/37-38. Richard was thirty-two. He was born 2 October 1452.

208/1st mar. n. Euripides, *Phoenisses*, 11. 524-5.

208/2nd mar. n. Cicero, *De Officiis,* III, 82; the line ending is ignored. Suetonius, *Julius, passim.*

209/1st mar. n. *Digest,* i, 3, 31: Ulpian, *Legem Iuliam et Papiam,* XIII.

209/2nd mar. n. Seneca, *Thyestes,* 214-5. The line ending is ignored.

209/3rd mar. n. This is not in Euripides, but in Seneca, *Phoenissae,* I, 664, where a line similar to this is given to Eteocles. In earlier versions the play was called *Thebaid,* and the line sometimes given to Polyneices: 'Imperia pretio quolibet constant bene'.

209/42-46. Edward III cannot be accused of complicity in the death of either his father or the Earl of Kent, since he was a child and under the control of his mother and her lover Mortimer. He punished the offenders when old enough to wield power in his own right.

209/7th mar. n. Seneca, *De Clementia,* I, xiii, 2: 'Scelera enim sceleribus tuenda sunt'.

210/3rd mar. n. Camden, p. 430 ('Cornavii'). There has been slight paraphrase to adapt to context, but no change of sense. There are scribal errors in Egerton one of them being, no doubt, 'purum' for 'puerulum'.

210/4th mar. n. Grafton, p. 228f and Holinshed, p. 553f, derived from Polydore, pp. 613f.

210/5th mar. n. Geronymo Çurita, *Anales de la Corona de Aragon* (Çaragoça, 1610), VI, ff. 42-42ᵛ and Esteuan de Garibáy y Çamàlloa, *D'el Compendio Historial de las Chronicas y Vniversal Historia de Todes les Reynos d'Espana* (Antwerp, 1571), II, 1448-50. Garibáy's account, using Polydore as a source, is closer to Buck's.

210/25 - 211/6. This incident occurred in 1506 and is recorded in *CSP* (Venice) I, 312ff and *CSP* (Spain) I, 385.

211/32-42. Holinshed, p. 536, notes that Henry kept his word about not putting Suffolk to death, 'keeping him in prison so long as he liued, and afterwards was beheaded vnder the reigne and commandement of his sonne'. This was in 1513. Brewer, *The Reign of Henry VIII* (London, 1884), I, 47f, observes that there is no contemporary notice of Suffolk's execution except in a letter of Peter Martyr where it is attributed to treasonable correspondence with his brother Richard, who was aiding France against England. A document on Richard de la Pole's activities quoted by Gairdner in *Letters and Papers,* I, 316, remarks prophetically on the danger for Edmund, in the hands of the king, should Richard go to France.

212/2-6. John de la Pole, Earl of Lincoln, was killed at the battle of Stoke, 1487, leading an army to support Simnel's uprising.

212/6-8. Buck's information probably came from Glover, p. 539: '*Katherine,* married to *William* Lord *Sturton,* widdow to the Lord *Grey,* and dyed in the Tower of London, in the 17. year of *Henry* the seauenth'. GEC, XII, pt. i, p. 304 refers to the marriage of Catherine Pole, daughter of the Duke of Suffolk to William, Lord Stourton, but a note indicates that this marriage has been doubted.

212/1st mar. n. Grafton, p. 79, from More, p. 3.

212/9-18. The Lady Anne's marriage to Thomas Howard, later 3rd Duke of Norfolk, was allowed by Henry VII in 1495, but they had been contracted under

Richard III. Henry would give his sister-in-law no dower, and the queen was forced 'from very shame' to settle an annuity on her from her private estate (Brenan, I, 119f). Catherine's marriage to William Courtenay, Earl of Devon, took place in 1495, not under Richard III, as Buck states. GEC, IV, 330, notes that this marriage made Henry VII jealous and suggests it as the reason for Courtenay's attainder and imprisonment for his alleged but unproved complicity in Suffolk's rebellion. Cecily was married to John, Viscount Welles, who was related to Henry VII, about 1487, and on his death she married Thomas Kyme, 'of whom nothing more is known' (GEC, XII, pt. ii, 450). Those who died unmarried were Mary (d. 1482), Margaret (d. 1472), and Bridget (d. 1517).

212/2nd mar. n. Polydore, p. 559. The reference to Book 25 is correct.

212/3rd mar. n. Glover, p. 205.

212/19-20. Although Buck does not mention Bacon, it seems likely from this and a few other references that he used Bacon's history of Henry VII, which says about the king's marriage relationship, 'he shewed himself no very indulgent husband towards her . . . . But his aversion toward the house of York . . . found place not only in his wars and counsels, but in his chamber and bed' (pp. 41f). 'Towards his Queen he was nothing uxorious; nor scarce indulgent; but companiable and respective, and without jealousy' (p. 242).

212/21-27. On his accession, Henry VII gave Elizabeth Woodville all possessions and rights of Queen Dowager (*Rot. Parl.,* VI, 288). Campbell, *Materials,* II, 148f records a document whereby all her lands and fees were taken from her in May 1487 and assigned to her daughter. She lived from then until her death in the Abbey of Bermondsey. The reason given by the chroniclers and thus possibly by Henry for this action is that she had submitted herself and her daughters into Richard's hands, contrary to her promise to Henry and his supporters (Polydore, p. 571). It is generally assumed — though this would be reason enough — that this was an excuse given to hide the real reason for her punishment, complicity in Simnel's rebellion (see Kendall, pp. 491f). MacGibbon (pp. 191ff) disagrees with the assumption that Henry deprived Elizabeth of her lands and confined her to Bermondsey after Simnel's rebellion. She had no motive, he says, to support Simnel and risk displacing her daughter. Henry VII treated for her marriage with James III and that of two of her daughters to James' sons, and she was afterwards at court in a position of dignity. MacGibbon suggests that it is more probable that she retired voluntarily and surrendered her estates in return for an annuity. She had a right of property at Bermondsey, being an heir to one of its benefactors. She died in 1492.

212/5th mar. n. Gainsford, p. 111.

212/6th mar. n. Joel, 1:4.

212/42-46. The execution of the Countess of Salisbury, who was born in 1473, occurred in 1541. According to GEC, XI, 401, 'In 1538 Henry VIII struck at the family of Pole, on account both of their descent from Edward IV's br. George, Duke of Clarence, and of the action of Card. Reginald Pole, who hoped that Paul III would publish a Bull of deprivation'. The countess was sent to the Tower in 1539, and in 1541, on the pretext of treasonable correspondence with her son Reginald, executed.

The Poles were attainted without trial in 31 Henry VIII.

212/47. Henry, Lord Montagu, the eldest surviving son of the Countess of Salisbury was executed in 1539, he and Henry Courtenay, Marquess of Exeter, having become 'victims of the King's fears that one of them might be chosen in his place if he were dethroned' (GEC, IX, 96). According to Pollard (*Henry VIII,* London, 1951, p. 299), he was probably the least guilty of all the Poles of treasonable activity against Henry VIII.

212/48 - 213/4. Reginald Pole, born in 1500, second or third son of the Countess of Salisbury, became Cardinal in 1536 and was Archbishop of Canterbury from 1556 until his death two years later. Henry VIII allowed him to go abroad to pursue his studies during the divorce proceedings, or which he knew Pole did not approve, thus saving his life. He remained abroad until after Mary's accession, working for the Papacy, often in danger from Henry's friends abroad. He was suggested by Chapuys to Charles V as a suitable candidate for the English throne (*Letters and Papers, Henry VIII,* VI, pp. 486f and VII, pp. 519f). He was attainted with the rest of his family in 1539.

213/5-8. A fugitive pretender in France, Richard de la Pole took over the title 'White Rose' and styled himself Duke of Suffolk even in his brother's lifetime and was backed by Francis I as candidate for the English throne. He was attainted in 1504 with his brothers William and Edmund and, with them, excepted from Henry VIII's general pardon. He fled abroad in 1501 and died in the Battle of Pavia, 1525.

213/14. I have been unable to locate this quotation.

213/22-23. Sources on Henry VII condemn his taxation above all else. His putting Warwick to death and his treatment of his wife (see above, notes 198/28-32 and 212/19-20) are other objections.

213/30-31. See above, text, pp. 87-9 and notes thereto.

214/mar. n. Curtius, VIII, viii, 11.

214/19-23. The story is that Edward the Confessor is said to have nominated William as his heir if he were to die without sons, and Harold, when William's prisoner, promised to help him to the throne, but broke his promise and seized the throne himself on the death of King Edward, refusing William's suit (Matthew of Westminster, I, 579 and 590f; William of Malmesbury, I, 278-80; Polydore, pp. 141-4). As for the barons' voiding William's claim, this is probably assumed from their acceptance of Harold as king. Matthew of Westminster, I, 589, says that Harold seized the throne, 'extorta fide a majoribus', and Polydore, p. 144, 'Non displicuit omnino id factum populo, qui plurimum spei in Haraldi uirtute habebat'.

214/27-38. The genealogical fervour of the Tudor and early Stuart period made it a practice to trace genealogy back as far as possible. In the Grenville copy of *Daphnis* in the British Library, Buck's genealogical tree traces the royal line from Egbert to Henry II.

214/39-43. See above, note 82/15-18.

215/1st mar. n. *Rot. Parl.,* VI, 270.

215/13. See text, pp. 87ff.

215/3rd mar. n. Buck is evidently confusing the names of Edmer and Ailred, two abbots of Rievaulx who wrote history. This material is not found in any of the present volumes of the Cotton collection, which contains only Ailred's histories of King David of Scotland and Henry II of England. But listed in early Cotton catalogues was a life of Edward the Confessor by Ailred. This is cited as missing in Casley's survey of the library. In an extant copy, B.L. MS. Arundel 63, Ch. 29, ff. 15ᵛ-16, entitled 'De anulo que*m* dedit beato ioh*anni* . . . ', contains this information.

215/4th mar. n. Hector Boethius, *Scotorum Historiae* (Paris, 1575), Bk. I, f. 2: 'Fuit is lapis cathedrae instar fatalis, vt qui vbicunque inueniretur, Scotis regnum portenderet'. Bk. XIV, f. 298: '. . . cathedram lapideam, quibus insidentes coronari Scotorum reges consueuerant, ē Scona Londinium secum attulit, atque in Vestmonasterio, vbi & hodie visitur, deposuit'. George Buchanan, *Rerum Scoticarum Historia* (Edinburgh, 1538), Bk. VIII, f. 76ᵛ: '. . . lapidem marmoreum rudem, in quo fatum regni contineri, vulgo persuasum erat, Londinum misit . . . .'

215/5th mar. n. Camden, p. 709, 'Rex Edwardus Primus Angli*ae* Westmonasterium deferendum curauit. De quo vaticinum vulgo iactitatum, quod cūm nunc fidem inuenerit, vt id genus paucula, subiungendum curaui'.

215/42-46. The existence at one time of this inscription is corroborated by William Brenchley Rye, *England as Seen by Foreigners* (London, 1865), p. 132, for the description of Westminster Abbey by Justus Zinzerling in 1610 notes that 'One of the curiosities is the stone on which Abraham [*sic*] rested; the chair or throne bears an inscription'. This does not prove that the inscription on the chair or stone was the same Buck quotes. That it gave the chair's legendary history is suggested by Zinzerling's association of it with Abraham, an error for Jacob. It is unclear in this recollection whether the inscription was on the chair or on the stone. That engraved on the chair is identified by Speed, p. 654, with the quotation Buck cites, text, p. 216 ('Ni fallat fatum Scotus . . .'). That this says nothing about the stone's Biblical association leads one to interpret Zinzerling's account as suggesting that there was a legend to this effect elsewhere in the vicinity of the chair. Buck had previously referred to the stone in *Daphnis:* 'You (most sacred Prince) the great IACOB, enthronized vpon the Patriarke *Jacobs* fatall stone, and vpon Saint *Jacobs* Festivall espoused solemnely faire *England* her selfe' (f. A3ᵛ).

215/6th mar. n. See above, note 215/4th mar. n.

216/3-4. Camden, p. 709 ('Perthia'): 'Ni fallat fatum, Scoti quocunque locatum / Inueniunt lapidem, regnare tenentur ibidem'. Buck, to make the prophecy seem to refer to James I, had made 'Scoti' singular.

216/6-7. Ecclesiastes 4:12 (Vulgate): 'Et si quispiam praevaluerit contra unum, duo resistunt ei; funiculus triplex difficile rumpitur'.

216/9-10. Luke 1: 32-33: 'Hie erit magnus, et Filius Altissimi vocabitur; et dabit illi Dominus Deus sedem David patris eius, et regnabit in domo Jacob in aeternum, et regni eius non erit finis'.

216/16-18. I Kings, 11.

216/19-20. Ecclesiasticus (Sirach), 10:8.

216/24-29. Gildas, *De Excidio Britanniae,* ed. Joseph Stevenson (London, 1838), *passim.*

216/29-31. Huntingdon, p. 173.

216/2nd mar. n. William of Malmesbury, I. 277.

216/3rd mar. n. B.L. MS. Cotton Vespasian A. XIX. The first sentence is from f. 113, the second from f. 110ᵛ. This work was listed among the entries in Cotton's library in all the earliest catalogues but is now erroneously described as lost. Buck used it in *Daphnis* as well. Camden quotes these passages (p. 104), placing the second one first, as Buck does, but Buck obviously derived his use of it from the original, since he gives no credit to Camden, and his 'humani cruoris' echoes the original, whereas Camden's 'sanguinis humani' is divergent. Moreover, Buck's pencilled 'X's in the margins throughout the manuscript, indicating his interest in certain passages, including the ones he quotes, reflect his practice in other books from which he derives information.

217/4-12. Polydore, p. 547. The brackets, one of which appears in Tiberius (the other would have appeared in a burnt out section) are Buck's indications of material he has added to the extract, otherwise closely followed.

217/13-19. See above, note 135/7 - 137/48.

217/33-50. See note 120/17-22 above. Francis Sandford, *A Genealogical History of the Kings of England* (London, 1677), p. 410, says: 'His Epitaph registered in a Book in the Colledge of Arms (differing not much from that mentioned in Mr *George Buck's* History of this King) . . . I have here inserted'. The differences between Sandford's and Buck's copies are slight, Buck's, despite scribal corruption, seeming in the main more accurate. Buck's is more favourable to Richard: 'iusta' is substituted in l. 2 for 'multa', 'certans' in l. 7 for 'merito', 'petita' in l. 14 for 'debita'. Because the manuscript is no longer extant and the epitaph is represented only in the Editor's copies, we cannot tell who made these alterations.

218/8-28. This epigram appears in Croyland, pp. 575f, with very few differences. A slight softening toward Richard appears in the substitution of 'Mundanam' in l. 16 for 'Ille trucem', but once again the loss of the manuscript and of Buck's original makes it impossible to determine responsibility for this divergence.

APPENDIX A: RICHARD'S DEFORMITY

Richard's physical appearance has always been a matter of dispute. No portrait shows him with anything but a not unattractive thin and serious face. Croyland suggests that it was pale (see note 127/50 - 128/3 above), and this is confirmed by Davydd Llwyd Llywelyn ab Gruffydd in his reference to 'little R' as 'pale and sad' (trans. introduction to Cothi, p. xxxvii). Rous (p. 216) and Polydore (p. 545) describe it as short and compact.

There is no evidence whatsoever of Richard's having been deformed. No contemporary writer alludes to a deformity, nor does any pictorial representation show signs of it. Even those contemporary writers hostile to Richard, including foreign ones who would have no excuse to fear printing the worst about him, mention nothing of a deformity. One would have expected it from Commynes, who had met Richard and who was so observant of appearances that he devotes a whole chapter to the subject of why it is not good for princes to meet, with examples based on physical appearance, and twice describes Edward IV. Nor is any such thing mentioned by Molines, whose ears were alive to scandal. Fabyan and Mancini, contemporaries of Richard's who had seen him in person and were both mildly hostile to him, say nothing. Nor does the Croyland continuator, who as a member of the Council certainly knew him. The exposure of his body after death (see above, note 120/17-22) should have been sufficient to settle the matter, but no one refers to it in this context. One may therefore conclude that a deformity, if one did exist, was so slight as not to be remarked in Richard's lifetime. It would have had to be slight indeed to have escaped comparison with his reputedly handsome brother Edward. The only writer contemporary with Richard who mentions any deformity is Rous, who does so only after Richard's death. Rous, who originated the tale that Richard was born with teeth and hair, eulogized him during his reign and after his death vilified him in the *Historia Regum Angliae* which he wrote for Henry VII. But the only deformity Rous mentions is an inequality of the shoulders (p. 216), and in the portrait of Richard which Rous executed, no striking deformity is seen. Richard is portrayed as short and slight but with erect posture, and his right shoulder appears slightly larger; but this may be due to error or attempt at perspective. More (p. 7) and Polydore (p. 565) both mention an inequality in the height of Richard's shoulders, Rous probably being their authority, but they disagree as to which shoulder it was. More makes Richard a hunchback as well and gives him a withered arm. Sir Richard Baker, a later chronicler, goes so far as to make Richard splay-footed and goggle-eyed (*A Chronicle of the Kings of England,* London, 1643, p. 137). We derive our usual picture of Richard's deformities from Shakespeare's play.

The withered arm story probably originated in More's reading literally, either intentionally or unintentionally, something which was stated figuratively in a common source used by him and Polydore (p. 543): that the current conflicts had sapped Richard's strength. It is quite possible that strenuous training in arms at an early age wrought a slight malformation so that the right shoulder either became over-developed or sagged. This may have made Richard appear stooped, giving rise to the legend of the hunched back. The term 'crouchback' or crookback' — which was applied to other mediaeval princes not documented as being hunchbacks — was applied to Richard by his enemies early in Henry VII's reign (Davies, p. 221). It could merely have indicated that he was somewhat stooped.

Most authors, deriving their description from Rous, speak of Richard's small stature, which accords with the information Buck cites (text, p. 129) from a conversation with Stow. This seems to be confirmed by the oration of the Scottish Ambassador Quhitlaw, quoted by Buck, text, p. 206, in which he cites a quotation to the effect that there has never been in so small a body so great a mind. The poem of Davydd Llwyd Llywelyn ab Gruffydd lends support, speaking of him as 'little R' and comparing him with his powerfully built brother Edward: 'How odious the vile cur to spy, / With withered shrank for brawny thigh'. This description is hardly meant to suggest that Richard had a withered leg: it merely indicates that he was, in comparison with his brother, slight. Richard's diminutive stature may have been overstressed for philosophical reasons, to make the traditional comparison of stature and soul.

On the other hand, Nicolas von Poppelau's description from his travel diary of his visit to England in 1484 (cited by Armstrong, in Mancini, pp. 136-8) describes him as three fingers (about two inches) taller than himself, but much thinner, with very delicate arms and legs. Armstrong suggests that if his arms were obviously delicate this might have accounted for the legend of the withered arm. Armstrong assumes that because von Poppelau was known to be remarkably strong, he was therefore undoubtedly tall (p. 137), an assumption which disregards the mechanics of physical movement. Von Poppelau implies in his description of Richard that he himself was thickset. A short, heavy man would have been in a better position than a tall man for balancing the heavy lance von Poppelau is renowned for carrying. Richard, two inches taller than a short and thickset man, could still have been considered short. Men who are short and slight but nevertheless possess unusual strength and stamina are by no means a physiological phenomenon (I cite myself as an example).

Besides Stow's account given by Buck, derived from people who had seen Richard, there are other *viva voce* reports. Walpole (p. 102) notes that 'The old countess of Desmond, who had danced with Richard, declared he was the handsomest man in the room except his brother Edward, and very well made'. This account is confirmed by two other sources, Sharon Turner, *Richard the Third, a Poem* (London, 1845), p. 277, and *Katharine Fry's Book,* ed. Jane Vansittart (London, 1966), p. 120. Both give the same information carried through independent reporters from the Countess of Desmond.

A commonplace of mediaeval and Renaissance superstition was the idea of the evil mind being accompanied by a warped body: it was natural that those who as part of the campaign against Richard portrayed his mind as warped should warp his body also. Holinshed states that 'the defects of fauour and amiable proportion, gaue proofe to this rule of physiognomie: "Distortum vultum sequitur distorsio morum" ' (p. 362). A Biblical reference may be at the heart of it: in Leviticus 21:16-23, we find that a man with a blemish or deformity — a crookback is specifically mentioned — 'shall not go in unto the vail, nor come nigh unto the altar, because he hath a blemish; that he profane not my sanctuaries'. Chambers in his biography of More, p. 79, reports an allegorical interpretation of the Queen of Sheba's treasures being borne to Solomon by camels: 'the camels must be the heathen . . . humpbacked by avarice and deformed by crime . . . .' *The Secret of Secrets,* of which there were numerous translations and imitations in the Middle Ages and in the fifteenth and sixteenth centuries, speaks of physiognomy in many places (*The Gouernaunce of Prynces,* trans. James Yonge, in *Three Prose Versions of the Secreta Secretorum,* I, ed. Robert Steele, EETS, extra ser. 74, London, 1898): 'cErtayn thynge hit is that the Sowle whyche Is the fourme of the body, sueth the kynde and the complexcion *and* the propyrteys of the body . . . . the Sow[l]e is the begynnynge *and* cause of al the natural mevynges of the body . . .' (p. 218). Signs of a shameless man are 'opyn eighyn and glysinynge, and the eighliddes full of blode *and* grete and shorte; Hey vprerid shuldris; the body Sumwhate Stowpynge' (p. 223); 'whan the shuldres bene moche vprerid, thei tokenyth orribill kynde *and* vntrouthe . . .' (p. 235). Especially to be avoided is one 'that . . . hath . . . the lymes dyfformyd out of kynde: Suche bene to enchue as enemys, for to wickidnesse they bene enclynet' (p. 232).

In popular ballads there are numerous examples of monstrous births which possess moral connotations of warning from God. Sixteenth century historians and chroniclers were avid in recording such monstrosities. We still find in film and comic strip the stereotype villain portrayed as deformed or foreign or both. A humped back seems to have had an association with the devil: says Harsnet in his *Declaration of Egregious Popish Impostures* (London, 1603), 'It was a pretty part in the old Church-playes, when the nimble Vice would skip up nimbly like a Iacke an Apes into the deuils necke, and ride the deuil a course'. This idea is echoed in Shakespeare's *Richard III* when little York says to his uncle, 'Because that I am little, like an ape, / He thinks that you should bear me on your shoulders' (III, i).

Richard's cognizance of the white boar fitted in well with the idea of his ugliness. Erasmus in his *Institutio Principis Christiani* (Basle, 1540), pp. 441f, quotes Platonic and Biblical metaphors of the wild beast for the tyrant and says that a tyrant should be depicted to a prince as a wild beast.

APPENDIX B: THE DEATH OF THE PRINCES

The death of the 'Princes in the Tower' has been the subject of greatest controversy in the story of Richard III, since it possesses the greatest emotional appeal and is most deeply shrouded in mystery and confused with conflicting reports. The only conclusions which can be drawn from available evidence seem to be (1) that rumours of their death were current at home and abroad during the reign of Richard III, but there is no proof of his guilt; (2) that Henry VII does not seem to have known what became of them, and no public statement was ever made by anyone who did know. One can do no more than marshal the evidence and appeal to plausibility. Various authors have pursued various theories as alternatives to the assumption of Richard's perpetration: Buck and Walpole that they survived abroad and Perkin Warbeck was in fact the Duke of York; Markham that Henry VII was the murderer; Kendall that Buckingham was the agent of their death; and Tucker that the Duke of Norfolk had the best motive (a theory initiated, but not published, by S.T. Bindoff). That one or both died a natural death is equally possible. It is also possible that they were shipped abroad secretly. During the time when they were known to be alive, there was a plot afoot to remove the daughters of Edward IV from sanctuary and send them abroad in disguise so that if anything should happen to the sons, the southern rebels could find in them a rallying point (Croyland, pp. 567f). There was a rumour in Henry VII's time that they were still alive after Richard's reign (More, p. 82; Polydore, p. 569). A plan of Richard's to send them away secretly might account for their being gradually withdrawn from public view until they were no longer seen, as both the Great Chronicle (p. 234) and Mancini (p. 92) report.

It could also be accounted for by their having become the focal point of the southern rebellion. Richard seems at first to have considered them harmless or to have tried giving the impression that he did. The wardrobe accounts for his coronation (Bod. MS. Gough Gen. Top. 5) enter in items 109 and 110 (f.12) a list of apparel and array 'To Lord Edward Son of late King Edward the fourth', and item 113 (f. 12) lists apparel and array for his henchmen. This material was actually delivered, indicating that Edward was intended to walk in Richard's coronation. By treating the children of Edward IV as no threat to him, Richard probably hoped to underplay their political importance. His plan failed when the southern rebellion used them as pawns. Croyland Chronicle (p. 567) — which never accuses Richard of their death — very plainly associates the spreading of the rumour with the calculated tactics of the rebellion. This form of propaganda made their removal necessary to Richard. He may simply have made their lodging in the Tower more obscure. The assumption that they could have remained in the Tower without public awareness is not far fetched. In Henry VII's time Lambert Simnel was set to impersonate the Earl of Warwick, then prisoner in the Tower, on the assumption that Warwick was dead.

Richard may have ordered the Princes to be secretly killed. One of his followers may have ordered them put to death without his advance knowledge to spare him responsibility. They could have died naturally. Buckingham and his mentor Morton could have had them sent abroad or put to death in order simultaneously to clear the way for another claimant — whether it was to be Buckingham himself or Richmond — and to throw suspicion on Richard. Buckingham's announcement of it was undeniably useful in concerting the rebellion, drawing the Woodville followers to the side of Richmond from their initial support of the Princes. Whatever did happen, Richard does not seem to have taken the rumours seriously enough to have shown the boys. Perhaps he wished to minimize their importance and avoid calling attention to them by seeming to ignore them. By acknowledging their death, if they were dead by any means, he risked throwing suspicion on himself. If he had sent them elsewhere, he would wish to conceal their whereabouts and consider the rumours advantageous in diverting enquiry. Of course he may not have known their whereabouts.

Before Richard's accession there was a fear that the Princes would be put to death. Mancini, who describes the events in England between Edward IV's death and Richard III's coronation says in December 1483, 'Non paucos homines in lacrymas et fletus [prorupisse] vidi, cum eius memoria fieret postquam a conspectibus hominum est amotus, et jam suspitio foret esse sublatum. An autem sublatus sit, et quo genere mortis nihil adhuc compertum habeo' (p. 92). Mancini reports also that young Edward's physician said the prince prayed daily, thinking he was near death. But GEC suggests that this indicates rather an awareness of fatal illness than of impending murder (XII, pt. ii, Appendix J, p. 33). In France in 1484 the Chancellor, addressing the Estates-General in a rhetorical diatribe against England, asks the audience to observe the fate of Edward IV's children: 'Aspicite, quaeso, quidnam post mortem regis Eduardi in ea terra contigerit, ejus scilicet jam adultos et egregios liberos impune trucidari et regni diadema in horum extinctorem, populis faventibus, delatum' (quoted Armstrong, in Mancini, introd., p. 22). Armstrong suggests that Mancini was the source of this information (p. 23). As we have seen, Mancini knew only that at the time of Richard's coronation people feared and suspected the death of the Princes, but he says he knows nothing of their end. In any case, the French address disrupts chronology for effect, having the murder take place before the granting of the crown to Richard.

Commynes states in one place that Buckingham was the murderer (II, 306) and in others that Richard was. He, too, is confused about chronology, saying Richard killed the princes, bastardized their sisters, then took the crown (I, 53f). One other foreign source from the early Tudor period is Valera, whose information comes from merchants in England at the time of Bosworth and thereafter. Writing to Ferdinand and Isabella, he recalls that Richard had the princes murdered during the life of Edward IV (Goodman and Mackay, p. 92). That this account not only wrenches chronology but shows strong colouring of Tudor myth discredits it. A survey of rumours current abroad during the late fifteenth and early sixteenth centuries, often uncertain, often far fetched, often conflicting with each other and with known fact, leads one to understand the outburst of *CSP* (Milan), p. 154, accompanying a (false) report of the death in battle of Clarence in 1471: 'I wish the country and the people were plunged deep in the sea, because of their lack of stability, for I feel like one going to the torture when I write about them, and no one ever hears twice alike about English affairs'.

Fabyan, a contemporary writing after the time but aware of popular rumour observes that feeling against Richard increased 'the more for asmoche as the common fame went that kynge Richarde hadde within the Tower put vnto secrete deth the .ii. sonnes of his broder Edwarde the .iiii.' (p. 670). The Great Chronicle is more detailed, saying that before Richard's accession the children were in royal lodgings, but after the Tower Council they were kept close. During the mayoral year concluding in October 1483, 'The childyr of kyng Edward were seen shotyng & playyng In the Gardyn of the Towyr by sundry tymys' (p. 234). This is followed by the statement,

> All the wyntyr seson of thys mayers tyme þe land was In good Quyet, But afftryr Estyrn much whysperyng was among the people þt The kyng hadd put the Childyr of kyng Edward to deth, and also that he hadd poysonyd the Quene his wyffe, and entend w^t a lycence purchasid to have maryed the eldest dowghtyr of kyng Edward.

Henry Tudor prepared to seize the throne 'Concideryng the deth of kyng Edwardys chyldyr, Of whom as than men fferid not opynly to saye that they were Rydd owth of this world' (p. 236). Chronology is extremely fuzzy. The rumour of the Princes' death and that of Queen Anne's death are placed in the same year, 1484, whereas the latter occurred in 1485, and the queen's death is placed before Buckingham's rebellion. It will be noted that particular stress is laid on the Princes' being dead before Henry VII decided to attempt the crown, as if a need for such certainty had been manifested.

Arnold's and Greyfriars' chronicles of the early Tudor period say only that Edward IV died, the Princes 'were put to silence', and Richard took the crown. Again the order of events is disarranged. Robert Ricart (*The Maire of Bristowe Is Kalendar,* ed. Lucy Toulmin Smith, Cam. Soc., 2nd ser. no. 5, London, 1872) has placed the murder in the second year of Richard's reign, but has had to add it in the margin as if, says the editor, he had forgotten it: 'And in this yere the two sonnes of King E. were put to scylence in the Towre of London' (p. 46). Rous has them die about the time of Richard's coronation and gives a rather oblique reference to the murder: 'ita quod ex post paucissimis notum fuit qua morte martirizati sunt' (p. 214). Henry's official panegyrists, André and Carmeliano are quite positive on the subject of Richard's having put the Princes to death. So it is the Welsh poet Dafydd Llwyd Llewellyn ab Gryffydd who welcomed Henry Tudor with a verse calling Richard 'a servile Boar who, in his wardship did imprison the sons of Edward, and kill his two nephews who were young. Shame on the hang-lipped Saracen for slaying angels of

Christ' (quoted Jones, p. 24).

So far there have been only vague and unspecific rumours. More, Polydore and their followers, however, give a more specific, though scarcely more credible tale. More's, highly circumstantial and totally incredible and inconsistent, is given with many qualifications. He begins by saying that covert dealing has obscured the truth and that he intends to 'rehearse you the dolorous end of those babes, not after euery way that I haue heard, but after that way y^t I haue so hard by suche men & such meanes, as me thinketh it wer hard but it should be true' (p. 83). He then relates, with circumstantial embellishments, the tale summarized by Buck (text, pp. 138f), whose inconsistencies and impossibilities are summed up by Kendall (pp. 471-81). The murder is the work of Sir James Tyrell, John Dighton, and Miles Forest. The cast is padded out by mention of a John Green; Sir Robert Brakenbury, Constable of the Tower; one William Slaughter or 'black wil', the Princes' keeper; an anonymous page who recommends Tyrell to Richard as prospective murderer while the latter is sitting on the privy; and an obscure and now conveniently dead priest who removed the bodies after Tyrell's agents had buried them. The murder, said to have taken place during Richard's progress, is described in detail as being performed by smothering. Forest is dead, Tyrell was executed for treasonable complicity in Suffolk's rising, and Dighton is still walking abroad unscathed (an odd fate for a regicide). The source of information is given as the confession of Tyrell and Dighton. Ignorance of the bodies' whereabouts is explained by the death of the priest, who reburied them. Hall finds it necessary to elaborate even further on this, adding that 'somme saye that kynge Richard caused the priest to take them vp and close them in lead and to put them in a coffyne full of holes hoked at the endes with .ii. hokes of yron, and so to cast them into a place called the Blacke deepes at the Thames mouth' (p. 378). Grafton copies this account. The tale gained credit through repetition.

Polydore is more circumspect, reporting that Brakenbury was sent a warrant for the Princes' death but delayed, and James Tyrell was then sent to execute the deed, 'sed quo genere mortis miselli pueri affecti fuerint, no*n* plane liquet' (p. 547), and Richard allowed the rumour of their death to spread. More's and Polydore's stories agree significantly only in the portrayal of Brakenbury, the time of the murder, and the accusation of Tyrell. Polydore, Henry VII's official historian, mentions no confession, no accomplices, and he describes the mode of murder as unknown. It would seem that Henry VII, finding on his hands a series of pretenders, felt the need of establishing the Princes' death more positively. Tyrell, a former follower of Richard, was conveniently executed for treason in 1502 (eleven to fifteen years before More wrote), making possible the circulation of a report that he had confessed in prison. How circumstantial and detailed this report was we cannot know. Clearly a real confession, had it existed, would have been published. It was a matter of greatest urgency to Henry VII to establish beyond doubt that the Princes were dead, for if they were alive, his repeal of the document declaring them illegitimate had made their claim supersede his own, and if they were known positively to be dead he would have been able to counter pretenders with proof. Consequently we must assume the confession was fictitious, and that Henry was forced to rely on spreading a rumour and letting it gather its own accretions. Rather awkward was the inability (despite the alleged confession) to produce the bodies, and equally awkward More's story of their secret removal. Obviously Henry could not afford to be too precise for fear of arousing questions which could not be answered.

Tyrell's responsibility for the murder is mentioned by Fabyan and the Great Chronicle, derived from the same source, the only independent historians which mention him in this capacity aside from the More-Polydore group. But they refer to his complicity — as indeed does More — as only one of many rumours. The Great Chronicle says 'Of which Cruell dede sir Jamys Tyrell was Reportid to be the doer, But oþer putt that wygth upon an old servaunt of kyng Rychardys namyd' (p. 237; no name is given). Grafton's continuation of Hardyng, written before he had discovered More, mentions that Tyrell was executed for treason but does not refer to him in connection with the murder (p. 585). The Tyrell confession story was simply added to the numerous rumours already circulating, and with so many in the air and each historian having to choose the rumour which best suited him, was often ignored. In an amazing list, More's nephew Rastell (p. 292) gives an idea of how many and what sort of rumours were abroad, omitting entirely to mention Tyrell, and in reading this we cease to wonder at More's confusion.

Bacon seems dubious about the story told by More: Tyrell and Dighton, he says, 'agreed both in a tale', the one given by More. 'Thus much was then delivered abroad, to be the effect of those examinations; but the King nevertheless made no use of them in any of his declarations. Whereby, as it seems, those examinations left the business somewhat perplexed'. Tyrell was beheaded later for other treasons, 'But John Dighton, who it seemeth spake best for the King, was forthwith set at liberty, and was the principal means of divulging this tradition' (Bacon, VI, 142f).

Henry was never able to do more than this. In his Act of Attainder passed against Richard he mentions the 'shedding of Infants blood' (*Rot. Parl.*, VI, 276), but is no more specific. This is a standard accusation against a 'tyrant'. Henry evidently did not know at this time whether or not the Princes were dead, but this general statement was a sure encouragement to the rumours of their death which had begun during Buckingham's rebellion and which he took care to keep alive. Possibly his delay in marrying and then crowning Elizabeth of York was partly due to a fear of her brothers' existence and possible resurgence. Perhaps this was a reason for the stress he laid on his right of conquest. Possibly, also, it was his reason for relegating Elizabeth Woodville — to get her out of the way in case Simnel, first announced in Ireland as a son of Edward IV, should actually be so and be subject to identification by his mother. His not confronting Perkin Warbeck with Richard of York's family may have emanated from the same fear that the Princes were still alive and Perkin might actually be York.

APPENDIX C: PERKIN WARBECK

The identity of Perkin Warbeck is still a mystery. No one knows even now whether or not he was the Duke of York. Both Gairdner and G.R. Elton (*England under the Tudors,* London, 1955) sum up well the arguments for imposture, pointing out that the disaffection of many of Henry's neighbour monarchs would have made them willing to support a scheme against him, whether or not their figurehead were a genuine heir to the English throne. The climate of domestic and foreign feeling was disposed to accept and encourage a pretender: Perkin was an important pawn in international politics.

Henry was extremely vague in his statements about Perkin, relying more on bravado and offhandedness than on circumstantial evidence (see Madden, p. 167). But, as Polydore admits, Henry, for all his underplaying, was frightened. Far from everyone's knowing Perkin to be an imposter, the tale was gaining so much credit in England that many of the chief magnates considered it true (Polydore, ed. Hay, p. 66), an observation Polydore lets slip in manuscript but alters in print. But he does not indicate that Henry made any genuine investigations to discover Perkin's origins. Hall adds an account of his sending spies to gather evidence, promising reward to the person who would solve the mystery of Perkin's origin (p. 465). If Henry did receive information from spies, they are as likely, for pay, to have manufactured as to have discovered it, and Henry as likely to have paid for manufactured information as for real. Foreign powers vied with each other in attempts to produce witnesses to Perkin's identity and to produce relatives for him. There is no serious evidence of his ever being confronted with any member of the Duke of York's family, though Henry seems to have given it out in intimate circles that he had been shown and failed to recognize certain of the duke's intimates. Raimondo de Soncino wrote to the Duke of Milan (*CSP*, Milan, pp. 329-31) that he had heard from Richmond Herald of an interview in a closed chamber, with only princes present, where Henry had asked Perkin if he recognized any of those present known to have been in close company with the duke in his childhood, and Perkin did not.

Henry seems to have wavered in certain of his statements about Perkin, notably in the fluctuation of his name between 'Warbeck' and 'Osbeck' and in identifying his father's profession. As for Perkin's own statements, we have, evidently invented by Polydore and embellished by his followers, an address to the King of Scots, in which he says Richard ordered the Princes to be murdered, but the prospective murderer misgave and killed only Edward, sparing York and transporting him out of the country (Polydore, pp. 596). But in his proclamation, of which there is a reliable record, he does not mention an attempted murder, or mention Richard at all, but says '. . . we in our tender age escaped by God's might out of the tower of London, and were secretly conveyed over the sea into other divers countries, there remaining certain years as unknown' (quoted by Spedding, Bacon, VI, Appendix II, p. 252). Polydore's statement loses credibility if we bear in mind that it is unlikely for the figurehead of the Yorkist movement, Perkin, to have cast aspersions on the last Yorkist king, to whose supporters he was bound to appeal.

A case can be made for the escape of one or both of the boys from the Tower, by Richard's or the Woodvilles' party or Buckingham and Morton's agency. If Perkin really was the Duke of York, then Richard's agency is suggested, since the 'confession' connects him with Sir Edward Brampton, a close associate of Edward IV who continued in the service of Richard III. On the other hand, the Woodvilles seem likely in that they would by preserving one of the boys be setting up a scheme to bring their family back to power.

The confession was evidently made, if at all, in private, as the report of Richmond Herald suggests and André seems to confirm, saying that Perkin, when he saw the king's clemency, confessed the imposture, and the king, to quell unrest, ordered the confession to be published (p. 72f). The publication of this seems to have been as sparse as that of Tyrell's 'confession'. Neither Fabyan nor Polydore mentions it. Hall is our sole authority for its text. Richmond Herald testifies to there having been copies made, as does the Great Chronicle (p. 284).It seems odd that none of these copies survives and that Polydore did not think the document worth attention. That there was a confession in existence is undeniable. Perkin read a confession on the scaffold and recited one before the Spanish Ambassador de Puebla and the Bishop of Cambrai (CSP, Spain, I, 185f). But the inconsistencies within the confession and with earlier statements made by and about Perkin, and also the complete disregard of its details by foreign powers and by Henry's official historian lead one to believe its authorship doubtful, its details unsupported by fact, and its recitation not voluntary.

Perkin's identity remains a mystery. Henry made no real effort to prove that he was Perkin Warbeck or that he was not York. The likeness to Edward IV is unquestionable, as shown by portraits. Madden observes the English character of his handwriting (p. 184). Flawless English cannot be accounted for by the experiences cited in the confession. His bearing remained dignified even in adversity, as Raimondo de Soncino testified to the Duke of Milan (CSP, Milan, p. 335). That an almost certainly spurious confession had to be made for him seems to indicate that he never broke down sufficiently to give a satisfactory confession which could have been simply verified, solving the matter. Yet he was sufficiently broken down to read a false confession. What pressure was brought to bear on him is not known, but even on the scaffold he was at Henry's mercy, since his wife was in Henry's power.

A case could be made for his actually being the Duke of York, but no one has satisfactorily treated this as yet. Another plausible theory is that he was an illegitimate son of Edward IV or some other member of the House of York. CSP (Milan) in 1468, speaking of the impending marriage of Margaret of York to the Duke of Burgundy, says that most people knew she had had love affairs, and 'indeed in the opinion of many she even has a son' (p. 124). The Milanese ambassador in Flanders wrote in 1495 to the Duke of Milan that the Emperor Maximilian told him Perkin Warbeck was the son of the Duchess of Burgundy and the Bishop of Cambrai, as he had been informed by Sir Robert Clifford (p. 292). This would explain why the Bishop of Cambrai asked to see him and why Perkin said in this interview that 'the Duchess, Madame Margaret, knew as well as himself that he was not the son of King Edward' (*CSP,* Spain, I, pp. 185f). Pollard (*The Reign of Henry VII,* London, 1913, I, xxii-xxiii) considers this a plausible explanation and wonders why if it were not true Maximilian would have repeated it about his wife's stepmother. It would also explain the humble foster parents, the aura of mystery, and Henry VII's unwillingness to publish the truth. And it would explain Perkin's willingness to adhere to a false confession, perhaps after he had confessed the truth to the king in private.

GLOSSARY

accabled (67)	overwhelmed
accoll (118)	embrace
acolasts (200)	prodigals
affied, affying, affiance (27, etc.)	trust(ed)
ambit (141, 152)	scope
appanage (20)	provision (land, office) for younger son of royalty
assentation (121)	assenting, flattery
Bashaes (42)	imperious people
battologies (7)	excessive and extensive repetitions
captate, -ion (35, 64)	endeavour to get
carnifices (105)	slaughterers
cognation (110)	relationship
commorient (141)	dying together
compatient (141)	sympathetic
copy (6)	copiousness
crapauds (38)	toads
deturpation (83)	making vile or base
disertly (27, etc.)	eloquently
emules (29)	rivals
facinorous (51)	excessively wicked
fastigious (86)	culminating
idoneous (193)	suitable
ierogliffs (175)	hieroglyphics, symbols
illuded (146)	mocked

inchantally (206)	by enchantment
leames (86)	drains
largitions (197)	bounties
mome (122)	dolt, fool
monomachy (104)	single combat
naves (48)	hubs
novercal (67)	stepmother-like
opiniasts (117)	opinionated people
palliardise (199 — 2)	debauchery
parergon, -a (56, 172)	digression
pasquillants (117)	writers of satire
patrociny (4)	patronage, protection
perduells (95, 96)	enemies
philautists (199)	self-lovers
plancentine (124)	ingratiating
posters (16, etc.)	descendants
precony (202, 203)	extolment
prosopolepsies (4)	partialities
quadruplators (193)	informers
refell (8)	refute
refricated (63)	restimulated
reginists (26)	queen's adherents
rhodomontados (26, 42)	extravagant boastings
ritrat (56)	portrait
sicaries (166)	assassins
sobriquets (9, etc.)	nicknames, epithets
suppeditated (6)	supplied
surquidry (101)	pride
tirociny (6, 9)	training, apprenticeship
truhanes (88, 192)	vagabonds
viaticum (121)	money or provision for travel
vitilitigators (120)	contenders
wast (140)	desolate

BIBLIOGRAPHY
LIST OF PRINTED SOURCES AND THESES

Adams, Joseph Quincy, 'Hill's List of Early Plays in Manuscript', *The Library*, XX (1939).

Albright, Evelyn May, *Dramatic Publication in England, 1580-1640*, New York, 1927.

Anglo, Sydney, 'The *British History* in Early Tudor Propaganda', *Bulletin of the John Rylands Library*, XLIV (1961).

———, *Spectacle, Pageantry, and Early Tudor Policy*, Oxford, 1969.

Armstrong, C.A.J., 'The Inauguration Ceremonies of the Yorkist Kings and Their Title to the Throne', *Transactions of the Royal Historical Society*, 4th ser. XXX (1948).

Bacon, Francis, *The Works of Francis Bacon,* ed. James Spedding, VI, London, 1858.

Bald, R.C., 'The *Locrine* and *George-a-Green* Title-Page Inscriptions', *The Library*, XV (1934).

———, 'A Manuscript Work by Sir George Buc', *Modern Language Review*, XXX (1935).

———, 'A Revels Office Entry', *Times Literary Supplement*, no. 1,311 (17 March 1927).

Bale, John, *Scriptorum Illustrium Maioris Britanniae*, Basle, [1557-9].

Beaumont, Francis and John Fletcher, *Comedies and Tragedies*, London, 1647.

Bellamy, J.G., 'Justice under the Yorkist Kings', *American Journal of Legal History*, IX (1965).

Benedict of Peterborough, *The Chronicle of the Reignes of Henry II and Richard I, A.D. 1169-1192*, 2 vols., ed. William Stubbs, R.S. 49, London, 1867.

Bennett, Josephine Waters, *The Evolution of the 'Faerie Queene'*, Chicago, 1942.

Bennett, R.E., *The Life and Works of Sir William Cornwallis*, unpublished doctoral dissertation, Harvard, 1931.

———, 'Sir William Cornwallis's Use of Montaigne', *PMLA*, XLVIII (1933).

Bentley, Gerald Eades, *The Jacobean and Caroline Stage*, 7 vols., Oxford, 1941-68.

Biographia Britannica, II, London, 1748.

———, II, corrected and enlarged by Andrew Kippis, London, 1780.

Black, Ira J., *A Study of Changing Historiographical Trends as Illustrated in the Medieval English Chronicles of Croyland Abbey*, unpublished M.A. thesis, Ohio State University, 1965.

Boethius, Hector, *Scotorum Historiae*, Paris, 1575.

Bouchard, Alain, *Les Grandes Cronicques de Bretagne*, n.p. [1517].

Bracton, Henricus de, *De Legibus et Consuetudinibus Angliae*, 6 vols., ed. Sir Travers Twiss, R.S. 70, London, 1878-83.

Brenan, Gerald and Edward Phillips Stratham, *The House of Howard*, 2 vols., London, 1907.

Brewer, J.S., *The Reign of Henry VIII*, London, 1884.

Brixius, Germanus, *Antimorus*, Basle, 1519.

[Brook, Ralph], *A Discoverie of Certaine Errours Published in Print in the Much Commended Britannia. 1594*, [London, 1596].

Brooks, F.W., *The Council of the North*, Historical Association Pamphlet 25, London, 1966.

Buchanan, George, *Rerum Scoticarum Historia*, Edinburgh, 1583.

B[uck], G[eorge], Knight, Δαφνις Πολυστεφανος.*An Eclog Treating of Crownes, and of Garlandes, and to Whom of Right They Appertaine*, London, 1605.

Buck, George, Gent., *The Great Plantagenet*, London, 1635.

_____, *The History of the Life and Reigne of Richard the Third*, London, 1646.

_____, *The History of the Life and Reigne of Richard the Third*, London, 1647.

_____, *The History of the Life and Reigne of Richard the Third*, London, 1973.

Calendar of Letters, Despatches, and State Papers, Relating to Negotiations between England and Spain, I, ed. G.A. Bergenroth, London, 1862.

Calendar of the Patent Rolls: 1461-7; 1467-77; 1476-85; 1485-94; 1494-1509, London, 1897-1916.

Calendar of State Papers and Manuscripts Existing in the Archives and Collections of Milan, I, ed. Allen B. Hinds, London, 1912.

Calendar of State Papers and Manuscripts, Relating to English Affairs, Existing in the Archives and Collections of Venice . . .' I: 1202-1509, ed. Rawdon Brown, London, 1864.

Calmette, Joseph, *Le Moyen Age*, Paris, 1948.

_____,et G. Périnelle, *Louis XI et l'Angleterre (1461-1483)*, Paris, 1930.

Cambrensis, Giraldus, *Topographica Hibernica*, V in *Opera*, ed. James F. Dimock, R.S. 21, London, 1867.

Camden, William, *Britannia*, London, 1600.

_____, *Britannia*, London, 1607.

_____, *Britain*, trans. Philemon Holland, London, 1610.

_____, *Remaines Concerning Britaine*, rev. ed., London, 1614.

Carte, Thomas, *A General History of England*, II, ii, London, 1750.

Casley, David, *A Catalogue of the Manuscripts of the King's Library: An Appendix to the Catalogue of the Cottonian Library; Together with an Account of Books Burnt or Damaged by a Late Fire*, London, 1734.

Catalogue of the Library of the Late Charles Yarnold, Esq., London, 1825.

A Catalogue of the Manuscripts in the Cottonian Library Deposited in the British Museum, London, 1802.

Cavendish, George, *The Life and Death of Cardinal Wolsey*, ed. Richard S. Sylvester, EETS 243, London, 1959.

Challen, W.H., 'Sir George Buck, Kt., Master of the Revels', *Notes and Queries* (1957).

[Chalmers, George], *An Apology for the Believers in the Shakspeare-Papers*, London, 1797.

————, *A Supplemental Apology for the Believers in the Shakspeare-Papers*, London, 1799.

Chambers, E.K., *The Elizabethan Stage*, 4 vols., Oxford, 1923.

————, Review of *The King's Office of the Revels 1610-1622, Review of English Studies*, I (1925).

————, *Thomas More*, London, 1935.

Chartrou, Josèphe, *L'Anjou de 1109 à 1151 - Foulque de Jerusalem et Geoffroi Plantagenet*, Paris, n.d.

Chrimes, S.B., *English Constitutional Ideas in the Fifteenth Century*, Cambridge, 1936.

————, *Lancastrians, Yorkists, and Henry VII*, London, 1966.

————, *Henry VII*, London, 1972.

Christ Church Letters, ed. J.B. Sheppard, Cam. Soc., 2nd ser. 19, London, 1877.

Chronicle of the Rebellion in Lincolnshire, 1470, ed. John Gough Nichols, in *The Camden Miscellany*, I, London, 1847.

The Chronicle of the Reigns of Henry II and Richard I, A.D. 1169-1192, ed. William Stubbs, 2 vols., R.S. 49, London, 1867.

Coggeshall, Radulphus de, *Chronicon Anglicanum*, ed. Joseph Stephenson, R.S. 66, London, 1875.

C[okayne], G[eorge] E[dward], *The Complete Peerage*, 13 vols., ed. Vicary Gibbs *et al.*, London, 1910-59.

Coke, Edward, *The First Part of the Institutes of the Laws of England*, 4 vols., ed. Frances Hargrave and Charles Butler, London, 1794.

Colie, Rosalie L., *Paradoxia Epidemica*, Princeton, 1966.

A Collection of Curious Discourses, [orig. ed. Thomas Hearne], 2 vols., London, 1775.

Commynes, Philippe de, *Mémoires*, 3 vols., ed. Joseph Calmette, Paris, 1924-25.

Conway, Agnes Ethel, 'The Maidstone Sector of Buckingham's Rebellion', *Archaeologia Cantiana*, XXXVII (1925).

Cornwallis, Sir William, *The Encomium of Richard the Third*, ed. A.N. Kincaid, London, 1977.

Cothi, Lewis Glyn, *The Poetical Works*, Oxford, 1837.

[*Croyland Chronicle*] in *Rerum Anglicarum Scriptorum Veterum*, I, [ed. William Fulman], Oxford, 1684.

Çurita, Geronymo, *Anales de la Corona de Aragon*, 6 vols., Çaragoça, 1610.

Davies, Robert, *Extracts from the Municipal Records of the City of York during the Reigns of Edward IV, Edward V and Richard III,* London, 1843.

De Ricci, Seymour, *English Collectors of Books and Manuscripts (1530-1930),* Cambridge, 1930.

Dos Santos, Domenigos Maurício Gomes, *O Mosteiro de Jesus de Aveiro,* Estudos de Historia (Ultramarina e Continental), Lisbon, 1963.

Du Boulay, F.R.H., *An Age of Ambition, English Society in the Late Middle Ages,* London, 1970.

Duff, E. Gordon, *Fifteenth Century English Books,* Oxford, 1917.

Dugdale, William, *The Baronage of England,* London, 1676.

————, *Monasticon Anglicanum,* VI, i, London, 1830.

Du Haillan, Bernard de Gerard, *L'Histoire de France,* [Paris], 1577.

Dunham, William Huse, Jr., *Lord Hastings' Indentured Retainers, 1461-1483,* Transactions of the Connecticut Academy of Arts and Sciences, 40, New Haven, 1955.

———— and Charles T. Wood, 'The Right to Rule England: Depositions and the Kingdom's Authority, 1327-1485', *American Historical Review,* LXXXI (Oct. 1976).

Du Tillet, Jean, *Recueil des Roys du France,* Paris, 1602.

Eccles, Mark, *Sir George Buc, Master of the Revels* in *Thomas Lodge and Other Elizabethans,* ed. Charles J. Sisson, Cambridge, Mass., 1933.

Edwards, J.G., 'The "Second" Continuation of the Crowland Chronicle', *BIHR,* XXXIX (1966).

Elton, G.R., *England under the Tudors,* London, 1955.

Emden, A.B., *A Biographical Register of the University of Cambridge to 1500,* Cambridge, 1963.

English Historical Scholarship in the Sixteenth and Seventeenth Centuries, ed. Levi Fox, London, 1956.

Erasmus, Desiderius, *Adagiorum Chiliades,* Basle, 1536.

————, *Institutio Principis Christiani,* Basle, 1540.

————, *Opus Epistolarum Des. Erasmi Roterodami,* 12 vols., ed. P.S. Allen, Oxford, 1904-58.

————, *Proverbs or Adages,* trans. Richard Taverner, facsimile of 1569 ed., ed. De Witt T. Starnes, Gainesville, 1956.

Evans, Howell T., *Wales and the Wars of the Roses,* Cambridge, 1915.

Evans, Joan, *A History of the Society of Antiquaries,* Oxford, 1956.

Excerpta Historica, compiled by Samuel Bentley, London, 1831.

Fabyan, Robert, *The New Chronicles of England and France,* repr. from Pynson's edition of 1516, ed. Henry Ellis, London, 1811.

Foedera . . ., compiled by Thomas Rymer, VII-XII, London, 1709-11.

Foxe, John, *The Ecclesiasticall Historie, Conteining the Acts and Monuments of Martyrs,* London, 1583.

Fry, Katharine, *Katharine Fry's Book,* ed. Jane Vansittart, London, 1966.

Fuchs, Leonhard, *De Historia Stirpium Commentarij Insignis,* London, 1551.

Fuller, Thomas *The Church History of Britain,* ed. J.S. Brewer, II, Oxford, 1845.

Fussner, F. Smith, *The Historical Revolution: English Historical Writing and Thought 1580-1640,* London, 1962.

Gainsford, Thomas, *The True and Wonderfull History of Perkin Warbeck,* London, 1618.

Gairdner, James, *History of the Life and Reign of Richard the Third,* Cambridge, 1898.

Garibay y Çamãlloa, Esteuan de, *D'El Compendio Historial de las Chronicas y Universal Historia de Todos los Reynos D'España,* II, Antwerp, 1571.

Gibbon, Edward, *Miscellaneous Works,* III, London, 1814.

Gildas, *De Excidio Britanniae,* ed. Joseph Stevenson, London, 1838.

Gildersleeve, Virginia Crocheron, *Government Regulation of the Elizabethan Drama,* New York, 1908.

[Glover, Robert], *The Catalogue of Honour,* ed. Thomas Milles, London, 1610.

G[odwin], F[rancis], *A Catalogue of the Bishops of England ,* London, 1601.

Goodman, Anthony and Angus MacKay, 'A Castilian Report on English Affairs, 1486', *EHR,* LXXXVIII (Jan. 1973).

Grafton, Richard, *Grafton's Chronicle; or, History of England,* 2 vols., London, 1809.

Grants, etc. from the Crown During the Reign of Edward the Fifth, introd. by John Gough Nichols, Cam. Soc., 1st ser. 60, London, 1854.

The Great Chronicle of London, ed. A.H. Thomas and I.D. Thornley, London, 1938.

Greg, W.W., 'Three Manuscript Notes by Sir George Buc', *The Library,* XII (1931).

Guicciardini, Ludovico, *Descrittione di Tutti i Paesi Bassi,* Antwerp, 1581.

Hall, Edward, *Chronicle,* ed. Henry Ellis, London, 1809.

Halsted, Caroline A., *Richard III, as Duke of Gloucester and King of England,* 2 vols., London, 1844.

Hanbury, H.G., 'The Legislation of Richard III', *American Journal of Legal History,* VI (1962).

Hanham, Alison, 'Hastings Redivivus', *EHR,* XC (Oct., 1975).

———, *Richard III and His Early Historians, 1483-1535,* Oxford, 1975.

———, 'Richard III, Lord Hastings and the Historians', *EHR,* LXXXVII (April, 1972).

Harbage, Alfred, *Annals of English Drama, 975-1700,* rev. S. Schoenbaum, London, 1964.

Hardyng, John, *The Chronicle of Iohn Hardyng . . . together with the Continuation by Richard Grafton,* ed. Henry Ellis, London, 1812.

Harington, John, *A New Discourse of a Stale Subject, Called The Metamorphosis of Ajax,* ed. Elizabeth Story Donno, London, 1962.

Hassall, W.O., *A Catalogue of the Library of Sir Edward Coke,* Yale Law Library Publications, 12, New Haven, 1950.

Hay, Denys, 'The Manuscript of Vergil's "Anglica Historia" ', *EHR,* LIV (1939).

————, *Polydore Vergil, Renaissance Historian and Man of Letters,* Oxford, 1952.

Haye, Jean de la, *Les Memoires et Recherches de France, et de la Gaule Acquitanique,* Paris, 1581.

Hazlitt, W. Carew, *Collections and Notes,* ser. 1, London, 1876.

————, *Hand-Book to the Popular, Poetical, and Dramatic Literature of Great Britain,* London, 1867.

Hervey, Mary F.S., *The Life, Correspondence and Collections of Thomas Howard, Earl of Arundel,* Cambridge, 1921.

Heuterus, Pontus, *Rerum Burgundicarum,* Antwerp, 1584.

The Historical Collections of a Citizen of London in the Fifteenth Century [Gregory's Chronicle], ed. James Gairdner, Cam. Soc., 2nd ser. 17, London, 1876.

Historie of the Arrivall of Edward IV in England, ed. John Bruce, Cam. Soc., 1st ser. 1, London, 1838.

Holinshed, Raphael, *Holinshed's Chronicles of England, Scotland, and Ireland,* 6 vols., London, 1807-8.

Hooper, Samuel, *A Catalogue of the Manuscripts in the Cottonian Library,* London, 1777.

Hope, W.H. St John, 'The Discovery of the Remains of King Henry VI in St. George's Chapel, Windsor Castle', *Archaeologia,* LXII (1911).

Hoveden, Roger de, *Chronica,* 4 vols., ed. William Stubbs, R.S. 51, London, 1868-9.

Howard, Henry, *A Defensatiue against the Poyson of Supposed Prophesies,* London, 1583.

Howard, Henry, *Indication of Memorials, Monuments, Paintings, and Engravings of Persons of the Howard Family . . . ,* Corby Castle, 1834.

Hume, David, *The History of England,* III, London, 1763.

Huntingdon, Henry of, *The History of the English,* ed. Thomas Arnold, R.S. 74, London, 1879.

Hutchinson, William, *The History of the County of Cumberland,* 2 vols., Carlisle, 1794.

Ingulph's Chronicle of the Abbey of Croyland with the Continuations by Peter of Blois and Anonymous Writers, trans. Henry T. Riley, London, 1854.

Ives, E.W., 'Andrew Dymmock and the Papers of Anthony, Earl Rivers, 1482-1483', *BIHR,* XLI (1968).

Jacob, E.F., *The Fifteenth Century, 1399-1485,* Oxford, 1961.

Jacob, John, *Publicanus Vindicatus,* London, 1654.

————, *et al.,* 'A Remonstrance of the Case of the late Farmers of the Customes, and their humble Petition to the Parliament', n.p., 1653.

James, Montague Rhodes and Claude Jenkins, *A Descriptive Catalogue of the Manuscripts in the Library of Lambeth Palace,* 2 vols., Cambridge, 1930-2.

Jenkins, Gladys, 'Ways and Means in Elizabethan Propaganda', *History,* new ser. XXVI (1941).

Jesse, John Heneage, *Memoirs of King Richard the Third and Some of His Contemporaries,* London, 1862.

Jones, W. Garmon, 'Welsh Nationalism and Henry Tudor', *The Transactions of the Honourable Society of Cymmrodorion* (1917-18), 1-59.

Kendall, Paul Murray, *Richard III,* New York, 1955.

————, ed. and introd., *Richard III, the Great Debate,* Folio Society, London 1965.

Kendrick, T.D., *British Antiquity,* London, 1950.

[Kennett, White] *A Complete History of England,* I and II, London, 1706.

[———— ,] *A Complete History of England,* 2nd ed., I, London, 1719.

Kincaid, Arthur Noel, 'The Dramatic Structure of Sir Thomas More's *History of Richard III*', *Studies in English Literature,* XII (1972).

————,'A Revels Office Scrap Deciphered', *Notes and Queries,* new ser. XIX (1972), 461-3.

Kingsford, Charles Lethbridge, *English Historical Literature in the Fifteenth Century,* Oxford, 1913.

Lander, J.R., 'Council, Administration and Councillors, 1461-1485', *BIHR,* XXXII (1959).

['Leicester's Commonwealth']: *The Copie of a Leter, Wryten by a Master of Arte of Cambrige, to His Friend in London; Concerning Some Talke . . . about the Present State, and Some Procedinges of the Erle of Leycester . . . ,* n.p., 1584.

Le Neve, John, *Fasti Ecclesiae Anglicanae,* 3 vols., Oxford, 1854.

Letters and Papers, Foreign and Domestic, of the Reign of Henry VIII, ed. J.S. Brewer, *et al.,* London, 1862-1932.

Letters and Papers Illustrative of the Reigns of Richard III and Henry VII, 2 vols.,ed. James Gairdner, R.S. 24, London, 1861-3.

Letters and Papers Illustrative of the Wars of the English in France, 2 vols.,ed. Joseph Stevenson, R.S. 22, London, 1861-64.

Levine, Mortimer, 'Richard III — Usurper or Lawful King?' *Speculum,* XXXIV (1959).

Levy, F.J., *Tudor Historical Thought,* San Marino, 1967.

Liber Eliensis, ed. E.O. Blake, Cam. Soc., 3rd ser. 92, London, 1962.

Livermore, H.V., *A New History of Portugal,* 2nd ed., London, 1976.

MacGibbon, David, *Elizabeth Woodville (1437-1492), Her Life and Times,* London, 1938.

McKisack, May, *Medieval History in the Tudor Age,* Oxford, 1971.

Macray, William Dunn, *A Register of the Members of St. Mary Magdalen College, Oxford,* new ser. I, London, 1894.

Madden, Frederic, 'Documents Relating to Perkin Warbeck, with Remarks on His History', *Archaeologia,* XXVII (1838).

———, 'Political Poems of the Reigns of Henry VI and Edward IV', *Archaeologia,* XXVII (1838).

Maitland, William, *The History and Survey of London,* 2 vols., London, 1756.

Malmesbury, William of, *De Gestis Regum Anglorum,* 2 vols., ed. William Stubbs, R.S. 90, London, 1887-9.

Mancini, Dominic, *The Usurpation of Richard the Third,* trans. and ed. C.A.J. Armstrong, 2nd ed., Oxford, 1969.

'The Manuscripts of the Corporation of Southampton and Kings Lynn', Historical Manuscripts Commission, 11th Report, Appendix, iii, London, 1887.

Marcham, Frank, *the King's Office of the Revels, 1610-1622,* London, 1925.

———, 'The King's Office of the Revels, 1610-1622', *Review of English Studies,* II (1926).

Marchegay and Salmon, *Chroniques des Comtes d'Anjou,* Société de l'Histoire de France, Paris, 1871.

Markham, Clements R., *Richard III: His Life and Character,* London, 1906.

Martin, Thomas, *The History of the Town of Thetford,* London, 1779.

Materials for a History of the Reign of Henry VII, 2 vols., ed. William Campbell, R.S. 60, London, 1873-7.

Memorials of Henry VII, ed. James Gairdner, R.S. 10, London 1858.

Meyer, Johannes, *Annales, sive Historiae Rerum Belgicarum,* Frankfurt, 1580.

Millican, Charles Bowie, *Spenser and the Table Round,* Cambridge, Mass., 1932.

Molinet, Jean, *Chroniques,* 3 vols., ed. Georges Doutrepont and Omer Jodogne, Brussels, 1935-7.

Monstrelet, Enguerran de, *Chroniques,* 3 vols., Paris, 1595.

More, Thomas, *The Correspondence of Sir Thomas More,* ed. Elizabeth Frances Rogers, Princeton, 1947.

———, *The History of King Richard III,* ed. Richard S. Sylvester, *The Complete Works of St. Thomas More,* II, New Haven, 1963.

———, *The Latin Epigrams of Thomas More;* ed. Leicester Bradner and Charles Arthur Lynch, Chicago, 1953.

———, *Latin Works,* Basle, 1563.

———, *Translations of Lucian,* ed. Craig R. Thompson, *The Complete Works of St. Thomas More,* III, i, New Haven, 1974.

———, *Workes . . . in the Englysh Tonge,* London, 1557.

Myers, A.R., 'The Character of Richard III', *History Today,* IV (1954).

———, 'Richard III and Historical Tradition', *History,* LIII (1968).

Newburgh, William of, *Historia Regum Anglicarum,* I and II in *Chronicles of the Reigns of Stephen, Henry II, and Richard I,* ed. Richard Howlett, R.S. 82, a & b, London, 1884-5.

Nicolas, Nicholas Harris, *Privy Purse Expenses of Elizabeth of York . . . ,*London 1830.

Original Letters Illustrative of English History, ed. Henry Ellis, 3rd ser., I of each ser., London, 1825-46.

Paradin, Claude, *Alliances Genealogiques des Rois et Princes de Gaule,* [Geneva,] 1606.

Paris, Matthew, *Chronica Majora,* 7 vols., ed. Henry Richards Luard, R.S. 57, London, 1872-83.

The Paston Letters, 4 vols.,ed. James Gairdner, Edinburgh, 1910.

Paston Letters and Papers of the Fifteenth Century, 2 vols., ed. Norman Davis, Oxford, 1971.

Peck, Francis, *Desiderata Curiosa,* II, London, 1732.

Plumpton Correspondence, ed. Thomas Stapleton, Cam. Soc. 4, London, 1839.

Pollard, A.F., *Henry VIII,* London, 1951.

———, 'The Making of Sir Thomas More's *Richard III',* *Historical Essays in Honour of James Tait,* Manchester, 1933.

———,*The Reign of Henry VII from Contemporary Sources,* 3 vols., London, 1913-4.

———, 'Sir Thomas More's "Richard III" ', *History,* XVII (1933).

Pollard, A.J., 'The Tyranny of Richard III', *Journal of Medieval History,* III (1977).

Pollard, A.W. and G.R. Redgrave, *A Short-Title Catalogue of Books Printed in England, Scotland, and Ireland and of English Books Printed Abroad 1475-1640,* London, 1950.

Portal, Ethel, M., 'The Academ Roial of King James I', *Proceedings of the British Academy,* VII (1915-16).

Pugh, T.B., 'The Marcher Lords of Glamorgan and Morgannwg, 1317-1485', *Glamorgan County History,* III, ed. T.B. Pugh, Cardiff, 1971.

Ramsay, James H., *Lancaster and York,* 2 vols., Oxford, 1892.

Rapin Thoyras, Paul de, *The History of England,* trans. N. Tindal, VI, London, 1728.

Rastell, John, *The Pastime of People,* ed. T.F. Dibdin, repr. from 1529 ed., London, 1811.

Reese, M.M. *The Cease of Majesty,* London, 1961.

A Report from the Committee Appointed to View the Cottonian Library, London, 1732.

Reynolds, E.E., *The Trial of St. Thomas More,* London, 1964.

Ricart, Robert, *The Maire of Bristowe Is Kalendar,* ed. Lucy Toulmin Smith, Cam. Soc., 2nd ser. 5, London, 1872.

[Ritson, Joseph], *Bibliographia Poetica,* London, 1802.

Roper, William, *The Lyfe of Sir Thomas Moore, knighte,* ed. Elsie Vaughan Hitchcock, EETS, orig. ser. 197, London, 1935.

Rotuli Parliamentorum . . . , 6 vols., London, 1767-77.

Roskell, J.S., 'William Catesby, Counsellor to Richard III', *Bulletin of the John Rylands Library,* XLII (1959).

Ross, Charles, *Edward IV,* London, 1974.

————, *The Wars of the Roses,* London, 1976.

Round, J. Horace, *Family Origins,* London, 1930.

Rous, John, *Historia Regum Angliae,* 2nd ed., Oxford, 1745.

————, [The Rows Roll or Warwick Roll], London, 1845.

Rye, William Brenchley, *England as Seen by Foreigners in the Days of Elizabeth and James the First,* London, 1865.

Sandford, Francis, *A Genealogical History of the Kings of England, and Monarchs of Great Britain,* London, 1677.

————, *The Life and Reign of Edward the Fourth,* 2 vols., London, 1923.

Scott, J.R., 'Letters Respecting Fauconberge's Kentish Rising in 1471', *Archaeologia Cantiana,* XI (1877).

The Second Maiden's Tragedy, 1611, ed. W.W. Greg, Malone Society Reprints, Oxford, 1909.

Serres, Jean de, *Inventaire General de L'Histoire de France,* 3 vols., Paris, 1600.

Shakespeare, William, *The Plays and Poems,* ed. Edmond Malone, I, ii, London, 1790.

————, *The Tragedy of Richard the Third,* ed. Horace Howard Furness, Jr., New Variorum Edition, 3rd ed., Philadelphia, 1908.

Sharp, Thomas, *A Dissertation on the Pageants or Dramatic Mysteries Anciently Performed at Coventry,* Coventry, 1825.

Smith, Thomas, *Catalogus Librorum Manuscriptorum Bibliothecae Cottonianae,* Oxford, 1696.

Speed, John, *The Historie of Great Britaine,* London, 1623.

Spelman, Henry, *Reliquiae Spelmanniae,* Oxford, 1698.

Sprott, Thomas, *Chronica,* ed. Thomas Hearne, London, 1719.

State Papers Published under the Authority of Her Majesty's Commission, I-XI: *Henry VIII,* London, 1830-1952.

The Statutes at Large, from the First Year of Edward the Fourth to the End of the Reign of Queen Elizabeth, II, London, 1770.

Stauffer, Donald A., *English Biography before 1700,* Cambridge, Mass., 1930.

The Stonor Letters and Papers, 1290-1483, 2 vols., ed. Charles Lethbridge Kingsford, Cam. Soc., 3rd ser. 29 and 30, London, 1919.

Stow, John, *The Annales of England,* London, 1601.

————, *The Annales or Generall Chronicle of England,* London, 1615.

————, *A Survey of London,* ed. Charles Lethbridge Kingsford, Oxford, 1908.

Strype, John, *Historical Collections of . . . John Aylmer,* London, 1701.

Tannenbaum, Samuel A., *Shakesperian Scraps and Other Elizabethan Fragments,* New York, 1933.

Tanner, Lawrence E. and William Wright, 'Recent Investigations Regarding the Fate of the Princes in the Tower', *Archaeologia,* LXXXIV (1935).

Thomson, J.F., 'Richard III and Lord Hastings — a Problematical Case Reviewed', *BIHR,* XLVIII (1975).

Three Prose Versions of the Secreta Secretorum, I, ed. Robert Steele, EETS, extra ser. 74, London, 1898.

Tucker, Melvin J., *The Life of Thomas Howard, Earl of Surrey and Second Duke of Norfolk, 1443-1524,* London, 1964.

Van Norden, Linda, *The Elizabethan College of Antiquaries,* unpublished doctoral dissertation, University of California at Los Angeles, 1946.

————, 'Sir Henry Spelman on the Chronology of the Elizabethan Society of Antiquaries', *Huntington Library Quarterly,* XIII (1949-50).

Vergil, Polydore, *Anglica Historia,* 2nd ed., Basle, 1555.

————, *The Anglica Historia of Polydore Vergil, A.D. 1485-1537,* ed. and trans. Denys Hay, Cam. Soc. 74, London, 1950.

————, *Three Books of Polydore Vergil's English History,* ed. Henry Ellis, Cam. Soc., 1st ser. 29, London, 1844.

Wagner, Anthony Richard, *A Catalogue of English Mediaeval Rolls of Arms,* 2 vols., Oxford, 1950.

————, *The Records and Collections of the College of Arms,* London, 1952.

Walpole, Horace, *Historic Doubts on the Life and Reign of King Richard the Third,* London, 1768.

Walsingham, Thomas, *Historia Anglicana,* 2 vols., ed. Henry Thomas Riley, R.S. 28, London, 1863-4.

————, *Ypodigma Neustriae,* ed. Henry Thomas Riley, R.S. 28(7), London, 1876.

Warkworth, John, *A Chronicle of the First Thirteen Years of the Reign of King Edward the Fourth,* ed. James Orchard Halliwell, Cam. Soc. 10, London, 1839.

Watson, Thomas, *The Ἑκατομπαθια or Passionate Centurie of Loue,* London, [1581].

Wendover, Roger de, *Flores Historiarum,* 3 vols., ed. Henry G. Hewlett, R.S. 84, London, 1886-9.

Westminster, Matthew of, *Flores Historiarum,* 3 vols., ed. Henry Richards Luard, R.S. 95, London, 1890.

Williams, D.T. *The Battle of Bosworth,* Leicester, 1973.

Wolffe, B.P., 'Hastings Reinterred', *EHR,* XCI (Oct. 1976).

————, 'When and Why Did Hastings Lose His Head?', *EHR,* LXXXIX (Oct. 1974).

————, *Yorkist and Early Tudor Government,* London, 1966.

Wood, Charles T., 'The Deposition of Edward V', *Traditio,* XXXVII (1975).

Worcester, William, *Annales Rerum Anglicanum* in II, *Liber Niger Scaccarii,* ed. Thomas Hearne, London, 1771.

Wormald, Francis and C.E. Wright, *The English Library before 1700,* London, 1958.

Zeeveld, W. Gordon, 'A Tudor Defense of Richard III', *PMLA,* LV (1940).

INDEX